The Financial System

Money,
Banking,
and the
U.S. Economy

Money, Banking, and the U.S. Economy

SEVENTH EDITION

Harry D. Hutchinson

University of Delaware

PRENTICE HALL, Englewood Cliffs, New Jersey 07632

Library of Congress Cataloging-in-Publication Data

Hutchinson, Harry D.
  Money, banking, and the United States economy/Harry D.
  Hutchinson. — 7th ed.
     p.   cm.
  Includes bibliographical references and index.
  ISBN 0-13-594466-X
    1. Banks and banking — United States.   2. Money — United States.
  3. Monetary policy — United States.   4. United States — Economic
  conditions — 1945 –   I. Title.
  HG2491.H8   1992
  332.1′0973 — dc20   91-24661
                                                              CIP

Editorial/production supervision: Eleanor Perz
Cover and interior design: Jerry Votta
Prepress buyer: Trudy Pisciotti
Manufacturing buyer: Robert Anderson
Supplements editor: David Scholder

Printed in the United States of America
10   9   8   7   6   5   4   3   2

ISBN 0-13-594466-X

Prentice-Hall International (UK) Limited, *London*
Prentice-Hall of Australia Pty. Limited, *Sydney*
Prentice-Hall Canada Inc., *Toronto*
Prentice-Hall Hispanoamericana, S.A., *Mexico*
Prentice-Hall of India Private Limited, *New Delhi*
Prentice-Hall of Japan, Inc., *Tokyo*
Simon & Schuster Asia Pte. Ltd., *Singapore*
Editora Prentice-Hall do Brasil, Ltda., *Rio de Janeiro*

Brief Contents

Contents

CHAPTER 15
Early Attempts to Explain the Value of Money — The "Old" Quantity Theory — 234

CHAPTER 16
The Simplified Theory of Income Determination — 250

CHAPTER 17
Investment Spending — 291

CHAPTER 18
The Rate of Interest — 306

CHAPTER 19
Review and Use of the Theory — The Keynesian Model — 335

Preface

This book is intended for use in undergraduate or survey M.B.A. courses in the economics of money and banking. Its scope and approach are more or less traditional, although it may lean more toward discussion of current issues in the field than the average text.

The first four chapters deal with the definition and components of the money supply, an overview of the role of the financial system in the economy, a description of financial markets, and a brief discussion of the characteristics of a number of the more important nonbank financial institutions.

Following this introductory section, the next three chapters deal more specifically with some of the current problems of depository institutions. First, there is an extensive, entirely new chapter devoted to a discussion of the savings and loan debacle of the 1980s. Then, Chapter 6 attempts a 100-year survey of federal banking legislation, while Chapter 7 deals with the ever-changing issues of bank regulation, concluding with an in-depth study of the structure, functions, and recent problems of the Federal Deposit Insurance Corporation.

From that point we go on to the business of commercial banking and the structure of the commercial banking system in the United States, concentrating on the dramatic changes that have occurred in the 1980s and 1990s. Then, in Chapters 9 through 13, we consider various aspects of the Federal Reserve System, including the instruments of monetary policy, the process of monetary policy formulation, and the nature of, and limits on, the creation of money in the United States. Chapter 14 concludes this primarily institutional section by dealing with the U.S. Treasury's impact on the money supply and derivation of the "Statement of Factors Affecting Depository Institution Reserves and the Monetary Base."

Chapters 15 through 22 are devoted to a consideration of monetary theory, beginning with the (pre-1930s) version of the quantity theory and progressing through a four-chapter development of an essentially Keynesian income-expenditure model. Following this, we allow for a variable price level by introducing aggregate demand and supply curves in Chapter 20, and then follow up with a thorough consideration of the modern monetarist viewpoint. Finally, in Chapter 22, some of the analytical devices developed to deal with such problems as inflation and stagflation are presented.

Chapter 23 gives consideration to transmission mechanisms connecting the money supply and economic activity, as well as a number of the alleged weaknesses of monetary policy. Chapter 24 deals with the prime alternatives to monetary policy as a stabilization device — fiscal policy, debt management, and incomes policies.

The concluding three chapters concentrate on international finance, including payment across national boundaries, exchange rate determination, the balance of payments statement, and the causes and significance of current account deficits and surpluses. Included in this section are thorough descriptions of the old gold standard, the International Monetary Fund, and the Bretton Woods "exchange rate system," as well as the so-called managed floating system in effect since 1973. Special emphasis is placed on the performance of the U.S. balance of payments during the 1980s and early 1990s.

Every textbook writer claims that his or her book is "written for the student." I can think of no satisfactory way of varying this familiar theme. Throughout, I have assigned the highest priority to keeping the discussion as clear and straightforward as the subject and my expository ability permit. Whether this effort will be a success, of course, only the student can judge. I simply attest that clarity has been my most important objective.

All teachers labor under certain preconceptions regarding the needs of their students. Mine include the belief that repetition of many fundamental principles already covered in the standard introductory course is a desirable and, indeed, necessary technique. For those students who really learned these basic tools in their first course, the cost involved in reviewing them once again is slight. For those who got through their principles course satisfactorily, but didn't quite fully grasp (or have already forgotten) such concepts as multiple credit expansion, the multiplier, or the balance of payments, repetition at this level is absolutely essential. Basically, I have tried to start "from scratch" in all areas, first recapitulating what is normally taught in the introductory course and then superimposing more advanced material on that base.

The major changes in this edition, as might be expected, have to do with the collapse of the savings and loan industry, the threat to the commercial banking industry, the troubles of the FDIC, and legislation, both proposed and actual, aimed at dealing with these problems. As this is being written, major new federal banking legislation is before the Congress, but forecasting exactly what will finally be passed is extremely hazardous.

I am indebted to many people for support, encouragement, and valuable suggestions for improvement. Especially helpful have been my colleagues Colleen Brickley and Don Puglisi, both of whom read extensive new sections and offered constructive criticism and suggestions. In addition, as always, I have benefited from suggestions from other users and from my students. To all of them, I am extremely grateful.

For any errors of omission or commission that remain despite our efforts to root them out, I follow long-established custom by accepting full responsibility. *Ite Caerulei!*

Money,
Banking,
and the
U.S. Economy

CHAPTER 1

What Is Money?

This is a book about money. Accordingly, logical order and the dictates of tradition require that we begin our discussion by defining the subject. *What*, precisely, *is money?*

On its face, the question may seem to be an absurdity and, indeed, something of an insult to the intelligence of the reader. "Surely," as one of my more outspoken students informed me recently, "everyone knows what money is. Is it really necessary to waste valuable class time discussing the obvious?"

The question is, of course, rhetorical. It is never necessary to "discuss the obvious." But that which appears obvious to some may not be so clear-cut to others. It is not a fact that "everyone knows what money is." For even if no one else had any doubts about it, monetary economists have been struggling for a number of years now to arrive at some consensus on the definition of money.

The problems show up at two levels. On the one hand, there are long-standing philosophical differences as to what constitutes the true "essence" of money. One group—undoubtedly the majority—argues that the distinguishing characteristic of money is its capacity to serve as a "generally accepted medium of exchange." Another group, however, sees the essential feature of money as its ability to serve as a "temporary abode of purchasing power—in which sellers of goods, services, or financial assets hold the proceeds in the interim between sale and subsequent purchase of other goods, services or assets." [1] This difference of opinion has never really been settled, but it has been neatly sidestepped by the monetary authorities who regularly collect and publish several different money supply series (labeled M1, M2, etc.), each aimed at satisfying the members of one of the two groups.

---

[1] *Improving the Monetary Aggregates*, report of the Advisory Committee on Monetary Statistics (Washington, D.C.: Board of Governors of the Federal Reserve System, 1976), p. 9.

The other problem — recently a much more vexing one — is that of deciding precisely where to draw the line separating those financial instruments that are money and those that are not. This task would be difficult enough to undertake in a static economy without change. But the unprecedented rate of financial innovation in the last 15 years has so severely magnified the problem that one high Federal Reserve official was led to observe, "I have concluded, most reluctantly, that we can no longer measure the money supply with any precision." [2]

In light of all this, we must recognize at the outset that defining money and agreeing on the financial assets that shall be counted as money is a complex and challenging task. Yet if we are to speak of the money supply, as indeed we must, meaningful communication requires that we agree on a single definition. The remainder of this chapter is aimed at that objective.

How Money Contributes to the Economy

Despite their many differences, virtually all economists agree that money must be defined functionally. That is, items that are to be considered money should be selected on the basis of the functions they perform rather than on such alternative characteristics as the identity of the issuer or the commodity of which they are made. We need, then, to consider carefully the particular functions that money does perform. Before doing so, however, it should be revealing to consider the difficulties inherent in an economy without money.

The Problems with Barter

If no money at all existed, each income recipient would necessarily have to be paid in kind — that is, in the form of his or her share of the actual goods that he or she had helped produce. If, for instance, one worked for a brewery, one's weekly paycheck might consist of 50 cases of beer.

Sounds great, you say? Don't be so sure. After the first couple of six-packs were consumed, most people would find it necessary to start bartering their remaining beer to others who happened to possess the food, clothing, fuel, and myriad other goods and services most of us choose to consume on a regular basis. The process of barter without money to serve as a common medium for which anything can be bought or sold would surely turn out to be a nightmare.

The problems encountered would be enormous. Not only would our beer peddler have to search out others who wished to trade off the things he or she wanted, but for a direct deal to be struck, these people would have to be people who desired to trade what they had for beer. To put it in the terms most commonly employed, exchange under barter conditions would require a *double coincidence of wants.* Not only must we find people who want our beer, but these same people must possess the things we want to trade for. Even if some sort of

[2] Frank E. Morris, "Do the Monetary Aggregates Have a Future as Targets of Federal Reserve Policy?" *New England Economic Review,* Federal Reserve Bank of Boston, March–April 1982, p. 5.

downtown marketing system were arranged to facilitate such exchanges, one can easily imagine the trading process taking as much of one's time as earning the beer in the first place.[3]

But that is not the end of it by any means. In a money economy, we tend to take for granted the role that money plays as a *numeraire* — a measuring device in terms of which the market worth of all goods and services is evaluated and can be compared. If there is no money to serve this function, the exchange value of every good or service must be expressed in terms of a certain number of units of every other one. If, for example, there were 1,000 different goods and services on the market, instead of 1,000 dollar prices being available to measure their relative market worth, *499,500 exchange ratios would be required!* Such a system would not only be a consumer's and accountant's nightmare — it would make efficient use of an economy's scarce resources a near impossibility.

It is fruitless to continue beating a dead horse. The inefficiency of an economy without money is probably quite obvious. To put the whole issue in a more positive vein, what are the social *merits* of money? In a phrase, an efficiently operating money system is a sine qua non for economic development and high living standards. It underlies and facilitates both specialization and capital formation — two essential ingredients of economic growth.

More than two centuries ago, Adam Smith emphasized the contribution that specialization can make to production levels. But specialization is the antithesis of self-sufficiency. As such, it makes *exchange* essential. Each specialist becomes dependent, not only upon all other specialist-producers, but upon the system that facilitates exchanging goods and services among them. Therefore, in a very real sense, money is an essential prerequisite to extensive specialization.

Capital formation, the process whereby new capital goods are produced, also depends heavily on a money system. Fundamentally, capital formation requires saving to release productive resources from the production of consumer goods and transference of those released resources to the building of plants, equipment, and other capital goods. All this could, conceptually, be accomplished without money, but it would be extremely difficult. In a barter system, the savers would be required to accumulate stocks of consumer goods and somehow make them available to investors who, in turn, would use them to pay the workers who build the capital goods. It could be done, but hardly extensively. How much simpler it is for the savers to save money income and lend *that* to the investors!

All this should make it clear why money was first created. It did not originate centuries ago with some farsighted government that saw the need for money and responded by offering it. Rather, it arose spontaneously out of the sheer necessity for a money substance to facilitate economic exchange. Governments now control the issuance of money, but they did not invent it, and some form of money would continue to be used with or without government involvement. In this area as much as in any other, "necessity" was truly the "mother of invention."

---

[3] Of course if the beer should become widely accepted as a medium of exchange as is reportedly the case on the South Pacific island of Yap, things would be easier. The Yapese even today use large stone wheels similar to millstones as their main form of money for large transactions. However, as *The Wall Street Journal* reports, "Stone wheels don't make good pocket money, so for small transactions, Yapese use other forms of currency, such as beer. Beer is proffered as payment for all sorts of odd jobs, including construction." *The Wall Street Journal*, March 29, 1984, p. 1.

The Functions of Money

What, specifically, are the functions performed by money? They consist, of course, essentially of overcoming the difficulties of a barter system. Traditionally, three main functions are considered.

Medium of Exchange   First and perhaps most important, money serves as a medium of exchange—as a vehicle through which the process of exchange among interdependent specialists is made possible. In this role, money serves as an essential lubricant that permits highly industrialized, intricately specialized economies to operate smoothly and effectively.

Unit of Account   In addition to its medium-of-exchange function, money serves as a *numeraire,* a sort of "value measuring rod," in terms of which the values of millions of goods and services can be expressed and compared. Students should recognize that this function is different from that of medium of exchange. Although in the United States today the dollar fulfills both roles simultaneously, this need not be the case. There have been a number of examples in history of one form of money fulfilling the medium-of-exchange function while an entirely different instrument played the role of unit of account in the public's calculations of value.[4]

Store of Value   Money that is spent is, of course, fulfilling the medium-of-exchange function. Obviously, however, a holder of money is free to "not spend" it — to retain it for any period of time desired as a store of value or a generalized, uncommitted claim to wealth.

    Money shares this role with a long list of other assets: stocks, bonds, real commodities, and many other items may also be considered appropriate forms in which to "store value." Sometimes, as in periods of falling prices, money is an extremely appropriate form in which to hold one's wealth. In inflationary periods, it is much less so. As we shall see, a significant portion of monetary theory and policy revolves around the public's decisions as to what portion of the money stock it chooses to hold as a store of value.

The Current Official Definition of Money in the United States

As noted earlier, most economists consider the medium-of-exchange function to be the critical one for distinguishing money from nonmoney claims. For them, the so-called "narrowly defined money stock" series entitled M1 is collected and reported on a monthly basis.

    For those who consider the essence of money to be its capacity to serve as a "temporary abode of purchasing power," broader series focusing more on the

---

[4] Some economists choose to list money's role as a *standard for deferred payments* as a separate function. Since this may be treated as simply a subfunction of its role as a unit of account, we do not list it separately here.

store of value function are needed. To satisfy this view, the Federal Reserve System regularly reports an M2 and M3 money stock.

Let us consider each of these in turn.

The Narrowly Defined Money Stock: M1

By all odds, the most widely used definition of money is *anything generally accepted as a medium of exchange*. Although in other times and other cultures many items have fulfilled this definition (such as, for example, gold, beads, cigarettes, and even stone wheels), until fairly recently in the United States the only things generally accepted as payment media were currency and coins in addition to demand deposits (i.e., checking accounts) held by the public at commercial banks. But although these items still dominate the M1 money supply (constituting nearly two-thirds of the M1 total in mid-1990), financial innovation and regulatory changes in the past two decades have complicated the issue markedly.

The Development of "Other Checkable Deposits"   In brief, what we have seen is that unprecedented and persisting inflation throughout the 1970s and early 1980s was accompanied by (indeed, in large part, *led* to) unprecedented rises in nominal interest rates. These high interest rates sharply raised the opportunity cost of holding noninterest-earning money balances. That, in turn, led financial institutions, ever alert to the public's desire to minimize the cost of holding transactions balances, to seek new financial arrangements that could accommodate such desires. Finally, these efforts at financial innovation tended to induce governmental regulatory reforms that have had the effect of legalizing several new types of "checkable deposits."

Perhaps the most important of these are the so-called "NOW accounts." Technically speaking, NOW accounts (or negotiable orders of withdrawal) are interest-earning savings accounts on which checks can be written.[5] The first NOW accounts were issued in 1972 by mutual savings banks in Massachusetts and New Hampshire where, under state law, they were declared legal.

After being upheld by the courts, the issuance of NOW accounts spread rapidly throughout New England. Within two years, in order to prevent a competitive advantage to mutual savings banks, all depository institutions in Massachusetts and New Hampshire except credit unions were authorized by Congress to issue NOW accounts. Then, in 1976, the same authority was granted to depository institutions in all New England states. Finally, after being legalized in still more states, Congress, in the Depository Institutions Deregulation and Monetary Control Act of 1980 (hereafter to be called the Monetary Control Act of 1980), authorized their issuance by all federally insured commercial banks, savings banks, and savings and loan associations throughout the country beginning in January 1981.

A second development of note was the authorization of so-called "ATS accounts" at commercial banks. ATS accounts (bank accounts offering "automatic

---

[5] For all practical purposes, NOW accounts could be considered checking accounts that pay interest, but since federal law still forbids payment of interest on regular checking accounts, they are technically considered savings accounts on which checks can be written.

transfer service") are arrangements whereby banks automatically transfer funds from interest-bearing savings accounts to checking accounts as checks are written. This, of course, permits the account owner to earn interest on his or her account — but to have it as readily available for spending purposes as a checking account. ATS accounts were initially authorized by bank regulatory agencies in 1978, challenged in the courts, but then made legal by the same 1980 Monetary Control Act that permitted nationwide NOW accounts.

Third, there was the development and subsequent legalization of "share draft accounts" issued by credit unions. These are arrangements whereby owners of interest-earning shares (accounts) at credit unions can write checks on them. They, too, were challenged in the courts, but ultimately were made legal by the Monetary Control Act.

The Specific Components of M1   Following a revision in 1980 that properly recognized the development of these new payment media, the M1 money supply currently includes the following:

1. **Currency and coins held by the nonbank public**
   Not included in M1 are currency and coins held by the U.S. Treasury, the Federal Reserve banks, and commercial banks.

2. **Demand deposits owned at commercial banks by the nonbank public**
   Not included in M1 are demand deposits *owned by* commercial banks, the U.S. Treasury, and foreign banks and official institutions as well as cash items in process of collection and Federal Reserve float.[6]

3. **Other checkable deposits, which include**
   a. NOW accounts at commercial banks and thrift institutions.
   b. ATS accounts at commercial banks and thrift institutions.
   c. Share draft accounts held at credit unions.
   d. Demand deposits (and outstanding traveler's checks) owned by the nonbank public and issued by depository institutions other than commercial banks.[7]

More Broadly Defined Money Stocks: M2 and M3

For those who consider the essence of "moneyness" to be a claim's capacity to serve as a "temporary abode of purchasing power," and to serve not only as a store of value but also to be readily convertible into a medium of exchange, additional claims must be included. To those who hold this view, the essence of an instrument's moneyness is thought to be its *liquidity*, which, in turn, largely determines its suitability as a store of value.

---

[6] Cash items in process of collection plus Federal Reserve float represents checks that have been deposited in one bank but have not yet been collected from the bank on which they are written. They are, of course, excluded to avoid double-counting a single demand deposit at two different banks.

[7] Mutual savings banks and savings and loan associations were authorized to issue demand deposits when related to newly authorized commercial loans in the Monetary Control Act of 1980 and the Garn-St Germain Act of 1982.

What is liquidity? An asset is said to possess *perfect* liquidity if it can be immediately converted into a fixed number of dollars without risk of loss.[8]

If our money concept were to be limited to assets possessing absolutely *perfect* liquidity, the items included would be precisely the same as those identified earlier as generally accepted media of exchange — coins, currency, and checkable deposits. Such a limitation would, of course, have the virtue of providing a not entirely unreasonable distinction between money and nonmoney assets. But the line of demarcation, if degree of liquidity is to be considered the distinguishing characteristic, is inevitably an arbitrary one. Consider, for example, the following list of assets:

1. Coins and currency
2. Demand deposits (checking accounts) and other checkable deposits
3. Passbook savings deposits at commercial banks
4. Savings deposits at savings and loan associations and mutual savings banks
5. Time certificates of deposit
6. Money market deposit accounts at depository institutions
7. Money market mutual funds
8. U.S. government savings bonds
9. Marketable U.S. government securities

As noted, only items 1 and 2 qualify as possessing perfect liquidity. Coins and currency *are* dollars, and checkable deposits obligate the depository institution to pay out cash at the owner's demand. But classifying these assets as money because they possess 100 percent liquidity while excluding several others that offer liquidity at somewhere around the 99 percent level certainly seems to involve drawing indefensibly fine distinctions.

Ordinary savings accounts at commercial banks, mutual savings banks, savings and loan associations, and credit unions are, in practice if not in law, as liquid as checking accounts. Although savings institutions have the legal right to make depositors wait for up to seven days after a withdrawal request before receiving cash, this right is almost universally waived.[9] The result is that both the depositors and the savings institutions have come to look upon these accounts, in practice, as being just as much withdrawable on demand as checking accounts.

In addition to regular savings accounts, the depository institutions also issue time certificates of deposit (CDs). These certificates, which usually offer a higher interest rate than do regular savings accounts, are most commonly sold in units of $1,000 or more and carry fixed maturity dates varying from 30 days to six years or more from date of issue.

The larger CDs (denomination sizes of $100,000 or more), designed primarily for business firms, are generally negotiable (i.e., can be sold from one owner to another). Holders of nonnegotiable CDs who find that they need their money in

[8] The phrase "without risk of loss" refers to dollars, not real purchasing power. For example, if a particular asset is of such a nature as to guarantee the holder immediate access to, say, $100, it has perfect liquidity even if the $100 may, as a result of inflation, have less real purchasing power than when the asset was initially purchased.

[9] Indeed, savings institutions are *required* to reserve this right but are under no obligation to enforce it.

advance of the specified maturity date can normally get it from the issuer, though only at the sacrifice of part of their interest income.[10]

How liquid are such time deposits? Not quite as liquid as regular savings accounts, of course, but nevertheless very highly liquid assets.

In practice, assets held in the form of shares of money market mutual funds or as money market deposit accounts are every bit as liquid as ordinary savings accounts. Indeed, along with the higher interest return they offer, their most attractive feature to most savers has been their high degree of liquidity. We shall have more to say about money market funds and deposits in the following pages.

The last two items — U.S. savings bonds and marketable U.S. government securities — are similar in that both are obligations of the U.S. Treasury and part of the national debt, but they are different in degree of liquidity. U.S. savings bonds (of which about $128 billion were outstanding in early 1991) are issued in the name of the initial purchaser and, as such, are nonmarketable; that is, they cannot be sold to someone else. On the other hand, savings bonds possess the unique advantage of being cashable (turned in to the government for repayment of principal plus a fixed amount of interest) at any time (after a short initial waiting period) before the actual maturity date. These bonds, then, would appear to be just about as liquid as regular savings accounts.

Marketable U.S. government securities, on the other hand (of which about $2.2 trillion were outstanding in early 1991), are substantially less liquid.[11] These obligations cannot be cashed in until their fixed maturity date. A holder of a marketable U.S. security who needs his or her money before the maturity date must sell it to someone else at the going market price. The market price of such securities is a variable amount that can, at any given time (depending largely on the behavior of interest rates and the length of time till maturity of the instrument), be above or below the par value of the asset. Marketable U.S. securities therefore, although still very liquid assets, are much less so than are U.S. savings bonds or time and savings deposits.

So where is all this leading us? Where do those who consider an asset's liquidity — or suitability as a "temporary abode of purchasing power" — as the essence of its moneyness draw the line between money and nonmoney items? What must be obvious by now is that *any* specific dividing line is bound to be somewhat arbitrary, and, indeed, in defining M2 and M3, the authorities were required to draw somewhat arbitrary distinctions.

The Specific Components of M2

The M2 money stock series includes all the instruments found in M1 plus the following highly liquid claims:

---

[10] Early withdrawal penalties of at least seven days' interest are required on withdrawals made within the first six days after deposit. Also, "nonpersonal" time deposits with maturities of at least 18 months are subject to a one-month interest penalty if withdrawn within the first 18 months.

[11] Marketable U.S. government securities include such instruments as (1) Treasury bills, with maturities varying from 91 days to one year; (2) Treasury notes, with maturities from 1 to 7 years; and (3) Treasury bonds, with maturities up to 30 years. In addition to savings bonds, over $800 billion of Treasury securities designed for government trust funds were also nonmarketable as of late 1990.

1. Savings deposits and "small" certificates of deposit (those in denominations of less than $100,000) issued by any depository institution
2. Money market deposit accounts
3. Money market mutual funds (except those designed for institutions)
4. Overnight repurchase agreements
5. Overnight Eurodollars

Perhaps it would be well to explain some of these components before proceeding. Many of them are the product of financial innovation in the 1970s and 1980s in response to an environment marked by soaring price levels and market interest rates along with governmental ceilings (called *Regulation Q* ceilings) on the interest depository institutions were permitted to pay to savings account and time deposit holders.

Consider, for example, *money market mutual funds (MMMFs)*. In the late 1960s and the 1970s when Regulation Q interest rate ceilings were being held well below comparable market rates, some managers of mutual funds (who were *not* subject to the Regulation Q ceilings) came up with the idea of offering small savers "shares" in mutual funds which were every bit as liquid as savings accounts but which offered much higher interest rates.

The idea was quite simple. The mutual fund managers (or investment companies as they are sometimes called) offered savers small-denomination "shares" which were withdrawable on demand, virtually riskless, and which paid an interest rate much higher than depository institutions were permitted to pay. The mutual fund then used the funds collected from a very large number of savers to purchase large-denomination "money market" instruments offering relatively high interest returns. These money market instruments, which were in general only available in denominations so large (e.g., in $100,000 units) as to be out of reach for individual small savers, consisted of highly liquid, very-short-term IOUs of firms and governments. We shall deal in more detail with money market instruments in Chapter 3.

Money market mutual funds grew rapidly in popularity in the late 1970s and early 1980s as evidenced by the growth in their total assets from $4 billion in 1978 to over $240 billion by late 1982. In large part, however, their gain came at the expense of commercial banks who were prevented by Regulation Q from offering competitive interest rates.

It was in response to this drain on commercial banks that Congress authorized the creation of *money market deposit accounts (MMDAs)* by depository institutions in 1982. These were designed to be directly competitive with money market mutual funds. That is, they offered the higher interest return made possible by their issuers purchasing money market instruments, they were withdrawable on demand, and they offered limited check-writing privileges.[12]

Overnight repurchase agreements, which are popularly referred to as RPs, are issued by commercial banks to companies other than depository institutions and money market mutual funds. Repurchase agreements typically arise in the following way. A corporation may have funds on deposit at a bank that it does not expect to need until the following day. It then arranges to use these funds to

---

[12] Only three checks per month can be written, however. On the other hand, these checks can be for any amount, and the accounts are insurable by the Federal Deposit Insurance Corporation.

"purchase" a U.S. security from the bank with the understanding that the bank will "buy" the security back on the following day. Such RP transactions are usually carried out in units of $1 million or more, and the corporation earns interest on the funds for a day at a rate approximately equal to the current federal funds rate.[13] Obviously corporations owning RPs consider them exceptionally liquid assets, since they guarantee a fixed amount of funds the following day.

Overnight Eurodollars are claims issued by Caribbean and London branches of U.S. banks to U.S. residents other than depository institutions and money market mutual funds. These particular Eurodollars are liabilities of banks located in the Caribbean and in London, the liabilities being denominated in dollars and payable in dollars on the following day. In effect, they represent readily available savings accounts that some U.S. residents hold there.

The Specific Components of M3

The M3 money stock includes all the instruments included in M2 plus:

1. Time deposits in denominations larger than $100,000 issued by depository institutions to anyone other than depository institutions, money market funds, the U.S. government, or foreign banks and official institutions.

2. Repurchase agreements with maturities of longer than one day (usually called *term RPs*).

3. Eurodollars with maturities of longer than one day.

4. Money market mutual funds available to institutions only.

Recent Money Supply Data

Table 1-1 shows actual data for the components of the M1, M2, and M3 money supply series as of April 1991. Figure 1-1 shows similar data graphically for January 1991.

Some Comments on the Composition of M1

It is worth noting that over one quarter of the M1 money supply is made up of currency and coins. Of that total, about 90 percent consists of Federal Reserve notes — paper currency issued by the 12 Federal Reserve banks — with the rest being coins.[14]

---

[13] The federal funds market will be discussed shortly. In actuality, the U.S. security simply serves as collateral for a loan that the corporation is making to the bank.

[14] Actually a fraction of 1 percent consists of other types of paper currency, most of which is currently being retired when the Treasury obtains it. Included are such time-honored types of currency as silver certificates, Federal Reserve bank notes, national bank notes, gold certificates, U.S. notes, and Treasury notes of 1890. Most of these still outstanding are undoubtedly being held by collectors.

TABLE 1-1 The U.S. money supply, April 1991 (billions)	
M1 components	
1. Currency and coins held by the nonbank public	$ 256.0
2. Demand deposits owned by the nonbank public	285.1
3. Other checkable deposits	311.8
M1 money supply total	$ 852.9
M2 components	
1. M1	$ 852.9
2. Savings accounts	428.5
3. "Small" time deposits	1,149.0
4. Money market deposit accounts	526.9
5. Money market mutual funds for individuals	371.2
6. Overnight repurchase agreements	49.0
7. Overnight Eurodollars	19.9
M2 money supply total	$3,397.4[a]
M3 components	
1. M2	$3,397.4
2. "Large" time deposits	503.4
3. Term RPs and term Eurodollars	150.7
4. Money market mutual funds for institutions	144.1
M3 money supply total	$4,180.8[a]

[a] Components of M2 and M3 may not add to total because deductions are made to estimate amount of demand deposits and cash held by thrift institutions to service time deposit liabilities and to estimate RPs and Eurodollars held by institution-only money market funds.
Source: Federal Reserve System.

Also noteworthy is the "other checkable deposit" portion which currently constitutes about 36 percent of M1. This total is particularly impressive when it is recognized that little more than a decade ago most of these payment methods did not even exist.[15]

One might well wonder why ordinary checking accounts, which pay no interest, still make up a larger part of the M1 money supply than the "other checkable deposits," which do. The answer is simple. First, business firms, which hold more than half the nation's demand deposits, are not permitted to own interest-earning deposits like NOW accounts. Second, most banks insist upon minimum balances in NOW accounts and some households find such a requirement sufficiently onerous to forgo willingly their use.

In looking at the breakdown of M1, it is instructive to consider the origins of our money supply. That is, what fraction of M1 was initially created by which institution? Table 1-2 reports the facts for mid-1990.

It is important to note, no doubt to the surprise of many people, that the U.S.

[15] NOW accounts were introduced in New England in 1972, but they became available nationwide only in 1981.

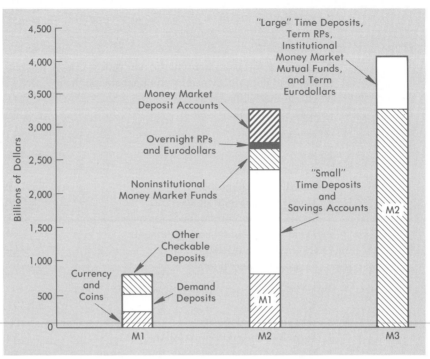

Source: Federal Reserve System.

FIGURE 1-1   Components of M1, M2, and M3, June 1990

Treasury has only the very minor role of providing the 2 percent of the nation's money supply made up of coins. And more important for our purposes, the dominating role of banks in providing money must be stressed. Despite recent innovations that have permitted savings and loan associations, mutual savings banks, and credit unions to join the money-creating game, commercial banks and the Federal Reserve banks still provide the vast majority. Indeed, in June 1990, 86 percent of the M1 money supply was the liability of these two banking institutions! Small wonder that in discussing money, we concentrate heavily on the Federal Reserve System and commercial banks.

TABLE 1-2   Percent of M1 provided by institution, June 1990

	Percent of M1
Coins—U.S. Treasury	2
Currency—Federal Reserve banks	26
Demand deposits—commercial banks	35
Other checkable deposits—commercial banks	25
Other checkable deposits—other thrifts[a]	12

[a] These include savings and loan associations, mutual savings banks, and credit unions.

Some Comments on the Pattern
of Money Supply Growth

As Figure 1-2 makes abundantly clear, the broader money supply series, M2 and
M3, has grown much faster than M1, especially since 1970. In fact, Figure 1-2
really *understates* this trend since the M2 and M3 series include the slower-
growing M1 totals. From 1970 to 1990 for example, M1 more than tripled while

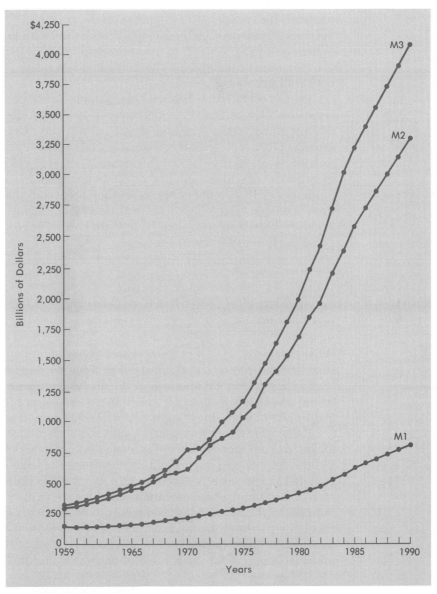

Source: Federal Reserve System.

FIGURE 1-2 Growth in the M1, M2, and M3 series,
1959–1990 (billions, seasonally adjusted)

M2 was almost five times greater. If the M1 component is excluded from the M2 series, however, the resultant "M2 minus M1" total rose sevenfold over the same period.

What are the causes of this relatively greater rate of growth in M2 and M3? It seems clear that once again high interest rates, financial innovation, and regulatory changes have played the lead role. High interest rates, of course, have lessened the attraction for noninterest-bearing cash and demand deposits, and although interest is paid on the "other checkable deposit" portion of M1, governmental regulation, for many of these years, held down the maximum interest rates payable on them to levels far below what had been available elsewhere. This tendency for spenders to economize on the traditional M1 type of transactions balances is evidenced by the fact that during the 1970s households cut "the ratio of their checkable deposits to their consumption spending by 18 percent," while "corporations reduced their checkable deposits relative to gross national product by 38 percent."[16]

On the other hand, financial innovations, made possible in many cases by regulatory change, have provided savers instruments offering them much higher interest along with a very high degree of liquidity. Examples abound, but the growth of RPs, money market mutual funds, and money market deposit accounts provide excellent illustrations. Incidentally, these developments have tended to increase the rate of growth of the M2 money stock in two ways. Not only have funds tended to flow out of M1 to M2, but also, funds that prior to these innovations had been used to purchase instruments not included in M2 or M3 (such as Treasury bills) began to flow back through the financial institutions, further pumping up the M2 and M3 totals.

Continuing Problems with the Definition of Money

What difference does it make how money is defined, one might well ask. The superficial answer is that we *must* define it for intelligible communication. If we would consider such things as how the money supply gets determined and how money affects our economic well-being, we must necessarily have a common conception of what this thing is that we are calling "money."

If that were the only reason it would not much matter what specific assets we included in our money concept as long as everyone understood what they were. But the definition of money and the decision as to what specific items are to be included in the series collected has a much more profound significance than merely facilitating communication. What we are really searching for, at least in the case of the M1 version, is a measure which bears a close and predictable relationship to important indexes of economic activity. We seek a concept with a measurable series that has some regular or at least predictable effect on such undeniably important variables as employment, production, and prices.

---

[16] See the excellent article, "Innovations in the Financial Markets," by Marcelle Arak in *Quarterly Review*, Federal Reserve Bank of New York, Winter 1981–1982.

It seems clear that the M1 series has long been intended to provide such a measure. The Federal Reserve System (Fed) has tried to include in that version of the money supply those assets that spenders look upon as their *transactions* balances. That is, these are assets that we believe people not only *can* spend (they are media of exchange) but that they *intend* to spend to finance transactions in the near future. Savings accounts and time deposits, though they *are* exceptionally liquid and *can* be withdrawn for spending easily, are thought to be somewhat more "firmly held." The thought is that they are not part of what the average spender considers his or her immediate "transactions balances."

If we really are successful in singling out the items people look upon as "transactions balances" to include in our M1 series and *if* those balances do bear some sort of reliable or predictable relation to total spending, then we have a measure well worth watching and controlling.

In recent years, however, concern has been raised about the M1 money concept on two fronts. First, it has been suggested that some of the items included may not really be transactions balances, while others may be inappropriately excluded. Second, it has been argued that even if we do indeed have the right items included to compose a "transactions balance" series, our experience in recent years indicates that there must have been a considerable change in the relationship between these transactions balances and total spending.[17]

The problems involved in deciding what to include and what to exclude are easy to understand. For a good many years prior to 1980, we thought we had a firm M1 definition when only currency, coins, and demand deposits were included. That comfortable state was upset, however, by the financial innovation that introduced NOW and ATS accounts and after a not inconsiderable lag, the Fed was forced to adjust by including them.

That 1980 revision did not end either financial innovation or our classification problem however. As we have seen, neither money market deposit accounts nor money market mutual funds are included in M1. The reason is that it is felt that most owners of MMDAs and MMMFs consider them, much like time deposits, to be a form in which liquid savings are held rather than immediately spendable transactions balances. But unlike time deposits, money market accounts offer limited check-writing privileges, a feature which surely makes their classification somewhat more tenuous. Certainly we cannot deny altogether the possibility that *some* money market account holders may consider them a part of their transactions balances.

On the other hand, there is the matter of NOW accounts. As we have noted, NOW accounts are currently included in the M1 series and that certainly seems the appropriate treatment. Surely the majority of NOW account owners consider them as much a part of their immediately spendable transactions balances as their noninterest-paying ordinary checking accounts. But once again there is room for reservation. It has been pointed out, for example, that the annual turnover rate of NOW accounts is many times less than that of ordinary checking accounts. While much of the explanation for this appears to lie in the fact that businesses cannot

---

[17] Two examples of such concern are "Measuring Money" by Carl E. Walsh, in the *Federal Reserve Bank of San Francisco Weekly Letter*, May 30, 1986, and "Should Money Be Redefined?" by Brian Mottey, *Federal Reserve Bank of San Francisco Weekly Letter*, September 5, 1986.

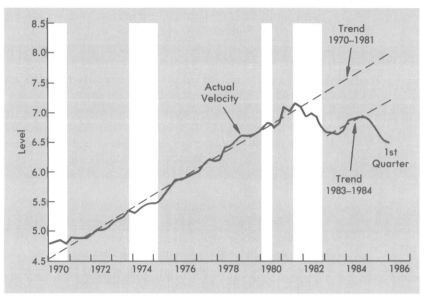

Source: Federal Reserve System.

FIGURE 1-3 Velocity of M1 (GNP/M1)

own NOW accounts, it is still possible that it may be partly because some NOW account owners consider them as savings rather than transactions balances.[18]

In any case, one thing became painfully clear in the 1980s. The relationship between M1 and the money level of GNP, which was a reasonably close one throughout the 1970s, fluctuated quite erratically during the 1980s. Figure 1-3, which depicts the velocity of spending M1 balances on GNP up through the mid-1980s, shows this quite vividly.

What this velocity behavior really shows seems to be a marked change in the relationship between the M1 series and nominal GNP (which, of course, reflects both production and prices). And that, in turn, means that to the extent the nation's monetary policy is aimed at controlling M1, with the ultimate intent of guiding money GNP, we have some real problems.[19]

We shall return to the behavior of velocity later in the section on monetary theory. At this point we can simply note that constructing a money series that bears a close and/or predictable relationship to the level of economic activity has proven to be a most difficult task.[20]

---

[18] For a balanced discussion of this point see Mottey, "Should Money Be Redefined?"

[19] Indeed the Federal Reserve's Open Market Committee has recognized these problems by downgrading M1 as a target in establishing monetary policy since the mid-1980s.

[20] One is reminded of the criticism of Friedman and Schwartz's *A Monetary History of the United States, 1867–1960* by James Tobin in a review article in 1965. Tobin asserts that ". . . Friedman and his followers seem to be saying: 'We don't know what money is, but whatever it is, its stock should grow steadily at 3 to 4 percent per year'." James Tobin, "The Monetary Interpretation of History," *American Economic Review*, June 1965, p. 465.

Review Questions

1. Carefully discuss the disadvantages of a barter economy.

2. "If Ms. Brown deposits $100 of cash into her checking account at a commercial bank, the effect on the M1 money supply is different from that which will result if she deposits the $100 into her savings deposit at a commercial bank. The two transactions, however, have the same effect on the M2 money supply." Explain.

3. If money is to be defined in accordance with the degree of liquidity of the asset, it is exceptionally difficult to draw the line between money and nonmoney assets. Discuss carefully.

4. What are the differences between U.S. savings bonds and marketable U.S. securities, and how do these differences affect their degree of liquidity?

5. Specify those checking accounts and currency that are *not* included in the M1 money supply definition.

6. Carefully identify share draft accounts.

7. If one wishes to study the M1 money supply, one must devote far more attention to the operations of banks than to the U.S. Treasury. Carefully explain why this is the case.

8. Nationwide authorization of NOW accounts and their inclusion into the M1 money supply definition tended to make M1 grow faster in recent years, relative to M2. Explain.

9. Identify the components of M2 and M3.

10. List and explain the functions of money.

11. Identify NOW accounts and ATS accounts.

12. Contrast money market mutual funds and money market deposit accounts.

13. "If M1 is intended to include all transactions accounts, there is room for doubt as to the appropriateness of the current treatment of money market accounts and NOW accounts." Explain carefully.

The Economic Role of Financial Institutions

"Economics," a student observed one day, "wouldn't be so bad if they'd get out of that oversimplified dream world they're always assuming and deal more directly with the real world we all live in."

Just so. It would indeed be nice to be able to start right off discussing the real world as it is, without reliance on the host of simplifying assumptions and models that appear to be the economist's stock in trade. But, of course, the modern industrialized economy is just too intricate and complex a mechanism to comprehend if approached directly as is. The result is that students find themselves confronting a whole series of dream worlds in which intentionally unrealistic simplifying assumptions have been made to bring out general relationships and principles that could not otherwise be understood.

The Circular Flow Diagram

One outstanding example of this technique of successive approximations of reality is the standard circular flow diagram of an economy encountered in nearly every introductory course. Figure 2-1 is such a diagram.

The purpose of this diagram is to present a bird's-eye view of how an economy gets real goods and services produced and purchased. Pedagogically, it is not only a perfectly valid device for its purpose but extremely useful.

But of course this diagram certainly does not claim to depict the real world. Rather, its prime function is to eliminate much of the complexity of reality, isolating the essence of the process whereby consumer goods are purchased by households in return for the income earned from productive services sold by households to the business sector.

The simplifying assumptions needed to come up with such a view of the

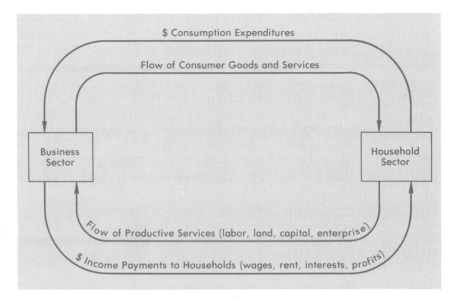

FIGURE 2-1 Circular flow diagram

economy are many. It ignores government, thereby not recognizing that part of householders' money income goes to pay taxes and part of their real income constitutes government services. It assumes a closed economy so that nothing is sold to or bought from foreigners. It ignores the many intrabusiness sector transactions that are an important part of the real-world economy. And finally, since all householders' income is assumed spent on consumption goods and nothing but consumer goods and services is produced, it admits no saving or investment.

Now such glaring omissions from the real-world scene are entirely appropriate when one's purpose is merely to obtain an overall view of the production-income generation process. But to assume no saving or investment is to ignore altogether that vast and intricate structure sometimes referred to as the financial sector on which much of the success of the goods-producing sectors heavily depends. To settle for that in a book which purports to be about money and banking would be unthinkable.

What the Financial Sector Does

The financial sector of the U.S. economy of the 1990s is a truly imposing one. As of the middle of 1990, it employed over 3 million people, a work force larger than the federal government or the entire transportation equipment industry and more than four times that of the entire mining industry or of the primary metals industry.[1]

[1] U.S. Department of Labor, *Employment and Earnings* (Washington, D.C.: Government Printing Office, June 1990).

What do all these people not directly involved in the making of final goods and services do? How can we justify the diversion of such a large segment of our limited human resources to "mere financial" dealings?

The answer of course is that an efficient financial industry is an essential prerequisite to a modern, highly specialized, mechanized economy. It provides the medium of exchange without which specialization could hardly exist. It provides a mechanism whereby any spending unit that does not choose to spend all its current after-tax income on consumer goods (that is, chooses to save) may conveniently make it available to other spending units who prefer to spend more than their current incomes. And, finally, in the process of accomplishing the latter, it makes available a procedure through which much of the nation's vital capital formation is financed.

We shall have much more to say in upcoming chapters about the process and effects of providing money for the economy. Let us turn now, however, to a brief consideration of the implications of the other functions of the financial sector.

Transferring Purchasing Power
from Surplus Spending Units
to Deficit Spending Units

In the circular flow diagram depicted in Figure 2-1, a closed and complete circle was accomplished by merely assuming that nobody chooses to save. Therefore, by assumption, if $1 trillion of income is received by households in income payments for productive services rendered, $1 trillion is spent by those households to buy all the output of business firms. Production at the $1 trillion level can therefore presumably be assured indefinitely, as we have simply assumed that whatever is produced is willingly purchased.

A nice world, perhaps, but not a world even remotely close to current reality. Pedagogical assumptions notwithstanding, everyone knows full well that some income recipients do save (spend less than their after-tax income) while others dissave, or deficit spend (spend more than their income). Within the household sector, young families and older, retired families typically dissave, while middle-aged families generally are net savers. On balance, the household sector as a whole typically saves, the business sector typically dissaves, and the government sector typically dissaves (although on those rare occasions when the government achieves a budget surplus, it is a net saver).

If, for example, the household sector in our circular flow diagram in Figure 2-1 should choose to save 10 percent of its $1 trillion of income, this means that only $900 billion is spent to buy the output of business. Taken by itself, the leakage in the income stream that this saving represents would tend—because of the unintended accumulation of $100 billion worth of business inventories it would cause—to lead to cutbacks of production, rising unemployment, and declining incomes.

But this result of saving is by no means inevitable. If by chance (and there is certainly no guarantee that this will happen) the business sector wishes to deficit spend by exactly $100 billion to purchase new capital goods (that is, to invest), and if, to finance such a venture, businesses are prepared to borrow the $100 billion that households have saved, then the potential unemployment may be avoided.[2] Indeed, in these fortuitous circumstances, *two* positive benefits to the economy will result from bringing the savers and investors together and permitting the former to finance the planned investment spending of the latter. Not only can this forestall potential unemployment in the short run, but it also can provide the economy with a larger stock of capital goods that, other things being equal, will expand productive potential in the future.

Clearly, the task of bringing together savers (those with surplus funds to lend) and investors (those who plan to deficit spend to purchase new capital goods) is an absolutely vital one. It is this extraordinarily important function that the financial sector performs.

> **The basic economic role and justification of financial institutions is to serve as middlemen between savers and investors, thereby facilitating the capital formation process.**

The Capital Formation Process

Before we proceed to a more detailed discussion of just how financial institutions carry out this basic function, it will be useful to digress briefly to consider further the capital formation process.

In the highly artificial Robinson Crusoe–type economy often visualized to simplify or throw into sharp relief some basic theoretical ideas, there is no financial mechanism to complicate the issue. Indeed one of the main purposes of such abstractions is to sweep aside the "veil" with which money and a financial system seem to distort and conceal the "real" economic developments underneath.

In the Crusoe-type economy where there is no money, the capital formation process is a very simple one. If Crusoe and Friday desire to raise their production of fish, they may consider it worthwhile to take several days off from actually fishing to produce a fishing net (a capital good). They realize, however, that they must continue eating while they construct the net. Consequently, they must produce an excess of consumer goods (fish, coconuts) to sustain themselves while working on their net. The act of building up this reserve stock of food is, in the purest sense, an act of *saving*—consuming less than the full amount of their income. It is this abstention from consumption that permits them to devote several days of their scarce labor supply to the construction of their net — an act of *investment*.

> **The fundamental "real" effect of saving, then, is the release of productive resources from the production of consumer goods.**

[2] Note that it is "ex ante" or "planned" investment that is referred to here, not "ex post" or "realized" investment. The latter equals saving, by definition, but planned investment and saving are equal only in equilibrium.

Investment, on the other hand, is the use of those released resources to produce a new capital good. In the Crusoe case, there is no money or financial structure to "muddy up the water" or obscure our vision of what goes on. The saving consists of stocking up real consumer goods, and the investment consists of building the capital good while living off these previously saved stocks.

In a money-using economy, things are more complicated. Suppose that we have an economy in which many people are specializing, so that exchange — and therefore money — is essential. In such a case, saving takes the form of people not spending all their money income to buy consumer goods. To keep it simple, let us assume that there are still no banks, so that each saver amasses, at least temporarily, a pile of cash.

Does this kind of saving have the same real effects as that of Crusoe? Of course. People who do not spend all their money incomes to purchase consumer goods thereby *release some productive resources*, which they *could* have tied up producing more consumer goods, for other purposes. Now if the money savings are lent to business firms that desire to purchase more capital goods, they may spend them to hire these released resources to build them. On the monetary level, money is saved, lent to investors, and spent by them to purchase capital goods. On the real level, productive resources are released by the savers' act of abstention, but they are rehired by the investors' act of investing.[3]

Incidentally, let us make one crucial distinction clear. Throughout this book, the word *investment*, as is customary in economics, is used to mean the *production of new capital goods*. Investment spending, then, consists of *expenditures to buy* newly produced capital goods. The purchase of securities such as stocks and bonds, on the other hand, is *not*, by our terminology, investment. However, since it is a common practice in everyday speech to refer to the purchase of securities as investment, we shall distinguish security purchase by calling it "financial" investment. But the word *investment* without a qualifying adjective should always be taken to mean the production of new capital goods.

For emphasis, let us restate the relevant definitions. In a money-using economy:

Saving — Not spending all of income to purchase consumption goods and services.
Investment Spending — Spending to purchase newly produced capital goods.

Now, as far as it goes, the preceding is all perfectly correct. But it glides over one major problem that cannot legitimately be ignored. Note that in an earlier paragraph we glibly stated that *if the money savings are lent to business firms*, all will be well. The extent to which, the ease with which, and the manner in which savings are made available to investors have to do largely with the development of the financial system.

---

[3] Note that we continue, for the present, the assumption that there is sufficient investment spending to absorb all the resources released by the saving, and thereby prevent unemployment.

Direct Finance via Sale of Primary Securities from Deficit Spending Units to Surplus Income Units

The simplest way in which a deficit spending unit (such as a business that needs to borrow to finance investment spending) can acquire the funds needed from surplus income units (savers) is by selling *primary securities* to them. Primary securities may be defined as claims issued directly by the deficit spending unit. They consist primarily of equities (stocks, which provide the buyer a part ownership in the firm), bonds (IOUs of the borrowers), and mortgages.

As a starting point, we might visualize the saving-investment process altering our circular flow diagram to look something like Figure 2-2.

Here we assume that householders spend only $90 billion of their $100 billion income to purchase consumer goods and services. Consequently — by definition — they save $10 billion. The $10 billion saved is then shown as being sent in to consumer goods-producing firms needing money in return for $10 billion of such primary securities as stocks and bonds. Within the business sector, at the same time, the consumer goods–producing firms spend the $10 billion they have raised from savers to purchase newly produced plant and equipment from capital goods–producing firms.

Figure 2-2 does constitute a rather neat way of altering the circular flow diagram to incorporate saving and investment but it is still far from a picture of reality. One serious problem is that it shows householders sending their savings directly in to business firms to purchase their securities. But, of course, savers do not really do this. What they actually do is work through such middlemen financial institutions as brokers and dealers.

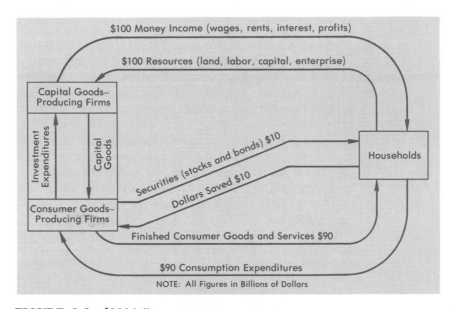

FIGURE 2-2 **$100 billion money income**

The Middleman Role of Brokers, Dealers, and Investment Banks

As noted, *brokers* and *dealers* function as key middlemen between savers and investors. Brokers play more of a pure middleman role in that they simply bring the buyer and seller of the primary security together (for a fee, of course) but do not themselves ever acquire legal title to the securities. Dealers, on the other hand, purchase primary securities outright from their issuers and then sell them to the ultimate lenders, bearing, in the process, the risk that they may not be able to find surplus income units willing to pay a price that guarantees them a profit.

Brokers and dealers operate in both the primary securities market and the secondary securities market. The *primary securities market* involves the initial sale of new securities by the deficit spending unit to the surplus income unit whereby the deficit spenders (e.g., investors) acquire the funds needed to purchase the desired capital goods. The *secondary securities market,* on the other hand, involves only the resale of securities (which have already been sold on the primary market) from one surplus income unit (saver) to another. A security sale on the secondary market simply transfers ownership of already outstanding securities, but provides no funds to deficit spending units.[4]

One type of broker-dealer firm of significance is the *investment bank.* Although investment banks now operate extensively in both the primary and secondary securities markets, their prime original function was in the primary market. That function is to aid the issuers of *new* primary securities such as corporations or governments in initially distributing them to surplus income units. The initial distribution of a block of new securities is a highly specialized business requiring sales outlets, capital, and expertise not normally possessed by the issuing organization. The natural result is to call in a specialist — the investment banker.

The investment banker acts as adviser to the security issuer as well as its retailer. At the outset he or she solicits business by going directly to those who need new capital and suggesting means of raising it, as well as negotiating for the right to handle the account. The firm or syndicate of firms that obtains the privilege of distributing the borrower's securities will usually underwrite the sale of the entire issue, assuring the issuer of the funds sought. When underwriting an issue, the investment banker purchases it outright, relying on his or her ability to resell the securities promptly to individuals and other financial institutions at a price high enough to cover the full original cost plus a return for services rendered. In this case, of course, the investment banker is performing as a dealer.

In other cases, such as when the security issuer is new and unknown or if for other reasons the resale of all the securities appear to be in some doubt, the investment banker may refuse to underwrite, agreeing instead to make a "best effort" to find buyers for the securities, but not purchasing them independently or making any guarantee of disposing of all of them. If the banker handles the distribution in this manner, the service performed is only that of a broker.

---

[4] The students must be cautious here, not to confuse *primary securities* with the *primary securities market.* Primary securities, as noted, are instruments such as stocks, bonds, and mortgages that are originally issued by deficit spending units. When initially sold (by the issuer), they are sold on the primary securities market. If they are subsequently sold by the initial buyer (a surplus income unit) to another surplus income unit, the sale is on the secondary securities *market* even though the securities *themselves* are still primary securities.

Success for an investment banking concern thus depends heavily upon two factors: the strength of its sales force and the extent of its access to short-term capital to enable it to "carry" a large issue until it is finally distributed.

The industry includes a number of firms that specialize solely in the investment banking business, plus a number of the larger commercial banks that, in addition to their other activities, operate investment banking departments. Commercial banks, however, have been permitted to provide an investment banking service only in the sale of U.S. government securities and general obligation issues of state and local governments since 1930s legislation barred them from doing so with business securities or state and local government revenue bonds.

The Supporting Role of Stock Exchanges

The willingness of savers to purchase new securities on the primary securities markets depends, in large measure, on the facilities available for selling them to someone else in the future, should the need arise. Providing these facilities (and thereby indirectly promoting the raising of new capital) is the function of over 6,000 broker-dealer firms who participate on the securities exchanges and the over-the-counter market. Investment bankers help to raise new capital for firms and governments. The securities exchanges and over-the-counter markets provide a marketplace wherein "old" securities may readily change hands on the secondary market.

Fundamentally, securities exchanges differ from the over-the-counter market only in that trading in securities listed on the exchange is carried out at auction at a central geographical location, whereas over-the-counter deals — primarily sales of the many securities that are not listed on the exchange — take place through brokers and dealers scattered throughout the nation.

A transaction on the floor of the exchange is initiated by a security owner who, desiring to buy or sell, contacts his or her broker. If the broker's firm is one of the hundreds of members of the exchange, the order is transmitted to the firm's representative on the floor. The representative then goes to the post on the floor, where securities are continuously auctioned off between buyers and sellers, and carries out the purchase or sale. If the broker is not a member of the exchange, the actual transaction must be carried out through a firm that is.

Over-the-counter transactions are often facilitated by the dealer's practice of carrying, on his or her own account, inventories of securities for sale, at a price, to the public. A few of the larger broker-dealer firms, primarily in New York City, act as wholesalers of over-the-counter securities, making continuous markets by standing ready to buy and sell at any time.

The Need For Financial Intermediaries

Direct finance — whereby brokers and dealers help to bring together surplus income units and deficit spending units — plays a very large role in the American economy. But if it were the only available method of bringing savers and investors together, there can be little doubt that a sizable proportion of the nation's savings would never find its way to the investors desiring to borrow it.

Why not? Think about it. If you save some money out of your income and the only avenue available to you to "put your savings to work for you" to earn some income is through purchase of stocks and bonds, how much of it would you commit in this manner? All of it? Careful now, you may want to give that a little more thought. What we are visualizing here is a world in which savers have only three forms in which they may hold their savings — money itself, stocks, and bonds.[5] Under such circumstances many savers might find it in their interests to hold a much larger proportion of their savings in money form than they do currently.

Why hoard money that pays no interest at all rather than lend it out and realize the interest, dividends, and possible capital gains that purchase of stocks and bonds would make possible? There are a number of rational reasons for such a course.

First, there's the matter of *liquidity*. Many people would like to have their savings in a form readily convertible to a more or less fixed number of dollars in case an emergency need or some special bargain opportunity arises. Stocks and bonds, which normally involve some default risk and also have widely varying market values, are usually fairly illiquid.

Second, there's the matter of *costs*. Brokers and dealers charge a fee for their services as middlemen. The minimum fee is often so high that small savers with minimal amounts to lend out would find a significant part of their interest and dividends absorbed by it.

Third, there may easily be a problem with the *minimum denomination sizes* in which many other income earning assets are available. The saver with only a few dollars per week available might have a difficult time finding primary securities that both meet his or her other needs and are available at a low enough unit price to permit purchase. It is true that many stocks have low unit prices but other — especially less risky and more liquid assets — often involve large minimum denomination sizes. A classic example of this is U.S. Treasury bills which, although short term, exceptionally liquid, and with essentially zero default risk, are available only in $10,000 units.

Fourth, sheer *lack of knowledge* about how to go about purchasing stocks and bonds, coupled with inability to evaluate the varying degrees of *risk* involved in the myriad stocks and bonds available, surely is enough to deter many savers.

Given a choice of holding their wealth only in the forms of money or primary securities, many savers — especially the millions of smaller savers — would undoubtedly opt to hold large portions in cash form. And such a development could make those savings unavailable to many potential investors who would like to use them to purchase additional capital goods. For the economy, as we have seen, such a situation could be extremely costly in terms of higher unemployment and lower capital formation rates.

---

[5] They may, of course, choose to hold real wealth also, instead of claims to wealth, but we are restricting the discussion here to claims only.

The Specific Functions of Financial Intermediaries

Fortunately the surplus income unit (saver) in the U.S. economy of the 1990s is not restricted to choosing between nonincome-earning money and direct ownership of primary securities as forms of wealth to hold. In addition, the saver can choose from among a wide range of asset forms issued by the *financial intermediaries.*

Financial intermediaries, as the name suggests, take a position between the ultimate lender (saver) and the ultimate borrower (investor). They acquire the savings of surplus income units by offering them *claims on themselves* (sometimes called "indirect" or "secondary" claims) that are of greater appeal (in terms of liquidity, denomination size, cost of acquisition, risk, and so on) than primary securities. Then they use the funds thus acquired to purchase the primary securities (stocks, bonds, mortgages) issued by the deficit spending units (the investors).

The student must be careful with the terminology here. Brokers, dealers, and investment banks are financial *institutions* that serve only as middlemen to bring savers and investors together. Financial *intermediaries,* on the other hand, are financial institutions that provide savers with claims more suited to their needs and tastes than primary securities.

A wide range of financial intermediaries designed to appeal to savers of practically any taste pattern exists. Those primarily interested in liquidity and safety will likely find such savings institutions as savings departments of commercial banks, mutual savings banks, savings and loan associations, and credit unions most attractive because the savings accounts they offer are highly liquid and, for the most part, insured against loss by the federal government. Having acquired the funds, these so-called thrift institutions then use them to purchase mortgages, bonds, and some other forms of business IOUs issued by investors.

Savers less concerned with liquidity and safety who have shied away from direct purchase of primary securities—because of lack of expertise, fear of the risk of "putting all their eggs in one basket," or prohibitive denomination sizes—may find mutual funds (a form of investment company) the type of financial intermediary that meets their needs. These institutions issue shares that constitute a claim against themselves (usually making it easy to purchase in small denomination sizes) and then use the proceeds to buy primary securities issued by a wide range of investors.[6]

Then, too, there are the financial intermediaries that offer savers specialized protection against the twin risks of dying too soon or living too long beyond their prime earning ages. In the former category are the life insurance companies that collect savings in the form of premium payments and then financially invest them in primary securities. In the latter category are pension plans, which collect

[6] In the previous chapter we learned that one type of mutual fund is the money market fund, wherein the primary securities purchased are predominantly short-term money market instruments. A different kind of mutual fund is one where bonds and/or common stock are the major financial investment.

savings via contributions from covered employees and their employers and then purchase a variety of primary securities.

An Overview of the Financial System

It may be of some benefit to illustrate these distinctions graphically. That is the objective of Figure 2-3. Here savers (on the right side) are depicted as splitting their net savings between the direct purchase of "new" primary securities

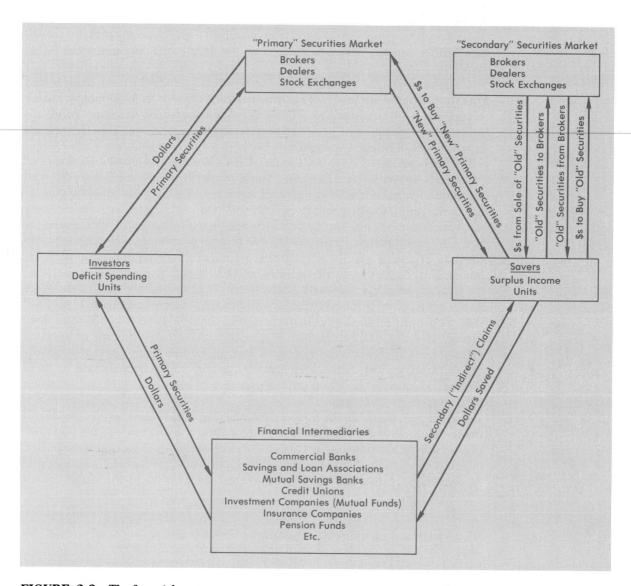

FIGURE 2-3   The financial system

(through brokers and dealers on the "primary" securities market), and the purchase of secondary "indirect" claims (from the financial intermediaries). Investors (on the left side) are shown as collecting needed funds via both the financial intermediaries and broker-dealer firms, issuing in return new primary securities.

In the upper right-hand corner an attempt is made to illustrate the flow of money and "old" securities on the secondary market. Here, householders who wish to buy "old" (previously issued and sold) securities from other householders through brokers and dealers on the stock exchanges carry out their wishes. While such exchanges of old securities do not directly contribute to real investment spending, the ready availability of such a secondary market undoubtedly does encourage more willing participation in the primary market.

The Growth of Intermediation

The process whereby an increasing proportion of overall investment in the economy is financed via the intermediaries is referred to as *intermediation*. Throughout most of the past half century, the U.S. economy has experienced rapidly increasing intermediation, as Table 2-1 and Figure 2-4 make clear.[7]

Note in Table 2-1 that commercial banks still dominate the financial industry, although the degree of dominance has been undercut somewhat by more rapid growth of some of the nonbank intermediaries in the past 40 years. Whereas in

TABLE 2-1 Total assets of selected financial institutions, 1950–1989 (billions of dollars)

Year	Commercial Banks	Savings and Loan Associations	Life Insurance Companies	Pension Plans	Mutual Savings Banks	Investment Companies	Credit Unions
1950	$ 168.9	$ 16.9	$ 64.0	$ 37.8	$ 22.4	$ 3.4	$ 1.0
1955	210.7	37.7	90.4	69.6	30.4	7.4	2.7
1960	257.6	71.5	119.6	108.2	39.6	19.5	5.7
1965	377.3	129.4	158.9	159.4	58.2	38.7	10.6
1970	576.2	179.2	207.3	262.0	79.0	54.7	17.8
1975	964.9	338.2	289.3	405.6	121.1	54.6	38.0
1980	1,537.0	630.7	479.2	859.1	171.6	138.3	71.7
1985	2,328.9	1,072.1	779.9	1,737.7	218.8	490.5	137.2
1989	3,249.6	751.6	1,303.7	2,685.3	498.5	553.9	183.7

Source: Federal Reserve System; Weisenberger Investment Company Service for Investment Co. data prior to 1985.

[7] Despite this long-run tendency, there were some shorter periods during the 1960s and 1970s that were characterized by *disintermediation*—a flow of savings away from intermediaries toward more "direct" finance. These periods were largely the product of the now defunct Regulation Q.

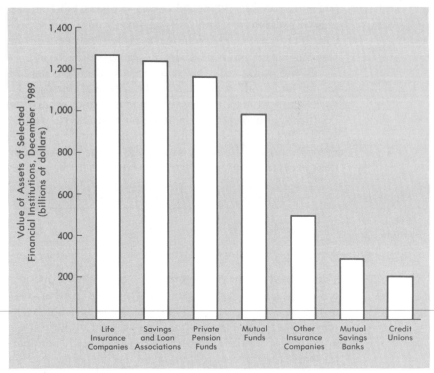

Source: Federal Reserve System.

FIGURE 2-4   **Value of assets of selected financial institutions, December 1989 (billions of dollars)**

1950, commercial bank assets substantially exceeded the assets held by all six of the nonbank institutions listed, by 1989 they were less than 60 percent of the size of those of their six competitors.

Review Questions

1. What economic functions are performed by the "finance" industry?

2. Despite their key role in the capital formation process, the financial intermediaries carry out a relatively small proportion of the nation's investment. Do you agree? Explain carefully.

3. Carefully explain why, in a fully employed economy, saving is an essential prerequisite to capital formation.

4. Distinguish "direct finance" from financing through financial intermediaries.

5. "If there were no financial intermediaries, it is likely that a substantial amount of the money saved would be hoarded rather than made available to investors." Do you agree? Explain carefully.

6. Carefully and completely explain *how* financial intermediaries help to prevent unemployment and increase the rate of capital formation.

7. Why does the statement "saving is an essential prerequisite to capital formation" only hold in an economy with full employment?

8. Distinguish brokers from dealers.

9. "The real, economic effect of saving (in a fully employed economy) is much more profound then merely seeing to it that investors have the money they need to carry out investment spending." Explain.

CHAPTER 3

The Purposes and Characteristics of Financial Markets

Financial markets exist to facilitate the purchase and sale of financial assets. It has become customary to draw a distinction between the *capital market* and the *money market*. The purpose of this chapter is to discuss the characteristics, participants, and functions of these two important types of financial markets.

Capital Market

Capital markets exist to facilitate the exchange of long-term financial assets. Traditionally, "long-term" has been taken to mean financial claims with maturity dates more than one year from the date of issue.

Actually most of our discussion in Chapter 2 was couched in terms of capital market transactions. It is in the capital market that deficit spending units in need of long-term funds find—directly or indirectly—surplus income units who can meet their needs.

Participants in the Capital Market

On one side of the capital market are those deficit spending units that need to obtain funds for periods longer than one year to finance spending in excess of their current incomes. In the main, these units include nonfinancial business firms (desiring to finance the purchase of plant and equipment), the federal government (that borrows to finance budget deficits), and state and local governments (that borrow to finance the building of such social capital as schools, roads, etc.).

On the other side are the surplus income units with funds available to lend out. The overwhelming majority of these funds in the U.S. economy come from the household sector. It is true, of course, that households also borrow to purchase houses and consumer durables. But even after allowing for this, the household sector as a whole is a net saver. Indeed, the household sector is the dominant supplier of funds on the capital market.

But as noted in the preceding chapter, only part of these household funds are *directly* made available to the deficit spending units on the other side.[1] Others come indirectly, through a variety of financial intermediaries. This is the case, as we have seen, because many householders find the secondary claims (time deposits, mutual fund shares, pension rights, etc.) issued by the intermediaries better suited to their needs. What happens here, of course, is that the intermediaries act as a conduit through which to pass these funds on to the deficit spending units.

Financial Instruments on the Capital Market

The financial instruments employed on the capital market are the primary securities referred to in Chapter 2. They are issued by the deficit spending units in return for the funds being raised. Specifically, they include corporate bonds, federal government securities, state and local government securities, corporate equities (or stock), and mortgages.

Table 3-1, which lists the estimated market value of the capital market's outstanding financial instruments as of early 1990, provides some perspective on its overall size.

Corporate Bonds   A corporate bond is a formal IOU of a corporation that guarantees its holder a fixed periodic interest payment plus repayment of the principal on a stated maturity date. The owner of a bond is a creditor of the corporation, and the corporation is required by law to pay all interest due each time period and to repay the full principal at the maturity date.

As with other securities, most corporate bonds are initially sold through

---

TABLE 3-1   Capital market financial instruments outstanding, March 1990 (billions of dollars)

U.S. government securities	$2,598.9
State and local government securities	792.1
Corporation and foreign bonds	1,602.2
Mortgages	3,568.9
Corporation stock	4,335.2

Source: Federal Reserve System.

---

[1] And even then, the middleman services of brokers and dealers are generally required.

TABLE 3-2   Holders of corporation bonds, December 1989 (billions of dollars)

Households	$ 117.2
Life insurance companies	520.4
Private pension funds	144.4
Other insurance companies	79.3
Mutual savings banks	11.5
State and local government pension funds	198.9
Mutual funds	74.1
Foreigners	188.3
Commercial banks	86.8
Savings and loan associations	48.8
Other	32.9
Total	$1,502.6

Source: Federal Reserve System.

brokers and dealers to individuals or financial intermediaries.[2] Although bonds can be, and are, resold on the secondary market, this is done rather infrequently. Most bonds are held to maturity by their original purchasers.

From the corporation's point of view, bonds have several advantages over stock as a source of external funds. One obvious one is the fact that interest paid to bondholders is treated as a cost and thereby deductible for purposes of computing the corporate profits tax. In contrast the dividends on stock are not deductible. Second, when inflation is expected, the commitment to make fixed dollar interest payments plus a fixed dollar principal repayment in the future means making progressively lower payments in real terms.

In recent years, as Table 3-2 makes clear, corporate bonds have had special appeal for life insurance companies, public and private pension funds, and foreigners.

U.S. Government Securities   There are three main types of U.S. government securities: Treasury bills, notes, and bonds. Treasury bills are short-term instruments with maturities between 90 days and 1 year and, as such, will be discussed later as money market instruments. Notes and bonds, on the other hand (which in early 1991 totaled just under $3 trillion), have maturities from 1 to 30 years.

Their advantage to buyers, of course, is the fact that they are free of default risk and that they are highly liquid. As Table 3-3 makes clear, the market for U.S. securities is a very broad one.[3]

---

[2] Those not distributed this way are "privately placed." This means that the entire issue is sold directly to a financial intermediary rather than being advertised for public distribution.

[3] It should be noted that the data in Table 3-3 include holdings of all Treasury debt, including Treasury bills. Also, it includes nonmarketable as well as marketable securities.

TABLE 3-3 U.S. government securities by holder, March 1990 (billions of dollars)	
U.S. government agencies and trust funds	$ 722.7
Federal Reserve banks	219.3
Commercial banks	182.0
Insurance companies	108.0
Other companies	95.0
State and local governments	338.0
Individuals	219.0
Foreigners	386.8
Other	811.1
Total	$3,081.9

Source: Treasury Bulletin.

State and Local Government Securities   State and local government securities are of two different types: general obligation bonds and revenue bonds. General obligation bonds are backed by the full taxing power of the issuing government. Revenue bonds, on the other hand, are generally issued to raise funds for a specific project that earns its own revenue. An example is a toll highway. These bonds are technically backed only by the revenue-earning capacity of the project being financed and not by the full taxing power of the issuing government.[4]

The chief attraction of state and local government securities (popularly referred to as "municipals") is the fact that the interest earned on them is exempt from federal tax. This tax-exempt feature permits them to be sold at interest rates lower than those required to sell taxable securities, thereby lowering state and local government borrowing costs. At the same time, however, it tends to limit the market for them to buyers who can benefit most from the tax-exemption feature. As Table 3-4 demonstrates, this has meant that commercial banks, property and casualty insurance companies, mutual funds, and high-income individuals have pretty much dominated the market for municipals.

Common Stocks   A holder of the common stock of a corporation, unlike a bondholder, is a part owner of the firm. As an owner, the stockholder is in the residual position with no fixed claims to either dividends or repayment of principal.

Common stock, of course, is a much riskier asset than a bond. If the corporation is highly profitable, the return to stockholders (in the form of both dividends and capital gains) can be much higher than that of bondholders. If it is unsuccessful, however, stockholders may get no return at all and even lose their original investment. In recent years, as is clear from Table 3-5, households and pension funds have been the dominant holders of corporate stock.

---

[4] Many governments, however, will choose to bail out a revenue bond issue with tax funds if revenues fall short rather than see it defaulted so the risk may not be as great as on first appearance.

TABLE 3-4   Holdings of state and local government securities, December 1989 (billions of dollars)

Commercial banks	$133.8
Property and casualty insurance companies	135.9
Households	348.5
Life insurance companies	9.2
Mutual funds	93.6
Nonfinancial corporations	9.0
State and local governments	12.2
Savings and loan associations	1.0
Mutual savings banks	1.7
Brokers and dealers	7.1
Other	9.0
Total	$821.2

Source: Federal Reserve System.

Although there is a secondary market for all capital market securities, that for equities—primarily the stock exchanges—is by far the most complete. As noted, this well-developed secondary market adds immensely to the attractiveness of stock. It must be remembered, however, that while the stock exchanges offer a ready market for the trading of stock of a listed corporation *at some price,* they do not protect the owner from the risk of substantial loss if the corporation itself has been unsuccessful.

Mortgages   A mortgage, of course, is a contract whereby the lender provides funds to finance the purchase of real estate in return for the borrower's promise to pay back the principal plus interest over a number of years.

As Table 3-6 indicates, the majority of mortgages are to finance the purchase

TABLE 3-5   Holding of corporate stock, market value, December 1989 (billions of dollars)[a]

Households	$2,613.1
Private pension funds	707.7
Life insurance companies	141.1
Mutual funds	239.5
State and local government pension funds	290.2
Foreigners	257.4
Other	133.1
Total	$4,382.1

[a] Totals include mutual fund shares.
Source: Federal Reserve System.

TABLE 3-6　Mortgages outstanding by type, December 1990 (billions of dollars)	
Single-family home mortgages	$2,690.7
Multifamily residential mortgages	300.2
Commercial mortgages	783.5
Farm mortgages	84.2

Source: Federal Reserve System.

of single-family homes. As of March 1990 over half of single-family home mortgages were being held by commercial banks, savings and loan associations, and mutual savings banks. Commercial mortgages, on the other hand, are owned primarily by life insurance companies and commercial banks, which as of March 1990 held over two-thirds of the total outstanding.

For many years the dominant suppliers of mortgage funds, aside from mortgage pools, have been savings and loan associations and commercial banks. This is still the case, as a glance at Table 3-7 makes clear. However, recent problems in the housing market and (*not* coincidentally) severe difficulties for many savings and loan associations have generated changes in practices and in regulation that are clearly harbingers of change for the future.

Money Market

The so-called "money market" serves a much different function from that of the capital market. While it still involves bringing together deficit spending and surplus income units, it does so for very different reasons.

Whereas the capital market exists primarily to assist the long-term financing of capital (and social) goods, the money market is a short-term market where

TABLE 3-7　Holdings of mortgages, December 1990 (billions of dollars)	
Savings institutions	$　841.8
Commercial banks	809.8
Life insurance companies	267.0
Mortgage pools	1,101.6
Governments	247.7
Households	590.6
Finance companies	48.8
Total	$3,858.6

Source: Federal Reserve System.

economic units with temporary surpluses of money are brought together with units incurring temporary shortages.

Families, businesses, and governments all find it necessary to hold a certain amount of money to bridge the gap between the receipt and the expenditure of income so as to permit a planned rate of expenditure unrestrained by the pattern of receipts. In the normal course of events, however, some units periodically find that they have accumulated more than they need for this purpose, while others periodically encounter temporary shortages. The prime function of the money market is to facilitate transactions between these two groups.

The transfer is accomplished via the use of a variety of short-term financial instruments issued by the borrowers. It has become customary to consider financial claims with a maturity of one year or less to be money market instruments, although the vast majority are 90 days or less. Among the more important money market instruments are U.S. Treasury bills, federal funds, negotiable certificates of deposit, banker's acceptances, commercial paper, and Eurodollars. These instruments are primarily the liabilities of the government, banks, or large business firms and, hence, involve only minimal default risk. Their liquidity is further enhanced by the fact that their short term forestalls major changes in value due to interest rate swings and that their markets are sufficiently broad to permit a large volume of transactions with only small effects on rates.[5]

Participants in the Money Market

The borrowers on the money market (sellers of money market instruments) include, among others, the U.S. Treasury, nonfinancial corporations, finance companies, commercial banks, and other depository institutions. The lenders (buyers of money market instruments) include some of the same institutions—such as commercial banks and nonfinancial corporations, plus such others as state and local governments, foreign banks, financial intermediaries, and (in large part, indirectly through financial intermediaries) individuals. Likely to appear on either side of the market depending upon the direction of monetary policy and a truly dominant factor on the market is the Federal Reserve System.

"Making the market," or playing the role of middleman, are a host of institutions including some of the largest commercial banks in New York, a group of 40-odd government securities dealers, a number of commercial paper dealers, and a variety of other specialized dealers and brokers.

Financial Instruments on the Money Market

As noted, money market instruments consist of a variety of claims with less than one year to maturity. As a rule, they are also easily marketable so that, to a holder, both their short term and their ready marketability provide them a very high

---

[5] This entire section owes a heavy debt to that excellent publication, *Instruments of the Money Market*, 5th ed., edited by Timothy Q. Cook and Bruce J. Summers and published by the Federal Reserve Bank of Richmond, 1981.

degree of *liquidity*. In this section, we shall briefly discuss the major characteristics of some of the more important money market instruments.[6]

U.S. Treasury Bills Without question, the most important money market instrument of all is the U.S. government *Treasury bill*. Treasury bills are the shortest-term U.S. security, and they, together with notes and bonds (discussed earlier under capital market instruments), make up the U.S. national debt.

Treasury bills are issued weekly in denominations of no less than $10,000 (although above the initial $10,000 minimum, they can be acquired in multiples of $5,000). At the weekly offerings, both 91-day and 182-day bills are offered, while on a monthly basis, bills with a one-year maturity are offered.

The interest rate paid on a Treasury bill issue is determined via competitive bidding. Persons or institutions desiring to make competitive bids state, in advance of that week's auction, the quantity of bills desired and the price they will pay. Since the bills always return $10,000 at maturity, the difference between that and the amount bid constitutes the interest earned for successful bidders.

Individuals desiring to purchase Treasury bills may do so on a noncompetitive basis by agreeing to accept the average interest yield arrived at by competitive bidders. Such noncompetitive purchases may be obtained directly from a Federal Reserve bank (where the auctions are held) by filing the appropriate form prior to the auction itself.

As Figure 3-1 shows, about one-fifth of the marketable U.S. securities held by private investors as of mid-1990 consisted of Treasury bills.

Federal Funds Depository institutions are required to maintain reserves to back up their outstanding deposit liabilities in the form of vault cash and/or as deposits at their district Federal Reserve banks.[7] Many years ago commercial banks with excess reserves (i.e., deposits at the Federal Reserve bank in excess of those required to back up their own outstanding deposit liabilities) began the practice of making overnight loans of excess reserves to other banks needing them. This was the beginning of the federal funds market.

Since these beginnings, the market has expanded enormously to include short-term loans of all "immediately available funds." Such immediately available funds include not only accounts at Federal Reserve banks but also "collected liabilities of commercial banks and other depository institutions."[8]

The majority of federal funds loans are overnight, with, for example, the Federal Reserve bank transferring ownership of the funds from the lending bank to the borrower for one day. On the following day, the transaction is reversed and the borrower pays interest at the federal funds rate.

The market now includes a number of large commercial banks with a standing offer to purchase all federal funds offered. Consequently, a ready market always exists for any such "immediately available funds."

---

[6] Although they constitute an important money market instrument, because they were discussed in Chapter 1, we will not reconsider RPs here.

[7] The depository institutions subject to these reserve requirements are commercial banks, savings and loan associations, mutual savings banks, and credit unions.

[8] Seth P. Maerowitz, "Federal Funds," in Cook and Summers, *Instruments of the Money Market*, p. 42.

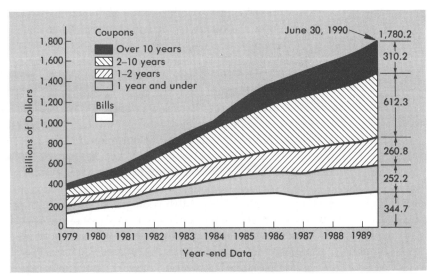

Source: Treasury Bulletin.

FIGURE 3-1   **Private holdings of treasury marketable debt by maturity**

Negotiable Certificates of Deposit   Negotiable certificates of deposit (CDs) are short-term certificates in denominations of $100,000 or more issued by commercial banks primarily to nonfinancial businesses who deposit funds with them.[9] These certificates, which are really a special form of time deposit, have maturities of from a minimum of 2 weeks to 12 months, with an average of around 3 months.

Certificates of deposit emerged as a significant source of bank funds and as an important money market instrument in the 1960s after an efficient secondary market for their resale developed. To be eligible for trading on the secondary market, CDs must be in minimum denominations of $1 million or more. As of April 1991, negotiable CDs issued by commercial banks totaled over $397 billion.

Banker's Acceptances   Banker's acceptances most commonly are created in the process of financing international trade. For example, a U.S. bank may issue a "letter of credit" on behalf of an American company planning to import goods. The letter of credit authorizes a foreign exporting company to draw up a "bill of exchange," calling for payment for the goods being sold, by the bank rather than the importing company. This bill of exchange is then sent to the U.S. bank that "accepts" this obligation to pay for the goods—usually within 90 days—by signing its acceptance on the face of the instrument. At this point the bill of exchange becomes an acceptance—a valuable document that is salable in the secondary market for acceptances. This market, located primarily in New York City, involves some 15 to 20 large firms, most of which also deal in U.S. securities.

---

[9] We ignore here CDs issued by thrift institutions, most of which are nonnegotiable, and Eurodollar CDs. For an interesting account on them, see Bruce J. Summers, "Negotiable Certificates of Deposit," in Cook and Summers, *Instruments of the Money Market*, pp. 73–93.

The acceptance market is much smaller than those for other instruments discussed, with only about $53 billion outstanding in early 1991.

Commercial Paper Commercial paper consists of short-term, unsecured IOUs issued by large, well-known corporations that are sold to dealers or directly to financial institutions. Among the issuers, financial companies were responsible for nearly 75 percent of the commercial paper outstanding in early 1991.

Commercial paper is generally offered in denominations of $100,000 or more and has a maturity date averaging about 30 days. While the issuers must be reasonably large and well known to command a market, the major buyers include money market mutual funds, large commercial banks, pension funds, state and local governments, and investment companies.

Commercial paper can be sold either directly to a buyer or to a dealer firm which resells it. The dealer firms are primarily large securities firms or components of bank holding companies that also deal in U.S. securities. The market has grown remarkably in recent years, almost doubling since 1985, reaching a total outstanding of about $600 billion by the beginning of 1991.

Eurodollars As stated in Chapter 1, Eurodollars are deposits, denominated in dollars, but held in banks outside the United States. For example, suppose that an Englishman is paid for goods sold to the United States via a mechanism that gives him a checking account in a U.S. bank. If he does not wish to convert this dollar deposit to pounds immediately, he may transfer ownership of it to his London bank in exchange for a dollar-denominated deposit claim against that bank that pays him interest. The London bank now possesses the deposit in the U.S. bank and may lend it out to any bank, foreign or American, or to any nonbank borrower.

Review Questions

1. Carefully distinguish between the capital market and the money market.

2. On the capital market, who are the most important participants and what are the major types of financial instruments used?

3. Distinguish among U.S. Treasury bonds, notes, and bills. Which type of U.S. security fits best in the money market?

4. Identify
   a. Federal funds
   b. Negotiable certificates of deposit
   c. Banker's acceptances
   d. Commercial paper
   e. Eurodollars

5. Distinguish the two major types of state and local government securities. What is the special attraction of all municipals to savers?

6. What are the most important financial instruments traded on the money market?

CHAPTER 4

Characteristics of Selected Nonbank Financial Institutions

Although our major emphasis in the remainder of this book will be on the nature, functions, and control of commercial banks, it will be useful to acquire at least a superficial understanding of the chief characteristics of some of the more important nonbank financial institutions. To that end, this chapter examines several of them.

To distinguish between commercial banks and the other major financial institutions used to be quite a simple matter. Although all perform the crucial role of middlemen between savers and investors and despite the fact that commercial banks have always carried out many of the same specific functions as other intermediaries, one function could always be singled out as being unique to commercial banks. That was the authority to accept and create demand deposits — money itself. Prior to the 1970s, exceptions to the rule that "only commercial banks can offer checking accounts" were so rare and unimportant that one could comfortably distinguish between commercial banks and other financial institutions on that criterion alone.

But all that began changing dramatically in the 1970s. NOW accounts were first issued in 1972 by a mutual savings bank in Massachusetts and soon spread to other states and other depository institutions. Shortly thereafter, in 1974, share draft accounts first appeared at credit unions and spread rapidly. Clearly, with developments such as these, the monopoly that commercial banks once had on the issuance of checking accounts has long since disappeared. These innovations, along with some others to be discussed in the paragraphs that follow, have been part of an ongoing process whereby all the depository institutions have tended to become more alike.

Despite these important changes, however, commercial banks still remain sufficiently dominant in the provision of checkable deposits to set them apart. For example, in January 1991, commercial banks were responsible for $491 billion of the total $594 billion of checking accounts and other checkable deposits in circulation — about 83 percent of the total. We shall rely on their continued dominance in this area as a distinguishing characteristic that still sets commercial banks sufficiently apart from the other financial institutions to warrant separate coverage. Here we consider some major characteristics of several nonbank financial institutions.

Savings and Loan Associations

Savings and loan associations (S&Ls) first appeared in the United States in 1831. Originally called "building and loan" associations, they were for many years truly voluntary associations devoted almost exclusively to the financing of home building. Over the years their operations formalized and they were brought under the regulatory control first of state governments and then under the federal government's control in 1933. At least until the 1980s, this regulation consisted primarily of directing savings and loan portfolio practices toward support of a firmly entrenched aspect of social policy in the United States — the encouragement of home ownership. As a result, saving and loan associations have long been considered highly specialized financial institutions, preoccupied almost completely with mortgages and financing the construction industry. And although the financial deregulation begun in 1980 has reduced this specialization somewhat, savings and loan associations have remained predominantly mortgage-granting institutions.

Like commercial banks, savings and loan associations can receive their charters from either federal or state governments. A federally chartered association becomes subject to the control and supervision of the Office of Thrift Supervision, a government agency with a relationship to savings and loan associations not unlike that of the Federal Reserve System to its member banks. Federally insured associations are required to join the Federal Home Loan Bank System. As of 1988 slightly more than half the 2,328 insured savings associations were state chartered, but the federally chartered associations, being larger on average, held almost 60 percent of the industry's assets.

All federally chartered associations are required to subscribe for the deposit insurance provided by the Federal Deposit Insurance Corporation. FDIC coverage, which offers insurance up to the limit of $100,000 per deposit, is also available to state-chartered associations.

A consolidated balance sheet for savings and loan associations (including some mutual savings banks) is shown in Table 4-1. What should be noted is the preponderance of mortgages among their assets and the dominance of savings accounts among their liabilities. The savings and loan industry encountered severe difficulties during the decade of the 1980s when their numbers fell from about 4,000 to around 2,500. This decline is still continuing during the 1990s. We shall consider the savings and loan industry's problems in detail in Chapter 5.

A glance at Table 4-2 makes clear that savings banks, like savings and loan associations, specialize in mortgage finance. Indeed, the distribution of assets and liabilities shown there is remarkably similar to that of the S&Ls.

What, then, does distinguish them? For many years the argument was that

TABLE 4-1   Consolidated balance sheet for Savings Association Insurance Fund – Insured institutions, January 1991[a] (billions)

Assets		Liabilities and net worth	
Mortgages	$ 624.6	Savings accounts	$ 823.5
Mortgage-backed securities	151.5	Borrowings	187.3
Commercial loans	23.7	Other liabilities and net worth	54.1
Consumer loans	46.6		
Cash and investment securities	140.6		
Other assets	77.9		
Total	$1,064.9	Total	$1,064.9

[a] Includes savings banks.
Source: Federal Reserve System.

savings banks were most concerned with the mobilizing of funds (savings) and the providing of a return to depositors and shareholders. They are thrift institutions first, and, by implication, housing financiers second. Savings and loan associations, on the other hand, were said to reverse these priorities, with home financing their central focus.

Whatever truth there may have been in such distinctions in the past, this has tended to become less and less accurate as the years have passed and in the 1990s it is entirely reasonable to look upon savings and loan associations and savings banks as essentially interchangeable.

Credit Unions

Credit unions are nonprofit, voluntary associations of people with a common bond that organize to collect savings deposits (more technically, "shares") from their members and put these deposits to work primarily via consumer loans to

TABLE 4-2   Consolidated balance sheet for Savings Association Insurance Fund – Insured federal savings banks, January 1991 (billions of dollars)

Assets		Liabilities and net worth	
Mortgages	$316.9	Savings accounts	$428.8
Mortgage-backed securities	79.5	Borrowings	102.3
Commercial loans	17.3	Other liabilities and net worth	36.3
Consumer loans	31.2		
Cash and investment securities	71.1		
Other assets	51.4		
Total	$567.4	Total	$567.4

Source: Federal Reserve System.

their own members. Originally organized in Germany as institutions to encourage thrift and to make available inexpensive loans to lower- and middle-income people, credit unions, while still small in absolute size, have shown among the most rapid rates of growth of all the financial institutions in the past quarter century. (See Table 4-3.)

The members of a credit union must share a common bond, such as working for a common employer, belonging to the same labor union or religious group, or living in the same area, although recently authorities have broadened the definition of "common bond" substantially.[1]

Credit unions can operate with either a federal or a state charter. Federal credit unions, which in recent years have controlled about two-thirds of the industry's total assets, are regulated and assisted by the National Credit Union Administration, a federal government agency set up for this specific purpose. Insurance, up to $100,000 per account, is provided by the National Credit Union Share Insurance Fund. Federally chartered credit unions are required to subscribe for this insurance, and, while many state CUs do also, many others are insured by agencies set up by the state that chartered them.

As noted, many credit unions offer their shareholders checking accounts in the form of *share draft accounts*. Share draft accounts are considered to be interest-earning savings accounts on which checks can be written, although, like NOW accounts, they are subject to the reserve requirements applied to transactions accounts by the Monetary Control Act of 1980.

Credit unions, while in the aggregate still the smallest of the thrift institutions, have been growing more rapidly than the others in recent years. There are a number of reasons for this rapid growth.

First, credit unions, being no longer subject to any Regulation Q-type con-

---

TABLE 4-3 Consolidated balance sheet for federally insured credit unions, December 1989 (billions of dollars)

Assets		Liabilities and net worth	
Cash and deposits	$ 38.5	Shares (deposits)	$187.0
U.S. government securities	12.1	Other liabilities	18.8
U.S. agency securities	6.3		
Mortgages	45.6		
Consumer loans	90.9		
Other assets	12.4		
Total	$199.7	Total	$205.8

Source: Federal Reserve System.

---

[1] For example, "Today, Groups from Feminists to Former Drug Addicts Have Their Own Credit Unions," *The Wall Street Journal*, June 22, 1977, p. 22.

trols on the interest paid on regular savings accounts, have tended to pay more than have competitive thrifts. But more than that, they have tended to charge somewhat lower rates on consumer loans to their members.

How can they do this? Credit unions have a number of cost advantages over their rivals. First, they often operate with significant subsidies, ranging from free services from volunteer officers to free office space and services such as payroll deduction provided by an employer. Second, their small homogeneous size often sharply reduces the cost in checking on the credit rating of prospective borrowers. Third, and perhaps most important, because of their nonprofit status, they pay no federal taxes.

Despite their impressive growth in recent years and recent legislation authorizing them to diversify their activities greatly, it does not seem likely that credit unions will ever challenge their rival thrifts in size. This is the case because despite the fact that the law now authorizes them to offer share drafts and credit cards and to finance mortgages, relatively few of them do so. Despite the fact that mortgages now comprise almost a quarter of their assets, most credit unions continue to function in accordance with their major original purpose — to serve small savers.

The major assets and liabilities of credit unions as of December 1989 are presented in Table 4-3.

Life Insurance Companies

Life insurance companies, which in the United States date back to 1759, sell substantially more than liquidity and an income on savings. It seems safe to argue that the vast majority of the savers who channel large portions of their incomes each year to life insurance premium payments do so more for risk protection than for direct income or liquidity.

To the policyholder, life insurance represents a type of protection, especially in the early years of family formation, that savings accounts or the direct or indirect purchase of stocks and bonds normally cannot provide. Savings, sent to the insurance company in the form of premium payments, do provide some liquidity for emergencies in the form of the policy's accumulated cash value or policy loans against it. But the prime motivating factor is undoubtedly the much greater face value of the policy available for the policyholder's dependents in the case of his or her untimely death.

This fact, plus the contractual nature of most of the premium payments and the substantially more liberal regulatory legislation, permits the insurance company portfolio manager a great deal more discretion than his or her counterpart in a mutual savings bank or savings and loan association.

Liquidity is a much less restraining influence. This is due partly to the fact that policyholders do not normally look upon their accumulated cash value as liquid savings to be drawn upon except in the direst of emergencies and partly to the fact that the annual inflow of funds to an insurance company is largely in the form of contractual premium payments — an inflow that can be depended on much more confidently than an inflow of savings deposits in other savings institutions.

TABLE 4-4 Assets of life insurance companies, December 1990 (billions of dollars)	
U.S. government securities	$ 180.2
State and local government securities	12.0
Corporate and foreign bonds	612.6
Mortgages	267.9
Corporation stock	128.6
Other assets	210.6
Total	$1,411.9

Source: Federal Reserve System.

As Table 4-4 indicates, life insurance companies are heavy purchasers of corporate bonds, with almost half of their total assets committed to such securities. The other major component of their portfolios is mortgages, which constituted just under one-fifth of their 1990 assets. Unlike the other major mortgage-granting institutions, it is interesting to note that life insurance companies specialize primarily in financing multifamily and commercial construction rather than single-family home building.

Investment Companies (Mutual Funds)

Investment companies sell shares to savers and then use the proceeds to purchase a wide variety of primary securities. To the saver, investment company shares constitute something of a middle ground between savings accounts on the one hand and the direct purchase of corporate or government securities on the other. As compared with savings accounts, some investment company shares have recently offered a substantially higher return with little loss of liquidity. Similarly, as compared with the direct purchase of securities, investment company shares offer a degree of diversification of risk that the small saver could hardly obtain on his or her own, plus the experienced market knowledge of a specialized management that makes the basic financial investment decisions.

There are two kinds of investment companies—closed end and open end. A closed-end company generally issues only a certain fixed amount of its own common stock and uses this, plus whatever additional capital is raised by borrowing, to purchase operating company securities. Its common stock is then bought and sold on the stock exchange, and the individual saver who wants to purchase more of it must do so from somebody else on the exchange. Similarly, a present owner of a share of a closed-end investment company can only "get his money out" by selling it to someone else on the exchange. Closed-end companies constitute only a very small fraction of the investment company industry, however, and we shall consequently ignore them in the remaining discussion.

An open-end investment company (popularly referred to as a "mutual fund"), on the other hand, will issue new shares of its own stock to anyone who

TABLE 4-5   Assets of all mutual funds
except money market funds, December 1989
(billions of dollars)

Cash and deposits	$ 8.5
Corporate stocks	239.5
U.S. government securities	120.0
State and local government securities	93.6
Corporate and foreign bonds	74.1
Other assets	19.4
Total	$555.1

Source: Federal Reserve System.

desires to purchase them. Consequently, the total assets of a successful open-end company tend to grow at the discretion of savers in contrast to the closed-end company, which maintains only a fixed amount of stock outstanding. (See Table 4-5.) A second major difference is that owners of mutual fund shares may redeem them for cash at any time by turning them in to the company. The amount paid for redemption depends upon the market value of the company's portfolio of securities at the time, which may, of course, be greater than or less than the amount originally paid in.

There is a mutual fund to suit almost any saver's preference. For those more interested in long-run growth of their wealth than in current return, there are a large number of *growth* funds that specialize primarily in common stock considered likely to provide significant capital appreciation. For savers looking for a bit less risk, there are what are called *balanced* funds with portfolios split between stocks and bonds. Those to whom a relatively high current income is paramount would find *income* funds an appropriate choice. Income funds, as might be guessed, tend to purchase stocks and bonds offering relatively high current dividends and interest but possessing relatively lower growth potential. And some high-income taxpayers would be likely to find the *municipal bond* (or *tax-exempt*) funds to their liking. These, as the name implies, specialize in the purchase of state and local government securities, the income from which is exempt from the federal income tax.

The newest, and in some ways most interesting, type of mutual fund is the *money market mutual fund* (MMMF). Introduced in 1972, MMMF assets had grown to about $4 billion by 1978. From that point they literally took off, exploding to well over $200 billion within the next four years.

What explained this remarkable growth? Without question Regulation Q-type interest rate ceilings, limiting the interest depository institutions could pay to their time depositors, played the leading role. Prior to the advent of money market mutual funds, Regulation Q ceilings discriminated sharply against small savers. For savers in sufficiently high income brackets to permit purchase of unregulated short-term instruments despite their imposing minimum denomination sizes (generally $10,000 and up), the governmentally imposed ceilings represented no barrier to the higher market returns available elsewhere in the money market. But for the majority of smaller savers who were unable to come

TABLE 4-6 Assets of money market mutual funds, December 1989 (billions of dollars)	
Time deposits	$ 41.2
Foreign deposits	26.4
Repurchase agreements	54.9
U.S. government securities	35.8
Commercial paper	186.6
Tax-exempt obligations	69.4
Other	13.8
Total	$428.1

Source: Federal Reserve System.

up with such large sums, few alternatives to the artificially low returns available at savings institutions existed.

Money market mutual funds offered small savers a way around these Regulation Q barriers. Generally speaking, one can join a MMMF for an initial minimum outlay of $500 to $2,000, after which additions can be made in very small amounts. In most cases, there is no charge for getting into or out of a fund. Once acquired, an account at a MMMF is exceptionally liquid. Not only can it be cashed in at any time without penalty, but in most cases shareholders are permitted to write checks on their accounts.[2]

When in late 1982 Congress authorized depository institutions to offer competing money market deposit accounts, there was some question whether money market mutual funds could survive the competition. Indeed, they did fall off sharply in 1983, but by the following year their assets topped $200 billion again, and in April 1991, they totaled over $370 billion. Table 4-6 shows the composition of their portfolios as of December 1989.

In conclusion, the following assessment seems reasonably safe. With Regulation Q phased out and money market deposit accounts definitely in, a prime reason for the rapid growth of money market mutual funds has been eliminated. But the money market fund has proved itself to be a viable institution performing a unique and valuable intermediary service. It appears likely to be with us for the indefinite future.

Pension Funds

In terms of total assets as well as rate of growth, pension plans rank among the most important of the financial institutions. As of the beginning of 1990, the value of the assets held by private and governmental pension funds exceeded $2.8 trillion.

[2] Most money market mutual funds limit check writing privileges to checks in excess of $500.

TABLE 4-7   Total assets of public and private pension funds, December 31, 1989 (billions of dollars)

All private pension funds		$1,901.1
Insured funds	737.6	
Noninsured funds	1,163.5	
All public pension funds		956.3
U.S. government	228.9	
State and local government	727.4	

Source: Federal Reserve System.

Pension funds can be conveniently divided into three categories. As Table 4-7 indicates, as of the end of 1989, those administered by the federal, state, and local governments held $956 billion of assets, private funds administered by insurance companies held $738 billion, and private "noninsured" funds, managed by trustees, held over $1,163 billion.

The federal government funds devote the majority of their assets to U.S. government securities, but all the others concentrate most heavily on corporate securities. The distribution of assets of the private noninsured funds as of December 1989 is shown in Table 4-8.

Finance Companies

Finance companies operate primarily at two levels. Consumer finance companies make personal loans directly to individuals, whereas business finance companies do their lending to, or on behalf of, business firms.

TABLE 4-8   Assets of private, noninsured pension funds, December 1989 (billions of dollars)

Cash and demand deposits	$ 6.1
Time deposits	52.3
Corporation stock	707.7
U.S. government securities	92.5
U.S. agency securities	50.3
Corporate and foreign bonds	144.4
Commercial paper	48.6
Mortgages	6.6
Other	55.0
Total	$1,108.5

Source: Federal Reserve System.

Consumer loans are generally quite small, with short maturities. Because the average size of a loan is so small, creating significant diseconomies of scale in terms of administration costs, and because the risk is large, consumer finance loans typically carry high interest charges. For example, the average interest rate charged by automobile finance companies on used car loans in February 1991 was 15.9 percent per year.

In addition to making personal loans, finance companies work through business firms to finance the sale of large consumer durables. In the sale of an automobile, for example, the finance company specifies the required down payment, the maturity, and the interest rate but allows the car dealer to draw up the necessary papers with the car buyer when an automobile is bought on credit. If the car buyer fails to keep up the payments, the most common procedure is for the finance company to repossess the car and resell it to the dealer for the unpaid balance of the loan.

Finance companies also provide funds directly to businesses to help them to carry their accounts receivable. This can take the form of a loan to the business firm, with its (the borrowing firm's) accounts receivable serving as collateral. In some cases, however, the finance company simply purchases the right to collect the borrowing firm's accounts receivable and then collects them itself. The customers who owed the borrowing company are generally notified that their obligation is now to the finance company.

In late 1990, the assets of all finance companies totaled over $500 billion, with about half being loans to business and the most of the rest loans to consumers. Of the former, more than half the total was for the purchase of automobiles.

Finance companies acquire most of their funds through the sale of long-term bonds but also rely heavily on the issuance of their own commercial paper and on bank loans. In late 1990, for example, their liabilities included about $239 billion in bonds issued and $149 billion in commercial paper, and $16 billion borrowed from banks. These sources were, of course, liberally supplemented by capital and surplus accounts of just under $42 billion.

Review Questions

1. What are the common characteristics of the so-called thrift institutions?

2. How might an increase in the use of adjustable rate mortgages help to ease the problems of U.S. thrift institutions?

3. Why has the mutual savings bank industry lost ground (relatively) to many other financial industries during the past 50 years?

4. How might the spectacular recent growth in credit unions be explained?

5. Carefully distinguish between investment companies and investment bankers.

6. How might one explain the rapid growth of money market mutual funds in the late 1970s and early 1980s? Do you believe that the removal of Regulation Q-type ceilings will eliminate the money market funds? Why or why not?

7. What legislation is most responsible for the emphasis on mortgages by savings and loan associations?

8. "The major problem of savings and loan associations in the 1980s was a mismatch in the maturities of their assets and liabilities." Explain carefully.

9. What developments have improved the profitability of the savings and loan industry since 1985?

10. Distinguish money market mutual funds from other types of mutual funds.

11. What was the role of Regulation Q in explaining the growth of money market mutual funds?

The Savings and Loan Debacle of the 1980s

Before we turn in the next six chapters to an intensive consideration of the commercial banking industry, it seems appropriate to devote one chapter to a detailed look at the causes and consequences of a financial disaster so vast and so costly as to be widely recognized as the most expensive in our nation's history. The disaster referred to, of course, is the near total collapse of the savings and loan industry.

Just how much will this debacle cost U.S. taxpayers? We will not know the exact cost for many years but the most widely accepted estimate as this is being written is $500 billion.[1]

Now in a period when we glibly speak of a $3 trillion national debt and a near $6 trillion GNP, it is extremely difficult for the average person to conceptualize the significance of a $500 billion hit on taxpayers. Perhaps the best way to put it into some kind of focus is to see how it compares with some other national totals.

One writer has put it this way:

> Why isn't anyone upset about this?
>
> Here are some other comparisons with that $500 billion bailout:
>
> The entire cost of World War II, in current dollars and including service-connected veterans' benefits, is about $460 billion. That's $40 billion less than the bailout.
>
> The cost of the Vietnam War, including benefits, stands at $172 billion. Korea was $70 billion. World War I was $63 billion. The Civil War was $7 billion — $1\frac{1}{2}$ percent of the cost of the savings-and-loan debacle.
>
> The National Cancer Institute spent $1.3 billion on cancer research last year. The National Institutes for Health spent $582 million on heart disease, $171 mil-

[1] This figure includes not only the cost of paying off insured depositors at failed savings and loan associations but also the interest cost incurred by borrowing most of that money now and paying it off over time.

lion on lung disease, $170 million on blood disease. Add them up: Less than one-half of 1% of the S&L money.

Why isn't anyone upset?

Across the country, corporations, foundations and individuals give away about $100 billion a year. In other words, if every charitable gift from every company, every foundation, every living human, and the will of everyone who died this year were earmarked to bail out the savings-and-loan industry, it wouldn't be enough to handle the cost even without worrying about the interest on that cost.

If you add up the budget of every state, you get total expenditures of about $450 billion, or at least you do if you add up the fiscal 1987 figures, the latest I could find. Again, less than the savings-and-loan bailout.

You get the idea. It's hard to find anything in this country — or in history — as costly as the savings-and-loan scandal. No war, no defense program, no social program, no other scandal has ever cost what this will cost.[2]

The Background to the Savings and Loan Crisis

As noted in the preceding chapter, savings and loan associations originated as institutions specializing in collecting savings via savings accounts and time deposits and channeling most of those funds to the financing of home building. Federal and state law and regulations essentially required this sort of specialization and, prior to the late 1970s and early 1980s, the industry flourished. Evidence to this effect is shown in Table 5-1. In fact, during the 1960–1975 period, the total assets of FSLIC-insured savings institutions nearly quintupled while those of commercial banks rose by a little over $3\frac{1}{2}$ times and those of life insurance companies and investment companies rose by only $2\frac{1}{2}$ times.

One small part of the reason for the early prosperity of savings institutions was the fact that the federal government's firm commitment to encouraging home ownership in the nation gave them an edge in attracting depositors. From 1933 until 1966, commercial banks were limited by the so-called Regulation Q in the interest they could pay to depositors while savings institutions were not.[3] Consequently, it was not uncommon for savings institutions to pay depositors 1 to 2 percent more than commercial banks.[4] And even after Regulation Q-type

---

[2] Michael Gartner, "Biggest Robbery in History — You're the Victim," *The Wall Street Journal*, August 9, 1990. While the quote does a good job of dramatizing the enormity of the cost of the savings and loan debacle, the reader must be cautious not to be misled. In the first place, note that the costs of past wars are reported in *current* dollar terms. That is, they are not adjusted for the difference in price levels in the different years. Second, the out-of-pocket costs of those wars listed probably do not include the interest cost involved in paying for them. A fairer comparison might have been with the most common current estimate of the out-of-pocket cost (not counting interest costs) of the savings and loan crisis — about $150 billion. Even with these adjustments, however, the cost of the crisis is staggering.

[3] In fact, however, during much of this period Regulation Q interest rate ceilings were essentially ineffective as ceilings because they were set above market rates. It was not until the mid-1960s that Regulation Q ceilings effectively prevented most commercial banks from paying depositors higher interest returns.

[4] See Norman Strunk and Fred Case, *Where Deregulation Went Wrong* (Washington, D.C.: U.S. League of Savings Institutions, 1988). Much of the material in this chapter is drawn from this ex-

TABLE 5-1 Selected data on FSLIC-insured savings institutions, 1960–1975

Year	Number of savings institution	Total assets (billions)	Return on equity (percent)
1960	4,098	$ 67.4	12.35%
1965	4,508	124.6	9.83
1970	4,365	170.6	8.02
1975	4,078	330.3	7.82

Source: Savings Institutions Sourcebook, United States League of Savings Institutions.

interest rate ceilings were imposed on savings institutions starting in 1966, they were permitted to pay $\frac{1}{4}$ to $\frac{1}{2}$ percent more than commercial banks.

But attracting depositors, while necessary, does not guarantee operation at a profit. Much more important ingredients of the favorable pre-1980s environment for savings institutions were the relatively low rates of inflation along with the associated low and stable rates of interest. Table 5-2 provides evidence of this. With economic conditions such as these, short-term interest rates (those savings institutions had to *pay* to depositors) were consistently well below long-term interest rates (those savings institutions *received* on their mortgages) so that the average savings and loan association was operated at a comfortable profit.[5]

TABLE 5-2 Rates of inflation and short-term interest, selected years

Year	Percent change in GNP deflator	Average Treasury bill interest rate
1950	2.0%	1.2%
1955	3.2	1.8
1960	1.6	2.9
1965	2.7	4.0

cellent study and from Michael Dotsey and Anatole Kuprianov, "Reforming Deposit Insurance: Lessons from the Savings and Loan Crisis" in the *Economic Review,* Federal Reserve Bank of Richmond, March–April, 1990.

[5] In fact, prior to passage of the Housing Act of 1968, savings and loan associations were prohibited from offering "deposits" with fixed interest rates. Instead savers got "share accounts" with a statement of "anticipated dividends." In effect, they could hardly lose because they only paid savers amounts which their earnings permitted. See Strunk and Case, *Where Deregulation Went Wrong,* p. 26.

The Decade of the 1980s —
S&L Disaster in Two Waves

Unfortunately for the savings and loan industry, as well as ultimately for the taxpayers, this comfortable and profitable environment could not be maintained into the decade of the 1980s. In fact, it turned out to be the most disastrous 10 years in the industry's history.

The problems that beset the industry arose in two waves with quite different core causes. As Table 5-3 makes clear, what we had were serious losses in 1981 and 1982, then a period of apparent recovery (capped by the second most profitable year in the industry's history in 1985), followed by a plunge into seemingly incalculable disaster in the final years of the decade.

The problem in 1981 and 1982 has been widely attributed to skyrocketing interest rates and the long-entrenched savings and loan practice of "borrowing short and lending long." This problem, which we shall consider in more detail in the next section, was thought to be short run and correctible once interest rates were brought down. And, indeed, in the mid-1980s that view seemed, for a while, to have been confirmed. But then in the last three years of the decade, the bottom fell out — this time because of a dramatic decline in the quality of S&L assets.

We shall consider these two "waves of failure" separately in the paragraphs that follow because, in fact, their core causes *were* different. Despite this separate treatment, however, it is important that the reader understand that the two periods of failure and loss are related if for no other reason than the fact that the 1981–1982 losses left many S&Ls in such a weakened condition as to be easy prey for later developments undermining asset values.

TABLE 5-3 Savings and loan industry failures and net income, 1980–1989

Year	Number of failures	Industry net income after taxes (millions)
1980	11	$ 781
1981	28	−4,631
1982	63	−4,142
1983	36	1,945
1984	22	1,013
1985	31	3,720
1986	46	132
1987	47	−7,779
1988	205	−12,057
1989	328	N.A.

N.A. = not available.

Source: Savings Institution Sourcebook for net income and *The Wall Street Journal*, November 2, 1990, for failures.

The First Wave — The Early 1980s

In the latter 1970s, for the second time in less than a decade, the OPEC countries quadrupled oil prices, and that, along with a probably excessively expansionary monetary policy earlier in the decade and well-entrenched inflationary expectations, combined to produce a wave of double-digit inflation. In response, beginning in 1979, the Federal Reserve System launched a strongly contractionary monetary policy aimed at bringing the inflation under control. Within a surprisingly short period of time the campaign succeeded but not without helping to precipitate a major recession and, along the way, pushing interest rates up to historic highs.

The result was that in the early 1980s (with the Regulation Q ceilings in process of being eliminated in accordance with 1980 legislation) savings institutions were forced to *pay* 11 percent to $11\frac{1}{2}$ percent to attract and keep the short-term funds depositors placed with them while *earning* substantially less than that on the long-term mortgages that dominated their portfolios. *New* mortgages, it is true, were paying $14\frac{1}{2}$ to 15 percent in 1981 and 1982. But the problem of "lending long" involved the fact that a large percentage of the mortgages owned by S&Ls in 1981 and 1982 had been granted 15, 20, and even 30 years earlier at fixed interest rates paying them 6 to 8 percent. There is just no way a savings institution can avoid losses if it is forced to pay 11 to $11\frac{1}{2}$ percent to its short-term depositors while earning only 6 to 8 percent on a large proportion of its assets!

Of course this mismatch in the maturity of savings institution assets and liabilities would not have been such a problem had the mortgages they owned been *adjustable rate mortgages (ARMs)* rather than fixed rate mortgages. Adjustable rate mortgages, of course, provide for periodic alterations in the rate of interest earned (charged) on outstanding mortgages as economic conditions and market interest rates change. Had the S&Ls of the early 1980s held a significant portion of their mortgages with adjustable rather than fixed rates, their income could have risen at rates more in line with their outgo. Unhappily, however, federally chartered savings institutions were forbidden from issuing adjustable rate mortgages prior to 1981. When the Federal Home Loan Bank Board finally authorized ARMs in April of that year, it was much too late to help with the S&L problems of 1981–1982.[6]

The Hopeful Mid-1980s

When the first wave of savings institution losses subsided in 1983, there was considerable reason for optimism about the future of the industry. And, as we have seen, the industry as a whole did record net profits from 1983 to 1986.

[6] Pressure from certain consumer groups and the National Association of Home Builders is said to have played a major role in blocking earlier authorization of ARMs. See Strunk and Case, *Where Deregulation Went Wrong*, p. 46. In addition, S&Ls were hurt by the fact that, prior to 1982, the courts refused to enforce "due on sale" clauses in mortgages. These clauses were intended to permit lenders to require repayment of the entire mortgage balance when a house was sold. Home owners selling houses with low fixed interest mortgages obviously could command higher prices if prospective buyers were able to assume the existing mortgage rather than being forced to refinance. But their gain, of course, came at the expense of the lenders. See Strunk and Case, pp. 47–48.

There were several reasons for guarded optimism. The economy recovered from the serious recession of 1982 and was launched on a long period of expansion. Of even greater immediate importance, interest rates fell sharply, markedly reducing the cost of S&L deposits. And the belated authorization of adjustable rate mortgages seemed likely to prevent redevelopment of the sort of crunch savings institutions had had to endure in 1981 and 1982.

In addition the Congress, in response to the "lending long and borrowing short" problem of the thrifts, passed two major pieces of legislation that were aimed primarily at authorizing greater diversification of savings institution assets. First the Depository Institutions Deregulation and Monetary Control Act of 1980 permitted them to make consumer loans, acquire commercial paper and corporate debt securities, and authorized more loans based on commercial real estate. This legislation was followed up by the Garn-St Germain Act of 1982, which expanded the authority for consumer and commercial real estate loans, among others.

Hopes were high that the worst was behind us. Sadly, however, these hopes turned out to be illusory.

The Second Wave — The Late 1980s

Although the savings and loan industry as a whole did earn net profits during the mid-1980s, that performance was, in fact, a highly misleading indicator of the true health of the industry. For the thrift industry of the mid-1980s was still littered with sick, undercapitalized, and all too often poorly managed firms that proved to be easy prey for a series of unfortunate economic developments. And this was the case despite (and partly *because of*) a set of regulators who seemed unwilling and/or unable to regulate, as well as a legislature and executive that seemed — for far too long — to devote more energy to wishing the problem away than to taking the painful action required to stop it before it got out of hand.

Economic Developments Undermining the Value of Thrift Assets   When oil prices are high, the oil-producing sectors of the country naturally benefit. Consequently in the early 1980s, with the OPEC nations propping oil prices way up, Texas, Oklahoma, and other oil-producing states in the U.S. southwest boomed. And since that boom caused the value of land, homes, apartment buildings, shopping centers, and the like to rise, the area's thrift institutions were more than willing to finance much of the construction underlying it.

But when the arbitrarily boosted oil prices collapsed at about the same time that severe droughts crippled the agricultural sector, the boom in the American southwest collapsed with them. Many businesses failed. Real estate values, which a few years earlier had seemed to be on a perpetual onward and upward course, plummeted. And that, of course meant that the market value of savings institution assets — primarily mortgages — plummeted too. The result was widespread insolvency among savings and loan institutions although, as we shall see, many were permitted to continue operating despite their failure.

Capital Requirements for Thrifts   Minimum capital requirements for depository institutions have two major purposes. First, by requiring that owners have a stake in the fortunes of the firm, it is hoped that they (owners) will act as a constraint on excessively risky or speculative behavior by the day-to-day managers. Second, capital requirements provide a cushion to protect the deposit insurance fund from loss. If, for example, there is a required capital-to-asset ratio of 6 percent, when the firm suffers losses, the first 6 percent of the decline in the value of its assets will deplete the owners' equity rather than using up any of the insurance fund's resources.[7]

In the case of the savings and loan industry, most of the original associations were "mutual" institutions—owned by their depositors, with no capital stock issued. The only way in which they could build up capital was via accumulation of retained earnings from years of profitable operation. Consequently, when the Federal Savings and Loan Insurance Corporation was established in 1934, the capital requirements it imposed on insured S&Ls had to be met, over time, via the accumulation of retained earnings.

The initial capital requirement required insured S&Ls to build up, via retained earnings, capital which was at least 5 percent of their deposits. They were given up to 25 years to build up to this required level and, in a significant concession made in 1972, were permitted to average their deposits over the preceding five years to compute their deposit base.[8] The extremely long period permitted to reach the 5 percent level plus the privilege of using the preceding five years' deposits as the base made these capital requirements relatively easy to meet. The result was that the savings and loan industry entered the decade of the 1980s with relatively low capital levels—a situation that was obviously worsened by the losses in 1981 and 1982.

Regulator Forbearance

There is rather general agreement that during the 1980s the major thrift institution regulators—the Federal Home Loan Bank Board and the Federal Savings and Loan Insurance Corporation—not only did not "crack down" on errant and ailing S&Ls sufficiently promptly or severely but, indeed, took quite a few steps in the other direction. Instead of quickly cracking down on excessively risky practices and promptly closing insolvent institutions, the thrift regulators treated their troubled charges with a remarkable degree of *forbearance*.

The Case for Regulator Forbearance

It is important to remember that financial institution regulators exist not merely to protect deposit insurance funds from loss but also to facilitate the efficient

---

[7] This, at least, would be their effect if the accounting measures used revealed the true economic value of the firm.

[8] It is interesting to note that the Federal Home Loan Bank Board attempted to establish requirements based on assets with the rate required varying with the risk of asset in the 1972–1980 period. Though abandoned in 1980, this effort preceded the risk-based requirements first imposed in the United States in December 1990.

performance of the financial services industry.[9] The ideal is to find a way of closing reckless or poorly managed institutions early while allowing well-managed companies that have encountered temporary reverses sufficient time to work their way back to solvency and profitability. For the latter, there is much to be said in support of a policy of regulator forbearance.

Consider, for example, the situation of a number of the nation's largest commercial banks who had made sizable loans to developing countries. When it became clear in the early 1980s that those countries were never likely to be able to repay the principal of the loans an overzealous regulator might have forced the banks to "realize" their losses immediately, thereby inflicting losses on them that could have seriously threatened their solvency and with it, the stability of the nation's entire banking system. Instead, the regulators showed forbearance, permitting the banks involved to recognize their losses over a number of years — a tactic which appears to have successfully avoided more severe problems.

Or, to put the case more in terms of the sort of problems faced by savings and loan associations, imagine a thrift with $2 million in outstanding deposits, $2 million in mortgages issued at 8 percent interest, and $200,000 in cash.[10] Such a firm would have a net worth of $200,000. If, however, mortgage rates should then zoom upward to 16 percent, the current *market* value of their mortgages (assuming they are 30 years from maturity) would fall to $1.14 million. If this firm should be declared insolvent and its assets sold under current circumstance, it could cost the insurance fund $660,000 to pay off the depositors fully. Clearly, if the firm is a well-managed one, it might be better to allow it to continue operating in the hopes that interest rates will fall again.

The point is that there *is* a case for regulator forbearance. But if that forbearance extends to the point of allowing poorly managed, overly speculative, seriously insolvent thrifts to continue operating, it can lead to disaster. It seems clear that that is what happened in the savings and loan industry in the 1980s. We turn now to consider the extent of that regulator forbearance.

Specific Examples of S&L Regulatory Forbearance in the 1980s

In fairness to the thrift regulators, it seems appropriate to distinguish between voluntary and involuntary forbearance. If the regulator could have closed an insolvent thrift but, instead, chose to alter rules or regulations to permit it to continue operating, the forbearance could be said to be voluntary. If, however, an otherwise insolvent thrift is permitted to continue operating because the insurance fund simply doesn't have enough money to pay off the insured depositors should the thrift be closed, then it is involuntary. In levying the responsibility for the S&L disaster, there is a strong case for attributing involuntary forbearance more to congressional and executive inaction than to regulator failure.

---

[9] This point is exceptionally well made by Leonard I. Nakamura in "Closing Troubled Financial Institutions: What Are the Issues?" *Business Review*, Federal Reserve Bank of Philadelphia, May–June 1990, on which much of this section is based.

[10] This example is taken from Nakamura, "Closing Troubled Financial Institutions," p. 20.

Voluntary Forbearance The Monetary Control Act of 1980 gave the Federal Home Loan Bank Board authorization to vary the S&L capital requirement (which had been fixed at 5 percent of deposits) between 3 percent and 6 percent. In response to the "first wave" of S&L problems, the Bank Board lowered the capital requirement to 4 percent in late 1980 and then down to 3 percent in December 1981.

In addition, the Bank Board switched from the so-called generally accepted accounting principles (GAAP) used to evaluate commercial banks to regulatory accounting principles (RAP). RAP accounting permitted S&Ls to count certain items as a part of their capital that GAAP accounting does not. The result was that a significant number of S&Ls that would have been declared insolvent with GAAP accounting were treated as solvent and allowed to continue operating. Table 5-4 illustrates the effect of this switch as of mid-1987. Note that on that date over 150 thrifts left open by RAP accounting would have been insolvent with the use of GAAP.

In retrospect it seems clear that regulator forbearance was carried too far. Too many insolvent and near insolvent thrift institutions were permitted not only to remain open, but to operate recklessly. However, as the decade rolled along and more and more thrifts became insolvent, the point was ultimately reached where—whether they would have been *willing* to close them or not—the regulators could not do so. This was because the FSLIC insurance fund lacked sufficient resources to permit them to pay off the insured depositors at insolvent thrifts. Once that point was reached, responsibility for allowing the debacle to continue rests with the legislature and executive who could have ended it earlier by providing the funds needed to close the sick S&Ls. At this point, in other words, the regulator's forbearance became involuntary.

TABLE 5-4 Savings institution net worth, June 30, 1987

Net worth as a percentage of assets	Using RAP Companies	Number of assets (billions)	Using GAAP Companies	Number of assets (billions)
Less than 0.0%	355	$ 95.4	506	$ 143.9
0.0 to 1.0	51	50.5	97	76.0
1.0 to 2.0	92	40.7	152	74.3
2.0 to 3.0	149	76.7	188	106.8
3.0 to 4.0	318	179.9	313	145.4
4.0 to 5.0	375	191.4	350	240.0
5.0 to 6.0	426	240.7	351	165.4
6.0 and over	1,381	376.3	1,190	299.8
All institutions	3,147	$1,251.6	3,147	$1,251.6

Source: United States League of Savings Institutions.

Other Contributing Factors

The "Moral Hazard" of Deposit Insurance

There are three main defenses against excessively speculative or risky behavior by banks and thrift institutions. First, there is the "market discipline" that *depositors* may exert with their freedom to withdraw their funds from a depository institution perceived as unsafe. Second, there is the potential influence of the *stockholders* who, while they still possess a positive net worth in the firm, will have reason to restrain the bank (or thrift) management from imprudent or over speculative activities. Finally, there are the *regulators* — in the case of the S&L industry, the Federal Home Loan Bank Board and the Federal Savings and Loan Insurance Corporation.

Unfortunately, however, establishment and implementation of deposit insurance have tended to undermine the "market discipline" of depositors. Federal deposit insurance was established in the 1930s in response to the "run on the banks" experienced then. While it did accomplish its goal of undercutting the mass hysteria of bank runs, it did so at a cost.[11] Since the federal government is assuring depositors that (at least up to the deposit insurance maximum) they cannot lose, they have no incentive to "discipline" their depositories by withdrawing funds no matter how recklessly they may behave.

What about stockholders as a restraining influence? Logically it would seem, the bigger the stockholder equity — that is, the more they have to lose — the more likely they are to do whatever they can to guide management into safe, prudent portfolio practices. But, alas, therein lies the rub. By the middle and later 1980s a very large number of savings and loan associations were already economically insolvent and hundreds more were tottering on the brink. These owners had already lost their financial stakes in their firms and could lose no more no matter how much the firm itself lost.

Under these circumstances, then, the full burden of disciplining imprudent depositories, ordering them to cease unsafe practices, and closing them when they became insolvent fell to the regulators. It proved to be too heavy a responsibility.

No matter how well meaning they may be, the fact is that regulators do not always have the information, the resources, or the expertise required to provide the oversight needed. Moreover, as we have seen, regulators may sometimes consider it appropriate to practice voluntary forbearance rather than to "crack down" promptly. And most devastating of all is that if the number of insolvencies has grown to the point that the insurance agency lacks sufficient funds to pay off their insured depositors should they be closed, the regulator has no choice but to allow them to continue operating.

So in the late 1980s the U.S. thrift industry looked something like this. Hundreds of already insolvent S&Ls were still open for business. On the one

---

[11] This section draws heavily on the excellent article by J. P. Barth, P. F. Bartholomew, and C. L. Labich entitled "Moral Hazard and the Thrift Crisis: An Analysis of the 1988 Resolutions," *Proceedings* of the 25th Annual Conference on Bank Structure and Competition, Federal Reserve Bank of Chicago, 1989.

hand, no matter how much more these firms lost from reckless ventures, their owners could lose no more. On the other there was the outside chance that a wild gamble financing some highly speculative undertaking just might succeed. If so, current management would be hailed as the financial geniuses who saved the firm and benefit accordingly. It was, in other words, a "no lose" situation for them.

But hold on. Where might an already insolvent S&L get the funds to lend out on such a wild gamble? And if, as was likely, the gamble failed who, if not the owners, would be the losers?

The answer to the first question, thanks to the existence of federal deposit insurance, is depositors anywhere. The answer to the second is the deposit insurance fund or, if it lacked sufficient funds, federal taxpayers.

All the sick thrifts had to do was offer depositors an interest rate somewhat higher than the going rate to attract their attention. They then were able to count on the aid of Wall Street investment firms who collected savings from people anywhere in the country, broke them up into $100,000 chunks, and sent them off as fully insured deposits in insolvent and near-insolvent thrifts in Texas, California, and wherever. These *brokered deposits* played a major role in the savings and loan debacle.[12] And then, when the vast majority of the wildly speculative ventures financed by these funds failed, the losses accumulated by the insurance fund and, ultimately, the taxpayers grew apace.

The Shortage of Properly Trained Auditors and Examiners at the Federal Home Loan Bank Board

The general philosophy of the government, especially in the late 1970s and early 1980s, was heavily in favor of reducing the role of government in the economy and speeding up the process of deregulation. This philosophy was reflected in the Monetary Control Act of 1980 and the Garn-St Germain Act of 1982, both of which were aimed at significant deregulation of the financial services industry. It was also reflected in the requirements for thrift financial reports and in the number and experience of thrift examiners available to the Federal Home Loan Bank Board (FHLBB).

As one example, in early 1984, the Bank Board eliminated its requirement of detailed monthly financial reports from S&Ls. In their place much briefer monthly reports were substituted and the more detailed report was due only quarterly. In a period when conditions could change dramatically in a matter of weeks, this curtailment of information turned out to be badly timed.

More serious was the FHLBB's shortage of qualified auditors and examiners during the decade. At a time when there was clear need for *more* examiners the

---

[12] As *The Wall Street Journal* put it: "It was a racket no one wanted to stop. Investors made money and, because Congress had raised deposit insurance to $100,000 per account in 1980, they didn't have to worry about what the thrifts were doing with their funds. Wall Street, led by Merrill Lynch and Co., made millions placing the money. Regulators looked the other way because the deposits kept many thrifts alive, postponing the day of reckoning." *The Wall Street Journal*, November 5, 1990, p. A6.

Source: J. R. Barth, P. F. Bartholomew, and C. L. Labich, "Moral Hazard and the Thrift Crisis: An Analysis of the 1988 Resolutions," p. 370.

FIGURE 5-1   **Thrift Regulators' Examination Staff, 1979 – 1988**

number of Bank Board examiners actually *fell* in every year from 1981 through 1984. This incredible fact is clearly shown in Figure 5-1, which also shows a marked improvement starting in 1985.

But numbers alone do not tell the whole story of regulator personnel weaknesses. The Bank Board also had great trouble attracting and keeping examiners with the experience to do the job. A major contributor to this problem was the relatively low salaries paid by the Federal Home Loan Bank Board. Information on comparative salaries at the major bank regulatory agencies in 1984 is presented in Table 5-5. A glance at these figures is all one needs to understand the Bank Board's difficulty in attracting and keeping experienced examiners.

Why the lower salaries for Bank Board examiners? The FHLBB, alone among bank regulatory agencies, was subject to civil service limits established by the Office of Personnel Management for the federal government as a whole. The

TABLE 5-5   **Salary comparisons of bank regulatory agencies, 1984**

	FHLBB	*Comptroller of currency*	*FDIC*	*Federal Reserve System*
Entry level	$14,390	$17,000	$17,750	$17,690
Average salary	24,775	30,764	32,505	37,900

Source: Strunk and Case, *Where Deregulation Went Wrong*, p. 141.

other three agencies were exempt from these limits.[13] It was not until mid-1985 that the Bank Board's examiner staff was moved from the Board, where their salaries were limited by civil service ceilings, to the individual Federal Home Loan Banks where they were not. Once that switch was made, salaries rose, and both the number and experience of examiners improved.

Laws Authorizing Thrifts to Broaden Their Portfolios

As we have seen, in the Garn-St Germain Act of 1982 the federal government authorized a broadening of the assets available for thrift purchase for federally chartered institutions. Among other things it authorized consumer loan up to 30 percent of assets, increased authority to make commercial real estate loans to 40 percent of assets, permitted non-real estate commercial loans up to 10 percent of assets, and eliminated certain limits on loan-to-value ratios, permitting some loans up to 100 percent of the value of the collateral.

By permitting wider diversification of their portfolios, it was hoped that these changes would help overcome the "lend long, borrow short" problem encountered in the early part of the decade. It is true that this permitted thrifts to purchase certain assets they were less familiar with and also true that some of these assets were riskier than the residential mortgages they had long been largely limited to. But the prospective gains seemed worth the risks, especially if more careful supervision was provided. As we have seen, however, they got less supervision so that some of these provisions turned out to contribute to later problems.

More serious was the even greater deregulation provided state-chartered thrifts in some of the states. Traditionally, the rules governing deposits at state-chartered (as well as federally chartered) thrifts were set by the FSLIC, but permissible portfolio practices for state-chartered institutions were controlled by state law.[14] In the 1980s states like Texas, California, and Florida authorized portfolio practices for their state chartered thrifts that encouraged much excessive risk taking. For example, Texas had no limits at all on the proportion of assets thrifts could devote to commercial real estate, consumer, or commercial non-real estate loans. Both Texas and California permitted extensive direct ownership of real estate by thrifts. Some states permitted major purchases of junk bonds. Many permitted purchases of a wide assortment of properties such as hotels, ski resorts, gambling casinos, and oil refineries through the use of "service corporations." [15]

In summary, this seems to be a case where the philosophy of a "dual" banking system — with both state-chartered and federally chartered institutions — failed us miserably. In retrospect, some states appear to have employed relaxed regulatory standards more to attract thrift institutions to their chartering agency than to serve the public better. In so doing, they also have contributed to the enormous losses of the S&L industry.

[13] Strunk and Case, *Where Deregulation Went Wrong*, p. 144.

[14] Ibid., p. 57.

[15] For details, see Strunk and Case, "Where Deregulation Went Wrong," pp. 56–73, and Barth, Bartholomew and Labich, "Moral Hazard and the Thrift Crisis," p. 382.

Summary — Who's Responsible?

The "blame" for the savings and loan fiasco is widespread. Certainly poor management and, in all too many cases, fraud played a part. Certainly also, the regulators at Federal Home Loan Bank Board and the FSLIC failed to discharge their responsibility satisfactorily. Certainly the "penny-wise, pound-foolish" policy of limiting the quantity and salaries of auditors was foolhardy. Certainly, in retrospect, it appears that some states went overboard with deregulation. But certainly the lion's share of the blame rests with an executive and a legislature who failed in their responsibilities. Rather than face up promptly to a nasty situation by providing the funds required to close the insolvent institutions promptly, they turned their backs and allowed them to take advantage of the moral hazard involved and make the losses much greater. We turn now, in the final section, to a consideration of the major legislation that was finally passed in 1989, to deal with the problems.

The Financial Institutions Reform, Recovery, and Enforcement Act of 1989

It was not until late 1989 that the Congress finally took definitive steps to deal with the S&L problem. This was done in the Financial Institutions Reform, Recovery, and Enforcement Act (FIRREA), more popularly (but erroneously) known as the "savings and loan bailout" bill. Congress had passed an earlier law in 1987 that authorized the borrowing of $10.8 billion to help refinance the FSLIC, thereby permitting the closing of some of the then insolvent thrifts, but it was not nearly enough to deal with the situation existing in 1987. And by 1989, of course, matters had gotten much worse.

In recognition of the failure of the major thrift regulatory agencies to satisfactorily carry out the task assigned them, the FIRREA abolished both the Federal Home Loan Bank Board and the Federal Savings and Loan Insurance Corporation. The regulatory responsibilities that had been entrusted to the FHLBB were turned over to the newly created Office of Thrift Supervision, while the deposit insurance function was shifted over to the Federal Deposit Insurance Corporation, which has long been responsible for insuring deposits in commercial banks.

The Office of Thrift Supervision

The newly created Office of Thrift Supervision (OTS) is a semi-autonomous agency within the Department of the Treasury.[16] It is headed by a director appointed by the president to a five-year term. The OTS director also serves as a member of the Board of the Federal Deposit Insurance Corporation.

---

[16] Its status within the Treasury is similar to that of the Office of the Comptroller of the Currency which charters and regulates national commercial banks.

The duties assigned to the OTS include

— chartering, regulating, and examining all federally chartered savings institutions

— regulating savings association holding companies

— establishing accounting standards for savings institutions that are *no less stringent* than the GAAP standards used by commercial banks

— establishing and implementing capital requirements for savings institutions that are *no less stringent* than those established for nationally chartered commercial banks

The Resolution Trust Corporation and the Resolution Funding Corporation

To deal with the large number of already insolvent S&Ls, the FIRREA also set up two temporary agencies. The Resolution Trust Corporation (RTC) was given the responsibility of taking over the failed institutions, selling their remaining good assets, and using those funds plus those provided by the Resolution Funding Corporation to pay off the insured depositors. The Resolution Funding Corporation was authorized to sell $50 billion of bonds to raise part of the money needed by the RTC. Both agencies are currently scheduled to cease operations on December 31, 1996.

The Restructured Federal Deposit Insurance Corporation

The FIRREA abolished the insolvent FSLIC and assigned the FDIC the responsibility of insuring deposits at thrift institutions.

The FDIC Board was reconstituted to include the FDIC Chairman (appointed by the president) the OTS director, the Comptroller of the Currency, plus two additional members to be appointed by the president to six-year terms.

The FDIC, itself, was broken up into two divisions — the Bank Insurance Fund, which handles the insurance for commercial banks, and the Savings Association Insurance Fund, which does so for savings institutions.[17]

Because of the depletion of the FSLIC insurance fund and a decline in the size of the FDIC fund, the act includes provisions for a substantial increase in premiums levied on insured institutions. Those levied on commercial banks were originally scheduled to increase over time from 8.3 cents per $100 of insured deposits in December 1989 to 15 cents per $100 by January 1991. However sharp losses to the FDIC fund from 1988 through 1991 forced use of emergency powers contained in FIRREA to raise them to 19.5 cents per $100 starting in January 1991 and further to 23 cents per $100 effective July 1, 1991.[18] Insurance premiums on savings associations, already at 20.8 cents per $100 of insured

---

[17] Many savings banks belonged to the FDIC long before FIRREA was passed.

[18] The FIRREA permits emergency increases in insurance premiums up to 32.5 cents per $100 of deposits so long as either fund is below 1.25 percent of insured deposits.

deposits in 1989, rose to 23 cents in December 1990, but then were scheduled to decline from 1993 to 1997 until they reached 15 cents per $100.

Other Features of FIRREA

In addition to the restructuring discussed, the FIRREA makes an attempt at undoing some of the deregulation carried out in earlier 1980s legislation. For example it requires thrift institutions to maintain 70 percent of their assets in the form of mortgage-related instruments, almost 80 percent of which must finance residential construction. Also, state-chartered associations are barred from acquiring assets not permitted to those with federal charters and must divest themselves of junk bonds by 1994.[19]

At this point it is too early to speculate on how effective FIRREA will prove to be. In any case the one thing that is certain is that more legislation affecting the financial services industry will be forthcoming in the 1990s. Certainly, much more than $50 billion will be needed to clean up the S&L mess.

Review Questions

1. Carefully distinguish the different causes of the two "waves" of thrift failure experienced during the 1980s.

2. The thrift practice of "borrowing short and lending long" led to trouble in the early 1980s. Explain.

3. How might more widespread use of adjustable rate mortgages have eased the thrift crisis in the early 1980s? Why weren't ARMs more widely used?

4. Carefully explain the case for some degree of "regulator forbearance." Distinguish voluntary and involuntary forbearance.

5. What effect did the substitution of regulatory accounting principles (RAP) for generally accepted accounting principles (GAAP) have on the savings and loan debacle? Explain.

6. Carefully explain what is meant by the "moral hazard" of deposit insurance.

7. What role did "brokered deposits" play in the thrift crisis?

8. How might one argue that deregulation was pushed too rapidly and too far in the case of the thrift industry during the 1980s?

9. What are the major provisions of the Financial Institutions Reform, Recovery, and Enforcement Act of 1989?

10. In your opinion, who is most responsible for the savings and loan fiasco of the 1980s?

[19] These, however, can be transferred to holding company affiliates.

Federal Commercial Bank Legislation: A Brief History

Although commercial banks are only part of the U.S. financial sector, they are probably the most important part. Consequently, we turn now to a brief consideration of the history of commercial banking laws.

It seems appropriate and meaningful to break up discussion of the past two centuries of bank legislation into three parts. First, we shall take a truly historical perspective by considering all the major banking laws passed prior to the Great Depression of the 1930s. That will cover the long period from 1791 until the 1930s and will involve consideration of the establishment of the First and Second Banks of the United States, a series of laws passed in the 1860s, and finally the Federal Reserve Act in 1913. Second, we shall focus on the bundle of banking laws that Congress passed in the 1930s in response to the Great Depression. In the main, these laws sharply increased the federal government's regulation of banks with the intention of preventing recurrence of the chaotic economic conditions of the early 1930s. Finally, we shall look at a series of laws passed during the 1980s, most of which involve efforts to undo some of the 1930s legislation and deregulate the commercial banking industry. These efforts continue, of course, into the 1990s.

From the Revolution to the Federal Reserve Act

When the Constitution was adopted in 1787, the only commercial banks in existence were state-chartered institutions. These banks were chartered by specific, individual acts of their state legislature, and they earned the bulk of their income from interest on loans to business. Since in those early days, the deposit habit had not yet been established (i.e., people would not willingly accept checks in payment), these state banks provided the proceeds of their loans in the form of *bank notes* — IOUs of the banks that promised to pay a specified amount of gold or silver to the bearer on demand and circulated freely as money. At the time, these bank notes constituted the nation's sole domestically issued currency supply.

In 1791, in response to the recommendations of Alexander Hamilton, the federal government chartered our first truly national bank, the First Bank of the United States, located in Philadelphia. It was a large bank relative to the size of the economy, and it dominated the banking scene from 1791 to 1811. Partially owned by the federal government, it performed some of the functions of a central bank, and it competed with state banks for ordinary commercial business. It handled the deposits of the federal government and also took upon itself the task of helping to ensure the convertibility of state bank notes. The latter function consisted of presenting state bank notes to the issuer with a demand for immediate payment in gold or silver.

The First Bank of the United States went out of existence in 1811 when Congress failed to renew its charter, but five years later, in 1816, the Second Bank of the United States was chartered for an additional 20-year period. The Second Bank followed policies similar to those of its predecessor, but some mismanagement, coupled with an unfortunate involvement in political matters, earned it the enmity of President Jackson as well as of the state banks. The result was that the bank's charter was allowed to lapse in 1836. For almost the next 30 years, the nation was served exclusively by state-chartered banks.

The period from 1836 to 1863, often referred to as the era of state banking, was, from the viewpoint of sound banking principles, a disastrous one. Despite two constructive developments early in the period, the general character of banking quickly degenerated to perhaps the lowest level in our history.[1]

On the good side of the ledger were the first faltering attempts at state regulation of banks in conjunction with the introduction of the *free-banking* principle and the institution of the nation's first system of *deposit (and note) insurance.*

It was New York State that pioneered deposit insurance starting as far back as 1829. This legislation, introducing as it did the need for control over the institutions offering the insured deposits, provided the entering wedge for state regulation of banks. It was buttressed shortly thereafter by Michigan in 1837 with the introduction of the free-banking principle. This principle, which authorized the charter of any banking company that could meet certain specified minimum conditions, not only eliminated the obvious political abuse associated with the old system, but also required more governmental regulation in establishing those "minimum conditions."

Despite these advances, the banking system, plagued with mismanagement, corruption, and just plain bad banking, sank to new depths. Banks with insufficient capital, overly speculative loans, and inadequate management were commonplace. Bank notes, promising to pay specie on demand, were often all but impossible to redeem as unscrupulous operators located redemption centers

---

[1] For a contrary view of the 1836–1863 period, see Arthur J. Rolnick and Warren E. Weber, "The Free Banking Era: New Evidence on Laissez-Faire Banking," *American Economic Review,* December 1983, pp. 1080–1091.

deep in the wilderness. As a consequence, such notes circulated at substantial and varying discounts, and the failure rate was abysmally high. With the nation's currency supply consisting almost entirely of state bank notes issued by banks scattered throughout the country, conditions were ideal for counterfeiters, and merchants found it necessary to purchase special compilations called "Counterfeit Detectors" to attempt to determine what currency was good and what was not.

The nation's monetary system was clearly a chaotic, deplorable shambles when the Civil War broke out. Indeed, it is something of a misnomer to call it a system at all. A significant proportion of the country's commercial banks were simply unsafe, and, although some states did attempt to exercise some restraint on their activities, the federal government had no control whatever. As a consequence, the nation's paper currency supply, which consisted primarily of state bank notes, was largely outside the control of federal authorities. And to top it all off, the bitter and costly war that began in 1861 not only had to be fought but also had to be financed. All these conditions combined to precipitate a major change in the nation's banking system with the passage of the National Bank Act of 1863.

The National Bank Act of 1863 and the 1863–1913 Period

The National Bank Act of 1863 did three things of significance.[2] First, it authorized the establishment of nationally chartered banks, to be approved and regulated by the newly established Comptroller of the Currency. Second, the newly authorized national banks were given the privilege of issuing, under strictly regulated conditions, a new form of paper currency called the National Bank note. Third, a prohibitive 10 percent tax was levied on the issuance of state bank notes by state-chartered banks.

The new national banks were, in general, much more strictly regulated than were state banks. To obtain a charter from the Comptroller of the Currency, a bank was required to meet minimum capital requirements, to refrain from making many loans then considered too speculative and risky, to subject itself to regular examination by the Comptroller of the Currency, and to maintain, at all times, specified reserves behind its deposits.[3]

The reserve requirements established were fixed by law (unlike today's situation whereby the Federal Reserve Board may vary the requirements within specified legal limits) and were higher for national banks located in large cities than for those in smaller localities. Specifically, national banks located in New York City, Chicago, and St. Louis were required to maintain a 25 percent reserve behind deposits, all in cash; national banks located in approximately the next 50 largest cities also had to meet a 25 percent reserve ratio but were permitted to hold half of it in checking accounts at national banks in New York, Chicago, or St.

---

[2] Actually, the provisions described in this section were included in several laws passed in the 1863–1865 period. For convenience, we shall combine them and refer to them all as provisions of the National Bank Act of 1863.

[3] There was, in those days, no distinction between demand and time deposits, so that all deposits were subject to the same reserve requirements.

Louis; all other national banks — the so-called ''country banks'' — had a 15 percent reserve requirement, three-fifths of which could be held on deposit at national banks in the larger cities.

The regulations governing the issuance of National Bank notes, the new paper currency authorized by the act, reflected the deep concern for safety that had been generated by conditions during the 1836 – 1863 period. Banks issuing National Bank notes were required to own, and pledge as security, U.S. government securities of at least equal value.[4] This requirement not only guaranteed the safety of these notes but, as we shall see, it severely limited the amount that could be issued.

The requirements for national banks, although hardly severe by today's standards, were in most cases substantially more rigorous than were those of the states, and it was all too apparent to Congress that the more lenient standards of the states would place nationally chartered banks at a serious competitive disadvantage. Consequently, it was decided to counter the threat of state banks by means of a 10 percent tax on their bank notes.

It seems clear that the real intent of Congress in levying this tax was the elimination of the state banks themselves. After all, the issuance of state bank notes (as the proceeds of loans made) was their main source of income. The 10 percent tax meant that a state bank seeking to net a 10 percent interest return on a loan would have to charge the borrower 20 percent! And since such a bank would be in competition with the newly authorized national banks with untaxed national bank notes to lend out, its future seemed dim indeed. As a matter of fact, state bank notes *did* quickly disappear from circulation and the number of state banks in existence fell from about 1,500 in 1862 to fewer than 250 in 1868.[5]

But the state banks themselves were saved from extinction by what was for them a fortuitous quirk of circumstances. Whereas in earlier years, borrowers from banks had generally insisted on currency as the proceeds of their loans and had received it in the form of bank notes, by the time the National Bank Act was passed, the advantages of deposits over currency had taken firm hold in the public's mind. And state banks found that they could continue to earn income by providing borrowers with newly created checking accounts rather than the bank notes that the new law virtually forbade. As a result, many state banks managed to continue to operate alongside the growing number of national banks, and within a few years, they once again exceeded the national banks in numbers.

The astonishingly rapid spread of the deposit banking habit among the American public in the late nineteenth century is clearly revealed in Table 6-1. The effect of that development on the mix of banks is evidenced by the fact that, whereas in 1870 only 325 state-chartered banks were competing with 1,612 nationally chartered ones, by 1910 the number of state banks had shot upward to 17,376 — two and a half times that of national banks.[6]

Deficiencies of the National Bank Act of 1863   The National Bank Act of 1863 solved some of our monetary problems, but, as is so often the case, it led to still

---

[4] In fact, initially National Bank notes could be issued in amounts equal to only 90 percent of the value of U.S. securities possessed by the issuer.

[5] *Banking Studies* (Washington, D.C.: Federal Reserve System, 1941).

[6] Carter H. Golembe and David S. Holland, *Federal Regulation of Banking 1983 – 84* (Washington, D.C.: Golembe Associates, Inc.), p. 7.

TABLE 6-1 Quantities of bank notes and bank deposits in circulation, selected years, 1834–1890 (millions of dollars)		
Year	Bank notes	Deposits
1834	$ 95	$ 76
1849	115	91
1855	187	190
1861	202	257
1870	336	775
1890	126	4,576

Source: American Bankers Association, *The Story of American Banking* (New York: American Bankers Association, 1963).

others. On the positive side, it did provide for the development of a more carefully controlled system of national banks, and it did, for the first time, concentrate control over the circulating currency in federal hands. And these were truly significant improvements. But as the nineteenth century drew to a close, it was clear that serious problems remained, some of them directly attributable to the act itself.

Four quite specific problems became increasingly evident as the twentieth century neared. It was these deficiencies that led to the passage of the Federal Reserve Act in 1913.

Rigidity and Inelasticity of the Currency Supply The deplorable situation that had been created by the widespread overissue of state bank notes was effectively eliminated by the 10 percent issue tax, but it soon became clear that the provisions for the issuance of National Bank notes were, in themselves, not entirely adequate.

The bank note problem under the National Bank Act, unlike in the earlier years, was not a matter of overissue. If anything, it was the other way around. National banks issuing notes were required to purchase and deposit, with the Comptroller of the Currency, U.S. government securities as backing for their outstanding notes. They were permitted to issue notes up to an amount equaling the par or market value (whichever was lower) of U.S. securities so deposited.

This requirement provided admirably for the safety of National Bank notes. However, by tying the quantity that could be issued directly to U.S. securities, the act overlooked the necessity of providing a currency supply that could expand and contract as the needs of trade required. When a bigger currency supply was needed, but no more U.S. securities were available, the economy's requirements could not be met.

And that is just about what happened. The value of U.S. securities outstanding fell from about $2.8 billion in 1866 to about $1.6 billion in 1890 as the federal government steadily reduced its debt during the period. Consequently, the base on which more National Bank notes could be issued was steadily declining at a time when the nation's economy was growing by leaps and bounds. In addition, during much of the period, U.S. securities were selling at substantial premiums and hence were not particularly desirable for bank purchase. The number of National Bank notes, which had totaled about $300 million in 1870, fell precipitously during the next 20 years.[7]

Nor was the long-run decline in the absolute volume of notes the only problem. A properly functioning currency supply should also expand and contract in volume in response to seasonal, cyclical, and panic-induced demands by the public. To employ the word that was popular then, the currency supply should be "elastic" with respect to the public's demands for it. Based as it was on U.S. securities, the supply of National Bank notes was, unfortunately, highly inelastic. In the words of the Comptroller of the Currency in 1914,

> Under the conditions existing, and which have existed for years past, the currency of the country under our national banking system has been entirely lacking in the element of elasticity which is so necessary to meet the requirements of business and the periodical demands for money and currency which come, especially in the great agricultural sections of the West and South.[8]

Problems Arising Out of Reserve Requirements   In addition to the currency issue problems, reserve requirements for deposits under the National Bank Act were the source of considerable trouble. As noted, the act permitted "country" banks to keep three-fifths of their reserves on deposit in large city banks and so-called reserve city banks (those located in the approximately 50 largest cities other than New York, Chicago, and St. Louis) to keep half of theirs on deposit in national banks in New York, Chicago, or St. Louis.

The problem these reserve arrangements created is perhaps best put in the words of the Comptroller of the Currency at the time of the passage of the Federal Reserve Act:

> A further weakness of the system which developed—and, with the expansion of our trade and industries, had become more evident and threatening—was the imperfect, inefficient, and unscientific method of handling our bank reserves. Under the national banking system the banks throughout the country have been accustomed to accumulate their reserve balances in the central cities of New York, Chicago, and St. Louis, where the national banks usually have allowed interest at the rate of 2 percent per annum, and sometimes more, to their correspondent national banks. To avoid loss from idle funds, these depository banks employed to a large extent the balances thus kept with them by putting the money out in call loans on bond and stock collateral. . . .
>
> When the banks throughout the country found it necessary to draw on their reserves in the large cities to meet the recurring seasonal demands of business, these large city banks, in turn, were forced to call in the broker's call loans, these calls resulting frequently in high money rates and declining security values, and sometimes in serious stringency, disturbance and panic, or alarm.[9]

[7] It should be noted that the rapid switch in public taste from notes to deposits during the same period kept this decline in currency supply from creating the havoc it might otherwise have caused.

[8] *Annual Report of the Comptroller of the Currency* (Washington, D.C.: Government Printing Office, 1914), p. 9.

[9] Ibid., pp. 9–10.

Thus, shortsighted reserve requirement arrangements contributed mightily to periodic financial panics. Ordinary seasonal demands for credit in the agricultural interior led to pressure on large-city banks, especially in New York City, which, in turn, created pressure on the stock market and all too often degenerated into an all-out financial panic. Allowing banks to hold required reserves on deposit at other commercial banks, it seemed, only provided a conduit through which disturbances in one sector could be transmitted to others with, all too often, disastrous results.

Lack of a "Lender of Last Resort" As the problems with reserve requirements made clear, one portion of the commercial banking system cannot readily "bail out" another part needing reserves, without risking its own liquidity position. Prior to the Federal Reserve System, banks under pressure in periods of crisis had no place to go other than to other banks under equivalent pressure to obtain needed funds.

What was sorely needed was a *central bank*—an institution in a position to make added reserve funds available to commercial banks in need, without draining funds from other banks. A "lender of last resort" to which the individual commercial banks or the banking system as a whole could turn was a vital necessity.

An Inefficient Check Collection System A fourth significant problem of the pre–Federal Reserve days was the extremely inefficient check collection system employed. Completed collection of checks written on out-of-town banks often took a week or more.

The procedure was often quite complicated. Smaller banks normally kept reserve and clearing balances on deposit at a "correspondent" commercial bank in a nearby large city. When a check written on a bank in another city was deposited, the recipient bank would normally send it to its correspondent for collection. If it happened that the big-city correspondent bank also held a clearing balance for the bank on which the check was written the process was simple: the clearing balance of one was increased and that of the other was decreased. But if, as was more often the case, the bank on which the check was written had clearing balances at a different correspondent bank, more complicated and more time-consuming methods were necessary.

Contributing greatly to the problem was the then common practice of many banks of deducting an *exchange charge* from the face value of all checks presented against them through the mails from out-of-town banks. Suppose, for example, that Mr. Jones wrote a $100 check on Bank X, payable to Mrs. Smith, who deposited it in Bank Y in a different city. Bank Y would then send the check in (through its big-city correspondent) for collection from Bank X. If the check were presented to Bank X by another bank in the same city, no exchange charge could be deducted. If, however, the check were received through the mails, from an out-of-town bank, Bank X might pay up only $99, keeping the $1 as an exchange charge, ostensibly to reimburse it for the cost and trouble of settling through the mails.

Naturally, banks with checks to be collected found it in their interest to seek means of avoiding the deduction of exchange charges. As one way to avoid them was to find a correspondent bank located in the same city as the payee bank, great efforts were made to do so. This sometimes meant a check would go through six or eight or even ten banks before completing the clearing process.

It was certainly an inefficient system, and one of the first actions of the Federal Reserve was to set up its own check collection facilities and to deny their use for checks written on banks that deducted exchange charges.

Although the nation suffered from these four problems for a number of years, it took the severe financial panic of 1907 to call forth positive steps toward fundamental reform. That experience led to a stopgap measure in 1908, the Aldrich-Vreeland Act, which set up, in turn, an important study group, the National Monetary Commission. Five years later, after much debate, the deliberations of the commission provided the basis for the Federal Reserve Act.

The Evolution of the Federal Reserve System

The Original Federal Reserve Act of 1913   As we have seen, the inelastic currency supply, inefficient check collection facilities, ill-designed reserve requirements, and other deficiencies of the National Bank Act of 1863 combined to produce a series of financial panics throughout the latter decades of the nineteenth century and on over into the first decade of the twentieth. This experience, in turn, prompted a searching study by the National Monetary Commission, whose report ultimately led to the passage of the Federal Reserve Act in 1913.

The Federal Reserve System originally established by that act was a far cry from the powerful central bank we know today. It consisted of 12 district Federal Reserve banks with considerable autonomy, along with a fairly weak seven-member coordinating group, the Board of Governors. As we shall see shortly, time and painful experience have since shifted the locus of power almost entirely out of the hands of the individual Federal Reserve banks into those of the Board.

More remarkable than the changes in structure, however, has been the evolution of the philosophy and objectives of the system. Whereas we now take for granted the goals of full employment, economic growth, and stable prices as almost the sine qua non of monetary policy, the framers of the original Federal Reserve Act made no mention of any of them. The act was intended, in its own words, "to furnish an elastic currency, to afford means of rediscounting commercial paper, to establish a more effective supervision of banking in the United States, and for other purposes." [10] It seems clear from this statement that the act was aimed primarily at the specific weaknesses that had cropped up under the national banking system rather than at the creation of a powerful new agency to stabilize the economy.

What were its specific provisions? It did require, as today, that all national banks join, while making membership voluntary for state banks. It borrowed from the National Bank Act the concept of differing reserve requirements for member banks in different-sized cities, but it specified that required reserves

---

[10] *Preamble*, the Federal Reserve Act.

must be kept on deposit in district Federal Reserve banks.[11] There was no provision for discretionary alteration in required reserve ratios by the Board. Open-market operations—today, by any measure, the most important of all monetary policy weapons—were essentially unknown.[12] For all practical purposes, the only discretionary monetary policy tool initially established by the act was the power to alter the Federal Reserve "discount rate," the interest rate charged by Federal Reserve banks on short-term loans of reserves to member banks.

The Commercial Loan (or "Real Bills") Theory   This limited reliance on discretionary monetary tools is explainable partially by the then widespread faith in a doctrine called the *commercial loan* (or "real bills") *theory*. The commercial loan theory centered on the belief that both the quantity and the quality of bank credit could be satisfactorily controlled if the basic legislation encouraged banks to restrict themselves largely to short-term (90 days in the general case) loans to business for the purpose of purchasing inventories. Such legislation, it was felt, would guarantee that banks would lend only for productive rather than speculative purposes and that an expansion in the quantity of bank credit would only occur when such an increase was needed to finance expanded trade. It was a soothing theory. Not only could we ensure that bank loans were sound and that bank credit would not expand to an inflationary level, but we could do so by law, thereby avoiding any heavy reliance on the discretion of policymakers.

The original Federal Reserve Act attempted to implement the commercial loan theory primarily through the discount mechanism.[13] It required member banks desiring to borrow reserves from their district Federal Reserve bank to turn over, as collateral for the loan, IOUs of businesses arising out of short-term loans the member banks had made to finance inventory purchases. Such IOUs came to be called "eligible paper," denoting the fact that they were initially the only assets eligible at the Federal Reserve's discount window. The idea was, of course, to restrict access to the discount window—and hence to the added reserves available there—to those member banks who "behaved themselves" by making loans consistent with the commercial loan theory.

The notion that it was possible to control both the quality and the quantity of credit automatically through laws requiring commercial banks to specialize in short-term inventory loans to business—the commercial loan theory—soon proved to be a fallacious one. For example, commercial loan adherents argued that restricting bank assets to short-term inventory loans would ensure the li-

---

[11] This was the case following a 1917 amendment. In the original act, vault cash also could be counted. From 1917 till late 1959, only deposits at the Fed could be counted. Since 1959, both vault cash and the member bank's Federal Reserve account have been acceptable.

[12] The Federal Reserve banks were given the power to purchase U.S. securities, but this was thought of primarily as a measure to permit them to earn income. The vastly more important effects of security purchases on member bank reserves, interest rates, and the money supply were simply not widely recognized or understood at the time.

[13] In addition, Federal Reserve notes, the new currency authorized by the act, could originally only be issued with a backing not only of gold but also of "eligible paper"—short-term IOUs of businesses acquired from member banks by the Federal Reserve banks through the discount facility.

quidity of banks because of the alleged *self-liquidating* character of loans secured by a firm's inventories. The idea was that a firm that borrowed to finance the purchase of its stock-in-trade would be in a position to repay the bank as soon as it had turned over that portion of its inventory. What was overlooked in the argument was the possibility of an economywide collapse of economic activity that would make it difficult or impossible for the borrower to sell his goods. In such a situation, short-term inventory loans derive their liquidity only from the fact that they can be discounted at the central bank—not through any inherently self-liquidating features.

Even more seriously misleading was the argument that tying discounts to short-term inventory loans would guarantee that the money supply could not be excessive. Commercial loan advocates argued that as long as access to the discount facility was limited to banks possessing "productive" short-term inventory loans, bank reserves and the money supply could only increase as the volume of physical production itself increased. Inflation, then, need not be a matter of concern.

But this, of course, misses the very essence of excess demand inflation. Once full employment is reached, firms bid against one another to obtain a larger share of the fixed supply of productive resources. As no more is to be had, the bidding simply forces prices up. As prices rise, the *dollar value* of each inventory acquisition necessarily rises. Firms, then, come to banks for ever-larger amounts of credit, and bank portfolios become stocked with more and more short-term commercial paper eligible for discount. The flaw in the commercial loan idea, of course, is that the quantity of short-term commercial loans does not only rise when real production rises; it also increases when the money value of production rises via inflationary price increases. And when this happens, far from preventing inflation, the commercial loan theory provisions actually feed it.

Fortunately for the nation, this belief in, and legislative reliance on, the commercial loan theory did not last long.

Changes in the Federal Reserve System Since 1913   It is perhaps one measure of the strength of the Federal Reserve Act that it has been able to weather successfully the test of time and evolve to handle ideas and objectives not even conceived of at the time of its passage.

The elements of the commercial loan theory embedded in the act disappeared fairly quickly, as did the notion of a decentralized system with 12 semiautonomous district banks.

It was in the 1930s, however, that the most far-reaching overhaul occurred. The agonizing experience of mass unemployment during the Great Depression and the spectacular bank panic of the early 1930s provided the impetus. Legislation enacted in the early and middle 1930s authorized variable reserve requirements, set up the FDIC, gave the Board of Governors of the Federal Reserve the power to establish margin requirements on the purchase of stock and ceilings on interest payable on savings accounts, and a host of other things. The most important change, however, was one of attitude and objective. No longer was the Federal Reserve System looked upon as an institution primarily concerned with correcting some deficiencies in the National Bank Act of 1863. It was now a powerful federal government stabilization agency charged with a crucial role in battling unemployment and inflation.

Banking Laws of the 1930s

We turn now to consider the set of banking laws "in and around" the decade of the 1930s. We use the phrase "in and around" because, along with the 1930s legislation, we want to include laws in 1927 and 1956 that reflect the same philosophy as the Banking Acts of 1933 and 1935. That philosophy, as one authority has put it, was to create for commercial banks "a regulatory (or government-fostered) cartel, complete with rigid entry barriers and regulations to prevent 'destructive' competition." [14]

The Background: Economic and Financial Conditions in the 1920s and 1930s

When one considers the state of the U.S. economy in the 1930s, it is not difficult to understand why Congress should have taken drastic steps. After all it was a decade in which economic activity virtually collapsed, with the unemployment rate varying, *for 10 long years,* between 14 and 25 percent. And one extremely important facet of that general decline (both as cause *and* effect) was the devastation of the commercial banking system.

Even before the onset of the Great Depression itself, the financial system was shaky. During the decade of the 1920s, an average of 600 banks failed each year. And this, it must be remembered, was before the existence of federal deposit insurance, with the result that many families lost their life savings. But even this performance pales into insignificance when compared to that of the early 1930s. From 1930 to 1933 over 9,000 banks failed—an average of 2,200 per year! Little wonder that Congress should have taken bold action to try to see to it that such devastation could never happen again.

The action taken, however, consisted primarily of a number of laws aimed at preventing what was looked at as "excessive and destructive" competition among commercial banks as well as between commercial banks and other financial institutions. In pursuance of that objective, legislation was passed that sharply limited interstate banking, instituted other barriers to entrance to the industry, placed ceilings on the interest banks could pay to attract depositors, and specifically forbid competition between commercial banks and certain other financial institutions. Let us look at some of these laws.

The McFadden Act and Bank Branching

State banks—those whose charter was issued by the state in which they operate—have always been subject to the branching regulations of that state. The majority of states today permit their state-chartered banks to open branches throughout the state. Some, however, limit intrastate branching to the same

[14] Franklin R. Edwards, "Can Regulatory Reform Prevent the Impending Disaster in Financial Markets," in *Restructuring the Financial System,* published by the Federal Reserve Bank of Kansas City, 1987, p. 7.

county or some other restricted area and a few so-called unit-banking states forbid any branches at all.

But, of course no state law can authorize its state-chartered banks to open branches in another state. So by the nature of the beast, interstate branching by state-chartered banks was illegal. But what about the national banks chartered by the federal government? What regulations governed their branching activities?

Although no law explicitly forbids branching by nationally chartered banks, the U.S. attorney general ruled in 1911 that the fact that the National Bank Act of 1863 had not specifically authorized branches meant that national banks were forbidden from branching at all. This ruling had obvious implications for the competitive position of national banks located in states that permitted some branching by their state-chartered banks.

In an effort to promote greater equity, Congress passed a law in 1927 called the **McFadden Act** that gave national banks the power to establish branches within the city in which they were located wherever state banks had similar powers. In the Banking Act of 1933, branching powers of national banks were broadened to permit the same degree of branching as that permitted state banks in their state.

Clearly the McFadden Act constituted a slight broadening in the branching powers of national banks. Yet in a strange twist of interpretation, it has come to be thought of as one of the two most important legislative barriers to interstate banking that have shaped our banking system. (The other, to be discussed shortly, is the Douglas Amendment to the Bank Holding Company Act of 1956.) The fact is that since state-chartered banks cannot branch over state lines and since the McFadden Act only authorizes nationally chartered banks to branch to the same degree as state banks, interstate banking via branching has long been illegal in this country.

The Bank Holding Company Act and the Douglas Amendment

The limitations on branching noted earlier stimulated interest in the use of the holding company device, especially in the so-called "unit" banking states where intrastate branching was prohibited.

A "pure" holding company is a corporation whose only asset is the voting stock of other corporations and whose only function is the control of the policies (via the voting stock owned) of other corporations. In the banking industry there are two types: multibank holding companies and one-bank holding companies. A multibank holding company, as the name implies, is a corporation that owns a controlling percentage of the stock of a number of commercial banks. A one-bank holding company, on the other hand, is a corporation that owns stock in a number of companies, only one of which is a commercial bank. We will consider the reasons for, and the implications of, the growth of bank holding companies in a later chapter.

The first significant legislation dealing with bank holding companies was the **Bank Holding Company Act of 1956.** That act requires all multibank holding companies to register with the Federal Reserve System (whether they are FRS members or not) and to submit to the regulatory actions of the Fed. Such regulation involves the power to approve or disapprove the establishment of new bank holding companies, acquisitions of new subsidiaries by existing bank holding companies, and to order divestment of certain nonbanking subsidiaries. Although one-bank holding companies were not made subject to regulation in the 1956 act, a sharp spurt in their growth in the late 1960s prompted Congress to bring them under FRS regulation also in the Bank Holding Company Amendments Act of 1970.

An important part of the Bank Holding Company Act worthy of note has come to be called the **Douglas Amendment.** This amendment makes it illegal for a bank holding company to acquire a commercial bank subsidiary located in a different state unless the laws of the state in which the subsidiary is located specifically invite out-of-state banking holding companies to enter. Since prior to 1980, no state had passed legislation inviting out-of-state bank holding companies in, the Douglas Amendment long served as a companion piece to the McFadden Act, effectively barring interstate banking, in this case, via the holding company device.[15]

The Bank Holding Company Act of 1956 and its Douglas Amendment consequently had two significant effects on the structure of the U.S. commercial banking system. First, by requiring that the bank holding company device be used only to acquire nonbanking subsidiaries whose function is "so closely related to banking or controlling banks as to be a proper incident thereto," it implicitly forbade use of the holding company device to mix commercial banking with such unrelated activities as industrial or commercial firms. Second, via the Douglas Amendment, it prevented the spread of interstate banking via the holding company device until a rash of state legislation in the 1980s rendered it ineffective.

The Banking Acts of 1933 and 1935

Although, as noted, the McFadden Act and the Bank Holding Company Act reflect the same general philosophy toward the regulation and "protection" of commercial banks, the main legislative reaction to the carnage of the Great Depression came during the 1930s in the Banking Acts of 1933 and 1935. This monumental banking legislation included the following key provisions:

1. Commercial banks were forbidden from paying interest on ordinary checking accounts.[16]

2. The Federal Reserve System was given the power to impose ceilings on the interest rates banks could pay on time deposits. This power was subsequently implemented through the Fed's Regulation Q.

3. In a section of the Banking Act of 1933 that has since come to be known as the **Glass-Steagall Act,** commercial banks were forbidden

---

[15] Actually, Maine did pass legislation inviting in out-of-state holding companies prior to 1980, but since it limited its invitation to bank holding companies from states offering a reciprocal invitation to Maine bank holding companies, and none did, its effect was nil.

[16] This prohibition is still in effect. Obviously, NOW accounts which do pay interest and do offer check-writing privileges are not considered "ordinary checking accounts."

from participating in the investment banking business and investment banks were prohibited from accepting deposits.[17]

4. The Federal Deposit Insurance Corporation was established to provide insurance for commercial bank depositors.

5. The Banking Act of 1935 specifically instructed bank chartering agencies to consider, among other things, the "convenience and needs of the community" before granting new charters.

6. The Board of Governors was given the power to vary required reserve ratios within prescribed limits and to set margin requirements on the purchase of stock.

With the possible exception of the establishment of the FDIC and the authorization of variable reserve ratios, all of these measures seem to reflect the conviction by Congress that the banking collapse of the early 1930s was brought about by excessively risky behavior on the part of bankers that resulted from overcompetition. The cure, as Congress in the 1930s saw it, was a series of government regulations aimed at preventing its reoccurrence.

1980s Banking Legislation: The Beginning of Deregulation

The regulatory structure established in response to the Great Depression worked reasonably well for nearly a half century. Each type of financial institution had more or less its own "turf" and was able to operate without much concern for competition. Commercial banks did their thing, thrift institutions did theirs, investment companies and investment bankers theirs, and so on. Within the commercial banking industry, both out-of-state competitors and price competition (via Regulation Q) were effectively barred.

As one authority put it,

> The result was to create an artificial financial structure characterized by thousands of small disparate financial institutions. We had institutions specializing in only mortgage loans, or consumer loans, or business finance, or trust services, and so forth. We had banks with thousands of branch offices, while others were prohibited from opening an office across the street from their main office. We had thousands of tiny institutions operating in insulated local markets, where competitors were unable to go, together with giant institutions operating in different cities, like they were on different planets of the solar system. . . . It was a regulatory-created and -nurtured edifice, not the child of natural market phenomenon, and it could only be sustained by protective regulation.[18]

---

[17] Banks were barred from dealing in or underwriting securities issued by corporations and so-called "revenue bonds" sold by state and local governments. Commercial banks are, however, permitted to underwrite and deal in U.S. government securities and "general obligation" securities of state and local governments.

[18] Edwards, "Can Regulatory Reform Prevent the Impending Disaster in Financial Markets," pp. 7–8.

But developments in the 1970s began to undermine the stability of this system. Rapid inflation and high, volatile interest rates made the return to financial innovators who could find ways around regulatory restraints more and more appealing. In addition, enormous technological changes in communications and information processing permitted a redesign of many financial assets that threatened to undermine financial intermediaries. And, as we went along, competition from foreign bankers, unrestrained by many of the prohibitions imposed on U.S. banks, began to make substantial inroads. It was clear that legislative changes were needed.

We turn here to take a look at some of those changes enacted during the 1980s. It should be stressed, however, that still more, possibly greater, legislation changes must be expected during the 1990s.

The Depository Institutions Deregulation and Monetary Control Act of 1980

The devastating experience of the 1930s and the conviction that its worst effects could have been prevented by the types of government regulation adopted in the mid-1930s stayed with us for a long time. Indeed, it was not until 1980 that serious new financial problems, brought on by financial innovation, rampant inflation, and skyrocketing interest rates, and to a certain extent compounded by certain regulatory measures instituted in the 1930s, convinced Congress to enact major changes. The result was the passage of the landmark Depository Institutions Deregulation and Monetary Control Act of 1980 (hereafter to be referred to as the MCA).

As its excessively wordy title suggests, the MCA of 1980 was a multipurpose bill aimed both at a degree of deregulation and at solidifying the Fed's power to control the money supply. Among its key provisions were the following:

1. It established uniform reserve requirements for transactions accounts and "nonpersonal" time deposits at *all* depository institutions, whether or not they are classified as commercial banks or are members of the Federal Reserve System. At the same time, in order to provide a "level playing field" as its proponents were fond of saying, it required the Fed to make its services available at a price reflecting true costs to all depository institutions subject to these reserve requirements.

2. It authorized all depository institutions to offer NOW accounts which previously had been legal only in selected northeastern states.

3. It authorized savings and loan institutions and mutual savings banks to further diversify their earning asset portfolios toward more business and consumer loans and relatively less dependence on mortgages.

4. It eliminated state usury laws (ceilings on interest rates that could be charged) on mortgages but gave the states a three-year period to reinstitute them if they chose.

5. It established a committee composed of the heads of most of the federal financial regulatory authorities and charged it with developing a plan for phasing out Regulation Q-type interest ceilings prior to April

1986. This assignment was accomplished as the law specified so that today there are no longer any governmentally imposed ceilings on the interest payable on time deposits or NOW accounts.

The Garn-St Germain Act of 1982

As had been the case in the 1930s and again in the 1960s, major banking reform requires not just one but a series of laws to achieve its goals. Accordingly, the MCA of 1980 was followed two years later by the Depository Institutions Act of 1982, more popularly known as the Garn-St Germain Act. Among the more important provisions of this law were:

1. It further liberalized the regulations governing thrift institutions earning asset portfolios, specifically with respect to commercial and consumer loans.
2. It permitted savings and loan associations to offer demand deposits when required as a result of business loans made.
3. It authorized issuance of NOW accounts to federal, state, and local governments.
4. It authorized (until 1985) in the case of failing banks or thrifts, mergers of banks with thrifts and, under certain conditions, interstate mergers.
5. It required the Depository Institutions Deregulation Committee to design and authorize a depository account for commercial banks and thrifts that would be directly competitive with money market mutual funds offered by investment companies — the money market deposit account.

The Competitive Equality Banking Act of 1987

The financial crisis faced by the FSLIC was the primary force impelling Congress to pass the Competitive Equality Banking Act of 1987. The bill, however, dealt with a wide range of banking issues.

Specifically, the 1987 law included the following major provisions:

1. The beleaguered FSLIC was authorized to raise $10.8 billion of additional capital over the next three years via the sale of bonds. This amount was obviously a pittance in comparison to the amount that organization needed.
2. Establishment of new nonbank banks after March 1987 was forbidden, and the activities and growth rate of the 160 nonbank banks in existence prior to March 1987 were constrained. Nonbank banks are commercial banklike institutions that have taken advantage of a legal loophole to evade intended regulation of commercial banks. They will be considered in depth in a later chapter.

3. Federal regulators were temporarily (until March 1988) forbidden from providing new authorization to banks to deal in insurance, real estate, or securities.

4. The Glass-Steagall Act's prohibitions on commercial banks engaging in an investment banking business were extended to apply to nonmember state banks.

Review Questions

1. Identify the First and Second Banks of the United States.

2. Discuss the problems with the nation's banking system that led to passage of the National Bank Act of 1863.

3. Identify the three main provisions of the National Bank Act of 1863 and then discuss the four major deficiencies of the act.

4. Identify "exchange charges" and explain how their widespread use under the National Bank Act of 1863 affected the check collection process.

5. Explain the commercial loan theory. In what respects was it implemented in the original Federal Reserve Act?

6. What were the major pieces of bank legislation passed during the 1930s?

7. Identify the McFadden Act and the Douglas Amendment.

8. Briefly identify the major provisions of the Monetary Control Act of 1980 and the Garn-St Germain Act of 1982.

9. What is the free-banking principle?

10. List and explain the major provisions of the National Bank Act of 1863.

11. "Although it seems evident that Congress intended to eliminate state banks with the National Bank Act of 1863, they didn't succeed." Explain.

12. In what sense might one argue that the supply of National Bank notes authorized by the National Bank Act was inelastic?

Bank Regulation and a Case Study of the FDIC

The banking legislation discussed in Chapter 6 makes it patently clear that the commercial banking industry is one of the most highly regulated industries in the economy. It is not hard to understand the reasons for this. After all, commercial banking is not just any old industry. It may be perfectly all right to permit the widget industry to expand or contract at will, or to disappear altogether for that matter, in the comfortable knowledge that no one will really be hurt except the stockholders and those people who happen to like widgets. But the commercial banking industry is something else.

Perhaps Paul A. Volcker, ex-chairman of the Board of Governors of the Federal Reserve System, said it best when he observed,

> Public policy has long recognized that commercial banks perform a unique and critical role in the economy and in the financial system. They are operators of the payments system; they are custodians of the bulk of liquid savings; they are the principal suppliers of short-term credit; and they are the critical link between monetary policy and the economy. Moreover, the fortunes of individual institutions are so intertwined that instability of one may infect another.[1]

In other words, the health of the commercial banking industry is of such overwhelming importance to the economy as a whole that it cannot be permitted to sink or swim on its own. It must be treated differently and subjected to special regulation.

In this chapter, we shall concern ourselves with the nature and effects of commercial bank regulation. First we shall identify the regulators and their

---

[1] Paul A. Volcker, Statement before the Subcommittee on Financial Institutions Supervision, Regulation and Insurance of the Committee on Banking, Finance and Urban Affairs, U.S. House of Representatives, April 17, 1985, reported in *Federal Reserve Bulletin*, June 1985, p. 424.

enforcement powers and then turn to a consideration of the major areas of federal regulation of commercial banks. Following that, we shall consider the structure, functions, and future of the Federal Deposit Insurance Corporation in more detail.

Bank Regulators and Their Powers

Who Are the Regulators?

The four main commercial bank regulatory agencies are the Comptroller of the Currency, the Federal Reserve System, the Federal Deposit Insurance Corporation, and 50 state regulatory commissions. In addition, on questions of bank merger, consolidation, and holding company acquisitions, the U.S. Department of Justice often exercises its considerable antitrust authority.

The Comptroller of the Currency   The Office of the Comptroller of the Currency (O.C.C.), as noted, was established more than a century ago as an integral part of the National Bank Act. Technically, the Comptroller's office is a part of the Treasury Department, but it operates pretty much as if it were an autonomous agency. The Comptroller himself for instance is appointed by the president to a five-year term from which, like the Board of Governors of the Federal Reserve, he may not be removed except for "cause." The O.C.C. finances itself from assessments levied on national banks.

Unlike the FRS and the FDIC, the Comptroller of the Currency operates strictly as a regulator, chartering national banks and examining and supervising those already chartered. The Fed, of course, is only a part-time regulator, being primarily occupied with the conduct of monetary policy. The FDIC, on the other hand, is a regulator only to the extent that its prime responsibility as an insurer demands it.

As a representative of the generally larger national banks, it should perhaps not be surprising that the Comptroller's office has tended to favor interstate banking and freer mergers while opposing such restrictions as the McFadden Act.[2] In these respects, the other regulators have tended to differ markedly.[3]

The Federal Reserve System   The Federal Reserve System, about which we have much more to say in a later chapter, controls and supervises the activities of all commercial banks belonging to the system. As a matter of law, all national banks must join the Federal Reserve (thus making them subject to control by both the Comptroller of the Currency and the FRS). State banks may join the Federal Reserve System if they choose. The approximately 1,000 state banks that have chosen to join are thereby subjected to the regulatory power of both the FRS and the state banking agency in their state.

[2] See Leonard Lapidus, *The Report of the Study of State and Federal Regulation of Commercial Banks* (Washington, D.C.: Federal Deposit Insurance Corporation, 1980), pp. 19–20.

[3] Ibid., p. 20.

The Federal Deposit Insurance Corporation   As we have learned, the Federal Deposit Insurance Corporation was established in 1933 as an important part of the thorough overhaul of banking legislation undertaken during the Great Depression. We will consider the structure and functioning of the FDIC in greater detail at the end of the chapter.

State Bank Regulatory Commissions   State-chartered banks that do not choose to join the Federal Reserve System — and as we have seen this constitutes a majority of the banks — are subject to the control and regulation of the state that issues their charter. Although it is difficult to generalize about 50 different sets of regulations, we can say that, in the main, state control is less stringent than is that of the Federal Reserve System.

Avoiding Unnecessary Duplication in Bank Regulation   It should be obvious from the foregoing discussion that not only is bank regulation a complex business in the United States but authority and responsibilities overlap in a number of areas. National banks, for example, are required to belong to the Federal Reserve System and to subscribe to FDIC coverage. They are thus technically subject to the regulations and supervision of three different agencies: the Comptroller of the Currency, the FRS authorities, and the FDIC authorities. State member banks are controlled by the Federal Reserve, the FDIC, and the regulations of the banking commission of the state in which they are chartered. Nonmember state banks are subject to regulation by their state banking commission and (except for the few who do not carry insurance coverage) the FDIC.

To minimize duplication of effort, especially with respect to actual examination of the banks themselves, a system has been worked out whereby bank examinations of one agency are accepted by others. The Comptroller of the Currency bears the brunt of examining national banks, making its findings available to the Federal Reserve and the FDIC. The Federal Reserve System carries out the actual examination of state member banks (along with the state banking commission, if they choose). These reports are also made available to the FDIC. The FDIC examines all insured nonmember banks (often in conjunction with the appropriate state authorities). Finally, state authorities alone are responsible for supervision and inspection of uninsured state banks. This distribution of authority plus some additional detail is depicted in Figure 7-1.

Despite these efforts to avoid duplication, the financial regulatory system has been subjected to severe criticism in recent years and proposals for reform abound. For example, one critic put it as follows:

> The aggressive, automated, diversified, multibillion-dollar companies that compete in today's financial services industry are regulated by agencies designed for the Civil War, the Panic of 1907, and the Great Depression. Regulatory techniques are outmoded and inconsistent. The system is characterized by overlapping authorities, duplicate controls, conflicts, and omissions. It is a disorderly structure, hard-pressed to cope with continuing changes in the industry.[4]

Among the major proposals for change in the structure of the regulatory system are: (1) consolidate all federal bank regulatory functions into one new

[4] Andrew S. Carron, *Reforming the Bank Regulatory Structure* (Washington, D.C.: The Brookings Institution, 1984). This staff paper is an excellent brief summary of the issue.

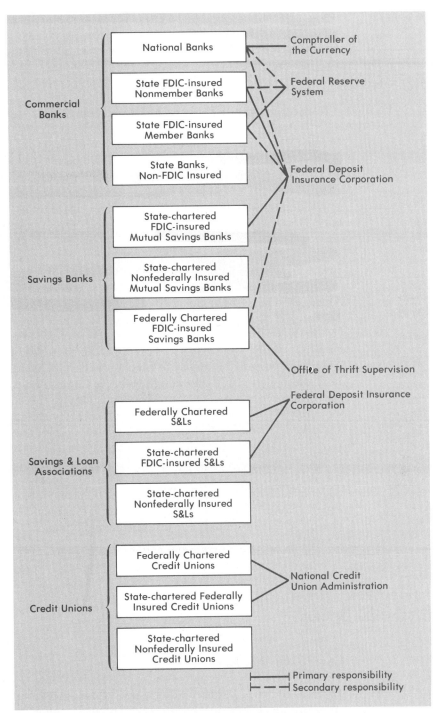

Source: Golembe and Holland, *Federal Regulation of Banking, 1983–84* (Washington, D.C.: Golembe Associates, Inc., 1983). Altered to include changes made by passage of FIRREA.

FIGURE 7-1 **Distribution of Federal Regulatory Authority**

agency; (2) convert the current regulation-by-industry system into a regulation-by-function one. This proposal would be especially helpful in overcoming current problems of unregulated competitors offering the same service as those that are regulated.

The Enforcement Powers of Bank Regulators

When a regulator encounters conditions it considers inappropriate, its first efforts to effect a cure may be by placing the bank on its "problem list." The bank can then expect more frequent and searching examinations and/or the extraction of a written agreement from the bank's managers pledging corrective measures.

When these milder measures appear or prove to be inadequate, the regulatory agencies are well equipped with more direct enforcement powers. First they may issue "cease and desist" orders requiring the bank to immediately stop an unsafe, unsound, or illegal practice. Second, they can, when deemed appropriate, levy civil money penalties ranging from $100 per day up to $10,000 per day on the offending bank as an institution and/or on its officers as individuals. Third, they possess the power to suspend and/or remove bank officers or directors subject to appropriate safeguards such as hearings for those suspended.

In the vast majority of cases, such measures have been sufficient to solve the problem. When they are not, however, the mere knowledge of the fact that regulators possess the power to revoke their charters and put them out of business is usually more than enough to bring them to heel. Strictly speaking, the power to revoke a bank's charter belongs only to the chartering agency — the Comptroller of the Currency or the authorized state agency. The Federal Reserve System and the FDIC, however, possess sanctions which for all practical purposes amount to the same thing. Although in a few states banks are permitted to operate without FDIC insurance coverage, to be competitive in most markets, it is essential. Therefore, if the FDIC threatens to withdraw a bank's insurance coverage, it is tantamount to putting it out of business. And if the Fed threatens to expel a bank from membership, though it technically could switch to a state charter and then reapply for insurance coverage, it is unlikely that it would be granted.

The Major Areas of Federal Regulation of Commercial Banks[5]

Control over Entry

To enter the corn industry all one need do is start raising and selling corn. To enter the banking business, things are a bit more complex. Under federal law it is illegal to accept deposits and conduct a commercial banking business before one

---

[5] The ensuing discussion is very strongly influenced by those outstanding publications, *Federal Regulation of Banking 1986–87* and *Federal Regulation of Banking 1983–84* by Carter H. Golembe and David S. Holland (Washington, D.C.: Golembe Associates, Inc., 1986 and 1983).

obtains a charter to do so from the Comptroller of the Currency or the appropriate state agency. Not only do both the chartering agencies specify certain explicit conditions (such as a capital requirement, to be discussed later), but both are required by the Banking Act of 1935 to consider "the convenience and needs of the community" before issuing a charter. Obviously, these legal requirements could and have acted as barriers to entry into the industry.

Capital Requirements

The so-called free-banking laws at both the federal and state levels have always specified a minimum dollar amount of capital needed before a charter may be granted. Although such limits are still on the law books, they have been permitted to become obsolete over the years and have been replaced by more meaningful supervisory rules based on the ratio of capital to assets, rather than simply dollar amounts of capital.[6]

In evaluating operating banks, the regulators have always considered the adequacy of their capital as a key indicator. Prior to 1981, however, no explicit capital-asset ratio was required, and the three federal regulators had no formal agreement to enforce common ratios on the three sets of banks they supervised.

Beginning in 1981, however, they began requiring explicit capital-to-asset ratios. From 1981 to 1985 the capital-asset ratios required by the three agencies were not the same. The confusion this created was finally eliminated in 1985 when the Federal Reserve System, the Comptroller of the Currency, and the Federal Deposit Insurance Corporation agreed on a common set of required capital-asset ratios. Under that agreement, banks were considered to have deficient capital if their *primary capital-to-asset ratio* was less than 5.5 percent and if their *total capital-to-asset ratio* was below 6 percent.[7] Banks not meeting the minimum capital requirements were normally warned by the appropriate regulatory agency and were given a period of time to correct the problem.

About the same time that the common capital-asset ratio was established, U.S. authorities entered into negotiations with financial officials from 11 other industrialized nations to establish common *risk-based* capital-asset ratios for all 12 nations.

Risk-based capital-asset ratios were needed, it was felt, to distinguish between those banks with relatively safe assets and those with relatively risky ones. The 12 participating countries were concerned at the fact that banks were acquiring more risky assets than previously as well as the fact that many of them were carrying out a greater proportion of risky "off-balance-sheet" activities.

After much debate and compromise the 12 nations reached an agreement—

[6] For example, current federal law requires minimum capital of $100,000 even though in practice the Comptroller of the Currency normally insists upon a minimum of $1 million of capital for a new charter. See ibid., p. 95.

[7] Primary capital includes the initial investment plus retained earnings plus capital reserves set up to absorb losses. Total capital includes primary capital plus preferred stock with a specified maturity date and subordinated notes and debentures (debt obligations of banks where the owners' claims are explicitly subordinated to depositors in case of insolvency and liquidation). For an excellent discussion of this matter, see R. A. Gilbert, C. C. Stone, and M. E. Treabing, "The New Capital Adequacy Standards," *Review*, Federal Reserve Bank of St. Louis, May 1985.

popularly referred to as the "Basle Agreement" — in June 1988 to establish common risk-based capital-asset ratios for all their commercial banks. Partial compliance with the terms of the agreement was required by December 1990, with full compliance by December 1992.[8]

The Basle Agreement contains two definitions of capital. "Core" (or tier 1) capital includes common and preferred stock plus retained earnings while "total" (or tier 2) capital includes everything in core capital plus subordinated debt and a limited amount of loan loss reserves.

Bank assets are separated into four risk categories. Assets such as U.S. government securities and mortgages guaranteed by the Government National Mortgage Association are considered to be riskless and are thus not counted at all in the asset portion of the required capital-asset ratio. General obligation municipal bonds, interbank deposits, and other guaranteed mortgages are treated as having a slight risk and included at 20 percent of their value. Municipal revenue bonds and first mortgages on private homes are included at 50 percent of their value, while all other assets are 100 percent counted. The result is, of course, that the fewer risky assets a bank has, the less capital it would be required to have to meet a given capital-asset ratio.

The terms of the Basle Agreement called for banks to achieve core capital equal to 3.25 percent and total capital, 7.25 percent of their risk-adjusted assets by December 1990. By December 1992 the core capital ratio is to be 4 percent and the total capital ratio 8 percent.[9]

In addition to the risk-based capital requirements established in the Basle Agreement, U.S. regulators have decided to keep a nonrisk-adjusted capital – total asset ratio requirement. Effective in January 1991, all federally regulated commercial banks were required to maintain core capital equal to at least 3 percent of their total assets.[10]

Controls over Types of Assets

Commercial banks are permitted under federal law to make loans and to purchase "marketable obligations . . . in the form of bonds, notes, and/or debentures." The quality of their loans is regulated by supervision. Bank examiners classify questionable loans into three categories. Those that appear to be inadequately protected are called "substandard." One step down are "doubtful" loans which the examiners feel are unlikely to be paid off in full.

Finally, the worst category of all are those designated as "loss loans." These are considered definitely uncollectible. Too many loans in any of these categories make a bank potentially subject to some of the enforcement procedures to be discussed later.

[8] For excellent discussions of the Basle Agreement, see William R. Keeton, "The New-Risk-Based Capital Plan for Commercial Banks," *Economic Review,* Federal Reserve Bank of Kansas City, December 1989, and R. Dan Brumbaugh, Jr., and Robert Litan, "The Banks Are Worse Off Than You Think," *Challenge,* January – February 1990.

[9] "Off-balance-sheet" activities are included among the assets with the same risk classification. For example, letters of credit to business firms would be included at 100 percent of their value while home equity credit lines would be counted at 50 percent.

[10] It should be noted that, in accordance with **FIRREA**, these requirements apply to savings institutions also.

In addition to classification by examination, bank loans are subject to other specific limitations. Unsecured loans to any one borrower, for example, may not exceed 15 percent of the bank's capital and surplus. Loans to an affiliate of a member bank (including its parent holding company) may not exceed 10 percent of its capital and surplus. Loans to such insiders as its officers, directors, or large stockholders may not be made on terms better than comparable loans to outsiders and, above a certain figure set by the appropriate regulator, may be subject to advance approval.

Control over Interest Rates

Over the years commercial banks have been significantly affected by two different types of interest rate controls. Usury laws, as one type, have been imposed by state legislation. These laws place a ceiling on the interest rates that banks may *charge* borrowers for such loans as mortgages or consumer loans. Economists are in general agreement that these laws not only serve no useful purpose but, when effective, tend to distort the allocation of credit and adversely affect consumer welfare. The typical reaction of banks constrained from charging the market rate on a mortgage by a lower usury ceiling has not been to grant the mortgage at the usury ceiling, but rather to simply cease granting mortgages altogether.

The other interest rate control was the implementation of Regulation Q–type ceilings on the interest rates banks were permitted to *pay* to their customers on time deposits. This, as noted in the preceding chapter, was authorized by the Banking Act of 1933 and was in effect until phased out in 1986 pursuant to the MCA of 1980. The decision to phase out Regulation Q ceilings came after widespread agreement was reached to the effect that the interest rate ceilings had (1) probably not contributed much to bank safety as intended and (2) tended to distort the allocation of credit and to discriminate against small savers.

Split Between Commercial and Investment Banking

As we saw in the last chapter, the portion of the Banking Act of 1933 popularly known as the Glass-Steagall Act was aimed at separating the commercial banking function from the investment banking function. It made it illegal for investment banks to accept deposits and for commercial banks to underwrite or deal in the sale of most securities.[11]

A variety of reasons has been cited for this legislation. Evidence of market manipulation in the securities industry prior to the stock market crash of 1929 played a role. The conviction that investment banking was too risky for commercial banks was a factor. Concern that a bank might abuse its powers by pushing the sale of securities of a shaky firm to whom it had made loans also entered in.

Whatever its original intent, the separation between commercial and investment banking was never complete. In the first place, the Glass-Steagall Act applies to banks that are members of the Federal Reserve System only. Conse-

---

[11] As noted earlier, commercial banks are permitted to deal in U.S. government securities and the general obligation issues of state and local governments.

quently, a nonmember state bank *can* have an investment banking form as an affiliate and conversely, an investment banking firm can own a nonmember commercial bank.[12] In addition, while the law does forbid member banks from underwriting or dealing in securities, it does not deny them the right to act as *brokers* in the sale of securities.

Although Congress seemed close to passing legislation repealing the Glass-Steagall Act in the late 1980s and 1990, it did not do so. Despite the absence of legislation on the matter, however, a series of Federal Reserve Board regulatory rulings from 1984 through 1990 went a long way toward cutting the heart out of Glass-Steagall. As one authority put it, "a continued nibbling away of the elements of separateness between commercial banking and investment banking does seem likely. . . . Indeed, it is not too farfetched to predict that Glass-Steagall will be no more effective in maintaining a separation between commercial and investment banking in a few years than the McFadden Act and the Douglas Amendment . . . have been in preventing interstate banking."[13]

In the main these rulings were based upon rather loose language in Section 20 of the Glass-Steagall Act, which states that "no member bank . . . shall be affiliated . . . with any organization *engaged principally* in the issue, flotation, underwriting public sale, or distribution at wholesale or retail or through syndicate participation of stocks, bonds, debentures, notes, or other securities" (italics added).

In permitting several large banks to underwrite sale of commercial paper, municipal revenue bonds, securitized mortgage debt, and corporate bonds and one bank to underwrite the sale of corporate stock, the Federal Reserve Board ruled that so long as the underwriting was carried out by a subsidiary within a bank holding company and so long as no more than 10 percent of the total revenue of that subsidiary was earned from the underwriting, the firm would not be considered *engaged principally* in underwriting and would not, therefore, be in violation of Section 20 of Glass-Steagall.

As a consequence, even without explicit legislation on the matter, the separation between investment and commercial banking seemed on the way out as we entered the 1990s. And, in addition, there seemed good reason to expect more explicit legislation to hasten the demise of Glass-Steagall.

Controls over Bank Structure

Finally, we should note once again the limitations on bank structure that have long been imposed by the McFadden Act and the Douglas Amendment. By limiting national bank branching privileges to those granted by the state in which the bank is located, the McFadden Act effectively barred interstate branching.

[12] Golembe and Holland, *Federal Regulation of Banking 1983–84*, p. 82. It should be noted that such commercial–investment banking affiliations must be carried out via the holding company device which makes them subject to the Fed's regulatory power. It is to avoid this control that some firms have taken advantage of a loophole in the Douglas Amendment to convert their commercial banking affiliate into a so-called "nonbank" bank. We shall learn more about the nonbank bank movement in a later chapter.

[13] George G. Kaufman, "The Securities Activities of Commercial Banks" in *Handbook for Banking Strategy*, R. Aspenwall and R. Eisenbeis, eds. (New York: John Wiley, 1984), pp. 696, 698.

The Douglas Amendment, at least until the 1980s, was almost equally successful in banning interstate banking via the holding company device. The result has been a commercial banking industry with a dramatically different structure than in most other industrialized countries. We shall look further into this matter in Chapter 8.

The Federal Deposit Insurance Corporation

Prior to the establishment of the Federal Deposit Insurance Corporation (FDIC) in 1934, there was ample reason for the American people to be uneasy about their commercial bank deposits. As we have seen, despite generally excellent economic conditions during the decade of the 1920s, an average of nearly 600 banks failed each year. And even that sorry performance was only a prelude of what was to come when the Great Depression arrived when failures shot upward to average over 2,200 per year from 1930 to 1933, culminating in an astronomical 4,000 in 1933 alone! Clearly action to restore faith in the banking system was sorely needed. It came, as we have seen, in a burst of legislation in 1933 which among other things authorized establishment of the FDIC in January 1934.[14]

Congress' intent in authorizing the FDIC is clear. Most obvious and visible was the desire to protect the savings of millions of individual depositors, thereby putting an end to the all-too-common personal financial tragedies inflicted by widespread bank failure. More fundamental from the social viewpoint, however, is the vast improvement it has brought about in the condition of the banking system as a whole. There are two important aspects of this more basic achievement.

First, because of the corporation's regulatory requirements and supervisory activities, the preponderant majority of the nation's commercial banks are probably safer than they might otherwise be. This is especially important because most of the nation's banks do not belong to the Federal Reserve System and, therefore, are not directly subject to that form of federal government regulation. The regulatory standards of the states vary widely, and it is fortunate that all but a handful of the nonmember state banks must meet the basic requirements of the FDIC in order to offer their depositors the advantage of deposit insurance.

Second, the very existence of deposit insurance has effectively eliminated, at its source, the bank panic and "run-on-the-bank" psychology that was so damaging to the entire economy in the 1920s and early 1930s. Bank panics are peculiar phenomena. In normal times, depositors prefer keeping the majority of their money balances in deposit form for the simple reason that payment by check is much more convenient. If, however, doubts develop regarding the basic sound-

---

[14] The FDIC offers insurance for deposits held at commercial banks and mutual savings banks. One year after the FDIC was authorized, Congress set up the Federal Savings and Loan Insurance Corporation (FSLIC) to provide similar insurance coverage for depositors in saving and loan associations. It was not until 1970 that provisions were made for equivalent insurance coverage for depositors in credit unions. That coverage was offered by the National Credit Union Share Insurance Fund. As we have seen the FSLIC was abolished in 1989.

ness of the banks, depositors naturally become concerned. If a few banks fail and their depositors are unable to redeem their deposits at full value, general concern rapidly deteriorates into panic. Depositors line up at their own banks in ever-increasing numbers, withdrawing cash to be sure that they "get theirs" before their bank too is forced to close its doors. And such panic philosophy tends to spread like wildfire until as happened in the early 1930s all banks, sound and unsound alike, find themselves facing liquidity crises that threaten their very existence.

But panics of this sort are entirely avoidable catastrophes. Ironically, the public only wants to withdraw cash at such times because it has developed the fear that it cannot get it. If people can be assured that they can convert their deposits to cash easily, they will not want the cash. The prevention of panics, then, is simple: Convince the public that it can always get its money and it will not rush to get it in the first place. And once bank panics consisting of such a "flight to cash" have been eliminated, the severe jolts to the economy that have resulted from the periodic disruption of credit and purchasing power attending them will be eradicated too. In this respect there can be no doubt that the FDIC, as of the present, has been an outstanding success.

As we moved into the 1990s, however, it was quite clear that some further significant revisions in the nation's deposit insurance system were on the horizon. Although the FDIC had avoided the total disaster that befell the FSLIC, it was forced to deal with such an upsurge of commercial bank failures as to markedly reduce the size of the bank insurance fund. What had to be recognized was the fact that, although commercial banks were in nowhere near as desperate a condition as the thrifts had been, the "moral hazard" created by the insurance existed for the FDIC too. We will consider some of the major proposals for revision of the deposit insurance system in the concluding section of this chapter.

The Structure of the FDIC

As we saw in Chapter 5, the FDIC is directed by a five-member board consisting of the FDIC chairman, the Comptroller of the Currency, the director of the Office of Thrift Supervision, and two other members, appointed by the president.

All commercial banks that are members of the Federal Reserve System are required to subscribe for FDIC coverage. In addition, the majority of states require their state-chartered nonmember banks to subscribe. Most of those few not required by law to offer FDIC insurance coverage find it next to impossible to compete without offering their depositors the advantage of deposit insurance.[15] The result is that over 99 percent of the banks containing over 99 percent of total deposits subscribe to FDIC coverage.[16]

Insured banks become subject to FDIC supervision and examination al-

---

[15] As we saw in Chapter 5, savings and loan association deposits are now insured by the FDIC. Most mutual savings banks already subscribed to FDIC coverage even before the FSLIC was abolished.

[16] Since, at least technically, deposits are insured only up to $100,000 per account, it is estimated that about 75 percent of the nation's deposits are fully insured.

though, as noted, the actual examinations are shared with the Office of the Comptroller of the Currency and the Federal Reserve System.

The FDIC operates two separate insurance funds—the Bank Insurance Fund and the Savings Association Insurance Fund.[17] The Bank Insurance Fund, which had assets totaling over $18 billion in 1987, has fallen rather sharply since then. The income of this fund consists of the amounts received from the annual premiums assessed on insured banks plus interest earned on the assets of the fund. When failure of insured banks requires the Fund to pay off its depositors, there is, of course, an outflow from the Fund. In 1988, 1989, and 1990, the outflow exceeded the income so that the Fund's net assets actually declined for the first time in FDIC history. Whether the increased premiums assessed on banks in the 1990s will be sufficient to reverse this trend remains to be seen. The Savings Association Insurance Fund, on the other hand, was just created so that, despite initially higher premiums than those on banks, it has not yet built up a fund of any significance.

FDIC Functions

The initial goal of the FDIC, of course, is to prevent bank failures, and its supervisory activities are pointed toward that objective. The FDIC employs over 1,500 bank examiners who conduct approximately 10,000 examinations and investigations annually. These examinations include a review of the bank's capital, the quality of its assets, its accounting procedures, and an assessment of its overall management. Bank officers are advised, warned, and/or disciplined as the results of these inspections dictate.

If difficulties persist, the troubled bank may attempt to stave off disaster by heavy borrowing from the Federal Reserve discount window. Sometimes, before failure actually occurs, the FDIC and other regulators are able to arrange a bailout via a merger with a stronger institution.

When despite all these efforts failure does occur, it is the chartering authority—the Comptroller of the Currency for a national bank or the appropriate state banking agency for a state bank—who is responsible for actually blowing the whistle and closing the bank. At that point, if the failed institution was federally insured, the FDIC becomes the receiver with authority to take over and dispose of the bank's assets while paying off its creditors to the extent required and possible.

In handling a failed bank, a key decision the FDIC must make is whether to employ the *deposit payoff* approach or the *purchase and assumption* approach.

The Deposit Payoff Approach   In the case of a deposit payoff, the FDIC begins to pay off insured depositors up to the limit of their insured coverage (maximum $100,000 per account), within a few days of the bank's closing. The payoff can take the form of a straight cash payment or, as is more common since the practice

---

[17] Actually a third insurance fund, called the FSLIC Resolution Fund, was also set up as a result of passage of the FIRREA. This fund inherited all the assets and liabilities of the insolvent FSLIC and is scheduled to be terminated when the assets are sold and the debts that had been incurred by the FSLIC are paid off.

was instituted in 1983, it can consist of simply a transfer of the insured deposit accounts to another, healthy institution.[18] Transferring the deposits has some advantages over a cash payoff in that it is often cheaper and "minimizes disruption to the closed bank's customers and to the affected communities."[19]

While insured depositors are promptly recompensed, those with accounts in excess of the $100,000 maximum become general creditors along with all other nondeposit creditors of the bank. General creditors have a claim only to whatever can be obtained from the sale of the failed bank's assets. Starting in 1984, however, the FDIC began making immediate partial repayments to holders of uninsured deposits in amounts based on the estimated present value of the assets to be liquidated.[20] This procedure is obviously advantageous to the owners of uninsured deposits, for it provides them at least a partial repayment much earlier than had been the case in the past.

The Purchase and Assumption Approach An alternative approach to dealing with a failed bank is through purchase and assumption. In this case the FDIC solicits bids from healthy banks to purchase the failed bank's assets as well as to assume responsibility for all (uninsured as well as insured) of its deposit liabilities. Since the value of the assets being purchased is bound to be less than that of the assumed deposit liabilities, the FDIC makes a cash payment to the assuming bank for the amount of the difference.

This process normally takes no more than three days and has the distinct advantage of preventing altogether the disruption of banking services to the depositors and community that can accompany a deposit payout. In addition, it has obvious benefits for large depositors who lose nothing regardless of the size of their deposits.

The Public Policy Issues Involved in the Method of Handling Failed Banks

In choosing between the deposit payoff and purchase and assumption approaches, the FDIC is required by law to select the method which will involve the least cost. The record shows that from 1934 through 1989, 1,112 of the 1,644 failures were handled by the purchase and assumption approach while the remaining 532 were dealt with through deposit payoffs. But the record also shows a clear-cut pattern with important implications. Almost without exception, large failed banks have been dealt with by a purchase and assumption transaction while smaller banks are more typically handled with deposit payoffs. Clear evidence of this bias is the fact that during the half century from 1934 to 1984, the 344 failed banks handled with deposit payoffs had average deposits of just under $6 million, while the 403 failed banks made subject to purchase and assumption averaged over $60 million in deposits.

---

[18] Obviously, the institution to which these deposit liabilities are transferred receives an equivalent value of assets to make the transfer acceptable.

[19] FDIC, *1984 Annual Report*, pp. 14–15.

[20] In 1984, for example, these payments made in 12 failure cases ranged from 40 to 75 percent of uninsured claims. FDIC, *1984 Annual Report*, p. 15.

This practice of discrimination by size of bank has led to criticism from two directions. In the first place, critics point out, it makes it almost impossible for smaller banks to attract large deposits, for since the purchase and assumption approach involves transferring *all* deposits of the failed bank (insured and uninsured alike) the effect is to provide 100 percent insurance for all deposits. The person or institution with over $100,000 to deposit would be foolish to put it into a relatively small bank where failure (and deposit payoff) could involve substantial loss when the loss would be avoided altogether if the failed bank were large.

Secondly, and more fundamentally, the de facto 100 percent insurance for all deposits at large banks is said to undercut seriously the effectiveness of so-called "market discipline" in restraining excessive risk taking by banks. Theoretically (if depositors are knowledgeable about and responsive to the degree of risk incurred by different banks), banks with the riskier portfolios would be required to pay higher interest rates to their depositors to compensate them for participating in a greater risk of failure. If such a "risk premium" is *not* paid, one might logically expect owners of deposits in excess of the legal $100,000 maximum to shop around for a safer place to entrust their funds. Consequently, either because payment of the "risk premium" increases their costs, or because of the fear of losing the accounts of their big depositors, such banks might be expected to follow less risky portfolio practices.

But if the insurance agency has established the practice of de facto 100 percent insurance coverage for all depositors in all large banks, risky or reckless portfolio practices are not "disciplined" either by the need to pay higher interest or by the risk of loss of deposits. The result is that the full burden of preventing the taking of undue risk falls on regulators and bank examiners.

In a sense, the FDIC is operating on the horns of a dilemma. While it would like to take steps to expose banks further to "market discipline," it is firmly committed to preventing the serious disruption to the banking system and the economy it feels sure would result from allowing a truly large bank to fail with substantial losses to holders of uninsured deposits.

The nature of this dilemma was clearly revealed in the handling of the huge Continental Illinois bank which was on the brink of failure in 1984. Rather than let it fail with attendant losses to large depositors, the federal government put up a whopping $4.5 billion to keep it afloat essentially as a government-owned bank. The FDIC made clear their reasons with the following statement:

> Permitting Continental to fail and paying off insured depositors was never a feasible option for the regulators. Insured accounts totalled only slightly more than $3 billion. This meant that uninsured depositors and other private creditors with over $30 billion in claims would have had their funds tied up for years in a bankruptcy proceeding awaiting the liquidation of assets and the settlement of litigation. Hundreds of small banks would have been particularly hard hit. Almost 2,300 small banks had nearly $6 billion at risk in Continental; 66 of them had more than their capital on the line and another 113 had between 50 and 100 percent.[21]

This bailout of Continental Illinois, and the FDIC's practice of using the purchase and assumption approach to handle the failure of large banks, has

---

[21] FDIC, *1984 Annual Report*, p. 4.

undoubtedly convinced large depositors that as long as they keep their accounts at large banks, they need have no worry about losses. And if that is the case, they have no incentive to exert "market discipline" on banks taking excessive risks.

The Recent Record of the FDIC

The achievements of the FDIC are indeed impressive. In its first 50 years of operation, bank failure averaged just over 16 per year—a sharp contrast to the yearly average of 600 in the prosperous 1920s. This dramatic improvement was undoubtedly due in part to the constructive role of the FDIC. Not only has it improved the quality of the nation's banks through its supervisory activities, but it has been extremely successful in improving the stability of, and confidence in, the nation's banking system. And all of this has been accomplished at modest cost. During its first half century, the net losses incurred in handling bank failures totaled just over $2.5 billion, a paltry sum when it is recognized that the value of insured deposits is now well over $2 *trillion*.

Despite this impressive long record of success, developments in the commercial banking industry and the behavior of the FDIC's insurance fund in the 1980s and early 1990s provide ample reason for concern for the future.

To begin with, bank failures, which had averaged only 5 per year from 1943 through 1981, suddenly shot up to average over 100 per year from 1982 to 1987, and then went on up to average nearly 200 per year from 1988 through 1990. The record of insured bank failures from establishment of the FDIC through 1990 is depicted in Figure 7-2.

If the banks failing were all small ones, the recent jump in their numbers would be a matter of relatively little concern to the FDIC or the economy. The fact is, however, that the recent failures have included some quite sizable banks, so that the cost of resolving them has been a matter of somewhat greater significance. Indeed, as a panel of experts recently put it, "What makes the current weakness in the U.S. banking system so troubling is that the problems now appear to be centered in the largest banks."[22]

Evidence of the increase in the size of bank failures in recent years is presented in Table 7-1. Adding to this evidence was the FDIC's forecast, in mid-1991, of the expected failure of 340 to 440 additional banks during 1991 and 1992.

Of course bank failures provide only a record of past problems. One index of potential future problems is the "problem bank" list.

During the regular periodic examination by regulators, each bank's condition is evaluated and rated on a five-point scale. Those receiving one of the two worst ratings are placed on the "problem list." In recent years, about 20 percent of banks placed on the problem list have failed within the next two years.[23] As Table 7-2 indicates, the problem list shot up from about 200 in the early 1980s to

---

[22] James R. Barth, R. Dan Brumbaugh, Jr., and Robert E. Litan, "The Banking Industry in Turmoil: A Report on the Condition of the U.S. Banking Industry and the Bank Insurance Fund," presented to the Financial Institutions Subcommittee of the House Committee on Banking, Housing and Urban Affairs, December 17, 1990.

[23] Ibid., p. 80.

Source: *Reforming Federal Deposit Insurance* (Washington, D.C.: Congressional Budget Office, 1990), pp. 142–143.

FIGURE 7-2   **Bank Insurance Fund Reserves Relative to Insured Deposits**

TABLE 7-1   Value of assets of failed banks, 1970–1990 (millions of dollars)

Year	Value of assets	Year	Value of assets
1970	$ 62.1	1981	4,859.1
1971	196.5	1982	11,632.4
1972	22.1	1983	7,026.9
1973	1,309.7	1984	3,276.4
1974	3,822.6	1985	8,741.3
1975	420.0	1986	6,991.6
1976	1,039.3	1987	6,850.7
1977	232.6	1988	35,697.8
1978	994.0	1989	29,168.6
1979	133.0	1990	16,000.0
1980	236.2		

Source: *Reforming Federal Deposit Insurance* (Washington, D.C.: Congressional Budget Office, 1990).

TABLE 7-2 Number of "problem banks," 1980–1990			
Year	*Problem banks*	*Year*	*Problem banks*
1980	212	1986	1,484
1981	223	1987	1,575
1982	369	1988	1,406
1983	642	1989	1,109
1984	848	1990 (June 30)	1,034
1985	1,140		

Source: Federal Deposit Insurance Corporation.

a peak of over 1,500 in 1987. Although the list had been pared back to under 1,100 by mid-1990, the increasing percentage of large banks included left the future no less ominous.

A final source of concern is the size of the FDIC's Bank Insurance Fund relative to the deposits insured. This fund, built up as we've seen from premiums levied on banks and accumulated interest, represents what is currently available to aid in resolving future failures. The size of the fund and its relation to the amount of insured deposits is reported in Table 7-3 and shown graphically in Figure 7-2. The absolute amount of the fund reached a peak in 1987 and, because of sizable bank failures recently, has fallen in each year since. The fund as a percentage of insured deposits has fared even worse. For most of the period up to 1985, it stayed close to 1.20 percent. Thereafter, however, it has fallen precipitously. And as of the time of this writing, the FDIC has predicted that the fund will fall by another $5–8 billion in 1991. To put the data in Table 7-3 in some sort of perspective, we might note that the now defunct FSLIC fund had reserves equal to 0.96 percent of its insured deposits as recently as 1983!

All this is disturbing, especially in light of the enormous losses so recently recorded by the savings and loan industry. And while no one believes that the commercial bank industry is in anything like the danger the thrift industry was a few years ago, some observers see additional reasons for concern.[24] It is noted, for example, that commercial banks have lost some of their highest-quality corporate borrowers in recent years because the "securitization" movement has made it easier for them to borrow directly through issuing commercial paper and bonds. As a result commercial banks have recently been making proportionately more real estate loans—especially the riskier commercial variety. Also, an increasing part of commercial bank portfolios are the sometimes quite speculative loans to finance leveraged buyouts.[25]

Finally, it must be recognized that the sharp reductions in the Bank Insurance Fund that occurred in 1988, 1989, and 1990 took place in an economy that was near full employment and still engaged in the longest peacetime growth period in our history. A look back at Table 7-1 will reveal the fact that (as the

[24] See, for example, the excellent article by R. Dan Brumbaugh, Jr., and Robert E. Litan entitled "The Banks Are Worse Off than You Think," *Challenge*, January–February 1990.
[25] Ibid., p. 9.

TABLE 7-3 Bank insurance fund, amount and percent of insured deposits, 1970–1990

Year	Bank insurance fund (millions of dollars)	Insurance fund as a percentage of insured deposits
1970	$ 4,380	1.253%
1971	4,740	1.265
1972	5,159	1.229
1973	5,615	1.206
1974	6,124	1.177
1975	6,716	1.180
1976	7,269	1.157
1977	7,993	1.154
1978	8,796	1.156
1979	9,793	1.211
1980	11,020	1.162
1981	12,246	1.238
1982	13,771	1.214
1983	15,424	1.216
1984	16,529	1.189
1985	17,957	1.194
1986	18,253	1.117
1987	18,302	1.103
1988	14,060	0.800
1989	13,210	0.700
1990	8,400	0.470

Source: Federal Deposit Insurance Corporation.

1973–74 and the 1981–82 data confirm) losses from bank failures typically rise during recessions. It is clear that the recession of 1990–91 has increased the FDIC's problems but it is too early at the date of this writing to say how much.

Proposals for FDIC Reform[26]

With the S&L debacle still freshly in mind and with problems in commercial banks clearly evident, major changes in the nation's deposit insurance program are assured. What is not certain, as this is being written, is the precise form those changes will take. We turn now to a brief consideration of some of the major proposals for reform.

---

[26] This section draws heavily on the excellent publication *Reforming Federal Deposit Insurance* (Washington, D.C.: Congressional Budget Office, 1990). See also Loretta J. Mester, "Curing Our Ailing Deposit-Insurance System," *Business Review*, Federal Reserve Bank of Philadelphia, September–October 1990.

Proposals Aimed at Increased Market Discipline

1. Reduce amount of deposit insurance. Many have pointed out that, to the extent that deposit insurance is aimed at providing protection for "small" depositors, the $100,000 maximum currently offered is more than is required. A cutback to $10,000 or $20,000 would not only expose the Insurance Fund to less potential loss but also would provide incentive for depositors with accounts in excess of the insured amount to exercise "discipline" on their banks by withdrawing funds if the bank's portfolio policies are perceived to be too risky.

The major objections to this proposal include the possibility that such withdrawals could trigger the sort of "runs" deposit insurance was intended to prevent and the fact that most depositors will be unlikely to possess the necessary information to judge the "riskiness" of their bank's practices.

An alternative method of reducing the level of deposit insurance would be to make the $100,000 limit applicable to each *person* rather than each *account,* thereby eliminating the current possibility of recovering much more than $100,000 of coverage by breaking one's wealth down into separate $100,000 accounts. A third possibility would be to copy the practice of several other countries that insure only 75 or 80 *percent* of a person's deposit up to a certain maximum. With this so-called co-insurance procedure, depositors will have even more incentive to "discipline" their depositories, since they will definitely suffer some loss if their bank fails. Both these latter two measures, however, are subject to the same disadvantages as the proposal to simply lower the dollar amount of insurance.

2. Require that uninsured creditors (including depositors with over $100,000) suffer a mandatory loss of some fixed fraction of their claims when a failed bank is assumed by another. This recommendation has come to be called the "haircut" proposal and is aimed at undercutting the worst effects of the "too big to fail" policy followed by the FDIC in the past. It would permit the regulator to continue its practice of handling big bank failures via the purchase and assumption approach, but it would mandate that uninsured creditors of such banks suffer a loss of perhaps 10 percent of their claims. The idea, once again, is to give such creditors an incentive to exercise "discipline" on their bank's portfolio policies.

3. Impose specific mandatory penalties on banks with low capital-asset ratios and require mandatory recapitalization and reorganization before owner's net worth reaches zero.[27] This proposal takes the position that the Insurance Fund (and the taxpayers) cannot lose so long as banks are closed while the losses can still be absorbed out of the owner's equity. The intent is not only to prevent loss to the taxpayers but to enlist the aid of the owners in disciplining bank management.

It would mandate specific penalties such as suspension of dividend payments and limits on growth when a bank's capital-asset ratio falls below certain levels. In addition, when that ratio reaches some critically low (but still positive) level, it would require that the bank be reorganized, merged, or closed altogether.

---

[27] For a description of such a proposal see Robert A. Eisenbeis, "Restructuring Banking," *Challenge*, January–February 1990.

The disadvantages of this proposal include the difficulty of measuring capital accurately and its rigidity. While it would forbid the sort of excessive "forbearance" shown the S&Ls, it would also forbid forbearance in situations in which it might be appropriate.

Proposals Aimed at Increasing the Regulators' Capacity to Supervise Effectively

1. **Switch to market value accounting.** One proposal that has gained considerable support is that, to the extent possible, banks should be required to report their assets in terms of market value rather than book value. The point is, of course, that book value accounting reports assets essentially at their historical cost rather than at the amount they would bring if they were sold in the market today. If the purpose of the regulator in requiring reports is to estimate the actual amount by which its assets exceed its liabilities, it seems clear that market value accounting is preferable. The main problem with this is the fact that it is not so easy to accomplish. Many bank assets are not regularly sold on the market so that arriving at a market value is a problem of considerable complexity.[28]

2. **Institute risk-based insurance premiums.** As we have seen, the current system assesses banks insurance premiums based only on the amount of their insured deposits. This proposal would levy higher premiums on banks with risky assets, not unlike the risk-based capital requirements that have been adopted. Alternatively, it might impose higher premiums on banks with low capital. The purpose, obviously, would be to induce banks to cut back on risks and/or increase capital. It might also be used to penalize (via higher premiums) those banks that rely heavily on brokered deposits.

On the negative side, it should be pointed out that differentiating degrees of risk of assets is a difficult task. In addition, since this would raise the costs of those institutions already incurring the greatest risk, it could have the unintended effect of pushing some of them over the brink into insolvency, thereby possibly placing a greater burden on the insurance fund.

3. **Increase the resources of the regulator.** Clearly, it would seem, the more and the better trained the bank examiners and auditors the FDIC has, the more thorough the job it can do in preventing loss.

4. **Increase the line of credit available to the FDIC from the Treasury.** As we have seen, a not inconsiderable part of the losses incurred in the S&L disaster came about because the FSLIC simply did not have enough funds to pay off depositors at already insolvent institutions. As a result, these "zombie" institutions were allowed to continue operating, attracting brokered deposits from around the country and using them to make ever riskier loans. And all the while, the losses grew larger.

This proposal is intended to permit quick closure of insolvent banks, without having to wait for Congress to pass explicit legislation authorizing the funds.

---

[28] For a statement on some of the problems, see A. N. Berger, K. A. Kuester, and J. M. O'Brien, "Some Red Flags Concerning Market Value Accounting," *Banking System Risk: Charting a New Course*, Federal Reserve Bank of Chicago, 1989.

A Final Comment on Reform   It is important to recognize that no matter what measures are taken to reform the nation's deposit insurance apparatus, problems must be expected if the industry itself should be chronically unprofitable. Consequently, any reform effort must go beyond the measures just discussed and include whatever legislation is needed to permit the U.S. commercial banking industry to compete effectively against its nonbank rivals as well as against banks from other countries. Among other things, this must involve reconsideration of the barriers set up by such measures as the McFadden Act, the Bank Holding Company Act, and the Glass-Steagall Act.[29] Indeed, as this is being written, Congress is debating sweeping legislation to not only reform the deposit insurance mechanism but, at the same time, to permit banks or their affiliates to sell insurance, deal in all types of securities, and branch freely over state lines.

Review Questions

1. Identify the four main bank regulators and comment on efforts currently made to avoid duplication of effort.

2. Explain how the "risk-based" capital requirements adopted in the Basle Agreement are applied.

3. "Even while the Glass-Steagall Act was still on the books, Federal Reserve regulatory rulings in the 1984–1990 period sharply undercut the separation between commercial and investment banking." Explain.

4. Distinguish the deposit payoff from the purchase and assumption approach. What public policy issues are involved in the choice between these two methods of handling failed banks?

5. Explain the dilemma confronting the FDIC in its attempt to impose market discipline on banks without permitting serious disruption to the system should a large bank fail.

6. Carefully discuss some of the major proposals that have been suggested for reforming deposit insurance.

---

[29] For an excellent statement to this effect, as well as a thorough review of the S&L crisis, see James Barth, *The Great Savings and Loan Debacle* (Washington, D.C.: American Enterprise Institute, 1990).

The Commercial Banking Business and the Structure of the Commercial Banking System

Our task in this chapter is twofold. First, we consider briefly the business of commercial banking. In this section we rely heavily on balance sheets to deal with such questions as: What are the objectives of the typical commercial banker and how does he or she go about pursuing them? Then we turn to a discussion of the structure of the U.S. commercial banking system, requiring in the process a consideration of the effects on that structure of some of the laws mentioned in Chapter 6.

An Introduction to Commercial Banking

The Balance Sheet of a Typical Commercial Bank

Table 8-1 depicts a consolidated balance sheet for all commercial banks in the United States as of December 1990. We shall use this picture of the entire banking system to get an idea of what a commercial bank does and of the importance of the various assets and liabilities to an average or typical commercial bank in this country.

One can obtain a superficial understanding of the basic nature of the commercial banking business simply by examining Table 8-1. Aside from their capital accounts and a limited amount of borrowing, commercial bank funds are raised by the issuance of two major liabilities: checkable deposits and time and saving deposits.

From the individual banker's point of view, demand deposit liabilities have the advantage of requiring payment of no explicit interest to their owners, but

TABLE 8-1 Consolidated balance sheet for all U.S. commercial
banks, December 1990 (billions of dollars)

Assets

Currency and coins		$ 31.9
Deposits at other U.S. banks		29.7
Federal Reserve account		23.7
Loans, total		2,306.4
Commercial and industrial	656.8	
Real estate	830.6	
Consumer	387.1	
All others	230.3	
Securities, total		602.8
U.S. government	436.9	
Other	165.9	
All other assets		396.0
Total assets		$3,390.5

Liabilities and capital accounts

Demand deposits and other checkable deposits	$ 638.1
Savings deposits	572.9
Time deposits	1,148.3
Borrowings	545.6
All other liabilities	265.0
Capital accounts	220.4
Total liabilities and capital accounts	$3,390.5

Source: Federal Reserve System.

the disadvantage of being legally payable in cash at the demand of the account
holders or transferable by check at any time to anyone else. Other checkable
deposits such as NOW accounts are also payable on demand even though they do
offer an interest payment to owners. Thus, the most attractive feature of checkable deposits to their owners—their perfect liquidity—represents a constant
threat to the bank issuing them. It must at all times be prepared to pay out
whatever amount of cash the owners choose to withdraw or transfer to another
bank. For if at any time the bank is unable to do so, it can legally be closed.

Time and savings deposits are a more costly source of funds to the banker.
The explicit interest payment on them is generally higher than that required on
NOW accounts and obviously higher than the zero interest payment required on
ordinary demand deposits. As we have seen, although the law requires bankers to
reserve the right to withhold payment on regular savings accounts for up to seven
days, the waiting period is almost universally waived, making savings accounts
almost as severe a liquidity constraint on commercial bankers as are checking
accounts. On the other hand, time deposits, especially certificates of deposit, can
only be cashed in before their maturity dates if an interest penalty of some
significance is paid. They therefore constitute slightly less of a withdrawal threat.

The exceptional degree of liquidity of their prime sources of funds distinguishes commercial banks from most other financial institutions and, rather obviously, involves a severe constraint on their use. Turning to the asset side of Table 8-1, it should not be surprising that commercial banks hold a much larger percentage of their assets in cash or near-cash form than the institutions considered in Chapter 4. In December 1990 their *primary reserves*—the sum of their vault cash, checking accounts at other commercial banks, and checking accounts at district Federal Reserve banks—totaled $85.3 billion, just over 2.5 percent of their assets.

Although these primary reserves are large in comparison with other financial institutions, when compared with commercial bank demand liabilities they are less impressive. In late 1990, for example, they constituted less than 14 percent of checkable deposits outstanding and less than 4 percent of total deposit liabilities. Clearly, the strongest of banks had nowhere near enough cash on hand to meet withdrawal demands had all its depositors chosen to demand payment at the same time.

Were the commercial banks therefore skating on thin ice in 1990 when these data were collected? By no means. Although the law requires payment of cash on demand to demand deposit owners, relatively few people exercise the privilege at any one time. A significant part of the art of commercial banking consists of knowing the habits of depositors (and the law) sufficiently well to keep the bank's primary reserve portion of its assets down to the minimum possible levels. For primary reserves, essential though they are for meeting the bank's liquidity and legal reserve requirements, are nonincome-earning assets. As private business concerns, commercial banks are understandably interested in putting all the assets they can into income-earning form.

The two basic types of *earning assets* of a commercial bank are loans and securities. In 1990, over 85 percent of bank assets were earning assets. We shall have more to say on this topic shortly. For the moment, let us simply note that a sizable amount of these, especially the $437 billion worth of U.S. government securities, are held partly as a sort of second line of defense against the possibility of unexpectedly large cash withdrawals (or losses to other banks). Assets held for this purpose are called *secondary reserves*. Although they normally yield somewhat lower interest returns than other earning assets, U.S. securities have the virtue of being quickly salable for cash should the amount of primary reserves on hand prove to be insufficient.

The Business of Commercial Banking

Much of our ensuing consideration of commercial banks will center on the activities and control of the banking system as a whole, as this more global approach seems the relevant one for our purposes. We would, however, be remiss if we were to turn directly to the subject of the control of the banking system without at least some preliminary comments on the banking business, as such, from the individual banker's vantage point.

Commercial banking, more so than many businesses, is an art that requires a peculiar blend of experience, insight, intelligence, and prudence. It is an exacting profession that requires successful practitioners to satisfy not only their own stockholders and depositors but also an imposing network of governmental regulatory agencies, as well as a general public that often looks with a jaundiced eye upon the caretaker of "other people's money." In no other business is a public image of integrity and prudence of greater importance.

At the risk of oversimplifying the problems confronting bankers, their primary responsibility might be viewed as maintaining a careful balance among *solvency, liquidity,* and *profitability.* This is a task of no small magnitude because, as is so often the case, there are inherent conflicts among the three objectives.

A bank is *solvent* if, given time, it can convert its assets into sufficient cash to meet at least all its outstanding liabilities. *Liquidity,* however, requires that it be able to pay cash *immediately,* when called upon to do so, for all of its demand liabilities. It is this latter requirement that forces the commercial banker into a pattern of portfolio management that is notably different from that of the other financial institutions. Although other institutions often *do* pay on demand, only commercial banks are faced with a preponderance of liabilities that are *legally* payable on the demand of the holder.

It should be made clear that a bank may be perfectly solvent without being sufficiently liquid. Given several weeks or months in which to dispose of its assets in an orderly fashion, it may be able to raise more than enough cash to meet all its liabilities. But the liquidity problem is a different kind of constraint. Claims for cash by its demand depositors must be met in full *immediately,* not within several weeks or months. And a bank that is perfectly solvent, in the sense that it could in time pay off all claimants, could easily be forced to close its doors because of illiquidity — inability to honor its promise to pay cash *on demand* to any checking account owner.

The third requirement, *profitability,* introduces new complications. Certainly a bank can maintain its solvency by purchasing only the safest of financial assets. At the same time it must make sure that a sufficient number of these safe assets are also liquid enough, that is, quickly convertible into a fairly fixed amount of cash, to meet the likely demand for cash. But it is precisely these assets, the safest and most liquid, that will earn the bank the lowest rates of return. After all, the safest, most liquid asset of all is cash, but a bank that held a portfolio composed entirely of cash would earn no income whatever and would quickly disappear from the scene.

The commercial banker, therefore, must walk a narrow line. He or she must balance the asset portfolio in such a way as to satisfy all three basic requirements. This is an essential part of the skill, the knowledge, the central art of banking.

The Task of Asset Management

Given a certain amount of funds, how does the commercial banker decide how to use them? How, that is, does a banker distribute those funds among the assets available to assure the firm of adequate profits along with liquidity and solvency? The question is a complex one and its solution obviously depends on a variety of factors.

For example, in 1947 U.S. commercial banks held 19 percent of their assets in the form of primary reserves, 25 percent in the form of loans, and an astounding 50 percent in securities. As Table 8-1 attests, 40-odd years later primary reserves were less than 3 percent, securities were only 18 percent, and loans led the parade at 68 percent!

Why such a difference? Obviously the 1947 distribution, coming as it did so soon after the end of World War II, was distinctly atypical. During the Great Depression of the 1930s through the war years, there had been relatively little private demand for credit compared with the enormous needs of the federal government. Consequently, commercial banks came out of the period with their portfolios overstocked with U.S. securities. In addition, exceptionally high legal reserve requirements and painful memories of the bank panic during the 1930s combined to keep primary reserves at abnormally high levels during the late 1940s.

Clearly, barring such unusual circumstances as these, the 1990 pattern, with loans the dominant earning asset and primary reserves held down to a minimum, is the more normal one. Let us turn now to a slightly more detailed consideration of the steps involved in asset management.

Assuring Liquidity The first priority is to guarantee adequate liquidity. As we have seen, this means committing a certain proportion of assets to the nonincome-earning, primary reserve category and a certain proportion to the highly liquid but relatively low-yielding form of secondary reserves — U.S. government securities.

The Loan Portfolio Once liquidity has been established, the banker is free to turn to the more agreeable task of maximizing profits. As Table 8-1 makes clear, this primarily means making loans. Until fairly recently the dominant type of loans were "commercial and industrial" loans to business. Now, however, real estate loans dominate. Reasons for this change include the decline of the longtime previous leader, the savings and loan industry, and the rapid spread of *securitization* of real estate loans. Securitization involves bundling together a large number of individual mortgage loans and then selling the package as a security like a bond. This development has made mortgages much more salable in the secondary market and has therefore markedly increased their liquidity.

Despite the ascendancy of mortgage loans, commercial and industrial loans retain an extremely important position in commercial bank portfolios. This is because commercial banks are almost unique in their suitability for serving the local business loan market. Most commercial banks are one-office, local institutions geared to specialize in loans to local business. Better than almost any other lender, they are in a position of knowing the credit needs of their locality. Perhaps more so than any other lenders, they feel it their purview — indeed, their responsibility — to fill those needs.

But there are sounder reasons than mere tradition for their concentration on business loans. Business firms typically keep their checking accounts at those banks that take care of their credit needs and these accounts are a most important source of funds for the bank.

In fact, it is a common practice for banks making such loans to require the borrower to maintain what is generally referred to as a *compensating balance* in its checking account as a precondition for granting the loan. For example, business borrowers are commonly required to maintain a checking account balance in the neighborhood of 10 percent of their unused credit line and 15 percent of the amount borrowed. The effect of such a requirement, of course, is to increase the effective yield on the loan well above the stated interest rate charged because the borrower is required to pay interest on the full amount of the loan even though he or she cannot use it all.

In recent decades, consumer loans have been competing with the business and mortgage loans for space in the commercial bank loan portfolio. Increasing commitments in these areas, the latter greatly enhanced by the widespread adoption of bank credit card plans with a national interchange, have provided healthy diversification in commercial bank portfolios and seem destined to continue.

The Securities Portfolio   Commercial bank security portfolios consist almost entirely of securities issued by the federal government and those issued by state and local governments.

Because they are the most liquid of all the earning assets, U.S. securities are held primarily as a secondary reserve, even though their interest yield is less than that of most loans. In addition, U.S. securities serve an important role as acceptable collateral for commercial bank borrowing from the Federal Reserve banks as well as required security for the acquisition of federal government demand deposits.

Although, as noted, U.S. securities equaled almost half of commercial bank assets immediately after World War II, they have fallen off steadily over the years. This decline represents, in large part, a return to more usual portfolio practices as the abnormal accumulation of governments acquired during that war have been replaced by loans. It reflects also the development of newer, more attractive sources of short-term funds, such as the federal funds market for liquidity purposes. Clearly, U.S. securities currently seem to represent a second-choice asset, since they tend to rise only in periods where bank reserves are plentiful and the demand for loans has fallen off.

State and local government securities, on the other hand, constituted a rapidly growing proportion of commercial bank assets — at least prior to the 1990s. First, the interest earned on these municipals is exempt from federal taxation. To commercial banks they therefore represent an important means of lowering the burden of the corporate income tax. Indeed, the evidence is clear that state and local securities have been the most important mechanism for tax avoidance employed by commercial banks in recent years.

Tax avoidance, however, is not the sole reason that commercial banks have expanded their portfolios of municipals. Commercial banks look upon it as something of an obligation to support area governments and generally will at least offer a bid on new issues. Such support, of course, is not entirely unrelated to the banks' desire to attract state and local government deposits. Second, as commercial banks are authorized to underwrite and deal in general obligation issues of state and local governments, those who do are in a strategic position to acquire attractive offerings for their own account. Finally, as the supply of municipals has increased, the secondary market for them — the market in which they may be resold before maturity — has improved substantially. This, of course, has made them much more liquid than they were previously.

The Task of Liability Management

For many years commercial banks were relatively passive about the acquisition of funds. Of course they made the obvious efforts to attract demand and time deposits, but most of the business of banking was viewed as properly allocating the funds available among competing assets.

This rather passive approach to the liability side of their balance sheets was possible and perhaps even appropriate in the first decade and a half after World War II. For during that period, demand deposits constituted a very large part of financial assets held by business, and bank portfolios were sufficiently over-stocked with U.S. securities to permit the financing of much of the expanding private demand for credit by unloading them.

By 1960, however, it was clear that commercial banks were failing to attract funds at a rate commensurate with the rest of the economy. Increasing sophistication and response to generally rising interest rates by corporate financial managers had led them to sharply reduce their holdings of demand deposits. Time deposits, on the other hand, were expanding rapidly, and commercial banks were falling behind, relative to the other financial institutions, in attracting them. To combat this development the commercial banks launched a massive and innovative campaign, beginning during the 1960s, to attract a larger share of the funds available. They did it by more extensive use of existing sources of funds, by developing new liability instruments with which to attract funds, and by competing vigorously, on a price basis, to attract a larger share. This effort has come to be called *liability management*.

Liability management has featured the development and refinement of a number of money market instruments discussed earlier. These include the broadening of the federal funds market, the borrowing of Eurodollars, and the development of the negotiable certificate of deposit and repurchase agreement, among others. This much more aggressive approach to commercial bank management has continued right on into the early 1990s.

The Structure of the U.S. Commercial Banking System

Over the years it has become customary to characterize the U.S. commercial banking system as unique in two important respects. First, it is a *dual banking system* wherein some banks are chartered and regulated by state governments while others are chartered and regulated by the federal government. Second, it is often described as a *unit banking system*, composed of many individual, one-office banks, rather than a few mammoth banking companies controlling extensive, nationwide systems of branch offices. Let us consider these two aspects of the nation's banking system in turn.

	State	*National*	
TABLE 8-2 Number of state and national commercial banks in the United States, 1860–1990			
Year	State banks	National banks	Total
1860	1,562	—	1,562
1865	349	1,294	1,643
1870	325	1,612	1,937
1875	586	2,076	2,662
1880	650	2,076	2,726
1885	1,015	2,689	3,704
1890	2,250	3,484	5,734
1895	4,369	3,715	8,084
1900	5,007	3,731	8,738
1905	9,018	5,664	14,682
1910	14,348	7,138	21,486
1915	17,748	7,597	25,345
1920	20,635	8,024	28,659
1925	19,573	8,066	27,639
1930	15,798	7,247	23,045
1935	9,752	5,425	15,177
1940	9,181	5,164	14,345
1945	8,994	5,017	14,011
1950	9,163	4,958	14,121
1955	9,024	4,692	13,716
1960	8,942	4,530	13,472
1965	8,989	4,815	13,804
1970	9,066	4,620	13,686
1975	9,888	4,744	14,632
1980	10,411	4,425	14,836
1985	10,104	4,968	15,072
1990	8,340	3,976	12,316

Source: Federal Reserve System.

A Dual Banking System

As noted in the preceding chapter, there are strong grounds for the belief that Congress's real purpose in levying a 10 percent tax on the issuance of state bank notes as part of the National Bank Act of 1863 was the elimination of state-chartered banks themselves. If so, as Table 8-2 makes clear, the effort failed.

Immediately after passage of the National Bank Act, the number of state banks in existence fell off precipitously. Within 10 years, however, saved from extinction by the public's widespread adoption of the checking habit, they began an impressive comeback. Before the turn of the century, state-chartered banks once again outnumbered national banks, and by 1920, they numbered well over

TABLE 8-3 National and state banks, number of banks and deposits, December 31, 1990

	National	*State*
Number of banks	3,976	8,340
Percentage of banks	32%	68%
Value of deposits	$1,374 billion	$964 billion
Percentage of total commercial bank deposits	59%	41%

Source: Federal Reserve System.

20,000. Although the number of national banks also grew rapidly through the early 1920s, they reached their high watermark at a level less than half that of state banks. Even though the total number of commercial banks has fallen off sharply since that time, state banks continue to outnumber national banks by over two to one.

One can, however, reach erroneous conclusions about the importance of state banks in the current banking scene by considering the number of banks alone. Despite the numerical dominance of state banks, the national banks are, on the average, much larger. The result, as is evident in Table 8-3, is that national banks currently control almost 60 percent of the total deposits at all U.S. commercial banks.

"Why," one might reasonably ask, "should the United States have a dual banking system anyway?" What advantage can there possibly be in maintaining two entirely different sets of regulatory agencies with different standards for chartering as well as for supervision?

One defender of the dual banking system has put it this way:

> Critics of the dual banking system sometimes regard it as little more than an arrangement under which commercial banks seek to play off one supervisory authority against another — or to escape strict regulation implemented at either level — and thereby to derive advantages which other highly regulated industries do not have.
>
> Such a criticism ignores the fact that the historic value of dual banking lies in its ability to provide an escape valve from arbitrary or discriminatory chartering and regulatory policies at either the state or Federal level. The possible intrusion of such inequities into either the chartering of banks or their regulation, with consequent implications for the allocation of credit among prospective borrowers, is an eventuality against which the strongest public safeguards should be erected.[1]

Critics of the system, on the other hand, see the dual banking system as an outmoded relic from the nation's past whose continued existence is explainable only on grounds of legislative inertia and the political power of states and state-chartered banks. In their view, protection for depositors, equity as between

[1] William J. Brown, *The Dual Banking System in the United States* (New York: American Bankers Association, 1968), p. 59.

banks, and the nation's economic welfare would all be better served by subjecting all commercial banks in the nation to a common set of federal government standards.

Whatever one's view on the justification for a dual banking system, it should be noted that its significance was greatly reduced by the Monetary Control Act of 1980 which applied uniform reserve requirements to all banks, regardless of their chartering institution.

A Unit Banking System

Another distinguishing characteristic of the U.S. commercial banking system is the fact that it is primarily made up of many single-office, unit banks, rather than the small group of vast branch systems typical in many other countries. It is not at all uncommon elsewhere for a mere handful of banking companies, each with hundreds of branches throughout the country, to dominate the entire nation's banking system. Table 8-4, which reports on the commercial banking structure in five countries, brings this point out clearly despite data that are a decade old. Note especially the last two columns. Whereas the average U.S. bank had fewer than three branches and served an average of 15,000 people, none of the other countries had fewer than 150 branches per bank and in none were fewer than a quarter of a million people served by each banking company.

What caused the U.S. banking system to develop along such dramatically different lines than those in other industrialized countries? The answer, of course, is that our laws shaped it.

Legislative antipathy to widespread development of branch banking and, for that matter, to large banks is rooted in our national heritage. Decentralization has long been considered a major virtue in economic life, correctly or not, and no potential concentration of power has been more feared by the American people and their representatives than that of the financial community—the "money lenders."

Although legislative prohibition has limited the development of branch banking and molded our banking system into a unique multifirm industry, it

TABLE 8-4　Commercial banking system structure, selected countries, 1982

Country	Number of commercial banks	Number of branches	Branches per bank	Population per bank
United States	14,451	39,784	2.7	15,676
Canada	11	7,414	674	2,221,636
United Kingdom	35	13,965	399	1,601,914
West Germany	243	40,767	164	254,156
Japan	86	13,334	155	1,378,825

Source: Federal Reserve System.

would be a mistake to conclude from this that the American banking industry is a real-world model of the economist's textbook version of pure competition. Let us turn now to consider some more detail about the makeup of the U.S. commercial banking system and how it got this way.

Concentration in the U.S. Commercial Banking Industry

Just how competitive is the U.S. banking system? Numbers alone shed little light on the issue. What had been a banking system of over 30,000 banks in 1921 had shrunk, largely as a result of failures in the 1920s and 1930s, to about 14,000 by 1940. It has fluctuated around that level ever since, until falling off a bit in recent years.

Now 14,000 firms in a single industry is an enormous number by almost any standard. It is far more than most other countries have. And, in comparison with other large industries in the United States, it is an equally impressive number. But the degree of competitiveness in an industry depends also on such matters as the size distribution within the industry and the size of the market within which competition can be effective. On both these grounds, the U.S. commercial banking system is less atomistic than the 14,000-firm figure might imply.

As is clear from Table 8-5, a relatively few large banks dominate the industry. For example, in 1989 the largest 2.6 percent of the nation's insured banks held almost 60 percent of the deposits of the entire system! At the other end of the spectrum, we find the smallest 60 percent of the banks — those with assets below $50 million — held just 8 percent of the total. Clearly within this industry there are significant differences in size and economic clout.

National data such as these, however, shed relatively little light on the degree of competition within the banking industry for the simple reason that the relevant market for many of the services of commercial banks is essentially local.

TABLE 8-5   Size distribution of insured U.S. banks, June 30, 1989

Size class (value of deposits in millions of dollars)	Number of banks	Percentage of banks	Percentage of deposits
$1,000 or more	353	2.6%	59.0%
500–999.9	240	1.8	7.1
100–499.9	2,193	16.3	18.5
50–99.9	2,610	19.4	7.7
25–49.9	3,399	25.3	5.2
10–24.9	3,450	25.7	2.5
0–9.9	1,197	8.3	0.3

Source: Federal Deposit Insurance Corporation, *Operating Banks and Branches Data Book*, June 30, 1989.

It matters little that there are 13,000 or 14,000 banks unless something can be said about the extent to which they compete directly with one another in the attraction of deposits and the making of loans.

What evidence do we have regarding the degree of competitiveness of the industry in this more specific, localized sense? One could show, for example, that in most metropolitan areas in the United States, three banks control a majority of the total deposits. And one might also present evidence showing a sizable number of one-bank towns in this country. But such evidence, while not without interest, fails to reflect the equally significant impact of such structural factors as the degree of branch banking and the extent of bank holding companies. And it also overlooks entirely the growing competition from other financial services institutions for business which used to be almost the sole preserve of commercial banks.

The Laws Limiting Branch Banking

The dual banking system itself imposes some limits on branching. Since more than half our banks are chartered by states, and since no state possesses the power to authorize one of its instrumentalities to operate in other states, interstate branching by state-chartered banks has never been legal.

But the limits have been even more stringent than that since, for many years, a number of states have curtailed *intra*state branching. As of 1990, for example, while 36 states permitted their state-chartered banks to branch statewide, 10 allowed only limited branching (such as within the city, county, or in contiguous counties), and the remaining four in the West or Midwest are classified as "unit" banking states, allowing no branching at all.

But what of the branching privileges of *nationally* chartered banks? They too are severely limited, primarily by the McFadden Act of 1927. The McFadden Act, as we learned in Chapter 6, authorized national banks to branch only to the same extent as the state banks in the state in which they are located. This had the effect of outlawing altogether the practice of interstate branching. The McFadden Act, then, provides much of the explanation for the data in Table 8-4.

Commercial Bank Holding Companies

There can be no doubt that state laws and the McFadden Act have sharply curtailed both intrastate and interstate banking via the branching device. However, branch banking is not the only mechanism available to banks desiring to expand geographically. Another is the holding company device.

Two different types of holding company structures have been employed in the commercial banking industry. One, the *multibank holding company*, is a holding company controlling a number of different banks. A major purpose of this use of the holding company device has been to evade the intent of restrictive branching laws. In fact, every state that limits intrastate branching permits the use of multibank holding companies.

The other type is the *one-bank holding company*, a holding company that controls a number of companies performing a variety of financial services, only one of which is a commercial bank.

One-bank holding companies have several advantages. First, they permit a holding company to engage in banking as well as in certain other related financial activities as long as the Board of Governors approves. Second, there are certain tax benefits to the one-bank holding company form. If at least 80 percent of the stock of the bank is owned by the holding company, the income of the bank that is subject to tax can be reduced by the amount of interest paid by the holding company on its debt. Third, they have long provided a device whereby a one-bank holding company could operate across state lines through nonbank subsidiaries.

The growth of holding companies in commercial banking in the past couple of decades has been little short of phenomenal. For example, in 1965 there were 550 one-bank holding companies and 53 multibank holding companies controlling another 468 banks. All told, however, these holding company-controlled banks held less than 13 percent of the industry's total deposits. Within 20 years that 13 percent had shot upward to more than 90 percent where it is today. Clearly, in the 1990s any bank *not* involved in a holding company structure is atypical and almost surely small.

As we learned earlier, the basic legislation dealing with bank holding companies is the Bank Holding Company Act of 1956. A key portion of that law, the so-called Douglas Amendment, was for many years the major barrier to interstate banking via the holding company device. To refresh the reader's memory, the Douglas Amendment made it illegal for a bank holding company to acquire a bank in another state. That is, such acquisition was declared illegal "unless the acquisition of such shares or assets of a State bank by an out-of-State bank holding company is specifically authorized by the statute laws of the State in which such bank is located." Since no state except Maine (and that, not until 1975) passed legislation authorizing out-of-state holding companies to come in until the decade of the 1980s, the Douglas Amendment served for many years as a companion piece to the McFadden Act in preventing interstate banking in the United States.

Interstate Banking: A Reality in the 1990s

Despite these legal limitations, a limited amount of interstate banking existed prior to the decade of the 1980s. Before passage of the Douglas Amendment, a number of bank holding companies were already engaged in interstate operation and were permitted to continue via "grandfather" clauses in the law. In addition, numerous foreign-owned banks also operate across state lines. Foreign banks were not subject to the McFadden Act prior to passage of the International Banking Act in 1978, and those already engaged in interstate banking prior to July 1978 were also "grandfathered."

In addition a large number of banks were already involved in a limited type of interstate banking through *loan production offices* and *Edge Act corporations*, both of which are exempted from the McFadden Act and Douglas Amendment.

Loan production offices consist of separate facilities established by a bank in other towns as well as in other states to seek out potential borrowers from the bank. These offices make contacts with borrowers and attempt to sell them on borrowing from their home office. When the actual loan is made, however, the bank itself completes the paperwork and issues the proceeds. In court decisions, loan production offices located in other states have been declared not to be official branches and, therefore, not forbidden by the McFadden Act.

Edge Act corporations are federally chartered banks explicitly authorized in the Federal Reserve Act to carry out a banking business related to financing international transactions. Like the international departments of large money market banks, Edge Act corporations deal in foreign exchange, and accept internationally related deposits. A bank in the interior of the country may well open an Edge Act corporation in New York City to help it with its international dealings. Though it may seem like a subsidiary or branch of its parent bank, as long as it limits itself to internationally related activities, it is exempt from the interstate prohibitions of the McFadden Act.[2]

The main movement toward truly widespread, nationwide interstate banking came almost entirely during the 1980s through state laws inviting out-of-state bank holding companies in, thereby dismantling the obstacle the Douglas Amendment had long imposed, and through widespread exploitation of a loophole in the Bank Holding Company Act via the so-called "nonbank bank" movement. Let us consider these two developments at some length.

State Laws and Interstate Banking

As we have seen, the Douglas Amendment forbade a bank holding company to acquire a bank in another state unless that state's legislature passed a law explicitly inviting in out-of-state holding companies. For almost two decades no state enacted such legislation. Then in 1975 Maine started the ball rolling with a law inviting out-of-state holding companies in, providing the home state of the holding company passed similar legislation inviting Maine's banks to come there.[3] This law, however, had no impact until the decade of the 1980s for the rather obvious reason that no other state passed such a law till 1982. But in that year the logjam broke, and the subsequent years of the decade have produced such an avalanche of state legislation that the barrier to interstate banking posed by the Douglas Amendment has now been rather thoroughly breached.

This legislation has taken a number of different tacks. Eighteen states have passed legislation only inviting in bank holding companies from their geographical region. These regional compacts were most prevalent in the Southeast and Midwest. Sixteen others have invited in out-of-state bank holding companies from any other state that reciprocates the invitation. Twelve have invited in out-of-state bank holding companies from any state whether or not it reciprocates. Only four states—Iowa, Kansas, North Dakota, and Montana—had passed no legislation to invite in out-of-state holding companies as of the early 1990s. The extent of these law as they are slated to take effect by 1993 is shown in

---

[2] On Edge Act corporations and loan production offices, see C. H. Golembe and D. S. Holland, *Federal Regulation of Banking, 1986–87*, (Washington, D.C.: Golembe Associates, Inc., 1986).

[3] Maine's reciprocity provision was dropped in 1984.

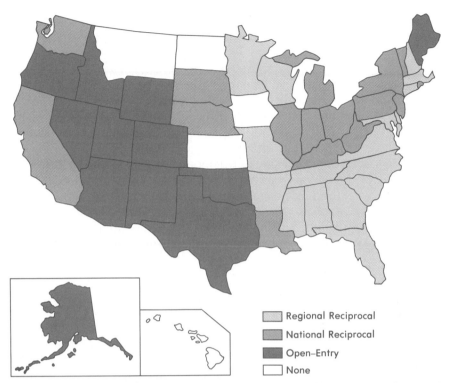

Regional Reciprocal
National Reciprocal
Open–Entry
None

Source: Robert T. Clair and Paula K. Tucker, "Interstate Banking and the Federal Reserve: A Historical Perspective," *Economic Review,* Federal Reserve Bank of Dallas, November 1989.

FIGURE 8-1   Interstate Banking Regulation in 1993

Figure 8-1. Clearly, widespread interstate banking via the holding company is a reality in the 1990s.

The Spread of "Nonbank" Banks

State legislation, it turned out, was not the only way around the constraints of the Douglas Amendment. Another method was through a loophole in the law.

The Bank Holding Company Act includes a rather specific definition of commercial banks, identifying them as financial institutions that both offer demand deposits and make commercial loans. The definition is reasonable enough, but the decision to include it in the law led to an important development often referred to as the "nonbank bank" movement.

If, to qualify as a commercial bank and therefore be constrained by the Bank Holding Company Act, an institution must both offer demand deposits *and* make commercial loans, then one that offers demand deposits but *does not* make commercial loans is *not* a "commercial bank" and *not* so constrained.[4] This loophole has been exploited to escape federal regulation in two important directions.

---

[4] The same loophole exists for the institution that makes commercial loans but does not offer ordinary demand deposits.

On the one hand, it has been used to skirt the Douglas Amendment's restriction on interstate banking via the holding company device. In addition, it has provided a way for retail, industrial, insurance, and investment companies—which, under the Bank Holding Company Act, are forbidden from entering the commercial banking business—to do so.

In light of the recent growth of state legislation authorizing widely expanded interstate banking, it seems unlikely that more extensive use of the "nonbank" bank device will be needed for bank holding companies desiring to extend their operations across state lines. Its use to permit companies otherwise forbidden from engaging in commercial banking to do so, however, continued to concern Federal Reserve officials as such well-known retailers as Sears and J. C. Penney, insurance companies such as Prudential and John Hancock, and brokerage firms such as Merrill Lynch and E. F. Hutton took advantage of the loophole in the 1980s. Finally, however, the Competitive Equality Banking Act of 1987 forbid establishment of any new nonbank banks and limited the growth of those already in existence.

Appendix: The Use of the T-Account

One all but indispensable tool in the study of commercial banks is the T-account, and, as we shall rely upon it heavily in future chapters, the student should take pains to see that he or she understands it thoroughly.

A T-account is intended to reflect the change in a bank's (or in the banking system's) balance sheet as a result of a single transaction. It is, of course, not the only way to show this. One could, by depicting a full balance sheet before, and a full balance sheet after, a transaction, accomplish the same purpose. And we shall, in some cases, use this more time-consuming method. But in most situations the T-account is preferable, and we shall employ it extensively in upcoming chapters.

A few examples should reveal the nature of this important tool. Suppose that Bank A, initially, is in the position reflected here:

Initial Balance Sheet of Bank A
(thousands of dollars)

Cash	$ 100	Demand deposits	$4,000
Federal Reserve Account	1,000	Time deposits	2,100
Loans	3,000		
Securities	2,000		

Now we are concerned with showing the effects of a single transaction on Bank A's balance sheet. Suppose, for example, that a depositor places $100 cash in his checking account. We could reflect the result of this transaction in either of two ways—by laboriously making up an entirely new balance sheet to incorporate the changes caused by the deposit or by using a T-account.

If we take the long way around, we would construct a balance sheet like the following:

Balance Sheet of Bank A after $100 Cash Deposit
(thousands of dollars)

Cash	$ 200	Demand deposits	$4,100
Federal Reserve Account	1,000	Time deposits	2,100
Loans	3,000		
Securities	2,000		

If we want to show the same thing in the simpler form of a T-account, however, we have simply

Bank A

Cash	+$100	Demand deposits	+$100

Note that in a T-account, only the asset or liability accounts affected by the transaction are written down, and each is accompanied by a plus or a minus sign to indicate whether the account was increased or decreased. Since a T-account shows changes in a bank's balance sheet, it must be balanced itself, with equal pluses (or minuses) on opposite sides, or with offsetting plus-minus entries on the same side.

To solidify the idea of the T-account and to provide some practice for the reader before we get to some more complicated uses, the following additional examples may be of some benefit.

1. Depositor withdraws $100 cash from his time deposit in Bank A.

Bank A

Cash	−$100	Time deposits	−$100

2. Bank A purchases a $100 U.S. security from a customer, paying the seller in the form of cash.

Bank A

Cash	−$100	
U.S. securities	+$100	

3. Bank A makes a $100 loan to a borrower, granting the proceeds in the form of an addition to her checking account.

Bank A

Loans	+$100	Demand deposits	+$100

4. A depositor at Bank A writes a $100 check on his checking account and deposits it in his time deposit at Bank A.

Bank A

		Demand deposits	−$100
		Time deposits	+$100

5. Bank A borrows $100 of reserves from its Federal Reserve bank.

Bank A

Federal Reserve account	+$100	Borrowings (notes payable)	+$100

6. A borrower from Bank A pays back a $100 loan from the bank by writing a check on her account there.

Bank A

Loans	−$100	Demand deposits	−$100

7. Bank A deposits $100 of vault cash into its checking account at its district Federal Reserve bank.

Bank A

Cash	−$100		
Federal Reserve Account	+$100		

Review Questions

1. "The exceptional degree of liquidity of their prime sources of funds distinguishes commercial banks from most other financial institutions and involves a severe restraint on their use." Explain.

2. Distinguish
   a. A T-account from a balance sheet.
   b. Primary reserves from secondary reserves.
   c. Asset management from liability management.

3. What are compensating balances? How might they affect the interest cost of a loan?

4. What are several reasons why commercial banks are heavy purchasers of state and local government securities?

5. Examine the pros and cons of the maintenance of the "dual banking" system.

6. Do you believe that the McFadden Act and other laws limiting branch banking in the United States contribute to a more competitive U.S. banking system? Why or why not?

7. What is the effect of the Douglas Amendment to the Bank Holding Company Act?

8. Write an essay discussing the nature of, and reasons for, the current trend toward interstate banking. Do you believe that it is a healthy trend? Why or why not?

9. Distinguish bank *solvency* from bank *liquidity*.

10. Contrast asset management with liability management.

11. The barriers against interstate banking were breached in the 1980s as a result of two major developments. What are they? Explain.

12. The nonbank bank movement not only permitted banks to evade geographical restrictions but also restriction on the type of industry that can acquire a banking subsidiary. Explain.

The Federal Reserve System — Structure and Functions

About 60 percent of the commercial banks in the United States are not members of the Federal Reserve System and, therefore, are not directly subject to the authority of that federal government agency. It would, however, be a gross error to conclude from this fact that the Federal Reserve authorities lack the power to exercise wide-reaching control over the nation's banking and monetary system. Not only do the banks that belong to the system hold almost 75 percent of the nation's deposits, but Federal Reserve actions have powerful direct and indirect effects on all banks — member and nonmember alike. For these reasons, as well as for the sake of brevity, we shall concentrate almost solely on the Federal Reserve System and its member banks in the remaining chapters of our institutional discussion.

The Current Structure of the Federal Reserve System

The Federal Reserve System consists of the rather complex structure sketched in Figure 9-1. Let us briefly discuss the various parts of the System, starting with the Board of Governors.

The Board of Governors

The Board of Governors of the Federal Reserve System consists of seven members, appointed by the president to 14-year terms. The seven governors are the top monetary authorities in the United States. Their power and prestige within the federal government are such as to rank them on a par with the most powerful

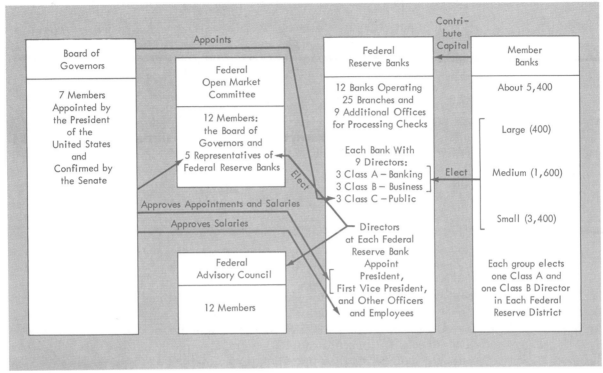

Source: Federal Reserve System.

FIGURE 9-1   **Structure of the Federal Reserve System**

of governmental officials. They are the architects of, and bear the final responsibility for, the nation's monetary policy.

It is they who have the power to alter reserve requirements (within the legal limits established by Congress) applying to depository institution deposits. It is they who "review and determine" (which, for all practical purposes, means "set") the discount rates charged by Federal Reserve banks on loans to depository institutions. It is they who set margin requirements on the purchase of securities. And it is they who compose a majority of the Federal Open Market Committee, which determines the extent and direction of the most effective monetary policy weapon of all — open-market operations. Without question, the governors are the nation's most powerful monetary authorities, and it is they who direct and control the activities of the rest of the system.

The "Independence" of the Federal Reserve   The Board of Governors is a strictly governmental agency concerned solely with the public interest. It does, however, maintain a unique status among governmental agencies in that it is, to a degree, insulated from and independent of much of the direct control by the president and Congress to which most other governmental agencies are subject.

The 14-year terms, for example, guarantee any member a tenure in office of longer duration than that of the president who makes the appointment. A member of the Board of Governors, not unlike a federal judge, may only be removed from office before the end of his or her term for "cause." Once appointed, he or she does not — as do cabinet members and other high officials — serve at the pleasure of the president. Consequently, in case of a difference in policy views, a Federal Reserve governor is free to pursue a monetary policy to which the president may be opposed without fear of dismissal.

In addition to this degree of protection from control by the executive, the Board of Governors also possesses an element of independence from legislative dictation that most other government agencies lack. This should certainly not be interpreted as implying that the Federal Reserve is *totally* independent of Congress. The Federal Reserve System was established by congressional action, and its structure, powers, and indeed its very existence are subject at all times to the legislative will.

Within the confines of existing law, however, the Federal Reserve System possesses a unique degree of freedom from congressional pressures simply because it earns its own income. Congress's power over the purse strings is, of course, among its most basic instruments of control. The majority of governmental agencies are required to come to Congress each year to request continuing financial support through appropriations. Officials of the Federal Reserve System also are obligated to appear regularly before various congressional committees to report on its activities. But unlike most others, they do not come, hat in hand, requesting the funds required to carry on for another year. Such appeals are unnecessary because the 12 Federal Reserve banks earn far more than enough income from their operations to pay all the Fed's expenses as well as all those of the Board of Governors. This, quite clearly, provides them with additional degrees of freedom.

The justification for this unusual degree of independence is a subject of dispute. On the one hand, it is argued that some such independence is needed to ensure that monetary policy and the public interest in a stable dollar are not dominated by the political interests of the executive departments, especially the Treasury. On the other hand, it is stressed that a sound governmental approach to cyclical and growth problems requires a degree of coordination among the various policy agencies, which the Federal Reserve System's independence may not always permit. Those who would reduce this independence argue that a democratic society requires that all elements of government entrusted with the determination of basic policy should be made directly responsible to the electorate or elected officials rather than insulated from such responsibility.

A note of caution, however, is in order here. It is true that the members of the Board of Governors and the Federal Reserve System as a whole possess a unique degree of independence within the government. It is also true that the independence they possess has, in the past, permitted them to defy the wishes of presidents as well as some powerful congressional leaders. But one must be careful not to carry the independence aspect to extremes. The Fed is certainly *not* an "autonomous fourth branch of government," wholly impervious to pressures from the executive and legislature. Indeed, some authorities have argued that, despite its technical independence, the Board of Governors tends to do pretty much whatever the incumbent administration wants. And even if that is not quite true, one can hardly ignore the fact that the Federal Reserve System with all its powers is the result of an act of Congress. It can hardly behave as if it were really independent of Congress when it knows that that body can take away all its authority whenever it chooses. Uniquely independent, yes. Completely independent, by no means.

The Federal Reserve Banks

When the Federal Reserve System was established, congressional fear of concentration of power led the legislature to set up 12 regional Federal Reserve banks rather than the single central bank typical of most other nations. The distribution of these banks within the 12 geographical Federal Reserve districts is depicted in Figure 9-2.

Ownership and Control of Federal Reserve Banks   The 12 Federal Reserve banks themselves are often referred to as "quasi-public" institutions. This means that, although they are entirely privately owned, they are operated with a view solely to public, governmental objectives.

All the stock issued by a Federal Reserve bank is owned by the privately owned member banks of its district. In addition, six of the nine members of each district bank's board of directors are selected by their member bank owners. But

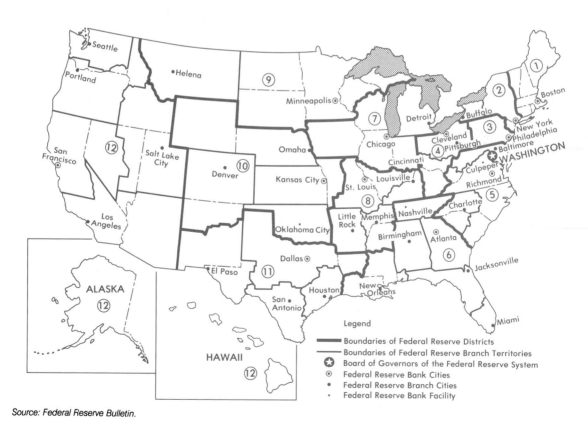

Source: Federal Reserve Bulletin.

FIGURE 9-2 The Federal Reserve System: Boundaries of Federal Reserve Districts and Their Branch Territories despite this 100 percent private ownership and seemingly effective private control of a majority of their directors, Federal Reserve banks today are, in most important respects, subject almost completely to the dictates of a strictly governmental agency, the Board of Governors in Washington.

The Board of Governors, for example, appoints the three remaining members (the so-called "Class C directors" mentioned in Figure 9-1) of each Federal Reserve bank's board of directors, one of whom is selected to be chairman of the board. In addition, the individual Reserve banks' directors have little direct say about such important matters as the setting of their own discount rates or the composition of their own security portfolios. Discount rates, though nominally set by the individual Reserve bank, are subject to review and determination by the Board of Governors. In actual practice, this results in the Board of Governors rather than individual Federal Reserve banks determining the rate. Similarly, the purchase and sale of U.S. securities, which make up nearly the whole of Federal Reserve bank earning assets, is subject to the complete control of the Federal Open Market Committee, a group dominated by the Board of Governors. As a result, the private owners and their six representatives on their Reserve bank's board of directors have little control over the most fundamental policy matters.

Earnings of Federal Reserve Banks   The public status of Federal Reserve banks is further reflected in their attitude toward, and disposition of, profits. Unlike other privately owned institutions, the Federal Reserve banks are governmentally oriented and thus view the making of a profit on their operations as an objective that is distinctly secondary to the goal of carrying out their public function. This is not to say that Federal Reserve banks do not attempt to minimize their operating costs and to "buy low and sell high" when altering their portfolio of assets. They do, and, as we can see, the result of their efforts yields them very large profits indeed. The point is that making a profit is not their goal. If faced with a choice between making a profit on a transaction and carrying out their public responsibilities as executors of the nation's monetary policy even though that required them to sell securities at a lower price than was paid for them, Fed banks would unhesitatingly choose the latter course.

Be that as it may, the Federal Reserve banks actually do earn very substantial profits from their operations which insulates the Fed somewhat from congressional dictation. Data for Federal Reserve bank earnings in 1990 are presented in Table 9-1.

As the table shows, most of the income of the Federal Reserve System accrues from interest earned on U.S. securities that have been acquired in the process of implementing open-market policy. A modest amount of additional income is earned from profits on the sale of services and interest on loans through the discount window.

It is very important for the student to realize that, although U.S. securities *are* the source of the bulk of Federal Reserve bank earnings, these assets were not acquired for this reason. Rather they were acquired in the process of carrying out monetary policy, and the purpose of their acquisition was to exert influence on the cost and availability of credit in the economy. The profit earned is purely a side effect of measures carried out for other reasons.

Nevertheless, substantial profits are regularly made by Federal Reserve banks, and it is interesting to note how they are distributed. In 1990, after paying

TABLE 9-1 Sources and disposition of Federal Reserve bank earnings, 1990 (millions of dollars)	
Income, by source	
Interest on U.S. securities	$22,746
Other income	729
Operating income	23,475
Total expenses	1,741
Net income	21,734
Additions to net income[a]	2,220
Total income available to distribute	23,954
Disposition of total income	
Dividends to member banks plus transfer to surplus	321
Paid to U.S. Treasury	$23,633

[a] Primarily results from increase in value of foreign currency.
Source: Federal Reserve Bulletin.

their total expenses of about $1.7 billion and an additional $0.3 billion in dividends and addition to surplus, the Fed returned the rest — over $23.6 billion — to the U.S. Treasury.[1]

"How," one might reasonably ask, "can they make so much income that, after paying all their expenses, all their dividends, and adding to their surplus, they still have over 90 percent of their *gross* revenue left to turn over to the Treasury? That sort of thing would be a startling accomplishment for any firm, let alone one that isn't even motivated by profit maximization."

The answer is a simple one. You too could show billions in profits if you had the powers of the Federal Reserve banks. Almost all their revenue was interest on their near quarter trillion dollar portfolio of U.S. securities. These securities — accumulated over the years through open-market purchases by the Fed — are acquired almost without cost because they, as the nation's ultimate monetary authority, possess the power to simply create whatever money is needed to buy them. We shall see how this is done later in our discussion.

Balance Sheet of Federal Reserve Banks   Probably the most fruitful way of learning about what Federal Reserve banks do is to study their balance sheets. For example, see Table 9-2.

[1] This payment to the Treasury is technically referred to as payment of "interest on Federal Reserve notes outstanding." Federal Reserve bank profits have regularly been so embarrassingly large that it was necessary to find a technicality in the law to authorize their return to the Treasury. Note what this means, however. Almost all the Fed's income comes from the Treasury in the form of interest on U.S. securities owned by Federal Reserve banks. The bulk of it, however — over 90 percent — is returned to the Treasury as "interest on Federal Reserve notes"! In a sense, then, one might argue that the portion of the national debt owned by the Federal Reserve System is virtually costless.

TABLE 9-2   Consolidated balance sheet of all 12 Federal Reserve banks, March 27, 1991 (billions of dollars)

Assets		*Liabilities and capital accounts*		
Gold certificates	$ 11.1	Federal Reserve notes		
Cash	0.7	Outstanding		$267.0
Loans	0.2	Demand deposits, total		33.9
U.S. securities	241.2	Depository institutions	$27.2	
Uncollected cash items	4.7	U.S. Treasury	6.2	
All other assets[a]	67.0	Foreign	0.3	
		Other	0.2	
		Deferred availability cash items		4.5
		Other liabilities		3.0
				5.5
Total assets	$313.8	Total liabilities and capital accounts		$313.8

[a] "Other assets" not separately listed include the special drawing rights certificate account, which is a claim on the International Monetary Fund transferred to the Federal Reserve banks by the U.S. Treasury; federal agency obligations, issued to aid farm and home loan programs, that are purchased by the Fed's open-market account; and a small total of banker's acceptances.
Source: Federal Reserve Statistical Release H.4.1.

The first asset, *gold certificates,* represents an item of considerable historical importance, although it currently has little significance to Federal Reserve banks. Gold certificates are issued by the U.S. Treasury, which is authorized by present law to print up one dollar in gold certificates for each dollar of gold owned. The gold certificates are then deposited in the Federal Reserve banks by the Treasury in return for an increase in the Treasury's checking account there.[2]

Until 1968 these gold certificates served as legal reserves for the issuance of Federal Reserve notes by the Federal Reserve banks. Under the law at that time, Federal Reserve banks were required to back up each dollar of Federal Reserve notes issued (remember, Federal Reserve notes make up the preponderant majority of the nation's currency supply) with 25 cents worth of gold certificates. Technically, then, the gold supply (which limited the gold certificate supply) placed an outside limit on the amount of Federal Reserve notes that could be issued.

In practice, however, the technical limit implied by that law was never permitted to become operable. Each time the limit was approached, Congress (wisely, it should be noted) changed the law, lowering the requirement.[3] In 1968 the last remaining legal tie between the U.S. gold supply and its money supply was abolished when the 25 percent gold certificate collateral requirement behind Federal Reserve notes was dropped.

[2] When the Treasury sells gold, it must withdraw an equivalent amount of gold certificates from the Federal Reserve banks. Actually these gold certificates currently are simply bookkeeping credits, not physical pieces of paper.

[3] In 1945, the requirement of a 40 percent gold certificate behind Federal Reserve notes and 35 percent behind member bank deposits was reduced to 25 percent behind both. In 1965 the 25 percent gold certificate requirement behind member bank deposits was dropped. Then, in 1968, the 25 percent requirement behind Federal Reserve notes was also abolished.

Consequently, the Federal Reserve's gold certificate account today has little meaning — legally or otherwise. The amount held is strictly a function of the size of the U.S. gold stock, and it has almost no significance for domestic policy considerations.

The *cash* asset account includes all currency and coins in the possession of the Federal Reserve banks, which are issued by, and are the liability of, the U.S. Treasury. This small account consists primarily of coins, although it also includes a limited amount of Treasury-issued currency such as U.S. notes. It is important for the reader to recognize that the bulk of the nation's currency supply — Federal Reserve notes — is *issued* by the Federal Reserve banks and, hence, shows up on the liability side of their balance sheet as "Federal Reserve notes outstanding."

Loans consist primarily of IOUs of depository institutions who have borrowed reserves from their district Federal Reserve banks via the "discount window." Most of these loans are very short term, issued in exchange for the borrowing bank's own promissory note, secured by U.S. securities.[4] Although seldom used in recent years, Federal Reserve banks may also make loans for up to 90 days to banks by discounting "eligible" paper or by accepting any other asset satisfactory to the Federal Reserve as security.

The largest and most important of Federal Reserve bank assets is the $241 billion portfolio of *U.S. securities.* These securities are, of course, initially issued by the U.S. Treasury to finance deficit spending by the federal government. Those held by the Federal Reserve banks are acquired as a result of the Fed's open-market operations, about which we shall have much more to say shortly. It should be noted, however, that the Fed's portfolio of U.S. securities is *not* purchased directly from the U.S. Treasury. Rather, the Federal Reserve buys them through middlemen securities dealers, from individuals or financial institutions that have previously acquired them from the Treasury. The Federal Reserve is prohibited from purchasing securities directly from the Treasury.

The final asset account, *uncollected cash items*, arises out of the check collection process, which we shall consider in detail shortly. In essence, this $4.7 billion account represents checks written on banks that have been received and/or sent out by the Federal Reserve but have not yet been received by, or collected from, the payee banks.

On the liability and net worth side, the $267 billion of *Federal Reserve notes outstanding* represents the majority of the nation's currency supply. It is a liability of the Federal Reserve banks, of course, because they are the issuing agents.

Among the demand deposits outstanding, those owed to the depository institutions constitute the bulk of the legal reserves that they, in turn, use to back up the demand and time deposits of their customers. The *U.S. Treasury demand deposit* is the checking account on which the Treasury writes virtually all the checks with which it makes payment for the goods and services the federal government purchases.

The *deferred availability cash items* is, like uncollected cash items on the asset side, a temporary account that arises in the process of check clearing and

---

[4] Actually such loans may be made even without the physical transfer of a promissory note, simply by a verbal agreement over the telephone. Member banks often store stocks of U.S. securities at their Federal Reserve bank so that they will be available to serve as security when borrowing becomes necessary.

collection. We shall deal with it shortly. Finally, the *capital accounts* represent the equity that the member bank owners have built up in their Federal Reserve banks by virtue of the requirement that they purchase stock in them.

The Member Banks

The base of the Federal Reserve System is composed of the member banks, consisting in December 1990 of 3,976 national banks, which are required to belong, plus 1,007of the larger state banks that have voluntarily chosen to join. The member bank undertakes certain responsibilities in return for the privileges of membership.

It is required to subscribe to stock in the Federal Reserve bank of its district in an amount equal to 6 percent of its own capital and surplus, although, to date, only half that amount must be paid in. The rest is subject to call. It must abide by a list of System regulations regarding its capital structure, its loans and invest-ments, its branch operations, its holding company operations, and the activities of its directors. It must submit, at the discretion of the Fed, to supervision and examination by Federal Reserve authorities. Finally, it must observe the reserve requirements set by the Federal Reserve for depository institutions with its deposit size.[5]

In return for these obligations, the member bank enjoys certain privileges. Its ownership of Federal Reserve bank stock entitles it to participate in the selection of six of the nine members of the board of directors of its Federal Reserve bank. In addition, it receives a safe 6 percent dividend on such stock owned.

Prior to passage of the Monetary Control Act of 1980, other unique advan-tages of membership in the system included the availability of emergency loans of reserves through the Fed's so-called discount window and access to the exten-sive check-clearing and collection facilities as well as the sophisticated wire transfer operation of the Federal Reserve System. While those services still exist, they are no longer either free or exclusively made available to member banks. For since all depository institutions have been made subject to the same reserve requirements, all now have equal access, at a price, to Fed services.

The Federal Open Market Committee

If there is any one group within which the basic decision of monetary policy is made, it is the 12-member Federal Open Market Committee. Its membership consists of the seven members of the Board of Governors plus five presidents of Federal Reserve banks. The president of the New York Federal Reserve Bank is a permanent member, and the four remaining positions are rotated among the presidents of the other Federal Reserve banks.

The Open Market Committee has sole responsibility for determining the direction and extent of the System's open-market operations. After carefully considering the economy's needs, it decides upon the type and scale of opera-

---

[5] Of course, since the passage of the Monetary Control Act of 1980, all depository institutions have the same reserve requirements, whether members of the Federal Reserve or not.

tions, and its decisions are binding on all Federal Reserve banks. If the Open Market Committee decides to sell, each Federal Reserve bank is *required* to make available for sale its proportionate share of the securities. Conversely, if the committee decides to buy, each Federal Reserve bank is required to make payment for its proportionate share of the total purchase.

We shall delve more deeply into the mechanics of open-market operations later. For the moment, it should simply be recognized that, as the one dominant tool of monetary policy is open-market operations, the Open Market Committee is an extremely important group.

The Federal Advisory Council

Of substantially lesser importance in terms of the actual determination of basic policy is the 12-member Federal Advisory Council. It consists of one representative from each Federal Reserve district, usually a commercial banker. It meets quarterly in, as its name indicates, a purely advisory capacity. It is intended to provide the Board of Governors direct access to the viewpoints of representative private bankers from around the country.

Functions and Objectives of the Federal Reserve System

Large governmental agencies generally do not have the privilege of working toward one single objective. The Federal Reserve System is no exception.

Its functions might most usefully be categorized into three groups. First, it carries out a variety of activities aimed at maintenance of a sound and effectively functioning money supply and commercial banking industry. Second, it acts as "fiscal agent" for the U.S. Treasury, aiding in the handling of Treasury cash balances, the collection of taxes, the sale and redemption of bonds, and the expenditure of funds.[6] Finally, and of greatest importance, it uses its arsenal of monetary policy weapons to pursue directly the basic social, but sadly, often conflicting, objectives of full employment, price stability, rapid economic growth, and balance-of-payments equilibrium.

Promoting Efficient Banking System and Effective Exchange Media

Included in the group of activities aimed at facilitating the effective operation of banks and the money supply are the following:

1. *Clearing and Collecting Checks.* A healthy proportion of the checks that are not strictly local are collected via the Federal Reserve banks, which make their collection facilities available to all depository institutions at a price covering cost.

---

[6] Acting as fiscal agent is *not* the same as carrying out fiscal policy. The latter is done by Congress.

The result is a highly efficient mechanism that greatly enhances the effectiveness of our main payments media. In addition to carrying out a major portion of the actual collecting chores, the Fed has also added immeasurably to the acceptability of demand deposits by requiring that all checks collected through its facilities be remitted at par by the bank on which they are written. This requirement has finally eliminated the practice of deducting exchange charges in the United States.

In the next chapter, we shall consider check collection procedures in some detail. For the moment it is sufficient to point out that the primary vehicles used by the Federal Reserve in the collection procedure are the banks' reserve accounts. The bank in which a check is deposited sends it in to its Federal Reserve bank, which completes the collection process by adding the amount of the check to that bank's reserve account, subtracting an equal amount from the reserve account of the bank on which it is written, and mailing the check on to the latter bank.

2. *Providing an Outside Source for Borrowing Additional Reserves*. One of the prime functions of a central bank is the provision of a source from which individual depository institutions in need can borrow additional reserves without, at the same time, reducing the reserves of some other commercial bank. The Federal Reserve's facilities for discounts and advances, popularly called the discount window, provide such a source. Indeed, as we have seen, this was one of the original purposes of the Federal Reserve Act.

Now that the restrictive notions involved in the commercial loan theory have been abandoned, a depository institution can borrow additional reserves from the Federal Reserve by offering virtually any sound asset it possesses as collateral. This is especially helpful to individual banks or groups of banks in particular areas that may be under some temporary but extreme pressure, as, for example, during a bank panic. It also helps banks that may have some difficulties immediately meeting changed conditions in the economy, or in the Federal Reserve's own regulations, make, with time, an orderly transition to the new circumstances. In fact, the discount window is the ultimate source of liquidity for the banking system.

3. *Issuance of an "Elastic" Currency—the Federal Reserve Note*. The Federal Reserve banks, as we have seen, provide the overwhelming majority of the nation's currency supply in the form of Federal Reserve notes. In doing so, they respond in an almost completely passive manner to the desires of the public for currency. That is to say, the quantity of Federal Reserve notes issues by the Fed tends to expand and contract as the public's desire for currency rises and falls.

A note of caution is in order here. The Federal Reserve System is by no means passive with respect to the total supply of money. Indeed, its main mission is actively to control this strategic quantity. If it passively permitted the total supply of money to expand and contract according to public desire, it would be defaulting on its primary task of stabilization.

It can, however, passively permit an expansion in the supply of Federal Reserve notes whenever the public desires to hold more currency *and fewer demand deposits*, without in any way abandoning its control over the total size of the money supply. And this is precisely what present law regulating the issuance of Federal Reserve notes permits.

When, as is true during the holiday season in December, the public develops a need for relatively more currency and relatively fewer demand deposits, checks are written at commercial banks for cash. The currency paid out, primarily Federal Reserve notes, comes, of course, directly from the vaults of commercial banks. These banks, however, must now replenish their vault cash to be prepared for further cash withdrawals. They do so by going to their district Reserve bank.

The banks obtain their needed supplies of currency by writing checks themselves, for cash, on their reserve accounts. If they possess sufficient excess reserves to do so without reducing their reserve accounts below prescribed levels, that is the end of the matter. If they do not have an adequate amount of excess reserves, they may, by pledging an acceptable asset as collateral, borrow the needed amount through the Federal Reserve's discount window.

Such borrowing for predictable seasonal needs is not often required, however, because the Federal Reserve authorities normally take steps through open-market purchases to provide added reserves in advance of the need.

From the Fed's point of view, requests from depository institutions for more currency are easily accommodated. As they are the issuers of Federal Reserve notes, they need only to have more of them printed. It is true that the law requires the Federal Reserve to back up Federal Reserve notes with collateral. This, however, presents no real problem. The collateral required may be "eligible paper," gold certificates, or U.S. securities. As Table 9-2 makes clear, the Fed currently holds almost enough U.S. securities to satisfy all collateral requirements. And if more were needed for such a purpose, almost any amount could be effortlessly acquired.

Conversely, when the public's desire for currency abates, such as normally occurs after the holiday season, the reverse process occurs. The public deposits the unwanted currency in checking accounts at depository institutions, and they, in turn, send the plethora of Federal Reserve notes back to the Federal Reserve banks in exchange for an increase in their reserve accounts there. The currency thus returned from circulation is then carefully examined by the Fed. Notes in good condition are stored for ultimate re-issue. Those not in good condition are simply destroyed.

This high degree of elasticity of our currency supply represents a marked improvement over the stringent note-issue restrictions existing under the National Banking System and is one of the major accomplishments of the Federal Reserve Act.

4. *Supervision and Examination of Member Banks.* In addition to concerning itself with the *quantity* of bank assets, a concern through which it controls the quantity of money, the Federal Reserve System must also consider the *quality* of these assets. It must be concerned not only with the extent of bank operations but with their soundness and prudence.

As we have seen, Federal Reserve authorities regularly examine the state-chartered banks that belong to the Federal Reserve System to determine and evaluate their assets and liabilities, their liquidity, their solvency, the quality of their management, and their compliance with established laws and regulations.

This function also includes supervising and overseeing the operations of bank holding companies, analyzing their annual reports, and passing on applications for new branches or mergers.

Aiding the Treasury

A somewhat different hat is worn by the Federal Reserve in its role as fiscal agent for the Treasury Department. In this capacity, the Fed performs many direct services for the Treasury, as well as aiding it in a more substantive manner when it offers a new issue of U.S. securities.

The services performed for the Treasury are many. The Federal Reserve banks hold Treasury checking accounts out of which most of the government's bills are paid. In addition, they supervise the *tax and loan accounts,* which are additional Treasury checking accounts held at a large number of commercial banks and savings institutions throughout the country. When the Treasury offers a new block of securities for sale, the Federal Reserve banks "disseminate information regarding the issues, accept tenders from customers, collect payments, credit the Treasury's account for the proceeds, and effect delivery of the securities." [7] When government securities mature, Federal Reserve banks redeem them. When U.S. saving bonds are issued, it is the Federal Reserve banks that do the job, and when they are cashed in, the Reserve banks handle the necessary transaction. It is evident that these direct services to the Treasury make up, in and of themselves, a formidable task.

But that is not the whole of the Federal Reserve System's responsibility vis-à-vis the Treasury Department. In addition to the preceding list of essentially administrative tasks, the Fed also undertakes to facilitate, in a more substantive way, the flotation of new Treasury securities. Specifically, it is its job to see to it that a new Treasury securities issue succeeds in the sense that there are sufficient buyers to take up the entire issue.

A responsibility of this type is extremely difficult to spell out specifically. Generally, it has required that the Federal Reserve act to maintain "orderly conditions" in the government bond market when new borrowing is under way. The meaning of "orderly conditions" is vague at best. The Federal Reserve usually offers a partial and temporary support to the government bond market at such times, perhaps involving the purchase of enough old U.S. securities to keep prices from being forced down too sharply by the new issue.

The very vagueness of this commitment to orderly conditions in the government bond market has, however, led to disagreement and friction between the two agencies that, in at least one famous incident, grew into a full-fledged public dispute.

Monetary Policy and Credit Control

Important as the other two groups of functions are, they are decidedly less important, in a relative sense, than the credit control function. When one thinks of monetary policy, one thinks not so much of *serving* the banking system as of *controlling* it. Here is the real raison d'être of the Federal Reserve System. This is its major function.

To put it all into one sentence, the primary function of the Federal Reserve

---

[7] *The Federal Reserve System, Purposes and Functions,* 7th ed. (Washington, D.C.: Government Printing Office, 1984), p. 111.

System is **to control the supply of money and credit and thereby regulate the cost of credit (the interest rate) in a manner that will affect aggregate expenditures in a direction that will contribute to the achievement of full employment, stable prices, rapid economic growth, and balance-of-payments equilibrium.**

The means available to System authorities for the pursuance of these goals are, of course, the traditional tools of monetary policy. They include such general credit control weapons as the power to alter required reserve ratios and discount rates and the authority to engage in open-market sale or purchase of U.S. securities. In addition, selective control over the use of credit for the purchase of stocks in the form of margin requirements is available as well as the somewhat vague and ill-defined policy popularly called *moral suasion.*

We shall postpone detailed consideration of these monetary policy tools to a later point. To provide a more thorough grounding for this task, let us turn once again to a discussion of some of the more technical aspects of commercial bank operations.

Review Questions

1. The Board of Governors of the Federal Reserve System is often said to be uniquely independent of both the executive and the legislature. Carefully explain the nature of this alleged independence and comment on its justification.

2. Do you believe that the Fed should be made more accountable to the president than is currently the case?

3. "The Federal Reserve banks are privately owned institutions that operate as if they were governmentally owned." Explain.

4. The Federal Reserve banks are permitted to earn enormous profits as a result of special powers granted them by Congress. Comment. Can you think of any problems that this arrangement might cause?

5. "Part of the nation's currency supply is an asset of the Federal Reserve banks, but even more of it is a liability." Explain.

6. Carefully explain how the nation's *currency* supply is determined. How would your answer differ if the question referred to the nation's *money* supply?

7. What is the composition of, and chief responsibility of, the Federal Open Market Committee?

8. Aside from carrying out monetary policy, what are the other functions of the Federal Reserve System?

9. Explicitly state the primary function of the Federal Reserve System.

Check Collection and Reserve Requirements

Any further description or evaluation of the credit control powers of the Federal Reserve System must be postponed until we learn more about the origin of that credit at the commercial bank level. This, in turn, requires familiarity with check collection procedures and some specifics of commercial bank reserve requirements, the tasks to which this chapter is devoted.

Check Collection

The simplest check collection procedure, of course, is that of a check that is written on and deposited in the same bank. In this case, all that is necessary is for the single bank involved to increase the account of the check depositor and decrease that of the check writer. No mechanism or collection agency is required because only one bank is involved. In most cases (approximately 75 percent by a recent estimate), wherein the check writer keeps his or her account at one bank and the check depositor banks at another, some procedures for settling the debt that arises between the two banks become necessary.

We shall consider, in turn, the means used to collect checks (1) written on one bank and deposited in a different bank in the same city, (2) written on one commercial bank and deposited in a different commercial bank in the same Federal Reserve district, (3) written on one bank and deposited in a different bank located in a different Federal Reserve district, and (4) written on an out-of-town bank and collected through facilities other than the Federal Reserve. Then, following a brief discussion of *Federal Reserve float*, we shall conclude the section with some observations on electronic funds transfer.

Check Collection Between Banks Located in the Same City — The Local Clearinghouse

Purely local checks, written on accounts at one bank and deposited in a different bank located in the same city, are collected at least once daily via the local clearinghouse.

A local clearinghouse is a voluntary organization of all the commercial banks in a particular community, set up for the express purpose of facilitating the clearance and collection of such purely local checks.

Its method of operation is quite simple. Each day at an agreed-upon hour, each local bank sends a messenger armed with all checks written on accounts at other local banks but deposited in its bank to the clearinghouse. Physically, the clearinghouse may be simply an office in one of the more conveniently located banks or, in the case of larger cities, a separate facility. Each bank messenger turns the checks collected over to the manager of the clearinghouse, whose function it is to make up a statement on the basis of which most of these interbank claims are canceled out.

Suppose, for example, in a three-bank town that the messenger from Bank X presents checks written on other local banks totaling $10,000, $7,000 of which are written on Bank Y and $3,000 of which are written on Bank Z; the messenger from Bank Y presents $4,000 of checks drawn on Bank X and $2,000 on Bank Z; and the messenger from Bank Z brings $5,000 worth of claims on Bank X and $3,000 on Bank Y. The clearinghouse manager would then make up a clearing statement resembling that in Table 10-1.

In this situation, as can be readily observed, Bank X has $10,000 of claims on other local banks, and other local banks have $9,000 on Bank X. Bank X is therefore said to have a *favorable clearing balance* amounting to $1,000. Similarly, Bank Z, which presents $8,000 of claims on the other two banks but has only $5,000 presented against it, has a $3,000 favorable clearing balance. Bank Y presents claims on Banks X and Z totaling $6,000 but is, in its turn, confronted with claims on it of $10,000. Bank Y, therefore, has an *unfavorable clearing balance* totaling $4,000.

Note that $24,000 of local checks are involved here but that a payment of $4,000 from Bank Y — $1,000 to Bank X and $3,000 to Bank Z — will be sufficient to settle accounts. The rest disappears through the simple process of cancellation. Bank X, for example, has given credit to its depositors for the $10,000

TABLE 10-1 Local clearinghouse statement

	Checks written on			Total checks brought
	Bank X	*Bank Y*	*Bank Z*	
Bank X brings	—	$ 7,000	$3,000	$10,000
Bank Y brings	$4,000	—	2,000	6,000
Bank Z brings	5,000	3,000	—	8,000
Total checks written on	$9,000	$10,000	$5,000	$24,000

in local checks deposited there. It is compensated by marking down other depositors' accounts by $9,000 (the checks presented against it at the clearinghouse) and receiving the $1,000 from Bank Y.

Although settlement can be made in a variety of ways, the $4,000 payment can be made quite simply by a telephone call to the Federal Reserve bank requesting an increase in Bank X's reserve account by $1,000, an increase in Bank Z's by $3,000, and an offsetting decrease in Bank Y's by $4,000.[1]

Collection of a Check Between Two Commercial Banks in Different Cities, but the Same Federal Reserve District

Only local checks can be collected through a local clearinghouse. When banks in different cities are involved, a different collection agency is required. One obvious collection agency is the district Reserve bank.

Suppose that Mr. Jones writes a $100 check on his account in a Reading, Pennsylvania, bank, payable to Firm X, which banks at a Philadelphia bank. How is this check collected?[2]

The check, deposited by Firm X in its Philadelphia bank, is sent by that bank to the Philadelphia Federal Reserve Bank, which serves both it and the Reading bank. The Philadelphia Federal Reserve Bank *collects* the check by increasing the reserve account of the Philadelphia bank by $100 and decreasing the reserve account of the Reading bank by a similar amount. The check is then sent to the Reading bank, which completes the collection process by marking down Mr. Jones's checking account by $100 and, at the end of the month, sending him the canceled check along with his monthly statement.

In terms of T-accounts, the transaction has the following effects:

Philadelphia Federal Reserve Bank

	Demand deposit of Philadelphia bank +$100
check	Demand deposit of Reading bank −$100

Reading Bank

Federal Reserve account −$100	Demand deposit of Mr. Jones −$100

Philadelphia Bank

Federal Reserve account +$100	Demand deposit of Firm X +$100

---

[1] One common practice, for example, is for all local banks to maintain a checking account at a single agreed-upon local bank (or out-of-town large-city correspondent). Again, settlement can be completed via a single telephone call from the clearinghouse manager.

[2] The process to be described in this section is an oversimplified version of the actual process. Despite its oversimplification, we shall use it as the basis for future examples that involve check collections. A more complete discussion of the actual process, including the complications introduced by time lags in the collection process, will be presented in the section entitled "A More Detailed Discussion of Check Collection—Federal Reserve Float."

Collection of a Check Between Two Commercial Banks in Different Federal Reserve Districts

Things become a bit more complicated when two different Federal Reserve districts are involved, for the rather obvious reason that the banks concerned do not carry Reserve accounts at a common Federal Reserve bank.

Suppose, for example, that our Mr. Jones in Reading (Philadelphia Federal Reserve district) makes out a check to pay a bill to Firm Y, located in New York City (New York Federal Reserve district). In this case, when Firm Y deposits the check in its New York bank, this bank sends it to the New York Federal Reserve Bank to initiate the collection process. The New York Federal Reserve Bank, as before, increases the reserve account of the New York bank, but this time it cannot collect from the bank on which the check is written. What solution exists for this problem?

For just such cases, the Federal Reserve System maintains an office in Washington called the *Interdistrict Settlement Fund.* Each of the 12 Federal Reserve banks maintains an Interdistrict Settlement Account at the Interdistrict Settlement Fund. Although strictly paper entries, these accounts function exactly as if they were checking accounts owned by the Federal Reserve banks whose function is to settle claims between districts.

On receipt of the check from Firm Y's New York commercial bank, the New York Federal Reserve Bank would, after increasing the bank's reserve account, send a wire to the Interdistrict Settlement Fund stating that it had received a check for $100 written on a bank in the Philadelphia Federal Reserve district. The Interdistrict Settlement Fund would respond to this by increasing the New York Federal Reserve Bank's Interdistrict Settlement Account and decreasing that of the Philadelphia Federal Reserve bank.

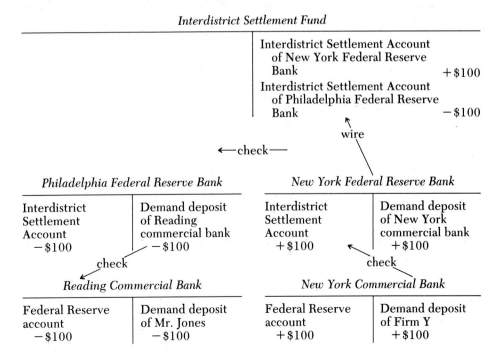

In the meantime the check would be sent directly from the New York Federal Reserve bank to the Philadelphia Federal Reserve bank where the latter would reduce the Reading bank's reserve account, as well as its own claim on the Interdistrict Settlement Fund, and then send it, at long last, to Reading.[3]

Collection of Nonlocal Checks Through Correspondent Banks

Although the Federal Reserve System clears billions of checks each year, an even greater number are collected outside the facilities of the system through correspondent banks. It has been estimated that the Fed's direct role in check collection reached its zenith in 1981 when it handled about 45 percent of all checks written. Since that time the percentage has fallen off to perhaps 35 percent. This decline in use of the Fed's collection facilities is the perfectly natural result of the fact that the Monetary Control Act of 1980 required the Fed to institute a charge for check collection instead of continuing to offer it as a free service.

There are a number of reasons for the extensive reliance on correspondent banks for check collection. These include the fact that correspondent banks are often closer and offer more rapid clearance than the appropriate Federal Reserve facility and that correspondent banks sometimes do not require their respondents to sort, code, and process checks as extensively as does the Fed. Thus, despite the fact that all depository institutions may have checks collected via the Federal Reserve mechanism by maintaining a clearing balance at a Federal Reserve bank, the majority rely more heavily on correspondent banks.

Nonlocal checks collected through correspondents can be handled in a variety of ways. If the bank on which the check is written and the bank in which it is deposited happen to have a common correspondent bank, collection simply requires the correspondent to shift its deposit obligation from the former to the latter bank. If the correspondent bank receives a check from one of its respondents written on a bank that does not have an account with it, it may give deposit credit to its respondent bank and send the check on to its own district Federal Reserve bank for collection. Or the correspondent bank may send it on to another commercial bank in which it and the bank on which the check is written both carry correspondent accounts.

A More Detailed Discussion of Check Collection — Federal Reserve Float

The preceding examples are perfectly adequate descriptions of the check collection process for most purposes. Indeed, in any future examples we may use in this book, we shall rely on them fully.

However, they are oversimplified rather than exact descriptions. And the oversimplification involved, although justified as a means of cutting out unnec-

---

[3] Each year Federal Reserve banks having had more claims on other district banks than have been presented against them at the Interdistrict Settlement Fund are "paid" for them by having U.S. securities shifted away from the other Reserve banks to them. It should be noted that an alternative procedure is for the bank in which the check is deposited to send it directly to the Federal Reserve bank of the bank on which the check is written.

essary detail, is seriously deficient in that it excludes explicit recognition of a rather significant concept—*Federal Reserve float.* This section is aimed at correcting that deficiency.

Let us refocus on the case of the check written on commercial Bank Y but deposited in commercial Bank X in the same Federal Reserve district.[4] In our earlier example of this case, we assumed that the bank sending the check in immediately got an addition to its reserves and that the bank on which it was written lost reserves as soon as the check reached the Federal Reserve bank. Now we must recognize that, strictly speaking, neither of these assumptions is correct.

When the bank in which a check is deposited sends it to the Federal Reserve bank, it does *not* immediately increase its Federal Reserve account but instead marks it up to a *temporary* account called its *Federal Reserve Collection Account.*

Thus the initial T-account effect would actually be

Commercial Bank X

Federal Reserve Collection Account	+$100	Demand deposit of check depositor	+$100

The important difference here is that the bank may *not* count its Federal Reserve Collection Account as a part of its legal reserves. When the check is received by the Federal Reserve bank, it, instead of immediately altering the reserve accounts of the two commercial banks involved, will indicate its receipt of the check by entering that amount in two temporary accounts entitled *uncollected cash items* and *deferred availability cash items*. The T-account effects would be

Federal Reserve Bank

Uncollected cash items	+$100	Deferred availability cash items	+$100

The *uncollected cash item* entry is a temporary account to denote the fact that the Federal Reserve bank will shortly (as soon as Bank Y receives the check) have a claim on Bank Y. When the bank on which the check is written receives it, the Federal Reserve bank will remove the *uncollected cash item* entry and, at that time, mark down the reserve account of Bank Y. Then, and only then, does that bank lose reserves from the check.

The *deferred availability cash items,* on the other hand, is a temporary account that recognizes that the Federal Reserve bank owes that amount to Commercial Bank X but that credit for additional legal reserves is being temporarily withheld—*deferred*—for a certain period of time.

Now the Federal Reserve bank maintains a time schedule for each bank in its district. This schedule categorizes each bank according to the *usual time it takes for a check to be delivered from the Federal Reserve bank to each particular bank.* If, for example, the normal time for delivery to Bank Y in our example were two

---

[4] Once again, to avoid unnecessary complication, we take an oversimplified example. The majority of checks cleared within the same Federal Reserve district currently provide credit within one day. Most of the Federal Reserve float we shall be concentrating on here arises out of interdistrict checks. Because such a transaction combines the complications of time lags with that of the Interdistrict Settlement Fund, our example will be restricted to an intradistrict transaction.

days, Bank Y would be in the "two-day" category. The significance of this category lies in the fact that any bank sending in a check written on Bank Y would know that, *whether the check was actually delivered to Bank Y in the usual time or not,* it could take credit for additional reserves automatically after waiting the prescribed two-day period.

In the usual case, the check *would* be received by Bank Y at the end of two days, in which case the following T-account entries would be appropriate:

Federal Reserve Bank

(5) Uncollected cash items	−$100	(3) Deferred availability cash items	−$100
		(4) Demand deposits of Bank X	+$100
		(6) Demand deposits of Bank Y	−$100

Bank Y

(7) Federal Reserve account −$100	(8) Demand deposit of check writer −$100

Bank X

(1) Federal Reserve collection account −$100 (2) Federal Reserve account +$100	

Entries (1), (2), (3), and (4) are necessary to recognize that, the scheduled time having elapsed, Bank X eliminates the temporary *Federal Reserve Collection Account* and takes credit for a $100 addition to its legal reserves, while the Federal Reserve bank eliminates the temporary *deferred availability item* account because the reserve credit to Bank X is no longer deferred.

Entries (5) and (6) are to take note of the fact that, as Bank Y has now actually received the check, the temporary *uncollected cash item* account can be eliminated and collection actually made by marking down Bank Y's reserve account. No "float" arises in this case.

There is, however, another possibility. If, after the scheduled two-day period has elapsed, Bank Y has for some reason *not yet* received the check, Bank X will automatically get its additional reserves (because the scheduled time period is up), but Bank Y will not yet lose any (because it has not yet, in fact, received the check).

In this case the T-account entries at the end of this two-day period would be

Federal Reserve Bank		*Bank X*	
	Deferred availability cash item −$100	Federal Reserve Collection Account −$100	
	Demand deposit of Bank X +$100	Federal Reserve account +$100	

For the moment (and until the check *is* actually received by Bank Y), the Federal Reserve's balance sheet still shows a $100 uncollected cash item, but no deferred availability cash item for this check. Also, for the same time period, *both banks are entitled to claim that $100 as a part of their legal reserves.* What has happened is that, because of the methods it uses to collect checks, the Federal Reserve has added to the banking system's total reserves just as surely as if it had made a loan to a member bank for $100. In this case, *Federal Reserve float* has arisen.

As this example illustrates, Federal Reserve float increases whenever a bank that has sent in a check for collection receives an addition to its reserves before the check actually reaches the bank on which it was written so that the latter's reserves can be correspondingly reduced. Such an increase, raising as it does the total legal reserves of the system, is conceptually precisely the same as a very short-term loan of reserves by the Fed.

For the System as a whole, the amount of Federal Reserve float can always be determined from the balance sheets of all Federal Reserve banks, as the excess of uncollected cash items over deferred availability cash items. For example, on March 27, 1991, uncollected cash items totaled $4.7 billion and deferred availability cash items totaled $4.5 billion. As of that date, therefore, Federal Reserve float totaled $0.2 billion.

Because they necessarily involve increases in total bank reserves, and therefore in the banking system's lending capacity, rises in Federal Reserve float are watched closely by Federal Reserve officials. Anything that slows down the normal delivery of checks—a rail strike, a crippling storm, or simply a big increase in check volume—can markedly raise bank reserves at least temporarily via this rather involved route and may require offsetting action.

It is important that the student familiarize himself or herself with the nature of Federal Reserve float and with the actual details of check collection. However, as specific detail can sometimes be a burden when considering other matters, we shall, in the remainder of this book, revert to the more simplified versions covered in the preceding sections. Specifically, in any future examples involving check collections, we shall ignore the "temporary" accounts just discussed and assume that reserve changes take place immediately.

Check Collection, Float, and the Monetary Control Act of 1980

Prior to the Monetary Control Act of 1980, member banks of the Federal Reserve System were subjected to substantially more rigorous reserve requirements than were applied to nonmember banks and other depository institutions. In an attempt to recompense them partially for this added expense, member banks were provided a number of services free of charge by the Federal Reserve System. When, however, the Monetary Control Act extended the same reserve requirements to all depository institutions, the main justification for these subsidized services to member banks was eliminated. As a result, the Monetary Control Act specifically required the Fed to (1) make such services as check collection, currency and coin provision, wire transfer, and securities safekeeping available to all depository institutions and (2) to sell such services to all users (including

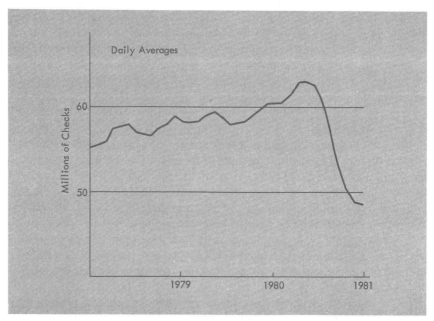

Source: Board of Governors of Federal Reserve System, *1981 Annual Report.*

FIGURE 10-1   Number of checks processed by the Federal Reserve System, 1979–1981

member banks) at prices that cover all costs including an estimate for the taxes and profits of a private supplier.

The most obvious result of this requirement is increased equity. If all depository institutions are to meet the same reserve requirements, all should have access to the discount window and to other Fed services on the same terms. But, in addition, charging explicit prices for such resource-using activities of the Fed has provided competition between the Fed and private sellers (e.g., correspondent banks) for the business and forces bank buyers to economize on the use of services heretofore considered "free goods." This should promote a more efficient use of resources in this area.

Charges for Federal Reserve check collection were introduced in mid-1981, and, as Figure 10-1 makes clear, the effect was as might have been expected: a significant reduction in checks processed through the Fed. Indeed, between 1980 and 1981, the number of checks collected via the Federal Reserve fell off by about 22 percent.

Another requirement of the Monetary Control Act was that, as soon as possible, the Federal Reserve was required to begin to charge for the heretofore interest-free loan of reserves provided the banking system when float arises. The Federal Reserve's initial response to this requirement was an intensive effort to reduce the size of the float. Beginning in 1980, the Board of Governors launched a program to reduce the level of float through improvements in the collection process. This plan reduced the size of float from a daily average of $4.2 billion in 1980 to a daily average of $1.8 billion during the second quarter of 1982. Further changes put the average level well under $1.0 billion by 1986. When float does arise, the most common procedure is to charge the payee bank (the bank in which the check was deposited) interest at the federal funds rate.[5]

Improving the Nation's Payment Mechanism: The Growth of Electronic Funds Transfer Systems

The sheer magnitude of the task of processing over 40 billion checks each year, plus the realization that this total has tended to double each decade, has forced the nation's monetary authorities into a series of measures aimed at speeding up the collection process and at reducing its enormous cost.[6]

The process of modernizing the check collection process began many years ago with the development of magnetic ink encoding of checks — an innovation that made possible the now almost universal practice of machine processing checks. It has continued more recently with the establishment of a number of regional check processing centers throughout the nation, and it goes forward at the moment with a series of efforts at the ultimate solution — replacement of paper checks altogether by systems permitting transfer of funds solely by electronic means.

What Is EFT?

In general terms, the movement toward development of an electronic funds transfer (EFT) system involves the substitution of electronic data processing and transmission for the current manual processing laboriously carried out primarily through paper checks. Preliminary steps toward establishment of a full-blown EFT system have included such measures as eliminating charges for, and expanding access to, the Federal Reserve's existing wire facilities for the transfer of funds. But the heart of the movement involves the spread of automated teller machines, point-of-sale systems, and automated clearinghouses.[7]

An *automated teller machine (ATM)* performs a number of banking services automatically either on or off the bank's premises. Among these services are the receipt of deposits, the dispensing of cash from demand and savings deposits, and making advances on credit cards. Access to the machine is via a card with magnetic strip and secret code number. Often the ATM is tied in to the bank's computer, permitting immediate alterations in the customer's account.

Point-of-sale systems (POS) are located in retail establishments and facilitate

---

[5] For an informative account of this issue see John C. Young, "The Rise and Fall of Federal Reserve Float," *Economic Review*, Federal Reserve Bank of Kansas City, February 1986.

[6] A recent estimate has placed the average real resource cost of payment by paper check at $0.68. See A. N. Berger and D. B. Humphrey, "The Role of Interstate Banking in the Diffusion of Electronic Payments Technology," in *Technological Innovation, Regulation, and the Monetary Economy*, C. Lawrence and R. Shay, eds. (Cambridge, MA: Ballinger Books, 1986).

[7] For a recent statement regarding EFT, see S. D. Felgram and R. E. Ferguson, "The Evolution of Retail EFT Networks," *New England Economic Review*, Federal Reserve Bank of Boston, July–August 1986. See also Michael C. Keeley, "A Cashless Society?" *Weekly Letter*, Federal Reserve Bank of San Francisco, April 15, 1988.

payment for goods purchased electronically. Also operated by the customer's card, these facilities perform services ranging from the authorization of checks or credit cards to transferring funds instantaneously (through the use of terminals tied in to the bank's computer) from the customer's to the store's account.

Automated clearinghouses (ACH) permit electronic clearing between banks. One of their most common uses is to make payroll payments directly to employees' banks without the use of checks. In this case, the employer places the payroll data on a computer tape and sends it to the (employer's) bank. Employees who are customers of the same bank have their accounts increased directly. Data as to amounts and banks of employees who bank elsewhere are then put on a magnetic tape that is delivered to the ACH. There a computer sorts out the information, bank by bank, and each other bank receives a computer tape listing the employees and the amount of their payment.

The Problems and Prospects of EFT Development   Several years ago it was generally thought that EFT systems would develop rapidly and smoothly, dramatically changing the nature of the nation's payments mechanism in short order. Indeed, if one considers the *value* of transactions, over 80 percent are already completed by some form of electronic funds transfer. On the other hand, if one focuses on the *number* of transactions, it is apparent that EFT has not yet really won the day, for as recently as 1987, "checks still handle over 300 times the number of payments that electronic payments do." [8] While EFT steadily gains wider acceptance, one is forced to the conclusion that the long-heralded "checkless society is still some distance away."

The hurdles to more rapid development have included a mixed bag of technological, cultural, and regulatory factors. While it seems clear that, given sufficiently extensive use, the electronic devices are capable of substantially reducing the average costs of payment, the initial outlays required are enormous. A large share of these costs would, of course, be fixed costs, so that — given very intensive use by the public — the cost per unit could be brought down to levels well below those of more conventional methods.

But the public's reception of EFT has been lukewarm, forestalling full realization of the significant economies of scale that are available. The reasons for public resistance are varied. Customs change slowly, and many people simply do not trust computers. In addition, there is considerable reluctance to give up the tried and true financial record that canceled checks provide. And many have expressed real concern that EFT data banks might ultimately collect so much personal information as to constitute a serious threat to privacy.

In one important respect, however, banking law has, at least up until quite recently, tended to "stack the deck" against EFT and in favor of paper checks. As we noted earlier, it has long been illegal for banks to pay explicit interest on checking accounts. But, especially when the Federal Reserve System was offering check collection free of charge to its member banks, checking accounts tended to be real money makers for banks. So they proceeded to subsidize

---

[8] Ibid., p. 1. A good illustration of the change is provided by the following two quotations from *Business Week* magazine. On August 4, 1975, *Business Week* reported, "Faster than any but the most optimistic thought possible, electronic banking is sweeping the country. . . . " Less than two years later, on April 18, 1977, the same magazine observed, "Suddenly it appears that the great electronic banking revolution that has been 'just around the corner' for a decade may never arrive at all."

checking accounts with *implicit* interest payments, not the least of which has been the provision of "free" checking.

But, as we have seen, the Monetary Control Act of 1980 has instituted some important changes. Now that banks must pay for the Fed's check collecting services, checking accounts are more expensive to administer and free checking is essentially on the way out. If these changes signal an end to the practice of subsidizing paper checks, and if EFT really can accomplish check collection at a much lower per unit cost than can the current manual system, the lower charges may well provide the incentive needed to change the public's attitude toward EFT markedly. It is not possible at this point to predict how rapidly EFT will grow. One can, however, be certain that it *will* continue growing.

By the beginning of the decade of the 1990s, the vast majority of the nation's depository institutions offered ATM facilities, and some 85 percent of these belonged to a network shared with other banks. In addition, the installation of POS systems was growing, and, by 1989, direct deposit of salary and pension payments equaled 40 percent of commercial payments handled by automated clearinghouses, half of social security payments, and two-thirds of federal salary payments.[9]

Federal Reserve System Reserve Requirements

Under current law, all depository institutions are required to back up their transactions accounts and their "nonpersonal" time deposits with a specified fraction of *total* or *legal* reserves. This requirement is, without question, the cornerstone of the Fed's power to control the money supply.

The applicable current law (the Monetary Control Act of 1980) identifies the depository institutions subject to reserve requirements as commercial banks (member and nonmember), mutual savings banks, savings and loan associations, and credit unions.[10] The "transactions accounts" behind which reserves are required include checking accounts, NOW accounts, ATS accounts, and share draft accounts. The "nonpersonal time deposits" subject to reserves are time deposits with maturities of less than two and a half years owned by anyone other than natural persons or sole proprietors.

The Monetary Control Act specifies the assets that qualify as *total* or *legal* reserves to include vault cash or checking accounts held at a district Federal Reserve bank.[11] Finally, the law sets up limits within which the Board of Gover-

---

[9] See *Annual Report*, Board of Governors of the Federal Reserve System, 1989. For an excellent summary of the EFT situation, see also Bruce J. Summers, "Electronic Payments in Retrospect," *Economic Review*, Federal Reserve Bank of Richmond, March–April 1988.

[10] Technically, the law covers all these institutions covered by, or eligible to apply for, federal insurance. See Charles R. McNeill, "The Depository Institutions Deregulation and Monetary Control Act of 1980," *Federal Reserve Bulletin*, June 1980.

[11] Accounts held by depository institutions at Federal Home Loan banks, the National Credit Union Administration Central Liquidity Facility, or correspondent banks count toward satisfying the reserve requirement if those institutions "pass through" such reserves to a Federal Reserve bank. Reserves are "passed through" if the correspondent bank or other authorized institution opens a dollar-for-dollar account at a Federal Reserve bank on behalf of its respondent bank.

TABLE 10-2   Legal limits to Board of Governors' authority
to vary required reserve ratios[a]

	Minimum	Maximum
Transactions accounts[b]		
0–$3.4 million[c]	0	0
$3.4–41.1 million[c]	3%	3%
Over $41.1 million	8	14
Nonpersonal savings and time deposits	0	9

[a] If five members of the Board of Governors vote to declare the existence of "extraordinary circumstances," the Board may impose any reserve ratio on any liability of depository institutions for 180 days.

[b] If five members of the Board of Governors vote affirmatively, the board may impose supplementary reserve requirements up to 4 percent on transactions accounts.

[c] The amount to which the zero and 3 percent bracket applies grows each year by 80 percent of the percentage change in total transactions accounts at all depository institutions. The figures in the table for these brackets are as of early 1991.

nors of the Federal Reserve System may alter the *required reserve ratio*. These limits are reported in Table 10-2.

There is, of course, nothing in the law to prevent a depository institution from holding *more* total reserves (i.e., vault cash and Federal Reserve account) than its outstanding deposits and required reserve ratios dictate. The institution that does so is said to have *excess* reserves—total legal reserves that exceed the minimum amount required to back up present deposit liabilities.

Perhaps a numerical example will help to clarify the terminology here. Suppose that Bank A happens to be a member bank for which the applicable required reserve ratios average out to 12 percent for transactions accounts and 3 percent for nonpersonal time deposits. Assume further that Bank A's balance sheet is

Bank A

Cash	$ 100	Transactions accounts (de-		
Federal Reserve account	250	mand deposits plus NOW		
Loans and securities	3,500	and ATS accounts)		$2,000
Other assets	1,150	Nonpersonal time deposits		2,500
		Other liabilities and net		
		worth		500

In that case its *total* reserves are $350 (the sum of its cash and Federal Reserve account). Its *required* reserves (the amount of total reserves the law requires it to have to back up its current outstanding transactions accounts and nonpersonal time deposits) equal $315—the sum of .12 × $2,000 and .03 × $2,500. Its *excess* reserves, therefore, equal $35.

The student should always remember the following simple relationship:

Total reserves ≡ Required reserves + Excess reserves

Given sufficient information to compute any two of these totals, the third is obvious.

Reserve requirements need not be met on a daily basis. Depository institutions have a two-week "reserve period," essentially ending every other Wednesday, within which they are required to maintain *average daily total reserves* equal to the required percentage of *average daily transactions accounts* outstanding during that period.[12] If, for example, average daily deposits during the period require average daily total reserves of $4 million, the requirement could be satisfied by a bank's holding average daily total reserves of $3 million for the first nine business days, as long as it had the $13 million needed on the tenth day to achieve the required $4 million average for the period.

What happens if a depository institution fails to meet the requirement? If the deficiency is minor—no more than 2 percent of the reserves required for the period—no penalty is assessed if it carries an equivalent amount of excess reserves the following period.[13] And even in the case of larger deficiencies, the Federal Reserve bank may waive any penalty depending on the circumstances. Where a penalty is assessed, the usual practice is to charge the offending institution a fine on the amount of the deficiency at a rate that is 2 percent higher than the current Federal Reserve discount rate. For more serious violators, the Fed may invoke "cease and desist" orders or, where appropriate, assess civil money penalties.

One final word of caution about the purpose of reserve requirements may be appropriate before we proceed. It is perhaps natural to think of required reserves as primarily a source of liquidity for the bank. Indeed, there can be little doubt that earlier reserve requirement legislation *was* aimed largely at providing liquid funds in case of sudden unexpected withdrawals. But those days have long since passed. Such a view constitutes a serious misconception regarding the major role of reserve requirements. After all, if the law requires that an institution *hold* a certain quantity of reserves, those reserves certainly are not available to pay out to meet cash demands.

Far from providing for bank liquidity needs, reserve requirements are the fulcrum or cornerstone on the basis of which our monetary authorities limit the supply of money and credit in the economy. And this is a much more important function than partially providing for bank liquidity.

Review Questions

1. Explain the operation of local clearinghouses. Why must the total of unfavorable clearing balances at any clearinghouse always equal the total of favorable clearing balances?

---

[12] Actually, average daily total reserves held during the two-week period between alternate Wednesdays must equal the required percentage of average daily transactions accounts held during the two-week period between alternate Mondays. The requirement is thus lagged for two days. Reserve requirements for time deposits are lagged for two weeks.

[13] Similarly, excess reserves in any period, up to a maximum of 2 percent of required reserves in that period, may be carried forward to apply to the following week's required reserves.

2. Carefully explain how the collection of a check written on a member bank in one Federal Reserve district and deposited in a member bank in a different district affects the balance sheets of the Federal Reserve banks involved.

3. Explain how Federal Reserve float arises. What is the significance of a sudden large increase in float?

4. Identify
   a. Interdistrict Settlement Fund
   b. Deferred availability cash items
   c. Point-of-sale systems
   d. Uncollected cash items

5. Explain carefully how the Monetary Control Act of 1980 has affected check collection and Federal Reserve float.

6. "In one important respect banking law has, at least up until quite recently, tended to stack the deck against **EFT** and in favor of paper checks." Why is this the case? What has happened "recently" to reduce this bias?

7. Carefully explain the reserve requirements applied to depository institutions including (a) the assets that can be counted as total reserves, (b) the legal limits to required reserve ratios, (c) the deposit liabilities behind which reserves must be maintained, (d) the reserve period over which the legal requirement is computed, and (e) the fundamental purpose of legally required reserves.

The Creation and Destruction of Money by Commercial Banks Under Simplified Conditions

In this chapter, we consider the process whereby commercial banks create and destroy money under the assumptions that no one withdraws cash, that no time deposits exist, and that the banks do not willingly keep excess reserves. These assumptions are, of course, far removed from reality, but they do serve the important function of providing us with the clearest possible preliminary view of the money creation process. A more realistic and much more complex discussion of the money supply expansion issue will be presented in Chapter 12.

The Fundamental Nature and Origin of Demand Deposits as Money

In one way, at least, it is unfortunate that the demand deposit portion of the money supply bears the name "deposit." The word "deposit" carries with it a connotation that can be seriously misleading to the introductory student. He or she is all too likely to leap to the seemingly logical conclusion that all demand deposits must necessarily have originated with the *deposit* of cash in a checking account somewhere, some time in the past.

Such a "money in the bank" view of demand deposits not only misconstrues their origin but also often leads to a distorted idea of the essence of demand deposits as money. The fundamental essence of demand deposits is the *debt of a bank*. It is the bank's debt that goes from person to person—settling transactions. The debt of the bank *is* the medium of exchange that performs the essential task of money regardless of its origin or whether any currency is involved.

Of course, demand deposits *can* originate from a depositor placing currency in a checking account, but this is the exception. Think for a moment about your own checking account. How often is it replenished by a direct deposit of currency? For most people, the answer is, "Seldom." Most people build up their balances by deposit of a check on another bank—the weekly paycheck from their employer or the student's monthly check from home. This simply consists of a transfer of a demand deposit from one bank to another. But where did that demand deposit really "originate? Is it likely that the check writer—your employer or your parents—originated it by depositing cash in their accounts? Not really. Chances are that they too received it in the form of a check.

The truth is, of course, that the bulk of the demand deposit portion of our money supply originates not from the deposit of currency but, rather, from commercial bank lending. It can, in fact, be said that *whenever a commercial bank makes a loan or purchases a security (from the nonbank public), it creates new money and thereby expands the nation's money supply.* Similarly, whenever a loan at a commercial bank is paid off or a security is sold (to a member of the nonbank public), money is thereby destroyed and the money supply cut. Let us see why this occurs.

How Banks Create and Destroy Money

Whenever a commercial bank makes a loan, it accepts the borrower's IOU, in return for which it makes available the proceeds of the loan in money form. Similarly, when a bank purchases a security from a member of the nonbank public, it adds the security to its portfolio and pays the seller with newly created money. In either case, the borrower (or the seller of the security) acquires claim to a new checking account, which the bank creates by simply writing it up on its books.[1] The T-account effects in these cases would be

Bank X Makes a Loan		*Bank X Buys a Security*	
Loans (borrower's IOU) +$100	Demand deposits (owed to borrower) +$100	Securities +$100	Demand deposits (owed to seller of security) +$100

In each case, the demand deposit created by the bank to complete the transaction constitutes a net addition to the nation's money supply, raising M1. Indeed the majority of the U.S. money supply originates in just this fashion.

Exactly the reverse occurs whenever bank loans mature and are paid off or when banks sell securities to members of the nonbank public. In this case, the borrower (or the purchaser of the security) must pay money into the bank, thereby removing it from circulation and reducing M1. In the most common

---

[1] Obviously the bank must possess sufficient reserves to permit this. The proceeds of a loan or the payment for a security *could*, of course, be made in the form of cash rather than a newly created demand deposit. This would be a most unusual procedure, since borrowers generally prefer the safety and convenience of a deposit. Even in this case, however, the money supply would rise, since cash that had been in bank vaults would then be in circulation.

situation, where payment is effected via a check written on an account at the bank being paid, the T-account effects are[2]

Loan at Bank X Paid Off	
Loans −$100	Demand deposits (of borrower) −$100

Bank X Sells a Security	
Securities −$100	Demand deposits (of buyer of security) −$100

The important thing for the student to bear in mind is the simple fact that **commercial banks cannot avoid raising the nation's money supply when they acquire more earning assets from the public.**

The Limits to Commercial Bank Money Creation, Assuming No Cash Drain, Time Deposits, or Desired Excess Reserves

At first glance, commercial banking would appear to be an absurdly lucrative business. After all, where else can a business manager create the "product" that provides his or her income—money for loan—by the mere stroke of a pen? What a wonderfully simple means of amassing profits! "Mr. Businessman, you give me your IOU for $100,000 and I shall reciprocate by giving you mine—in the form of a checking account—for the same amount, *provided* that you agree to pay me back an additional $10,000 in interest for doing so." What a seemingly effortless way of earning a living!

But alas, the road to riches for the commercial banker is not really all that easy. It is true that bankers have every reason for desiring to expand their loans, thereby expanding the money supply by an equivalent amount—for when they can do this, they do indeed raise their income. But their ability to do so is limited on a number of fronts and for a variety of reasons.

We turn now to a consideration of the limits to the lending (and money creating) capacity of commercial banks. We shall approach this topic in three steps. First, our focus will be restricted to the individual commercial bank and the limitations on its ability to create more money. Then, we switch to a consideration of the banking system as a whole under the highly oversimplified assumptions of no cash drain and no time deposits and no desired excess reserves. Third, in the next chapter, we attempt a closer approach to reality by relaxing our assumptions and admitting cash drain, time deposits, and desired excess reserves into the picture. Throughout this chapter and the next, to keep the discussion as simple as possible, we focus only on commercial banks and only on the demand deposit component of transactions accounts.

---

[2] If the borrower pays off the loan with cash—an unlikely possibility—the money supply is still reduced by the amount of the payment, since cash that was in the public's hands then disappears into the bank vaults (where it is no longer counted as part of M1).

The Single Commercial Bank
in a Many-Bank System

The individual commercial bank, as a profit-seeking institution, has a natural desire to maximize its ownership of earning assets — loans and securities. Because, as we have just seen, such assets can be readily acquired by the simple act of creating more demand deposits, an obvious question arises. What keeps commercial banks from expanding the money supply to infinite proportions in their quest for added profits? What limits the individual bank's money creation?[3]

To begin with, any issuer of demand deposits must be prepared, as a matter of law, to pay *cash on demand* to any depositor who requests it. Consequently, *even if there were no required reserve ratio at all,* commercial banks could not freely expand loans (and demand deposits) without limit. As long as people desire to hold their money partly in the form of demand deposits and partly in the form of cash, any expansion in the former will surely induce an increase in the latter. If, for example, a bank possesses $1 million in cash and has, at the moment, $40 million of demand deposits outstanding, the $1 million may be just adequate to meet usual demands for cash on the part of the holders of the $40 million. Any increase in loans (and therefore in demand deposits) in this case would consequently raise the demand deposit total, and the attendant risk of cash withdrawal, to a level at which $1 million in cash would be insufficient. Such a bank, then, would be unable to grant more loans.

The risk of cash withdrawal, however, is not the most important limitation on the single bank's loan expansion potential. Far more confining is the restriction that is imposed by the combination of the *required reserve ratio* and the *likelihood that borrowers of newly created deposits will write checks on them that will be deposited in other banks.*

Let us revert, once again, to an example. Suppose that Bank X, subject to a required reserve ratio of 20 percent, has the following assets and liabilities:

Bank X

Cash	$ 10,000	Demand deposits	$600,000
Federal Reserve account	125,000	Other liabilities and net	100,000
Loans and securities	560,000	worth	
Other assets	5,000		

Assuming no nonpersonal time deposits, Bank X has excess reserves totaling $15,000 ($135,000 minus 20 percent of $600,000). The very existence of excess reserves indicates unused lending power available to the bank. We can assume that, as a profit-maximizing institution, Bank X will want to exploit its full lending (and interest-earning) capacity. Just how far can it go?

If the required reserve ratio were the only limitation, it seems clear that, at least initially, it could *legally* lend an additional $75,000 — for if a 20 percent

---

[3] While the physical act of creating added deposits *is* essentially costless, servicing those deposits (and attracting the reserves that permit them) does, of course, involve real marginal costs, which certainly could make some loans losing propositions. If such costs were to be the effective limit on loans, however, they would result in banks retaining excess reserves — a possibility that we have assumed away.

required reserve ratio means anything, it signifies that each dollar of reserves can, at maximum, back up $5 of demand deposits. Therefore $15,000 of excess reserves can be used *legally* to back up $75,000 of additional demand deposits. But hold on a bit!

No banker can afford to be satisfied with considering only what is legal today without some concern with what is likely tomorrow. And the truth is that if Bank X *should* lend out an additional $75,000 on the basis of its present $15,000 of excess reserves, it will certainly be in trouble tomorrow.

Let us take a long look at the consequences of a single bank lending out, as in this case, an amount equal to five times its excess reserves. Immediately after the loan is granted, Bank X's balance sheet would be altered to look like this:

Bank X

Cash	$ 10,000	Demand deposits	$675,000
Federal Reserve account	125,000	Other liabilities and net	100,000
Loans and securities	635,000	worth	
Other assets	5,000		

Bank X is, for the moment at least, within the limits of the law, as its $135,000 of total legal reserves are exactly 20 percent of its outstanding demand deposits. But it had better beware the future.

The borrower of the $75,000 can certainly be expected to begin writing checks on his newly created account almost immediately. After all, who borrows money at interest without the intent of spending the money? Bank X must count on $75,000 worth of checks being written in short order.

Now the important question is, "Where will those checks end up?" If they are redeposited by the check recipient into accounts at Bank X, Bank X will lose no reserves and be in no difficulty. If, however, they are deposited in a *different* bank, then Bank X can expect to lose $75,000 of reserves as a result of their collection through the Federal Reserve.

Which eventuality is most likely? The answer is obvious. Bank X is only one out of more than 12,000 commercial banks in this country—any of which might receive the check—so the odds on its returning to Bank X are prohibitively small. And if the likely thing happens and $75,000 of checks are written, deposited in a different bank, and collected via the Federal Reserve, Bank X would quickly find itself in the following position:

Bank X

Cash	$ 10,000	Demand deposits	$600,000
Federal Reserve account	50,000	Other liabilities and net	100,000
Loans and securities	635,000	worth	
Other assets	5,000		

Its total legal reserves are reduced to $60,000, while its required reserves are $120,000. It has a $60,000 deficiency, which, if not made up shortly, will lay it open to fines or other penalties. Clearly, no single bank would knowingly place itself in this situation.

For the reasons just discussed, individual commercial banks making loans must *expect* to lose reserves shortly in the amount loaned. Consequently, the prudent banker must limit his or her lending (and money creating) activities to a scale that will preclude the embarrassment and expense of a reserve deficiency. The only completely safe practice is to limit new loans to the *amount of the bank's excess reserves* rather than a multiple of them. This is, in fact, the usual custom of commercial bankers.

If Bank X should follow the "working rule" of lending just the amount of its excess reserves, $15,000, the expected loss of reserves that follows the granting of the loan will not leave it with a reserve deficiency. Immediately after making the loan, its balance sheet would be

Bank X

Cash	$ 10,000	Demand deposits	$615,000
Federal Reserve account	125,000	Other liabilities and net	100,000
Loans and securities	575,000	worth	
Other assets	5,000		

Then, after the borrower writes checks, the recipient deposits them in a different bank, and they are collected via the Federal Reserve, it would be left with

Bank X

Cash	$ 10,000	Demand deposits	$600,000
Federal Reserve account	110,000	Other liabilities and net	100,000
Loans and securities	575,000	worth	
Other assets	5,000		

Its remaining reserves of $120,000 are just sufficient to meet the requirements of the law, and it can go on about its business. Its prudence, in limiting its loans to the amount of its excess reserves, has paid off.

Summing up, the individual commercial bank is limited in its lending and money-creating activities by (1) the likelihood of cash withdrawal and (2) the legal reserve requirement, coupled with the likelihood that it will quickly lose reserves (to other commercial banks) in the full amount of any loan it makes. To protect against either or both of these threats, the single commercial banker in a many-bank system can safely lend out only the amount of his or her excess reserves.

The Commercial Banking System, Assuming No Cash Withdrawal, Time Deposits, or Desired Excess Reserves

No one bank can safely expand the money supply by more than the amount of its excess reserves. But if we widen our horizon to encompass all 12,000-plus commercial banks — the banking system as a whole — we find, not surprisingly, that potential expansion is considerably enhanced. With each single bank along the way expanding to its safe maximum, the sum created by all is bound to be greater.

In this section, for simplicity, we assume that banks have no desire to hold on to any excess reserves and that depositors are satisfied to keep checking accounts in that form, withdrawing no cash and converting no demand deposits to time deposits. Once a demand deposit is created via the loan process, it is assumed to stay in that form.

With these simplifications, which will be dropped in the next chapter, the results are apparent. Unlike the single-bank case, when loans are made and checks are written on the newly created deposits, there is no loss of reserves *for the system as a whole.* This is because the loss of reserves by the bank that made the loan is exactly offset, from the vantage point of the system as a whole, by the gain of reserves on the part of the bank in which the checks are deposited.

If, in this case, the banking system starts out with excess reserves of $15,000, and none of these reserves can be lost *to the system* through cash withdrawal, through conversion to time deposits, or through transfer to another bank, then the maximum possible expansion of deposits and loans is only reached when every dollar of excess reserves is used to support its maximum permissible amount of demand deposits.

If, for example, the required reserve ratio is 20 percent (one-fifth), this means that at maximum each $1 of reserves may support $5 of deposits. Consequently, $15,000 of excess reserves could, at the extreme, back up five times that amount, or $75,000 of new demand deposits. If the required reserve ratio were 10 percent (one-tenth), each dollar of reserves would back up $10 of deposits, and $15,000 of excess reserves would not be "used up" until $150,000 of demand deposits had been created. Finally, a 25 percent (one-fourth) required reserve ratio would imply that each dollar of reserves can support $4 of deposits, so that $15,000 of excess reserves would be sufficient to back up $60,000 of additional deposits.

It is not coincidental that in each of the preceding examples, the maximum possible expansion of demand deposits by the banking system as a whole equals the *reciprocal of the required reserve ratio times its excess reserves.* Under the assumptions we have made, that is the formula for computing maximum potential deposit (and loan) expansion for the banking system as a whole.

To compute maximum potential deposit and loan expansion by the entire commercial banking system (assuming no cash withdrawal, no conversion to time deposits, and no desired excess reserves):

$$\frac{1}{\text{Required reserve ratio}} \times \begin{array}{c}\text{Excess reserves}\\ \text{of system}\end{array} = \begin{array}{c}\text{Maximum possible}\\ \text{expansion of demand}\\ \text{deposits and loans}\end{array}$$

Some memorization of pat formulas is useful for handling economic issues, but memorization alone is sterile without a thorough understanding of the logic that lies behind the formulas. Let us take a brief look beyond the mere mathematics of the final outcome, to the *process* whereby this result may be achieved.

Suppose, for example, that we have a banking system in which no bank has excess (or a deficiency of) reserves except Bank A, which, at the moment, is in the following condition:

Bank A

Cash	$ 50,000	Demand deposits	$2,000,000
Federal Reserve account	380,000	Other liabilities and net	300,000
Loans and securities	1,800,000	worth	
Other assets	70,000		

If the required reserve ratio for all banks is 20 percent, Bank A (and the banking system as a whole) has $30,000 of excess reserves. Of course, we know immediately that, given these facts, the banking system as a whole can increase loans and demand deposits by $150,000 before the expansion limit is reached. Then, and only then, will every dollar of reserves be backing up its legal limit of $5 of deposits. Then, and only then, will every dollar of excess reserves have been used up in the sense that it will have become part of the required reserves.

But our interest here is in the *process* by which this limit is approached. It all starts, of course, in Bank A, the only bank with the present capacity to grant additional loans. As a single bank, Bank A, for reasons discussed earlier, will find its ideal combination of profitability and safety by following the working rule of lending out an amount just equal to its excess reserves. The T-account effects of its doing so will be

Bank A

Loans	+$30,000	Demand deposits	+$30,000

It is to be expected that the borrower will then write checks on his or her newly acquired account and that the recipient of those checks will deposit them in another bank. If the other bank is Bank B, it can be expected to send the checks in for collection immediately via the Federal Reserve. The effects of this step are

Bank A		*Bank B*	
Federal Reserve account −$30,000	Demand deposits −$30,000	Federal Reserve account +$30,000	Demand deposits +$30,000

Now the wisdom of Bank A's forbearance in lending only the amount of its excess reserves becomes evident. The expected has happened, and it has lost reserves equal to the loan granted. But, because it retains $400,000 of legal reserves, it is still able to support the remaining $2 million of demand deposits. It has done all the money creating it could and is now safely out of the picture.

But whereas Bank A has lost all *its* excess reserves, the banking *system* has not. The $30,000 of reserves, lost by Bank A, have been gained by Bank B. And now Bank B is in a position to grant a loan.

Bank B, which started with no excess reserves, has now received a $30,000 boost in its total reserves and an equivalent increase in its demand deposit liabilities. Remembering that $6,000 of the added reserves are required to back up the added deposits, we see that Bank B now has excess reserves of $24,000. It can, therefore, safely lend that amount.

Bank B

Loans	+$24,000	Demand deposits	+$24,000

At this point, $54,000 of newly created money exists. The $30,000 created by Bank A is still held as a deposit in Bank B, and an additional $24,000 has just been created by Bank B. As before, the borrower can be expected to write checks on the $24,000, and the checks will in all likelihood be deposited in a different bank (Bank C), which will, in turn, send them through the Federal Reserve collection facilities.

Bank B		Bank C	
Federal Reserve account −$24,000	Demand deposits −$24,000	Federal Reserve account +$24,000	Demand deposits +$24,000

Bank B loses $24,000 of the $30,000 of reserves it originally acquired, but the $6,000 it retains is sufficient to back up the $30,000 demand deposit that is still there. As before, however, another bank has gained the lost reserves. And, as the $24,000 of added total reserves provides Bank C with $19,200 of *excess* reserves (added total reserves, $24,000, minus 20 percent of added demand deposits, $4,800), this bank can now add further to the credit and money supply:

Bank C

Loans	+$19,200	Demand deposits	+$19,200

At this point, $73,200 of new money exists, $30,000 created by Bank A and still in Bank B, $24,000 created by Bank B and now in Bank C, and $19,200, just created by Bank C. Bank C will shortly lose $19,200 of reserves and deposits and Bank D will gain them. Bank D will then have excess reserves of $15,360 and will lend that much. It, in turn, will lose that amount to Bank E, which will then be in a position to create an additional $12,288, and so on. It is hardly necessary to continue with this description, the future course of which must be obvious by now.

Note that at each step along the way, individual commercial banks add to the money supply 80 percent of the amount added by the preceding bank. What we have, then, is a process in which, if the original excess reserves are represented by x, money is created in the following amounts:

	Bank A		Bank B		Bank C		Bank D	
Amount of new money created	x	+	$.8x$	+	$.8(.8x)$	+	$.8[.8(.8x)]$	etc.

This series of money supply additions clearly make up an infinite geometrical series, the formula for the addition of which is

$$\frac{1}{(1 - \text{The common multiple})} \times \text{The first term in the series}$$

or, in this case,

$$\frac{1}{(1-.80)} \times \text{Initial excess reserves} = \frac{1}{.20} \times \$30{,}000 = 5 \times \$30{,}000 = \$150{,}000$$

Since, in this simplified case of banking system expansion, the denominator (1 minus the common multiple) must always equal the required reserve ratio, the mathematics and logic underlying the formula used earlier become clearer. What we now know is that the formula

$$\frac{1}{\text{Required reserve ratio}} \times \text{Excess reserves} = \begin{array}{l}\text{Maximum possible expansion}\\ \text{of demand deposits}\\ \text{and loans}\end{array}$$

is simply the formula for summing the additions to the money supply that occur

TABLE 11-1 Summary of process of demand deposit expansion by entire banking system, no cash or time deposits

Banks	New money created by	New loans made by	Newly created demand deposits retained by	Original excess reserves used up as required reserves by
A	$ 30,000	$ 30,000	—	—
B	24,000	24,000	$ 30,000	$ 6,000
C	19,200	19,200	24,000	4,800
D	15,360	15,360	19,200	3,840
E	12,288	12,288	15,360	3,072
F	9,830	9,830	12,288	2,458
G	7,864	7,864	9,830	1,966
H	6,291	6,291	7,864	1,573
I	5,033	5,033	6,291	1,258
J	4,026	4,026	5,033	1,007
K	3,221	3,221	4,026	805
L	2,577	2,577	3,221	644
M	2,062	2,062	2,577	515
N	1,650	1,650	2,062	412
O	1,320	1,320	1,650	330
P	1,056	1,056	1,320	264
Q	845	845	1,056	211
All other	3,377	3,337	4,222	845
Total by banking system as a whole	$150,000	$150,000	$150,000	$30,000

over time at Banks A, B, C, D, and so on, in amounts making up a geometric progression. The process of expansion just described is depicted in tabular form in Table 11-1.[4]

Commercial Bank Adjustment to Reserve Deficiencies

As we have just seen, commercial banks typically respond to excess reserves by acquiring more earning assets, thereby raising the money supply to the limit permitted by the required reserve ratio.[5] Let us now consider the other side of the coin. How do commercial banks adjust to reserve deficiencies?

A Single Bank with a Reserve Deficiency

We begin with the case of a single bank. Assume, for example, that Bank A is currently in the following position:

Bank A

Cash	$ 50,000	Demand deposits	$2,250,000
Federal Reserve account	375,000	Other liabilities and net	750,000
Loans and securities	2,200,000	worth	
Other assets	375,000		

If the required reserve ratio is 20 percent for demand deposits, Bank A clearly has a reserve **deficiency** totaling $25,000. Such a situation cannot be permitted to continue indefinitely. Bank A obviously must take some action to correct it.

Now it must be remembered that the reserve requirement is a *ratio*. A $25,000 deficiency can be eliminated either by obtaining $25,000 of additional legal reserves or (if RRR = 20 percent) by reducing demand deposits by $125,000, or by some combination of the two. Of course, the acquisition of more reserves is normally preferable, and a commercial bank can opt for this solution in a number of ways. It could sell some of its U.S. securities, borrow reserves on the federal funds market, or borrow them through the Fed's discount window. Let us consider these options in turn.

Sale of U.S. Securities   One possible method is via the sale of some of its secondary reserves, its short-term U.S. securities. If our Bank A can find a buyer for $25,000 worth of U.S. securities, its reserve deficiency will probably be erased.

---

[4] Some students may recognize the arithmetical equivalence of the so-called "money multiplier" (1/RRR) with the expenditure multiplier (1/MPS) normally encountered in introductory courses. The two are arithmetically identical, both being the formula for summing an infinite geometric series.

[5] Under the conditions assumed in this chapter.

Three possible sales must be considered—to another commercial bank, to a member of the nonbank public, and to a Federal Reserve bank.

If another commercial bank should purchase them, the normal means of payment between banks will provide Bank A with additional reserves at the expense of the purchasing bank, as the following T-accounts illustrate.

Bank A		*Commercial Bank* *Purchasing Securities*	
U.S. securities −$25,000		U.S. securities +$25,000	
Federal Reserve account +$25,000		Federal Reserve account −$25,000	

If the purchaser is a nonbank financial institution such as an insurance company, or any other member of the nonbank public, payment would normally be made by a check written on an account at another commercial bank, the collection of which would, once again, raise Bank A's reserve account by the requisite amount while lowering that of the other bank.

Bank A		*Bank on Which* *Check Is Written to* *Purchase Securities*	
U.S. securities −$25,000		Federal Reserve account −$25,000	Demand deposits of purchaser −$25,000
Federal Reserve account +$25,000			

Finally it is conceivable that Bank A might sell its U.S. securities to a Federal Reserve bank. If so, the T-account effects would be

Bank A		*Federal Reserve Bank*	
U.S. securities −$25,000		U.S. securities +$25,000	Demand deposit of Bank A +$25,000
Federal Reserve account +$25,000			

Of course it must be remembered that this last option—selling U.S. securities to the Federal Reserve System—involves a Federal Reserve *open-market purchase*. Such a transaction would only be carried out at the initiative of the Federal Reserve System when it considered it appropriate to raise the banking system's reserves. The Fed does not purchase securities simply to bail out individual commercial banks in need.

Borrowing Federal Funds   An attractive alternative to the sale of U.S. securities would be borrowing the needed reserves on the *federal funds* market. Federal funds, as noted earlier, consist of excess reserves in the form of deposits in the district Federal Reserve bank, which are lent by one bank to another. Typically, federal fund transactions take the form of an unsecured 24-hour loan.[6] Arrangements are agreed upon by telephone between the lending bank and the borrowing bank (often referred to as the "selling" bank and the "buying" bank) and confirmed later by telephone and/or mail. The actual transfer of the reserves is normally accomplished via a phone call or telegram from the lending bank to the Federal Reserve bank, instructing the latter to transfer the agreed-upon amount from its reserve account to that of the borrower. In the most usual case (a one-day loan), the Federal Reserve bank will reverse the transaction on the following day. Payment of interest for the loan — at the going *federal funds rate* — is normally made by wire transfer the next day.

The T-account effects of borrowing federal funds, for Bank A, might thus be

	Bank A	Bank That Lends Excess Reserves	
Federal Reserve account +$25,000	Federal funds purchased +$25,000	Federal Reserve account −$25,000 Federal funds sold +$25,000	

The federal funds market has grown rapidly in size and sophistication in the past decade. Originally a market only among larger banks, it has more recently expanded to include most of the nation's banks. The increasing participation of smaller banks is partly a result of the development of large-bank intermediaries or brokers that "make a market" in federal funds for those who wish either to borrow or to lend. The reduction in the minimum-size transactions unit from $1 million to as little as $25,000 has also helped to open the market to much wider participation, although transactions through brokers more typically have a minimum denomination size of $25 million.

In addition, the essentially short-term nature of the market makes it almost ideal for handling many of the day-to-day changes involved in bank reserve management. Most small banks could not afford the skilled and specialized personnel required to keep their reserves fully used at all times by purchasing other earning assets. The federal funds market, therefore, provides access to income that might otherwise be forgone.

For a bank with a reserve deficiency, the short term of federal funds transactions has a special appeal. U.S. securities, although highly liquid, are generally sold through dealers who charge a commission for the service. Often it is cheaper to pay a federal funds rate that is higher than the interest forgone on the U.S. security if the added reserves are only needed temporarily, for the full cost of the security sale includes not only the interest forgone but the commission charge by the dealer.

---

[6] Although most federal funds transactions are still of a specified, very-short-term maturity, recent years have seen increasing use of open-ended transactions wherein the borrowing bank is authorized to continue to use the funds for an indefinite period until notified to the contrary by the lending bank. In addition, some federal funds transactions have had specified maturity dates of up to one year.

Borrowing Through the Federal Reserve Discount Window A third source of funds for a bank with a reserve deficiency is the discount window of its Federal Reserve bank. It will be recalled that one of the original purposes of the Federal Reserve was to set up a "lender of last resort" to which individual member banks in temporary need could turn.

The T-account effects of this solution would be

Federal Reserve Bank		*Bank A*	
Loans + $25,000	Demand deposit of Bank A + $25,000	Federal Reserve account + $25,000	Notes payable + $25,000

Although on the surface this might well seem the most desirable "way out" of all for our Bank A, it has not been of great significance in recent years. We shall dig more deeply into this issue in Chapter 13. For our present discussion, we need only note that two reasons for the relative unattractiveness of the discount window have been advanced. On the one hand, it has long been argued that member banks are traditionally reluctant to be in debt to the central bank and only turn to the Fed as a last resort. On the other hand, it has been persuasively argued that the Federal Reserve's Regulation A, which has governed the administration of the discount window, has worked so as to in effect refuse many potential member bank borrowers access to loans. In any case, borrowing from the Federal Reserve has not been of great importance in recent years.

The Banking System with a Reserve Deficiency

Just as there is a difference in the expansion potential of a single bank and the entire banking system when excess reserves exist, so too there is a difference in the alternatives available to the single bank and the system when reserves are deficient.

Consider the following. Assume that the Federal Reserve System has been implementing a severely contractionary monetary policy for some time. In fact, let us assume that this policy has been so effective that Bank A has the same $25,000 deficiency assumed before but in this case no other bank has any excess reserves. The result, of course, is that the deficiency confronted by Bank A is also a deficiency for the banking system as a whole. What can Bank A and the system as a whole do to come within the requirements of the law?

To begin with, it cannot borrow federal funds or sell securities to other banks, for none of them has the excess reserves needed to permit it. In addition, since we have assumed that it was Federal Reserve policy that created this reserve deficiency, it seems unrealistic to expect that the Fed would ease things by buying securities from Bank A or making a loan of added reserves through the discount window.[7]

---

[7] It should be noted that we are making extreme assumptions here. Even with a *very* contractionary monetary policy, the Federal Reserve System is unlikely to go so far as to force an outright reserve deficiency for the banking system as a whole. It is also unlikely that it would ever refuse to

With all these possibilities ruled out, Bank A has only a couple of options left. It can sell U.S. securities to a member of the nonbank public (such as, for example, an insurance company) or it can allow loans coming due to be paid off, without reissuing them. Let us see how each of these approaches would work.

If it sold $25,000 of U.S. securities to an insurance company and the insurance company paid by check on its account at Bank B, the T-account effects would be

Bank A		Bank B	
Federal Reserve account +$25,000 U.S. securities −$25,000		Federal Reserve account −$25,000	Demand deposit of insurance company −$25,000

So where does this leave us? Bank A has eliminated its reserve deficiency, but what of the system as a whole? Specifically, what about Bank B, which had neither an excess nor a deficiency of reserves before this transaction? Clearly, Bank B has inherited most of the reserve deficiency Bank A has just escaped. Its *required* reserves are reduced by $5,000 (20 percent of $25,000) because its demand deposits are down by $25,000, but its *total legal* reserves are down by a full $25,000, so it now has a $20,000 reserve deficiency.

Now of course Bank B can get out from under the same way Bank A did — by selling a $20,000 U.S. security to a member of the public. But when it does so, assuming that the buyer of the securities pays by check on his or her account at Bank C, Bank C ends up with $20,000 fewer demand deposit liabilities and $20,000 less reserves — a reserve deficiency of $16,000.

If this game of "hot potato" is carried on until no bank in the system has any reserve deficiency, we end with a multiple contraction that is exactly the reverse of the multiple expansion discussed earlier. The end will only come when the banking system has unloaded a total of $125,000 of U.S. securities to the public so that demand deposits are reduced by a full $125,000. *Not* coincidentally, that represents the reciprocal of the required reserve ratio (5) times the original reserve deficiency ($25,000).

Nor would the result be any different if instead of reacting to the reserve deficiency by selling securities, the banks in difficulty had allowed loans reaching maturity to be paid off without reissuing them. For this approach — like the sale of securities to the public — does not result in the banking system acquiring more reserves. Rather it "works" by reducing the deposits that reserves are required to back up. And this will only eliminate a $25,000 reserve deficiency when those deposits have been reduced by a full $125,000 (assuming a required reserve ratio of 20 percent, of course). This result is shown in the following T-account.

Bank A			
Loans	−$125,000	Demand deposits	−$125,000

provide temporary help to individual banks via the discount window. We made these assumptions, not to describe reality, but for pedagogical reasons.

Summary

This chapter has endeavored to explain how, under the unrealistic assumptions of no cash drain, no time deposits, and no desired excess reserves, commercial banks expand and contract the nation's money supply as they go about their business of attempting to maximize profits. Given the assumptions made, we have seen that the only limit on money supply expansion by the banking system as a whole is the required reserve ratio. Further, we have learned that the existence of fractional (below 100 percent) reserve requirements permits the banking system as a whole, though not any one bank, to create new money in an amount that is a multiple of excess reserves.

Specifically, we have seen that, given the simplifying assumptions used,

1. A *single bank* with excess reserves can safely make new loans and create new money in an amount equal to

$$1 \times \frac{\text{Excess}}{\text{reserves}} = \frac{\text{Maximum safe increase}}{\text{in loans and demand deposits}}$$

2. The *banking system* with excess reserves can make new loans and create new money in an amount equal to

$$\frac{1}{\text{RRR}} \times \frac{\text{Excess}}{\text{reserves}} = \frac{\text{Maximum possible increase in}}{\text{loans and demand deposits}}$$

3. A *single bank* with a reserve deficiency has a variety of means of eliminating its deficiencies without the necessity of a reduction in the money supply.

4. The *banking system* with a reserve deficiency must reduce its loans or securities to eliminate the deficiency if the Federal Reserve System will not provide it more reserves. This must be done by an amount equal to

$$\frac{1}{\text{RRR}} \times \frac{\text{Reserve}}{\text{deficiency}} = \frac{\text{Necessary reduction in loans}}{\text{or securities and in demand deposits}}$$

Review Questions

1. Show appropriately labeled T-accounts depicting the effect on commercial banks (and the money supply) of a commercial bank
   a. Making a loan to a member of the public.
   b. Purchasing a U.S. security from a member of the nonbank public.

c. Having a loan made earlier to a member of the public paid off via a check.

d. Selling a U.S. security to a member of the nonbank public.

2. Explain carefully why a single bank in a many-bank system cannot safely make new loans in an amount larger than its excess reserves.

3. Assume that the banking system as a whole has the following consolidated balance sheet and that the required reserve ratio for demand deposits is 15 percent while that for time deposits is 5 percent.

Cash	$ 50,000	Demand deposits	$1,000,000
Federal Reserve account	180,000	Time deposits	1,000,000
Loans	1,500,000	Other	250,000
Securities	500,000		
Other	20,000		

a. What are the excess reserves of the banking system?

b. Assuming no cash drain, no change in time deposits, and that the banks do not willingly hold any excess reserves, what is the maximum increase in the money supply that the system can now create?

4. Carefully discuss the avenues open to a single bank with a reserve deficiency for eliminating that deficiency.

5. "If a single bank has a $100,000 reserve deficiency, the sale of $100,000 of U.S. securities to the nonbank public will normally (but not always) eliminate the deficiency. Such action will not, however, eliminate a $100,000 reserve deficiency of the banking system as a whole."

a. Using T-accounts, show how such a sale by Bank A would normally eliminate its deficiency. Under what circumstance would it *not* do so?

b. Explain carefully why such a sale could not eliminate the banking *system's* deficiency.

6. "If the banking system as a whole has a reserve deficiency and cannot acquire more total reserves, the result must be a multiple contraction of demand deposits and loans or securities." Explain.

7. What are federal funds?

CHAPTER 12

The Determinants of the Money Supply

A solid basis for understanding complex institutions sometimes necessitates suppression of the details of the real-world situation to isolate and magnify main underlying causal mechanisms. Such is the case with commercial banking.

For purposes of throwing into bold relief the central fact that multiple credit creation results from fractional reserve banking, the oversimplified version presented in the preceding chapter probably does a better job than a more detailed, realistic discussion. But if the ultimate objective is to consider practical policy measures in a going economy, some of the more important complicating factors must be reinjected into the picture.

The Federal Reserve's Board of Governors, for example, can hardly carry out its real-world obligations by blandly assuming—without further concern for what, in fact, *will* happen—that with a 20 percent required reserve ratio, $1 billion of excess reserves will produce a $5 billion rise in the money supply. This result will be realized only if the public withdraws no cash and converts no demand deposits to time deposits, and if the banks are unwilling to carry any excess reserves. If the public or the commercial banks should happen to be so uncooperative as to violate these assumptions, then the $5 billion money supply increase simply will not come about. The Board of Governors must be concerned not with what would be if the world fit the assumptions, but with what *will* happen in the world that exists.

The fact is that people *do* typically desire to hold more currency when their checking accounts increase. They *do* tend to convert some of their added demand deposits into time deposit form as their wealth grows. And banks *do*, depending on conditions, sometimes willingly retain some excess reserves rather than lend "up to the hilt." Our task in the first section of this chapter is to take explicit account of these complexities and their effect on the system's money-creating potential.

The Money Creation Capacity of the Banking System Under More Realistic Conditions

Given excess reserves, commercial banks, as we have seen, have every incentive to expand their earning assets. In the process, the borrowing members of the public receive, as the proceeds of the loans, newly created demand deposits. But once the loans are made and the new checking accounts are credited to the public, it is the public and not the banks who will determine, according to its preferences, whether those funds will remain in demand deposit form, be converted to currency, or be transferred into some near-money form such as time deposits.

The public, of course, has its preferences and freely exercises them. While most transactions are settled by check, currency or coin is more convenient for a wide variety of others, and depositors quite naturally have no compunction about withdrawing, in cash form, the amount required to meet such needs. Similarly, even though regular checking accounts may possess superior liquidity, they pay no explicit interest.[1] Depositors consequently regularly transfer some funds out of checking and into savings accounts to bolster their incomes.

Both these actions, of course, reduce the banking system's money-creating powers. If the system starts with $100,000 of excess reserves and a 20 percent required reserve ratio, it can create new demand deposits totaling $500,000, *provided that each dollar of those excess reserves is available to back up its full complement of $5 worth of demand deposits.* But if, along the way, the public is going to take actions that "use up" those reserves in other ways, the result will be quite different. After all, a dollar withdrawn in cash form takes away a reserve dollar that *could have* supported $5 in demand deposit form. And a dollar required to back up time deposits is simply not available to back up demand deposits. Allowing for cash drain and conversion to time deposits can only reduce the size of the system's so-called "money multiplier" to something less than the reciprocal of the required reserve ratio.

A Numerical Example of the Process of Expansion, Assuming Cash Drain and Time Deposits

Let us assume the following conditions hold in the banking system:

1. The banking system has $100,000 of excess reserves, all initially held by Bank A. (We retain, for the moment, the assumption that banks will not willingly keep excess reserves in that form.)
2. The required reserve ratio for demand deposits—henceforth symbolized as R_d—is 16 percent.

[1] To simplify, we assume no NOW or ATS accounts in this chapter.

3. The required reserve ratio for time deposits — henceforth symbolized as R_t — is 5 percent.

4. The public's relative preference for the three assets — demand deposits, cash, and time deposits (which we shall henceforth refer to as the public's "preferred asset ratio") — is such that for every added $5 worth of demand deposits willingly held, it insists upon holding an additional $4 of time deposits and an additional $1 of currency and coins. In essence, this means that when the banks provide the public with $10 of new demand deposits, the public will withdraw $1 in cash and transfer $4 into savings accounts, retaining only $5 of the demand deposits initially received in that form.

Now let us trace through a few steps of the process whereby expansion might occur under such conditions. Initially, Banker A with $100,000 of excess reserves will, as before, lend the maximum safe amount, $100,000. In doing so, of course, $100,000 of new demand deposits are created as the proceeds of the loan:

<table>
<tr><td colspan="2" align="center">*Bank A*</td></tr>
<tr><td>Loans   +$100,000</td><td>Demand deposits   +$100,000</td></tr>
</table>

Again, precisely as in the preceding chapter, the borrower can be expected to write $100,000 of checks payable to a creditor, who will deposit them in his or her bank (Bank B). When Bank B sends them through the Federal Reserve for collection, the effect will be

<table>
<tr><td colspan="2" align="center">*Bank A*</td><td colspan="2" align="center">*Bank B*</td></tr>
<tr><td>Federal Reserve account
−$100,000</td><td>Demand deposits
−$100,000</td><td>Federal Reserve account
+$100,000</td><td>Demand deposits
+$100,000</td></tr>
</table>

Up to now nothing is altered from the simpler case in Chapter 11. Now, however, we must introduce the effects of the new assumptions applied by the public's preferred asset ratio. If the depositor in Bank B is an "average" member of the public, he or she is unwilling to keep all the new funds in demand deposit form. Rather, $10,000 will be withdrawn in cash and $40,000 will be transferred to a time deposit account (leaving only $50,000 in demand deposits). The effects on Bank B of this transaction are

<table>
<tr><td colspan="2" align="center">*Bank B*</td></tr>
<tr><td>Cash   −$10,000</td><td>Demand deposits   −$50,000</td></tr>
<tr><td></td><td>Time deposits   +$40,000</td></tr>
</table>

And what is Banker B's reserve position now? Notice that, whereas he or she originally received a $100,000 increase in total reserves, the cash withdrawal has reduced that by $10,000. And of the $90,000 remaining, $8,000 (.16 × $50,000) is required to back up the $50,000 of demand deposits still there and

$2,000 (.05 × $40,000) is required to back up the $40,000 time deposit. Consequently, Banker B now has *excess* reserves of $80,000 on the basis of which more loans can be made. Banker B can now safely lend that amount.

Bank B			
Loans	+$80,000	Demand deposits	+$80,000

If, as before, checks are written on the full $80,000, deposited in another bank (Bank C), and collected via the Federal Reserve, the effects are

Bank B		*Bank C*	
Federal Reserve account −$80,000	Demand deposits −$80,000	Federal Reserve account +$80,000	Demand deposits +$80,000

Once again, at this point the owner of the $80,000 demand deposit in Bank C converts it to the forms and in the proportions desired. He or she withdraws $8,000 in cash and transfers $32,000 to his or her savings account (leaving $40,000 of demand deposits, $32,000 in time deposits, and $8,000 in cash, exactly the 5 to 4 to 1 ratio desired).

Bank C			
Cash	−$8,000	Demand deposits	−$40,000
		Time deposits	+$32,000

And now what is Bank C's reserve position? The net addition to its total reserves is $72,000 ($80,000 minus the cash withdrawal of $8,000). Its added required reserves are $8,000 (.16 × $40,000 plus .05 × $32,000). Consequently, Bank C now has $64,000 of excess reserves to support another loan of that amount.

There is no point in continuing this example. Obviously the same process repeats itself over and over again until ultimately, at the limit, all the original $100,000 of excess reserves is "used up" — either by becoming required to back up the growing demand and time deposit liabilities or by being lost entirely to the banking system via cash withdrawals. But how can we add up the results of this more complex series of events?

The Demand Deposit Multiplier with Cash Drain and Time Deposits

What we need is a **demand deposit multiplier,** an expression that tells us the maximum number of dollars of new demand deposits that can be supported by each dollar of excess reserves. In the simpler case considered in the preceding chapter, we came up with a demand deposit multiplier equal to $1/R_d$. If R_d (the required reserve ratio applying to demand deposits) is 20 percent, this multiplier simply recognizes that for each $1 of demand deposits created, 20 cents worth of the original excess reserves are "used up" by becoming reserves.[2] This, of course, produces a multiplier of 5.

The situation is more complex, but the principle is the same where cash drain and time deposits are admitted. Here, for each added dollar of demand deposits created and held by the public, excess reserves are "used up" as required backing not only for demand deposits but also for time deposits. And still more is lost to the system altogether via the cash withdrawal. In the example used in the preceding section, for instance, for each additional dollar of demand deposits created and held, 16 cents of the original excess reserves is shifted to the required reserve category to back it up ($R_d = 16$ percent). And since the public adds 80 cents to its time deposits for each added $1 of demand deposits (recall the assumption that the public insists upon $4 in added time deposits for each $5 in added demand deposits — 80 percent as much) and the required reserve ratio for time deposits, R_t, is assumed to be 5 percent, another 4 cents ($.80 \times .05$) of the original excess reserves is required to back up the new time deposits. Finally, with the public desiring to add to its cash an amount equal to 20 percent of its added demand deposits, the creation of an added dollar of demand deposits generates a 20 cent loss of reserves via cash withdrawal. So how does all this add up? Each one dollar of new demand deposits created and held leads to the "using up" of a total of 40 cents worth of the original excess reserves. It follows from this that each $1.00 of excess reserves is sufficient to permit the addition of $2.50 to the quantity of demand deposits. The demand deposit multiplier, then, is $2\frac{1}{2}$.

All this can, of course, be more simply represented in arithmetic terms. The formula for the demand deposit multiplier is

$$\frac{1}{R_d + c + (R_t \times t)}$$

where

R_d = required reserve ratio behind demand deposits

R_t = required reserve ratio behind time deposits

c = the amount of cash desired by the public, *for each dollar of demand deposits desired*

t = the amount of time deposits desired by the public, *for each dollar of demand deposits desired*

In the example used in the preceding section $R_d = 16$ percent, $R_t = 5$ percent, $c = \frac{1}{5}$ or .20, and $t = \frac{4}{5}$ or .80. We thus have a demand deposit multiplier equal to[3]

$$\frac{1}{.16 + .20 + (.05 \times .80)} = \frac{1}{.40} = 2\frac{1}{2}$$

---

[2] In the simplified case from Chapter 11, what we have termed the *demand deposit multiplier* is also the *money multiplier*, since under the assumptions employed there the entire money supply consisted of demand deposits.

[3] Note particularly that c and t are *fractions* that must be computed from the public's preferred asset ratio. In the example employed, we assume that the public chose to hold demand deposits,

Now to compute the maximum increase in demand deposits created and held by the public, we merely need multiply the multiplier by the excess reserves possessed by the system:

$$\frac{1}{R_d + c + (R_t \times t)} \times \text{Excess reserves} = \begin{array}{c} \text{Maximum possible}\\ \text{increase in demand}\\ \text{deposits by the banking}\\ \text{system}^4 \end{array}$$

From this result, it is a simple matter to compute the other changes of interest to us. The demand deposit multiplier, $2\frac{1}{2}$, times the initial excess reserves of $100,000 tells us that when the expansion process is completed, the demand deposit liabilities of the banking system will be increased by $250,000.

To compute the resulting added time deposits, we merely multiply t (desired time deposits as a fraction of desired demand deposits) by the amount of additional demand deposits:

$$t \times \Delta \text{ Demand deposits} = \Delta \text{ Time deposits}$$
$$.80 \times \$250,000 = \$200,000$$

Total cash withdrawn by the public is simply c (desired cash as a fraction of desired demand deposits) times the amount of additional demand deposits:

$$c \times \Delta \text{ Demand deposits} = \Delta \text{ Cash held by public}$$
$$.20 \times \$250,000 = \$50,000^5$$

And what about the change in the money supply? If we assume, for simplicity, that none of the time deposits created are checkable deposits (such as NOW accounts or ATS accounts) so that changes in the M1 money supply must be composed of changes in demand deposits or cash held by the public, the money supply increases by $300,000. This, of course, is simply the sum of the increase in demand deposits and cash in the hands of the public.

Finally, we can compute the change in loans of the banking system by adding

---

time deposits, and cash in a 5 : 4 : 1 ratio. Thus, since it chooses to hold $1 in cash for each $5 in demand deposits, c equals $1/$5, or .20. And since it chooses to hold $4 of time deposits for each $5 of demand deposits, t equals $4/$5, or .80.

[4] This, of course, is the maximum demand deposits *after* the public has put its assets in the desired proportion. Many more demand deposits are actually created when loans are made, but many of them are given up in favor of cash or time deposits.

[5] Note that when demand deposits have risen by $250,000, time deposits by $200,000, and the publicly held currency supply by $50,000, all the $100,000 of excess reserves we started with have been "used up" either as required reserves to back up deposits or withdrawn altogether from the banks. The cash drain uses up $50,000 of it, and the other $50,000 [(.16 × $250,000) + (.05 × $200,000)] has become required to back up the new deposits.

together the changes in demand deposits, time deposits, and cash — a total of $500,000.[6]

The effects of the entire process on the banking system's balance sheet in T-account form would be

Banking System

Cash	−$50,000	Demand deposits	+$250,000
Loans	+$500,000	Time deposits	+$200,000

The Effect of Desired Excess Reserves

Up to now we have assumed that banks do not willingly hold on to any excess reserves, preferring instead to maximize their earning assets and the deposit liabilities that come along with them. But this may not always be the case.

Why might banks choose to retain some excess reserves, thereby forgoing potential income? Because the commercial bank operates in an uncertain world in which contingencies abound. It must be ready to pay cash on demand to any of its depositors, and required reserves are not available for that purpose. It may quite reasonably feel that the greater its deposit liabilities, the greater its exposure to sudden, unexpected cash withdrawals. And, of course, it may be that the added revenue derivable from further loans does not justify the added costs incurred in the process.

Whatever the reason for holding them, what is the effect of desired excess reserves on the system's expansion potential? Simply to reduce it by precisely the same degree as would an equivalent rise in the required reserve ratio. After all, whether reserves are held as a matter of law or of bank preference, their limiting effects are similar. Suppose, for example, that we assume that the banks in the case considered choose to hold excess reserves equal to 10 percent of their demand deposit liabilities, and we symbolize that as x. Then the demand deposit multiplier would become

$$\frac{1}{R_d + c + (R_t \cdot t) + x}$$

where x = the number of dollars of excess reserves willingly held by banks, expressed as a fraction of their demand deposit liabilities.

Substituting in the numbers assumed, we have

$$\frac{1}{.16 + .20 + (.05 \times .80) + .10} = \frac{1}{.50} = 2$$

Inclusion of the desired excess reserve variable reduces the demand deposit multiplier from $2\frac{1}{2}$ to 2. Clearly the same result would have been produced by an increase in the required reserve ratio to 26 percent.

---

[6] What really happens here is that, during the process of expansion, banks lend $500,000 and create a full $500,000 of demand deposits. But the public, unwilling to hold all its added assets in demand deposit form, withdraws $50,000 of cash and transfers $200,000 to time deposit accounts.

The Money Multiplier with Cash Drain, Time Deposits, and Desired Excess Reserves

The expression we have derived thus far

$$\frac{1}{R_d + c + (R_t \cdot t) + x}$$

tells us the increase in *demand deposits* that can be obtained from each dollar of excess reserves possessed by the system. It is but a short step from this to derive a **money multiplier,** an expression for the increase in the *money supply* derivable from each dollar of excess reserves.

The change in the money supply, of course, is simply the sum of the change in demand deposits and the change in cash held by the public.[7] The cash component, we have seen, can easily be computed by c times ΔDD, which is equivalent to

$$c\left[\frac{1}{R_d + c + (R_t \cdot t) + x} \times \text{Excess reserves}\right]$$

or

$$\frac{c}{R_d + c + (R_t \cdot t) + x} \times \text{Excess reserves}$$

The change in the entire money supply then equals

$$\underbrace{\frac{1}{R_d + c + (R_t \cdot t) + x} \times \text{Excess reserves}}_{\text{Change in demand deposits}} \quad \text{plus} \quad + \quad \underbrace{\frac{c}{R_d + c + (R_t \cdot t) + x} \times \text{Excess reserves}}_{\text{Change in cash}}$$

which combines to

$$\boxed{\frac{1 + c}{R_d + c + (R_t \cdot t) + x} \times \text{Excess reserves} = \text{Change in money supply}}$$

The expression on the left, the *money multiplier,* can be used to compute the change in the money supply that results from any dollar of excess reserves obtained by the banking system. Obviously it constitutes a powerful tool of analysis in that it reveals much about the determinants of the nation's money supply.

---

[7] This is true, of course, only if we once again assume no NOW or ATS accounts.

The Money Multiplier and the Monetary Base

Since the commercial banking system can only create new money on the basis of excess reserves, it is important that the student understand the logic and limits of the expansion process in those terms. But necessary as it is, the "money multiplier times excess reserves" formulation is something less than an ideal device for revealing the specific role played by the monetary authorities in control of the money stock.

The point is that although the monetary authorities do not really *directly* determine the banking system's excess reserves, they *are* directly responsible for issuing the nation's entire stock of currency and coins and for altering the size of commercial bank Federal Reserve accounts. But when they raise either of these, there is no assurance that the total effect of their efforts will be reflected in increased excess bank reserves, primarily because some of them may immediately be required reserves and others may be withdrawn from the system altogether. Clearly, we will be better able to evaluate the role of government in the money determination process if we can recast the terms of our money expansion formula in such a way as to permit us to apply the money multiplier directly to specific actions of the monetary authorities themselves.

This we can do by employing the concept of the *monetary base.* **The monetary base includes all currency and coins in circulation — in the hands of the nonbank public as well as the vaults of depository institutions — plus the sum of Federal Reserve accounts owned by depository institutions.**[8] The monetary base, or "high-powered money" as it is sometimes called, not only is directly controllable by the monetary authorities (the Federal Reserve System and, to a much lesser extent, the U.S. Treasury) but is the ultimate base of the nation's money supply. Indeed, the money multiplier times the monetary base always, by definition, equals the money supply. That is,

$$\frac{1+c}{R_d + c + (R_t \cdot t) + x} \times \frac{\text{Monetary}}{\text{base}} = \text{Money supply}$$

Let us see why this must be so. The monetary base, B, consists of total depository institution reserves, TR, plus cash in the public's hand, C. By definition, therefore,

$$B = TR + C$$

[8] Some economists prefer to call this total the "source base." To the total of currency in circulation and Federal Reserve accounts, they would add a small additional total called the "reserve adjustment." The reserve adjustment is intended to permit changes in required reserve ratios to be reflected not only in the size of the money multiplier but also in the size of the monetary base. See Leonall C. Andersen and Jerry L. Jordan, "The Monetary Base — Explanation and Analytical Use," *Review*, Federal Reserve Bank of St. Louis, August 1968. For an updating of the concept, see also R. A. Gilbert, "Revision of the St. Louis Federal Reserve's Adjusted Monetary Base," *Review*, Federal Reserve Bank of St. Louis, December 1980.

Now, in equilibrium, all depository institution reserves are either required or willingly held as excess reserves. That is,

$$TR = (R_d \cdot DD) + (R_t \cdot TD) + (x \cdot DD)$$

Required	Required	Desired
reserves	reserves	excess
behind	behind	reserves
demand	time	
deposits	deposits	

where DD stands for transactions accounts and TD stands for nonpersonal time deposits.

Substituting the second expression into the first, we have

$$B = (R_d \cdot DD) + (R_t \cdot TD) + (x \cdot DD) + C$$

Now, defining t and c as before, we know that

$$TD = t \cdot DD$$

$$C = c \cdot DD$$

Therefore, we can say,

$$B = (R_d \cdot DD) + (R_t \cdot t \cdot DD) + (x \cdot DD) + (c \cdot DD)$$

Factoring out the DD, this becomes

$$B = [R_d + (R_t \cdot t) + x + c]DD$$

If we now divide both sides by the terms in the brackets, we get

$$\frac{1}{R_d + c + (R_t \cdot t) + x} \cdot B = DD$$

To put this in terms of the money supply, rather than demand deposits, we must recall that the money supply, M, equals transactions deposits, DD, plus cash in the hands of the public, C. Therefore,

$$M = DD + C$$

and, since $C = cDD$, we have

$$M = DD + cDD$$

and, factoring out the DD

$$M = (1 + c)DD$$

Now, multiplying both sides of the expression derived by $(1 + c)$, we have

$$\frac{1 + c}{R_d + c + (R_t \cdot t) + x} \cdot B = M$$

That is, the money multiplier times the monetary base equals the money supply. And if this is correct, the same thing must hold for *changes* in the monetary base:

$$\frac{1 + c}{R_d + c + (R_t \cdot t) + x} \cdot \Delta B = \Delta M$$

An Aside: The Difference Between the Money Multiplier Related to Changes in Excess Reserves and Changes in the Monetary Base

It may seem incongruous to the reader that, whereas earlier we stated that the money multiplier times excess reserves produces the change in the money supply, we are now saying that the same multiplier times the change in the monetary base (clearly a total that can be quite different from excess reserves) equals the change in the money supply. Can both these uses of the money multiplier possibly be correct? Indeed they can.

Consider what each form tells us. The "money multiplier times increase in excess reserves" formulation tells us how much new money the banking system is capable of creating if it is provided with a given amount of excess reserves. The "money multiplier times increase in the monetary base" formulation, on the other hand, tells us how much new money will result (whether directly created by the banking system or not) from a given increase in the monetary base.

Many Federal Reserve monetary actions affect excess reserves and the monetary base identically, so that no conflict arises. This is true, for instance, of an open-market purchase from the commercial banks and of a Federal Reserve discount. In both cases, the Fed provides the selling (or borrowing) bank an increase in its Federal Reserve account in the amount of the purchase (or discount), and since there is no accompanying change in the bank's deposit liabilities, the entire rise in the monetary base takes the form of excess reserves. Any increase in the money supply that results in these cases must come entirely from the banking system creating new money on the base of its newly acquired excess reserves.

In other cases, though, there appears to be a difference. By way of example, let us assume that the Federal Reserve purchases $120 million of U.S. securities from members of the nonbank public, paying by check. When the check is deposited in the seller's account at a commercial bank and collected via the FRS, the T-account effect on that bank will be

Bank of the Seller of the Securities

Federal Reserve account	+$120 million	Demand deposits	+$120 million

Now assume that $R_d = 20$ percent and $c = .20$ (and, for simplicity, that there are no time deposits or desired excess reserves, so that t and x are both zero).

Under these assumptions, the money multiplier — $(1 + c)/(R_d + c)$ — equals 3. The open-market purchase has increased the monetary base by $120 million, so that the "money multiplier times increase in the monetary base" formulation tells us that the Federal Reserve's action will ultimately lead to a rise in the money supply of 3×120, or $360 million.

But what about the "money multiplier times change in excess reserves" formulation? With a required reserve ratio of 20 percent, the increase in excess reserves resulting from the open-market purchase is $96 million ($24 million being required to back up the new $120 million deposit acquired by the seller of the securities). But the money multiplier (3) times the increase in excess reserves ($96 million) seems to say that the increase in the money supply will be only $288 million.

Which formulation is wrong? Neither. They simply represent different answers to different questions. The "money multiplier times change in excess reserves" formulation tells you, quite correctly, how much new money the banking system can create *if given $96 million of excess reserves.* The "money multiplier times change in monetary base" formulation, on the other hand, tells you, quite correctly, how much new money will ultimately result from a $120 million open-market purchase.

Notice that if one follows the assumptions throughout, there is no conflict. Assuming that the original seller of the securities is an average member of the public (with $c = .20$), she will not be willing to keep all her $120 million proceeds in checking account form. Rather, she will write a $20 million check for cash, leaving herself with the desired $100 million of demand deposits and $20 million of cash. This action would reduce the bank's excess reserves to $80 million ($120 million minus $20 million lost via cash withdrawal and another $20 million required to back up the remaining $100 million of deposits). On the basis of these excess reserves, the banking system can create new money equal to $3 \times \$80$ million, or $240 million. And that $240 million created by bank loans, added to the $120 million still possessed by the seller of the securities, gives us the same $360 million total money supply change the other formulation gave us.

What it comes down to is this. If one is interested solely in the amount of new money that *the banking system* can create in the process of making loans, the "money multiplier times excess reserves" formulation will do the job nicely. If, however, one is interested in the total change in the money supply that will result from specific actions by the monetary authorities, the "money multiplier times monetary base" formulation is the one required. This is the case because the latter formulation automatically adds together both the new money created by bank loans and *any other new money resulting from the monetary action itself.* As pointed out in the previous example, the open-market purchase itself resulted in the seller of the securities acquiring $120 million of new money and then the banks, making use of the $80 million increase in excess reserves provided them, added $240 million more through making loans.

Summary

The formula derived in this chapter,

$$\frac{1+c}{R_d + c + (R_t \cdot t) + x} \times \text{Change in the monetary base} = \text{Change in the money supply}$$

is an exceptionally effective mechanism for organizing discussion of the determinants of the nation's money supply. The next two chapters will focus on the methods whereby the nation's monetary authorities attempt to control the money supply through altering the monetary base or the money multiplier.

Review Questions

1. Briefly explain how cash drain, an increase in time deposits, and the holding of desired excess reserves reduces the maximum demand deposits a banking system can support.

2. Carefully explain *why* the sum of the increase in demand deposits and time deposits, plus the cash withdrawn from the banking system, necessarily equals the maximum possible increase in loans for the system.

3. What are the components of the monetary base? What is the significance of the monetary base?

4. Assume an economy in which $R_d = 13$ percent and $R_t = 7$ percent. The public insists upon holding $.75 in cash and $5.00 in time deposits for each $5.00 of demand deposits, and the banks insist upon holding excess reserves equal to $2\frac{1}{2}$ percent of *all* outstanding demand deposits. Assume further that the initial balance sheet for the commercial banking system is as follows:

Cash	$ 30,000	Demand deposits	$1,000,000
Federal Reserve account	165,000	Time deposits	1,000,000
Loans and securities	1,900,000	Other	100,000
Other	5,000		

Compute the changes the banking system would be required to make to fit the conditions given and show the banking system's balance sheet after it has completed all necessary adjustments.

5. Assume a banking system in which the following conditions hold:
   a. $R_d = 15$ percent and $R_t = 5$ percent.
   b. The people insist upon holding $3.00 in time deposits and $.50 in cash for every $5.00 in demand deposits they will hold.
   c. The banks insist upon holding $2 in excess reserves for every $100 *increase* in demand deposit liabilities above $400,000 (but none for the first $400,000).
   d. The banking system's initial balance sheet is

Cash	$ 12,000	Demand deposits	$400,000
Federal Reserve account	69,000	Time deposits	240,000
Loans and securities	600,000	Other	60,000
Other	19,000		

Compute the data required to show the position of the banking system after it has expanded to the limits permitted it by the given conditions. Enter the appropriate figures for each account in a balance sheet for the banking system after it has adjusted to the conditions given. Prove that your answer is correct by showing that all the initial excess reserves are now used up as required reserves, desired excess reserves, or withdrawn from the banks in cash.

6. Assume an economy in which $R_d = 16$ percent and $R_t = 5$ percent, and in which the public chooses to hold $1.00 in currency and $4.00 in time deposits for every $5.00 in demand deposits it will hold. Assume further that banks choose to hold no excess reserves ($x = 0$). Now the Federal Reserve carries out an open-market purchase from the nonbank public in the amount of $100 million. This initially raises the banking system's total reserves by $100 million and its outstanding demand deposit liabilities by $100 million.

   a. Using the change in the monetary base resulting from this open-market purchase and the demand deposit multiplier, compute the change in the banking system's demand deposits that will result.

   b. Assuming that the member of the nonbank public who sold the securities to the Fed subsequently converts the $100 million into the proportions indicated by c and t, compute the excess reserves available *after* this conversion. Then multiply the demand deposit multiplier times the result. Add this to the demand deposits retained by the seller of the securities.

   Your answer for the total demand deposit expansion should be the same for (a) and (b).

7. Carefully explain the significance of the difference in the result given by multiplying the money multiplier times the change in monetary base and the result given by multiplying the money multiplier times the change in excess reserves.

The Major Monetary Policy Tools

Even a casual inspection of the money supply formula derived in the preceding chapter reveals that if the Federal Reserve System is to control the nation's money supply, it must do so via alterations in the monetary base and/or the required reserve ratios, since the remaining elements of the money multiplier, c, t, and x, are directly determined by the public and the commercial banks.

This chapter considers the tools of monetary policy available to the Fed and their implications for control of the nation's money stock.

General versus Selective Controls

It has become customary to separate the various monetary policy tools into two categories, general and selective. *General* (or *quantitative*) *credit controls* are those that, when implemented, alter the total supply of credit available to borrowers in general without singling out for discriminatory treatment (intentionally at least) any particular group of borrowers that desires credit for a specific purpose. The total supply of credit may be cut, for example, but it is the "credit market" rather than the monetary authorities that determines which particular potential borrowers are rationed out. *Selective* (or *qualitative*) *credit controls,* on the other hand, are specifically aimed at altering the quantity of credit available for specified groups of borrowers that are borrowing to finance the purchase of a particular item, or selected group of items.

Included in the Federal Reserve's arsenal of general credit controls is the power to alter required reserve ratios and discount rates, as well as open-market operations. At the present time, there is only one specifically selective control on the books—the power to set margin requirements on the purchase of stock.

TABLE 13-1 Legal limits to Board of Governors' authority to vary required reserve ratios

	Minimum	*Maximum*
Transactions accounts		
0–$3.4 million	0	0
$3.4–$41.1 million	3%	3%
Over $41.1 million	8	14
Nonpersonal savings and time deposits	0	9

However, in the past, the purchase of real estate and of selected consumer durable goods on credit has been controlled, and we shall comment briefly on those efforts at selective control.

General Monetary Policy Tools

The Power to Alter Required Reserve Ratios

The original Federal Reserve Act allowed the Board of Governors no discretion in the area of reserve requirements. It set up fixed required reserve ratios for the member banks in each group and specified the member bank assets that could be counted as legal reserves.

It was in 1933 that Congress first gave the Board of Governors temporary authority to alter required reserve ratios, and in 1935 this temporary power was granted on a permanent basis. But prior to 1980, the Fed's reserve requirements applied only to commercial banks that were members of the Federal Reserve System (FRS).

With the passage of the Monetary Control Act of 1980, as we have seen, FRS reserve requirements were extended to all depository institutions issuing transactions accounts or nonpersonal time deposits. Table 13-1 repeats the current legal limits on the Board of Governors' authority to alter required reserve ratios.

The Effects of Altering Required Reserve Ratios A numerical example may help to illustrate the potency of this credit control tool. To keep things as simple as possible, let us assume that commercial banks are the only depository institutions, that demand deposits are the only transactions accounts, and that all time deposits are nonpersonal so that reserve requirements apply. Assume further that initially the consolidated balance sheet of all commercial banks is as given here:

All Commercial Banks

Cash plus Federal Reserve account	$ 80	Demand deposits	$400
Other assets	920	Time deposits	400
		Other liabilities and net worth	200

Now, suppose that $R_d = 14$ percent, $R_t = 6$ percent, and the public's preferred asset ratio is $1 in time deposits (t = 1.0) and $.20 in cash (c = .20) for each $1 in demand deposits. Finally, let us assume that banks desire to hold no excess reserves (x = 0).

Given all these assumptions, we know that (1) the public must currently be holding $80 of cash (since that is 20 percent of its demand deposit holding); (2) the monetary base is $160 (sum of total bank reserves and cash held by public); (3) the "money multiplier" must be 3: 1.2/[.14 + .20 + (1 × .06)]; and (4) the maximum possible money supply is $480 (money multiplier times monetary base), which just equals the current money supply. Under current conditions, in other words, the money supply cannot be increased.

But suppose now that Fed economists determine that a recession is developing and that moderating its effects requires an increase in bank loans and the money supply. What could the Board of Governors do?

It could, if it chose, cut the required reserve ratio for demand deposits from 14 percent to 8 percent and also cut that for time deposits from 6 percent to 2 percent. Let us consider the effects of such a change.

Employing the assumptions already made, such action would raise the money multiplier from 3 to 4: new multiplier equals 1.2/[.08 + .20 + (1 × .02)]. This larger multiplier times the monetary base of $160 produces a possible money supply of $640, a money stock increase of $160.[1]

But this increase in the money supply and in bank lending capacity is not the only effect of lower required reserve ratios, for increasing the supply of bank credit (i.e., loanable funds) will tend to affect the *price of loanable funds* in the same direction as would any increase in supply. The price of loanable funds, the interest rate, will tend to *fall*. And such reductions in interest rates will tend to encourage prospective investors to borrow and spend. Thus, cuts in required reserve ratios tend to affect demand in two ways. Not only do they make loanable funds more readily available for investors, but they tend to make them cheaper as well.

The reverse, of course, is also true. *Increases* in required reserve ratios tend to *reduce* the size of the money multiplier (and *cut* excess reserves) leading to *reductions* in the availability of loanable funds, *reductions* in the potential money supply, and *increases* in interest rates. All these effects, in turn, tend to cut, or hold down on, spending with borrowed funds.

Evaluation of Variable Reserve Ratios as a Stabilization Device   Whatever else might be said about it, one thing is clear: the power to alter required reserve ratios is a very potent weapon. With demand deposits and other checkable deposits currently over the $700 billion mark, each 1 percent cut in the ratio releases over $7 billion of excess reserves, thereby providing the basis for an expansion in loans and money supply several times that amount. Although the numerical example considered in the preceding section is an extreme one (in practice, the Fed would be more likely to alter reserve ratios by 1 or 2 percent at most), it does serve to illustrate the potency of this particular element of monetary policy.

[1] Note that the effect could also be put in terms of excess reserves. With $R_d = 8$ percent and $R_t = 2$ percent, required reserves are $40, so that excess reserves are $40. The money multiplier (four) times the excess reserves created by the cut in R_d and R_t equals $160.

But despite its power, the Fed has not tended to rely heavily on varying reserve ratios to combat the ups and downs of the regular business cycle. Why is this the case? The Commission on Money and Credit made the following observation more than three decades ago:

> While changes in reserve requirements are a powerful instrument of credit control, they are awkward and cumbersome in comparison with open market operations and present difficult problems of adjustment for many medium-sized and small banks. . . . The Commission believes that the power to change reserve requirements should be used only sparingly and favors major reliance on the use of open market operations for countercyclical adjustments.[2]

There have been several major objections to relying on changes in reserve requirements for the day-to-day implementation of monetary policy. First, this particular credit control tool lacks flexibility. Unlike open-market operations, which can be carried out every day and easily reversed when necessary, changing reserve ratios is only feasible several times per year at best. And precisely because they are changed only infrequently, reserve ratio changes tend to receive considerable press and public notice. Thus they carry with them definite so-called *"announcement effects"*—psychological reactions by the banks and the public to Federal Reserve actions. We shall have more to say about announcement effects in discussing discount rate changes. For the moment, it should be noted that some authorities feel that such reactions to monetary policy moves may tend to undercut the intent of the policy.

In light of these problems, the Fed has tended to rely more heavily on its other general credit controls, especially open-market operations, for the implementation of the bulk of its countercyclical monetary policies. The power to alter reserve ratios (especially to *raise* them) has, despite its acknowledged potency, been held largely in reserve in case a real emergency requiring restriction arises. In fact, since the current reserve requirement rules were established in 1980, there have been only three modest changes in the reserve required behind time deposits and none in that behind transactions deposits.

The "Discount Window" and the Power to Alter the Federal Reserve Discount Rate

As we have seen, one major reason for establishing the Federal Reserve System in the first place was to provide an outside source of reserves from which banks in temporary need might borrow. The facility set up to serve this purpose has come to be called the Fed's "discount window" and the interest rate charged on such loans, the discount rate. Although the power to alter the discount rate is generally considered to be the monetary policy weapon, let us first consider the evolution of the discount facility itself.

The Evolution of the FRS Discount Mechanism   In accordance with the framers' faith in the commercial loan theory, the original Federal Reserve Act attempted

---

[2] Commission on Money and Credit, *Money and Credit* (Englewood Cliffs, NJ: Prentice-Hall, 1961), p. 67.

to tie member bank borrowing from the Fed directly to the volume of short-term commercial loans. This was accomplished by requiring that member banks desiring to borrow reserves from their district Federal Reserve bank pledge, as collateral for the loan, the IOUs that they (the member banks) had acquired from businesses that had borrowed from them. Such short-term IOUs, dubbed "eligible paper" in the original act, were initially the only form of collateral that a member bank was entitled to use to borrow through the Fed's discount window. The thought was, of course, that all would be well if the acquisition of additional reserves through the discount window was limited by the volume of short-term commercial loans that the banks had made.[3]

As we have seen, the commercial loan theory was ill conceived and did not last long. Indeed, within a very few years, the collateral eligible for borrowing through the discount window was broadened to include U.S. securities and then later in the 1930s further liberalized to include "any asset acceptable to the lending Federal Reserve bank."

This liberalization of collateral requirements for discounts did much more than sound the death knell of the commercial loan theory. More germane to our current topic, it brought to an end the early practice of relying on collateral eligibility requirements as the prime means of limiting access to the discount window.

It was clear, of course, that *some* method was required to limit member bank borrowing from the Federal Reserve. Unrestrained, easy access to borrowed reserves could not be permitted to offset completely efforts at restrictive monetary policies. In the years since eligibility requirements were abandoned as the prime rationing device, the Fed had depended in varying degrees on two means of limiting access to the discount window: the discount rate and authoritative, nonprice rationing. We consider the discount rate shortly; let us look now at the nonprice rationing methods used by the System.

Loans from Federal Reserve banks have always been clearly designated as a privilege available to banks, not a right. Over the years, the Fed has made various efforts to spell out the circumstances under which a member bank might expect to be accommodated at the discount window and the circumstances under which it should not. Currently these conditions, the rules under which the discount window is administered, are spelled out in the Fed's *Regulation A*.

Under Regulation A any depository institution subject to the uniform reserve requirements established in the Monetary Control Act of 1980 may borrow through the Fed's discount window.[4] It is expected, however, to do so only as a last resort, after all "reasonable alternative sources of funds . . . have been fully used." Federal Reserve credit is *not* to be used as a substitute for capital, nor is undue use to be made of such credit "for the speculative carrying of, or trading in

---

[3] Originally, the common practice was for a district Federal Reserve bank actually to purchase a business's IOU from the borrowing bank by "rediscounting" it. This consisted of giving the borrowing bank the face value of the IOU minus the discount rate charged. In recent years, all discount window borrowing has been via an *advance*, where eligible paper is merely pledged as collateral rather than purchased.

[4] It should be noted that Regulation A also permits a Federal Reserve bank, after consultation with the Board, to extend credit to individuals or nondepository business firms "in unusual and exigent circumstances" where it is clear that "credit is not available from other sources and failure to obtain such credit would adversely affect the economy."

securities, real estate, or commodities or for any other purpose inconsistent with the maintenance of sound credit conditions."[5] Also considered inappropriate would be borrowing to take advantage of a favorable spread between the federal funds rate and the discount rate as well as borrowing by a net seller of federal funds.[6]

On a more positive note, discount window credit is available to depository institutions in two different categories: adjustment credit and extended credit.

Adjustment credit dominated until recent years. Its purpose is to protect banks against "sudden, unforeseen deposit outflows,. . . temporary and unexpected difficulties in obtaining funds from other sources, and, in some circumstances . . . unexpected increases in loan demand."[7] Such borrowing is generally very short term, often just overnight. As might be expected, adjustment credit tends to increase during periods of protracted contractionary monetary policy.

Extended credit is available for somewhat longer periods. It is made available for seasonal purposes to smaller banks without effective access to national money markets who can demonstrate seasonal patterns in deposits and loans that create a need. Extended credit is also available for other than seasonal purposes. For instance, it has been used to aid depository institutions experiencing unusual liquidity strains due to exceptional circumstances and to tide over savings institutions suffering from a temporary mismatch in the time structure of their assets and liabilities.[8]

The T-account Effects of a Federal Reserve Discount or Advance   Once the Federal Reserve agrees to a member bank's application for a loan, the procedures are simple. Normally the borrowing bank signs an IOU, pledging some of its U.S. securities as collateral for the loan.[9] The proceeds of the loan, of course, take the form of an increase in the borrower's Federal Reserve account. The T-account effects are as follows:

Federal Reserve Bank		*Borrowing Bank*	
Loans (the IOU signed by borrowing bank) +$100	Deposit of borrowing commercial bank +$100	Federal Reserve account +$100	Notes payable +$100

The major effect of the transaction is to increase the monetary base (and the borrowing bank's excess reserves) by the full amount of the discount. Temporary

[5] Board of Governors of the Federal Reserve System, "Advances and Discounts by Federal Reserve Banks—Regulation A," *Federal Reserve Bulletin*, September 1980, p. 757.

[6] For an excellent account see David A. Mengle, "The Discount Window," *Economic Review*, Federal Reserve Bank of Richmond, May–June 1986.

[7] Board of Governors of the Federal Reserve System, *The Federal Reserve System: Purposes and Functions* (Washington, D.C.: FRB, 1984), p. 60.

[8] On extended credit see Gordon H. Sellon, Jr. "The Role of Extended Credit in Federal Reserve Discount Policy," *Economic Review*, Federal Reserve Bank of Kansas City, May 1985.

[9] Actually, this degree of formality is not really required. A request to borrow can be made by letter, wire, or telephone. In addition, many banks have their district Federal Reserve bank hold some of their U.S. securities for safekeeping so that the needed collateral is already there.

though it is, the result is to permit a potential money stock increase equal to the money multiplier times the increase in base that it generates.

Altering the Discount Rate as a Stabilization Weapon   As noted, the interest rate charged for these loans of reserves is called the Federal Reserve *discount rate*. Technically, each district Federal Reserve bank sets its own discount rate, and the Board of Governors reviews and determines the rates set. In fact, however, the individual Reserve banks have relatively little autonomy in this decision. In practice, the Board of Governors effectively controls the rates.

System authorities are free to set whatever discount rate seems appropriate. Discount rate increases are generally considered contractionary monetary measures (holding down on spending for new goods and services), while decreases are thought of as expansionary (encouraging an increase in such spending). To understand better the issues involved, let us consider the likely transmission mechanism between a rise in the Fed's discount rate and its intended cut in aggregate demand. How, in other words, are discount rate increases expected to work?

First, since the increase makes reserves borrowed from the Fed more expensive than before, it may be that some banks that would have borrowed before the rise will decide not to now. If this is the case, the discount rate increase will have prevented the increase in the system's reserves (or in the monetary base) that would have occurred in its absence.

But that isn't all. If the banks that refrained from borrowing because of the higher discount rate still need additional reserves, they will have to turn elsewhere to get them. They may, for instance, attempt to borrow federal funds instead. But if they do, they are adding to the demand for an existing supply of federal funds and the result will surely be a rise in the federal funds interest rate. Or they may raise the reserves needed by selling a short-term U.S. security, part of their secondary reserves. But this approach, by adding to the supply of such securities seeking a buyer, will lower the price of U.S. securities, thereby raising the effective interest yields being earned on *them*.[10] Either way, the increase in the Fed's discount rate has led to increases in *other* short-term interest rates. And since, via arbitrage, such a change will tend ultimately to raise all short-term rates, prospective spenders may be induced to cut back on their spending with borrowed money because of the higher cost.

That, at least, is how a discount rate increase is *supposed* to work and, indeed, to some degree it probably does. But even if it does, there are solid reasons for doubting its potency as a stabilization weapon.

One serious problem with the scenario just sketched is its implication that in periods of rising interest rates, it is the rises in the Fed's discount rate which *cause* other short-term rates to rise. But a check of the record quickly refutes this. In recent years, most discount rate increases have been technical adjustments to bring the discount rate into line with other short-term rates. Instead of the discount rate forcing other rates upward, the direction of causation has been pretty much the other way around. The comparative data in Table 13-2 show essentially the same story. Instead of *leading* other interest rates, the discount

---

[10] We shall see in Chapter 18 why a fall in the market value of a bond necessarily implies a rise in the interest yield earned on it.

TABLE 13-2 Comparative short-term interest rates
1966–1989 (percentage)

Year	Banker's acceptances	Federal funds	U.S. 91-day Treasury bills	Federal Reserve discount rate[a]
1966	5.36	5.11	4.85	4.50
1967	4.75	4.22	4.29	4.50
1968	5.75	5.66	5.34	5.50
1969	7.61	8.22	6.67	6.00
1970	7.31	7.17	6.39	5.50
1971	4.85	4.66	4.33	4.50
1972	4.47	4.44	4.07	4.50
1973	8.08	8.74	7.03	7.50
1974	9.92	10.51	7.84	7.75
1975	6.30	5.82	5.80	6.00
1976	5.19	5.05	4.98	5.25
1977	5.59	5.54	5.27	6.00
1978	8.11	7.93	7.19	9.50
1979	11.04	11.19	10.07	12.00
1980	12.72	13.36	11.43	13.00
1981	15.32	16.38	14.03	12.00
1982	11.89	12.26	10.61	8.50
1983	8.90	9.09	8.61	8.50
1984	10.14	10.22	9.52	8.00
1985	7.92	8.10	7.48	7.50
1986	6.39	6.80	5.98	5.50
1987	6.75	6.66	5.78	6.00
1988	7.56	7.57	6.67	6.50
1989	8.87	9.21	8.11	7.00

[a] Discount rate in effect at end of year. All other figures are averages for the year.
Source: Federal Reserve Bulletin.

rate has tended to *lag* behind. A similar pattern is revealed by Figure 13-1 where we note that the discount rate has exceeded the federal funds rate only during recession periods (see 1971, 1975, 1980, and 1982). Note also that whenever the federal funds rate has risen sharply, the discount rate has been well below it.

Note one final point about the data in Table 13-2 and Figure 13-1. In years when short-term interest rates were peaking (check, for example, 1969, 1974, 1981), discount rates not only lagged other rates but show up as a real bargain. What, one is tempted to ask, kept member banks from taking advantage of these "bargain" rates and borrowing heavily from the Fed rather than obtaining their reserves at higher cost elsewhere?

First, it should be recognized that member bank borrowing did, indeed, rise during these years to take advantage of the spread. Excessive borrowing, however, was probably prevented by Regulation A and by the alleged reluctance of commercial bankers to be in debt to the central bank.

According to the "reluctance" theory, bankers will normally only borrow from the Federal Reserve as a last resort when other, more desired sources of funds are relatively inaccessible. Its prime implication is that the discount rate need not be above other rates to prevent overuse of the discount facility.

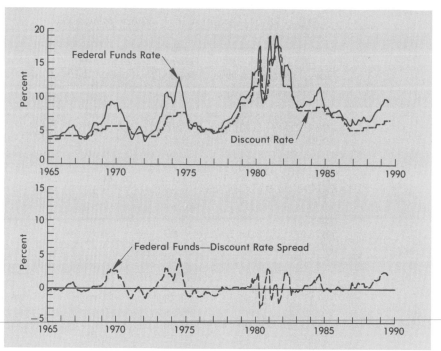

Source: E. J. Stevens, "Setting the Discount Rate," *Economic Commentary,* Federal Reserve Bank of Cleveland, July 15, 1989.

FIGURE 13-1   The federal funds rate and the discount rate, 1965–1990

There is undoubtedly real substance to the reluctance theory, but it is difficult to conceive of that alone as being sufficient to prevent overuse of Fed credit when the spread is as large as it was in 1970, 1974, and 1981. Undoubtedly, the nonprice rationing implied by the rules of Regulation A played a major role also.

Announcement Effects   Most authorities are agreed that discount rate increases, though working in the proper *direction* to restrain excessive spending, probably make only a very slight contribution toward combating inflationary pressures. Somewhat more emphasis has been placed by some upon the psychological announcement effects of a change in the discount rate.

The argument runs something like this. Unlike open-market operations, which are being carried on continuously, discount rate changes are only made periodically. When such changes are made, especially when they involve a change of *direction,* they are widely interpreted as a signal or indication of the Board of Governors' thinking and of the future course of monetary policy. A rise in the discount rate after a series of reductions, for example, may well indicate that the Board foresees some inflationary pressure and can be expected to use its general credit controls to make credit (and bank reserves) harder to get in the near future.

The effect of such a signal of the Federal Reserve's future intentions will depend upon a number of factors. Those who would rely on it as a helpful development see bankers reacting to the likelihood of a shortage of reserves in the future by slowing down on current loan commitment in order to conserve elbow room for making loans to important customers later on when additional reserves will be difficult to obtain and when the interest return will be more favorable than it is today. If this is the reaction of lenders, the announcement effect of the rise in the discount rate does promote the objectives of the Federal Reserve. Credit extension is slowed down, as is desired.

Critics, however, see some potential problems with this mechanism.[11] If bankers interpret the increase in the discount rate as a one-shot affair, to be followed in the future by lower rates, it will be in their interest to lend more now, taking advantage of the temporarily higher return available. And if they do so, the expectational effects of the discount rate rise are perverse, encouraging rather than restricting current inflationary pressure.

Nor is that the end of it. There is no reason to assume that reaction to the announcement of a discount rate increase will be restricted to lenders. After all, borrowers and spenders, also armed with expectations about the future, read the newspapers too. And if borrowers and spenders interpret a rise in the discount rate as a heralding of future inflationary pressure, they may well borrow and spend more now, because of it, to beat the rise in borrowing costs and prices that is coming in the future. To the degree that this is the case, the discount rate signal has even more seriously perverse effects.[12]

One final word on announcement effects is in order. Although their *direction* may be the subject of debate, their *existence* can hardly be questioned. In recent years, mere speculation in the financial press regarding prospective discount rate change has seemed at times to be sufficient to give the stock market reasonably severe jolts. And rightly or wrongly, stock market analysts have attributed these responses to the discount rate.

Conclusion — Evaluation of the Discount Mechanism As these comments indicate, the power to alter the discount rate is regarded as an extremely weak stabilization weapon by the majority of authorities. Indeed one distinguished economist years ago was so disenchanted with the whole mechanism as to propose outright elimination of the discount window itself.[13]

Although most economists share the conviction that the power to alter the discount rate is an exceptionally ineffective weapon in the monetary policy arsenal, few would concur in the proposal to close the window altogether. Indeed, given the upsurge in bank failures recently and the precarious condition of many of the nation's remaining savings institutions, one might well argue that the discount facility as the ultimate guarantor of the banking system's liquidity is an indispensable part of the economy's "safety net." In addition, some have argued that the fact that individual banks have a temporary source of borrowed reserves permits the Federal Reserve to make freer use of more powerful tools of credit restraint, such as open-market operations, than might be the case if the discount

---

[11] See, for example, W. L. Smith, "The Instruments of General Monetary Control," *National Banking Review*, September 1963, pp. 59–64.

[12] Discount rate increases are sometimes used as a signal for a quite different purpose — to indicate to other countries and speculators the nation's intention to clamp down on domestic inflation for balance-of-payments reasons. Discussion of international factors is postponed until later chapters.

[13] M. Friedman, *A Program for Monetary Stability* (New York: Fordham University Press, 1959).

window, serving as a sort of "safety valve," did not exist. Finally, alterations in the discount rate are sometimes useful to deal with balance-of-payments problems. That is, a rise in the discount rate may be used not just to reduce domestic demand, but also to raise short-term interest rates generally as a means of attracting short-term foreign capital to this country (or keeping that which is already here from leaving).[14]

Open-Market Operations

Open-market operations are by a wide margin the most important of the arsenal of monetary policy weapons. These can be defined as **purchases or sales of U.S. securities by the Federal Reserve System (on the secondary market) for the purpose of increasing or decreasing the amount of bank reserves (the monetary base).**

Policy in this area is determined by the Federal Open Market Committee, which normally meets about every six weeks in Washington. The committee, as noted earlier, includes the seven members of the Board of Governors plus five Federal Reserve bank presidents. It should be noted that although only the official committee members can vote, all 12 Federal Reserve banks normally send representatives who participate in the discussions. Once the FOMC has reached a consensus, it transmits its orders in the form of a "directive" to an official with the title of *System Account Manager*, who operates out of the New York Federal Reserve Bank.

The basic responsibility of the System Account Manager is to carry out the orders of the Federal Open Market Committee—to do the buying when purchases are decreed and to do the selling when the reverse is called for. Put this way, the account manager may appear to have a purely perfunctory task, that of buying or selling when he is told to do so. Actually this is far from the truth; his is an exacting position requiring an inordinate amount of skill and knowledge of the securities market, in addition to considerable discretion and judgment. Instead of simply being instructed to buy or sell securities, he is typically provided with the target ranges for the various money supply series and is expected to carry out whatever purchases or sales he feels are necessary to hit those targets.

For example, the directive issued by the FOMC in its July 1990 meeting said in part

> The Federal Open Market Committee seeks monetary and financial conditions that will foster price stability, promote growth in output on a sustainable basis, and contribute to an improved pattern of international transactions. In furtherance of these objectives the Committee reaffirmed at this meeting the range it had established in February for M2 growth of 3 to 7 percent, measured from the fourth quarter of 1989 to the fourth quarter of 1990. The Committee also retained the monitoring range of 5 to 9 percent for the year that it had set for growth of total

---

[14] For other commentaries on the discount mechanism, see Daniel L. Thornton, "The Discount Rate and Market Interest Rates: What's the Connection?" *Review*, Federal Reserve Bank of St. Louis, June–July 1982; and Gordon H. Sellon, Jr., "The Role of the Discount Rate in Monetary Policy: A Theoretical Analysis," *Economic Review*, Federal Reserve Bank of Kansas City, June 1980.

domestic nonfinancial debt. With regard to M3, the Committee recognized that the ongoing restructuring of thrift depository institutions had depressed its growth relative to spending and total credit more than anticipated. Taking account of the unexpectedly strong M3 velocity, the Committee decided to reduce the 1990 range to 1 to 5 percent.[15]

In the concluding section of this chapter, we return to the issue of FOMC policy directives, concentrating specifically on the committee's designation of targets for the System Account Manager. For the present, let us ignore this issue and concentrate on the mechanism through which the directives are implemented.

If the Federal Open Market Committee has given orders that require the purchase of securities, their intent is to increase the quantity of commercial bank reserves. The account manager, who operates in New York for the obvious reason that it is the location of the market for U.S. securities, carries out these orders through 42 major government securities dealers in the city.[16]

The government securities dealers are middlemen who bring together buyers and sellers of U.S. securities. They offer a ready market for government obligations by regularly quoting "bid" and "ask" prices on federal government obligations. As middlemen, they purchase securities with the intent of reselling them to institutions and individuals who desire them as a part of their regular portfolios, although they also hold some for their own accounts; when they sell, they acquire most of the securities ultimately from the same types of institutions and individuals. Their income is earned primarily for their services of bringing buyer and seller together.

When the Federal Reserve's system account manager is given orders requiring purchase of securities, all the major government securities dealers are contacted by telephone and comparative bids are obtained. The dealer or dealers offering the lowest price then are generally awarded the business. Conversely, in the case of an open-market sale, the dealer or dealers offering the highest price would normally be the successful bidders.

The System Account Manager acts on behalf of all 12 Federal Reserve banks, which have no discretion regarding their own individual participation in the operation. When the account manager buys securities, the total increase in the Fed's portfolio of securities is apportioned among all the Reserve banks. Similarly, if in pursuance of orders from the Open Market Committee, the account manager sells securities, the individual Federal Reserve banks' portfolios of U.S. securities will each be proportionately reduced, regardless of their own desires in the matter.

On the other hand, it is important to understand that no compulsion whatever applies to the commercial banks. The term "open market" implies that the Federal Reserve buys or sells at a price that is attractive enough to convince someone to enter into a deal voluntarily. If the Fed is buying and the commercial banks do not choose to sell, they cannot be compelled to do so. In such a situation the System Account Manager would simply have to offer a high enough price to

---

[15] *Federal Reserve Bulletin*, October 1990, p. 845.

[16] As of mid-1989.

convince a member of the nonbank public to sell. Who the seller happens to be is a matter of little moment to the Federal Reserve, for the monetary base (and total bank reserves) will be increased by the amount of the purchase regardless.

Mechanics of an Open-Market Purchase   The actual mechanics of the purchase go something like this. The dealer purchases the U.S. securities from the ultimate seller by means of a check written on his or her account at a member bank. The Federal Reserve, in turn, pays the dealer for the securities via an officer's check, which it makes up on itself and which the dealer firm can be expected to deposit in its checking account at a member bank. The result is that the Federal Reserve has the securities, the ultimate seller of the securities has an increase in his or her checking account, and the commercial banks have more reserves.

The U.S. securities purchased to carry out open-market policy, it should be understood, are *not* "new" U.S. securities issued by the U.S. Treasury to finance current deficit spending. The Federal Reserve System is constrained by law from purchasing "new" securities directly from the Treasury. Rather, open-market purchases are carried out in the secondary market and the securities are bought through dealers from commercial banks or the nonbank public (individuals, nonbank financial institutions, other corporations, and so on). Such transactions, then, simply involve a transfer of ownership of already existing U.S. securities, and the U.S. Treasury (though it is, of course, the original issuer) does not enter into the picture at all.

Because the market for U.S. government securities is complex, and because it is not uncommon for students to confuse the roles of the Federal Reserve System and the Treasury, it is suggested that the reader take the time to study Figure 13-2. This graphic constitutes an attempt to separate the primary and secondary markets for U.S. securities and to illustrate the roles of the Fed and Treasury in each.

The immediate result of an open-market purchase differs slightly depending on whether the ultimate seller of the securities is a commercial bank or a member of the "nonbank public." If we ignored the intermediate role played by the dealer, the T-account effects of a purchase from a commercial bank would be as follows.[17]

Federal Reserve		*Commercial Bank*	
U.S. securities +$100	Demand deposits of commercial banks +$100	U.S. securities −$100 Federal Reserve account +$100	

[17] In fact, the securities dealers help disperse the effects of open-market operations throughout the country. Although the immediate effects of an open-market purchase are entirely on the reserves of New York City banks, the securities dealers generally borrow from banks throughout the country to raise the funds needed to purchase the securities they are selling to the Fed. When the Fed then pays the dealers for the securities, the dealers, in turn, must repay the banks from which they borrowed. This spreads new reserves widely. See Paul Meek, *Open Market Operations*, Federal Reserve Bank of New York, 1985.

Primary market (Where U.S. securities are initially issued)		Secondary market (U.S. securities that have been sold in the past on the primary market are resold from one owner to another)	
Seller	Buyers	Sellers	Buyers
U.S. Treasury All U.S. securities are originally issued by the U.S. Treasury. These securities are issued to: (1) Raise money to finance deficit spending (when, for example, expansionary fiscal policy is being employed) This will raise the national debt. (2) Raise money needed to pay off holders of old U.S. securities that have reached their maturity date. This is called "refunding" and it does not affect the level of the national debt. *Note:* The Federal Reserve System does *not* buy U.S. securities directly from the U.S. Treasury.	1. Households 2. Nonfinancial companies 3. Nonbank financial companies 4. State and local governments 5. Foreigners 6. Commercial banks	1. Households 2. Nonfinancial companies 3. Nonbank financial companies 4. State and local governments 5. Foreigners 6. Commercial banks 7. Federal Reserve System When the FRS sells, this constitutes an "open-market sale" which will reduce total bank reserves by the amount of the sale. { (items 1–5) The "nonbank" public }	1. Households 2. Nonfinancial companies 3. Nonbank financial companies 4. State and local governments 5. Foreigners 6. Commercial banks 7. Federal Reserve System When the FRS buys, this constitutes an "open-market purchase" which will raise total bank reserves by the amount of the purchase. { (items 1–5) The "nonbank" public }

Note: The U.S. Treasury is not normally involved in the secondary market. The level of national debt is not affected by transactions on the secondary market.

FIGURE 13-2 Markets for U.S. government securities

In this case, the monetary base (and total bank reserves) have gone up by the amount of the purchase (making possible, of course, a future expansion in the money supply by some multiple of this amount). Commercial bank *excess* reserves also rise by the amount of the purchase, but the purchase itself (as distinct from subsequent actions banks may take as a result of it) has no immediate effect on the money supply.

If, on the other hand, the ultimate seller is a member of the nonbank public (say, for example, an insurance company), the T-account effects, again ignoring the transactions of the dealer middleman, would be

Federal Reserve		*Insurance Company's Commercial Bank*		*Insurance Company*	
U.S. securities +$100	Demand deposits of commercial banks +$100	Federal Reserve account +$100	Demand deposit of insurance company +$100	U.S. securities −$100 Checking account at commercial bank +$100	

In this case, it is assumed that the Federal Reserve pays the insurance company (the ultimate seller) with a $100 check (written on itself). The insurance company then deposits its check in its account at its commercial bank, which sends it in for collection to the Federal Reserve and receives payment in the form of an increase in its Federal Reserve account.

As before, the monetary base (and, of course, total member bank reserves) is increased by the full amount of the purchase. In this case, however, the immediate effect on *excess* reserves and the money supply is somewhat different from that when commercial banks were the sellers. For here the money supply is increased by $100 as a direct result of the purchase itself (the new demand deposit obtained by the insurance company). And since this new demand deposit necessitates setting aside part of the bank's new Federal Reserve account as required reserves, *excess* reserves go up by something less than $100. (For example, if R_d equals 20 percent, the increase in excess reserves is only $80.)

The differences in the two cases, however, are of no real significance. What really matters is that, no matter who the seller is, a **Federal Reserve open-market purchase always increases the monetary base (and total bank reserves) by the amount of the purchase.** This, in turn, provides the basis for an increase in the money supply equal to the money multiplier times the change in the monetary base. And that expansion in money and loans, in its turn, leads to lower interest rates.

The interest rate effects of an open-market purchase are twofold: an initial reduction caused by the purchase itself plus further cuts later caused by the expansion in credit permitted by the increased reserves.

The initial cut comes about as a direct result of the purchase of securities. If the account manager sets out, for example, to purchase $2 billion of U.S. securities during a given week, he is not likely to find sellers willing to offer such a large amount at the current market price. This is no problem for the account manager, of course; all he needs to do is pay a slightly higher price to induce enough sellers to part with the necessary volume.

Such action, of course, tends to raise the market value of U.S. securities. If a security has been selling for $1,000 and paying the holder an interest return of $100 per year, its effective yield was 10 percent per annum. If a Federal Reserve open-market purchase now raises that market value to, say, $1,050 (still paying the holder the fixed $100 per year), the yield, expressed as a percentage of its new, higher market value is now closer to 9.5 percent. Interest returns on Treasury securities are thus immediately reduced by the purchase.

Ultimately, further interest rate cuts can be expected as the banks make use of their now more plentiful reserves to expand the money and credit supply. Such an increase in the supply of credit or, alternatively, in the supply of "loanable funds," together with an unchanged demand for loanable funds will quite naturally lead to a fall in the price of loanable funds — the rate of interest.

Mechanics of an Open-Market Sale　If the Open Market Committee sees a need for credit restraint and calls, accordingly, for a policy involving open-market sales, the reverse of this operation is in order. The System Account Manager would contact all government security dealers asking for the prices they would offer to take the quantity of securities for sale. The dealers, in turn, would quote prices that would seem to them low enough to enable them to resell the securities to ultimate holders and still earn a return for their intermediary service. When the sale is made, the dealers would pay the Federal Reserve with checks on their accounts at commercial banks but would then be repaid by checks written by the ultimate purchasers on their own checking accounts.

If the T-account effects involving the security dealers' role were once again ignored, the effect of a Federal Reserve sale to a commercial bank would be

Federal Reserve		*Commercial Bank*	
U.S. securities −$100	Demand deposits of commercial banks −$100	U.S. securities +$100 Federal Reserve account −$100	

The monetary base and total as well as excess reserves are reduced by the full amount of the sale, while, for the moment at least, there is no effect on the money supply.

If the ultimate purchaser turns out to be a member of the nonbank public (once again we will assume it to be an insurance company), the T-account effects of the sale are

Federal Reserve		*Insurance Company's Commercial Bank*		*Insurance Company*	
U.S. securities −$100	Demand deposits of commercial banks −$100	Federal Reserve account −$100	Demand deposits of insurance company −$100	U.S. securities +$100 Checking account at commercial bank −$100	

In this case, it is assumed that the insurance company pays the Federal Reserve with a check written on its account at a commercial bank. The Federal Reserve then collects the check by marking down the Reserve account of the bank on which it is written by $100. The monetary base and total reserves are cut by the full amount of the sale. Here, however, the money supply is immediately cut by $100, so excess reserves go down by only $80 (assuming a 20 percent reserve ratio) and required reserves are reduced by $20 because of the elimination of the insurance company's checking account. In both cases, however, the removal of $100 of total reserves from the bank reduces the (potential) money supply by the money multiplier times the amount of the sale.

In summary, **when the Federal Reserve sells U.S. securities, the monetary base and total bank reserves are cut by the amount of the sale no matter who buys.** This cut reduces the (potential) money and credit supply by that amount times the money multiplier. Finally, there is upward pressure on interest rates — initially because the open-market sale lowers U.S. security prices thereby raising the yield on them and later because the supply of credit (or loanable funds) is reduced relative to the demand.

The Advantages of Open-Market Operations   Open-market operations unquestionably bear the bulk of the burden of carrying out monetary policy. The main reasons for their primacy are clear. To begin with, the initiative for their implementation is entirely in Federal Reserve hands and not, as with the discount mechanism, partly with the banks. Second, with the U.S. security portfolio of nearly $250 billion and the ability to purchase any desired amount more if conditions warrant, the FRS has sufficient power to alter bank reserves within any desired limits via the weapon. Third, the open-market device is a model of flexibility. Because it is used continuously, it does not carry with it the psychological announcement effects that accompany alterations in the discount rate or required reserve ratios. Consequently, it is entirely feasible to "operate by feel," buying today and then reversing to a sale tomorrow if conditions warrant. Open-market operations can be made as powerful as a sledgehammer or as discriminating as a surgeon's scalpel. In an area replete with controversy, there is remarkable unanimity with respect to the preeminence of open-market operations among monetary policy weapons.

Selective Credit Controls

If the government should take action to reduce sharply the supply of eggs produced in the United States, the price of eggs would have to rise, assuming a free, competitive market. As fewer eggs would be available, some people who would have eaten them under the old conditions would now be unable to do so. But the mechanism for determining which particular consumers get "cut out" of the egg market would be the impersonal one of the price system. Those who are unwilling (or unable) to pay the higher price, we say, are "rationed out" by the increase in price.

Contrast this situation to one in which the government simply decreed that all consumers living in New York City would have to go without eggs next year. Here, as before, government action has had the effect of cutting out certain people from egg consumption, but whereas in the former case, the government does not specify the particular individuals who will do without (leaving it to the forces of the market to determine that), in the latter case it does.

This comes pretty close to illustrating the difference between general credit controls and selective ones. Under general credit controls, government action may be taken to reduce the total supply of credit available, but the credit market determines which particular credit users will have to do without. Under selective credit controls, government takes action to alter the amount (or terms) of credit available for specific groups of people who desire to use it for a particular purpose.

In past years Congress has given the Board of Governors authority to impose selective credit controls on three different groups of credit users: those who purchase securities on credit, those who purchase consumer durables on credit, and those who buy real estate with borrowed funds. As of today, the authority with respect to real estate and consumer durables has lapsed, leaving margin controls on the purchase of stock as the only selective control now available to the Board.[18]

The Power to Set Margin Requirements on the Purchase of Stock

In 1934 the Securities Exchange Act gave the Federal Reserve's Board of Governors the authority to set margin requirements on the purchase of stocks. Acting on this basic legislative authority, the Board of Governors subsequently issued Regulations T and U, specifying the details of the control. Briefly, the board is empowered to specify what proportion of the purchase price of stocks may *not* be borrowed from brokers or commercial banks.[19] If, for example, the margin requirement is at 65 percent, banks and brokers that lend money for the purpose of financing stock purchases may only lend 35 percent of the purchase price. Alternatively, a 65 percent margin requirement indicates that the buyer of stock must put up 65 percent of the purchase price in cash.

Experience in the 1920s and early 1930s, of course, provided the background and impetus to the initial margin requirement legislation. The stock

---

[18] This represents a quite narrow view of selective credit controls. One might reasonably call any policy that attempts to channel credit into, or out of, a particular use a selective credit policy. Such a definition would therefore include many other measures, such as several mortgage interest subsidy programs, portfolio limitations restricting savings and loan associations primarily to mortgages, ceilings on FHA and VA mortgage interest, and usury laws. For an excellent survey of the entire subject, see *Studies in Selective Credit Policies*, edited by Ira Kaminov and James M. O'Brien, Federal Reserve Bank of Philadelphia, 1975.

[19] More specifically, Regulation T controls loans for stock purchase from security brokers and dealers to purchasers; Regulation U has to do with loans for *any* commercial bank to either brokers or purchasers of stock. In addition, Regulations X and G place limitations on credit granted for security purchase by lenders other than banks, brokers, and dealers as well as on the borrowers themselves.

market boom of the 1920s was generously fed by bank credit. Purchases of stock on very thin margins (with the bulk of the purchase price borrowed) were common. Inevitably, this meant that the safety of a significant proportion of bank loans depended on fluctuations in stock prices. When the stock market crash came in 1929, the rapid decline in market prices quickly wiped out the equity of many owners, leaving the banks (and many brokers who had in turn borrowed from banks) with collateral that was decreasing in value at an alarming rate. Chaos followed. Banks were forced to sell the securities to attempt to meet their commitments to depositors, with the effect of depressing the stock market still further while pouring more fuel on the fires of the bank panic that ensued. It was indeed a time for action, and among the many laws passed in response to the crisis was the one granting the authority to set margin requirements.

Entirely aside from the general philosophical issues regarding selective controls, a number of problems have emerged concerning the implementation of margin requirements. In theory, at least, control is effected through the lender, who is expected to determine the intended use of the funds that he or she is lending. Generally this problem is simplified by the fact that when stocks are to be purchased, the stock itself composes the collateral for the loan.

Weaknesses of Margin Requirements   A number of leakages in the network of control have appeared over the years. To begin with, a borrower may deny any intention of purchasing stocks with his or her borrowed funds, pledge other assets as collateral for the loan, but then go ahead and buy stocks anyway. Or the borrower may purchase stocks with cash he or she would normally use to purchase materials and supplies and then borrow money to finance the materials and supplies purchased, pledging the stocks he or she already has as collateral for the loan. In addition, lenders other than commercial banks and brokers, who are not subject to margin requirements, may increase their security loans when brokers and commercial banks are being held down by high margin requirements. And, indeed, some of these nonregulated lenders may be getting the funds they lend to finance security purchases from commercial banks themselves.

Despite these weaknesses in practice, many authorities feel that margin requirements serve a useful purpose.[20] That purpose, however, is not the same as for general credit controls. Although a tightening of general credit controls may combat rises in the *general* price level, there is considerable doubt that increases in margin requirements accomplish the same results, for they are aimed, as their name indicates, *selectively* at one segment of the economy. If they are successful, they clamp down on excessive speculation in the stock market and stock price increases, but there is little reason to believe they have much effectiveness in combating general inflation of the prices of goods and services. After all, holding down on the use of credit to purchase stocks does not in any way cut the quantity of credit available to buy other things. And it is quite likely that the credit that would, in the absence of margin requirements, have been used to purchase stocks may now be used to purchase something else.

---

[20] Approval, however, is far from unanimous. See, for example, Thomas G, Moore, "Stock Market Margin Requirements," *Journal of Political Economy*, Vol. 74, No. 2 (1966).

The Power to Limit the Use of Credit by Buyers of Real Estate and Consumer Durable Goods

During World War II, the Board of Governors was given the power to limit the credit that could be granted on the purchase of a number of major consumer durable goods. Although this authority ended in 1947, it was granted again during the Korean war starting in 1950. In addition, 1950 saw the first grant of authority to the Board of Governors to control credit used to finance the purchase of real estate.[21] Authority for both controls lapsed in mid-1952, and the board now has no power in either area.

Consumer credit controls were enforced on a specific list of major consumer durable goods. They took the form of minimum down payment requirements coupled with maximum repayment periods for the amount borrowed. For example, during much of World War II, minimum down payments of $33\frac{1}{3}$ percent and maximum repayment periods of 12 months were enforced on an extensive array of consumer durables. Controls over the use of credit in the purchase of real estate limited the size of the mortgage that could be granted to a specified percentage of the market value of the home and also set up maximum terms for the length of the mortgage.

Although both these efforts at selective controls now fall in the category of history, debate over the wisdom of their possible use in peacetime continues. This is especially true with respect to controls over consumer credit, which some have suggested should be given to the Federal Reserve on a standby basis, to be used when conditions warrant. Those favoring such authority cite the destabilizing role that they believe consumer credit has played in business cycles in recent years. Opponents counter with the arguments that extension of selective controls in peacetime is inimical to the philosophy of a free enterprise, consumer-directed economy and that they are unlikely to accomplish their intended goal in any case.[22]

Moral Suasion

In addition to the general and selective credit control devices, notice should be taken of the rather vague, ill-defined area usually referred to as *moral suasion.* Properly speaking, moral suasion is not really a *control* device at all, as it involves voluntary cooperation by, rather than coercion of, the member banks. It might

---

[21] Actually the control over real estate credit was shared by the Board of Governors and the Housing and Home Finance Administration.

[22] For excellent brief surveys of selective credit controls, see James M. O'Brien, "Can Credit Controls Be Controlled?" *Business Review,* Federal Reserve Bank of Philadelphia, January 1972; and Arnold Dill, "Selective Credit Controls: The Experience and Recent Interest," *Monthly Review,* Federal Reserve Bank of Atlanta, May 1971. For a more thorough review of the entire area, see Kaminov and O'Brien, *Studies in Selective Credit Policies.*

best be described as an attempt on the part of Federal Reserve authorities to persuade banks to voluntarily tailor their lending policies to the desires of the Fed, thereby reducing the need for more overt credit control measures.

This attempt to persuade comes through many channels. During the periodic examinations made of state member banks, discussions with bank officers often turn to the Fed's overall aims in credit policy. At periodic banquets and meetings held for bankers in their district, representatives of the Reserve bank hammer away at the reasons for, and wisdom of, recent policy actions. In their frequent publications, the Board of Governors and the 12 Federal Reserve banks carry the message very much farther. Much of this, it is true, might well be put under the heading of mere public relations, but the most sanguine supporters of moral suasion claim that it accomplishes much more. If bankers do respond to these many appeals to "do right" as far as credit is concerned, the burden that must be borne by the other tools of monetary policy is proportionately reduced.

For all the natural appeal of the voluntary way of doing things, it seems fair to observe that, barring some unusual and compelling incentive to cooperate, the moral suasion approach probably, in and of itself, accomplishes little. However, our experience with it during the Korean war provides some basis for optimism in times of national emergency.

At that time, at the urging of the Federal Reserve, the credit industry, including nonbank leaders as well as commercial banks, set up the National Voluntary Credit Restraint Committee. The purpose of the committee was to draw up a set of standards, specifying those uses of credit that were in the national interest and those that were not. The entire approach was voluntary, but there is considerable evidence that the committee elicited widespread cooperation among lenders and that the Federal Reserve's task of controlling credit expansion was thereby measurably relieved.

However, this experience cannot be taken as evidence of the peacetime effectiveness of moral suasion. The Korean war provided a sufficient sense of national emergency and patriotic fervor to partially modify the normally powerful drive to maximize profits. It is impossible to say what the future will hold, but there can be little question that the voluntary approach is less effective without some special incentives to help modify actions aimed at profit maximization.

The Process of Monetary Policy Formulation

The fundamental decisions that establish the direction and extent of the nation's monetary policy are hammered out at the regular meetings of the Federal Open Market Committee. As noted, these meetings are attended not only by the 12 voting members of the committee but also by officials from the seven Federal Reserve banks not currently represented on the FOMC. Although the future course of open-market operations is the prime concern, decisions regarding the use of all the monetary policy tools are made during the course of their deliberations.

At the meetings, participants are provided with extensive background data, including forecasts of production, prices, employment, and so forth, arrived at by a combination of the judgment of the Board's staff and the output of Fed's large econometric model of the economy. With this impressive array of information as the basis, the committee then sets out to determine policy.

The ultimate objectives of monetary policy have long been considered to include price stability, fuller employment, and reasonably rapid economic growth. Despite the arguments of some authorities in the late 1980s that price stability should be recognized as the sole responsibility of the Fed, most economists seem content to retain the multiple goals suggested.

But the Fed's monetary policy instruments—principally open-market operations—obviously do not work *directly* on these ultimate goals. What is needed for policy formulation, then, is the identification of certain *intermediate targets* which are reasonably closely linked, through some logical cause and effect transmission mechanism, to the ultimate production, employment, and price-level goals. And, to ensure adequate control over these intermediate targets, it has been considered necessary to identify specific so-called *operating targets* that not only can guide the intermediate targets but can, in turn, be effectively guided by such monetary policy instruments as open-market operations.[23]

What we have then, is a monetary policy formulation process which looks much like the following schematic sketch:

Monetary Policy Instruments (Open-Market Operations) —control→ Certain Operating Targets —which control→ Certain Intermediate Targets —which are closely related to→ Ultimate Goals: Price Stability Full Employment Rapid Economic Growth

As underlying conditions and our understanding of how the economy works have changed over the years, both the operating targets and the intermediate targets have changed. Throughout the 1950s and much of the 1960s, the intermediate target employed appears to have been the volume of bank credit while the operating target seems to have been a combination of "free reserves" and "money market conditions."

Free reserves can be defined as excess reserves minus reserves borrowed from the Fed. Money market conditions was simply technical jargon referring to an array of short-term interest rates the FOMC was endeavoring to control.[24] That is, during the 1950s and 1960s, the formulation of monetary policy was as follows:

1950s and 1960s

Open-Market Operations —were aimed at controlling→ Money Market Conditions and/or Free Reserves —which were thought to control→ The Volume of Bank Credit —which was aimed at→ Price Stability Full Employment Rapid Growth

[23] This discussion relies heavily on the excellent article by Ann-Marie Meulendyke entitled "A Review of Federal Reserve Policy Targets and Operating Guides in Recent Decades," *Quarterly Review*, Federal Reserve Bank of New York, Autumn 1988. See also H. Robert Heller, "Implementing Monetary Policy," *Federal Reserve Bulletin*, July 1988.

[24] See Benjamin M. Friedman, "The Inefficiency of Short-Run Monetary Targets," *Brookings Papers on Economic Activity*, Vol. 2, 1977, pp. 297–298.

During most of this period, therefore, low and/or falling short-term interest rates were taken as evidence of an easy or expansionary monetary policy while high and/or rising rates were accepted as evidence of a tight or contractionary monetary policy.

In retrospect, it seems clear that this early preoccupation with interest rates as the main operating target for monetary policy resulted partly from concern for the stability of financial institutions and partly from early Keynesian views on the efficacy of monetary policy as a weapon in the nation's stabilization arsenal. Since some early Keynesians viewed fiscal policy as very potent and monetary policy as working (altering aggregate demand) only as a consequence of very large changes in the interest rates, it was hardly surprising that the former was relied upon to control aggregate demand, whereas the latter was looked upon more as a device for maintaining stability in financial markets.[25]

By the latter 1960s, however, an unfortunately pro-cyclical fiscal policy along with accelerating rates of inflation forced a reevaluation of the practice of relying so heavily on market interest rate behavior as the operating target to guide monetary policy. Although other issues played a role in this change, the most important was probably that played by inflationary expectations.[26]

The point here is a simple one. If rising market interest rates are accepted as evidence that a restrictive monetary policy has been implemented, policymakers may interpret what is actually an expansionary (inflationary) monetary policy as a contractionary one. This is because when lenders have come to expect a rise in the price level, they will tack an inflationary premium on to the real rate of interest that they will accept. If, for instance, the market rate of interest rises from 10 percent to 12 percent such behavior could very well signify (or, indeed, result from) an *expansionary* monetary policy. This would be the case if at the same time the expected inflation rate rose by 5 percent, implying that the real rate of interest actually *fell* by 3 percent.

As a result of considerations such as these, significant changes began to appear in FOMC directives to the System Account Manager. First, in 1966 the Open Market Committee, though still couching its directives primarily in terms of effects on money market conditions, began to add a "proviso clause" to take explicit account of money supply changes. For example, the directive from the FOMC meeting of July 18, 1967, stated that open-market operations were to be conducted

---

[25] See Gordon H. Sellon, Jr., and Ronald L. Teigen, "The Choice of Short-Run Targets for Monetary Policy," *Economic Review*, Federal Reserve Bank of Kansas City, May 1981, for an especially lucid account. See also Stephen H. Axilrod, "Monetary Policy, Money Supply, and the Federal Reserve's Operating Procedures," *Federal Reserve Bulletin*, January 1982; and Benjamin M. Friedman, "Time to Reexamine the Monetary Targets Framework," *New England Economic Review*, March–April 1982.

[26] A factor of real significance in the movement away from interest rates and toward the money stock as the appropriate target for monetary policy was the opposition of the monetarists, who gained considerable strength during the 1960s. Although we shall consider the monetarist viewpoint in some depth in Chapter 21, it should be noted at this point that one need not subscribe to the entire monetarist position to accept their belief that the prime monetary policy target should be a money aggregate rather than interest rates. See William Poole, "Rules of Thumb for Guiding Monetary Policy," *Open Market Policies and Operating Procedures,* Board of Governors of the Federal Reserve System, 1971; and Richard G. Davis, "Implementing Open Market Policy with Monetary Aggregate Objectives," *Monthly Review*, Federal Reserve Bank of New York, July 1973.

with a view to maintaining about the prevailing conditions in the money market; but operations shall be modified insofar as the Treasury financing permits to moderate any apparent tendency for bank credit and money to expand more than currently expected.[27]

Then in 1970 a further shift in emphasis appeared wherein directives began to be written primarily in terms of effects on the money supply and bank credit, with "money market conditions" in the secondary or proviso role. For example, the directive of April 7, 1970, stated that

> To implement this policy, the Committee desires to see moderate growth in money and bank credit over the months ahead. System open market operations until the next meeting of the Committee shall be conducted with a view to maintaining money market conditions consistent with that objective.[28]

It was not, however, until the mid-1970s that Congress made this movement toward explicit recognition of monetary aggregates as intermediate targets for monetary policy mandatory. First, in a 1975 Congressional Resolution and then in the Full Employment and Balanced Growth Act of 1978, Congress required the Fed to publicly announce its targets explicitly in terms of annual percentage rates of growth in the money supply. For about a decade, then, the Federal Reserve System has been announcing and pursuing explicit money supply growth rates. But this has not really meant that interest rate targets have been altogether abandoned. In fact, until October 1979, the Fed saw fit to pursue its money supply growth targets indirectly via control of the federal funds interest rate.

The result of all this was that the monetary policy formulation process throughout most of the 1970s was as follows:

1970s

Open-Market Operations	were aimed at → controlling	the Federal Funds Interest Rate	which was — thought to → control	The Money Supply M1, M2, M3	which was — aimed at →	Price Stability Full Employment Rapid Growth

How well did this approach work? Not well enough, as its abandonment in October 1979 clearly attests. The problem was that although the Fed was able to control the federal funds rate very effectively, the hoped-for close link between it and the resultant money supply did not materialize. In fact, as Table 13-3 makes clear, despite the FOMC's success in hitting its federal funds rate targets, the growth in the money supply during 1977 and 1978 markedly exceeded its target range.

It was this failure to control the money supply plus the widespread conviction that the excessively expansionary monetary policy was a major contributor to the accelerating inflation at the time that led to a dramatic change in monetary policy targeting in October 1979.

Led by Chairman Paul Volcker, the FOMC at that point made a firm commitment to bring the price level under control. To do that it recognized that it would

[27] "Record of Policy Actions of F.O.M.C.," *Federal Reserve Bulletin*, November 1967.

[28] "Record of Policy Actions of F.O.M.C.," *Federal Reserve Bulletin*, July 1970.

TABLE 13-3   Money supply growth and inflation, 1977 and 1978

Year	FRS target range for M1 (%)	Actual change in M1 (%)	Rise in consumer price index (%)
1977	4.5–6.5	7.9	6.8
1978	4.0–6.5	7.2	9.0

not only have to constrain the money supply but that it would have to do so convincingly enough to undercut the public's well-entrenched inflationary expectations. Accordingly, it abandoned the federal funds rate as its "operating target" and adopted in its place the quantity of "nonborrowed reserves." The result was that from October 1979 until September 1982 the monetary policy formulation process was essentially the following:

1979–1982

| Open-Market Operations | were aimed at controlling | → | Nonborrowed Reserves | which was thought to control | → | The Money Supply M1, M2, M3 | which was aimed at | → | Price Stability Full Employment Rapid Growth |

The upshot of all this was that monetary policy formulation during that three-year period worked as follows. The FOMC established target ranges for the rate of growth in M1, M2, and M3 from the fourth quarter of each year to the fourth quarter of the next year.[29] Subsequently, at each Open Market Committee meeting, the FOMC established "short-run" (two- to three-month) targets for M1 and M2 that were considered appropriate to stay within (or return to) the annual growth rates established. In essence, the System Account Manager was then directed to aim at maintaining a level of nonborrowed reserves (total reserves minus those borrowed through the discount window) sufficient to achieve the desired short-run rate of growth in M1 and M2. The federal funds rate, which previously had been constrained within a very narrow range, was now permitted to vary as much as 4 to 5 percent during the month, and even if it strayed outside this range, the account manager was usually advised only to "consult" with the committee.

Following these procedures from 1979 through 1982, the Federal Reserve System was able to bring down the rate of growth of the money supply quite substantially. From annual M1 growth rates of around 8 percent in the latter 1970s, it fell to $7\frac{1}{2}$ percent in 1980, 5 percent in 1981, and about 6 percent over the first three quarters of 1982. As a partial consequence (the absence of massive supply shocks such as rocked the economy in the mid- and late 1970s helped enormously too), the annual rate of inflation fell from around 12 percent in 1980 to around 4 percent by 1982.

But, of course, the FRS was unable to overcome the inflation problem without contributing at the same time to development of the worst recession since the

[29] A target was also set for the rate of growth of a broader aggregate called "bank credit."

decade of the 1930s. That recession, coupled with the uncertainty introduced by financial innovation, precipitated further changes in monetary policy formulation in 1982. First, about midyear, the FOMC announced its willingness to permit M1 to grow at rates "somewhat above the target ranges" for the rest of the year. Then in the October 1982 meeting, the committee went further by failing to specify *any* short-run target for M1.

The reason for this notable deemphasis of the M1 target was a large and unprecedented decline in velocity which all but destroyed the heretofore reasonably close relation between the M1 money supply and the level of total spending. Related undoubtedly to the widespread financial innovation that typified the early 1980s, that erratic velocity behavior presaged still another change in monetary policy targets.

Although the FOMC reinstituted M1 targets starting in early 1983, it tended to treat them rather casually throughout much of the decade. For example, despite establishing an M1 target range of from 3 percent to 8 percent for the period from the fourth quarter of 1984 to the fourth quarter of 1985, it permitted the actual M1 total to shoot upward by over 12 percent during the period. And in 1986, with the target still set at the 3 percent to 8 percent range, the actual annual rate of increase for M1 was over 15 percent! And, when the time for setting the 1987 money supply targets came at the February 1987 FOMC meeting, the Committee once again declined even to set a target range for its M1 series. It seemed apparent that the Committee was satisfied to allow extraordinary increases in M1 so long as sharp decreases in the velocity of spending were expected to, in large degree, neutralize them. As the Federal Reserve Bank of New York put it, "In deciding not to set a target range for M1 growth, the Committee continued to view the relationship between M1 and economic activity as too unreliable to warrant reliance on this measure as a guide for the conduct of monetary policy." [30]

What had happened, then, was a breakdown in the relationship between the intermediate target, the money supply, and the ultimate policy objectives. This necessitated one more alteration in the policy formulation process. From late 1982 until the early 1990s, that process has been as follows:

1982–1991

| Open-Market Operations | were aimed at controlling | → | Borrowed Reserves | which was thought to control | → | M2 and M3 plus other indicators | which was aimed at | → | Price Stability Full Employment Rapid Growth |

As one authority put it, "The immediate operating targets have, in a sense, come full circle since the 1950s: the FOMC initially targeted free reserves and then shifted to federal funds rates, to nonborrowed reserves, and most recently to borrowed reserves, a measure similar in many ways to free reserves.[31]

What is clear is that control in a dynamic, ever-changing economy is an extremely difficult task and that monetary policy continues to involve as much art as science.

[30] "Monetary Policy and Open Market Operations During 1989," *Quarterly Review*, Federal Reserve Bank of New York, Spring 1990, p. 52.

[31] Meulendyke, "A Review of Federal Reserve Policy Targets," p. 7.

Review Questions

1. a. Assume that initially the banking system has total reserves of $30 billion and that outstanding demand and time deposit liabilities are $100 billion each. If $R_d = 25$ percent and $R_t = 5$ percent, confirm that there are no excess reserves.
   b. Now, assuming that $c = .20$ and $t = 1.0$, compute the monetary base.
   c. If R_d is now reduced to 15 percent, use the (new) money multiplier to compute the change in money supply made possible by the required reserve ratio change.

2. If the required reserve ratio is raised, trace through, in step-by-step fashion (i.e., via the transmission mechanism), exactly how such a measure would be expected to affect aggregate expenditures.

3. Specifically, how *might* an increase in the discount rate tend to cut aggregate expenditures?

4. "In the early days of the Federal Reserve System, authorities relied upon eligibility requirements to limit access to the discount window. More recently, Regulation A has been relied on to do this job." Explain.

5. The announcement effects of discount rate changes may either reinforce or work against the intent of the policy. Explain.

6. Explain *two* ways in which an open-market purchase may affect interest rates.

7. Show by the use of appropriately labeled T-accounts for the commercial banks and the Federal Reserve banks the effects of a $100 million open-market purchase from the commercial banks and from the nonbank public. In each case, indicate the effect *of the purchase alone* on total reserves, excess reserves, and the money supply.

8. Write an essay comparing the relative advantages and disadvantages of the three general credit controls of the Federal Reserve.

9. "All Federal Reserve open-market operations are carried out in the secondary, rather than the primary, securities market." Why is this the case?

10. Opponents of selective credit controls often argue that such controls interfere with consumer choice in the allocation of the nation's resources. Develop this point.

11. Why did the FOMC tend to allow M1 to greatly exceed its targets in several years during the 1980s?

12. Distinguish between adjustment credit and extended credit in terms of the discount facility of the FRS.

13. Explain, as completely as you can, the Fed's current procedures for formulating monetary policy.

Other Determinants
of the Money Supply

The money supply, as we have seen, depends upon the size of the money multiplier $(1 + c)/[R_d + c + (R_t \cdot t) + x]$ and of the monetary base. The essence of monetary policy is the Federal Reserve's power to alter the size of the multiplier (by varying R_d and R_t) and/or the monetary base (by implementing any of its three general credit controls).

But while the Fed is the sole institution whose main responsibility is control of the money supply, it by no means is the only one whose actions actually *do* affect it. There are three other groups in the economy whose activities, though primarily motivated by other considerations, do, in fact, affect the money supply: the nonbank public, the commercial banks, and the U.S. Treasury Department.

It should already be clear how the nonbank public can do this. Any change in its so-called "preferred asset" ratio will, by altering c or t, obviously affect the size of the money multiplier and, therefore, the size of the money supply a given monetary base can support. Similarly, any change in the banking system's desire for excess reserves (i.e., in x) will alter the money multiplier.

The effects of Treasury actions on the money supply are somewhat more complex, and most of this chapter will focus on them. All the factors affecting the size of the monetary base are summarized at the end of the chapter.

Effects of Treasury Activities

The U.S. Treasury, of course, is primarily charged with meeting the nation's fiscal needs. At the risk of oversimplifying what is actually a monumental task, this responsibility might be said to boil down to seeing to it that the federal government always has on hand the funds that are necessary to carry out the spending programs set up by Congress.

This alone involves a number of fundamental duties, including collection of taxes, borrowing by sale of government securities when required spending exceeds tax revenue, handling the cash balances of the federal government including those arising from a tax surplus, and refunding the outstanding federal debt when necessary. Each of these duties provides the Treasury with major areas of discretion, such that the impact on the economy of handling the job one way or the other must be given careful consideration.

For example, if a deficit must be financed, it makes a difference what type of securities is sold. If a tax surplus is in the offing, different ways of disposing of it will have substantially different impacts on the economy. If a sizable portion of the national debt is approaching maturity and there is no tax surplus available to meet the bill, the choice of the type of new obligation to sell to obtain the needed funds can be crucial. And even the apparently simple decision of determining the location of the Treasury's cash balances involves matters that are by no means inconsequential.

In this section, we shall consider the consequences for bank reserves and the money supply of several of the more important Treasury activities. Specifically, we shall look at the effects of changing the location of Treasury cash balances, the effects of financing deficits and disposing of surpluses in various ways, and the effects of refunding the existing national debt.

The Location of Treasury Cash Balances — Tax and Loan Accounts

One very important task of the Treasury is the management of its cash balances, the handling of which can markedly affect commercial bank reserves. These balances consist, beyond a small amount held in the form of currency and coins, primarily of checking accounts at the 12 Federal Reserve banks and at over 15,000 depository institutions designated as special depositories.[1]

Treasury deposits held at commercial banks and the other depository institutions are called tax and loan accounts. As the name implies, these accounts are used to receive funds being paid to the federal government by taxpayers as well as by those who are lending money to the government, through the purchase of U.S. securities.

Depository institutions holding tax and loan accounts must pay interest on them. The Treasury, in turn, pays for services performed by the depository institutions on a flat fee per-item basis.[2]

Why, the reader may ask, does the Treasury keep checking accounts at commercial banks and other depository institutions *as well as* at Federal Reserve banks? Why not simplify matters by keeping all its demand deposits at the Federal Reserve? A moment or two of reflection will clear up this matter.

---

[1] A depository institution can qualify as a "special depository," thereby becoming eligible to hold tax and loan accounts, by pledging certain specified securities as collateral and by being recommended by the Federal Reserve bank in its district.

[2] For an explanation see William N. Cox, "Changes in the Treasury's Cash Management Procedures," *Economic Review*, Federal Reserve Bank of Atlanta, January–February 1978.

When taxes are paid in by the public or when loan funds are made available to the government, the taxpayer (or security purchaser) generally writes a check on his or her account at a commercial bank to make payment. If these funds were deposited directly into the Treasury's accounts at the Federal Reserve, the immediate effect would be to reduce bank reserves and the money supply by that amount, as the following T-accounts indicate:

Federal Reserve Banks		*Commercial Banks*	
	Demand deposits of commercial banks −$100 Demand deposit of U.S. Treasury +$100	Federal Reserve account −$100	Demand deposit of taxpayer −$100

When the Treasury spends out of its accounts at Federal Reserve banks, the effects on the money supply and bank reserves are, of course, the other way around. The Treasury makes out a check payable to some member of the public who deposits it in his or her account at a commercial bank and the collection process raises bank reserves:

Federal Reserve Banks		*Commercial Banks*	
	Demand deposits of commercial banks +$100 Demand deposit of U.S. Treasury −$100	Federal Reserve account +$100	Demand deposit of person paid by Treasury +$100

If the money collection and money disbursement sides of Treasury operations were always perfectly coordinated, their opposing effects on reserves and the money supply would offset one another, so that no major disturbance would be forthcoming. But, unfortunately, no such neat offset occurs. Treasury receipts, both from taxes and from security sales, arrive in an uneven pattern throughout the year, bulking particularly large on April 15 when settlement for the personal income tax is due and at the end of each quarter when corporate payments come in. Treasury spending patterns, on the other hand, are much more evenly distributed throughout the year. Without tax and loan accounts this failure of Treasury income and outgo to mesh perfectly would subject the banking system to constant disruption in the form of substantial net losses of reserves around the end of each quarter, offset only over time by government spending.

It was for the purpose of minimizing the disturbing effects of Treasury operations on the banking system that the tax and loan accounts were established. Under this arrangement, most taxes (and loan funds) are paid in initially to a tax and loan account, usually at a commercial bank. As this simply represents a change in the ownership of demand deposits still in commercial banks, no loss in bank reserves results.

The Treasury, however, does not choose to subject itself to the administrative chaos that might be involved in making its disbursements directly out of the tax and loan accounts located at over 15,000 different depository institutions. Therefore, its expenditures with rare exceptions are made through checks written on its accounts at Federal Reserve banks. This source is regularly replenished, as expenditures are planned, by transfer of the necessary amount from the tax and loan accounts to accounts at the Fed. As a general rule, an attempt has been made to keep Treasury accounts at Federal Reserve banks at around the $5 billion level, although periodically they may be much larger.

To illustrate how all this works, assume that the Treasury collects $10 billion in tax payments on April 15, and that those funds are then spent at a rate of $500 million per day for the next 20 days. On April 15, when the taxes are paid, the checks would be immediately redeposited into Treasury tax and loan accounts in commercial banks, with T-account effects as follows:

Commercial Banks

	Demand deposits of taxpayers −$10 billion
	Demand deposits of U.S. Treasury in tax and loan accounts +$10 billion

Note that the collection of this large quantity of tax funds has no effect whatever on bank reserves (or the monetary base) as it would have had the checks been deposited in Treasury accounts at Federal Reserve banks.[3]

Now, on April 16 and each day thereafter, the funds about to be spent are transferred out of tax and loan accounts at depository institutions into Treasury accounts at Federal Reserve banks:

Federal Reserve		*Commercial Banks*	
	Demand deposits of commercial banks −$500 million	Federal Reserve account −$500 million	Demand deposits of U.S. Treasury in tax and loan accounts −$500 million
	Demand deposits of U.S. Treasury +$500 million		

and the Treasury then immediately spends the funds:

Federal Reserve		*Commercial Banks*	
	Demand deposits of U.S. Treasury −$500 million	Federal Reserve account +$500 million	Demand deposit of those paid by the Treasury +$500 million
	Demand deposits of commercial banks +$500 million		

[3] Lest the seriousness of such a sudden reserve drain be underestimated, it should be noted that a $10 billion reserve loss would reduce depository institution reserve accounts by over 15 percent!

The result is that the reduction in bank reserves is very short-lived, being replenished almost immediately by the spending of the funds. As a consequence, the potential destabilizing effect on bank reserves that could result from the fact that tax collection and spending are not well coordinated is avoided.

The Monetary Aspects of Fiscal Policy: Effects on Bank Reserves and the Money Supply of Alternative Means of Financing Deficits and Disposing of Tax Surpluses

A common practice in introductory economics courses is to distinguish sharply between monetary policy and fiscal policy. The former is generally defined as action by the Federal Reserve System to alter the quantity of bank reserves and the potential money and credit supply so as to ultimately affect the level of aggregate expenditures in the necessary direction for stability and growth. Fiscal policy, on the other hand, is usually described as alterations in tax and/or expenditure programs by Congress, also aimed at promoting stability and growth via effects on aggregate expenditures.[4]

Such distinctions are useful for throwing into broad relief the central difference between two techniques. Valuable though it may be to emphasize the conceptual differences between them, it is important to recognize that a single policy action can often involve them both.

This is particularly true of fiscal policy, the implementation of which is the particular responsibility of the Treasury Department. If, for example, Congress cuts taxes to raise demand, the *fiscal* policy effects of the action have to do with increased consumption and investment spending by those groups whose disposable incomes have been increased by the tax cut.

But that is not all there is to it. If the tax cut has reduced governmental revenue below its expenditures, it is the task of the Treasury to raise the funds needed to cover the deficit. The particular means it chooses to carry out this responsibility are matters that can also affect the money supply and bank reserves. And the overall effect of the deficit on aggregate expenditures will depend, to some extent, on these decisions.

The Financing of a Budget Deficit

When the expenditure and tax laws enacted by Congress result in a budget deficit, it is the Treasury's responsibility to provide the money not raised by taxation. Although in theory small deficits might be financed on a very-short-

---

[4] In this section, we shall oversimplify by ignoring the tax and loan accounts, assuming for the moment that both tax and loan funds are deposited directly in the Treasury's Federal Reserve account. The complexity that this simplification overcomes is considerable and the final effects on bank reserves and the money supply of each operation are unchanged in any case.

term basis by drawing down balances already held by the Treasury at its special depositories or at Federal Reserve banks, such expedients are, for obvious reasons, strictly limited. Financing deficits of any significance requires the Treasury to sell new U.S. securities to borrow the needed funds. And the monetary effects of such security sales will differ, depending upon the identity of the purchasers.

Borrowing by Sale of New U.S. Securities to the Nonbank Public

If the Treasury should finance a deficit by sale of securities to members of the nonbank public, the operation (once the funds are spent) has no net effects on the money supply, bank reserves, or monetary base.

Effects of Treasury selling new U.S. securities to nonbank public and depositing the proceeds in their Federal Reserve accounts:

Federal Reserve		*Commercial Banks*	
	Demand deposits of commercial banks −$100	Federal Reserve account −$100	Demand deposits of buyers of the securities −$100
	Demand deposits of U.S. Treasury +$100		

Effects of Treasury spending the funds:

Federal Reserve		*Commercial Banks*	
	Demand deposits of U.S. Treasury −$100	Federal Reserve account +$100	Demand deposits of those paid by government +$100
	Demand deposits of commercial banks +$100		

Although the sale of the securities and transfer of the proceeds into the Treasury's Federal Reserve account reduces both the public's money supply and the banking system's reserves, the subsequent deficit spending pumps the money right back out into the public's hand and the reserves right back to the commercial banks. Consequently, we can conclude that *financing deficit spending via sale of U.S. securities to the nonbank public has no net monetary effects.*

Borrowing by Sale of New U.S. Securities to the Commercial Banks

The monetary effects are only slightly different if the securities are sold to commercial banks. In this case, the T-account effects of the sale of the securities are

Federal Reserve		*Commercial Banks*	
	Demand deposits of commercial banks −$100	U.S. securities +$100	
	Demand deposits of U.S. Treasury +$100	Federal Reserve account −$100	

When the borrowed funds are subsequently spent, the effects are

Federal Reserve		*Commercial Banks*	
	Demand deposits of U.S. Treasury −$100	Federal Reserve account +$100	Demand deposits of those paid by the government +$100
	Demand deposits of commercial banks +$100		

Here, when the banks buy the securities, they pay the Treasury with a check on their Federal Reserve account. This half of the transaction cuts the banking system's total reserves but has no effect on the money supply. However, when the funds are spent by the Treasury (assuming that those paid by the government deposit their checks in commercial banks), the banks' total reserves are restored to their original level while the money supply is increased.

One would be tempted to conclude that this method of financing a deficit is more expansionary than the preceding example because it increases the money supply. Such a conclusion, however, does not really seem warranted. Note that there is no change in the monetary base involved here. The transaction does not really put the banking system in a position to create any more money than it could have before. All that has happened is that excess reserves that the banking system already had have been used up (i.e., turned into required reserves) by the expansion in demand deposits.

Borrowing by Sale of New U.S. Securities to the Federal Reserve System

In theory, if not in practice, there is a third possibility. The Treasury might finance the deficit by selling its securities to the Federal Reserve banks.

But we must tread carefully here for, as we saw in the last chapter, the Federal Reserve banks are forbidden by law from purchasing new U.S. securities from the U.S. Treasury.

What we need to understand at this point is what the monetary effects *would be* if such a practice *were* legal. Once that is illustrated, it should be easier to see why the law forbids it.

Let's consider the T-account effects that would occur if the Fed *could* buy new U.S. securities from the Treasury.

Federal Reserve buys the securities:

Federal Reserve		Commercial Banks
U.S. securities +$100	Demand deposits of U.S. Treasury +$100	No effect

Treasury spends the proceeds:

Federal Reserve		Commercial Banks	
	Demand deposits of U.S. Treasury −$100	Federal Reserve account +$100	Demand deposits of those paid by the government +$100
	Demand deposits of commercial banks +$100		

Note that in this case the sale of the securities reduces neither the money supply nor bank reserves. Since the act of spending the newly borrowed funds does raise both total reserves and the money supply, the result is that the entire procedure would be strongly expansionary.

The law essentially forbids this because it would have precisely the same monetary effects as if the federal government ran the printing presses to raise the money needed to cover budget deficits. That this is the case should not be surprising. After all, if the Treasury could raise the money it needs to finance deficit spending by simply calling on another government agency to create it for them, what difference does it make whether that agency is the Bureau of Engraving or the Federal Reserve System? Consequently, it was long ago decided that when the federal government spends more than it takes in via taxes, it should, to guard against the possibility of hyperinflation, be forced to borrow the deficit from someone other than itself. Both running the printing presses and borrowing from the Fed are forbidden.

Considering all this, what can we conclude about the monetary effects of different means of financing budget deficits? Given the legal prohibition against the Treasury borrowing from the Fed, it seems fair to say that whether the Treasury finances deficits by borrowing from the commercial banks or from the nonbank public, the monetary effects are minor. Neither, after all, alters the monetary base.

The Disposition of a Tax Surplus

On those rare (indeed, almost forgotten) occasions when tax revenues are in excess of government expenditures, the Treasury's area of discretion has to do with the handling of the tax surplus. Two major possibilities present themselves. The Treasury might simply hoard the surplus, either in its tax and loan accounts or in its checking account at the Federal Reserve. Or it may use it to retire a portion of its outstanding debt.

If a tax surplus is held in a tax and loan account at commercial banks, its collection will reduce the money supply but leave the monetary base, total bank reserves and excess reserves unaffected.[5] If, however, the surplus is transferred to the Treasury's Federal Reserve account, and hoarded there, its effect will be to lower the money supply, bank reserves, and the monetary base by the amount of the surplus and excess reserves by a lesser amount, the magnitude of which depends on the required reserve ratio. The second alternative is clearly more contractionary than the first.

The hoarding of tax surpluses is reasonable economically, depending on the state of the economy, but this practice could be hazardous politically. When a large national debt on which interest is accruing exists, it is extremely difficult to justify holding a tax surplus when it might be used to reduce the level of debt. Consequently, the usual practice of the Treasury is to employ surpluses to retire outstanding securities.

Using Tax Surplus to Retire Securities
Held by Nonbank Public

If a tax surplus is used to retire maturing U.S. securities held by the nonbank public, neither the money supply nor bank reserves are altered. The collection of the tax surplus cuts both the money supply and the total reserves, but the use of it to retire securities held by the public pumps that money and those reserves right back to the public and the banks.

When the tax surplus is collected and deposited in the Treasury's Federal Reserve account,

Federal Reserve		*Commercial Banks*	
	Demand deposits of commercial banks −$100	Federal Reserve account −$100	Demand deposits of taxpayers −$100
	Demand deposits of U.S. Treasury +$100		

When the funds are used to retire maturing securities held by the nonbank public,

Federal Reserve		*Commercial Banks*	
	Demand deposits of U.S. Treasury −$100	Federal Reserve account +$100	Demand deposits of owners of maturing securities +$100
	Demand deposits of commercial banks +$100		

[5] Because the money supply excludes Treasury deposits, it is reduced by the collection of the surplus. However, the amount of demand deposits behind which commercial banks are required to maintain reserves is unchanged, so that, despite the drop in the money supply, as defined, required reserves are unchanged.

From this we can conclude that collecting a tax surplus and using it to retire maturing securities held by the nonbank public has no net monetary effects. Neither total reserves, the monetary base, nor the money supply is altered as a result.

Using Tax Surplus to Retire Securities Held by Commercial Banks

A tax surplus used to retire maturing U.S. securities held by the commercial banks would reduce the money supply but would leave total member bank reserves and the monetary base unchanged. That is, the collection of the tax surplus reduces demand deposits of taxpayers and (when the Treasury deposits the funds in its Federal Reserve account) total bank reserves by the full amount of the surplus. Subsequently, when the surplus is spent to retire bank-held securities, the total reserves are restored to the banks, but demand deposits remain below their original level. In T-accounts we have the following:

1. Collection of tax surplus and deposit in Treasury's Federal Reserve account:

Federal Reserve		*Commercial Banks*	
	Demand deposits of commercial banks −$100	Federal Reserve account −$100	Demand deposits of taxpayers −$100
	Demand deposits of U.S. Treasury +$100		

2. The tax surplus is used to retire maturing securities held by commercial banks:

Federal Reserve		*Commercial Banks*	
	Demand deposits of U.S. Treasury −$100	U.S. securities −$100	
	Demand deposits of commercial banks +$100	Federal Reserve account +$100	

Note once again that despite the fact that the money supply is reduced in this case, it is scarcely more contractionary than the preceding example where the money supply was unaffected. The difference is that, in this case, since demand deposits (and, therefore, required reserves) are reduced while total reserves are unchanged, *excess* reserves are *increased*. By any reasonable assumptions, one would have to expect the banking system subsequently to make new loans (creating new money) on the basis of these excess reserves, thereby restoring the money supply to its original size.

Using Tax Surplus to Retire Securities
Held by the Federal Reserve Banks

Finally, a tax surplus could be used to retire U.S. securities held by the Federal Reserve banks themselves. This approach, as the following T-accounts demonstrate, will result in a reduction of both the money supply *and* total commercial bank reserves (as well as the monetary base) by the amount of the surplus. It does so because this use of the surplus funds restores neither the public's demand deposits nor the commercial banks' reserves that were drained away in tax collection.

1. Collection of tax surplus and deposit in Federal Reserve:

Federal Reserve		*Commercial Banks*	
	Demand deposits of commercial banks −$100	Federal Reserve account −$100	Demand deposits of taxpayers −$100
	Demand deposits of U.S. Treasury +$100		

2. Use of tax surplus to retire U.S. securities owned by the Federal Reserve banks:

Federal Reserve		*Commercial Banks*
U.S. securities −$100	Demand deposits of U.S. Treasury −$100	No effect

Note that the monetary effects of this method of handling a tax surplus are exactly equivalent to those that would result from the Treasury's collecting the tax surplus and hoarding it all in its checking account at the Federal Reserve. Clearly, if the purpose of collecting the tax surplus is to reduce an excessive level of aggregate demand to combat inflation, using it to pay off Federal Reserve–held securities or hoarding it in the Treasury's Federal Reserve account will be preferable (cut aggregate demand more) to the other possibilities discussed. This is so because both the fiscal *and* the monetary effects of the action are contractive.

An Aside: Fiscal Policy Measures May
Affect Aggregate Expenditures Even
When There Are No Monetary Effects

Before proceeding to a consideration of the monetary effects of other Treasury actions, let us pause to try and head off a common misperception. As we have seen, neither deficit spending financed by selling securities to the nonbank public nor collection of a tax surplus used to retire securities held by the public alter the money supply. But despite the absence of monetary effects, such fiscal policy measures *may* affect the level of aggregate expenditures. What the student must guard against is erroneously equating "money supply" with "income."

Let us illustrate the problem by referring to the collection of a tax surplus and use of it to retire maturing U.S. securities held by the nonbank public. For example, if the tax surplus was created by an increase in tax rates, it constitutes a contractionary fiscal policy measure aimed at lowering aggregate expenditures.

The problem is simply that some students look at the T-accounts for these transactions and say, "Such a thing cannot change spending. After all, all the government is doing is taking the money out of one group's hands (the taxpayers) and turning around and putting the same money back into the hands of another group (the bondholders). Any cut in consumer spending by taxpayers would be expected to just be offset by an increase in spending by the bondholders, so the measure cannot have any net effect on aggregate expenditures."

Sound persuasive? To many people it does, but in this form it involves an improper identification of money with income. Let's look at the two sides of this transaction more closely. If taxes are increased, the result is a reduction in taxpayers' *income*. This, in turn, means that they will cut their consumption spending somewhat since consumption spending depends on income. However, when the Treasury turns around and uses the tax surplus to retire maturing securities, does this correspondingly raise bondholders' incomes? Not really. It is true they receive the money but that is only in exchange for the bonds that have matured. The bondholders have simply had the *form of their wealth changed*. They now have more money and fewer bonds, but they do not have either more income or more wealth. Therefore, there is no obvious reason why they should raise their consumer spending.

Our point here is not to take a position on the much-debated issue of the effectiveness of fiscal policy. One could raise several legitimate reservations about the effectiveness of fiscal policy measures. What we *are* concerned with is that the student not dismiss fiscal policy on the illegitimate grounds of identifying the *stock* of money with the *flow* of income.

Treasury Debt Refunding

One of the Treasury Department's weightier responsibilities is the refunding of debt that matures each year when no tax surplus is available to retire it. This, of course, requires the sale of new securities to raise the funds with which to retire those coming due. The Treasury, as the issuer, is free to tailor the type and maturity of the new issue to its desires. Certain types of securities especially appeal to particular groups of lenders, so the Treasury, in designing the nature and special characteristics of the new issue, can reasonably effectively determine the security's purchaser.

This, too, provides a means of altering the monetary base and the money supply, and the possibilities are many. By way of example, assume that $100 million of securities held by the Federal Reserve are approaching maturity and that the Treasury chooses to raise the funds to pay them off by selling an equivalent amount of new securities to the nonbank public. The effects of these transactions are shown as follows in T-account form.

1. Sale of new U.S. securities to the nonbank public and deposit of funds in the Treasury's Federal Reserve account:

Federal Reserve		*Commercial Banks*	
	Demand deposits of commercial banks −$100	Federal Reserve account −$100	Demand deposits of security purchasers −$100
	Demand deposits of U.S. Treasury +$100		

2. Use of the newly borrowed funds to retire maturing U.S. securities held by the Federal Reserve:

Federal Reserve		*Commercial Banks*
U.S. securities −$100	Demand deposits of U.S. Treasury −$100	No effect

The result of this particular refunding operation is to reduce both the money supply and the monetary base by the full amount of the refunding operation, a monetary effect that is sharply contractionary.

We shall not take the time here to go through the monetary effects of all possible refunding combinations. This is an exercise that the student might prefer to work out on his or her own. It is clear, however, that substantial increases or decreases in the economy's liquidity are possible via the debt refunding mechanism.

Defensive Versus Dynamic Monetary Policy

Monetary policy, as one authority put it, has its *defensive* and *dynamic* aspects.[6]

Defensive policy is under way when the Federal Reserve System, for example, employs open-market operations to combat or offset an undesired change in the monetary base or money supply that has come about as a result of activities by the public, the commercial banks, or the Treasury such as those just described. *Dynamic* policy, on the other hand, involves the use of monetary policy weapons,

[6] Robert V. Roosa coined these appropriate terms in his excellent monograph entitled *Federal Reserve Operations in the Money and Government Securities Markets,* published by the Federal Reserve Bank of New York in 1956.

not just to prevent unfavorable changes but rather to promote actively desired positive changes. Many of the more serious problems encountered by the Fed in achieving its short-run money supply targets arise out of its inability to anticipate changes in conditions originating with actions by the public or Treasury and calling for defensive policy.

It cannot be overemphasized, however, that despite all this, it is still the Fed that holds the whip hand in determination of the money supply. It is true, for example, that alterations in the location of Treasury checking accounts *can* affect commercial bank reserves, but the very existence of the tax and loan accounts represents an attempt by the Treasury to avoid such changes. The money supply *can* be increased in cases of deficit spending, but this will only happen if the securities are sold to commercial banks and even then, the banking system's excess reserves are cut. The monetary base *can* be decreased if a tax surplus is collected and used to retire securities held by the Federal Reserve, and a variety of effects on bank reserves is possible with debt refunding. But the Fed can, whenever it chooses, offset such results with open-market operations. Clearly, despite the wide-ranging capacities of the public and the Treasury to affect the size of the nation's money stock, the ultimate monetary power rests with the Fed.

Summary — Sources and Uses of Bank Reserves and the Monetary Base

In the past few chapters, we have considered a wide range of activities by the public, the commercial banks, the Treasury, and the Federal Reserve itself that affects the nation's money supply. Obviously, it would be convenient if we could consolidate all these into a single neat statement that summarizes all the factors affecting bank reserves and the monetary base. Fortunately such a statement exists, and Table 14-1 reports the data for the averages of daily figures for the week ending March 27, 1991.

Table 14-1, the result of a complex process of consolidation and cancellation of all the items in the balance sheets of the Federal Reserve banks and the Treasury monetary accounts, itemizes all the factors affecting depository institution reserves at the Federal Reserve. On the left side, under the heading "Factors Supplying Reserve Funds," are reported all the items whose increase (decrease) raises (lowers) the size of depository institutions' Federal Reserve accounts. On the right above the double line and entitled "Factors Absorbing Reserve Funds" appear all the items whose increase (decrease) lowers (raises) depository institution reserves. The sum of items 1 through 4 on the left side minus the sum of items 5 through 9 on the right, then, equals depository institution deposits at Federal Reserve banks (item 10).

The appendix to this chapter contains a detailed explanation of the derivation of this table. For those who choose not to become involved in this much detail, a few definitions of the items listed may suffice to bring out its essence.

Federal Reserve credit outstanding reflects the sum of the items that supply

TABLE 14-1 Factors affecting the reserves of depository institutions, week ended March 27, 1991 (millions of dollars)

Factors Supplying Reserve Funds			*Factors Absorbing Reserve Funds*	
1. Federal Reserve credit outstanding		283,727	5. Treasury cash	622
U.S. securities[a]	244,084		6. Treasury deposits at Federal Reserve banks	6,131
Loans	174		7. Other deposits at Federal Reserve banks (except depository institutions)	3,284
Float	270			
Other FRS assets	39,201			
2. Gold stock		11,058	8. Other Federal Reserve liabilities and capital	8.549
3. Special drawing rights certificate account		10,018	9. Currency in circulation	286,030
4. Treasury currency outstanding		20,546		
			10. Depository institution reserve balances with Federal Reserve	20,734

[a] Includes federal agency securities.
Source: Federal Reserve System Release H.4.1.

bank reserves that are under the direct control of the Federal Reserve System. Dominant, of course, if the Fed's portfolio of U.S. securities resulting from open-market purchases.

The *gold stock* constitutes the total gold supply owned by the U.S. Treasury.[7]

The *special drawing rights certificate account* is an asset of the Federal Reserve banks that results from the Treasury "monetizing" special drawing rights received from the International Monetary Fund. From the Fed's point of view, this account has the same source and significance as gold certificates. (Special drawing rights are more fully explained in Chapter 27.)

Treasury currency outstanding includes all the U.S. currency and coins held by the nonbank public, the commercial banks, the Federal Reserve banks, and the Treasury itself, except Federal Reserve notes.

Treasury cash constitutes all currency and coins (including any uncoined silver bullion) held by the Treasury in its own vaults.

Currency in circulation consists of all currency and coins held outside the Treasury and the Federal Reserve banks. It therefore includes Federal Reserve notes and currency and coins issued by the Treasury that are held by the commercial banks and by the nonbank public.

[7] Valued at the "official" gold price of $42.22 per ounce rather than at the free-market price many times higher.

TABLE 14-2   Factors affecting depository institution reserves March 28, 1990, and March 27, 1991 (billions of dollars)

Factors Supplying Reserve Funds	3-28-90		3-27-91		Change	
1. Federal Reserve credit outstanding		268.0		283.7		+15.7
U.S. securities	234.6		244.1		+19.5	
Loans	2.2		0.2		−2.0	
Float	0.2		0.3		+0.1	
Other Federal Reserve assets	41.1		39.2		−1.9	
2. Gold stock		11.1		11.1		0
3. Special drawing rights certificate account		8.5		10.0		+1.5
4. Treasury currency outstanding		19.8		20.5		+0.7
Factors Absorbing Reserve Funds						
5. Treasury cash		0.5		0.6		+0.1
6. Treasury deposits at Federal Reserve banks		5.5		6.1		+0.6
7. Other deposits at Federal Reserve banks (except depository institutions)		2.8		3.3		+0.5
8. Other Federal Reserve liabilities and capital		9.1		8.5		−0.6
9. Currency in circulation		257.0		286.0		+29.0

So much for definitions. How does one read and interpret such a table as that presented in Table 14-1? Let us use the changes from March 28, 1990 to March 27, 1991 as an example with the data as reported in Table 14-2. What does this tell us about the changes over that 12-month period?

Note that the dominant factor supplying additional reserve funds for depository institutions during that year was open-market operations, which provided just under $20 billion of added reserves. With one exception, most of the other factors changed only slightly. That one exception, however, was a whopping $29 billion increase in currency in circulation.

The upshot is that from March 28, 1990 to March 27, 1991, reserve balances held with Federal Reserve banks fell by over $11 billion.

Appendix: Derivation of the "Factors Affecting Depository Institution Reserves" Statement

The "Factors Affecting Depository Institution Reserves" statement is published weekly by the Federal Reserve system as Release H.4.1 and appears monthly in the *Federal Reserve Bulletin*. As noted, it results from a process of consolidation and cancellation of the items in the consolidated balance sheet of all Federal Reserve banks and of a partial balance sheet containing the U.S. Treasury's monetary accounts. Let us trace through the derivation of this very important statement for September 30, 1976.

The consolidated balance sheet for all Federal Reserve banks for September 30, 1976, was as follows:

Consolidated Federal Reserve bank balance sheet, September 30, 1976 (millions of dollars)

Assets		Liabilities and Capital Accounts	
1. Gold certificates	$ 11,598	8. Federal Reserve notes outstanding	$ 79,674
2. SDR certificate account	800	9. Deposits of member banks	26,220
3. Cash	370	10. Deposits of U.S. Treasury	13,296
4. Loans (discounts and advances)	322	11. Deposits of others	1,417
5. U.S. securities[a]	103,507	12. Deferred availability cash items	4,771
6. Cash items in process of collection	7,768	13. Other liabilities	1,205
7. Other assets[b]	4,638	14. Capital accounts	2,420
	$129,003		$129,003

[a] Includes federal agency securities held.
[b] Includes acceptances held.

The Treasury monetary accounts as of the same date were

Treasury monetary accounts, September 30, 1976 (millions of dollars)

15. Gold stock	$11,598	18. Gold certificates	$11,598
16. Treasury currency outstanding	10,742	19. Treasury currency outside Treasury	10,380
17. Federal Reserve notes held in the Treasury	134	20. Treasury cash	496
	$22,474		$22,474

To aid the reader in understanding the following derivation, it may be useful to begin with some definitions.

Treasury currency outstanding (item 16), it will be recalled, includes all paper currency and coins issued by the Treasury that are held by anyone in the economy, including the nonbank public, the member banks, the Federal Reserve banks, and the Treasury itself. (Except for some $300-odd million of U.S. notes, all paper currency issued by the Treasury is currently in process of retirement.) Of the $10,742 million of Treasury currency outstanding, for example, $362 million was held by the Treasury itself (item 16 minus item 19), $370 million was held by the Federal Reserve banks (item 3), and the remaining $10,010 million was held by the member banks and public.

Treasury currency outside the Treasury (item 19) includes, as its title indicates, all Treasury currency outstanding not held by the Treasury. It includes the $10,010 million held by the member banks and public plus the $370 million held by the Federal Reserve banks.

Treasury cash measures the amount of funds the Treasury has at its disposal without writing checks on its Federal Reserve or tax and loan accounts. Thus it was composed of the $362 million of Treasury currency held by the Treasury plus the $134 million of Federal Reserve notes in Treasury vaults.

Deriving the "Factors Affecting Depository Institution Reserves" statement first requires combining the statements of the Federal Reserve banks and of the Treasury monetary accounts. This, of course, can be simply done by listing all the assets from both statements on one side and all the liabilities and capital accounts from both on the other. That is,

a. $(1) + (2) + (3) + (4) + (5) + (6) + (7) + (15) + (16) + (17)$
$\equiv (8) + (9) + (10) + (11) + (12) + (13) + (14) + (18) + (19) + (20)$

Since we are interested in isolating the determinants of reserve accounts at the Fed, it will be useful to rearrange the preceding definitional identity to read

b. $(9) \equiv [(1) + (2) + (3) + (4) + (5) + (6) + (7) + (15) + (16) + (17)] - [(8)$
$+ (10) + (11) + (12) + (13) + (14) + (18) + (19) + (20)]$

From here on the procedure is simply to consolidate the items in the awkward expression (b) so as to reduce them to the minimum number of basic determinants. This involves four operations:

1. Consolidating items 6 and 12 and replacing them with the positive item "float."
2. Consolidating items 3, 8, 17, and 19 and replacing them with the negative item "currency in circulation."
3. Eliminating gold certificates from each side, items 1 and 18.
4. Consolidating items 13 and 14 into "other Federal Reserve liabilities and capital."

Let us run through these four adjustments, one by one. Since Federal Reserve float is the difference between cash items in process of collection and deferred availability cash items, we can easily amend expression (b) by subtracting item 12 from item 6 and entering the positive result as float—a factor supplying reserve funds.

c. $(9) \equiv [(1) + (2) + (3) + (4) + (5) + (7) + (15) + (16) + (17) + \text{F.R. float}] - [(8) + (10) + (11) + (13) + (14) + (18) + (19) + (20)]$

Next we can consolidate four more of our original items into a single entry entitled "currency in circulation" if we add items 8 and 19 and subtract from this the sum of items 3 and 17. What this step gives us is the amount of currency and coins held outside the Treasury and Federal Reserve banks. This, of course, is currency and coins held by the nonbank public and the member banks — a total defined earlier as currency in circulation. With the adjustment, we have

d. $(9) \equiv [(1) + (2) + (4) + (5) + (7) + (16) + \text{F.R. float}] - [(10) + (11) + (13) + (14) + (18) + (20) + \text{Currency in circulation}]$

Next, since items 1 and 18 both represent gold certificates, with oppposite signs, they can be eliminated, producing

e. $(9) \equiv [(2) + (4) + (5) + (7) + (15) + (16) + \text{F.R. float}] - [(10) + (11) + (13) + (14) + (20) + \text{Currency in circulation}]$

Finally, we replace the sum of items 13 and 14 with the single item "other Federal Reserve liabilities and capital" on the negative side and wind up with

f. $(9) \equiv [(2) + (4) + (5) + (7) + (15) + (16) + \text{F.R. float}] - [(10) + (11) + (20) + \text{Other F.R. liabilities and capital accounts} + \text{Currency in circulation}]$

Expression (f) represents the irreducible list of factors affecting member bank reserve accounts, which makes up the statement we set out to derive. When the positive factors on the right side of the identity sign in expression (f) are listed on the reserve-supplying side and the negative factors are listed on the reserve-absorbing side, we have

Factors affecting bank reserves, September 30, 1976 (millions of dollars)

Factors Supplying Reserve Funds		*Factors Absorbing Reserve Funds*	
5. U.S. securities owned by Federal Reserve banks	$103,507	20. Treasury cash	$ 496
4. Loans to member banks by Federal Reserve banks	322	10. Treasury deposits at the Federal Reserve	13,296
7. Other Federal Reserve assets	4,638	11. Other deposits at Federal Reserve banks (except member banks)	1,417
15. Gold stock	11,598		
2. Special drawing rights certificate account	800	Other Federal Reserve liabilities and capital accounts	3,625
16. Treasury currency outstanding	10,742	Currency in circulation	89,549
Federal Reserve float	2,997		

What specifically does the table tell us? Since the sum of the "Factors Supplying Reserve Funds" was $134.6 billion and the sum of the "Factors Absorbing Reserve Funds" was $108.4 billion, it tells us that on September 30, 1976, the value of bank deposits at Federal Reserve banks was $26.2 billion.[8] In addition, it tells us that the monetary base as of September 30, 1976, was $115.7 billion, a figure easily computed by adding the currency in circulation item to member bank deposits at the Fed.

Review Questions

1. What is the fundamental purpose of Treasury tax and loan accounts?

2. When the Treasury sells U.S. securities to finance a deficit and then spends the proceeds, the national debt increases and the money supply may also increase. When the Federal Reserve sells U.S. securities, however, the national debt is unaffected and the money supply normally falls. Carefully explain the difference in these two cases.

3. When the Treasury sells U.S. securities to finance deficit spending, the effects on bank reserves and the money supply will differ depending on to whom the securities are sold. Using appropriately labeled T-accounts, illustrate these differences when the securities are sold to the public, the commercial banks, and the Federal Reserve.

4. If the Congress raises taxes to produce a budget surplus, contrast the monetary effects involved when the surplus is (a) hoarded in tax and loan accounts, (b) hoarded in the Treasury's account at Federal Reserve, (c) used to retire maturing securities held by the nonbank public, (d) used to retire maturing securities held by the commercial banks, (e) used to retire maturing securities held by the Federal Reserve banks.

5. If, as during World War II, we are already at full employment but the Treasury is required to finance large budget deficits, what method of financing the deficits seems most appropriate? Explain carefully.

6. Using appropriately labeled T-accounts for the commercial banks and the Federal Reserve banks, illustrate the effects of the Treasury borrowing $100 million from the nonbank public and then using the proceeds to retire maturing securities held by the Federal Reserve banks. What is the effect of this on the monetary base and the money supply?

---

[8] Total member bank reserves on September 30, 1976, were $34.6 billion, since, in addition to the $26.2 billion of deposits at the Fed, member banks held vault cash (which is a part of the currency in circulation total in the table) totaling some $8.4 billion. It should be recognized that, since these data precede the Monetary Control Act of 1980, the resulting reserve figure is that for member banks only.

7. Suppose you know that during a certain period Federal Reserve float rose by $1 billion. U.S. securities held by the Fed rose by $5 billion, Treasury currency outstanding went up by $1 billion, Treasury deposits at the Fed rose by $3 billion, and currency in circulation went up by $3 billion. What would be the net effect of all this on member bank deposits at the Fed? How about the net effect on the monetary base?

8. Carefully explain why the Treasury is not permitted to finance deficit spending by sale of new U.S. securities to the Federal Reserve System.

9. Using appropriately labeled T-accounts for commercial banks and the Federal Reserve, show the effects of the Treasury collecting a $100 billion tax surplus and using it to retire securities held by the nonbank public. Now explain how this policy measure may cut aggregate expenditures even though the money supply is unchanged.

Early Attempts to Explain the Value of Money — The "Old" Quantity Theory

In this section, we switch our focus from institutional to theoretical matters. Armed with our technical knowledge of what *makes* the money and credit supply change, we must now come to grips with the far more significant question of what *difference* it makes if the money and credit supply *does* change. To be more specific, to what degree and in what circumstances do changes in the money and credit supply affect, for good or ill, our major economic goals of maximum production, full employment, stable prices, and rapid economic growth?

The answer to this question lies squarely within the bailiwick of economic theory, the subject of Chapters 15 through 22. To deal adequately with the effect of changes in the money supply on our economic goals, we will, in the following chapters, be concerned with building up via income determination, monetary, and interest rate theories a "model" of the economy through which we can trace the effect of changes in monetary and other variables.

We begin, in this chapter, by considering two earlier attempts to explain the determinants of the value of money. Ever since certain items became generally acceptable as mediums of exchange, people have been curious about the determinants of their acceptability and purchasing power. If a tailor sells a suit for $200 he is giving up an item with obvious utility in return for what may be a few scraps of paper. Why should he be willing to do this? What determines how many "scraps of paper" he can get for the suit? Why are people willing to accept money for goods and what determines the value of this money (or its reciprocal, the price level)?

The Commodity Theory

One early answer to questions such as these came from the so-called "commodity theorists." In their view, the source of money's acceptability and value was the commodity value of the money substance itself. Money was freely accepted because the commodity of which it was made (or into which paper money was convertible) had significant value in some nonmoney use. Our tailor willingly gives up the suit because he receives in its stead a commodity (gold perhaps?) of equal (or greater, to the tailor) value.

Specifically, the value of money (or its reciprocal, the price level) was said to vary directly with the quantity of the commodity of which it was made (or backed). Hence to the commodity theorist, the more gold there was in or "behind" each dollar, the greater the value of the dollar and the lower the price level.

Now to the modern reader, long since accustomed to nonconvertible paper money, such a theory may sound incredibly naïve. And though it would, indeed, be naïve to apply it in this form to today's world, some defense of the earlier commodity theorists seems in order.

It should be noted that the first monies *were* commodities — commodities that evolved naturally to their money use. There can be little doubt that these commodity monies *were* acceptable in exchange largely because of the nonmoney value of the commodity itself. And it seems reasonable to assume that their purchasing power — the amount of goods and services obtainable for each money unit — *would* tend to vary directly with the quantity of the commodity. Consequently, *many years ago* the commodity theory undoubtedly was a fairly reasonable and at least partly valid hypothesis.

Time and changing customs, however, have a sneaky way of playing tricks on long-established truths. A combination of government issue, the legal tender power, and, most important of all, a growing willingness among the public to accept certain tokens at an exchange value far exceeding their commodity value, has long since cut the ground out from under the commodity theory. It is certainly no longer true, and has not been so for many years, that the acceptability or value of money is determined by the commodity of which it is made (or backed).

But the idea died hard and, indeed, in the general public's mind is probably not completely dead yet. How often does one hear, even today, statements that imply that the value of the American dollar is somehow directly and fundamentally derived from the gold held in Fort Knox?

These myths from the past appear to possess remarkable staying power, the facts notwithstanding. Even though the U.S. Treasury has refused to exchange gold for dollars held by Americans since 1933, the idea that the Treasury's gold hoard "gives the dollar value" has persisted. Let us be done with this fiction. The dollar today is a fiat currency, the acceptability and value of which depends in no way on a commodity backing, gold or otherwise. The value of the dollar depends on a far more substantial foundation than that relatively insignificant stock of glittering yellow metal stored in Fort Knox.

The Basis of Money's Acceptability

But all this is simply negative. If people do not accept money because of the commodity value of the substance of which it is made, why do they accept it? Why should people be willing to give up goods and services of obvious utility and value in return for mere "scraps of paper"? The answer seems obvious. These "scraps of paper," if they function as an effective money, must also have utility.[1]

The seller of goods is a demander of money. If Mr. Jones is willing to part with x bushels of wheat for $100, he is not only supplying x bushels of wheat; he is also demanding $100 of money, which he is willing to hold for some period of time. Hence we can reasonably speak of a demand for money that, as in the ordinary theory of demand, is based on utility.

What utility does the possession of money provide? First, and most distinctive, money acts as a *medium of exchange.* Mr. Jones will accept $100 for his wheat because he knows that the $100 is generally acceptable to other sellers who have goods and services he wants to purchase. Possession of the $100 permits him to obtain what he wants when he wants it without all the inconvenience of barter.

But that isn't all. Money also serves reasonably well, along with a number of other items, as a *store of value.* Mr. Jones may not, at the moment, desire to purchase any goods and services. He may prefer to bide his time, retaining *command* over goods, without any immediate commitment to one or another. In this case, he may choose to hold on to the money rather than some other form of wealth.[2]

The "Old" Quantity Theory

Although the commodity theory explanation of the value of money long seemed to have strong appeal for the general public, it never attracted substantial support from economists. For many years, the majority of economists espoused a quantitative rather than a qualitative explanation of the value of money. This took the form of the time-honored **quantity theory of money.**

As does the commodity theory, the quantity theory traces its origin back many years. Unlike the commodity theory, however, the quantity theory has been able to adapt itself over the years. As cruder versions have been challenged and discredited, newer, more sophisticated hypotheses have been developed to replace the old. If long survival under constant attack can be taken as a measure of the strength of an idea, the quantity theory must be awarded an honored position in economic thought. For, albeit in a form much altered from that of its origin, the quantity theory continues today to be a lively source of debate among monetary theorists.

As its name implies, the quantity theory, in all its versions, looks to the quantity of money as the main causal determinant of changes in the price level. If the theory is valid, its implications for monetary policy are indeed enormous. For, as we have seen, the quantity of money is subject, given sufficient skill by the monetary authorities and a stable institutional environment, to reasonably pre-

---

[1] Of course, to function as an effective money, the legal tender power helps, custom helps, and limitation of supply is absolutely essential.

[2] As we shall see, holding wealth in money form has certain advantages over holding it in other forms. It also has its disadvantages.

cise control. If the price level should be responsive in a predictable degree to the supply of money, knowledge of the relationship would obviously be invaluable to policymakers.

Of course, none of the versions of this theory has been so naïve as simply to posit the proposition that, without some logical behavioral process, prices automatically follow the money supply, willy-nilly. Developed by brilliant theorists, all quantity theories worthy of the name have attempted to explain the process — the causal sequence — whereby a larger money supply leads to higher prices.

But theorizing about relationships in a complex economy requires order and simplification to avoid a hodgepodge of confusing detail. It requires, among other things, a simplified framework of the economy within which the important variables stand out as clearly as do superhighways on a large-scale road map. In a phrase, what is needed is a way of looking at the economy that will screen out the unnecessary detail and provide the foundation for the construction of a cause and effect theory.

Each version of the quantity theory has relied upon a variant of either the *equation of exchange* or the *cash balance equation* as its way of looking at some of the important variables in the economy. As these equations are the frameworks upon which the quantity theory is built, we shall consider them in the next section before discussing the theory itself.

The Equation of Exchange

The *equation of exchange* is simply a complicated way of stating an obvious truth. Starting from the unassailable proposition that for every dollar spent by a buyer, a dollar is received by a seller, we can proceed without difficulty to the equally obvious statement that, for any given group (assuming, of course, no transactions outside the group) during any given time period, the dollar value of all newly produced goods and services purchased equals the dollar value of all newly produced goods and services sold.

Although it may seem absurd to stress such an obvious identity as "amount bought equals amount sold," that is really all the equation of exchange says. The equation itself is

$$MV \equiv PQ$$

where

M = the average supply of money during the period

V = the number of times per period (i.e., the rate at which) the average dollar is spent to purchase newly produced goods and services (for short, V can be called the *actual velocity*)

P = the average price of all newly produced goods and services sold during the period

Q = (quantity) the number of physical units of newly produced goods and services sold during the period

So what does this fancy equation really say? The left side, MV, clearly equals the dollar amount spent on newly produced goods and services during the period, whereas the right side, PQ, just as clearly equals the dollar amount received for selling them. Because the equation is a truism — true, by definition, under any and all conditions — we have used an identity sign ($\equiv$) rather than a simple equals sign.

But, the reader may be thinking, of what use is it to dress up an obvious identity in this form when everyone already grants that the amount bought equals the amount sold? The answer to this question is very simple. When we break total expenditures down into the two components M and V, we have spotlighted two variables — the money supply and the rate of spending it — that do fluctuate and that do affect the level of expenditures. And when we break down the other side (which obviously is equal to GNP) into a P and a Q component, we are separating out two variables — the price level and the level of physical output — that have obvious implications for economic welfare.

Nevertheless, it is a fact that the identity MV $\equiv$ PQ is, as such, merely a sterile framework. It is not a theory. It does not say that MV *causes* PQ, nor does it imply the reverse causation. The quantity theory, as we shall see, *is* a cause and effect theory that uses the equation of exchange as a framework. But the equation itself says no more than that the amount bought equals the amount sold.[3]

The Cash Balance Equation

While most earlier American economists were looking at things in terms of the equation of exchange, their counterparts in England, especially at Cambridge University, were coming to essentially similar conclusions by the use of a slightly different equation. This has come to be called the cash balance equation (sometimes referred to as the "Cambridge equation").

The cash balance equation is

$$M \equiv kPQ$$

where M, P, and Q are defined exactly as in the equation of exchange and k is *the period of time (expressed as a fraction of time period) people hold on to the average dollar before spending it to purchase newly produced goods and services.*

Obviously the only difference between the cash balance equation and the equation of exchange is the use of k instead of V. Let us look at the relationship between these two variables. Algebraically, the relationship is a simple one. Since MV $\equiv$ PQ, V $\equiv$ PQ/M, and since M $\equiv$ kPQ, k $\equiv$ M/PQ. Clearly, V and k are simply reciprocals of one another.

But arithmetic aside, what is the *logic* of the relation between the two? Suppose, for example, that the time period is one year and V is 4. This means, of course, that the average dollar is spent four times per year on new goods and services, or every three months. That in turn means that the average dollar is *held*

---

[3] Another version of the equation of exchange is the so-called transactions version wherein all transactions are considered rather than just spending on newly produced goods and services. In this case, the equation is usually written as MV $\equiv$ PT, and V, P, and T are defined in terms of all transactions rather than restricted to expenditures on GNP.

for three months before it is spent. And if it is held for three months, it is held for one quarter of the time period. Clearly, k therefore equals one fourth.

The equation of exchange, as we have seen, is an identity that merely expresses the fact that the amount spent on new goods and services equals the amount received from selling them. Is there a similar commonsense explanation of the identity expressed by the cash balance equation?

Indeed there is. The left side, M, of course, equals the average supply of money in existence during the period. But what about the right side, kPQ? Although it may not be intuitively obvious, this expression measures the amount of money people actually held (willingly or unwillingly) during the period. So the equation itself simply states the obvious truism that the amount of money in existence during the period was equal to the amount people and institutions actually held.

Equilibrium Conditions
versus Definitional Identities

As definitional identities, neither the cash balance nor the equation-of-exchange approach adds much of significance to our understanding of the working of the economy. As long as V and k are defined in terms of what people *do* with money rather than with what people *desire* to do with it, the equations are sterile truisms offering, in and of themselves, no insight into the forces that lead to economic change. Unless we know whether or not people are actually spending money at the rate they desire to (or actually holding the size of money balances they wish to), we cannot say whether we have an equilibrium situation that will tend to be maintained or a disequilibrium situation that portends change.

Consider, for example, an analogous case familiar to all students of introductory economics — the case of the market for a single good. Suppose the demand for and supply of Product X are as follows:

Market for Product X

Quantity demanded	Price	Quantity supplied
10	$5	50
20	4	40
30	3	30
40	2	20
50	1	10

If the market price is at $3, we say we have equilibrium because the quantity demanded equals the quantity supplied. Or, alternatively, $3 is the equilibrium price because at that price what people *desire to do*, they *do do*. The quantity that buyers *want* to buy is 30 units, and they do so. The quantity that sellers *want* to sell is 30 units, and they do so. Since neither buyers nor sellers are forced to do something they do not want to do, there is no force (in the form of frustrated buyers or sellers) tending to cause a change. This is the essence of equilibrium.

But what is the situation if the market price is, say, $4? At that price the amount sellers *desire* to sell is 40 units, but the amount they actually do sell is only 20, since that is all buyers will take at $4. At $4, then, even though the quantity *actually sold* equals the quantity *actually bought* (as, of course, it always must by definition), the quantity that sellers *desire to sell* exceeds the quantity that buyers *desire to buy.* We have, therefore, a disequilibrium situation in which sellers — barred from doing what they want to do at the market price — will take action that will tend to change the price.

In the case of the market for a single good, to say that the quantity bought equals the quantity sold is to state a *definitional identity* that holds at any price, equilibrium or not. To say that the quantity demanded equals the quantity supplied, however, is to state an *equilibrium condition* — one that holds only at the equilibrium price where buyers and sellers can do what they desire to do.

Now all of this is perfectly analogous to the equations just introduced. If MV equals PQ (or M equals kPQ), all we know is that the amount spent equals the amount received (or that the supply of money in existence was held by someone). But that situation holds for *any* values of the variables in the equations. What it does not tell us is whether this is an equilibrium situation that can be expected to continue or a disequilibrium one in which spenders (or money holders) are being frustrated. If one of disequilibrium, dissatisfied spenders (or money holders) will take action (just as dissatisfied sellers did in the Product X case at the $4 price), which will tend to change the values of some of the variables (just as the price fell in the Product X case).

How can we change our equations so as to put them in the form of *equilibrium conditions* rather than mere *definitional identities?* What we need is a behavioral variable couched in terms of what people *desire* to do rather than what they *actually* do. *Equilibrium* can then be defined as a situation in which people are actually doing what they desire to do, so that there is no dissatisfaction causing changes.

To put our equations in the form of equilibrium conditions, what we need is to redefine V in terms of the rate people *desire* to spend on new goods and services and to redefine k in terms of the fraction of the time period people *desire* to hold the average dollar before spending it. This is done now with a prime added to distinguish desired V and k from actual. That is,

V′ = (desired velocity) the number of times per period people *desire* to spend the average dollar on newly produced goods and services

k′ = the fraction of the time period people *desire* to hold the average dollar before spending it on newly produced goods and services

Using these new definitions for V′ and k′, we now have two new equations, each of which is an equilibrium condition rather than a mere definitional identity. What does MV′ = PQ say? It says that "equilibrium will be reached when *desired* spending on newly produced goods and services equals the amount produced." Note that this is nothing more than a restatement of the old, familiar equilibrium production condition — total desired spending equals production.[4]

---

[4] For future reference, let us establish one more point about the left-hand side of the equation of exchange, if V′ is defined as desired velocity:

And what about the cash balance equation presented in the form of an equilibrium condition? What does $M = k'PQ$ say? Now that k' has been defined in terms of money holders' *desires*, the right side of this equation can quite properly be labeled the *demand for money*. So the equation $M = k'PQ$ says that "in equilibrium the supply of money (M) equals the demand for money (k'PQ)."

Let us illustrate what we have via an arithmetical example, using the cash balance form of equation. Suppose that initially $M = \$200$, $k' = \frac{1}{5}$, $P = \$2.50$, and $Q = 400$. Under these conditions, we are at equilibrium because

$$M = k'PQ$$

which means → the supply of money equals the demand for money which requires also that → actual k equals desired k'.

Now suppose the Federal Reserve authorities make use of their monetary policy weapons to increase the supply of money to $240. Immediately after such action we have a disequilibrium situation wherein

$$M > k'PQ$$

which means → the supply of money exceeds the demand for money which requires that → actual k > desired k'.

Now, how can people respond to a disequilibrium situation in which the supply of money they *must* hold (and cannot, in the aggregate, change) exceeds the quantity they *desire* to hold under current circumstances? They will respond, of course, by attempting to unload the unwanted, excess money balances. This, of course, does not imply that they will act irrationally by throwing unwanted money balances away. Rather, they will "unload" them by spending them to buy products or securities.

The reader should note, however, that while such spending gets rid of the unwanted money balances of the spender, it in no way reduces the money supply the community as a whole holds. This is so, of course, because any money spent by Mrs. A is necessarily acquired by Mr. B (the seller of the goods or securities).

Despite this, as we shall see, these efforts to unload unwanted money balances *will* lead to changes in the economy that ultimately must move it toward a new, different equilibrium position.

$$MV' = \frac{\text{Total intended expenditures on newly}}{\text{produced goods and services}} = C + I + G$$

Total intended or desired spending on new goods and services can be broken down in two different ways. In the equation of exchange, it is broken down in a way that spotlights the money supply and the rate at which it is spent. Another method of breaking down the same total is by spending groups — consumption spending, investment spending, and government spending on goods and services. Although we shall not make much of this relationship now, the student should bear it in mind when we come to the next chapter and the Keynesian theory of income determination. As we shall see, the basic difference between those who choose to use the equation of exchange and those who adhere to the theory to be discussed in Chapters 16 through 19 is that while the former find it more useful to emphasize the money supply — velocity breakdown of total expenditures — the latter group considers a breakdown by spending groups more fruitful. We return to this comparison later. Let it simply be observed at this point that both approaches are useful; neither is wrong.

The Advantages of the Cash Balance Equation

It should be clear by now that there is no fundamental difference between the equation of exchange and the cash balance equation approaches. V and k are simply the reciprocals of one another. It is, as one distinguished authority once put it, merely the difference between "money resting" and "money on the wing."

Yet despite their formal similarity, the cash balance approach seems to have been the forerunner of many more pathbreaking ideas in monetary economics than its alter ego, the equation of exchange. The reasons for this are not altogether clear, but in retrospect it seems apparent that the cash balance way of looking at the economy led to the asking of more fruitful questions.

The velocity concept has always seemed somewhat mechanistic. It was rather difficult to conceive of people spending their money at a rate other than that desired. On the other hand, it was much easier to imagine people having cash balances larger or smaller than desired. Similarly, although the reasons for changes in desired velocity proved difficult to come up with, it was just a bit easier to conceptualize changes in desired cash balances.

Perhaps the most important difference between the two is that the cash balance equation is conveniently arranged in supply and demand terms, which provided a better mesh with general economic theory. For the left-hand side, M is the supply of money while the right, k'PQ, is just as surely the demand for money. This format led theorists of the cash balance orientation to focus on the question, "What determines the demand for money?" It has turned out to be a most useful approach.

The Essence of the "Old" Quantity Theory

Whatever the relative merits of the different equations, one point should be clearly understood. Neither of them is a theory. Neither of them, in and of itself, sheds any light on cause and effect in the economy. They do provide a useful means of organizing some of the economy's key variables, but it remains for the theoretician to provide hypotheses regarding the nature of cause and effect relationships between the variables. To say that MV *equals* PQ is merely to present an obvious truism. No theory is involved. To say, however, that MV' *causes* PQ is to promulgate a theoretical hypothesis arguing that M and/or V' are active variables and that P and/or Q are passive ones; that although a change in MV' can cause a change in PQ, no change in PQ can come about without alterations in MV' being the causal force.

All versions of the quantity theory have argued that M is a key causal variable and that P (or PQ) is a passive one that results from the level of M. All have also looked upon V' (or k') as being, if not absolutely fixed, at least reasonably stable and/or predictable. Over the years, however, the several versions of the quantity theory have differed notably in detail and degree of sophistication. In this chapter, we shall deal only with the older (pre-1930s) versions of the quantity theory. The "modern" quantity theory associated most prominently with the name of

Professor Milton Friedman and the monetarist school will be discussed in a later chapter.

The Key Assumptions for the "Old" Quantity Theory   The usefulness and relevance of a theory depend upon the simplifying assumptions underlying it as well as upon the internal logic of the reasoning involved. In the case of the older versions of the quantity theory, the underlying assumptions are absolutely crucial to the argument, and we must look at them carefully.

In the first place, in complete accord with other elements of classical employment theory, it was assumed that a free enterprise economy contains within it a mechanism that will reasonably promptly restore those conditions necessary for full employment when any tendency toward a deficiency of demand arises. Full employment was considered the norm. This was the result of their faith in "Say's Law."

Temporary divergences from the full-employment state were admissable, of course, but these were looked upon as so readily correctable that major periods of long-run mass unemployment need not be a source of concern.

The important significance of the full-employment assumption for our purposes is its effect on the level of production. If we can count on reasonably full employment most of the time, the main reason for short-run, drastic changes in output (Q in the equation of exchange) is removed. Over time, of course, output will grow as the labor force, capital equipment, and technology grow, but these factors take effect slowly and rather steadily over longer time periods. Output may grow at 3 to 4 percent per year, but this kind of change is both steady and predictable. The likelihood of shorter-run drastic changes in Q, such as the 25 percent reduction that occurred during the Great Depression of the 1930s, was ruled out by assumption. Hence it was argued that Q, although not absolutely fixed, would change very little, and predictably from year to year.

Second, the quantity theory rested on some key assumptions regarding the nature and determinants of V' (or k'). It too was considered to be a constant, or nearly so. The logic behind this assumption merits rather careful consideration.

Let us first look at it from the cash balance approach:

$$M = k'PQ$$

Because the right side of this equation denotes the demand for money, the cash balance theorists focused on the question, "Why should rational people demand money? They can't eat it. It pays them no interest return. What rational reasons are there for people willingly accepting and holding money?"

One answer was easy to come up with. People are willing to accept and hold money because it facilitates exchange. Barter, the exchange of goods for goods, is unwieldy and difficult. It is much simpler to accept income in the form of a medium of exchange and then spend it gradually throughout the pay period to acquire the goods and services one desires.

People, in other words, willingly hold some money to finance transactions (consumer expenditures) that they need to make between paydays. There is, to put it in the terminology of one famed Cambridge economist, a *transactions* demand for money.

Now what determines the size of this transactions demand for money? Pretty clearly, the level of income itself. If the only reason for willingly holding money is to finance consumer expenditures between paydays, the level of consumer expenditures dictates the amount of money that will be held. And the level of income pretty well determines the amount of consumer expenditures.

People, then, do willingly hold money, but only to bridge the gap between paydays. What they hold, they intend to spend before the following paycheck gives them a new supply. If Mrs. Jones receives $2,000 on the first of each month, she holds that money only to finance expenditures during the month so that by the end of the month she has no money left. Indeed, if the only reason for holding money at all is to finance expenditures, it would be irrational not to spend it all before the next check comes in. Holding money *during* the month makes sense because it is needed to facilitate transactions, but holding it longer than that is irrational.

Now all this may bother the alert reader. Suppose that Mrs. Jones wants to spend only $1,600 of her $2,000 paycheck on consumer goods and save the extra $400. Isn't it possible that she may choose to keep the $400 saved in money form? Isn't it conceivable, in other words, that money may be demanded as an asset — as one way in which wealth may be held over time? If so, there would be *two* sources of demand for money. Some would be held to facilitate transactions during the pay period, and an additional amount could be kept, perhaps over a number of pay periods, as a means of storing wealth along with stocks, bonds, and other assets.

Although some earlier economists did recognize the possibility of an asset demand for money, the strict early quantity theorists considered this irrational behavior. If a person is accumulating wealth, they reasoned, and has a choice between holding it in the form of securities on which interest is earned and holding it in the form of money, which pays no interest, he or she would be foolish to choose money. Holding money as a store of wealth seemed irrational, as doing so meant forgoing the income that could be earned by purchasing securities.

The result was that to these quantity theorists *the only rational demand for money was a transactions demand.* People will accept and hold only as much money as they need to facilitate upcoming expenditures.

The implications of all this for V' (or k') were profound, for it led the quantity theorists to look upon V' as pretty much of a constant also, changing little in the short run.

If people hold money only to finance expenditures, what can cause changes in the quantity demanded? Except over the long run, only changes in the level of income itself. It was recognized that changes in the financial structure, in the efficiency of check collection, and in payment habits *could* alter the amount of money needed to finance transactions of a given size, but these things change only slowly over long periods and in a shorter-run context could be properly ignored. The demand for money, then, was thought to be a constant fraction (k') of the level of income (PQ). If it takes $100 of money balances to finance the purchase of $300 of goods and services, it will take $200 of money to finance a $600 income. (k' is a constant fraction, one-third.)

Let us now sum up this section. The key assumptions of the older quantity theory were

1. *The level of income (and, hence, Q in the equation) was considered essentially a constant in the short run.*

2. *Desired velocity, V' (and its reciprocal k') was considered essentially a constant in the short run.*

Following directly from the two assumptions just discussed, the quantity theory argues that

---

The price level is determined by the money supply. Changes in the money supply cause equal proportionate changes in the price level in the same direction.

The Approach to a New Equilibrium Under a Crude Version of the "Old" Quantity Theory   Let us return to a numerical example to illustrate the process through which the quantity theory conclusion might be reached. Assume, as before, that we start from an equilibrium position in which $M = \$200$, $k' = \frac{1}{5}$, $P = \$2.50$, and $Q = 400$. Now suppose that the Fed upsets this equilibrium by increasing the money supply to $240. That is,

Initial equilibrium situation	Situation immediately after money supply increase
$M = \$200$	$M = \$240$
$k' = \frac{1}{5}$	$k' = \frac{1}{5}$
$P = \$2.50$	$P = \$2.50$
$Q = 400$	$Q = 400$

Immediately after the Federal Reserve increases the money supply, the demand for money is $200 ($\frac{1}{5} \cdot \$2.50 \cdot 400$) and the supply is $240. People, therefore, are currently holding $40 more in money balances than they desire to hold under these conditions. What can they do about this unsatisfactory situation?

Individuals can, of course, attempt to correct it by unloading some of their excess money balances by, for one example, spending them on consumer goods. If they should do this, note again that the entire community's money supply does not change, since the excess balances have merely been transferred to the seller of the consumer goods. And if the quantity theorists' assumptions about the stability of Q and k' hold, they do not change either.

What does? The price level, of course. If the initial disequilibrium *does* generate a rise in consumption spending (as the way of unloading excess money balances), the result must be a rise in aggregate demand. And if, in accordance with the quantity theorists' assumption, we are already at full employment so that Q cannot rise in response, P must rise.

By how much must the price level rise? It must continue rising so long as the disequilibrium situation created by excess money balances remains. But note that the rise in prices itself will ultimately wipe out the disequilibrium. As prices rise, the money value of income (PQ) rises. Since more money is needed to finance a higher dollar value of transactions, eventually the rise in prices transforms the new money into *desired* money balances. This will be the case when P has risen to $3, at which point

---

New equilibrium

M = $240
k' = $\frac{1}{5}$ i.e., M = k'PQ
P = $3.00 $240 = $\frac{1}{5}$ × $3 × 400
Q = 400

At this point the quantity theory has worked itself out. **A 20 percent rise in the supply of money has led to a 20 percent rise in the price level,** just as the theory says.

A More Realistic Explanation of the "Old" Quantity Theory Process   Even if one should grant the key quantity theory assumptions of stable V' and Q, the preceding explanation is excessively oversimplified. It does not necessarily follow that a public that holds excess money balances will choose to spend the excess on added consumer goods.

People generally increase their purchases of consumer goods only when an increase in their income or wealth permits it and excess money balances are *not* the same as excess wealth or income. The money supply, for example, may have been increased through a Federal Reserve System open-market purchase that does not directly and immediately change the amount of the public's wealth or income. Is there a more realistic means of tracing through the process of the quantity theory working itself out?

Of course there is. People with excess money balances may choose to buy existing securities rather than consumer goods. But this does not change the quantity theory conclusion in any way. The increased demand for securities will raise security prices, and this, in turn, lowers interest rates.[5] Lower interest rates will permit an increase in spending on those goods most dependent on borrowed money, especially capital goods.

So we are back where we were before. The rise in the money supply ultimately causes a rise in the demand for goods and services, which, in turn, raises prices. And once again, a new equilibrium will only be reached when prices have risen by the same percentage as did the money supply.

The Validity and Importance of the "Old" Quantity Theory

How valid is the "old" quantity theory as an explanation of actual price-level movements in the United States? Although over time the money supply and prices have tended to move generally in the same direction, the relationship is far from the close one the theory would imply.

---

[5] The inverse relationship between bond prices and interest rates will be examined in Chapter 18.

TABLE 15-1 Income velocity since World War II[a]

Year	V	Year	V
1947	2.04	1969	4.58
1948	2.30	1970	4.58
1949	2.31	1971	4.66
1950	2.46	1972	4.70
1951	2.67	1973	4.98
1952	2.73	1974	5.16
1953	2.83	1975	5.31
1954	2.77	1976	5.52
1955	2.94	1977	5.70
1956	3.06	1978	5.92
1957	3.24	1979	6.18
1958	3.17	1980	6.32
1959	3.46	1981	6.61
1960	3.56	1982	6.49
1961	3.58	1983	6.32
1962	3.78	1984	6.60
1963	3.85	1985	6.25
1964	3.94	1986	5.76
1965	4.08	1987	6.02
1966	4.35	1988	6.19
1967	4.32	1989	6.54
1968	4.37		

[a] Figures prior to 1959 are computed from a slightly different definition of money.

First, contrary to the key assumption of a relatively stable Q over time, we observe that real GNP (the closest approximation of Q available) has tended to vary markedly in both the short and the long run, especially during the Great Depression of the 1930s and during a number of post–World War II recessions.

Second, the assumption of a relatively stable desired velocity (or k′) seems also to be at variance with the facts, especially if the money measure employed is the narrowly defined M1 variant. As Table 15-1 clearly reveals, V not only has risen dramatically since World War II, but it has tended to level off or fall during most post–World War II recessions. Such behavior hardly supports the contention that M alone causes P![6] In addition, in the 1980s it was especially erratic.

All in all, although there is a very rough similarity between money supply and price-level movements over time, the "fit," as illustrated in Figure 15-1, is sufficiently imprecise as to invalidate the "old" quantity theory.

Finally, it should be made clear that even a much closer correlation between the money supply and the price level than has actually existed would not prove the quantity theory. For the quantity theory not only says that money and prices will move together but also says that the money supply is the *causal* factor. A quantity theorist of the vintage discussed in this chapter must show not only that

[6] It should be noted, however, that if the M2 money definition is used, the resulting velocity figure is far more stable, at least during the last two decades.

Source: Robert L. Hetzel, ''A Primer on the Importance of the Money Supply,'' *Economic Review,* Federal Reserve Bank of Richmond, September–October 1977.

FIGURE 15-1   M1 and prices, 1956–1978

the price level rises by 20 percent when the money supply goes up 20 percent but also that the latter *causes* the former. If it could be shown that a rise in the price level makes necessary and therefore calls forth equivalent increases in the stock of money, the quantity theory is in trouble.

Few, if any, economists today subscribe to the quantity theory as discussed in this chapter. Yet, as noted earlier, the quantity theory has displayed remarkable resilience. Just as many were prepared to retire it permanently to a place in history, a new version, in very much altered form, has arisen to challenge economists and policymakers.

The ''modern'' quantity theory, originally fostered primarily by a highly respected group of economists at the University of Chicago, has become a center of controversy in the past three decades. In a sense, it and its policy conclusions are a reaction to the new orthodoxy that came along with the Keynesian ''revolution,'' just as Keynes's momentous contributions represented an attack on the classical theory of which the ''old'' quantity theory was a part.

In deference to the actual chronological development of these ideas, we shall not go into the modern quantity theory at this point. Instead, let us turn now to the Keynesian revolution, returning later, in Chapter 21, to consider the rebirth of the quantity theory philosophy.

Review Questions

1. ''To say that $MV \equiv PQ$ is simply to state an obvious truism; to say that $MV' = PQ$, however, is to state an equilibrium condition.'' Explain carefully.

2. Contrast the equation of exchange and the cash balance equation when

each is stated in the form of an equilibrium condition. In this form, what does each equation say?

3. Carefully explain the logic of (as distinct from the algebra of) the relation between V and k.

4. Identify and explain the two key assumptions underlying the conclusions reached by the "old" quantity theorists.

5. What is the basic conclusion of the "old" quantity theory?

6. "If M = $200, k' = $\frac{1}{5}$, P = $2.00, Q = 400, and we know that 400 is the full-employment level of production, we must expect inflation to result." Explain carefully.

7. If M = $500, k' = $\frac{1}{4}$, P = $2.00, and Q = 1,000, how would you characterize the situation of the economy? Now if the Fed should carry out open-market purchases that increase M to $600, what is the situation immediately after the money supply has been increased? Explain, using quantity theory assumptions, what people are likely to do about this disequilibrium situation that will ultimately produce a new equilibrium. What will be the sizes of the four variables in the new equilibrium situation?

The Simplified Theory of Income Determination

Introduction: The Classical Backdrop and Its Overthrow

Besides the quantity theory, classical economic theory (pre-1935) contained a body of reasoning that led many of its earlier followers to believe that there existed, within a free enterprise economy, a mechanism that would swiftly, surely, and automatically restore full employment whenever the ugly specter of involuntary unemployment reared its head. Hence the long-cherished philosophy of *laissez-faire*—let the economy alone.

The Classical Theory

The main mechanism involved was thought to be the rate of interest. Briefly, and in highly oversimplified form, the classical argument ran this way:

1. The very process of producing any given value of goods leads to an equivalent amount of income being earned by *someone* for producing them. (If $500 billion worth of goods are produced, $500 billion of income is earned for producing them.)

2. Ignoring government and foreign trade, the recipients of this income must dispose of it either by spending it to buy consumer goods or by not spending it on consumer goods. If we define *saving* as income received but not spent on consumer goods, all income is either consumed or saved. (Suppose, of the $500 billion income, that $400 billion is spent on consumption and $100 billion is saved.)

3. What is needed to keep the following period's production at the same high $500 billion level is for everything produced this period to be sold. Demand, therefore, must total $500 billion.

4. In addition to the $400 billion of consumer expenditures, the other element of demand that is needed to ensure that there is the $500 billion of total spending required to purchase all $500 billion of goods produced is *investment spending*, that is, spending by business to purchase newly produced capital goods. In our example, $100 billion of investment spending along with the $400 billion of consumer spending would be required to produce the needed $500 billion of demand. Note that as long as spending by investors just equals the saving ("not spending" by consumers), we can be sure that there is sufficient total spending to purchase everything produced.

5. What is needed then is something that will cause investment spending to be as large as saving. The required mechanism is the rate of interest.

   a. The rate of interest is determined where the quantity of funds supplied by savers equals the quantity of funds demanded by investors.
   b. Because people only save money (refrain from consumption) in order to receive the reward of interest (hoarding is irrational), the higher the interest rate, the larger the quantity that will be saved. (The savings *schedule* will be positively sloped with respect to the rate of interest.)
   c. Because interest is one of the costs that a business must incur to invest, the quantity invested will be larger, the lower the rate of interest. (As shown in Figure 16-1, the investment schedule will be negatively sloped with respect to the rate of interest.)

6. With this setup (and assuming that the interest rate is a flexible price), a deficiency of demand to buy what has been produced cannot exist for long. For, if saving *should* exceed investment, the rate of interest will be bid down, and this

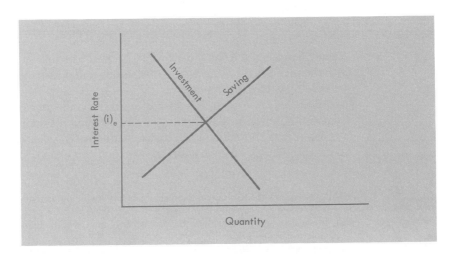

FIGURE 16-1 Classical interest rate determination

movement in the interest rate will at one and the same time expand the quantity invested and lower the quantity saved until the two come together.

Consequently, movements in the rate of interest will keep investment equal to saving, which, in turn, guarantees that everything produced is bought, so that producers need not lay off workers because of unsold inventories from this period's production.[1]

Keynes and His Attack on the Classicals

It was a rosy picture. But it turned out to be a misleading theory, because it did not really fit the facts. It did not accord with our experience in the real world. Through the many years during which the classical theory dominated thinking, there were challengers, some of them very important. But the final overthrow of the heart of the structure, at least in England and the United States, awaited the Great Depression of the 1930s and the publication of J. M. Keynes's *General Theory of Employment, Interest and Money* in 1936.

It did not take an economist to recognize, in the early 1930s, that something *must* be wrong with a theory that argues that full employment is the norm and unemployment simply a temporary interruption that will soon be automatically eliminated by movements in the interest rate. When upwards of one-fourth of the labor force is pounding the pavements seeking nonexistent jobs, the man on the street, being unencumbered with the niceties of theory, saw clearly that something pretty fundamental was wrong. So, too, did the already famous British economist, John Maynard Keynes.

After a long struggle to break out of the well-worn track of classical reasoning, Keynes consolidated his new ideas into his now renowned *General Theory*. In it he confessed that his work was the result of "a struggle of escape from habitual thoughts and modes of expression. . . . The difficulty lies, not in the new ideas, but in escaping from the old ones, which ramify, for those brought up as most of us have been, into every corner of our minds."[2]

Keynes leaves no doubt about the purpose of his study. It is, on the one hand, to expose the fallacies of the classical theory and, on the other, to construct a new framework, a new theory, to replace it. No fence straddler, he boldly states in his first chapter that the classical analysis is valid only in very special circumstances "which happen not to be those of the economic society in which we actually live, with the result that its teaching is misleading and disastrous if we attempt to apply it to the facts of experience."[3]

With this statement as a springboard, Keynes goes on to point out specific fallacies in the classical reasoning and to develop his own framework of analysis. It is essentially this framework that we call here the *theory of income determination* and to which we turn shortly.

---

[1] This description of the classical ideas is admittedly highly oversimplified and should not, by any means, be taken as a complete description. It is included here for pedagogical, rather than analytical, reasons, and it omits much of the classical argument, not the least of which is the assumption of flexible wages and prices.

[2] J. M. Keynes, *General Theory of Employment, Interest and Money* (London: Macmillan, 1936), p. viii.

[3] Ibid., p. 3.

Before doing so, it should be pointed out that the theory that will be developed in chapters 16 through 19 should not be taken to be an exact reproduction of Keynes's *General Theory*. His famous volume is now nearly 60 years old and has had to weather the storm of controversy its author expected. As is true of all new ideas, substantial portions of what Keynes said have been deleted, and many things he did not foresee have been added. What we will be exploring, then, is not *Keynes's theory* but what has now come to be accepted as an important, integral part of economic theory. We are concerned, not in evaluating Keynes, but in making use of his major contributions to our discipline.

Let us now turn from the background and the developers of the theory of income determination to the theory itself.

The General Approach

The *theory of income determination* is just what its name implies — an attempt to say something about how the level of income and production gets determined in a modern capitalistic economy. But its implications run deeper. If we can develop a theory that tells us how the level of production is determined, and what can make it change, we shall be in a position to go further and say something about what determines the level of employment, prices, and the like. Our goal, then, is to develop a theoretical framework that will permit us to discuss, in an organized fashion, the factors that affect our ability to achieve the generally accepted economic goals of full production, full employment, and stable prices.

We start off with the rather commonsense view that, because in a free enterprise economy, producers can only be expected to produce that which they can sell, the level of intended expenditures on newly produced goods and services is the main direct determinant of the level of production.[4]

Now, as pointed out earlier, there are two alternative ways of looking at total intended expenditures on newly produced goods and services, or *aggregate expenditures* as we shall refer to it. One could take the equation of exchange approach and break aggregate expenditures down into the components of M and V'. Or, if it appears to provide a better insight into the causation involved, the alternative of subdividing aggregate expenditures by spending group can be adopted. The Keynesian theory of income determination is built around the latter alternative.

Simplifying Assumptions

To keep our analysis within manageable proportions, some simplifying assumptions are necessary. For the time being, we will be talking about an economy in which the following complications are ruled out by assumption:

---

[4] This is, of course, a relatively short-run viewpoint. In the longer run, one would have to consider not only the determinants of the level of spending but also the quantities and qualities of productive factors available and the state of technology. We are, in what follows, assuming these factors to be essentially fixed, thereby bypassing discussion of the area that has come to be called economic growth.

1. There are no exports or imports. (We deal with a "closed" economy.)
2. There is no business saving. (There are no depreciation allowances or corporate retained earnings.)
3. All taxes are personal taxes and all are "lump-sum" taxes, which do not vary as income varies. (There are no business taxes, no income taxes, and no social security taxes.)
4. The government makes no transfer payments. (All government expenditures are to purchase newly produced goods or current productive services.)
5. Neither investment spending nor government spending varies with the level of income. (The size of each is determined autonomously by something other than the level of income, and changes in the income level have no effect on the amount of either.)
6. If the economy is at less than the full-employment level of output, increases in aggregate expenditures will raise only production and employment, but not prices. (This, of course, is by no means true of the "real world" and we assume it for pedagogical reasons only.)
7. The rate of interest is assumed to be fixed and invariant.[5]

Definitions and Symbols

It is essential that the student be completely familiar with the definitions and symbols that will be employed. The most important of these are

1. *Consumption expenditures* (C) — spending by households to buy newly produced consumer goods and services.
2. *Investment expenditures* (I) — *intended* spending, primarily by business, to buy newly produced capital goods and additions to inventory.

Note two things about this definition. First, expenditures to buy already existing capital goods or to buy stocks and bonds (sometimes referred to as *financial* investment) are *not* investment as we are using the term. Second, increases in inventories that were *unintended* (those that arise simply because everything produced could not be sold) are not a part of investment. In other words, when the word "investment" appears without a qualifying adjective, it refers to *planned* or *intended* investment, not *actual* or *realized* investment.

3. *Government expenditures* (G) — spending by all levels of government to purchase newly produced goods or current productive services. This would include purchasing government goods from private business firms as well as purchasing the current productive services of government employees. It would *not* include government transfer payments, which are ruled out by assumption.
4. *Taxes* (T) — the portion of personal income received by individuals that

[5] The significance of this assumption will be made clear later on, in Chapter 19.

must be paid to the government in taxes. (Remember, these are *not* income taxes.)

5. *Saving* (S) — that portion of income received by individuals (personal income) that is neither paid in taxes nor spent to purchase consumer goods during the period. Alternatively, because personal income minus taxes equals disposable income, saving can be defined as that portion of disposable income not spent to buy consumer goods during the period.

It is extremely important that the student recognize that we are defining *saving* negatively. Saving is not something individuals *do* with their income; it is something they do *not* do.

Perhaps this point can best be illustrated by example. Suppose that an individual receives $5,000 of personal income. Out of this he is required to pay $800 in taxes, leaving him $4,200 in disposable income. If he now decides to spend $3,500 to purchase consumer goods, his saving, *by definition,* is $700. This is the amount of his personal income he does *not* spend on taxes or consumption. (Or, again, it is the portion of disposable income not spent on consumption.)

What *does* he do with the $700 that we are calling saving? We do not know, but he may do *anything* with it except pay taxes or buy consumer goods. He may, for example, put it in a savings account at a bank. He may lend it to someone in return for an IOU. He may buy stocks or bonds. He may simply hoard it in money form, either in the cookie jar at home or in a checking account at his bank. He could use it (although this is rare) to buy a piece of equipment for his business. In this case he is both a saver *and* an investor. Or, to carry the illustration to absurd lengths, he may even *lose* the money. The point is, so long as he receives income that he does *not* use for taxes or consumption spending, no matter what he *does* do with it, that portion of his income is, *by definition,* saved.[6]

6. *Total production* or *total income* (Y) — the total value of new goods and services produced during the period. Obviously, this equals gross national product. (It should be noted that, because of the simplifying assumptions under which we are working, personal income is also equal in amount to GNP.)

The Nature of the Economy Being Considered

It does very little good to simply memorize definitions and simplifying assumptions and attempt to go on from there with the analysis. Much more fruitful is a careful attempt to conceptualize the nature of the economy that the simplifying assumptions produce. What is the nature of the economy we are considering?

First, it is an economy in which all the income resulting from production (GNP) is received by individuals as personal income in the form of wages, rent, interest, or profits.

$$Y \equiv GNP \equiv PI$$

[6] The use of money that has been saved to purchase securities or capital equipment does not constitute dissaving. The student must be careful not to equate saving with hoarding.

This results from assumptions 2, 3, and 4. It will be remembered that, in the national income accounts, GNP and PI are related in the following manner:

Gross national product	*minus*	Depreciation allowances
	equals	Net national product
	minus	Indirect business taxes
	equals	National income
		⎰ Social security taxes
	minus	⎱ Corporate profits taxes
		⎱ Corporate retained earnings
	plus	Government transfer payments
	equals	Personal income

Simplifying assumption 2 eliminates depreciation allowances and corporate retained earnings. Assumption 3 rules out indirect business taxes, social security taxes, and corporate profits taxes; and assumption 4 eliminates government transfer payments. The result is that, in the economy we are assuming, there is no difference in amount between GNP and PI. If $500 billion of production takes place, $500 billion is assumed received by individuals as personal income.

Now, since disposable income is defined as personal income minus personal taxes, the following relationship also holds, by definition:

$$Y \equiv GNP \equiv PI \equiv DI + T$$

All disposable income is (as a result of our definition of saving) either spent on consumption or saved. Consequently, as $DI \equiv C + S$ and $Y \equiv DI + T$, by substitution we have

$$Y \equiv C + S + T$$

This simply says that we have defined things so that all the income earned from production in any time period is spent on consumption, saved, or paid in taxes to the government.

When goods are produced and put up for sale, they meet a demand called total intended spending, which is composed of three kinds of spending: consumption, investment, and government. A fourth potential demand by foreigners is ruled out by the first simplifying assumption. Consequently, we can say

$$\text{Total intended spending} \equiv C + I + G$$

The Definition of the Time Period

One final conceptual problem must be cleared up before we can proceed. This concerns the definition of the time period. In the real world, of course, production, the receipt of income, and the spending of it make up a continuous process not really divisible into discrete, finite time periods. Nevertheless, it will be convenient to break up this real world sequence into arbitrary time periods.

We assume that the first thing that happens during our time period is that producers turn out the period's output of new goods and services—GNP. Second, during the same period, an equivalent amount of personal income is paid out in the form of wages, rent, interest, and profits. Third, the recipients of this income split it up among consumption, saving, and taxes. Finally, at the end of the period, the goods produced at the beginning are put on the market for sale. There they are met with a demand composed of consumption, investment, and government spending.

The second period begins once again with the production of goods and services. The amount produced in the second period depends, however, on the sales experience of producers in the previous period.[7] In other words, time is arbitrarily being broken down as follows:

$$\text{Period 1}$$
$$\overbrace{\text{Production}_1 \rightarrow \text{Income}_1 \rightarrow \text{Spending}_1}$$

$$\text{Period 2}$$
$$\overbrace{\text{Production}_2 \rightarrow \text{Income}_2 \rightarrow \text{Spending}_2}$$

The more detailed schematic picture contained in Figure 16-2 may be helpful in visualizing it. Note that although production, income, and $C + S + T$ are all equal by definition, total spending does not have to equal production. Indeed, it is differences between the amount produced and the amount willingly purchased that provide the motive force for production changes from period to period.

Conditions for Stable, Rising, and Falling Production

Now that the nature of the model is clear (if it is not, go back over the preceding section carefully before going on), we can proceed to consider the circumstances under which production will rise, fall, or stay the same from period to period. Actually, this is a simple, commonsense matter.

---

[7]Technically speaking, we are relying on a "production lag" to separate our time periods. We assume that the production that takes place in period 2 is determined on the basis of sellers' experience during period 1. An alternative method would involve reliance on an "expenditure lag" wherein, as is indicated,

$$\text{Period 1}$$
$$\overbrace{\text{Expend}_1 \rightarrow \text{Production}_1 \rightarrow \text{Income}_1}$$

$$\text{Period 2}$$
$$\overbrace{\text{Expend}_2 \rightarrow \text{Production}_2 \rightarrow \text{Income}_2}$$

income earners are assumed to be paid for work done in period 1 in that same period but cannot use their income until the following period.

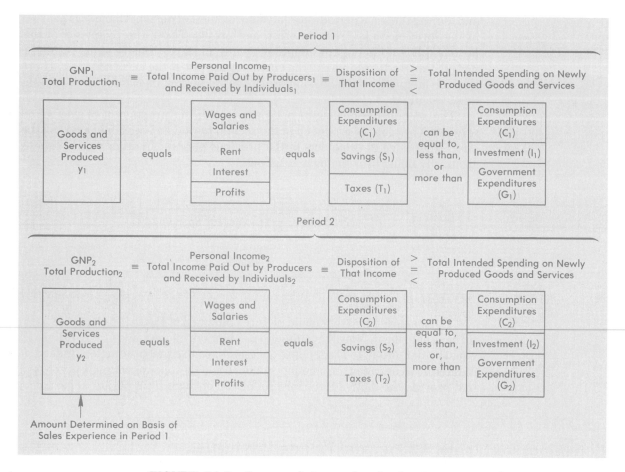

FIGURE 16-2   Conceptual picture of production, income, expenditure process

Production and Total Intended Spending

Under what circumstances will the level of production set in period 1 be continued in the following period? [8] The answer results from simple logic. It makes sense to argue that if the goods and services produced in period 1 are all sold to buyers (consumers, investors, and the government) during the period, producers have reason to be satisfied with period 1's production level and to continue it in the following period. If, in other words, total intended spending in period 1 $(C_1 + I_1 + G_1)$ just equals production, everything produced is bought. Producers' inventories neither rise because of a disappointing sales experience nor fall because of an unexpectedly heavy demand. There is, therefore, no reason to alter production schedules for the next period. The *equilibrium* level of production has been achieved.

[8] It should be repeated here that we assume that idle resources are available and that prices are rigid. In addition, it is assumed for this chapter that interest rates are fixed at a given level.

Equilibrium, of course, means a stable situation—a position *toward which* forces are pushing the production level.[9] It is a production level that, once achieved, will tend to be maintained.

Equilibrium Condition (condition under which production will stay the same in period 2 as in period 1):

$$\text{Total intended spending}_1 = \text{Production}_1$$

But now suppose that sales experience is disappointing. What if total spending during the period is *less* than enough to buy everything produced? If, for example, producers set their production schedules at a $500 billion level but find that the three spending groups purchase at only the $450 billion level, what then? If this is the case, producers find themselves with an unintended rise in their inventories amounting to $50 billion worth of unsold goods. It is certainly not difficult to predict the result. Production in period 2 will undoubtedly be scaled down to permit a "working off" of these excessive inventories. To state it more specifically,

---

Condition for Falling Production (condition under which production will be reduced from period 1 to period 2):

$$\text{Total intended spending}_1 < \text{Production}_1$$

Finally, what is to be expected if expenditures exceed producers' expectations? What is $500 billion of goods and services are produced in period 1, but buyers purchase $550 billion? Such an experience is a happy one for sellers who find that they have sold not only everything produced during the period but $50 billion more out of their inventories on hand. The only logical response to this sellers' market situation is to raise production schedules in the following period to meet the higher demand.[10]

Condition for Rising Production (condition under which production will be raised from period 1 to period 2):

$$\text{Total intended spending}_1 > \text{Production}_1$$

---

[9] This is true, at least, of a *stable* equilibrium position, which is the only case we shall consider.

[10] In fact, of course, they may be raised further than that. Producers may choose not only to meet the demand but also to build their depleted inventories back to the desired size.

Fundamental Conditions in
Terms of $I + G$ and $S + T$

It is sometimes useful to state these three conditions in a different way. The student should learn both, but it is important that he or she recognize that they are simply alternative ways of saying the same thing. The logic — the "why" — of the three conditions, however they are stated, remains the same as that just discussed.

Let us use a numerical example to illustrate the alternative approach. Suppose that production in period 1 is $500 billion. It is then definitionally true that the total income earned is $500 billion. It is also definitionally true that the sum of $C_1 + S_1 + T_1$ is $500 billion. Finally, let us suppose that taxes equal $70 billion and consumption spending, $380 billion, so that saving, by definition, is $50 billion. We have, then, a situation such as

	PI_1		
GNP_1	(Income	C_1	$380 billion
(Production) $\equiv$	earned$_1$) $\equiv$	S_1	50 billion
$500 billion	$500 billion	T_1	70 billion
			$500 billion

As $C_1 + S_1 + T_1$ is, by definition, always equal to production in period 1, there is no reason why we cannot use the former total, rather than the latter, in our fundamental conditions. And, as total intended spending in period 1 is nothing but the sum of expenditures by the three spending groups, it is optional whether we use the total figure or the sum of its components, $C_1 + I_1 + G_1$.

We can, then, restate our fundamental conditions in the following way:

1. Condition for stable production as between periods 1 and 2 — when $C_1 + I_1 + G_1 = C_1 + S_1 + T_1$
2. Condition for rising production as between periods 1 and 2 — when $C_1 + I_1 + G_1 > C_1 + S_1 + T_1$
3. Condition for falling production as between periods 1 and 2 — when $C_1 + I_1 + G_1 < C_1 + S_1 + T_1$

Indeed, we can go one step farther. Recognizing that the same quantity on each side of an equality or inequality sign can be dropped without altering the sense of our statements, we can eliminate consumption spending and end up with

> 1. Equilibrium condition $\rightarrow I_1 + G_1 = S_1 + T_1$
> 2. Condition for rising production $\rightarrow I_1 + G_1 > S_1 + T_1$
> 3. Condition for falling production $\rightarrow I_1 + G_1 < S_1 + T_1$

One fact here can hardly be overemphasized. The student who commits these three conditions to memory without taking the slight time and trouble required to understand their commonsense logic is doing himself or herself a great disservice. If the student does not "see" that the condition $I_1 + G_1 > S_1 + T_1$ is simply another way of expressing the fact that total spending exceeds production, he or she is missing, at the outset, the fundamental commonsense logic of the entire theory of income determination. If the student simply memorizes, he or she ends up with a strictly mechanistic picture of our theory, which bars him or her from a true appreciation of its usefulness.

The Determinants of Consumption and the Consumption Schedule

Demand, it would seem, plays the key role. If total spending exceeds production, production (and employment along with it) will rise. Conversely, total spending lower than production means falling production (and, presumably, increasing unemployment). If C, I, and G can be kept at appropriate levels, some of our more serious economic maladies can be kept under control.

The logical next step in our inquiry seems clear. We must give some consideration to the determinants of the components of total spending. What causes C, I, and G to be high or low — to rise or fall?

Actually in the present chapter we shall attempt only a part of the job. We shall deal with the determinants of consumption but, for the present, treat investment and government spending as "given." To employ the usual economist's parlance, we shall assume that both investment and government spending are autonomous variables, dependent on determinants other than the level of production and income with which we are primarily concerned.

We might, for example, assume that government spending depends entirely on the state of the nation's foreign affairs, without any relationship whatever to the level of income within the country. Similarly, it could be argued that investment spending depends completely on future expectations and not at all on the present income level.[11]

The result is that frequent statements such as the following will be encountered: "Investment is $100 billion and government spending, $85 billion." The student should interpret this as meaning that future expectations cause I to settle at $100 billion while foreign affairs cause G to be $85 billion; that changes in the nation's income level will in no way affect these figures; and that they will remain fixed at these levels until expectations and/or foreign affairs change.

The Determinants of Consumption Spending

What determines the nation's total consumption spending? Why does Country A spend $500 billion to purchase consumer goods while Country B spends only $100 billion? Why does Country A spend $500 billion on consumption in one year and then $600 billion in the next year?

---

[11] Neither of these assumptions is completely realistic, of course. They are made only to simplify the analysis.

Our concern here is for the determinants of the nation's *total* consumption spending, but any individual consumer could, from personal experience, come up with an acceptable list. To some degree, our knowledge of these determinants depends on commonsense reasoning from individual experience and to some degree on careful statistical investigation of the past. In any case, it seems clear that the following are among the most important:

1. *Level of Income.* One of the cornerstones of Keynesian theory is the observation that the most important determinant of consumption spending (and of saving) is the current level of income received and available to spend. The importance of this to Keynes was twofold. First, it denied the classical assumption that the interest rate was the major factor determining the quantity saved (and consumed). Second, much of the usefulness of the Keynesian multiplier rests on the stability of the relationship between income and consumption.

A priori, it seems obvious that consumption should vary with income. And the relationship, statistical investigation shows, *is* very strong, but it is not perfect. One explanation for the imperfect correlation of consumption and income is that other factors besides income influence consumption spending. Some of these other factors are listed in the discussion that follows.

A second possible explanation, put forth by a number of economists, is the possibility that it may not be so much the current, *absolute* level of income that determines consumption as some *relative* or *permanent* concept of income.[12] Perhaps consumers respond more to their income relative to others or to their income relative to the income they have become accustomed to in the past. Perhaps they decide their consumption spending more on the basis of what they consider to be their lifetime, permanent income than on current short-run changes therein. We shall not delve further into these theories here, but they are of great importance in modern consumption theory.

2. *Consumer Expectations Regarding Future Prices, Incomes, and Availability of Goods.* A rational person who confidently expects future prices to be higher will have a strong incentive to spend a larger percentage of his or her income on consumer goods now, while prices are still relatively low, than he or she would in the absence of such an expectation.

Similarly, a person who expects his or her income to be higher in future years would be quite within the bounds of logic to spend a larger percentage of his or her income on consumption now than he or she would if such a rise in income were not expected.

Finally, as appears to have been the case in past wartime periods as well as during energy shortages, if people expect that because of wartime priorities or foreign embargos such things as automobile tires and gasoline may not be freely available for some time, they are motivated by personal self-interest to stock up now on those goods they expect to need.

---

[12] See, for example, J. S. Duesenberry, *Income, Saving and the Theory of Consumer Behavior* (Cambridge, MA: Harvard University Press, 1949); M. Friedman, *A Theory of the Consumption Function* (Princeton, NJ: Princeton University Press, 1957); and A. Ando and F. Modigliani, "The Life Cycle Hypothesis of Saving: Aggregate Implications and Tests," *American Economic Review,* March 1963.

3. *Real Value of Consumers' Liquid Wealth.* Other things equal, the person (or society) who possesses a large amount of liquid wealth will be free to spend a larger percentage of his or her income on consumption than he or she would if it were necessary to build up, via saving, a contingency reserve fund. (Note that the real value of wealth can rise either because people acquire more claims to wealth like money and bonds, or because with the same number of claims, the price level falls. We deal with the effects of a variable price level in a later chapter.)

4. *Community's Present Stock of Consumer Durables.* Presumably the greater the stock of consumer durables now held by the public, and the newer these goods are, the less the need for consumers to buy more. This, then, would be a negative variable, causing consumption spending to vary inversely to it, other things being equal.

5. *The Age Composition of the Population.* Since it is a well-known fact that, on average, younger people (just establishing family units) and older, retired people are by necessity relatively heavy spenders with little opportunity to save while middle-aged people (who have already paid for their homes and/or have educated their children) tend to be relatively heavy savers, the age composition of the population goes a long way toward determining the split between consumption and saving.

6. *Social Customs and Attitudes Toward Saving.* Other things being equal, the attitude of the public toward the virtues of saving will certainly matter. One would expect, for example, a community whose social mores classify saving as a highly ranked virtue to spend less on consumption than another community similar in all respects except this sociopsychological bent toward saving.

7. *Level of Personal Taxes.* The total income earned (or GNP) is not all available to be spent as the income earners choose. Out of gross income (which, recall, equals personal income in our oversimplified world), the government takes a chunk in the form of taxes. Thus the higher the level of personal taxes, the lower the level of both consumption and saving (and vice versa).

The Consumption Schedule Defined

As is true for all economic variables, the nation's consumption spending is affected by many factors. Yet, if we are to deal with consumption analytically, we must devise a method of expressing these many interrelationships in a simplified manner. The method traditionally used in economics is the consumption schedule (or function).

A nation's consumption schedule presents *the amounts that will be spent on consumption at all possible levels of income, other determinants (besides income) being considered fixed.* In short, the consumption schedule shows how the national total of consumption spending will change if the nation's income (and nothing else) is varied.

How might one obtain the data for a consumption schedule? Because it deals with what people *will* do in the future, the only fully appropriate technique available would be a survey asking people what their intentions are.

Suppose, for example, that we have a nation of 1 million families and we ask each family (or some statistically appropriate sample) the following questions: "Assuming that your expectations, wealth, ownership of consumer durables, taxes, and attitude toward thrift (the *non*income determinants of consumption) stay as they are now, how much will you spend to buy consumer goods next week if your income is 0? How much will you spend if your income turns out to be $100? How much if it is $200? $300? $400? $500? "

While such a survey is conceivable, almost surely our respondents would want to know whether the reference is to income before or after taxes. Let us take care of that problem first by assuming that the government collects $100 in taxes, leaving the people with disposable income exactly $100 less than GNP. Now we can put our survey question in terms of after-tax income (that is, in terms of consumption spending out of disposable income).

When the survey is completed, we could then total up the responses received for each income level and draw up a table such as Table 16-1.

The consumption schedule—the relation between income and consumption—could be either columns 1 and 4 (relation between GNP and consumption) or columns 3 and 4 (relation between DI and consumption). Although either relationship could be used, let us concentrate on the relation between GNP and consumption.[13]

If it seems strange to single out one determinant of consumption—income—and hold all others fixed, the student might well recall the concept of the market demand for a single product. Whereas the quantity consumers are willing

TABLE 16-1 Numerical example of consumption schedule (millions of dollars)

1	2	3	4	5
Possible alternative levels of GNP	*Taxes*	*Possible alternative levels of disposable income*	*C*	*S*
$ 0	$100	−$100	$ 50	−$150
100	100	0	100	−100
200	100	100	150	− 50
300	100	200	200	0
400	100	300	250	50
500	100	400	300	100
600	100	500	350	150
700	100	600	400	200

[13] A word of caution is in order here. A consumption schedule shows the relation between various possible amounts of total (national) GNP and total (national) consumption. The numbers in the schedule are presumed to be national aggregates. They do *not* compare the consumption spending of different families at different income levels.

and able to purchase of a good depends not only on its price but also on consumer tastes, incomes, expectations, and the like, the demand curve assumes that all the determinants except price are fixed and then shows the relation between price and the quantity demanded. A change in any of the determinants other than price, we say, will shift the demand curve itself.

This concept, familiar in the case of the market demand for a good, is precisely paralleled by the consumption schedule. Here, too, we select the one determinant that seems most important and assume the others fixed. Here, too, a change in the main variable (income) will lead to a different amount consumed but will not change (shift) the consumption schedule itself. This is perfectly analogous to a change in price changing the quantity demanded but not shifting the demand curve itself. It will be well worth the reader's time to think through the similarities in these two important economic tools before proceeding.

Methods of Expressing a Nation's Consumption Schedule

Assuming that we have made our survey and have aggregated the responses received, there are three alternative methods for expressing the consumption schedule. We can (1) report the data, as in Table 16-1, in tabular form, (2) show the results geometrically as a line in a graph, or (3) express the relationship algebraically in an equation.

Consumption Function as a Table — The APC, APS, MPC, and MPS

Using the data from Table 16-1, the consumption (and saving) schedule could simply be reported as follows:

GNP	C	S
$ 0	$ 50	−$150
100	100	−100
200	150	−50
300	200	0
400	250	50
500	300	100
600	350	150
700	400	200

If one already has all the figures that make up the consumption and saving schedule, one needs nothing else for a full picture. However, there are several expressions that partially reflect the *nature* of the relation between income and consumption which may be used to describe that relationship. These are the average propensity to consume, the average propensity to save, the marginal propensity to consume, and the marginal propensity to save.

1. *Average Propensity to Consume.* This may be defined as "consumption expressed as a fraction of income."

$$APC = \frac{C}{GNP}$$

In the example, the figures are such that the APC is different at each level of GNP. For instance, when GNP is 200, the APC is $\frac{3}{4}$; when GNP is 400, the APC is $\frac{5}{8}$; and when GNP is 600, the APC is $\frac{7}{12}$. As common sense would seem to dictate, the APC (fraction of GNP consumed) falls as income rises.

2. *Average Propensity to Save.* The APS is "saving expressed as a fraction of income."

$$APS = \frac{S}{GNP}$$

It, too, changes as income changes, becoming larger as income rises. It is $\frac{1}{8}$ when GNP is 400, $\frac{1}{5}$ when GNP is 500, and $\frac{1}{4}$ when GNP is 600.[14]

3. *Marginal Propensity to Consume.* The MPC is actually a more important concept for our analysis than the APC. It can be defined as "the *change in* consumption expressed as a fraction of the *change in* GNP."

$$MPC = \frac{\Delta C}{\Delta GNP}$$

We have chosen figures for our numerical example in the table that, unlike the APC, result in the same MPC at all income levels. Note that between any two GNP levels chosen, the MPC is .5. Every $100 *change* in GNP calls forth a $50 *change in* consumption spending in the same direction.

There are two reasons for the use of an example with a constant MPC. First, this comes reasonably close to reality. Attempts to measure the U.S. consumption schedule have revealed an MPC that changes little when income changes except at the highest income levels. Second, the constant MPC assumption greatly simplifies the upcoming analysis. For both reasons, we retain this feature in future examples.

4. *Marginal Propensity to Save.* The MPS is defined as "the change in saving, expressed as a fraction of the change in income." The numerical example shows

---

[14] Note that because we are using GNP as our measure of income, the APC and APS do not total to 1 as they would if we employed the relation between the disposable income and C and S. This is because part of GNP goes to the government in the form of taxes.

FIGURE 16-3   The consumption function

that every $100 rise in GNP calls forth a $50 increase in saving. The MPS, then, is .5.[15]

$$MPS = \frac{\Delta S}{\Delta GNP}$$

Graphical Representation of the Consumption Schedule   An alternative method of representing the results of our survey is via a graph. The consumption schedule can be simply plotted in a two-dimensional diagram as in Figure 16-3.

With expenditures measured off on the vertical axis and GNP on the horizontal (the units on each axis being identical), each dot in Figure 16-3 represents the amount of consumption spending at a particular GNP level. The eight dots, then, represent all the data included in the numerical table. When they are joined together by the line labeled C, we have a complete graphical representation of the community's consumption schedule.

The dot on the vertical axis, of course, shows the amount of consumption (50) when GNP is zero. The *slope* of the line, measured as the vertical "rise" divided by the horizontal "run," is equal to $\Delta C/\Delta GNP$ — or the MPC. Hence, we can say that the larger the MPC, the steeper the consumption function.

Algebraic Representation of the Consumption Function   Anything that can be depicted by a straight line has an equation of the form $y = a + bx$ and can be

---

[15] The MPC plus the MPS *do* total 1 in this case, but only because our example assumes that taxes are a lump-sum $100, not related to the income level. If there were an income tax in the picture, part of any change in GNP would be taken in this form of increased income taxes. In that case one would need the sum of the MPC, the MPS, and the marginal propensity to tax, to equal 1.

stated algebraically. For the consumption function we have been working with, the equation is

$$C = .5 \, GNP + 50$$

Obtaining the equation from the table is a simple matter. The constant term is always the amount of consumption at zero GNP. The coefficient of the GNP variable (.5 in our example) is always equal to the marginal propensity to consume.

Changes in the Equilibrium Level of Production: The Multiplier Concept

A Numerical Example

Earlier we learned that when $I + G > S + T$ (that is, total spending exceeds production), production and income must rise. We are now prepared to tackle that more difficult question of *how much* production and income will rise before equilibrium ($I + G = S + T$) is restored.

The answer is inherently tied in with the consumption function concept just discussed. That is, *because* consumption spending gets bigger when income rises, and *because* consumption spending is a part of total spending requiring further rises in production and income, any initial rise in spending will set off a whole chain of events in the economy, which will raise production and income by some multiple of the original increase.

Perhaps a numerical example with two different economies is the best way to make the point. Suppose we look, simultaneously, at Economies A and B, in Tables 16-2 and 16-3.

It may help at this point to recall the simplifying assumptions under which we are working. Total production churns out an equal amount of income. This income is partly dispersed in the payment of taxes (which are assumed to be a fixed amount, not varying with income). The amount left after taxes is Disposable Income, which households either consume or save. The amount they choose to spend on consumption, together with investment and government spending, make up total intended spending. Consequently, for Economies A and B, column 1 is production and the sum of columns 4, 6, and 7 is total intended spending.

To determine the equilibrium level of production in Economy A, we can either find the place where total spending just equals production or employ the equivalent alternative of locating the point where $I + G = S + T$. The student should verify independently the fact that Economy A's equilibrium level is $300. Note also that at any level of production less than $300, more will be bought than is produced; while at any production level above $300, there will not be enough spending to purchase everything turned out.

In Economy B, for precisely the same reason, the equilibrium level of production is $400. In this case also, any level of output less than $400 will be faced with a demand that absorbs more than the amount produced, whereas a produc-

TABLE 16-2 Economy A (MPC = ½)

1	2	3	4	5	6	7	8
Possible levels of production	"Lump-sum" taxes collected	Possible levels of disposable income (1-2)	Consumption expenditures	Saving (3-4)	Investment spending	Government spending	Total intended spending (4+6+7)
$100	$50	$ 50	$100	-$ 50	$45	$55	$200
200	50	150	150	0	45	55	250
300	50	250	200	50	45	55	300
400	50	350	250	100	45	55	350
500	50	450	300	150	45	55	400
600	50	550	350	200	45	55	450

TABLE 16-3 Economy B (MPC = ¾)

1	2	3	4	5	6	7	8
Possible levels of production	"Lump-sum" taxes collected	Possible levels of disposable income (1-2)	Consumption expenditures	Saving (3-4)	Investment spending	Government spending	Total intended spending (4+6+7)
$100	$50	$ 50	$75	-$ 25	$45	$55	$175
200	50	150	150	0	45	55	250
300	50	250	225	25	45	55	325
400	50	350	300	50	45	55	400
500	50	450	375	75	45	55	475
600	50	550	450	100	45	55	550

tion level of over $400 will be so high that the spending propensities in the economy will not be enough to buy it all.

Finally, it should be noted that the two economies are exactly alike in all but one respect—their consumption functions. The citizens of Economy B are clearly the "bigger spenders," with a marginal propensity to consume of .75 rather than the .50 that is the case for Economy A. The explanation for this difference is to be found in the other, *nonincome* determinants of consumption discussed in the previous section.

Solving Algebraically for the Equilibrium Level

When complete tables are given, as in this case, one can simply read off the equilibrium production level by locating the point at which total expenditures equal production. Such a procedure is not always possible, however, especially in the classroom where time limitations may not permit the copying of long columns of numbers on the chalkboard.

Fortunately there is an alternative means of computing the equilibrium production level. In Table 16-2, the following information is given for Economy A:

$$C = .5 \, GNP + 50$$

$$I = 45$$

$$G = 55$$

The condition for equilibrium production, we know, is production equals total intended spending, which can be written as

$$GNP = C + I + G$$

By substituting the given information for C, I, and G into the equilibrium condition, we can solve for the equilibrium GNP:

$$GNP = C + I + G$$

Substituting,

$$GNP = .5 \, GNP + 50 + 45 + 55$$

Solving,

$$.5 \, GNP = 150$$

$$GNP = 300$$

The same thing can be done for Economy B. We are given the following information:

$$C = .75 \, GNP^{16}$$

$$I = 45$$

$$G = 55$$

[16] In this case, because consumption falls by $75 for every $100 drop in GNP, consumption spending will be zero at zero GNP, so that we have no constant term in the consumption function.

Plugging these data into the equilibrium condition, we have

$$GNP = C + I + G$$
$$GNP = .75\ GNP + 45 + 55$$
$$.25\ GNP = 100$$
$$GNP = 400$$

Graphical Presentation of the Same Data

While we are about it, let us see how the data for Economies A and B might be depicted graphically. Figure 16-4 refers to Economy A; Figure 16-5 is for Economy B.

FIGURE 16-4 Determination of equilibrium — Economy A

FIGURE 16-5 Determination of equilibrium — Economy B

In both diagrams, the elements of total expenditures (C, I, and G) are measured off vertically, and the level of income earned appears on the horizontal axis. The line labeled *C* in each is the consumption function that corresponds to the data from columns 1 and 4 in Tables 16-2 and 16-3. The line labeled C + I results from adding the amount of investment spending (here, $45 at all levels of income) to the amount of consumer spending at each income level. The C + I + G, or total spending line, is computed by adding the $55 of government spending to the C + I total at each level of income. The dashed 45° line is the locus of all points equidistant from the two axes. As one axis measures production and the other total expenditures, it should be clear the 45° line contains all points of equilibrium.

There is in each graph only one level of production that satisfies the conditions for equilibrium. That is where the C + I + G line crosses (equals) the 45° line. Here, and only here, the amount being produced is all willingly bought by spenders. Here, and only here, does total intended spending equal production.

The Multiplier, Initiated by a Rise in Investment

Now suppose that each of our two economies has reached the equilibrium level of production — A at $300 and B at $400. What effect will a $50 rise (to $95) in the level of investment spending have?[17]

The initial impact is obvious. In each economy, total spending will, in the first instance, exceed production by $50. That is, Economy A will find that its $300 production rate encounters $350 of expenditures while in Economy B the $400 of goods turned out will be met by $450 worth of spending. In both cases, inventories will be drawn down, and therefore production in the following period can be expected to rise.

The question we are concerned with here is, "By *how much* must the level of production rise before it reaches a new equilibrium level?"

The Multiplier Process

It is not difficult, with the aid of Tables 16-2 and 16-3, to determine the new equilibrium levels for Economies A and B. If, in Economy A, investment rises to $95 and government spending remains at $55, their total is $150, and equilibrium requires that saving plus taxes (remember, equilibrium is where I + G = S + T) also equal $150. Such a position is only reached when production has risen by $100, to $400. Similarly, in Economy B, when the sum of investment and government spending rises to $150, what is needed to restore equilibrium is a rise in S + T to the same point. This would require a rise there by $200 to a new equilibrium production level of $600.

Because a $50 rise in investment forces production up by $100 in Economy A, we say the *multiplier for that country is 2*. Because a $50 rise in investment spending leads to a $200 rise in Economy B's equilibrium level of output, we say that the *multiplier for that nation is 4*.

[17] The reader should note that we are referring to a permanent rise in the level of investment, not just a rise for a single period. The assumption is that investment rises to $95 and stays there rather than falls back to $45 in the following period.

TABLE 16-4 The movement toward equilibrium of Economy A (MPC = $\frac{1}{2}$)

	Time period						New equilibrium
	1	2	3	4	5		
Production and income	$300	$300	$350	$375	$387.50	→	$400
C	200	200	225	237.50	243.75	→	250
I	45	95	95	95	95	→	95
G	55	55	55	55	55	→	55
T	50	50	50	50	50	→	50
S	50	50	75	87.50	93.75	→	100
Total spending	300	350	375	387.50	393.75	→	400

But this is all too automatic. Simply reading results from tables does nothing to make clear the logical causation involved in the *process* by which production is forced up. We need to take the time to ferret out the economic logic involved instead of turning the whole thing into sterile arithmetic. We need, in other words, to deal with the "whys" of the multiplier process. *Why* does production in Country A rise by double the initial rise in investment? *Why* does production in Country B rise by twice as much as that in Country A? What is the *process* that we refer to as the multiplier, and why does it operate as it does?

Let us concentrate first on Country A. If the only change in spending propensities that takes place is a $50 rise in investment, why is a $50 rise in production not sufficient to restore equilibrium?

Table 16-4 provides us with a period-by-period picture of the multiplier process. Within each time period, it is assumed that the total income earned from production is all disposed of by paying taxes, spending on consumption, and saving. Second, it is assumed that the level of total spending (sum of C, I, and G in any period) determines the level of production in the following period. That is, we are assuming that producers always adjust their production levels to the level of the *previous* period's demand.[18]

In period 1, the production of $300 is met by equivalent level of spending, so that there is no reason for changing production levels in period 2. As between periods 1 and 2, Economy A is at equilibrium. In period 2, the $300 of earned income is again split among taxes ($50), consumption ($200), and saving ($50). But in this period, investors suddenly decide that they want to increase their purchases of capital goods from the old level of $45 to the higher level of $95. Thus, aggregate expenditures in period 2 turn out to be $350, although production was only $300 (I + G > S + T by $50). Consequently, inventories of sellers in period 2 are drawn down, and we expect them to raise production in the following period. By assumption, we take the amount of this production rise to be $50, so that production (and income earned from production) in period 3 is $350.

[18] This is not the only possible assumption or even necessarily the most likely one, but *some* assumption must be made. The fact is that whether producers anticipate by raising production to a *higher* level than the previous period's demand, the final equilibrium level is unchanged. We adopt this assumption as the most convenient one for purposes of exposition.

Up to this point, the multiplier process has not entered the picture, but it begins to show up in period 3. Here, $50 of added income is earned and, as we assume taxes do not rise, it is all available to recipients as disposable income to spend on consumption or save. How do they split this new income? The marginal propensity to consume of one half tells us that half of it will be spent on consumption and half will be saved. Consequently, consumption spending in period 3 rises by $25 to $225 and saving goes up to $75. The result (of the additional consumption spending) is that once again total spending ($375) exceeds production ($350). The $50 rise in production that took place in period 3 was not enough to restore equilibrium because demand in the form of added consumer spending rose still higher. This is the heart of the multiplier idea.

Assuming once again that producers react to the disequilibrium of period 3 by raising period 4's production by the amount of the excess demand experienced in period 3, production will go up to $375. Once again, however, the $25.00 of added income earned as a result of this production boost leads to a $12.50 rise in consumption and an equal rise in saving. Total spending in period 4 is thus $387.50 while production is only $375.00.

There is no need to carry the discussion further. The point is that, via some such process, *production must keep on rising until it is so high that the sum of taxes and saving is enough to equal the higher level of I + G.*

The multiplier effects show up in periods 4, 5, 6, 7, . . ., where production is pushed up beyond the $350 level, because the added income earned from additional production leads to additional consumption spending. The multiplier then results entirely from the fact that a **rise in production leads to a rise in income, which leads to a rise in consumer spending, which, in turn, causes production to be raised further in the following period, and so forth.**

Table 16-5 provides the same period-by-period picture of the rise to the new equilibrium in Economy B. Why is the multiplier larger in this case? Why does production rise further before reaching the new equilibrium? Because here, consumers who get added income spend a larger portion of it, thus adding more to aggregate expenditures in each period and, consequently, more to production. Or, to approach it from the other direction, saving rises less rapidly here as income rises (the MPS is smaller). As equilibrium requires that saving rise by

TABLE 16-5   The movement toward equilibrium of Economy B (MPC = $\frac{3}{4}$)

	Time period						New equilibrium
	1	2	3	4	5		
Production and income	$400	$400	$450	$487.50	$515.60	→	$600
C	300	300	337.50	365.60	386.70	→	450
I	45	95	95	95	95	→	95
G	55	55	55	55	55	→	55
T	50	50	50	50	50	→	50
S	50	50	62.50	71.90	78.90	→	100
Total spending	400	450	487.50	515.60	536.70	→	600

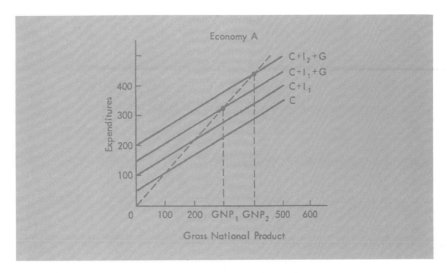

FIGURE 16-6   Effect of multiplier — Economy A

enough to offset (equal) the higher level of investment that started it all, the lower the marginal propensity to save, the greater the rise in income required to call forth the necessary amount of saving.

The multiplier and its workings can also be visualized in graphical terms, as Figures 16-6 and 16-7 indicate. In each of these graphs, the rise in investment spending is indicated by the vertical distance between the $C + I_1 + G$ line (where $I_1 = \$45$) and the $C + I_2 + G$ line (where $I_2 = \$95$). The change in the equilibrium level of production and income is the horizontal distance between GNP_1 and GNP_2, which, in turn, are located by the points where $C + I_1 + G$ and

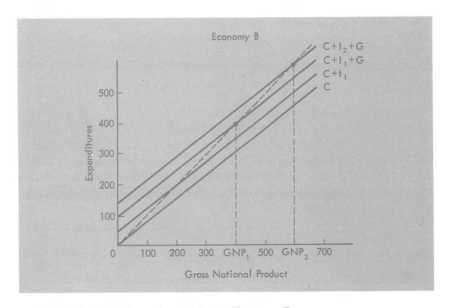

FIGURE 16-7   Effect of multiplier — Economy B

FIGURE 16-8   The process of the multiplier

C + I$_2$ + G cross the 45° line. The multiplier is the horizontal distance between GNP$_1$ and GNP$_2$ in each case, divided by the vertical distance between C + I$_1$ + G and C + I$_2$ + G.

The period-by-period working out of the multiplier presented in numerical form in Table 16-4 for Economy A is shown graphically in Figure 16-8.

In time period 2 (Table 16-4), total spending turns out to be AC, but production is only AB. As a result, production is pushed up in time period 3 to JD (to an amount equal to AC — the previous period's demand). Total spending in period 3, however, turns out to be JE (because of the induced rise in consumption). Consequently, production must be raised again in time period 4 — to KF. This still does not produce equilibrium, however, because spending in period 4 has risen to KG. The cumulative rise continues, as in Table 16-4, until GNP reaches 400.

Multiplier Definitions

Up to this point we have been discussing the multiplier *process* without ever defining the multiplier itself. Let us turn to the definition.

The multiplier is simply a number that, multiplied times any change in autonomous spending, gives the change in the equilibrium level of production. That is,

		Initial		Change in
Multiplier ×		change in	=	equilibrium
		autonomous spending		level of production

Note two things. Although in the example for Economies A and B, it was a rise in the investment spending part of total spending that triggered the multiplier, the same thing would have resulted had government spending or the level of the consumption function initially risen by $50. The multiplier is a general concept that works no matter what form the initial change in spending takes.

Second, the multiplier is reversible. An initial *decline* in C, or I, or G will set off a multiplied *decline* in GNP for reasons exactly the reverse of those just discussed.

It should be clear to the student who followed the examples given that the *size* of the multiplier is inherently tied up with the size of the MPC and the MPS in the economy. Specifically, the multiplier equals[19]

$$\frac{1}{1 - \text{MPC}} \text{ or } \frac{1}{\text{MPS}}$$

Why does $1/(1 - \text{MPC})$ give you the multiplier? Mathematically, the multiplier process makes up an infinite geometric series, the sum of which can always be obtained by multiplying the first term in the series by the reciprocal of 1 minus the common multiple.

If the MPC were .5, for example, and investment spending initially rose by $1, production would rise, over time, by the following amounts:

$$\$1 \rightarrow 50¢ \rightarrow 25¢ \rightarrow 12\tfrac{1}{2}¢ \rightarrow 6\tfrac{1}{4}¢ \rightarrow 3\tfrac{1}{8}¢, \text{ and so on}$$

Note that each additional increase in production is one half of that of the preceding period. We thus have an infinite geometric series in which .5 is the common multiple. The *sum* of this series (at the limit) can be obtained by taking $1/(1 - \text{common multiple})$ times the initial increase. This is precisely the multiplier formula, as the MPC *is* the common multiple.

Less formally, why should the multiplier equal $1/\text{MPS}$? Suppose the MPS were one-fifth. If investment spending should rise by $10 (so that $I + G > S + T$ by $10 initially), how can the equilibrium production level be restored? Clearly, if investment is assumed to stay at its higher level and G and T are fixed, the only thing that can restore the equilibrium situation ($I + G = S + T$) is a $10 rise in saving. Now what does an MPS of one-fifth really mean? Simply that it takes a $5 rise in income to cause people to save $1 more. So how much must income rise to induce people to save the added $10 needed to restore equilibrium? Clearly enough, it must rise by $50, or $5 \times \$10$.

[19] A little caution is in order here. In this example, *because we have assumed lump-sum taxes,* MPC + MPS = 1, so that $1/(1 - \text{MPC})$ and $1/\text{MPS}$ are simply alternative expressions of the same thing. If an income tax were included in the picture, $1/(1 - \text{MPC})$ would still be the correct formula for the multiplier, but the alternative expression would have to be $1/(\text{MPS} + \text{MPT})$, where the MPT is the marginal propensity to tax. The student will be well advised to stick to $1/(1 - \text{MPC})$, which is correct with or without an income tax (and so long as the consumption is the only expenditure element related to income).

The Algebraic Solution Again

Referring once again to the data for Economy B in Table 16-3, one can easily compute the change in equilibrium production levels via simple algebra.

It will be remembered that the initial given conditions for Economy B were

$$C = .75 \text{ GNP}$$

$$I = \$45$$

$$G = \$55$$

so that the initial equilibrium GNP was $400. We are concerned with computing the change in GNP if investment should be raised to $95 (by $50).

There are two very simple methods for obtaining the answer. One may simply plug the *new* data into the equilibrium condition and solve. Thus we have

$$C = .75 \text{ GNP}$$

$$I = \$95$$

$$G = \$55$$

Equilibrium condition:

$$\text{GNP} = C + I + G$$

Substituting,

$$\text{GNP} = .75 \text{ GNP} + \$95 + \$55$$

$$.25 \text{ GNP} = \$150$$

$$\text{GNP} = \$600$$

A $50 rise in investment spending raises the equilibrium GNP by $200.

Alternatively, one might use the multiplier to get the answer. It will be remembered that the coefficient of the GNP term in the consumption function is the MPC. In this case the MPC is .75.

The multiplier is $1/(1 - \text{MPC})$. The multiplier in Economy B, then is $1/(1 - .75)$, or 4. Consequently, we can quickly compute the *change* in the equilibrium GNP by

	Multiplier	Initial Change in Investment	Change in Equilibrium GNP
	4	$\times$ +$50	= +$200

The Multiplier, Initiated by a Rise in Government Spending

Perhaps it is unnecessary to make the point specifically, but the student should keep in mind that the multiplier is a *general* concept. The multiplier process can just as readily be set off by a rise in government spending as by a rise in investment, and a cut in government spending may initiate the same sort of downward multiplied spiral as a cut in investment.

Referring once again to Economies A and B in Tables 16-2 and 16-3, a $50 rise in government spending, rather than in investment, would, other things being equal, lead to the same final results. The only difference for Economy A would be that $50 of the $100 rise would be accounted for by government, rather than investment spending. The same may be said of the $200 rise in Economy B. A student can hardly understand the theory underlining fiscal policy until he or she recognizes the part the multiplier process plays in it.

The Multiplier, Initiated by an Upward Shift in the Consumption Function

It was pointed out earlier that there are a number of determinants of consumption, including not only income but wealth, stock of consumer durables, consumer expectations, taxes, and the like. The latter are assumed constant when any consumption function is drawn and a change in any of them shifts the level of the consumption function.

Clearly, consumption spending can rise either because income has risen, permitting increased consumption, or because one of the other determinants has changed, leading to greater consumption spending (and less saving) than before at *every* income level. It would be convenient to be able to distinguish verbally between these two possibilities.

Such a distinction is possible with the aid of the familiar economic terms *autonomous* and *induced*. An *induced* change in consumption spending may be defined as a *change in consumption spending that is caused by a change in income.* The multiplier effect is a result of induced consumption spending.

On the other hand, *an increase in consumption spending that occurs because of an upward shift of the consumption function itself* (which has, in turn, been caused by changes in consumer expectations, wealth, and so forth) may be referred to as an *autonomous* rise in consumption.

Perhaps the distinction can be made clear with an example. Suppose we are dealing with a country in which, at the moment, the consumption function is

GNP	Consumption spending
$ 0	$ 50
100	100
200	150
300	200
400	250
500	300
600	350

If, because of a rise in investment or government spending, income should be increased, consumption spending would also rise. Such an increase would be an induced rise in consumption caused by *a movement along a given consumption function.*

On the other hand, if consumer expectations should change so that the entire consumption function is raised, as shown in the following table, the $50 rise in consumption spending is autonomous.

GNP	Consumption spending (before change in expectations)	Consumption spending (after change in expectations)
$ 0	$ 50	$100
100	100	150
200	150	200
300	200	250
400	250	300
500	300	350
600	350	400

The difference between an induced rise and an autonomous rise in consumption is illustrated further in Figure 16-9.

Now although induced changes in consumption *are* the heart of the multiplier process, autonomous changes in consumption can, exactly like investment and government spending, *set off* the multiplier. Suppose we illustrate by assuming an economy whose equilibrium is upset by an upward shift of the consumption function itself from $C = .5 \, GNP + \$50$ in period 1 to $C = .5 \, GNP + \$100$ in period 2.

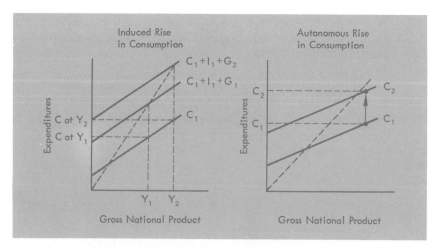

FIGURE 16-9   Autonomous versus induced changes in consumption

TABLE 16-6 Movement toward equilibrium after rise in level of consumption function

	Time period						New equilibrium
	1	*2*	*3*	*4*	*5*		
Production and income	$300	$300	$350	$375	$387.50	→	$400
C	200	250	275	287.50	293.75	→	300
I	45	45	45	45	45	→	45
G	55	55	55	55	55	→	55
T	50	50	50	50	50	→	50
S	50	0	25	37.50	43.75	→	50
Total spending	300	350	375	387.50	393.75	→	400

Table 16-6 and Figure 16-10 show the result. In period 1, equilibrium has been achieved. In period 2, however, there is an autonomous rise in consumption by $50, which is the result of an upward shift of the consumption function itself (accompanied by an equivalent downward shift in the saving function). This autonomous rise in consumer spending, then, leads into the same multiplied expansion as before. The rise in consumption spending in period 2 is autonomous; the *further* rise in consumer spending in succeeding periods is *induced*.

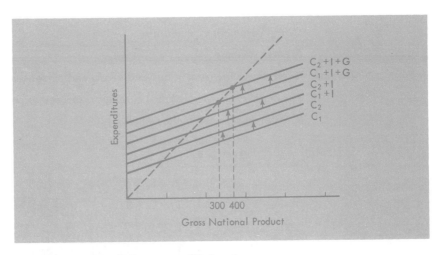

FIGURE 16-10 Effect on equilibrium income level of upward shift of consumption function

Appendix: Computing Equilibrium Income Levels Under More Realistic Assumptions

The simplifying assumptions under which we have been operating up to now were designed to ease computational burdens while still permitting the essential structure to show through, but such oversimplification is only useful for pedagogical purposes. The very simplicity of our assumptions often disturbs the literal, practical-minded student searching for answers to real-world problems.

In this appendix, we relax some of our more unrealistic assumptions and work through a number of problems that may be of interest. The main tool will be elementary algebra, but along the way we refer to the effects of certain changes on the graphs we rely upon exclusively in upcoming chapters.

New Assumptions   We shall begin with an economy in which

1. There is a personal income tax.
2. Corporations do accumulate retained earnings (i.e., there *is* business saving).

Aside from these two changes, all assumptions will remain as before.

Symbols and Definitions   The following symbols will be employed:

Y_g = gross national product, net national product, or national income

Y_p = personal income

Y_d = disposable income

C = consumption expenditures

I = investment expenditures

G = government expenditures

T = tax revenue

S = total saving (sum of business saving and personal saving)

S_b = business saving (retained earnings expressed as percentage of GNP)

S_p = personal saving by households

Definitional Relationships

$$S \equiv S_b + S_p$$
$$Y_d \equiv C + S_p$$
$$Y_p \equiv Y_d + T$$
$$Y_g \equiv Y_p + S_b \equiv Y_d + T + S_b$$
$$Y_g \equiv C + S_p + S_b + T$$
$$Y_g \equiv C + S + T$$

All these relationships follow directly from definitions used in arriving at the national income accounts aggregates. It will be easier to keep the national income account "ladder" in mind than to attempt simply to memorize these.

$$C + S + T \equiv Y_g \equiv \text{Total production}$$
$$C + I + G \equiv \text{Total spending}$$

Numerical Example — Initial Conditions   Assume an economy in which the following conditions hold initially:

$$C = .8Y_d + 15$$
$$I = 65$$
$$G = 80$$
$$T = .2Y_g \text{ (implying an income tax rate averaging 20 percent of GNP)}$$
$$S_b = .05Y_g$$

Consumption Out of Disposable Income Versus Consumption Out of Gross National Product   The alert student will note that the consumption function given relates consumer spending to disposable income rather than to GNP, as was the case earlier in the chapter. As this may be the source of confusion, let us look at these relationships more carefully. Selected data fitting the given conditions are presented in the following table.

Y_g	$S_b(.05Y_g)$	$T(.20Y_g)$	Y_d	$C(.8Y_d + 15)$
100	5	20	75	$60 + 15 = 75$
200	10	40	150	$120 + 15 = 135$
300	15	60	225	$180 + 15 = 195$
400	20	80	300	$240 + 15 = 255$
500	25	100	375	$300 + 15 = 315$

By definition, Y_d equals Y_g minus business saving and taxes. Disposable income available to people to use as they choose is what is left out of Y_g *after* businesses take out the amount they choose to save and the government collects its tax revenue. People receive Y_d, out of which they spend a part on consumption, and save the rest (S_p).

But all this is more than a bit confusing. There are two income aggregates — Y_g and Y_d. Consumption is obviously related to both. Doesn't this give us *two* different consumption functions and *two* different MPCs? Which is the *right* one for which purpose? The question deserves careful consideration.

If the consumption function is being used as a reflection of a psychological propensity by consumers, clearly the relationship between consumption and disposable income is the appropriate one. Certainly personal behavior is better reflected by relating consumption to the income people are free to dispose of as they choose than to a more all-inclusive income concept such as GNP. So it is entirely in order to present the consumption function as it is, in terms of disposable income.

What *about* the relation between consumption and GNP? Does it have any significance at all? Indeed it does! When one uses the conventional income determination graph, the consumption function drawn is the relation between C and GNP. When one uses the MPC to compute the multiplier, it is $\Delta C/\Delta GNP$ that is used, not $\Delta C/\Delta DI$. Finally, when one sets out to determine the equilibrium production level in a numerical problem, the first task is to convert the consumption function from its relationship to DI to a relationship to GNP.

This is not difficult. It simply requires figuring the relation between DI and GNP and then substituting in the given consumption function. For example we know that, by definition,

$$Y_d = Y_g - (S_b + T)$$

Substituting given data for S_b and T, we have

$$Y_d = Y_g - (.05Y_g + .20Y_g)$$
$$Y_d = Y_g - .25Y_g$$
$$Y_d = .75Y_g$$

Now as we know that disposable income is 75 percent of GNP, we can substitute this in the given C function and solve.
Given

$$C = .8Y_d + 15$$

from above,

$$Y_d = .75Y_g$$

Substituting,

$$C = .8(.75Y_g) + 15$$
$$C = .6Y_g + 15$$

We now have a consumption function relating consumer spending to GNP. If we were to draw a consumption function in the conventional income determination diagram, it is $C = .6Y_g + 15$ that we would plot, *not* $C = .8Y_d + 15$.

Suppose that we want to compute the multiplier for this economy. The formula, it will be recalled, is $1/(1 - MPC)$, but *which* MPC shall we use — the .8 contained in the function related to disposable income or the .6 just computed? The MPC out of GNP, .6, is the appropriate one for figuring the multiplier.[20] Hence the multiplier in this economy is $2\frac{1}{2}$, *not* 5.

Computing the Initial Equilibrium GNP   Now that we have consumption in terms of GNP, computing the initial equilibrium in our given economy is simply a matter of substitution into the equilibrium condition.

---

[20] Conventional symbols often used in economics are b for the MPC out of DI and t for the income tax rate. The multiplier for an economy with an income tax (but no business saving) is then $1/[1 - b(1 - t)]$. The careful reader will recognize that $b(1 - t)$ is simply the MPC out of GNP.

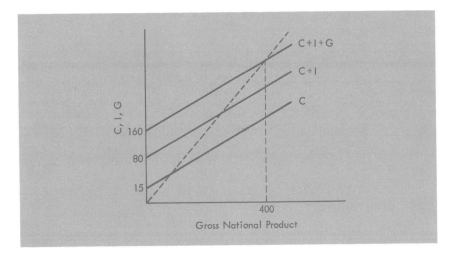

FIGURE 16-11 Initial equilibrium income

The equilibrium condition is

$$Y_g = C + I + G$$

Substituting,

$$Y_g = .6Y_g + 15 + 65 + 80$$
$$.4Y_g = 160$$
$$Y_g = 400$$

The initial equilibrium level of GNP is 400. In graphical terms, all this would look like Figure 16-11.

Effect of a Rise in Investment   Suppose that investment rises by 20 (to 85). What will be the effect on the equilibrium GNP? The answer can be obtained either by plugging the new investment figure into the equilibrium condition or by using the multiplier. We shall go through both.

We now have given

$$C = .6Y_g + 15$$
$$G = 80$$
$$I = 85 \text{ (up 20 from 65)}$$

Substituting,

$$Y_g = .6Y_g + 15 + 80 + 85$$
$$4Y_g = 180$$
$$Y_g = 450$$

FIGURE 16-12   Rise in equilibrium income
resulting from investment increase

Alternatively, we could use our knowledge of the multiplier to get the answer. The multiplier equals $1/(1 - .6) = 2\frac{1}{2}$.

		Change in
Multiplier	Change in I	Equilibrium GNP
$2\frac{1}{2}$	$\times$ (+20) =	+50

The equilibrium GNP rises by 50, from 400 to 450. Graphically, this looks like Figure 16-12.

Effect of a Rise in Government Spending   Going back to the original conditions with an initial equilibrium GNP of 400, what will be the effect of a fiscal policy change in which government spending is increased by 40 with no change in taxes?

Substituting into the equilibrium condition, we have

$$C = .6Y_g + 15$$
$$I = 65$$
$$G = 120 \text{ (up 40 from 80)}$$
$$Y_g = .6Y_g + 15 + 65 + 120$$
$$.4Y_g = 200$$
$$Y_g = 500$$

Using the multiplier, we have

		Change in
Multiplier	Change in G	Equilibrium GNP
$2\frac{1}{2}$	$\times$ (+40) =	+100

The graph of this is given in Figure 16-13.

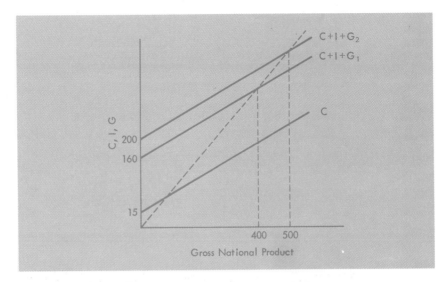

FIGURE 16-13   Rise in equilibrium income resulting
from rise in government spending

Effect of a Cut in Income Tax Rate   Suppose that a different form of fiscal policy is used to raise GNP. Let us assume, again starting from the initial situation, that the income tax rate is cut in half, from 20 percent of GNP to 10 percent of GNP. What will this do?

This type of change poses a different problem. The cut in income taxes, of course, is expected to raise GNP by permitting consumption spending to rise, but how do we compute how much the increase is?

Clearly, as a tax cut means that the government is taking less out of GNP and leaving more money in disposable income form, the tax change alters the consumption function. The first step is to compute the *new* relation between consumption and GNP.

We have given

$$C = .8Y_d + 15$$
$$S_b = .05Y_g$$
$$T = .10Y_g \text{ (down from } .20Y_g)$$

Definitionally,

$$Y_d = Y_g - (S_b + T)$$

Substituting,

$$Y_d = Y_g - (0.5Y_g + .10Y_g)$$
$$Y_d = .85Y_g$$

Substituting in the given C function,

$$C = .8(.85Y_g) + 15$$
$$C = .68Y_g + 15$$

FIGURE 16-14   Rise in equilibrium income resulting
from income tax rate cut

The tax cut has altered the consumption function by raising the MPC out of
GNP from .60 to .68. This means that the multiplier is larger and, graphically, the
consumption line is steeper. (Remember, the slope of the C function in the graph
is the MPC out of GNP.)

The effect of the tax cut on GNP can now be readily computed from the
equilibrium condition.[21]

$$Y_g = C + I + G$$
$$Y_g = .68Y_g + 15 + 65 + 80$$
$$.32Y_g = 160$$
$$Y_g = 500$$

Graphically, as shown in Figure 16-14, the income tax cut case is a bit
different. Because the immediate effect is to raise the MPC out of GNP, the slope
of the consumption function is increased. The total spending line, then, is also
steepened.

Summary   Although many more examples could be worked through, what we
have covered should be sufficient for our purposes. Perhaps a summary of the
effects of, and approach to, other possible changes would be useful.

---

[21] It can also be computed by use of the multiplier, although with added complications. The
multiplier—using the *new* MPC out of GNP—is now $1/(1 - .68)$, or $1/.32$. The initial rise in aggregate expenditures permitted by the tax cut is a rise in consumption spending of 32. (Under the
original conditions, GNP was 400 and the tax rate was 20 percent, so tax revenue was 80. The
halving of the tax rate thus initially raises disposable income by 40, out of which consumers spend
8/10, or 32, and save the rest.) The multiplier, $1/.32$, times the initial increase in consumption of
32, produces a rise in the equilibrium GNP of 100.

A change that raises (lowers) any of the constant terms (I, G, or the constant term in the consumption function) will simply raise (lower) the level of the total spending line without affecting its slope (the MPC). Such problems can be solved by substituting the new data directly into the equilibrium condition or by using the (old) multiplier.

However, if the change involved affects the income tax rate, the percentage of business saving, or the MPC out of disposable income, the solution is more complicated. A cut (rise) in the income tax rate or in the percentage of business saving, or a rise (fall) in the MPC out of disposable income, will steepen (flatten) the consumption function. Consequently, in any of these cases, it will first be necessary to compute the new relation between consumption and GNP. This *new* consumption function can then be substituted into the equilibrium condition, or the *new* multiplier can be employed.

Review Questions

1. What mechanism did the classical economists think would guarantee that any level of output would generate sufficient demand to buy it all? Explain.

2. What is the *significance* of the equilibrium level of production? What *conditions* must be fulfilled for the economy to be at equilibrium as it is defined in this chapter?

3. Carefully explain the *logic* of the *process* we call the multiplier.

4. List and explain the determinants of the level of the consumption function. Is the money level of income one of them? Explain why or why not.

5. If $C = .8 \text{ GNP} + 30$, investment spending is $80, and government spending on goods and services is $50, what is the equilibrium level of GNP?

6. Explain the difference between an *autonomous* rise and an *induced* rise in consumption.

7. For each of the following changes, indicate the effect on the equilibrium GNP and briefly explain:
   a. The MPC is .75 and G and lump-sum T are both increased by 100.
   b. People decide to save $100 more than before at every level of GNP.

8. Assume an economy in which
   a. Individuals dissave (negative personal savings) by $30 at zero DI and save $20 for each $100 increase in DI.
   b. There is an income tax with a rate equal to 15 percent of GNP plus a lump-sum tax equal to $25.
   c. Business savings is 5 percent of GNP, investment spending is $70, and government spending is $100.
      (1) Compute the equilibrium GNP.
      (2) Compute the new equilibrium GNP if now taxes are cut to

.10 GNP + 20 and government spending is cut by 32 (to 68). (Can you do this by use of the multiplier?)

(3) Draw an income determination graph that depicts the situation in (1). Indicate the amounts of the vertical intercepts of the C line and the C + I + G line. Now draw in the new C lines and new C + I + G lines for the conditions in (2). Indicate the new vertical intercepts. What are the slopes of the C + I + G lines in (1) and in (2)?

9. "If when GNP falls from 500 to 400, taxes fall from 60 to 55 and saving falls from 80 to 60 (and the marginal propensity to invest is zero) we can be sure that the multiplier is 4." Explain, making it clear that you understand why the reciprocal of the MPS cannot be used to compute the multiplier in this case.

10. Assuming that the following conditions hold, compute the equilibrium level of GNP and indicate the slope and vertical intercept of the total expenditures line.

   a. Individuals dissave (negative personal saving) by $30 at zero DI and save $20 for each $100 increase in DI.

   b. There is an income tax with a rate equal to 15 percent of GNP plus a lump-sum tax equal to $25.

   c. Business saving is 5 percent of GNP, investment sending is $70, and government spending is $100.

Investment Spending

Introduction

Mastering economic theory is not unlike erecting a building. Even the finest of superstructures will produce a faulty finished product if the foundation is weak. We should, therefore, make sure that the essence of Chapter 16 is clearly in mind before plunging more deeply into the analysis.

We have seen that the modern theory of income determination rests upon the basic assumption that it is the level of expenditures to purchase newly produced goods and services that determines how much will be produced. More specifically, we have argued that production will tend toward the level where total intended spending just equals production—the equilibrium level.

Of the three elements of total intended spending—consumption, investment, and government spending—only consumption has thus far been carefully considered. We have seen that whereas many factors affect the level of consumer spending, income is by far the most important, so important, in fact, that we refer to the relation between income and consumption as a functional relationship, the consumption function.

The existence of the so-called multiplier in the economy is, indeed, due primarily to the fact that consumption spending is so heavily dependent on income. Any autonomous rise in consumption, investment, or government spending, we have argued, will not only cause production to rise but, by causing rises in income, will induce further rises in consumption spending, so that before a new equilibrium position is reached, production will have risen by a multiple of the original increase.

Multiple changes in the level of production and income (and, indirectly, in employment and/or prices), then, can emanate from autonomous changes in any of the three elements of aggregate expenditures. What we need to know more about are the possible causes of the autonomous changes that initiate these cumulative income changes.

We already know something about the causes of autonomous changes in consumption spending. Consumer expectations, consumer wealth, the existing stock of consumer durables, taxes, and so on, all can, by changing, cause autonomous consumption changes. In actuality, although these factors *can* be important in initiating income changes, they generally are not. Consumption spending, in the long run at least, is a relatively stable, passive portion of total spending, changing in significant amount only when income does.

Not so for the other two elements. Both investment spending and government spending can be highly volatile, setting off repeated cumulative changes in the nation's income in one direction or another. We must, if we are to be able to say much about the economy, know more about them and the causes of their erratic behavior.

Unfortunately, not much can be said from the economic point of view about the determinants of government spending. At least not in the context in which we are considering it. The level of such spending is so heavily dependent on essentially noneconomic factors such as international affairs and domestic politics that a discussion of economic determinants hardly seems warranted. We will, therefore, pass it by with the important and obvious reminder that as one of the major tools of fiscal policy, government spending can and does have significant effects on the level of income.

This leaves investment, possibly the most volatile of the elements of total spending. The remainder of this chapter considers the determinants of the level of investment spending, the causes of its volatility, and the effects of its erratic behavior on the level of income in the economy.

The Determinants of the Level of Investment Spending

Investment spending, the reader will remember, has been defined as "intentional spending to buy newly produced capital goods." The question before us is, "What causes such spending to be large or small?"

If one were to start out and, reasoning from sheer common sense, list the factors that would appear to affect the level of investment spending, the list would be imposing. Among others, the following would certainly be included:

1. Expected future levels of demand (to buy products produced on machines bought today).
2. Expected future wage and material costs (to purchase the labor and materials needed to operate the machine, or to use instead of the machine).
3. Expected future added tax liability to be incurred as a result of selling the goods produced by the machine.
4. The current price of the machines to be bought.

5. The interest cost of borrowing the money to buy the machine (or to forgo the potential interest return on one's own money used to buy the machine).

6. Future consumer tastes (will they shift away from products that can be produced on the machines available to be purchased?).

7. The pace of technological change (will a better machine soon make those available now obsolete?).

8. The gambling spirit of entrepreneurs.

9. The existing stock of capital goods.

There can be no doubt that each of the factors on this partial list plays a role in the determination of the level of investment spending in any period. The problem that confronts us is, "How can all these factors be organized to develop a reasonably accurate, yet not too unwieldy, theory?"

Essentially what economists have done is to cover almost all these individual determinants under the unquestionably vague phrase "business managers' expectations of future profits." We say that the level of investment spending today depends upon "business managers' expectations of future profits," which, in turn, depends on almost all the factors in the foregoing list. But such sweeping generalities, though formally correct, are not very helpful for purposes of analysis. We need to see how all these variables can be systematically handled.

The Investment Decision — the Variables Involved

It should help to clarify matters if we attempt to follow through the logical thought process of an individual business manager considering the purchase of a particular machine.

Suppose that Mr. Jones is trying to decide whether to buy a certain machine, the price of which is $21,000, for his business. If he is a profit maximizer, what does he consider in arriving at his decision?

He knows that if he buys the machine and uses it in production, his total revenue will increase. The machine will add to his ability to produce and, assuming that he can sell this added output, its use adds to his firm's gross income. That's the good side of it. On the negative side, he realizes that certain added costs will accrue from buying and using it. His costs will be increased not only by the initial price of the machine but also by the interest cost he incurs to finance the purchase and by the added labor, material, and tax costs that will necessarily be encountered to operate it. Presumably, his decision on whether to purchase it will rest on the balance of good versus bad. If it is expected to add more to his revenue than to his costs, he can increase his profits by buying it. On the other hand, if expected costs from buying and using it exceed expected added revenue from selling the goods produced on it, he will forgo the opportunity.

It is apparent that the investment decision is full of "ifs." Our business manager must first estimate the expected added revenue as a result of purchasing the machine. What does such an estimate entail? It requires that he guess at

1. The physical productivity of the machine per year.
2. The economic life of the machine (which involves a guess at how soon his competitors may come up with a better machine which will make this one obsolete).
3. Consumer demand for the product produced on the machine (which involves not only a forecast of consumer tastes but also an estimate of the course of the business cycle).

Fraught with difficulty though it may be, no investment will be made by a profit maximizer without, explicitly or implicitly, considering all these imponderables. Let us assume that our Mr. Jones has done so and has come up with a "best guess" that the annual added total revenue he will derive from selling products produced on the machine is $25,000. Furthermore, he expects this added revenue to continue for two years, the expected useful life of the machine.

Now let us consider the negative side. Mr. Jones *knows* that buying and operating the machine will add to his yearly costs by the following amounts:

1. The initial cost of the machine, $21,000, spread over two years, or $10,500 per year.
2. The interest cost involved in financing the purchase, which we shall for the moment assume to be $2,100 per year. Note that he bears this cost whether or not he pays that amount out of pocket to a lender from whom he borrows. For if he uses his own funds, tying them up in the purchase of this machine means he is forgoing that amount of interest income he *could earn* by lending his money to someone else.

In addition to evaluating these known costs, he will have to resort once again to his engineers, accountants, or crystal ball to obtain a best guess at others. Suppose that he does so and comes up with the following estimates:

1. Labor cost incurred to operate and maintain the machine each year $5,000
2. Cost of material fed into the machine each year $3,500
3. Increased annual taxes incurred as a result of added goods sold and/or profit made $3,400

Now if we put all his estimates together, this would appear to be the picture:

Expected added annual revenue		$25,000
Minus: Expected added annual costs		24,500
Original cost of machine (depreciation)	$10,500	
Interest cost	2,100	
Labor and material cost	8,500	
Taxes	3,400	
Expected added annual profits		$ 500

In this case the purchase of the machine would appear to be advisable, yielding an addition to profits of $500 for each of the next two years. It would seem that, to maximize his profits, Mr. Jones must make the investment.

But hold on. We have omitted something that is absolutely crucial to the investment decision. The $500 expected annual net profit figure we have come up with may be Mr. Jones's "best guess," but it is, at best, a guess. Mr. Jones *thinks* that this $500 is the greatest likelihood, but, as any business manager must, he knows that there is some (lesser) chance that if he buys the machine he will lose money. Can the risk involved be ignored altogether by assuming that Mr. Jones will always act on his best guess despite his being aware that things might turn out differently?

That depends on how much of a gambler Mr. Jones is. Let us suppose, for purposes of argument, that whereas a $500 annual profit is most likely (there being 50 chances out of 100 that this will be the result), there are also 5 chances out of 100 that he will lose $1,000 per year, 20 chances out of 100 that he will just break even, 20 chances out of 100 that he will make an annual profit of $1,000, and 5 chances out of 100 that he will make $2,000 profit per year.

If that is the case, his outlook on the likely profitability of the investment would look something like that in Figure 17-1. This, of course, is a probability distribution that in this case turns out to be a symmetrical curve.

The problem facing Mr. Jones has now been complicated. Would he be as willing to accept this set of probable results as a *certain* $500 profit per year? It all depends on his makeup. If he is a relatively conservative man, he would prefer a certain $500 to this range of possibilities, even though the chances of loss may appear to be offset by equal chances of larger gain. In such a case, the risk involved is a positive detriment that would lessen the chance of his buying the

FIGURE 17-1 Probability distribution of profit prospects for potential investment

machine. If, on the other hand, he is a gambler by nature, he might conceivably prefer this set of probabilities to a certain $500, putting more store in the possibilities of greater profit than in the equal likelihood of loss.

There is no safe way of characterizing all business managers with respect to their attitude toward the risk involved. However, it would seem that most would be on the conservative side, preferring a certain $500 to the range of probabilities shown in Figure 17-1. If that is the case for Mr. Jones, we had better take account of his aversion to risk in his investment decision.

Suppose that, to cover his risk, Mr. Jones insists that his best guess on the profitability of a $21,000 investment be at least $1,000 per year. If this is the case, that $1,000 *risk allowance* will have the same effect in deterring his purchase of the machine as would an additional out-of-pocket cost of $1,000. There is no reason we cannot consider it explicitly as another cost, like wages, interest, and so on, that must be covered.

Now that we have all the data needed, what about the $21,000 machine? Will Mr. Jones go ahead and buy it or not? The answer, of course, is that he will not. When the risk allowance of $1,000 is added to the other costs, totaling $24,500, we end up with expected annual costs of $25,500 and expected annual revenue of only $25,000. Purchase of the machine would be a losing proposition (or at least would not pay enough to be worth the risk involved).

The Marginal Efficiency of Investment

Logically, the investment decision in the preceding example is sound. If expected added annual revenue exceeds expected added annual cost (including risk allowance), the machine will be purchased by a profit maximizer. If cost exceeds revenue, it will not.

But economists for years have had a somewhat different way of manipulating these cost and revenue figures. It involves the concept of the *marginal efficiency of investment*. Let us see what is involved.

The marginal efficiency of investment may be defined as *the rate of discount that will equate expected annual net revenues to the present cost of the machine*. In somewhat less exact terms, the MEI may also be described as the *expected rate of return on an investment (with interest not being included as one of the costs)*.

Symbolically, the MEI of any given prospective investment project can be determined from the following expression:

$$C = \frac{R_1}{(1 + r)} + \frac{R_2}{(1 + r)^2} + \cdots + \frac{R_n}{(1 + r)^n}$$

where

C = the original cost of the machine

R_1, R_2, etc. = the expected annual net revenue computed by subtracting all costs except interest and depreciation from expected annual gross revenue

r = marginal efficiency of investment

In the example, we have the following:

C = $21,000
R₁ and R₂ = $12,100

Expected annual gross revenue		$25,000
Expected annual costs (excluding depreciation and interest)		12,900
Labor and materials	$8,500	
Taxes	3,400	
Risk allowance	1,000	
		$12,100

Substituting these figures into the formula, we get

$$\$21{,}000 = \frac{\$12{,}100}{(1+r)} + \frac{\$12{,}100}{(1+r)^2}$$

Solving for r, we get .10. Therefore, this machine has an **MEI** of 10 percent.

Now all this may seem a little strange to the reader, especially the fact that interest and depreciation costs are not included in the computation of expected net revenue. Do we really ignore these costs when computing the **MEI**? If so, what good is it?

The answer is no and yes. We do *not* exclude depreciation when computing the **MEI**. After all, the full depreciation cost is simply the price of the machine, included as C in the formula.

On the other hand, the interest cost *is* excluded in the computation of the **MEI**. But this is not to say that it is omitted entirely from consideration in the investment decision. It is simply brought in at a different point.

In our example, the machine has an **MEI** of 10 percent. But this does *not* say that the machine is expected to yield a clear profit of 10 percent per year. What it says is *if you do not consider the interest cost*, the machine is expected to yield 10 percent. Consequently, we can never tell whether an investment will be profitable or not by considering the **MEI** alone. We must consider it *in comparison* with the one cost it does not take into account—the interest rate.

Our machine has an **MEI** of 10 percent. It will add to profits and be undertaken only if the one cost not yet considered—the interest cost—is less than 10 percent.

We conclude, then, that all capital goods for which the MEI (expected rate of return, not including the interest cost) exceeds the rate of interest must be bought in order to exploit all profit opportunities.

The Marginal Efficiency of Investment Schedule for the Economy as a Whole

At any point in time, many potential investments are under consideration by many different firms throughout the economy. Although the estimating approach may be different from that just described, presumably each investment project has, to the business manager considering it, an expected rate of return.

Suppose that we were to carry out a gigantic survey of all business managers asking each to list investments being contemplated and the **MEI** for each. If we should then add up all the responses received for the economy as a whole, we might end up with a result something like the following:

Dollars worth of investment projects (billions of dollars)	*With an MEI (expected rate of return) of at least*
$10	20%
15	18
20	16
25	14
30	12
35	10
40	8
45	6
50	4
55	2

Such a result could equally well be expressed graphically, as in Figure 17-2.

Why do we end up here with a downward sloping curve? Why do we imply with our example that the marginal rate of return to be expected from $40 billion worth of investment is less than that to be expected from $20 billion worth?

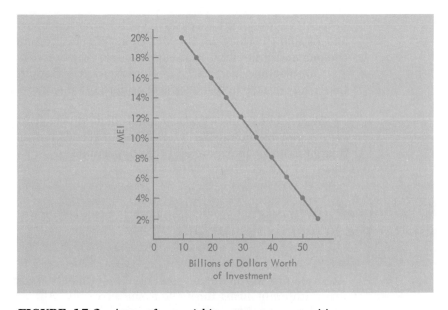

FIGURE 17-2 **Array of potential investment opportunities**

Because each investment figure includes the value of all the projects with a higher rate of return plus the value of additional projects that are expected to realize the lower rate. For example, when investment is pushed from $30 billion to $35 billion, the marginal expected rate of return falls from 12 percent to 10 percent. The investment projects that can be expected to yield at least 12 percent total up to $30 billion, but the total for which a return of at least 10 percent is expected is $5 billion higher because it includes both the $30 billion for which a 12 percent return is expected plus the additional $5 billion worth of projects for which returns of 11.5 percent, 11 percent, 10.5 percent, and 10 percent are expected.

The curve we have in Figure 17-2, however, is not an investment demand schedule. It is nothing more than a cumulative array of prospective investment projects with their expected rates of return computed without considering the interest cost. Alternatively, it tells us that there exists at the moment $10 billion worth of potential investment projects with an expected rate of return (not deducting interest cost) of 20 percent *or more,* that there are $15 billion worth of potential investment projects with an expected rate of return (not deducting interest cost) of 18 percent *or more,* and so on.

To convert Figure 17-2 into an investment demand schedule, we need to bring in explicit recognition of the one cost not yet accounted for up to now. That cost, is, of course, the rate of interest. As noted earlier, any investment expenditure involves an interest cost, whether explicit or implicit. If the investor borrows the money to buy this machine externally from a lender on the capital market, his interest cost is, of course, the amount the lender charges him. If, however, he uses internally generated funds such as his own retained earnings to buy the machine, he does not avoid an interest cost. The difference is that in this case his interest cost is an implicit rather than an explicit one. It is the interest return he *could* have earned from his retained earnings had he lent them out to someone else and charged the going rate of interest, rather than tying them up in the purchase of a machine. This form of interest cost — the opportunity cost of using his own funds — is just as real as any other.

Let us bring the interest cost into our example by using the vertical axis (which, in Figure 17-2, is already in percentage terms) to measure off *both* the MEI *and* the market rate of interest. This is done in Figure 17-3.

Note that the curve labeled MEI in Figure 17-3 is exactly the same curve (from exactly the same source) as the curve in Figure 17-2. It, like the curve in Figure 17-2, tells us the MEI of various levels of investment spending.

Now suppose that the market rate of interest (the level of which is, of course, subject to manipulation by the Federal Reserve System) happens to be 10 percent, as indicated by the dashed horizontal line at the 10 percent level. What does Figure 17-3 now tell us? It says that if the business managers in this economy are profit maximizers, they will buy exactly $35 billion worth of capital goods. That is, they will purchase all capital goods for which the MEI exceeds the rate of interest, for so long as the MEI exceeds the interest rate, a profit is realizable on the purchase. *Profit maximizers, then, must carry investment up to the point where the MEI is driven down to equal the rate of interest* to exploit all profit opportunities.

Suppose, for example, that the money to purchase machines must be borrowed externally so that there is an explicit interest payment to a lender of 10

FIGURE 17-3   Marginal efficiency of investment schedule

percent. So long as buying a machine will bring in a rate of return (not allowing for interest cost) of *more* than 10 percent, a profit can be realized on it.

Or consider the possibility that the money needed to buy capital goods is already available in the form of accumulated retained earnings. Then what Figure 17-3 tells us is that business managers have two alternatives. They can put their money into buying machines and realize the rates of return shown on the MEI curve, or put it into buying bonds or other financial assets and realize the market interest rate of 10 percent. If this is their choice, it is obvious that (with the first $35 billion of their retained earnings) they will do better to buy capital goods.

Note now the effect of a reduction in the market rate of interest to, say, 6 percent. This lower interest cost will make an additional $10 billion of investment projects profitable (that is, those between $35 billion and $45 billion). Conversely, an increase in the rate of interest from 10 to 12 percent would cut back on investment spending by $5 billion (because now the investment projects between $30 and $35 billion are not profitable enough to cover all costs including interest).

Before proceeding, one word of caution is in order. All references to the rate of interest in this chapter should be interpreted as referring to the *real* rate of interest — the rate of interest adjusted to eliminate the effects of inflation. If, for example, the market rate of interest rises from 10 to 15 percent in a year in which the rate of the price-level increase goes up 5 percent, the *real* rate of interest (the *real* cost of borrowing money) has not risen at all.

Determinants of the Level
of the MEI Curve of the Economy

For the student who followed through on the logical thought process of our mythical Mr. Jones in arriving at the **MEI** for his particular $21,000 investment, most of the factors that determine the level of, or cause shifts in, the economy's **MEI** curve will be apparent. Anything that raises expected revenues would raise the **MEI** (and tend to shift the curve out to the right), and anything that raises costs (except the rate of interest) would lower the **MEI** (and tend to shift the curve to the left). Nevertheless, because we are now talking about the determinants of the level of the entire **MEI** curve for the economy as a whole rather than the considerations behind one prospective investment for one business manager, we had better list some of the more important determinants.

1. *Technology.* There can be no doubt that technological progress, whether in the form of development of new methods of production or new products, has profound effects on the level of the **MEI** curve. Although there may be exceptions, we will assume that improvements in the state of technical knowledge tend to raise the **MEI** curve—that is, shift it to the right.

2. *Stock of Capital Goods on Hand.* To the degree that the stock of capital goods in the economy increases more rapidly than do the other factors of production, we will, other things being equal, encounter diminishing marginal physical productivity of capital. Consequently, the larger the stock of capital goods already on hand, relative to the other productive factors, the farther to the left is the **MEI** curve.

3. *Tax Policy.* Just as Mr. Jones's decision was affected by the level of taxes he expected to have to pay, so must the outlook of all prospective investors be influenced by tax policy. This applies not only to corporate profits tax rates, business property taxes, and excise taxes but also to less obvious factors such as changes in the rate at which depreciation is permitted for tax purposes. Clearly any tax change that has the effect of reducing taxes on the income earned from successful investment would, other things being equal, tend to shift the community's **MEI** curve to the right.

4. *Business Managers' Psychology.* Because investment spending is entirely an activity that pays off only in the future, its volume is inevitably influenced by the psychology of investors. Even the hard economic facts that underlie the estimate of the rate of return from an investment are colored by the psychological makeup of those who make the investment decisions, because further expectations involve a degree of crystal ball gazing that, by its very nature, cannot be based entirely on economic fact. If the investor group is composed primarily of gamblers, the risk allowance will be smaller and the resulting **MEI** curve will lie farther to the right than if investors are extremely cautious by nature.

5. *Social and Political Atmosphere.* Just as the interpretation of economic facts is influenced by psychology, so must it be affected by apparent changes in the social or political structure within which the economy functions. Rationally or irrationally, the illness of a president, the election of a seemingly hostile Congress, the

intensification of social problems—all will affect business managers' expectations. In large part, of course, the effectiveness of such developments as determinants of investment depends upon the effect they appear likely to have on such fundamental economic facts as tax policy and the like. Nevertheless, they would seem to be sufficiently different in origin to justify a separate listing.

This is hardly an exhaustive list, but it does include some of the most important determinants of the **MEI** curve's level. A change in any one will alter the expectation of return from investment all along the line, thereby raising or lowering the **MEI** curve itself.

The Significance of the Slope (or Elasticity) of the MEI Curve

Although there can be no doubt that the **MEI** curve slopes downward to the right, there is considerable doubt and disagreement as to how *rapidly* it falls. In this section, we shall say what we can about the actual slope (or elasticity[1]) of the **MEI** curve and then explore its implications.

Is the usual **MEI** curve for the American economy relatively steep or relatively flat? The truth is, we do not really know. Extensive efforts have been made to find out, but as yet there appears to be no conclusive proof one way or the other. Some scholars have attempted to get at the issue via the survey technique in which business managers are asked the relative importance of various factors as determinants of investment. Although the survey results almost unanimously reveal the interest rate as a factor of generally minor importance, this approach falls short of conclusively demonstrating that the **MEI** curve is inelastic. Other investigators have employed econometric techniques with indifferent success. Others with and without resort to empirical evidence have theorized that such things as risk allowances, corporate profits taxes, and short payoff periods make for an inelastic investment demand curve.

Perhaps continued effort along these lines will pay off with more definitive results in the future. Until that point is reached, however, an agnostic view appears most appropriate. We just do not know how elastic or inelastic the **MEI** curve is.

But the question is a vitally important one, especially in its implications for the effectiveness of monetary policy. If it could be shown that the **MEI** curve was highly elastic (relatively flat) over most of its range, this would be equivalent to saying that slightly lowering the rate of interest (with a given **MEI** curve) will make profitable and call forth substantial amounts of additional investment spending. A highly inelastic **MEI** curve carries exactly the opposite implications. Let us look at Figure 17-4 to examine this point.

In the graph on the left, we have drawn a relatively flat **MEI** curve to represent a high degree of elasticity. On the right, the fairly steep curve is intended to

[1] Although the slope and elasticity of a demand curve are not identical, with the exceptions of the limiting cases of perfectly elastic and perfectly inelastic curves, we shall oversimplify here by ignoring the difference. Specifically, we refer to a relatively steep **MEI** curve (or a steep portion of an **MEI** curve) as inelastic and to a relatively flat curve (or portion thereof) as elastic.

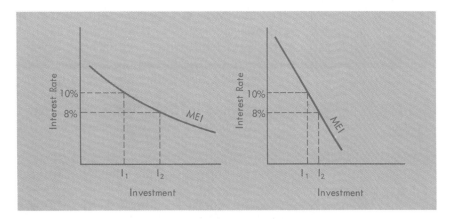

FIGURE 17-4 Effects of differing degrees of elasticity on MEI curves

depict a case of low elasticity. It can be seen that a reduction in the interest rate from 10 percent to 8 percent permits a relatively large increase in the volume of investment in the elastic case, but only a small increase where the **MEI** is quite inelastic. An easy money policy designed to raise total spending via a lowering of interest rates would clearly be more successful, the more elastic the **MEI**. The same reasoning applies, of course, to the effectiveness of interest rate increases induced by a tight money policy.

Before leaving this area, note that the statement "investment is highly elastic with respect to the rate of interest" is not necessarily the same thing as arguing that the interest rate is *important* as a determinant of the level of investment. Perhaps another example will help to make the point.

In Figure 17-5 we have drawn a pair of MEI curves that are highly elastic over most of their ranges. Suppose that, initially, the MEI curve applicable for our economy is MEI_1 and that the rate of interest is 10 percent. This would mean that the volume of investment spending would be I_1. Now, suppose that Federal Reserve policy lowers the interest rate to 8 percent to combat a developing

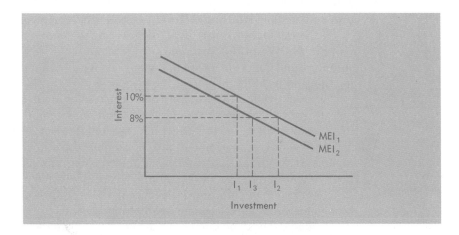

FIGURE 17-5 MEI elasticity partially offset by shift of curve

recession. *If the MEI curve itself does not shift*, the reduction in interest rates will permit a substantial increase in investment spending up to I_2. But, in fact, there is good reason to expect a shift in the curve itself as business managers' expectations are adversely affected by the developing recession. If the MEI curve shifts to the left to MEI_2 at the same time as the interest rate is reduced, the new volume of investment will be I_3, a very slight increase. Thus we have a situation wherein, even though investment is highly elastic with respect to the rate of interest, changes in the other factors (business managers' expectations) that affect investment work in the opposite direction and keep investment from rising substantially.

The reverse, of course, is also possible. If the MEI curve is highly elastic and monetary policy raises interest rates to combat a developing inflation (the purpose being to cut investment spending), the elasticity of the investment demand curve does not guarantee that investment spending will be diminished. For the optimism generated among business managers by the boom conditions may be reflected in an upward shift of the MEI curve itself, producing a smaller decrease in investment than a stable, elastic curve would lead one to expect. Indeed, there may even be an increase.

If, in fact, shifts in the MEI curve itself are so frequent and significant as to swamp the effects on investment of interest rate changes, then one must conclude that even if the MEI *is* elastic, interest may not be an important factor in determining investment. This possibility partially motivated our earlier statement that replies to surveys by business managers to the effect that interest was not an important factor do not necessarily prove that the MEI curve is inelastic.

Summary

We have now what amounts to half a theory. We have seen that given the rate of interest, the marginal efficiency of investment schedule will tell us the volume of investment at which producers will maximize expected profits. This volume of investment spending, along with the level of government spending and the consumption function, will permit us to determine the equilibrium level of production and income. All this can be expressed graphically, as in Figure 17-6.

If the rate of interest is given to us as i_0, the volume of investment spending will be $0I_0$. When this volume of investment is added (vertically) to the consumption and government spending curves, we find that the equilibrium level of income and production is $0Y_0$.

Of course different assumptions for the curves involved would give us different answers. If business managers' expectations became worse, the MEI curve itself would shift to the left, in which case an interest rate of i_0 would produce a smaller volume of investment and, consequently, a lower equilibrium level of income. If one of the determinants of the consumption schedule, such as income taxes or consumer expectations, should change from what is depicted to produce a higher or steeper consumption function, the equilibrium level of income would be higher, even with the same level of investment.

A good deal can be said about the economy with the aid of this "half model"

FIGURE 17-6 Combining MEI and income determination diagrams

alone. But we must go further. To complete the picture, we need to know how the rate of interest is determined. This is the subject of Chapter 18. Once it is completed, we will have covered all the pieces of our simplified model of the economy and will be in a position to go ahead in Chapter 19 and use it in its entirety.

Review Questions

1. Make a list of all the factors discussed in this chapter, an increase in which will lower the **MEI** of a single potential investment project. What will these changes do to the level of the **MEI** curve?

2. Carefully explain why profit-maximizing business managers will carry investment spending up to the point where the **MEI** just equals the interest rate rather than stopping at a point where the **MEI** is much higher than the interest rate. Can you relate this to a single business manager's output decision and the comparison of marginal revenue and marginal cost?

3. List and explain the major factors that could cause a nation's **MEI** curve to shift to the right.

4. "It is a fact that in year 1 the interest rate was 8 percent and the volume of investment spending was $80 billion. Then in year 2 the interest rate was 12 percent and investment spending rose to $160 billion. This proves that the **MEI** curve for that nation must have had a positive slope." Do you agree? Explain why or why not. What impact would it have on your explanation if you knew that the price level rose by 50 percent from year 1 to year 2?

5. If the Fed is trying to raise aggregate demand via reductions in interest rates, would it prefer a steep or a flat **MEI** curve? Explain.

CHAPTER 18

The Rate of Interest

What determines the rate of interest is a question over which economists have struggled for many years. This debate still goes on, but, fortunately, enough solid ground of agreement has been established to permit a fairly confident discussion of where we now stand and how we got there.

This chapter is divided into two main sections. After some brief introductory comments limiting the area of discussion, we consider the first of two current approaches to the theory of interest. Called the *loanable funds theory*, this approach is a modification of the classical explanation of the rate of interest.

Following the loanable funds discussion, we consider the *liquidity preference theory* of interest. This approach is another one of the contributions of J. M. Keynes, and we give it fuller consideration because of the facility with which it fits into the complete Keynesian model.

Limitations to the Area of Discussion

It is a gross oversimplification to speak of *the* rate of interest, since there are many different rates of interest ruling in any economy at any given time. What do we mean by *the* rate of interest?

The rate of interest should be taken to mean the rate of return paid to a lender who has lent his or her money for a long period of time by a borrower for whom the chances of default are extremely remote. For instance, the return on a long-term, virtually riskless security would provide a good measure of what we mean by *the* rate of interest. There is no better example than the interest paid on a long-term U.S. government security.

What about all the other rates being paid? At any one time, even if we had already determined *the* rate of interest to be 10 percent, one could find examples of a whole structure of rates ranging from perhaps 5 percent to as high as 40 percent or more. What explains the divergencies from our "pure" 10 percent rate?

To answer such questions adequately, we would have to become deeply involved in a complicated discussion of the structure of interest rates. This, we shall not do.

Suffice it to say that interest rates above and below the pure rate are largely explainable by differences in the term of the loan, the costs of collection, the risk involved, and the expectations of the parties (especially in regard to future price changes). In the discussion that follows, we ignore such differences and concentrate on the forces that determine the pure long-term "riskless" rate of interest.

The Loanable Funds Theory of Interest

The explanation of interest that has perhaps the greatest appeal to common sense is the loanable funds theory. It considers the interest rate, reasonably enough, to be simply *the price paid for the right to borrow and use loanable funds*. With this straightforward definition of interest as the focus, it then becomes necessary to consider the components that determine that price — the demand for and supply of loanable funds.

The Classical Theory Background to Loanable Funds

The loanable funds interest theory is a logical extension and modification of the much older classical theory of interest. It may therefore be useful to consider the classical theory briefly first.

One of the oldest areas of dispute in interest theory has to do with the ultimate determinants of interest. Is the interest rate a *real* or a *monetary* phenomenon? Does it depend entirely on real variables within the economy or can it be permanently altered by mere monetary manipulations?

The classical answer to this question was clear-cut. To the classical economists, money was only a veil that partially concealed but did not really alter any of the basic real forces in the economy. This was as true of their interest theory as of other elements of their elegant structure.

Their reasoning ran something like this. Interest is what must be paid for the right to borrow money. But this amount is a price that, like all other prices, is determined by demand and supply. The demand for borrowed money comes almost entirely from business managers, who desire to use the funds to purchase capital goods. The supply, on the other hand, comes from individuals who, having decided not to spend all their income on consumption, have some left over in the form of saving, available to lend out.

We must look behind these surface phenomena for a fuller understanding. The amount of borrowed money demanded by business managers depends es-

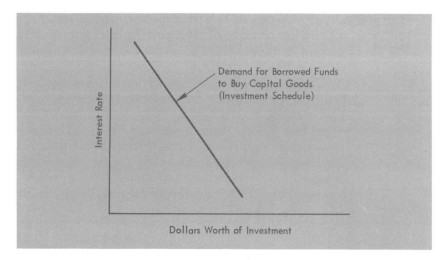

FIGURE 18-1   Demands for funds for investment

sentially on the marginal productivity of capital goods. If the productivity of any added machine is expected to be high enough to more than cover the interest cost of financing its purchase, it must be bought to maximize profits. However, additional capital goods when combined with the other factors of production will produce diminishing marginal productivity. Therefore, more such goods will be bought only at lower rates of interest because their lower productivity will not cover higher rates. That is to say, the demand for borrowed funds (reflecting, as it does, the diminishing productivity of capital) will look like that in Figure 18-1.[1]

On the other side of the market, the supply of funds made available by savers is motivated by the opportunity of receiving interest on funds not spent for consumption. Actually, as noted earlier, it was argued that it is irrational for people to refrain from spending their income on consumption (and suffer the disutility associated with such abstinence) and then hoard the saved money. For any rational person would prefer some interest return on his or her savings to none. Therefore, as it is the reward of interest that motivates saving, the higher the rate of interest, the greater the quantity we can expect to be saved. The supply of savings, then, would look like that in Figure 18-2.

As the supply of funds to be lent out at interest comes from saving and the demand for funds to borrow comes from investors, their price — the rate of interest — will settle at an equilibrium level at which saving and investment are equal. This equilibrium rate of interest is shown in Figure 18-3 where demand and supply intersect.

In summary, then, the classical economists considered the rate of interest to be entirely a real phenomenon reflecting the real disutility suffered by savers as a result of their abstinence, on the one hand, and the real marginal productivity of capital goods, on the other.

[1] The classical investment schedule is related to, but not quite the same as, the Keynesian **MEI** schedule discussed in the preceding chapter.

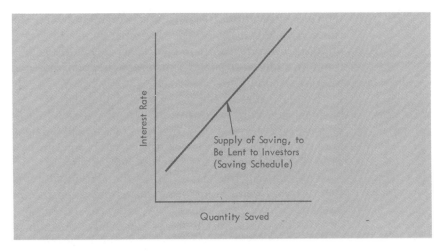

FIGURE 18-2 Supply of funds from saving

Reformulation into the
Loanable Funds Theory

There is much that is appealing and much that is correct in the classical interest theory. But it has not stood up under the test of time, partly because of institutional and structural changes in the economy over the years and partly because of flaws in the underlying assumptions.

In the first place, critics asked, is saving out of current income really the only source of funds to be lent out (and therefore to affect the interest rate)? What about banks? Certainly as creators of money (and not simply middlemen), they

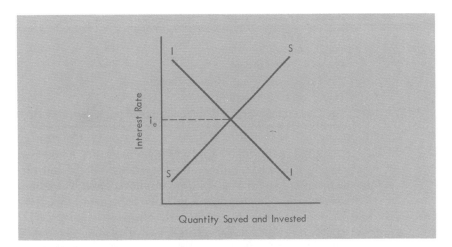

FIGURE 18-3 Classical equilibrium interest rate

lend money *in addition* to what savers save. And while we're about it, how about those savers? Is it really true that what is saved is *always* lent out at interest? Suppose savers *do* choose to hoard part of what they save in year 1 and then lend it out (in addition to year 2's saving) in the following year? Won't this affect the interest rate in both years?

Second, what of the other side of the market—the demand side? True, business investors do borrow much of what is lent, but are they the only borrowers? Surely we know that the government has been a significant borrower in recent decades. And for that matter, consumers are by no means all net savers. They, too, borrow and pay interest.

Questions such as these led to the reformulation of the classical interest theory into a more complete explanation called the *loanable funds theory of interest.*

The loanable funds theory, as noted, takes the interest rate as "the price that must be paid for the right to borrow and use loanable funds." To explain that price, one need only look at the components of the demand for, and supply of, loanable funds.

On the supply side, saving is still considered an important component.[2] Now, however, the contribution of banks and possibility of hoarding or dishoarding are also taken into account.

Components of Supply of Loanable Funds

1. Gross saving out of current income
   plus
2. New money created by banks (or minus money destroyed)
   plus
3. Dishoarding—lending of funds saved in previous years but hoarded then (or minus hoarding)

Let us consider a numerical example. Suppose that in year 1, the following events occur:

Total income received	$800 billion
Total consumption spending	700 billion
Therefore, total saving	100 billion
Total amount lent out by savers at interest	75 billion
Therefore, total hoarding	25 billion
Total new money created by banks in making loans	50 billion

What is the total supply of loanable funds made available in year 1? Pretty clearly it is $125 billion. Banks put in $50 billion of newly created money. Consumers saved $100 billion, but not all of it was lent out. The $25 billion that was hoarded during year 1 must be subtracted to arrive at the correct figure.

[2] Unlike the classical theory, however, there is no assurance that the quantity saved is larger the higher the interest rate. Some people save without reference to the interest rate, and some may even save *more* the *lower* the rate of interest.

Suppose now in year 2 that

Total income received	$900 billion
Total consumption spending	800 billion
Therefore, total saving	100 billion
Total amount lent out by savers at interest ($100 billion from this year's saving, plus the $25 billion that was hoarded in year 1)	125 billion
Therefore, total dishoarding	25 billion
Total new money created by banks in making loans	50 billion

In year 2, the supply of loanable funds totals $175 billion — $100 billion from year 2 saving, $50 billion from banks, and $25 billion from lending out money saved and hoarded last year.

So much for the supply side. What makes up the demand for loanable funds? Who demands the right to borrow and use the funds that savers, dishoarders, and banks make available?

Components of Demand for Loanable Funds

1. Business demand to finance the purchase of capital goods (investment)
   plus
2. Government demand to finance deficit spending (or minus government tax surplus)
   plus
3. Consumer demand to finance consumer purchases on credit

An increase on the part of any of these three groups of borrowers in their demand for loanable funds would, other things equal, raise the rate of interest. Similarly, a decrease in any of the components of the supply of loanable funds — less saving, more hoarding, or a cut in the money supply — would raise the rate of interest.

Graphically, the loanable funds theory of interest might appear as in Figure 18-4, where S equals saving, DH stands for dishoarding, ΔM represents an increase in the money supply, I equals demand by business for funds to finance investment, G_d stands for the government budget deficit, and C_d represents gross consumer borrowing. Note that the diagram assumes that dishoarding will occur at high interest rates and hoarding will be likely at low rates. The equilibrium rate of interest, as pointed out, is determined where the *demand for loanable funds forthcoming from business, government, and consumers equals the supply of loanable funds made available by savers, dishoarders, and the banks.*[3]

The Loanable Funds Theory and "Crowding Out"   Before turning to a consideration of the liquidity preference theory of interest, it might be useful to discuss how the loanable funds theory can be used to illustrate a current issue of consid-

---

[3] Note that the saving schedule has been drawn here with a positive slope reflecting a higher quantity saved at higher rates of interest. This classical-like assumption is *not* necessarily descriptive of reality.

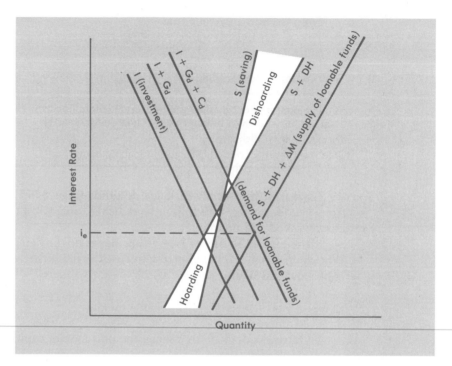

FIGURE 18-4   Graphical representation of loanable funds theory of interest

erable significance — the so-called "crowding out" effect of government deficit spending.

The crowding out effect is the tendency for the government, in the process of borrowing to finance deficit spending, to force up interest rates and thereby cut back on the volume of investment spending.

Crowding out, when it occurs, has two somewhat different impacts on the nation's economic welfare. First, it can undermine the effectiveness of discretionary fiscal policy. If, for example, the problem is excessive unemployment and expansionary fiscal policy is being employed to moderate it, the initial objective is to raise the level of total spending. This would be pursued, of course, by cutting taxes and/or raising the level of government spending. If, however, financing the deficit caused by the fiscal action results in a reduction in the investment spending portion of aggregate expenditures, this obviously reduces the expansionary impact of the policy. Thus, it weakens our ability to stabilize the economy via fiscal policy.

But crowding out can affect our long-run production potential as well as our shorter-run stabilization capabilities. If, for instance, deficit spending is carried out when the economy is at or near its full employment level of output, the increased government or consumer spending (permitted by lower taxes) can only come at the expense of investment spending. Therefore, the net effect is that the economy produces more government or consumer goods and fewer capital goods.[4] And this, of course, reduces our productive potential and future living standards.

[4] This result need not occur if there are large amounts of unemployed resources available. It *must* occur if there is no unemployment.

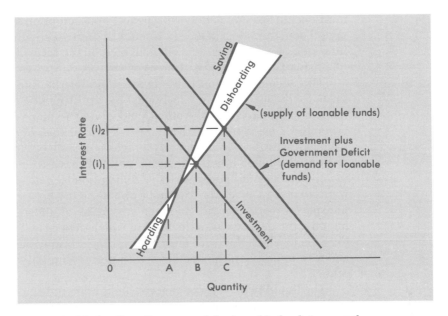

FIGURE 18-5   Crowding out and the loanable funds interest theory

The crowding out effect is easy to demonstrate using the loanable funds theory of interest. To make the diagram even simpler, however, let us assume that there is no consumer borrowing and no change in the money supply. This leaves us with a supply of loanable funds consisting entirely of saving plus or minus dishoarding or hoarding and a demand for loanable funds coming only from investors and the government. Consider Figure 18-5.

Note that had there been no government deficit to finance, the entire demand for loanable funds would have come from business investors with the result of an equilibrium interest rate of $0(i)_1$ and an amount spent on capital goods of $0B$. When the government enters the market for loanable funds to finance its deficit, however, the demand for loanable funds is shifted out to the right and the equilibrium interest rate is bid up to $0(i)_2$. At this higher interest rate, however, only $0A$ funds are borrowed for investment purposes with the remaining AC used by the government. The net effect is that AB of potential investment spending has been crowded out by the government's borrowing.

The Liquidity Preference Theory of Interest

When J. M. Keynes wrote his epic *General Theory,* he concocted an interest theory with an entirely different approach. As a longtime Cambridge economist, he was accustomed to thinking in terms of the demand for *money* rather than the quite different demand for loanable funds we have been discussing. To the Keynes of the *General Theory,* interest *is the price that must be paid to get people to forgo willingly the advantages of liquidity.*

Income recipients, Keynes pointed out, must make two decisions. First, they must decide how much they will spend on consumption and how much they will save. Then, they must decide how much of their saved funds they will lend out at interest and how much they will hold on to in the form of (perhaps temporarily) idle money.

This second decision is the crucial one for the interest rate. Lending out saved funds (such as by buying bonds) has the attraction of returning an interest income to the saver. On the other hand, giving up money in return for bonds or other IOUs has a real disadvantage—a loss of *liquidity*. Possession of money balances provides the holder advantages not available to the bondholder. The person who holds bonds but no money will have to go through the trouble, inconvenience, and perhaps risk of selling bonds to get money when he or she wants to make a purchase. The money holder is in a better position to take care of unexpected contingencies and take advantage of unexpected bargains. Consequently, the decision as to the form in which savings will be held is an economic decision in which the saver must contrast the attractiveness of an interest return and less liquidity on the one hand with perfect liquidity and no interest on the other.

The liquidity preference theorist looks upon the equilibrium rate of interest as **that rate that will cause people willingly to hold the existing supply of money.** There are, as we shall be discussing in more detail, two prime reasons for holding money. Some money must be held to finance expenditures on goods and services between paydays. Second—and this is the crucial matter—other amounts of money will be held willingly as an asset, beyond transactions needs, because the advantages of liquidity seem to outweigh the advantages of an interest return.

Clearly, this latter portion of the demand for money will vary inversely with the current rate of interest. If the rate of interest being paid to those who give up liquidity (and buy bonds) is very low, many people will find the advantage of holding money superior to the low return paid for parting with liquidity. The quantity of money demanded will thus be large. Conversely, if the current rate of interest is relatively high, the advantage of giving up liquidity by buying bonds is relatively greater. The quantity of money demanded will be small.

But let us not overlook one fact. The supply of money that exists (and that *must* be held, either willingly or unwillingly) is determined by the monetary authorities. If the current rate of interest is quite high, people will choose to hold relatively less money and more bonds. In fact, they may not *want* to hold all the money that exists under such conditions, but they have no choice. They (as a group) *must* hold all the money that the Federal Reserve has foisted upon them. If they do not *willingly* hold all this money, their individual efforts to get rid of the excess will tend (in a manner we describe shortly) to lower the rate of interest.

Similarly, suppose that the current rate of interest is very low, so that people desire to hold large amounts of money (the liquidity advantage exceeding the advantage of a small interest return). If the Federal Reserve is keeping the money supply at a low level, there may be less money in existence than people would *like* to hold. Consumers as a group cannot change the supply of money that exists but, as individuals, each can *try* to acquire more. These efforts, we shall see, will tend to raise the rate of interest.

In essence, then, the liquidity preference theory says that **the interest rate is determined by the demand for and supply of money.** If the demand for money (the amount people would willingly hold) exceeds today's supply of money, the interest rate will rise because of people's efforts to acquire more. If the supply of money that exists is greater than the demand for money (the amount willingly held), the efforts of people to get rid of the excess will force the interest rate down. **The equilibrium rate of interest, then, is that rate of interest at which people willingly hold (i.e., demand) exactly the supply of money that exists.**

One word of caution before we look more deeply into the demand for money. This theory is different from the loanable funds theory. The student should be careful *not* to identify the supply of loanable funds with the supply of money. They are two different animals. Similarly, the demand for loanable funds is quite different from the demand for money.

The Demand for Money

Much of the first 14 chapters was devoted to discussing the determinants of the supply of money. We need not repeat that material here. But our coverage of the demand for money thus far has been, to say the least, highly superficial. We have, as yet, done little more than allude to the fact that there is some sort of inverse relationship between the level of the interest rate and the quantity of money demanded. We must do better than that. We must know more about this demand for money.

When Keynes introduced his liquidity preference theory, he argued that there were three rational motives for holding (demanding) money. He entitled these the *transactions, precautionary,* and *speculative motives.* In our discussion, we shall ignore the precautionary motive[5] and deal separately with the transactions and speculative demands.

The Transactions Demand for Money   All of us have some need to hold money balances for some period to cover our requirements for cash for spending between paydays. We define *transactions balances* in just this way — *money, held in cash form temporarily, for the purpose of financing needed expenditures for goods and services between paydays.*

Transactions balances constitute assets held in noninterest-bearing (or, if in NOW accounts, low-interest-bearing) money form simply because of *convenience.* If, for example, a person is paid $1,500 on the first of each month and has every intention of spending all that income on consumer goods during the month, it would be *most* unusual for him or her to buy a $1,500 bond with it or put it in a savings account or even a money market fund to maximize interest earnings. Why? First, because he or she is unlikely to earn any interest, even in a savings account, if the money is needed in less than 30 days. Second, even if interest *could* be earned on it, the paltry return for such a limited time period would hardly be worth the time and trouble of dealing with the savings institution every day or so to draw out what is needed to spend that day.

All of us carry *some* transactions money balances to bridge the gap between the periodic receipt of income and the more or less continual expenditure of it.

---

[5] The precautionary motive holdings consist of money balances held, over and above those needed to finance transactions or take advantage of speculation on movements in the interest rate, to cover contingencies such as accident and sudden illness. We do not treat this motive separately because its determinants are quite similar to the transactions demand.

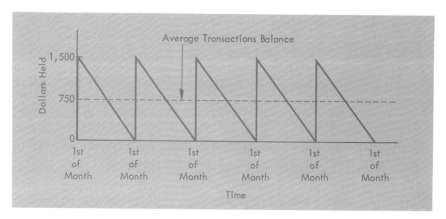

FIGURE 18-6   Transactions balances over time

Any person with change in pocket or purse, or a positive balance in a checking account, has a transactions demand for money if those are funds he or she counts on spending before the next paycheck arrives.

Probably the best way to look at the transactions demand for money is via the simple diagram in Figure 18-6. We depict there the transactions balances held by a man who is paid $1,500 per month, on the first of each month, and who spends that money at a constant rate throughout the month, ending up with a zero balance at the end of the month. Such a person has, on the average, $750 of transactions balance — $1,500 on the first of the month, $1,450 on the second, $1,400 on the third, and so forth, until, on the thirtieth, he spends his last $50.

If so prudent a spending pattern seems hardly applicable to anyone we know, we can just as easily depict by the same device the more familiar case (to most of us) of the person who spends most of her income shortly after payday. Suppose that our subject receives $1,500 on the first of each month but spends $1,300 of it in the first day, spreading the other $200 out equally over the remaining 29 days of the month.

Such a person's transactions balances are depicted in Figure 18-7. She, of course, has a much smaller average demand for transactions money than does her more "prudent" counterpart. On the average she holds somewhat less than $150 for transactions purposes — $1,500 the first day, $200 on the second, about $193.10 on the third, and so forth, spending her last $6.90 (approximately) on the thirtieth day.

It should be clear that all of us have some (however small) transactions demand for money. And, although it is equally obvious that we differ widely in the size of our individual transactions demands, it is not individual differences that most concern us in the task at hand. What is more important for our purposes here are the determinants of the size of the transactions demand for the nation as a whole. What kinds of changes in the economy could significantly increase or decrease the entire nation's transactions demand?

Determinants of the Quantity of Money Demanded for Transactions Purposes in the Nation as a Whole   The most obvious determinants are four: the public's payment habits, the degree of vertical integration of production, the development of

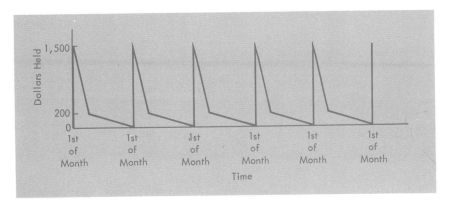

FIGURE 18-7   Transactions balances over time

the economy's financial system, and the level of income.[6] Let us discuss these in order.

Suppose that our prudent individual, who, it will be remembered, received $1,500 each month and spent it all with the unbelievable regularity of $50 per day until his balance was exhausted on the thirtieth day, is notified by his employer that henceforth he will be paid twice monthly, on the first and fifteenth. What effect, if any, will such a speeding up of his paydays have on his transactions demand?

Figure 18-8 depicts the situation. His previous payment and spending pattern is shown by the solid line and the new "two paydays per month" arrangement by the broken line. Assuming that he remains prudent and continues to spend just $50 per day, it is readily apparent that his average transactions demand for money has been cut in half. Whereas before he willingly held, on the average, $750 in transactions balances, now he finds he can get along just as well with a mean balance of $375.

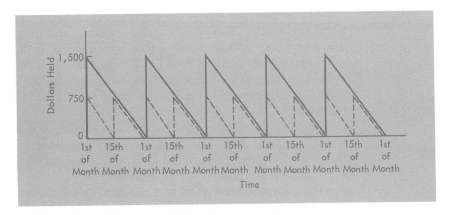

FIGURE 18-8   Transactions balances over time —
effect of reduction in payment period

[6] Another determinant, the rate of interest, will be considered shortly.

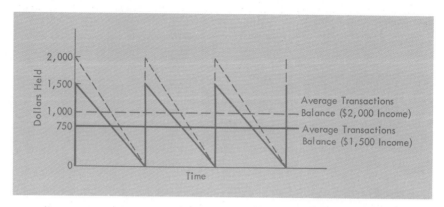

FIGURE 18-9   Transactions balances over time — effect of rise in income

If such a speedup in payment habits occurs throughout the economy, the result is clear. A smaller stock of money will suffice to do the same work as one twice as large. In terms of the equation of exchange, because money sits idle for a shorter period of time, on the average, the velocity of spending is raised. The same level of spending (MV) is thereby obtainable with a smaller supply of money. We can say then that *a speedup in payment habits tends to reduce the transactions demand for money,* whereas a slowdown in frequency of payment would raise the transactions demand.

The second determinant is the *degree of vertical integration of production.* If there is little vertical integration of production, each step in the productive process being carried out by separate firms, each firm must carry some transactions cash balance. If, on the other hand, production is carried on from raw material to finished product within the same highly integrated firm, there exists at least the possibility that a smaller total transactions balance will be needed to finance the entire process.

Third, the *development of the country's financial system* or, more specifically, *the availability of credit,* will certainly be a determining factor. A highly developed financial system, wherein opportunity to borrow funds to finance needed purchases is easily and economically available, will permit an individual to get along on a substantially smaller cash balance than is the case where it is very difficult to obtain credit. Consider, for example, the effects of the credit card in reducing the need for transactions money balances. The more highly developed the financial system, other things being equal, the lower the transactions demand for money.

Finally, *the level of income* itself is surely a quite important determinant. This is simply to say that the higher a person's income, the greater his transactions and therefore the greater his need for transactions cash balances. The point can perhaps be best illustrated as in Figure 18-9.

Here the solid lines, as before, indicate the fluctuation in cash balances under the assumptions that our subject's monthly pay is $1,500 and that he spends it evenly over the month. If his monthly income should now be raised to $2,000 and he should still choose to spend it all at a steady rate before his next payday, his transactions balance would behave in a manner depicted by the broken lines. Clearly the rise in income raises his transactions demand for money. With a

$1,500 monthly check, his average transactions balance is $750, whereas, with $2,000, the average for the month rises to $1,000. And, in this case, what is true for the individual would appear also to be true for the nation as a whole. The quantity of money demanded for transaction purposes for the community as a whole will surely rise as the nation's income (GNP) rises. For the more income we have, the more spending we do, and hence the larger transactions balances we need to facilitate that spending.

In summary, we can say the quantity of money demanded for transactions purposes will tend to be larger

1. The less frequently people are paid.
2. The less the vertical integration of industry structure.
3. The harder it is to borrow funds needed for spending.
4. The higher the level of income.

The Transactions Demand-for-Money Curve   Although all four of these factors affect the size of the transactions demand, the first three would appear to change only slowly over the long run. That is, a change in payment habits, degree of vertical integration, or maturity of the financial structure will certainly affect the transactions demand *when they change,* but all three normally change only slowly over a long period of time. Hence, within any short-run context, these three are not likely, *in fact,* to cause significant changes in the size of the transactions demand. The level of income, on the other hand, is subject to significant short-run as well as long-run changes. The result is that, in practice, the quantity of money demanded for transactions purposes changes, in the short run, largely in response to changes in the level of income (GNP).

To take account of these considerations, we depict the transactions demand for money graphically in Figure 18-10. Here the level of income is measured off on the vertical axis and quantity (of transactions funds demanded) on the hori-

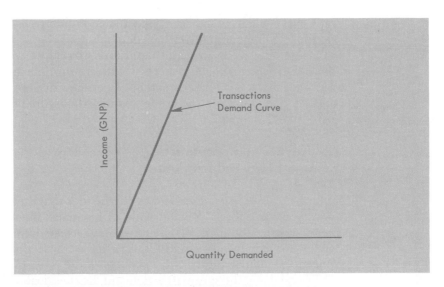

FIGURE 18-10   **Transactions demand-for-money curve**

zontal axis. The transactions demand curve itself is upward sloping, indicating that the quantity of transactions balances demanded rises as income rises. *The degree of slope depends on the other three determinants.* For example, the effect of a speedup of payment habits, further vertical integration, or a significant advance in the nation's credit facilities would be to *steepen* the curve itself. Opposite changes in any of these three would have a tendency to move the curve to a flatter position.

We have, then, in Figure 18-10, a curve that tells us how, with a given set of payment habits, vertical integration, and financial system, the quantity of money demanded for transactions purposes varies with the level of income.

The Transactions Demand and the Quantity Theory   There was nothing revolutionary or even novel about Keynes's transactions demand for money. Indeed, if we were to stop here, we would be right back in a crude quantity theory world.

The student will remember that the early quantity theorists held that V' (or k') was essentially a constant because the only rational reason they could accept for holding money was to finance upcoming expenditures — the transactions demand, pure and simple.

True, they recognized that changes in payment habits, integration, or the financial structure would tend to change V' (k'), but only slowly in the long run. In the short run, the only factor that could change the quantity of money demanded was a change in money income itself.

What Cambridge economist Keynes was arguing in his discussion of the transactions demand for money was completely in keeping with views that had held sway for years. Take, for example, the cash balance equation:

$$M = k'PQ$$

What does it really say? In equilibrium, the supply of money (M) must equal the demand for money ($k'PQ$). If, as quantity theorists assumed, k' is a constant, then the quantity of money demanded for transactions purposes varies only as the level of money income (PQ) varies. If we were to plot this demand for money in a graph, we would have something like that in Figure 18-11 where the line depicts the demand for money and its slope depends upon the size of k'. As k' was thought to change only when long-run determinants such as payment habits and the financial structure change, it seemed quite appropriate for the quantity theorists to assume that k' (V') was essentially a constant in the short run. And if k' is a constant (and Q is also), the crude quantity theory follows by definition.

The Keynesian Speculative (or Asset) Demand for Money

Keynes, however, was not content with the idea that the demand for money was entirely a transactions demand. One of his major innovations in the *General Theory* was the argument that there was also a speculative demand for money, a demand for money balances in addition to the transactions demand, that results from speculation about the future course of the rate of interest.

In explaining the speculative demand, Keynes dealt with a model in which it was assumed that savers have only two forms in which to hold wealth — long-

FIGURE 18-11   Transactions demand curve related to quantity theory

term bonds and money. By so limiting the options of savers, Keynes not only departed sharply from reality as we know it but also opened himself to challenge. Later on, we consider some of these challenges. For the moment, however, let us accept Keynes's initial assumptions.

Relation Between Bond Prices and Interest Rates   To understand fully the speculative demand for money a la Keynes, we must do some preliminary spadework on the relation between bond prices and interest rates.

To keep the discussion as simple as possible without sacrificing anything fundamental, we work with an example in which the bonds involved are *perpetuities*—bonds that have no maturity date. The borrower (issuer of the bonds) agrees to pay interest to the holder forever, but the principal is never to be paid back. In such a case, the only way a bondholder can get the principal back (hopefully) is by selling the bond to someone else.

Suppose we take, for our example, a bond that was originally issued by the lender at a par value and purchase price of $1,000. The bond carries a coupon rate of 8 percent, which is to say that the issuer agrees to pay, in perpetuity, 8 percent of the par value of the bond ($80) annually to the holder. Let us also assume that the market rate of interest, which we shall define as the *rate of interest being paid elsewhere in the economy on securities of a risk similar to this one*, was also 8 percent when the bond was originally issued.[7] These figures are listed in the first line of Table 18-1.

---

[7] This is simply a commonsense assumption. If the market rate of interest had been 9 percent when the bond was originally issued, no rational lender would have bought it at par because, by definition, similar investments were available that paid more. On the other hand, if the market rate of interest had been 6 percent, the issuer of this bond would be foolish to attach a coupon rate of 8 percent to his obligation. Presumably he could, in such a case, attract borrowers by paying less. Simple logic leads us to expect the coupon rate of a newly issued bond to approximate the market rate of interest.

TABLE 18-1   An example — the relation between interest rates and bond prices

Date	Par value	Coupon rate	Coupon payment	Market rate of interest	Market value of bond
When issued	$1,000	8%	$80	8%	$1,000
After interest rates rise	1,000	8	80	10	800
After interest rates fall	1,000	8	80	5	1,600

Now the par value, coupon rate, and coupon payment are printed on the face of the security and, as such, cannot change while the bond is outstanding. The issuer is committed to paying $80 per year to the holder, regardless of any other changes in the economy.

The market rate of interest and the market value of the bond, however, are something else again. The former, as we know, can easily change as a result of changes in money supply, saving, investment, hoarding, dishoarding, and the like. Our task is to understand how such changes in interest rates relate to changes in bond prices.

Suppose, in our example in Table 18-1, that five years after the bond is issued, the market rate of interest rises from 8 percent to 10 percent. At what price can the holder of the bond sell it? Clearly, no rational person would be willing to pay $1,000 for it, as this would be tantamount to accepting an $80-per-year income when otherwise similar alternatives are available paying $100 per year. If an actual return of 10 percent on a bond of similar risk is available elsewhere, the maximum price for which our bond can be sold to rational people is $800 (.10X = $80). That is, because $80 is all that this bond pays, the rational purchaser will be willing to pay an amount that "$80 is 10 percent of," and no more.

The holder of the bond will suffer a $200 capital loss if he or she sells it after the market rate of interest rises to 10 percent. A rise in the rate of interest has thus been reflected in lowering bond prices.

If we look further into the future, say, ten years from the date of issue, and assume that by that time the market rate of interest has fallen to 5 percent, we get the reverse result. Now the holder of this bond paying $80 per year can expect to find a buyer who will pay substantially *more* than the $1,000 par value. For if 5 percent is a prospective buyer's best alternative, he or she should be willing to pay up to $1,600 to acquire our bond (.05X = $80). In this case, the seller of the bond realizes a handsome capital gain.

Though the case of a bond with a fixed maturity date requires more complicated arithmetic, it is no different in principle.[8] By way of summary, we can say that **whenever interest rates fall, bond prices rise, and vice versa.**

---

[8] In the case of a bond with five years until maturity, for example, the present value can be computed from the formula

$$V = \frac{R}{1+i} + \frac{R}{(1+i)^2} + \frac{R}{(1+i)^3} + \frac{R}{(1+i)^4} + \frac{R}{(1+i)^5} + \frac{P}{(1+i)^5}$$

This relationship is purely arithmetical and should be interpreted as definitional rather than as a cause and effect proposition. To say that interest rates rise is just another way of saying that bond prices fall. To say that bond prices rise is just another way of saying that interest rates have fallen. We shall therefore use them interchangeably.

An Example of the Advantage of Holding Speculative Balances   Let us get back to the speculative demand for money. If people confidently expect the rate of interest to rise in the near future, they are, according to Keynes, perfectly justified in holding idle (speculative) money balances over and above their needs for transactions and precautionary purposes for that period. Indeed, they would be irrational if they did not do so.

It is a simple matter to demonstrate the point. Suppose that Miss Jones expects the interest rate to rise from the present 8 percent level to 10 percent within six months. If we return to the example from Table 18-1, she would have to pay $1,000 for the bond if she should buy it today while the market rate is still at 8 percent, but if her expectations turn out to be correct, she can buy it six months from now for $800. Of course, by holding idle money for the six-month period, she would be forgoing an interest return of $40 (half a year's interest).[9] But there is certainly nothing irrational about giving up $40 interest return to be able to save $200 on the purchase price of the bond! Clearly there is logic in a speculative demand for money.

The Community's Speculative Demand for Money   Granting that holding idle money for speculative purposes makes sense, what determines the size of this demand on the part of the community as a whole? Obviously, the more people who expect interest rates to rise, the greater the speculative demand. But this

---

where

$$R = \text{annual coupon payment}$$

$$V = \text{present market value of the bond}$$

$$i = \text{market rate of interest}$$

$$P = \text{par value of the bond, to be repaid at maturity}$$

The expression can be reduced to

$$V = \frac{R}{i}\left[1 - \frac{1}{(1 + i)^5}\right] = \frac{P}{(1 + i)^5}$$

Our example of perpetuity, in which the interest is paid forever [so that $k/(1 + i)^5$ becomes infinitely small and the last term, $P/(1 + i)^5$, is zero], reduces the formula to $V = R/i$. As the limiting case, the change in present value resulting from any given change in the rate of interest will always be larger for a perpetuity than for the more realistic case of a bond with a fixed maturity date. Also, the closer the bond is to the maturity date, the less the change in its market price that will result from an interest rate change.

[9] Of course it would not really be necessary to forgo an interest return altogether. Her most likely course would be to hold her funds in a NOW account or a money market deposit account (a part of M2) while awaiting the expected change in bond prices. Since bond yields are normally higher than these more liquid alternatives, she would still be forgoing some interest return.

does not advance us very far, as it leaves unanswered the fundamental question, "What leads people to expect changes in interest rates?"

One way of approaching this more fundamental question is to consider people's ideas regarding the *normal range* of interest rates. Our ideas of *high* or *low* interest rates are usually formulated in light of our recent experience. If we have become "used to" interest rates that have varied from 2 to 6 percent, we tend to think of 6 percent as pretty high and 2 percent as quite low. If, on the other hand, we have become accustomed to rates varying from 5 to 15 percent, 12 or 13 percent does not seem unusually high and anything below 6 percent appears to us as quite low.

People's conceptions of what the normal range of interest rate fluctuation *is* must certainly form part of the basis for their expectations of *changes* in rates. For example, if people, because of their recent observations, form the judgment that interest rates normally fluctuate within a 2 to 6 percent range, the existence of an 8 percent rate would lead them to expect, almost compellingly, a drop in rates. An 8 percent interest rate appears abnormally high and they expect a fall. Similarly, an actual 1.5 percent rate appears abnormally low, leading them to expect an increase.

The same thing applies to the whole community. If the entire community feels that 5 percent is as low as interest rates are going to get and 15 percent is as high as they are likely to go, when interest rates actually reach (or perhaps even surpass) 15 percent, everyone will expect them to fall. If, on the other hand, interest rates actually get down to (or below) 5 percent, everyone will expect them to rise.

Under such circumstances, we should expect rational people to hold *no* speculative money balances when the interest rate is 15 percent, because at such a level they unanimously expect bond prices to *rise,* and they will go out and buy them now rather than wait. Conversely, when the rate of interest is down to 5 percent, we can expect people to hold very large speculative money balances because all look for interest rates to rise (bond prices to fall), and it will be preferable to hold their saving in money form until they do.

Following this logic, it would appear that the community's speculative demand for money will vary inversely with the rate of interest. At rates that are low relative to recent experience, the quantity demanded for speculative purposes will be large; whereas at rates that are high relative to recent experience, speculative balances will be small.

Of course, our discussion thus far oversimplifies greatly. No individual is quite sure just where the upper and lower interest rate limits are. Although one may feel that the normal range is 5 percent to 15 percent, one is not quite certain, for example, that rates will not start rising again after dipping to 6 percent. Therefore, instead of holding no speculative balances until a 5 percent interest rate is reached, one may hold *some* at 6 percent, but even more at 5 percent, where the likelihood of a rise is even greater. If the rate of interest should actually reach 4 percent, and this is so low that people are positively convinced it *must* rise, then they will rationally hold *all* added wealth in idle speculative balances, betting on a drop in bond prices, which appears all but certain.

Then, too, it is a gross oversimplification to talk as if all people were alike, with exactly the same interest rate expectations. Some may look upon 5 percent as the "lowest possible rate" but others may consider 6 or 7 percent as the floor and choose to hold speculative balances when those market rates are realized.

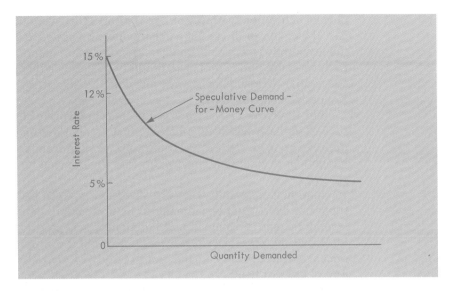

FIGURE 18-12 Speculative demand-for-money curve

Similarly, for the individual who considers an existing rate of 15 percent to be the highest possible, it would be irrational to hold any speculative money balances. Not so, however, for his neighbor who feels that interest rates may rise as high as 17 or 18 percent.

What kind of speculative demand for the nation as a whole would result if all individuals behaved this way? Clearly the quantity of money demanded for speculative reasons would vary inversely with the rate of interest. The demand for speculative balances would look something like that in Figure 18-12.

Here we depict a situation in which no speculative funds are held when the interest rate reaches 15 percent, presumably indicating that when interest rates are that high, *no one* expects a further increase and, therefore, no one holds any speculative money balances. At a rate of 12 percent, however, some few people expect a rise in interest rates, so there is a small positive quantity demanded. The lower the interest rate, the more people come to expect a rise; consequently, the greater the quantity of speculative funds demanded. By the time the rate of interest gets down to as low as 5 percent, according to Figure 18-12, *everyone* is convinced that interest rates must rise, so that the speculative demand becomes infinite. This area (the flat portion) of the speculative demand-for-money curve has been given the name *liquidity trap* and has a significance to which we return shortly.

Post-Keynesian Amendments and Additions to the Demand-for-Money Concept

Some have argued that the liquidity preference theory of interest was the key contribution of the Keynesian revolution. Certainly it was of major significance. If the demand for money (and hence V′) is subject to so unstable a determinant as people's expectations, then we must be much less certain about the effects of a change in the money supply on expenditures than were the early quantity theorists. If changes in M can be partially offset by opposite changes in V′, then the money supply is a less all-important variable and monetary policy is a substantially less sure policy tool. The liquidity preference theory of interest, with the speculative demand for money playing the star role, was certainly a major Keynesian contribution.

But the *General Theory* was a pioneering work of the 1930s and Keynes's successors have had over a half century to comprehend, ponder, debate, and improve upon his theoretical framework. A significant portion of this later work has gone into amending his insights into the demand for money.

Revision in Transactions Demand   To Keynes, as to his classical predecessors, the prime short-run determinant of the transactions demand for money was the level of income. This much is still generally accepted.

However, several writers have pointed out the importance of another determinant of transactions demand, not stressed by Keynes.[10] The new variable is the rate of interest itself.

To relate the size of transactions balances solely to the level of income to be transacted, these writers point out, is to make the determination of these active balances all too mechanistic. To say that there are always x dollars in transactions balances when income is y dollars is equivalent to saying that transactors have no decision to make and no alternatives to consider.

Clearly, within limits at least, this is not the case. Any money held, whether in the form of transactions or asset balances, *could* be lent out at interest. If a person has made the decision to hold an average of $500 in transactions balances to finance upcoming consumption expenditures, she has presumably decided that the interest return she could earn on it by lending it out for a few days or so is not worth the trouble, cost, and inconvenience of doing so. To deposit one's money in a savings account on day 1 and then withdraw it for spending on day 3 or 4 is more bother than the few cents of interest sacrificed is worth.

This may be so when the rate of interest is 5 percent, but does the same thing necessarily follow when it has risen to 10 percent? And if a 5 percent return on $500 for a week doesn't seem worth two trips to the bank, would the same thing be true if what was being sacrificed was 5 percent of $1 million for a week?

Certainly rational people must consider the opportunity cost of their transactions balances. Although it may normally be convenient to hold an average of $500 in transactions balances to finance $2,000 of expenditures per month, a doubling of the rate of interest may be sufficient incentive to cause a transactor to make those two trips to the savings bank or calls to the money market fund and cut her average transactions balance substantially.

These considerations are especially pertinent in the case of huge business firms and state and local governments whose financial managers handle immense cash balances. When large transactions balances are involved, potentially large amounts of interest are being sacrificed. As interest rates rise, the sophisticated

[10] See, for example, A. H. Hansen, *Monetary Theory and Fiscal Policy* (New York: McGraw-Hill, 1949); W. J. Baumol, "The Transactions Demand for Cash: An Inventory Theoretic Approach," *Quarterly Journal of Economics*, November 1952; and James Tobin, "The Interest Elasticity of Transactions Demand for Cash," *Review of Economics and Statistics*, August 1956.

financial managers of big institutions find it more and more in their interests to take the trouble required to economize on their transactions balances. For, in these cases, even one day's interest lost may be a substantial amount. There is solid evidence that corporate and government financial managers do, indeed, tend to pare the size of their transactions balances when interest rates rise. And because more than half the money supply is held by business, such actions will likely have a significant impact on the community's total transactions demand.

The upshot of all this is that it appears that the transactions demand for money varies positively with the level of income and negatively with the rate of interest.

This amendment to the Keynesian framework is of major significance. The speculative demand for money and its negative relation to the rate of interest had long been considered a crucial element of Keynesian theory and its associated policy positions. This was so because the Keynesian case for a variable velocity and for fiscal policy as a stabilization weapon rested heavily on an inverse interest rate–demand for money relationship. Recognition of the fact that the transactions demand for money *also* varies inversely with the rate of interest relieved Keynesian theory and policy of a possibly unwarranted reliance on the speculative demand for money. The result is that whether or not one accepts Keynes's speculative demand as a major factor, the total demand for money varies inversely with the rate of interest. And that is a crucial corollary to the Keynesian policy positions.

Revision in Speculative (or Asset) Demand   The Keynesian speculative money demand depended heavily on the concept of a "normal" range of interest rates. Only if the interest rate was below normal, and therefore expected to rise, was it rational to hold speculative money balances.

According to Keynes,

1. People hold speculative money balances because of expectations of interest rate increases (and accompanying capital losses on bonds).

2. The quantity of speculative money balances demanded is larger, the lower the interest rate (that is, the speculative demand curve has a negative slope) because, the lower the rate, the more intense the expectation of a rise becomes.

3. The *level* of the speculative demand curve for money depends on the range over which people consider interest fluctuations to be *normal*. If, for example, the normal range in the public's mind were from 2 percent to 6 percent, the curve would become flat at 2 percent and cut the vertical axis at 6 percent. If, on the other hand, the public's ideas of normality should change to the point where they consider 4 percent an unusually low rate and 10 percent a high one, the speculative demand curve would shift to the higher limits set by the 4 percent and 10 percent figures.

Some post-Keynesians, while accepting the validity of the concept of an asset demand for money (a demand for money in excess of that needed to finance transactions), have expressed reservations with regard to Keynes's heavy dependence on speculation as its raison d'être.

It has been pointed out, for example, that one can explain the existence and negative slope of the asset (speculative) demand-for-money curve without any reliance at all upon the concept of a normal range of interest rates. Even if the public has no prior conceptions of the likely direction of movement of interest rates, the mere knowledge that they are likely to change in either direction will be sufficient to produce a downward-sloping asset demand-for-money curve.[11] The argument is a fairly simple one.

When one buys a bond (instead of holding asset money balances), one obtains the advantage of interest but incurs the disadvantages of illiquidity. Among the disadvantages of illiquidity is the risk that interest rates will rise, causing capital losses to the holder.

Now no one can be *sure* that the rate of return will move in one certain direction, but one can be confident that it will change — up or down. Even if one thinks that there is as great a chance that interest rates will fall (conferring capital gains) as that they will rise (inflicting capital losses), one can hardly be indifferent to the risk that they may rise.

Suppose, for example, that an investor is faced with the following decision. He has $100 that he can keep in money form or use to purchase a $100 bond paying 5 percent. If he keeps the $100 (and the price level is constant), he is certain of what he will have. If he buys the bond *and if the interest rate doesn't rise and cause a capital loss,* he will have $105 next year. But that "if" is not a small one.

Suppose that our investor feels that it is most likely that the interest rate will stay about where it is but that there are equal (smaller) probabilities that it will change (up or down) by 1 percent. The most likely case is that it will not change, so that the $5 of interest return will be clear gain. Does this mean that he will give up the certainty of holding money to buy the bond?

Not necessarily. The small (equal) chance of capital gain or loss arising out of an interest rate fall or rise involves some degree of risk. And although the 5 percent interest return is a "good" thing favoring purchase of the bond, the risk of interest rate change is a "bad" thing opposing its purchase (favoring the holding of idle money instead).

At low rates of interest, the "bad" thing (risk) may well be dominant, so that large money balances will be held. As the interest rate rises, however, the return compensates more and more for the risk involved, so that more bonds will be purchased and less idle money will be held. It is therefore rational to hold asset money balances even without any conception of a normal interest rate level. And, following this logic, the asset demand-for-money curve will be negatively sloped, indicating larger asset money balances at lower interest rates.

Nor, in the opinions of many, is the level of the asset demand-for-money curve adequately explained by the range of the public's interest rate expectations. For one thing, we could expect the quantity of money held as an asset to be smaller, at any given rate of interest, the greater the variety (i.e., for other than transactions purposes) of near-monies available. Surely, it has been argued, a community whose claims to wealth consist of nothing but money and highly illiquid bonds will find a need to hold a larger percentage of its wealth in the form

---

[11] See J. Tobin, "Liquidity Preference as Behavior Toward Risk," *Review of Economic Studies,* February 1958.

of money than another community in which many diverse near-monies, issued by a variety of financial institutions, are available to compete with money as a means of satisfying this desire for liquidity. Keynes, of course, assumed a world in which the only financial assets available were bonds and money. Clearly such an assumption does not fit our current scene, and the argument here is that the existence of near-monies makes a significant difference.

Finally, it has been pointed out that the community's wealth must also be considered as a factor determining the level of the asset demand-for-money curve. Certainly a wealthier community that is attempting to maintain a portfolio of assets that, in some sense, satisfies its relative desires for liquid and illiquid assets can be expected to demand more money (and other assets too) to hold than a poorer community with similar tastes and expectations.

Once these amendments and additions are made to the Keynesian arguments, we have an asset demand-for-money curve that will lie farther to the right:

1. The greater the community's wealth,
2. The less the variety of other liquid assets available, and
3. The higher the range of interest rates the community looks upon as normal.

The curve will be steeper,

1. The wider the range over which the average person expects interest rate fluctuation, and
2. The greater the divergence of opinion among the public as to the normal range of interest rates. For example, if half the population considers 1 percent a normal low and 6 percent a normal high, while the other half considers 5 percent the likely low and 10 percent the high, the community's asset demand for money will be steeper (stretching from 1 percent to 10 percent) than if everyone agreed on a range from 1 percent to 6 percent.

The Total Demand for Money

Now we must bring our two pieces together. The total demand for money is the sum of the transactions demand and the asset (speculative) demand, and our main task here is to combine the two, both conceptually and graphically.

We concluded earlier that the quantity of money demanded for transactions purposes changes primarily as a result of changes in the level of income.[12] The quantity demanded for asset purposes, on the other hand, varies with the rate of interest. How can we depict these two in the same two-dimensional graph?

Figure 18-13 deals with this problem. In part (a) the transactions demand is drawn; in part (b) the asset demand is reproduced. In part (c) the two are combined to form the **total** demand for money.

---

[12] For simplicity's sake, we ignore the fact that the transactions demand is also related to the interest rate.

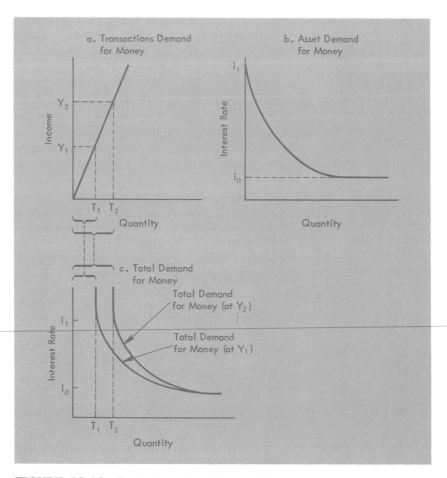

FIGURE 18-13   Derivation of total demand-for-money curve

Because there is no way to show variations in three variables (interest rate, income level, and quantity of money demanded) in a two-dimensional diagram, explicit reference to one must be eliminated. Our choice, as indicated by Figure 18-13c, is to eliminate income and plot the total demand-for-money curve with the vertical axis measuring off changes in interest rates and the horizontal axis, quantity demanded.

How then do we take account of the unquestioned fact that changes in the level of income, by changing the quantity of money demanded for transactions purposes, will change the total demand for money? Very simply.

As Figure 18-13 shows, we must draw a new total demand-for-money curve for each level of income. For example, in part (a), when the level of income is Y_1, the quantity demanded for transactions purposes is T_1. For this particular income level, a fixed number of dollars is demanded for transactions purposes. We take account of that amount in part (c) by the dashed vertical line labeled T_1. Then, to form the total demand for money, we simply "add on," horizontally, the additional quantities demanded at various rates of interest for asset purposes. The result is the *total demand for money when the level of income is at Y_1.*

If the level of income should rise to Y_2, a whole new total demand-for-money curve is required. Such a change in income would raise the amount demanded for transactions purposes to T_2 in part (a), which, in part (c), is reflected by the dashed vertical line labeled T_2. When the (assumed unchanged) asset demand is added to this larger transactions demand, the result is a higher total demand-for-money curve, labeled "Total Demand for Money" (at Y_2).

We arrive then, at a diagram in which changes in the level of income shift the entire total demand-for-money curve and changes in the rate of interest (by altering the quantity demanded for asset purposes) change the quantity demanded via movements along a given demand curve.

The Demand for Money, the Supply of Money, and the Equilibrium Rate of Interest

Now that we have made our way through the reasoning that underlies the concept of demand for money, we are prepared to put it together with the supply and discuss the determination of the equilibrium rate of interest.

Supply and demand are shown together in Figure 18-14. The supply of money, being a certain number of dollars at any point in time, is shown as a vertical line.[13] In the diagram, the equilibrium rate of interest is i_e.

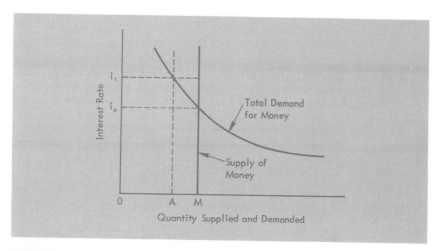

FIGURE 18-14 Supply and demand for money —
the equilibrium rate of interest

[13] The vertical line for the supply of money implies an assumption that the supply of money is autonomously determined by the monetary authorities and does not vary with the rate of interest. Recent research indicates that this is not entirely accurate. The monetary authorities can determine the amount of bank reserves, but the money supply depends also on what banks do with reserves. There are some indications that the money supply actually gets larger at higher interest rates as banks find lending more rewarding. This is a matter of some significance, as it tends to influence the potential effectiveness of both monetary and fiscal policy.

Why must the rate of interest tend toward the point where the demand for money equals its supply? Suppose that, for the moment, the actual market rate is i_1. At this rate, the quantity of money people *desire* to hold for transactions and asset purposes (read off the total demand-for-money curve) is less than the supply that exists (which they *must* hold). Consequently, some people hold some money *unwillingly* (specifically, the amount AM at i_1).

Now no person needs to hold on to money that he or she does not want to hold. But, short of giving or throwing it away, what can a person *do* with money he or she does not want to hold? One answer, of course, is to spend it to buy bonds.

What will be the effects of unwanted cash being spent to buy bonds? Assuming that the supply of bonds available is unchanged, the immediate result can only be a rise in their prices. But, as we have seen, higher bond prices are equivalent to lower interest rates. The market rate of interest will thus be forced down by the price rise. For how long must this process of buying more bonds with unwanted cash, raising bond prices, and lowering interest rates continue? Clearly, until there is no more unwanted cash to keep it going. A look at Figure 18-14 will show that this point will only be reached when the market rate of interest has fallen from i_1 to i_e. Here, equilibrium is restored in the sense that people willingly hold in their transactions and asset balances all the money that exists.

Perhaps one more example will help to clarify this point. Suppose, as in Figure 18-15 that the rate of interest is originally at the equilibrium level of i_1, and that the Federal Reserve, in pursuance of a tight money policy, upsets this equilibrium by reducing the supply of money from S of M_1 to S of M_2.

Immediately after the cut in money supply, individuals find themselves (at the relatively low i_1 interest rate) desiring to hold more money in their transactions and asset balances than there is money to be held. What can they do about this kind of frustration? *Individuals* can accumulate larger cash balances not only by cutting back on their purchases of bonds but also by offering for sale some of the bonds they already own. Such action, of course, does nothing to increase the

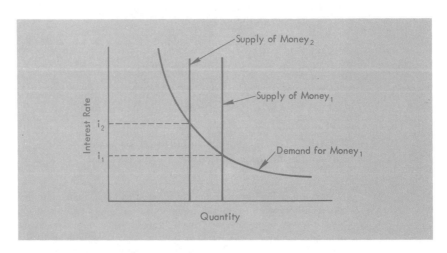

FIGURE 18-15   **Effect of reduction in money supply**

supply of money for the community as a whole (merely transferring the shortage from one person to another), but it will have the effect (via lowering the demand for, and raising the supply of, bonds on the market) of lowering bond prices and raising interest rates. When interest rate i_2 is reached, we again have equilibrium because now people only want to hold the smaller money supply that exists.

Review Questions

1. Contrast the *loanable funds* and *liquidity preference* theories of interest.

2. "An increase in dishoarding affects interest rates in the same direction as an open-market purchase by the Fed." Do you agree? Explain.

3. What are transactions money balances? Carefully explain how each of the following affect the slope of the transactions demand for money curve:
   a. Payment habits
   b. The availability of credit
   c. The degree of vertical integration of production

4. Explain carefully how and why the current rate of interest might affect the quantity of money demanded for transactions purposes. How might an inverse relation between the rate of interest and the quantity of money demanded for transactions purposes affect the degree of effectiveness of a contractionary monetary policy? Explain.

5. "If the only reason people willingly held money was for transactions purposes, and the quantity demanded was not affected by the rate of interest, one of the key assumptions of the 'old' quantity theory would be valid." Explain.

6. Verbally and graphically explain (using the liquidity preference theory of interest)
   a. How a law outlawing the credit card might affect interest rates.
   b. The process whereby the interest rate would move from the old to the new equilibrium level.

7. Verbally and graphically explain (using the liquidity preference theory of interest)
   a. How a decrease in the level of GNP would affect interest rates.
   b. The process whereby the interest rate would move from the old to the new equilibrium level.

8. Carefully explain the logic of an asset demand for money as well as why the quantity of money demanded for asset purposes would be expected to be larger at lower interest rates.

9. What would be the significance, for expansionary monetary policy, of the economy being currently in a "liquidity trap"?

10. Using an appropriately labeled diagram depicting the loanable funds theory of interest, illustrate how government borrowing may crowd out investment spending.

11. Explain what will happen to the level of the total demand for money curve as a result of
    a. A rise in GNP.
    b. A speedup in payment habits.
    c. A reduction in the level of the range of interest rates considered normal.

12. List all the determinants of the level of the asset demand-for-money curve.

13. Speculate on the likely impact on the effectiveness of monetary policy of the quantity of money *supplied* being directly related to the rate of interest. Can you think of any reason why the quantity of money supplied *might* vary positively with the rate of interest? (Remember "desired" excess reserves?)

Review and Use of the Theory — The Keynesian Model

The three previous chapters were intended to serve as building blocks. Each has concentrated on developing one part of the Keynesian theory of income determination. The task that remains is to assemble the pieces to construct a single, usable, theoretical framework.

Our approach will be two pronged. First, we shall review and summarize the important ideas developed in Chapters 16, 17, and 18, winding up with a graphical model of the economy that encompasses them all. Then, we go to some lengths to demonstrate how such a model can be used as a framework for analyzing the effects of various changes in the economy on its performance.

Summary of the Parts and Development of the Whole

A Review

We started off in Chapter 16 with a discussion of the immediate determinants of the level of production and income. We observed first that production tends to rise whenever total spending exceeds production, that production will fall whenever total spending falls short of production, and that a change in either direction will stop only when income and production reach the equilibrium level where spending just equals production.

When we looked at this mechanism in more detail, we saw that all-important total spending level was composed of consumption spending, investment spending, and government spending. Assuming as a first approximation that investment and government spending were autonomously determined by factors other than income, we concentrated on the determinants of consumption. Here we

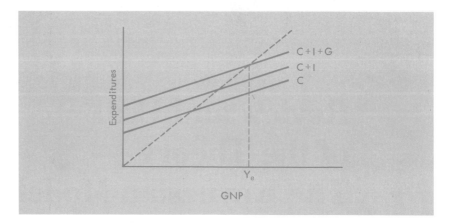

FIGURE 19-1   Equilibrium income determination diagram

concluded that given consumer expectations, wealth, and the like, consumption spending varies with the level of income. These considerations provided us with the basis for producing Figure 19-1 to depict the determination of the equilibrium level of production.

What this diagram tells us is that given the amount spent by government and investors, if we survey the public so that we know how much it will spend on consumption at various levels of income, we can from these three pieces of information figure out the equilibrium level of production and income.

Of course, the amount spent on investment is not a given datum. Consequently, we went on in Chapter 17 to investigate the investment decision somewhat more thoroughly. Here we developed an investment demand schedule, entitled the marginal efficiency of investment schedule, the level of which depended mainly on business managers' expectations of the future profits to be had by investing. This **MEI** curve, we said, tells us how much investment spending there will be at various rates of interest. The two diagrams together (as in Figure

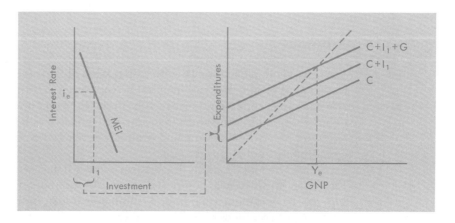

FIGURE 19-2   MEI and income determination diagrams combined

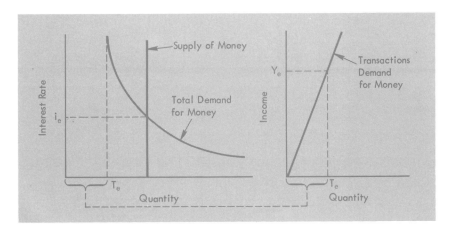

FIGURE 19-3 Interest rate determination

19-2), then, provided us with a more complete picture than Figure 19-1 does alone.

Here we were able to say, given the rate of interest, that investment spending will be so and so much and that it, along with government spending and the consumption function, will determine the equilibrium income level.

This led us finally to investigate what determines the rate of interest. To fit in more easily with our analysis, we chose to emphasize the liquidity preference theory of interest, wherein interest rates depend on the demand for and supply of money. Here we saw that the demand for money is composed of two parts, the transactions and asset demands. The size of the transactions demand depends, most importantly, on the level of income, whereas the quantity demanded for asset purposes varies inversely with the rate of interest. The two together make up the total demand for money, which, along with the supply of money, determines the equilibrium rate of interest.

Thus we have made a complete circle. In Figure 19-2, constructed on the basis of Chapters 16 and 17, we say *"given the rate of interest,* the MEI schedule plus the consumption schedule and government spending *will tell us the equilibrium level of income."* In Figure 19-3, based on Chapter 18, we say *"given the level of income,* we can compute the quantity of money demanded for transactions purposes, which, along with the asset demand and the supply of money, *will tell us the equilibrium interest rate."* Clearly, these two parts of the analysis are interdependent and need to be combined for a complete theory. That is precisely what we plan to do next.

The Four-Diagram Model

Figure 19-4 presents the full theory in diagrammatic form. It includes nothing we have not discussed before, the only new feature being the fact that we have combined it all into one four-diagram model.

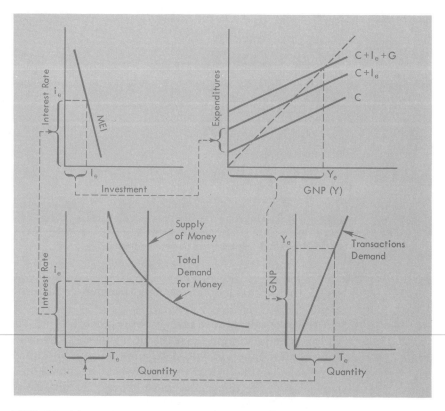

FIGURE 19-4   An economy in "general" equilibrium

Figure 19-4 is drawn to show an economy in **"general"** *equilibrium*. That is to say, the equilibrium level of income determined in the upper right-hand drawing calls forth (in the lower right-hand drawing) a quantity of money demanded for transactions purposes, which, along with the asset demand and money supply (lower left-hand drawing), determines an equilibrium rate of interest that permits a level of investment (upper left-hand drawing) consistent with the level of income with which we started. This is a long and, perhaps, tortuous statement, but it will bear study.

What we have now is a new situation. Whereas in Chapter 16 we could speak of the equilibrium level of production in terms of the single condition, *total spending equals production,* and in Chapter 18 we could consider the equilibrium rate of interest as wherever *the demand for money equals the supply of money,* now things are more complicated. Now that we are considering both the goods market and the money market in one interdetermined whole, *general* equilibrium requires that all three of the following conditions be met:

1. Aggregate expenditures equal production.
2. Demand for money equals supply of money.

3. The production level and interest rate levels must be "consistent" with one another.[1]

If, for example, the rate of interest at which the demand for money equals the supply of money is one that will shortly cause investment spending to change, then the production level must change too. This would *not* be a state of general equilibrium. Only when there is no tendency toward change in any part of the four-diagram model do we have general equilibrium.

The Determinants of the Slopes and Levels of the Curves

The purpose of the four-diagram model is to provide us with a framework for analyzing the economic effects of any one of a large number of initial changes. The initial changes that this model equips us to deal with are changes in the determinants of the levels and/or slopes of the curves. To facilitate the task coming up in the next section, let us complete our review by listing in one place most of the determinants discussed in Chapters 16, 17, and 18. It will be convenient to handle this in outline form, starting first with the curve in the lower right-hand sector and working our way around clockwise.

Some Major Determinants of Slopes and Levels of Curves in the Four-Diagram Model

A. Determinants of Slope of Transactions Demand-for-Money Curve
   1. Frequency of payment habits — a speedup would steepen the curve
   2. Development of financial structure — further development would steepen the curve
   3. Degree of vertical integration of industry — the greater the integration, the steeper the curve

B. Determinants of Level of (Total) Demand-for-Money Curve
   1. Transactions demand, which is larger the higher the level of income
   2. Level of speculative (asset) demand, which will be higher the higher the range of interest rates people feel is normal, the larger the community's wealth, and the smaller the choice of other highly liquid assets

C. Determinants of Position of Supply-of-Money Curve
   1. Federal Reserve policy
   2. Treasury policy
   3. Public's preferred asset ratio
   4. Commercial bank policy as to desired excess reserves

D. Determinants of Level of MEI Curve
   1. State of technical knowledge — curve usually raised by technological innovations

---

[1] It is implicitly assumed that when the money market is cleared (i.e., when the demand for money equals the supply of money), the bond market is also cleared.

2. Stock of existing capital goods — curve is usually lower the more capital goods there are because of diminishing marginal productivity
3. Level of business taxes — curve is generally higher, the lower the business taxes
4. Degree of optimism or pessimism of business managers regarding future profit prospects — the more optimistic, the higher the curve

E. Determinants of Level of Total Spending (C + I + G) Curve
  1. Level of investment, which depends on the MEI and interest rate
  2. Level of government spending on goods and services, which is considered autonomous — that is, determined by noneconomic factors
  3. Level of consumption function, which depends, in turn, on
    a. Consumer expectations
    b. Consumer wealth
    c. Consumer tastes (attitudes toward virtues of savings)
    d. Level of personal taxes
    e. Stock of consumer durables already on hand
    f. Age composition of the population

Examples of Use of the Complete Theory Using the Four-Diagram Approach

We are now prepared to make use of our model. Before tracing through a number of specific examples, however, it might be helpful to provide some ground rules to facilitate the use of the four-diagram framework.

We always start off with an economy in general equilibrium in the sense in which this condition is pictured in Figure 19-4. That is, we shall assume that prior to a change in one of the curves, the equilibrium rate of interest determined in the lower left-hand graph is consistent with the equilibrium level of income determined in the upper right-hand graph and vice versa.

Then we assume a change in conditions that changes the level or slope of one of the curves and attempt to trace the effects of that change on the economy, until a new general equilibrium position (where once again the rate of interest is consistent with the level of income, and vice versa) is reached.

The first task will be to locate the curve (or curves) affected by the assumed change in conditions. Once the nature of this original shift is determined, its effects should be traced through the four diagrams in a *clockwise* direction. That is to say, if the initial change affects the rate of interest determined in the lower left-hand graph, the effect of this on the volume of investment in the upper left-hand graph should be read off next, followed by a determination of the effect of this change in investment on the equilibrium level of income in the upper right-hand graph, and so on.

As we shall soon see, it will be necessary to "go around" our four-diagram model more than once before a new, internally consistent equilibrium is reached. To facilitate discussion, we shall refer to these circuits of our model as "rounds." The end of a "round" will be assumed to have been reached each time we determine a new level of income in the upper right-hand graph.

For example, if our initial change were in the lower left-hand graph, the rate of interest would be affected first. This would, in turn, affect the level of investment, which would then alter the level of income in the upper right-hand graph. At this point we have completed round 1 of the change toward a new equilibrium. The effect of this change in income on the transactions demand for money, its subsequent effect on the total demand for money and the interest rate, this secondary effect on investment, and finally on the level of income, will be referred to as round 2 of the complete change. And so on.

The Effects of an Increase in the Supply of Money

Suppose that the initial equilibrium of the economy is disturbed by a Federal Reserve open-market purchase from the nonbank public. This, of course, has the immediate effect of moving the money supply line out to the right (to S or M_1, in Figure 19-5).

Such a change, other things being equal, will tend to lower the rate of interest from i_0 to i_1. At this lower rate of interest, the upper left-hand graph tells us, the amount spent on investment will rise from I_0 to I_1. Going on over to the upper right-hand graph, we then see that, given the MPC (slope of consumption func-

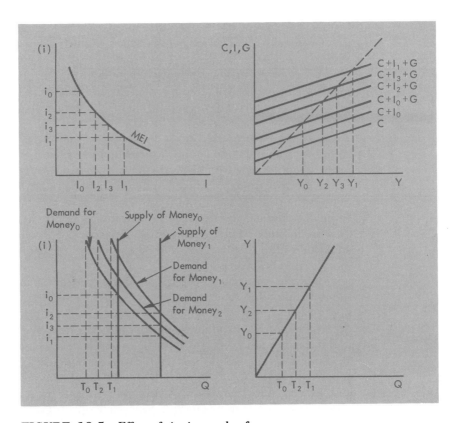

FIGURE 19-5 Effect of rise in supply of money

tion), such a rise in investment will raise the level of income from Y_0 to Y_1. This is the end of round 1, and, as can easily be seen, the open-market operations have had the initial effect of raising the level of income.

But that is not the end of the adjustment, since a new general equilibrium has not yet been achieved — interest rate level i_1 and income level Y_1 are *not* consistent with one another. The increase in people's incomes (from Y_0 to Y_1) generated in our "round 1" result will mean that they will now need larger transactions money balances to finance a higher level of transactions. Consequently (in what we shall refer to as a "round 2" adjustment), the quantity of money demanded for transactions purposes must rise from T_0 to T_1. And this, in turn, will push the total demand-for-money curve (lower left-hand graph) out to the right from D for M_0 to D for M_1. Such a shift will raise the rate of interest somewhat, from i_1 to i_2 (but i_2 will almost certainly still be lower than i_0). The higher rate of interest will cut back investment from I_1 to I_2, which, in turn, will reduce the level of income from Y_1 to Y_2 (Y_2 will still be higher than the original equilibrium of Y_0).

We have now completed round 2 and it can be seen that its effects are to offset partially the effects of round 1. The first round, considering the direct effects of the increased money supply, raised the income level of Y_1, but the second round, which takes account of the increased transactions demand called forth by that rise in income, operates, in lesser degree, in the opposite direction.

And even yet we are not through. There is a third round to be considered. The reduction in income (from Y_1 to Y_2) will lower the transactions demand once again (from T_1 to T_2), which will lower the total demand for money (from D for M_1 to D for M_2) and lower the rate of interest (from i_2 to i_3). This will permit a rise in investment (from I_2 to I_3), which will raise the level of income again, this time to Y_3.

We need go no further with the detailed description of this adjustment process, although it will be apparent to the alert reader that further rounds would be necessary before a new equilibrium in which the rate of interest and the level of income are consistent would be reached.

Indeed, if we carried on with the same approach through several more rounds, the approach to equilibrium taken by the level of income and the rate of interest would appear to be an oscillating one such as depicted in Figure 19-6.

In Figure 19-6a, Y_0 is taken to be the initial equilibrium level of income. Y_1 depicts the rise we get in round 1 as a result of increase in money supply. Then round 2 brings us back down to Y_2, and round 3 raises income once again to Y_3. This oscillating process continues through successive rounds at lesser and lesser amplitude until finally a new equilibrium level of income consistent with the interest rate is approached.

Similarly, in Figure 19-6b, the route apparently followed by the rate of interest is sketched in. The increased supply of money initially lowers the rate of interest from i_0 to i_1. The higher level of income permitted by i_1, however, raises the transactions demand for money in round 2, producing i_2. This then gives way in the third round to i_3, and so forth.

Now as Figures 19-5 and 19-6 make amply clear, tracing the adjustment process through all the way to a new general equilibrium would be a cumbersome and, indeed, impossible task. Fortunately, for our purposes, completing round after round after round is neither necessary nor desirable.

We need not go beyond two rounds to generalize about the ultimate general equilibrium effects on income and interest rate. If the given change in conditions

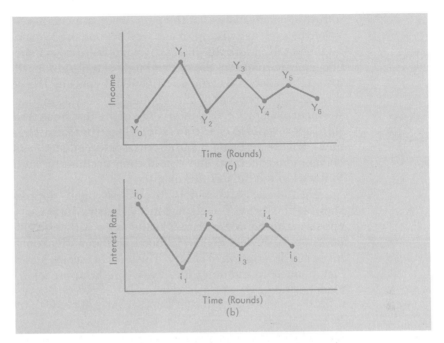

FIGURE 19-6 Path of income and interest rate changes through time assumed in four-diagram model of the economy

is such as to raise (lower) the level of income in round 1, unless very peculiar circumstances exist, the effect of round 2 will be to lower (raise) income to a point below (above) that reached in round 1 but still above (below) the original level. Future rounds will simply cause further fluctuations *within the limits reached in rounds 1 and 2.* The new general equilibrium results, then, would normally be

1. Higher (lower) than the original equilibrium.
2. Lower (higher) than the income after round 1.
3. Higher (lower) than the income after round 2.[2]

An Important Note of Caution

Before we proceed, it is most important that the student recognize that the "round-by-round" adjustment process just sketched is by no means a literal description of the path that the economy *actually* follows in response to a change in underlying conditions. Rather it represents a strictly pedagogical device whereby we are attempting to highlight some of the causal relationships involved in the adjustment process.

To discuss the adjustment of the economy to a change in conditions, one has essentially three choices. First, to trace the process of change, one might develop

[2] The same generalization holds for the interest rate. If the effect in the first round is to lower (raise) it, it will be raised (lowered) somewhat in the second round and then lowered (raised) again in the third. In equilibrium, it will be lower (higher) than originally but higher (lower) than after the first round.

a truly dynamic analysis of the path of adjustment. Such an approach, however, would be extremely complex and well beyond the scope of this book. Second, one might largely ignore the *process* by which adjustment occurs, choosing instead to concentrate solely on the old and new equilibrium positions involved. This approach, of course, has the advantage of bypassing the complexities involved in discussing the process of change, but this very advantage necessitates the omission of explanatory causal interconnections that some would consider essential. A third approach is to create an artificial (and unrealistic) description of the adjustment process to bring out the causal interconnections that *do* exist when the economy moves from one equilibrium position to another. This is the course followed in the bulk of this chapter.

The four-diagram models' "round-by-round" approach has the advantage of showing the "whys" of change more clearly. But it carries with it the hazard of appearing to say more than it really does. Although it is extremely useful as a pedagogical device, Figure 19-6 and the round-by-round approach must *not* be taken as a description of reality. The level of income and rate of interest do not, in fact, bounce up and down like a yo-yo in the approach to a new general equilibrium position.

Determinants of the Effectiveness of Changes in Money Supply in Affecting the Level of Income

As we observed earlier, the main function of the Federal Reserve System is to control the supply of money to contribute to price stability and full employment. In other words, the Fed attempts to use its controls over the money supply to hold down on inflationary rises in income in boom periods and to contribute to increases in income (in the form of increased production and employment) during recessions.

Having just discussed the process through which changes in the money supply affect the level of income, some consideration of the determinants of the *magnitude* of the effect of money supply changes on income levels may well be in order.

As a policy weapon, money supply changes are intended to work via their effect on the level of spending. A cut in the money supply is successful as a contracyclical tool to the degree that it cuts or holds down total spending. Conversely, an increase in the money supply, in the same context, is successful to the degree that it raises or holds up total spending. Our question here is, "Under what conditions will changes in the money supply be most effective in achieving their goal of affecting total spending and GNP?"

Possible Effects on Interest Rates   Let us look at it first from the point of view of expansionary monetary policy—a rise in the supply of money. If such a policy is to affect total expenditures and income levels, it must first lower the interest rate.[3]

---

[3] It should be observed that, according to the modern monetarists, money supply increases may raise aggregate demand directly as asset holders seek to trade off the new, unwanted money for other assets, as well as indirectly via an initial lowering of the interest rate. This point of view will be considered in a later chapter.

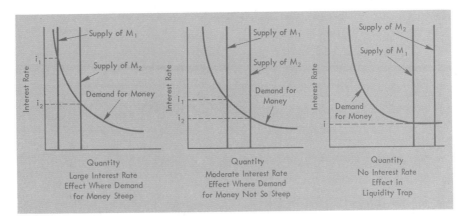

FIGURE 19-7   Effect of slope of demand-for-money curve
on the amount of interest rate change

How effective it will be will depend, in part, on *how much* the interest rate is lowered as a result of any given money supply increase. Clearly, this in turn depends partly upon how high interest rates already are. As Figure 19-7 shows, if interest rates are currently near the top of their normal range, that portion of the demand-for-money curve will normally be very steep and money supply increases will tend to cause relatively large interest rate declines. If, on the other hand, the interest rate is already so low that many people expect increases, the relevant portion of the demand-for-money curve may be relatively flat and money supply increases will elicit only moderate reduction in the interest rate. The extreme situation would be if there existed, and we were in, a perfectly horizontal portion of the demand-for-money curve (the liquidity trap). Here, expansionary monetary policy would be useless, since money supply increases would be completely absorbed into speculative balances, permitting no decline in interest rates whatever.[4]

We can conclude, therefore, that **money supply changes will have more desired effect on interest rates the steeper the slope of the total demand-for-money curve in the area affected.**

Possible Effects on Investment   But even if the interest rate is reduced, success is not guaranteed. The drop in interest rates is not the end, but merely a means to the end. The goal here is to raise production and employment, and the hope is that the reduction in interest rates will permit such a rise. Now it is true that, to some extent, lower interest rates will encourage more spending by anyone who spends with borrowed funds. Not only business investors but also government and consumers make use of borrowed funds to finance their spending. But the latter two groups seem to be usually insensitive to the interest rate as a cost factor and we shall oversimplify here by assuming that they do not react at all. This leaves us with only business investors to consider.

How much more investment spending can be expected consequent to a given drop in the interest rate? It all depends on the slope of the MEI curve. If the MEI

[4] It should be noted that empirical investigation has found no evidence of a true liquidity trap in the United States.

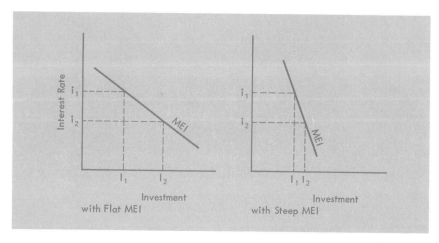

FIGURE 19-8 Effect of slope of MEI curve on the amount
of change in investment spending

curve is relatively steep, investors are not very responsive to interest rate declines and investment will not rise much. Conversely, a flat MEI curve indicates a
situation wherein an interest rate decrease will permit a sizable rise in investment
spending. Figure 19-8 illustrates the two possibilities.

Our conclusion is that **money supply increases (and consequent interest rate
declines) will lead to larger increases in investment spending the flatter the MEI
curve in the area affected.**

Effects on Equilibrium Income Levels   If a money supply increase has lowered
interest rates and that, in turn, has raised investment spending, then we can
expect (consider the upper right-hand diagram in Figure 19-5) a rise in the
equilibrium level of income. How large a rise in GNP will result from a given
increase in investment spending depends, of course, on the size of the multiplier.
Since the multiplier is larger, the larger the MPC, and since the MPC *is* the slope
of the consumption function, we can say **the steeper the consumption function
(and consequently the steeper the C + I + G line), the larger the rise in GNP
that will result from a given money supply increase.**

**Effect of the Slope of the Transactions Demand-for-Money Curve on the (Undesir-
able) Second-Round Effect**   Finally, we must consider the potential effects of
round 2. If the money supply increase has succeeded in raising GNP in the first
round, it will lead to an increase in the quantity of money demanded for transactions purposes at the beginning of the second. And since any such increase must
ultimately lead to some rise in the total demand for money, some rise in interest
rates (barring a liquidity trap), and some cutback in investment spending, it is an
undesirable change tending to offset some of the desired effects on GNP
achieved during the first round. *(The second round always works to undercut
somewhat the effects of the first round.)* Consequently, to maximize the desired
effect of a money supply change on GNP, it is preferable to minimize the unfavorable second-round effect.

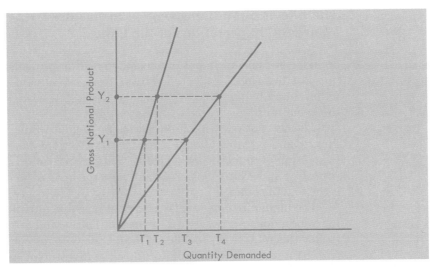

FIGURE 19-9 Effect of slope of transactions demand-for-money curve on undesirable "second-round" effects

What slope of the transactions demand-for-money curve will minimize these undesirable second-round developments? A steep curve, because the steeper the transactions demand curve, the smaller the increase in the quantity of money demanded for transactions purposes that will result from any given first-round GNP increase. We can therefore conclude **the rise in the general equilibrium GNP that will result from an increase in the money supply will be greater the steeper the transactions demand-for-money curve.** This is illustrated in Figure 19-9. Note there that with the steeper curve, a rise in GNP from Y_1 to Y_2 will increase the quantity demanded by only T_1T_2, whereas with the flatter curve, the increase is the much larger amount, T_3T_4.

The effects of the slopes of all these curves on the effectiveness of money supply changes in altering GNP are summarized in Table 19-1.

TABLE 19-1 Determinants of the effectiveness and/or ineffectiveness of money supply changes

Changes in the money supply will have greater effects on income if	*Changes in the money supply will be relatively ineffective in changing income if*
1. The total demand-for-money curve is steep in the affected area.	1. The total demand-for-money curve is flat in the affected area.
2. The MEI curve is flat in the affected area.	2. The MEI curve is steep in the affected area.
3. The consumption function is steep.	3. The consumption function is flat.
4. The transactions demand-for-money curve is steep, leading to small offsetting second-round effects.	4. The transactions demand-for-money curve is flat, causing a large offsetting second-round effect.

The Effects of an Improvement in Business Managers' Expectations of the Future

Suppose because of important technological improvements, for example, that business managers' expected returns from investment are sharply increased. Other things being equal, what changes could this be expected to bring about in the economy?

Clearly, the most likely initial major impact would be an **MEI** curve shift upward and to the right. As Figure 19-10 shows, this would permit an initial rise in investment spending from I_0 to I_1. This in turn would raise total expenditures (from $C + I_0 + G$ to $C + I_1 + G$) and raise the level of income from Y_0 to Y_1. This is the end of round 1.

The higher income level would then raise the quantity of money demanded for transactions purposes to T_1 from T_0. This would raise the total demand for money (from D for M_0 to D for M_1) and raise the rate of interest to i_1. A higher interest rate would cause some cutback in investment spending (from I_1 to I_2), which would, in turn, lower total expenditures and the level of income from Y_1 to Y_2. This marks the end of round 2.

If we should follow this process on to its conclusion at a new stable equilibrium, we would find that the level of income would be somewhere between Y_1 and Y_2. In any event it would be higher than Y_0. The rate of interest would finally end up higher than i_0, but somewhat lower than i_1.

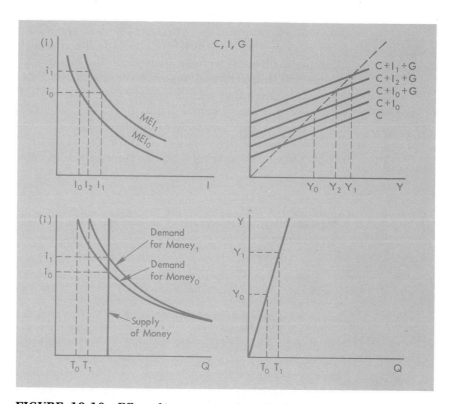

FIGURE 19-10   Effect of improvement in technology

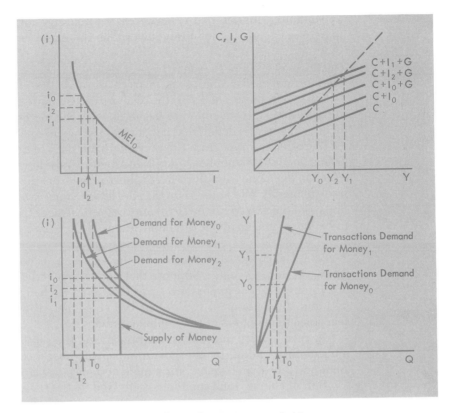

FIGURE 19-11   Effect of speedup in payment habits

The Effects of a Speedup in Paydays

Although it is hardly a very likely change in the short run, it will nevertheless be instructive to trace through the effects of a change in payment habits. Suppose, for example, that all business firms suddenly started paying weekly rather than monthly salaries.

As seen in the preceding chapter, such a change will reduce the need for transactions balances, thereby increasing the slope of the transactions demand-for-money curve in the lower right-hand graph (from transactions demand for M_0 to transactions demand for M_1) in Figure 19-11. This, at income level Y_0, will lower the quantity of money demanded for transactions purposes from T_0 to T_1.

The result of the cut in the transactions demand will be a shift in the total demand for money to the left (to D for M_1) and a fall in the rate of interest (from i_0 to i_1). The lower interest rate permits a rise in investment (from I_0 to I_1), which, in turn, raises the level of income from Y_0 to Y_1.

In round 2, the quantity of money demanded for transactions purposes rises from T_1 to T_2, the total demand for money rises from D for M_1 to D for M_2, and the rate of interest comes back up to i_2. The higher interest cuts back investment to I_2, which lowers the level of income from Y_1 to Y_2. If this were followed through, the general equilibrium level of income would be between Y_1 and Y_2

(and definitely higher than Y_0), whereas the final equilibrium interest rate would be between i_1 and i_2, definitely lower than the initial level of i_0.

The Effect of a Cut in Personal Taxes, Creating a Government Deficit   Our four-diagram model also equips us to trace through the effects of a fiscal policy measure, but, as we shall see, the analysis can be more complicated. The additional wrinkle introduced here has to do with the method used by the government to finance the deficit that it incurs (or the means of disposing of the surplus).

We already know, from Chapter 14, that if the Treasury finances a deficit by selling bonds to the nonbank public and then spends the proceeds, there is no net effect on the money supply, whereas borrowing from the banks will increase the stock of money. We noted then that the latter course would be the more expansionary of the two. With the aid of our theoretical model, we are now in a position to be more specific about the implications of these two alternatives.

Treasury Deficit Spending Financed by Borrowing from the Nonbank Public — No Change in Money Supply   Suppose that a government deficit is created by means of a (lump-sum) cut in personal taxes (assuming unchanged government spending) and the amount of the deficit thereby created is raised by sale of U.S. securities to members of the nonbank public.

In such a case, the sale of the bonds cuts the public's money supply, but immediate spending by the government will raise it again by an equivalent amount. Hence, on balance, *the supply of money is unaffected.*

But, of course, total spending is affected by the tax cut. By cutting personal taxes, the government permits a larger slice of gross income to go to individuals in the form of Disposable Income. They, in turn, can be counted on to spend a substantial part of it on additional consumption. Graphically, then, the first important effect on our four-diagram model will be to shift the consumption function and the total spending line to the higher level of $C_1 + I_0 + G$,[5] as in Figure 19-12. The upward shift will be by somewhat less than the amount of the tax cut so long as the MPC is less than 1.[6]

The initial rise in consumption permitted by the tax cut plus the additional induced rises in consumption caused by the multiplier will drive income up from Y_0 to Y_1. In short order, then, we complete round 1. The fiscal policy has had its desired effect by raising spending and income (and, it is hoped, employment along with them).

But, unfortunately, round 2 will have effects on the rate of interest that will, to some degree, offset part of the rise in income. The increase to Y_1 will raise the quantity of money demanded for transactions purposes from T_0 to T_1; this will raise the total demand-for-money curve to D for M_1 and raise the interest rate from i_0 to i_1. The higher interest rate will cut investment spending back to I_1, which will lower aggregate demand from $C_1 + I_0 + G$ to $C_1 + I_1 + G$ and reduce

---

[5] As we are not assuming that taxes are related to income, we can show this effect with a parallel upward shift of the consumption schedule. If the cut had been in income taxes, the consumption schedule would become steeper, with a larger multiplier.

[6] In cases of fiscal policy, confusion can be avoided by starting the analysis in one of the two top diagrams—with the initial effects of the tax or government expenditure change, and then considering the effects on the money supply, if any, in round 2.

FIGURE 19-12   Effect of deficit spending —
deficit borrowed from nonbank public

the income level to Y_2. Further revolutions will culminate in a new equilibrium level somewhere between Y_1 and Y_2 and a new equilibrium interest rate between i_0 and i_1.

What are the implications of all this in so many words? Simply this. The reduction in taxes is successful in raising the level of income, but part of the "good" effects on total spending are undercut because the government has financed its deficit in a manner that raised interest rates and cut back on private investment. This tendency for the intended effects of a fiscal policy measure to be undercut because the interest rate changes induced by the financing of the government's deficit affect investment spending in the opposite direction is the same *crowding out* effect we first encountered in Chapter 18 while considering the loanable funds theory of interest. The only difference is that in this case we are employing the liquidity preference theory of interest.

The magnitude of the crowding out effect is the subject of substantial current debate. Although the majority of the economics profession appears to retain the conviction that it does not eliminate all the intended effects of a fiscal policy measure (as depicted in Figure 19-12), some monetarists maintain that it does and that, consequently, fiscal policy measures that involve no money supply changes are totally ineffective.

We shall have more to say about this issue in the chapter on monetarism. For now, it is important for the student to recognize that the conclusion generally reached in the introductory macroeconomics course to the effect that "if the multiplier is 4 and government spending is raised by 10, the equilibrium GNP will rise by 40" only holds if the effects on total spending of financing the deficit (our second-round effects) are ignored.[7]

Treasury Deficit Spending Financed by Borrowing from the Banks — Rise in Supply of Money   Suppose, in contrast to the case just discussed, that the deficit created by the tax cut is financed by sale of U.S. securities to the banks rather than to the public. In this case, as pointed out earlier, the money that the government borrows is newly created by the banks and, when spent, the money supply of the public rises.

In terms of our four-diagram model, we again start in the upper right-hand graph, showing the upward shift in the $C + I + G$ line and the rise in income caused by the tax cut. In Figure 19-13 income rises initially from Y_0 to Y_1.

As before, the higher income level will require more money for transactions purposes, which, in turn, will raise the demand for money from D for M_0 to D for M_1. But here we encounter something new. By selling bonds to the banks, the government has also produced a rise in the supply of money — from S of M_0 to S of M_1. Unlike the situation in which the bonds were sold to the public, the effect

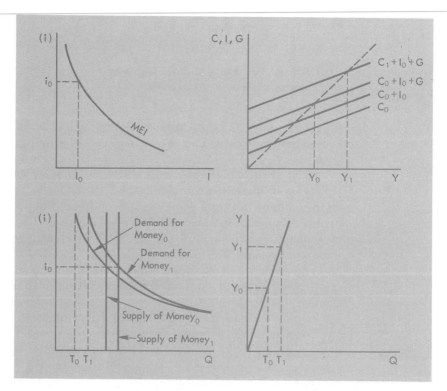

FIGURE 19-13   Effect of deficit spending — deficit borrowed from banks

[7] That is, as we see in the following section, unless the deficit is financed in a manner that increases the money supply.

(if any) on the rate of interest during this second round is indeterminate. In Figure 19-13, we have drawn the relevant schedules so that the changes in the supply of, and the demand for, money exactly offset one another but, of course, this need not always be the case. The interest rate could rise slightly if the increase in demand exceeded that in supply or fall slightly if the reverse occurred.

So far as general conclusions are concerned, one thing can be said with some assurance. When the deficit is financed via sale of bonds to the banks, the increase in the supply of money that accompanies it will certainly keep the rate of interest from rising as much as it would have had the bonds been sold to the nonbank public with the money supply unchanged. Consequently, private investment spending will be cut back less than in the former case and the final equilibrium level of income *must* be higher. Crowding out, in other words, must be less.

This, then, tells us something more specific about the merits of different methods of handling fiscal policy. If deficit spending is carried out with the express purpose of raising total spending and income, it is better to borrow the deficit from the banks than from the public because the former course will be less likely to raise interest rates and cut back on private investment spending.

These results also permit us to make some generalizations regarding the best means of financing deficits when the purpose of the deficit spending is *not* to raise aggregate demand. Take the case of an all-out war effort (such as World War II) where we are already at full employment but the government deems it necessary to operate at a substantial deficit because of very heavy military expenditures.

In such a situation, increases in total spending drive money income up by means of inflationary price rises (in the absence of direct controls over prices). Anything that can be done to hold down on the inflationary rise in aggregate expenditures will be helpful.

Clearly the inflationary pressure will be lessened if the deficit is financed by borrowing from the nonbank public rather than the banks. Why? Because that course will result in a rise in the rate of interest (demand for money rises but supply does not), which will have the favorable effect of cutting private investment somewhat. If the deficit were financed via sale of bonds to the banks, the increased demand for money, caused by the rise in income, might well be offset by the increase in the supply of money, forestalling any rise in interest rates. Borrowing from the nonbank public is, thus, less inflationary.

The Effect of a Reduction in Government Expenditures, Creating a Tax Surplus

One further example of the operation of our model may be useful. Suppose that the government, to combat inflationary pressures, cuts government spending without reducing taxes, thereby creating a tax surplus. As in the previous case (where we had to specify how the deficit was financed), we cannot really spell out the effects unless we are told what the government does with its tax surplus. The purpose of the policy is presumably to cut spending and prevent further price increases, but its effectiveness will depend partly on the disposition of the surplus. To be truthful, however, it should be recognized that this version of the Keynesian model is an awkward one to use for considering contractionary policy.

In order to do so, one is forced to interpret the first-round decline in nominal GNP as reflecting a desired cut in the price level rather than an undesired cut in real output and employment. If the reader can stretch his or her credulity sufficiently to accept this interpretation, we shall return to our story.

The fact is that the use of the tax surplus—that is, the determination of whose securities it shall be used to pay off—plays a role in the overall effectiveness of the policy.

Treasury Tax Surplus Used to Retire Securities Held by the Nonbank Public—No Change in Money Supply The reduction in government spending affects the upper right-hand graph by reducing total spending and, hence, the money level of income (from Y_0 to Y_1 in Figure 19-14). This, in turn, reduces the quantity of money needed for transactions purposes and cuts the total demand for money (from D for M_0 to D for M_1).

As the paying off of bonds held by the public places the surplus money collected in taxes back into circulation, the money supply is unaffected and the rate of interest must fall. Such a fall will permit more investment spending (from I_0 to I_1), and this increase will raise the C + I + G line back up a bit, offsetting, to some degree, the intended contractionary effects of the surplus.

Treasury Tax Surplus Used to Retire Securities Owned by the Banks—Money Supply Is Cut Where the intent of the policy is to cut total spending and combat

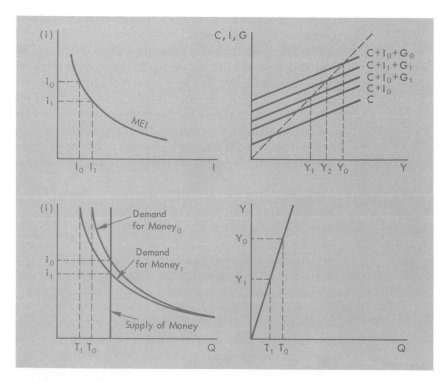

FIGURE 19-14 Effect of tax surplus used to retire bonds held by nonbank public

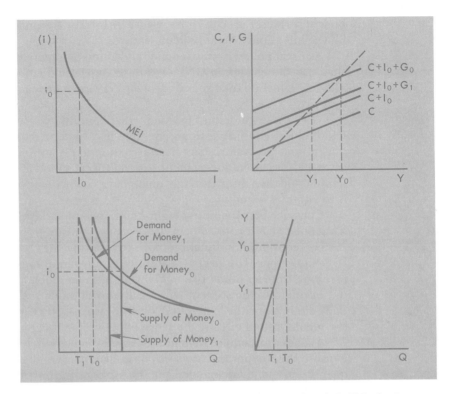

FIGURE 19-15   Effect of tax surplus used to retire bonds held by banks

inflation, more desirable results will be forthcoming from using the tax surplus to retire securities held by the banks. This is because in this case the money supply is reduced (see Figure 19-15).

Once again the cut in government spending reduces total spending and the money level of income. This will lower the need for transactions balances and lower the demand for money. In contrast to the previous case, however, the lower demand for money need not lead to a reduction in interest rates and an undesirable rise in investment spending. For here the cut in the demand for money may be completely offset by the cut in the supply of money, and interest rates can thus remain unchanged. The result must be a greater net reduction in total spending (and, presumably, in inflationary pressure) than is obtainable where the surplus is used to retire publicly held securities.

Determinants of the Effectiveness of Pure Fiscal Policy in Altering GNP

The examples considered in the last few pages provide an ideal background for summarization regarding the conditions most favorable to effective fiscal policy measures. These, then, can be readily compared with those pertaining to monetary policy, as listed in Table 19-1.

For this purpose, "pure" fiscal policy measures will be defined as alterations in government expenditures and/or taxes *without any change in the money supply*. The creation of budget deficits financed by sale of securities to the public or budget surpluses used to retire securities held by the public would consequently fill the bill as pure fiscal policy measures.

As fiscal policy is most commonly aimed at affecting the nation's GNP, we shall use the change in GNP as the measure of effectiveness. The greater the ultimate effect on total spending and GNP, the more successful the fiscal policy measure.

With these guidelines in mind, what conditions—what slopes of curves—will be most conducive to an effective fiscal policy measure? For purposes of illustration, we shall restrict our discussion to expansionary fiscal policy (cut in taxes and/or rise in government expenditures) aimed at raising GNP. (The student should then think through, on his or her own, the reverse case where the aim is to cut total spending.)

Consider first the upper right-hand, income determination diagram where fiscal policy has its first impact. Here a **steep consumption function is desirable.** A steep consumption function indicates a larger MPC, which, in turn, means a large multiplier. The larger the multiplier, the larger the desired change in GNP resulting from an initial rise in G or cut in T. So much for round 1.

In round 2, the student will recall, developments will be unfavorable, partially diminishing the first-round, desired rise in GNP. Consequently, the smaller the second-round effects, the more effective the fiscal policy measure.

A steep transactions demand-for-money curve will be most favorable. This is because the steeper the transactions demand curve, the smaller the increase in quantity of money demanded for transactions purposes as a result of the first-round rise in GNP. The smaller this increase is, the less the rise in the total demand-for-money curve in the lower left-hand diagram and the smaller the unfavorable second-round effects.

With any given rise (shift to the right) in the total demand-for-money curve, **the interest rate will rise less, the flatter the total demand-for-money curve.** This is illustrated in Figure 19-16.

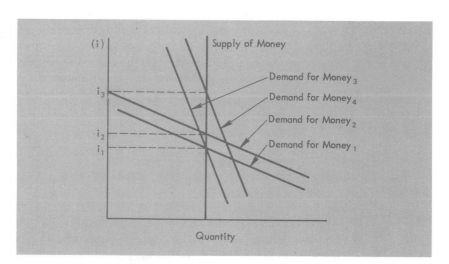

FIGURE 19-16   **Effect on interest rate of slope of shifting demand-for-money curve**

TABLE 19-2   Determinants of the effectiveness of "pure" fiscal policy measures

Fiscal policy will have greater effects on GNP if	*Fiscal policy will have smaller effects on GNP if*
1. The consumption function is steep.	1. The consumption function is flat.
2. The transactions demand-for-money curve is steep.	2. The transactions demand-for-money curve is flat.
3. The total demand-for-money curve is flat.	3. The total demand-for-money curve is steep.
4. The MEI curve is steep.	4. The MEI curve is flat.

Here, if the demand-for-money curve should shift to the right from relatively flat D_1 to D_2, the interest rate rises only from i_1 to i_2. If, however, the original demand-for-money curve were the relatively steep D_3 curve, a shift to the right (equivalent to the shift between D_1 and D_2) to D_4 would raise the interest rate all the way up to i_3. As a rise in the interest rate has unfavorable effects, a flat demand-for-money curve is preferable.

Finally, turning to the upper left-hand diagram of the four-diagram model, **fiscal policy will be more effective the steeper the MEI curve.** Any change in investment resulting from interest rate changes will come in round 2, and the effects on total spending will be the opposite of those desired. A steep MEI curve will mean very little cutback in investment spending because of a rise in interest rates. For an expansionary fiscal policy measure, this is desirable. All this is summarized in Table 19-2.

Note that in comparing Table 19-2 with Table 19-1 monetary and fiscal policy are both more effective the steeper the consumption function and the steeper the transactions demand-for-money curve. Monetary policy, however, requires a steep total demand-for-money curve and a flat MEI curve; fiscal policy is most effective if these two curves are of the opposite slopes. These differences should be kept in mind, when we consider the monetarist position.

An Alternative Geometric
Approach — IS and LM Curves

In attempting to illustrate a complicated set of relationships geometrically, one is often confronted with difficult choices. On the one hand, it is useful to have all the pieces of the theory explicitly exposed so that changes and interconnections can be clearly seen. This is the virtue of the four-diagram approach.

But virtue has its price, and the student who has carefully worked through the examples presented in the preceding section will be keenly aware of the price of the four-diagram framework. It is a most cumbersome apparatus, hardly efficient for repeated chalkboard use in the classroom.

Is there a simpler geometric construct that can be used to represent all this? There is indeed. All the curves involved in the upper two diagrams can be collapsed into a single line, typically designated as an IS curve. Similarly, all the curves included in the bottom two diagrams can be represented by a single LM curve. In fact, the IS–LM method is, by all odds, the dominant geometric representation of Keynesian theory now commonly employed.

Our task in this section is twofold. First, we investigate the derivation of IS and LM curves; then, we shall illustrate their use.

Derivation of IS and LM Curves

IS Curves   An IS curve may be defined as **a curve that shows the various possible equilibrium levels of income that would result from various given rates of interest.**

It should be clear by now, focusing on the top two diagrams of the four-diagram framework, that each rate of interest permits a given level of investment spending, which, along with C and G, leads to a certain equilibrium level of income. In Figure 19-17, for example, relatively low interest rate i_1 produces investment spending I_1, which, along with C and G, establishes income level Y_1. Higher interest rate i_2 permits less investment, I_2, which in turn leads to lower income level Y_2. And so on.

The IS curve involves no more than a line that shows all the possible interest rate–income combinations. Its derivation can be shown as in Figure 19-18.

Here the MEI curve (with a lump-sum amount of government spending added to it) is shown in the lower-right diagram. The upper-right diagram is simply a 45° line with $I + G$ on the horizontal axis and $S + T$ on the vertical. The upper left is the saving plus taxes schedule related to the income level.

Starting in the lower-right corner, if the interest rate is i_1, this will permit $I + G_1$. Going up to the upper right, we know that, in equilibrium $I + G$ equals

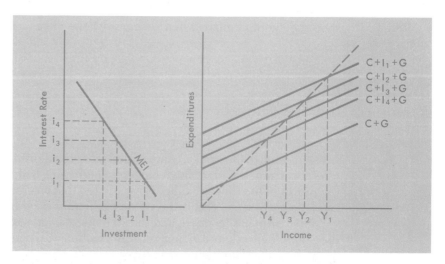

FIGURE 19-17   IS curve — interest rates and income levels

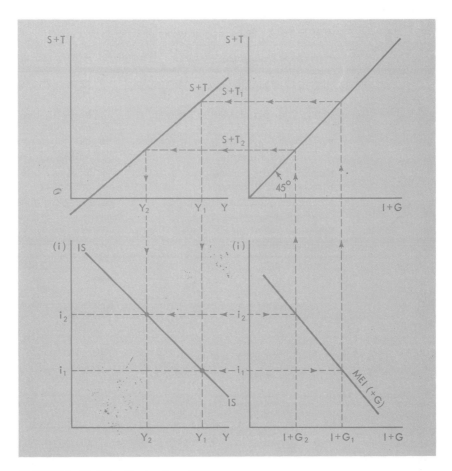

FIGURE 19-18 Derivation of IS curve

S + T, so that we will have to have saving plus taxes of $S + T_1$. Finally, in the upper left, for saving plus taxes to be at the $S + T_1$ level, we must have an income level of Y_1. (The $S + T$ schedule is, of course, directly derived from the consumption function. In this example, we simply use the $I + G = S + T$ form of the equilibrium condition rather than total spending equals production condition used in the upper right-hand part of the four-diagram model.) This gives us the first dot on the IS curve — interest rate i_1 — which will lead to income level Y_1.

The same procedure is then followed starting from interest rate i_2. This produces $I + G_2$, which means that we must have saving plus taxes equal to $S + T_2$. This level is only reached when income is at level Y_2. We have a second dot depicting another interest-income relation. When these dots (and, conceptually, many more similar ones) are joined together in a line, we have an IS curve.

Now, before proceeding, the student should think through what we have done. This IS curve represents the results of a given MEI curve, a given quantity of government spending, and a given consumption schedule (which implies a given tax rate). A change in any of these underlying functions will change the IS curve itself.

TABLE 19-3   Some major causes of shifts in IS curves

Initial cause	*Effect on IS*
1. Rise in G or parallel rise in MEI curve	1. Shifts to right by initial amount times multiplier
2. Fall in G or parallel fall in MEI curve	2. Shifts to left by initial amount times multiplier
3. Parallel rise in consumption function (fall in S + T function)	3. Shifts to right by initial amount times multiplier
4. Parallel fall in consumption function (rise in S + T function)	4. Shifts to left by initial amount times multiplier
5. Steepened (flattened) slope of MEI curve	5. Steepens (flattens)
6. Steepened (flattened) slope of consumption function	6. Flattens (steepens)

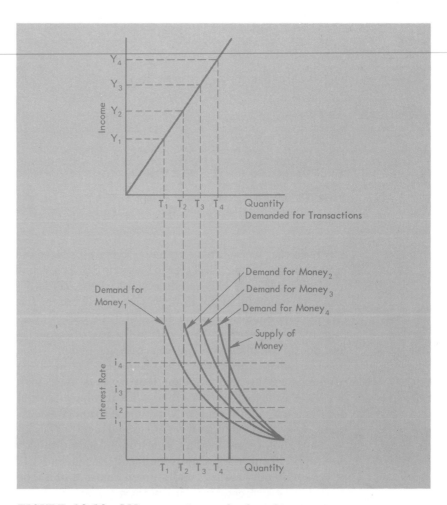

FIGURE 19-19   LM curve — income levels and interest rates

For example, a lump-sum rise in government spending or a parallel shift to the right in the MEI curve will shift the MEI (+G) curve (Figure 19-18) to the right by that amount. If the effect of this is followed through Figure 19-18, it will be apparent that the original change, plus the effects of the multiplier that enter the picture in the upper-left diagram, will shift the IS curve to the right by an amount equal to the original change in G (or I) times the multiplier.

To shorten the discussion, some of the main causes of shifts in the IS curve are listed in Table 19-3. The student should be cautioned, however, that this is not a table simply to memorize. If the IS–LM framework is to be used, it will be well worth the effort to trace through the derivation in each case.

LM Curves The LM curve shows **various possible equilibrium rates of interest that would result from alternative given levels of income.** This curve represents everything in the two bottom diagrams of the four-diagram framework. It recognizes, as in Figure 19-19, that for every level of income there is a different transactions demand, which in its turn produces a different rate of interest.

The complete derivation of an LM curve is depicted in Figure 19-20, which can perhaps most logically be interpreted as starting in the upper-left diagram

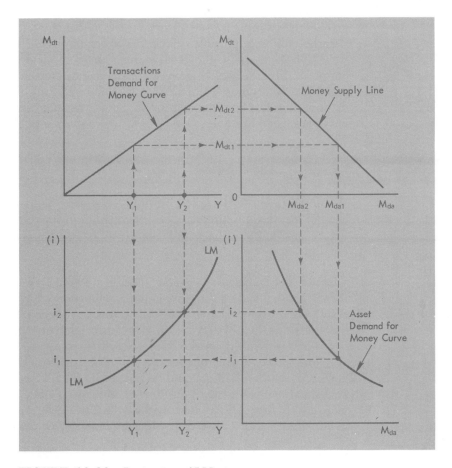

FIGURE 19-20 Derivation of LM curve

TABLE 19-4 Some major causes of shifts in LM curves

Initial cause	Effect on LM
1. Rise (fall) in supply of money	1. Shift to right (left)
2. Rise (fall) in level of asset demand-for-money curve	2. Shift to left (right)
3. Steepening (flattening) of transactions demand-for-money curve (as drawn in Figure 19-19)	3. Flattening (steepening)
4. Steepening (flattening) of asset demand-for-money curve	4. Steepening (flattening)

where a transactions demand-for-money curve is depicted. (Note that the axes are reversed compared with earlier transactions demand curves used.) The upper-right diagram depicts (by its distance out from the origin) the given supply of money. The lower right, of course, is the asset demand-for-money curve.

If the level of income is Y_1, then $0M_{dt1}$ of the money supply is needed for transactions purposes, leaving $0M_{da1}$ available as asset balances. For people willingly to hold that amount of asset money, the asset demand curve tells us that the interest rate must be as low as i_1. If income is Y_2, on the other hand, $0M_{dt2}$ of the given money supply is used up as transactions balances, leaving only $0M_{da2}$ to be absorbed for asset purposes. This will be accomplished at interest rate i_2.

The LM curve, like the IS curve, rests on a complicated base. The underlying curves in this case are the transactions demand-for-money curve, the asset demand-for-money curve, and the supply of money. If any of these changes its level or slope, the LM curve changes also. Some possible causes of shifts in the LM curve are listed in Table 19-4.

Use of IS–LM Curves

When the IS and LM curves are drawn together, their intersection shows the level of income and rate of interest needed to produce general equilibrium. In Figure 19-21, then, the equilibrium level of income is Y_e, and the associated equilibrium rate of interest is i_e.

Effect of Rise in Supply of Money If the Federal Reserve institutes an "easy money" policy, raising the money supply while everything else is unchanged, the results are routinely shown in IS–LM terms. In Figure 19-22, the money supply increase shifts the LM curve to the right and this lowers the rate of interest from i_1 to i_2 while raising the level of income from Y_1 to Y_2.

Note, however, the effects of a different situation. If the asset demand-for-money curve had had a liquidity trap in it, the LM curve would have been horizontal over that range of interest rates too. (Trace it through and see for yourself.) In that case, as Figure 19-23 illustrates, the easy money policy would fail to affect interest rates or the income level.

Effect of a Cut in the Income Tax Rate with the Deficit Financed by Sale of Bonds to Public Suppose that the income tax rate is cut (with government spending unchanged) and the deficit thereby created is financed by borrowing from the

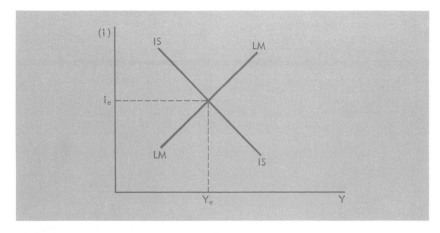

FIGURE 19-21 Equilibrium with IS–LM curves

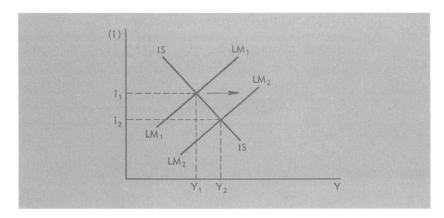

FIGURE 19-22 Change in equilibrium from shift in LM curve

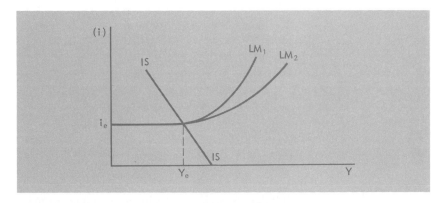

FIGURE 19-23 Equilibrium in the liquidity trap

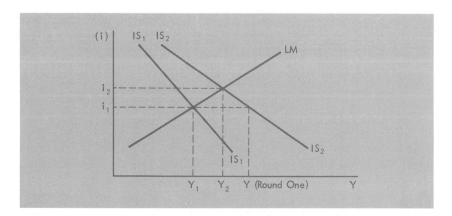

FIGURE 19-24   Income tax cut with no change in money supply

nonbank public (so that there is no change in money supply). How is this shown with IS and LM curves?

It will be recalled that a lower income tax rate produces a steeper consumption function. Such a change (because it increases the multiplier) would flatten (and raise) the IS curve. This would tend to raise the equilibrium income level (from Y_1 to Y_2 in Figure 19-24) and raise the equilibrium rate of interest. Note that the round 1 increase in Y (labeled Y, round 1) is cut back in succeeding rounds by interest rate increases, to Y_2.

Effect of Cut in Income Tax with Deficit Financed by Sale of Bonds to Banks   Once again, let us contrast the fixed money supply case to one depicting an increase in money. If the government deficit created by the cut in income taxes were financed by sale of securities to the banks, the supply of money would be raised.

The IS – LM result is shown in Figure 19-25. Again, the IS curve flattens (and rises) as a result of the tax cut. Here, however, the money supply increase shifts

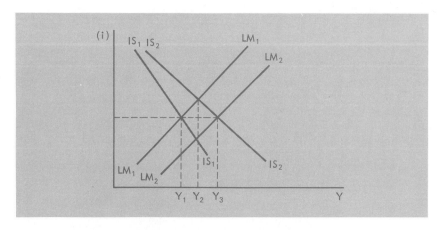

FIGURE 19-25   Income tax cut with money supply increase

the LM curve to the right also, producing a larger rise in income (from Y_1 to Y_3) and, in this particular case, no rise whatever in the rate of interest. The money supply increase, by keeping the rate of interest down, permits a larger increase in income than if the money stock were held constant. The increase is larger by an amount equal to $Y_2 Y_3$.

Conclusion

The four-diagram framework and the IS–LM approach are alternative means of presenting the same ideas. The former has the advantage of revealing more clearly the underlying interconnections that lead to change, although the latter is geometrically simpler.

One should not be misled, however. Geometrical simplicity does not imply theoretical simplicity. The innocent-appearing IS and LM curves involve exactly the same complexities as their components. To use IS and LM curves with under-standing and facility, one must already have worked through their underpinnings quite thoroughly.

Appendix: Algebraic Presentation

As every line has an equation, the theoretical model sketched out in this chapter can also be presented algebraically. This appendix may be looked upon as simply a continuation of the appendix to Chapter 16, supplemented by the material added in Chapters 17 and 18.

Let us begin by assuming an economy in which the following conditions hold initially:

$C = .625Y_d + 100$	(The consumption function in terms of disposable income)
$T = .2Y_g$	(An income tax with an average tax rate equal to 20 percent of GNP)
$I = 40 - 200i$	(A straight-line MEI curve negatively sloped with respect to the interest rate)
$G = 60$	(Government spending a constant, autonomously determined)
$M_s = 91$	(The money supply a constant, autonomously determined)
$M_{dt} = .2Y_g$	(The transactions demand for money equal to 20 percent of GNP)
$M_{da} = 20 - 100i$	(The asset demand for money a straight line, negatively related to the interest rate)

Equilibrium Conditions

1. Production equals total spending, or

$$Y_g = C + I + G$$

2. Supply of money equals demand for money, or

$$M_s = M_{dt} + M_{da}$$

3. Level of income and rate of interest must be consistent.

Computing Initial Equilibrium
Income and Interest Rate Levels

Putting Consumption in Terms of GNP   By definition, if there is no business saving,

$$Y_d = Y_g - T$$

Substituting,

$$Y_d = Y_g - .2Y_g$$
$$Y_d = .8Y_g$$

Substituting in C function,

$$C = .625(.8Y_g) + 100$$

Therefore,

$$C = .5Y_g + 100$$

Solving for Equilibrium in the Goods Market (Getting Equation for IS Curve)   The equilibrium condition is

$$Y_g = C + I + G$$

Substituting,

$$Y_g = (.5Y_g + 100) + (40 - 200_i) + 60$$
$$Y_g = .5Y_g - 200i + 200$$
$$.5Y_g = 200 - 200i$$
$$Y_g = 400 - 400i \text{ (equation for IS curve)}$$

Solving for Equilibrium in the Money Market (Getting Equation for LM Curve)   The equilibrium condition is

$$M_s = M_{dt} + M_{da}$$

Substituting,

$$91 = .2Y_g + (20 - 100i)$$
$$.2Y_g = 71 + 100i$$
$$Y_g = 355 + 500i \text{ (equation for LM curve)}$$

Solution for Initial "General" Equilibrium in Economy The income level and interest rates are compatible only at the levels where the IS and LM curves intersect. Therefore, we have equilibrium condition

$$IS = LM$$

Substituting,

$$400 - 400i - Y_g = 355 + 500i - Y_g$$
$$900i = 45$$
$$i = .05$$

The initial equilibrium interest rate equals 5 percent. Substituting 5 percent in LM equation (or IS),

$$Y_g = 355 + 500(.05)$$
$$Y_g = 355 + 25$$
$$Y_g = 380$$

The initial equilibrium GNP equals 380.

Computing Effect of Cut in Money Supply on GNP and Interest Rate

Now suppose that the economy has achieved its equilibrium positions of 380 and 5 percent and the monetary authorities apply a "tight money" policy consisting of a cut in the money supply to 82 (by 9). What will such a policy do to GNP and the interest rate?

Computing New LM Equation As the only change is in the money supply, the IS curve is unchanged. Equating the new money supply with the demand for money, we have

$$82 = .2Y_g + 20 - 100i$$
$$.2Y_g = 62 + 100i$$
$$Y_g = 310 + 500i \text{ (new LM curve)}$$

Computing New Equilibriums

$$IS = LM$$
$$400 - 400i = 310 + 500i$$
$$900i = 90$$
$$i = .10$$

The new equilibrium interest rate is 10 percent.

Substituting the 10 percent interest rate into the LM equation,

$$Y_g = 310 + 500(.10)$$

$$Y_g = 360$$

The new equilibrium GNP level is 360.

The Approach to the New Equilibrium by "Rounds"

This same change can be shown in rounds as in the early part of the chapter where the four-diagram approach was used.

Note that each value in Table 19-5 is computed directly from the given equation. The only complication is for the transactions demand for money, which is always based on the *previous* round's level of income. This treatment follows the discussion in the body of the chapter exactly.

Several significant items show up when the data are presented in this form. In the first place, note the crucial role played by asset money balances. In the new equilibrium, only $4 of the original $9 cut from the money supply comes out of transactions balances; the other $5 is drawn out of asset balances by the rise in the interest rate. If there had been no asset money balances and the entire money supply reduction had been withdrawn from transactions balances, income would have been reduced by a full 45—a figure directly reflecting the fact that each dollar in transactions balances supports a 5 in income. This would be a "crude quantity theory type" world in which money supply changes lead to equal proportional income changes.

Second, the data make clear that when the money market is included in the model, the simple multiplier used in Chapter 15 is inadequate to compute the change in equilibrium GNP. Note that in round 1, the rise in interest to 14 percent cut investment spending by 18. This, in turn, led to a cut in the GNP level (after the first round) of 36. As the MPC in this economy is 0.5, the multiplier is 2, and 2 times the initial cut in investment is, indeed, 36. But of course that's only

TABLE 19-5   Round-by-round approach to general equilibrium

	Initial equilibrium	End of round 1	End of round 2	End of round 3	End of round 4		New equilibrium
M_s	91	82	82	82	82	→	82
M_{dt}	76	76	68.8	74.56	69.95	→	72
M_{da}	15	6	13.2	7.44	12.05	→	10
i	5%	14%	6.8%	12.56%	7.95%	→	10%
C	290	272	286.4	274.88	284.10	→	280
$I + G$	90	72	86.4	74.88	84.10	→	80
Y_g	380	344	372.2	349.76	368.20	→	360

the beginning of the story. The later effects on the demand for money, and hence the rate of interest, are not taken into account by the simple multiplier.[8] One of the main reasons for bringing the money market and interest rate determination into the picture is to illustrate how it operates to cut down on the size of the simple multiplier.

The note of caution made earlier regarding the round-by-round approach to a new general equilibrium should be repeated here. This section and the data in Table 19-5 are included for pedagogical reasons only. In no sense does the real world follow such an adjustment path.

Computing Effects on GNP and Interest Rate of Fiscal Policy Measures

Returning to the original conditions, under which, it will be recalled, the IS equation was $Y_g = 400 - 400i$, the LM equation $Y_g = 355 + 500i$, the equilibrium GNP, 380, and the equilibrium interest rate 5 percent, let us compute the effects of certain fiscal policy measures.

Rise in Government Spending Financed by Borrowing from Nonbank Public Suppose that in an effort to raise employment and production, the government now raises its spending by \$9, borrowing the proceeds from the public.

The increase in government spending changes the IS equation because, of course, government spending is now \$69 rather than \$60. Thus we have

$$Y_g = C + I + G$$
$$Y_g = (.5Y_g + 100) + (40 - 200i) + 69$$
$$.5Y_g = 209 - 200i$$
$$Y_g = 418 - 400i \text{ (new IS equation)}$$

As the deficit is financed by sale of bonds to the public, the money supply is, of course, not changed. The LM equation therefore stays the same:

$$Y_g = 355 + 500i \text{ (LM equation)}$$

---

[8] The multiplier that takes account of the monetary sector changes is

$$\frac{1}{1 - b(1 - t) + (x \times y/z)}$$

where b = MPC out of DI, t = income tax rate, x = coefficient of interest term in investment equation, y = coefficient of income term in transactions demand-for-money equation, and z = coefficient of interest term in asset demand-for-money equation. With the given numbers, we have

$$\frac{1}{1 - .625(1 - .2) + (-200 \times .2/-100)} = \frac{1}{1 - .5 + .4} = \text{a multiplier of } 1.0/.9$$

This multiplier times the initial cut investment — $1.0/.9 \times 18$ — gives us a cut in the GNP of 20.

Solving by means of simultaneous equations, we get new equilibrium values for GNP and the interest rate of

$$Y_g = 390$$
$$i = 7\%$$

Note that the expansionary fiscal policy has had its desired effect of raising the income level. However, in the process, the interest rate is also increased, and that holds the income expansion well below the rise of 18 that the simple multiplier would have predicted.

Rise in Government Spending with Deficit Financed by New Money If the $9 of added government spending should be financed by sale of bonds to the banks, the effects are markedly different. For in this case the money supply goes up by $9 at the same time government spending rises. We have what is in effect an expansive fiscal policy aided by an expansive monetary policy.

Once again the rise in government spending gives us an IS equation of

$$Y_g = 418 - 400i$$

In this case, however, the LM equation is also altered by the increase in money supply from 91 to 100. To get the new LM equation, we have

$$\text{Supply of money} = \text{Demand for money}$$
$$100 = .2Y_g + (20 - 100i)$$
$$.2Y_g = 80 + 100i$$
$$Y_g = 400 + 500i \text{ (new LM equation)}$$

Solving now for the equilibrium income and interest rate levels, we get

$$Y_g = 410$$
$$i = 2\%$$

The important thing to note here is that the increase in the supply of money kept the interest rate from restricting the expansive effect of the fiscal policy, so that Y_g rose substantially more than in the preceding example. Indeed, in this example the increase in the supply of money had so much more weight than the rise in demand caused by the increase in Y_g that the equilibrium interest rate actually went *down*, permitting investment spending to rise also. This latter result should not be taken as necessarily typical. It is simply the result of the particular set of equations we chose to assume initially. The student will recall that in a case such as this, depending upon the particular circumstances, the interest rate may fall, rise, or stay the same. The important point is that it winds up at a lower level than in the preceding example and hence the income level rises more.

Review Questions

1. Indicate the slopes (flat or steep) of the MEI curve and of the total demand-for-money curve that are most conducive to money supply changes having a large effect on total expenditures and, in each case, briefly explain why.

2. If it is desired to raise GNP by $25 billion and the MPS is .4, explain the circumstances that must hold for a $10 billion rise in government spending on goods and services to accomplish the desired goal. (Assume that the government budget is balanced before the rise in G.)

3. Carefully explain *why* fiscal and monetary policy require different slopes in some of the curves in the four-diagram model to have the greatest effect on GNP.

4. Explain the significance of the slope of the transactions demand-for-money curve to the effectiveness of money supply changes aimed at raising GNP.

5. Explain what would be the implications for expansionary pure fiscal policy if bond prices were already at the lowest levels the public considers possible.

6. In the context of the four-diagram model of the economy, carefully explain how the method used to dispose of the tax surplus will affect the effectiveness of a fiscal policy measure aimed at cutting total expenditures.

7. Assume that initially we are at general equilibrium. Then the Fed carries out open-market sales to the banks. This produces an initial disequilibrium in the money market that will cause money holders to react in such a way as to cause changes that will ultimately restore equality between the demand for, and supply of, money.

   Using only the liquidity preferences theory of interest, explain the process whereby people may react to the initial disequilibrium as well as why they will be satisfied when the new equilibrium is reached.

8. "Contractionary fiscal policy is less effective, the higher the interest rates already are and the more responsive investors are to changes in interest rates." Do you agree? Explain carefully why this is or is not the case.

9. Using the full four-diagram model of the economy as a framework for your reasoning, indicate in each case (a) the curve (or curves) initially affected by the changes given, (b) the type of effect on the curve or curves (i.e., steepened, flattened, shifted right or left, shifted up or down), and (c) the effect on the general equilibrium GNP and rate of interest (i.e., increased, decreased, indeterminate).
   a. The public's conception of the normal range of interest rate fluctuation changes from a range of 3 to 8 percent to a range of 6 to 11 percent.
   b. The personal income tax rate is reduced and the budget deficit thereby created is financed by selling new U.S. securities to the banks.

    c. Corporate profit taxes are cut and the budget deficit created is financed by sale of new U.S. securities to the public.

    d. Personal taxes are raised from .15 GNP + 20 to .20 GNP + 30 and the tax surplus thereby created is used to retire maturing U.S. securities held by the banks.

    e. A natural disaster destroys half the nation's stock of capital goods and consumer durable goods.

    f. The government lowers business taxes and finances the deficit thereby created by selling U.S. securities to the nonbank public.

    g. Government spending is raised by $20 billion and lump-sum taxes are increased by $20 billion to finance it.

    h. Businesses increase the fraction of GNP that they withhold in the form of business saving.

10. "If the personal income tax rate is cut and the deficit thereby created is financed by sale of U.S. securities to the public, when the new general equilibrium position is reached the aggregate expenditures line will be steeper but will have a lower vertical intercept." Carefully explain why this must be the case.

11. "If government spending is raised by $10 billion, it will cause the IS curve to shift to the right by $10 billion." Do you agree? Explain why or why not.

12. Using IS and LM curves, illustrate and discuss the effects on GNP and interest rates of an increase in lump-sum taxes with the tax surplus used to retire securities held by the banks.

13. What would be the effect on the slope of its LM curve if, in a particular economy, a liquidity trap existed at interest rates below 4 percent? Using IS and LM curves, illustrate the comparative effectiveness of pure fiscal policy and monetary policy if carried out within the liquidity trap.

14. What is the connection between the slope of the total demand-for-money curve and the slope of the LM curve; between the slope of the MEI curve and the slope of the IS curve? In both cases, explain carefully.

Aggregate Demand, Aggregate Supply, and a Variable Price Level

Introduction

The Keynesian model, as depicted in the four-diagram or IS–LM framework, provides us a reasonably clear picture of some of the more important interconnections between spending and production as well as between the "goods" and "money" markets. One glaring omission, however, limits its applicability. This is the implicit assumption of a stable price level.

The student will recall the simplifying assumptions made in introducing Chapter 16. There we assumed that increases in intended spending did not affect prices until the full-employment level of output was achieved, after which further rises in spending could only raise the price level.[1]

This assumption can be illustrated with a diagram like Figure 20-1 in which the price level is measured off on the vertical axis and output (real GNP) is measured off horizontally.

The implications, of course, are that if we are currently producing any amount less than 0A (which is assumed to be the full-employment level of output), rises in total intended spending will have the favorable effect of raising output but no unfavorable inflationary effects. Once we have reached the 0A level of output, on the other hand, increased spending can only raise prices since we have already reduced unemployment to its minimum. As a corollary, these assumptions imply that there exists an ideal level of total spending for stabilization policymakers to shoot at, where we will suffer neither inflation nor unemployment.

[1] The full-employment level of output is commonly referred to as the level of output at which the "natural" rate of unemployment has been achieved. The natural rate of unemployment is generally taken to mean the fraction of the labor force unemployed when total spending has been raised far enough to just eliminate cyclical unemployment, leaving only frictional and structural unemployment.

FIGURE 20-1

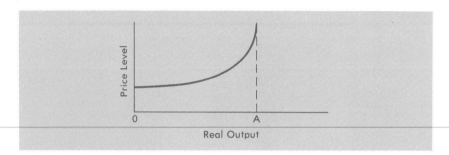

FIGURE 20-2

One does not need to be an economist to recognize how unrealistic these assumptions are. Indeed, if asked to resketch the line drawn in Figure 20-1 to accord more fully with real-world experience, almost anyone would eliminate the kink where output 0A is first achieved and insert instead an upward sloping line such as the one in Figure 20-2.

Such an adjustment obviously recognizes that the approach to the full-employment level of output produces a mixed bag of results, the rise in real output being accompanied by increasing inflation.

The purpose of this chapter is to recast our discussion by introducing the effects of a variable price level. We do so with the aid of *aggregate demand* and *aggregate supply* schedules. Let us turn now to consider these new concepts.

An Aggregate Demand Curve

Definition

An aggregate demand curve shows how the aggregate quantity of goods and services demanded varies as the price level varies, assuming all other factors influencing the amount demanded (aside from the price level) are fixed.

An aggregate demand curve, then, is conceptually identical to a demand-for-a-single-good curve, the only differences being that the aggregate demand curve

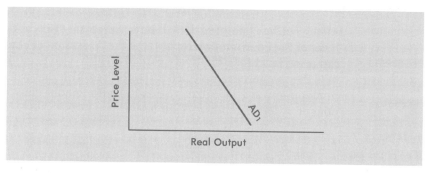

FIGURE 20-3

shows how the quantities demanded for *all* newly produced goods and services vary as the overall *price level* varies, rather than how the quantity demanded for a *single* good varies as *its* price varies.

In graphical form, the typical aggregate demand curve looks like AD_1 in Figure 20-3.

Why Does the Aggregate Quantity Demanded Rise as the Price Level Falls? (Why Is the Aggregate Demand Curve Down Sloping?)

The reader will no doubt recall from microeconomics that the quantity of a single good that is demanded rises as the price falls because of the substitution and income effects. That is, as the price of good A falls, people want to buy more of it both because the fall in its price causes a shift away from substitute goods toward the now cheaper good A and because that lower price raises the real purchasing power of buyers' fixed money incomes. These reasons for the so-called "law of demand" are not applicable to explain the negative slope of an *aggregate* demand curve, however, so we must first consider what *does* cause a lower overall price level to be associated with a higher aggregate quantity demanded.

Two relationships are most important: the *interest rate effect* and the *wealth effect*. Let us consider these in turn.

It will be recalled that the quantity of money demanded for transactions purposes is directly related to the money level of GNP. The lower the price level, the lower the money level of GNP and, therefore, the lower the quantity of money demanded for transactions purposes. This causes a fall (shift to the left) in the total demand for money and that, in its turn, lowers the equilibrium rate of interest. Finally, given the **MEI** curve, the lower interest rate permits a rise in the investment spending component of aggregate demand.

Symbolically, then, the interest rate effect is:

Price Level	Q of Money Demanded for Transactions Purpose	Tot D for Money	Interest Rate	Investment Spending Part of Total Spending
↓	↓	↓	↓	↑

The wealth effect (or, as it is sometimes called, the "real balance" effect) is somewhat less complex. It will be recalled that one of the determinants of the level of the consumption function is the real value of consumers' wealth. When the price level falls, the real value of wealth with fixed dollar value (such as, to take the simplest example, a $100 bill) rises. This, in turn, shifts the consumption function upward, causing a rise in the autonomous consumption spending component of total spending. That is,

| Price Level | Real Value of Some Forms of Wealth ↑↓ | Consumption Function ↑ | Consumption Spending Component of Total Spending ↑ |

From this, we must recognize that every total spending $(C + I + G)$ line assumes a given price level. At a lower price level, I will be higher (via the interest rate effect) and C will be higher (via the wealth effect) so that the level of the $C + I + G$ line will be higher for two reasons. In turn, the aggregate quantity demanded as read off the aggregate demand curve will be higher by the multiplier times the sum of the rises in autonomous C and I.

Suppose, in Figure 20-4, that initially we were in equilibrium with price level P_1 and real GNP level Q_1, and that something then causes the price level to fall to P_2. In the upper diagram, the total intended spending line will shift up (via the interest rate and wealth effects) by AB to $C_2 + I_2$. This will initially cause total intended spending to exceed production (at Q_1) by AB which will trigger a multiplied rise in production to Q_2. At Q_2, the total intended spending $(C_2 + I_2)$

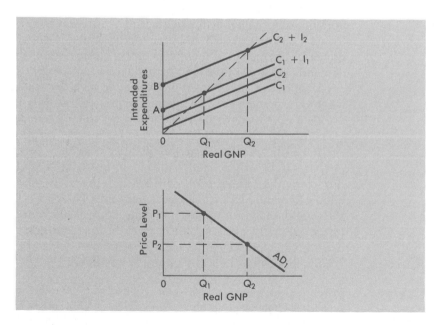

FIGURE 20-4

will once again equal production (so that inventories are no longer being drawn down). Note that in the bottom diagram, the aggregate quantity demanded has increased by the full Q_1Q_2.

What Can Cause Shifts in the Level of the Aggregate Demand Curve?

What are the determinants of the *level* of the aggregate demand curve? What will cause the aggregate demand curve itself to shift to the right or left? The answer is anything which changes the level of the $C + I + G$ curve *except a change in the price level*.

The economy's aggregate demand curve will be shifted by any change in autonomous spending that is not a result of the wealth effect or interest rate effect as discussed. Although not all inclusive, Table 20-1 lists some of the more important determinants of the level of the aggregate demand curve.

To illustrate these effects, consider the expansionary fiscal policy measure depicted in Figure 20-5. Here, it is assumed that government spending on goods and service is raised by **AB** and that this causes the equilibrium production level to rise by Q_1Q_2, or by the multiplier times **AB**.[2]

Note that the effect is to cause the aggregate quantity demanded to rise by the change in G times the multiplier, *at every price level*, thereby shifting the aggregate demand line to the right to AD_2. An expansionary monetary policy measure such as a rise in the supply of money which lowers interest rates enough to permit a rise in investment spending of **AB** would have precisely the same effect on the economy's aggregate demand curve.

TABLE 20-1 Some determinants of level of aggregate demand curve

Factors that will shift aggregate demand curve to right	*Factors that will shift aggregate demand curve to left*
1. Cut in personal taxes which shifts consumption function upward.	1. Increase in personal taxes which shifts consumption function downward.
2. Rise in government spending on goods and services which shifts $C + I + G$ line upward.	2. Cut in government spending on goods and services which shifts $C + I + G$ line downward.
3. Improvement in expected profits from investment which shifts **MEI** curve to right and raises investment spending.	3. Deterioration in expected profits from investment which shifts **MEI** curve to left and cuts investment spending.
4. Increase in supply of money which lowers interest rates and permits a rise in investment spending.	4. Cut in supply of money which raises interest rates and causes a cutback in investment spending.

[2] To minimize the complications, we assume that the deficit is financed with new money so that there is no second-round interest rate increase and, therefore, no crowding out.

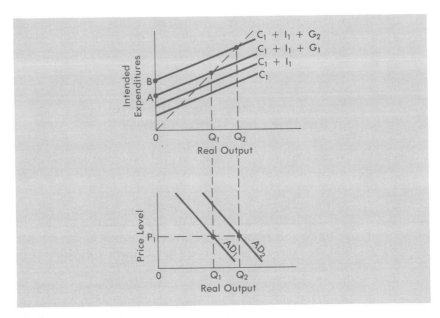

FIGURE 20-5 Effect of a rise in government spending on aggregate demand curve

The Aggregate Supply Curve

The aggregate demand curve, of course, shows only how the aggregate quantity demanded by the three spending groups varies as the price level varies. That is, it shows how the aggregate amount buyers *want to buy* changes as the price level changes. Whether buyers will be able to actually buy the amount they want depends upon suppliers, and to consider their behavior, we need an aggregate supply curve.

Definition

An aggregate supply curve shows how the aggregate quantity of real output supplied varies as the price level varies, assuming all other factors (except the price level) affecting the quantity supplied are fixed.[3]

Graphically, we assume that the aggregate supply curve is shaped roughly as is the curve sketched in Figure 20-6 with a nearly horizontal segment (AB) at low

[3] Many economists refer to the curve we define here as the *short-run* aggregate supply curve to recognize the fact that each short-run aggregate supply curve assumes given resource prices (such as wage rates) and that such resource prices will, after some lag, tend to rise (fall) if the current level of output is above (below) the so-called potential level. In this approach, the long-run aggregate supply curve is considered to be a vertical line at the potential level of output. In the next section, we introduce the potential level of output, but we will not use the short-run and long-run distinctions.

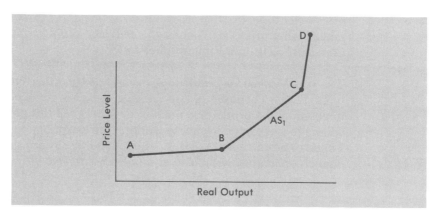

FIGURE 20-6

levels of output, an upsloping segment (BC), and finally a near-vertical segment (CD) as we approach the maximum amounts of output that current techniques and resource quantities permit.

What Explains the Slope of the Aggregate Supply Curve?

Since the aggregate supply curve depicted in Figure 20-6 has three distinct segments with quite different slopes, we must consider the explanation for the slope of each segment separately.

The Near-Horizontal (or "Keynesian") Segment (A to B) The implication of the nearly horizontal segment of the aggregate supply curve is that, in this range, producers are willing to supply more with little or no rise in the price level.

At these very low levels of output, the economy is assumed to be in depression or severe recession with large numbers of unemployed workers and considerable unemployed capital available. Furthermore, it is assumed that many of the workers and machines currently idle are just as productive (i.e., can turn out just as many units of output per hour) as those now working. Consequently, when more workers are hired to raise output, *cost per unit of product does not rise* and, as a result, revenue per unit, or price, does not need to go up either.

The Intermediate Upsloping Segment (B to C) Once the economy has recovered from the depths of recession (and reached point B), however, conditions change. By this point it is assumed that the most productive of the unemployed resources have already been put back to work and that those still available are capable of producing fewer units per hour than those presently employed.

Production can be increased beyond point B via either of two routes. Current employees can work overtime and be paid time and a half or some of the still unemployed can be added to the payrolls. Assuming a constant wage rate per hour, either approach will raise cost per unit of product and necessitate a higher price level to justify the production. To put it as simply as possible, in the BC range higher prices are required to convince suppliers to incur the higher costs they must incur in raising production.

The Near-Vertical (or Classical) Segment (C to D)   Once output has been raised to point C, the economy is approaching the outright limits on output that are imposed by the production possibilities curve. At this point, virtually everyone willing to work has a job and is working the maximum desired number of hours. Efforts to produce more merely lead to bidding already employed workers from one job to another with little or no increase in real output being realized.

What Can Cause Shifts in the Aggregate Supply Curve?

As before, we can say that a change in any factor affecting the aggregate quantity supplied, except for a change in the price level, will shift the aggregate supply curve to the right or left. Three such factors should be noted.

A Change in Resource Prices   Each aggregate supply curve assumes a given set of resource prices. The most important resource price is the wage rate of labor but the interest rate and the price per unit of essential materials are also significant.

Clearly, a rise in a resource price will raise the cost of any given amount of output, thereby shifting the aggregate supply curve up and to the left. Consider the graph depicted in Figure 20-7.

If we have been producing an output of 0A with aggregate supply curve AS_1, the price level required to convince sellers to offer 0A is $0P_1$. If wage rates now rise, the effect can be looked at in either of two ways. In order to make sellers willing to continue offering 0A of output, the price level would have to rise to $0P_2$ to cover the increased cost. Conversely, if the price level stays at $0P_1$, real output

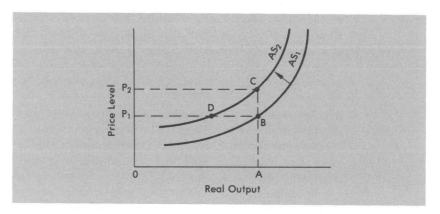

FIGURE 20-7   Effect of a rise in a resource price

would have to be cut back by DB, resulting in the layoff of those workers whose output per hour is not high enough to justify keeping them employed at the higher wage rate. Obviously, a cut in the wage rate would shift the aggregate supply out to the right for the opposite reasons.

A Change in Technology   An improvement in technology would tend to shift the aggregate supply curve out to the right. This is the case because a technological improvement usually implies a less costly way of producing any given amount. Note that both an improvement in technology and a reduction in resource prices shift the aggregate supply line down and to the right because both permit production of any given amount at lower cost.

A Change in the Quantity of Resources   An obvious addition to the list of aggregate supply shifters is the quantity of resources available. Just as an increase in resources shifts a nation's production possibilities curve out to the right, it also shifts its aggregate supply curve out to the right.

Aggregate Supply, Aggregate Demand, and the "Potential" Level of Output

Now that we have introduced aggregate demand and aggregate supply, let us put them together along with the concept of the "potential" or "full-employment" level of output and consider equilibrium production levels.

We begin with a definition of the full-employment or potential level of output. Economists have long recognized that it would be impossible and probably undesirable to attempt to achieve a zero level of unemployment. If the economy is to remain free and flexible, and we are to avoid the problems of accelerating inflation, some (hopefully small) fraction of the labor force is always going to be unemployed or "between jobs" for frictional and structural reasons. As a consequence, the full-employment level of output has come to be defined, not as the level of output where *all* unemployment is eliminated, but rather as the level of output at which *cyclical* unemployment has been eliminated, even though joblessness (some estimate 5 to $5\frac{1}{2}$ percent of the labor force) still exists for frictional and structural reasons.

Suppose that we have an economy in which aggregate demand happens to equal aggregate supply exactly at this potential level of output. We then have an *equilibrium* level which happens also to be a *full-employment* one. Consider Figure 20-8.

If we let the vertical line represent the full-employment level of real output, one can readily see that the forces of the market, as expressed via the aggregate demand and aggregate supply curves, will push us toward the fortuitous equilibrium output level that produces full employment. We have an output of $0Q_1$ and a price level of $0P_1$ and everything is fine. But what can we expect if the aggregate demand curve shifts?

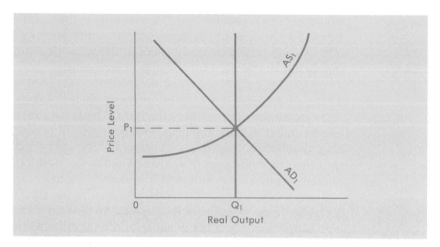

FIGURE 20-8

The Price System's Automatic Reaction
to a Rise in Aggregate Demand:
An Inflationary Gap

Let us trace through the economy's automatic response to a rightward shift in the aggregate demand curve, which, as we have seen, could be caused by a change in any one of a number of basic determinants. Look at Figure 20-9.

If we start, as before, at $0Q_1$ and $0P_1$ as a result of AD_1 and AS_1, we initially have equilibrium at full employment. If, however, the aggregate demand curve now shifts to the right to AD_2, it is clear that initially at price level $0P_1$ the aggregate quantity demanded, $0Q_2$, exceeds the aggregate quantity supplied, $0Q_1$. Such a shortage would lead sellers to produce more, raising the quantity

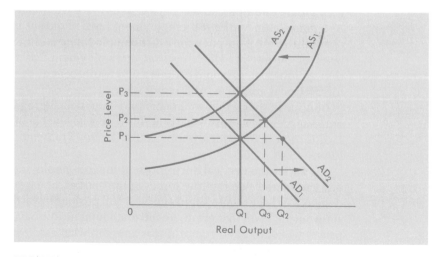

FIGURE 20-9

supplied. In the process, however (since we are in the intermediate upsloping segment of the aggregate supply curve), employers are forced to hire less productive workers, which raises per-unit production costs and requires a rise in the price level. As the quantity supplied is rising, the higher price level it requires will simultaneously lead to a cutback in the aggregate quantity demanded from $0Q_2$ to $0Q_3$. This movement along the AD_2 curve is a consequence of reductions in autonomous consumption and investment spending caused by the wealth and interest rate effects discussed earlier.

However, the adjustment is not completed at $0Q_3$ and $0P_2$. With the economy heating up, employers for some period of time in the short run — perhaps until current labor union contracts expire — will have had the advantage of rising prices with fixed money wages. These employers will begin competing for the scarce labor supply by offering higher money wage rates. But since money wage rates are a key resource price, this step in the adjustment will shift the aggregate supply curve up and to the left. And that, in turn, will further raise prices while reducing real output below the $0Q_3$ level. Since an excess demand for labor exists at all levels of real output beyond $0Q_1$, money wages must continue rising, and therefore the aggregate supply curve must continue shifting leftward, until AS_2 is reached. At that point a new long-run equilibrium is reached at which real output is back at $0Q_1$ and the price level has been raised to $0Q_3$.

Now let us step back and make some important observations regarding the inflationary process just sketched.

1. An inflationary gap caused by excess aggregate demand is self-limiting (i.e., will tend automatically to close itself) so long as it is not kept open by recurring increases in demand.

2. Real output can be increased to above the full-employment level only temporarily, and then, only at the cost of a rise in the price level.

3. During the process of adjusting to excess aggregate demand (specifically, during the shift back to the left of the aggregate supply curve), the economy will undergo a period of what has come to be called *stagflation* where unemployment and the price level are both rising at the same time.

The Price System's Automatic Response to a Fall in Aggregate Demand: A Recessionary Gap

Is there a comparable automatic mechanism tending to eliminate a *deficiency* in aggregate demand and the recessionary gap it creates? If so, the knowledge would be extremely important since it could put an end to all the debate as to when and how public policy should be used to combat recession and excess unemployment. Let's take a look, using Figure 20-10 as the basis for our consideration.

Suppose the initial equilibrium price and real output levels are $0P_1$ and $0Q_1$ as determined by the intersection of AD_1 and AS_1. Then assume that there is a cutback in spending that shifts the aggregate demand line back to AD_2. Initially, at price level $0P_1$, there is a surplus since the aggregate quantity supplied (read

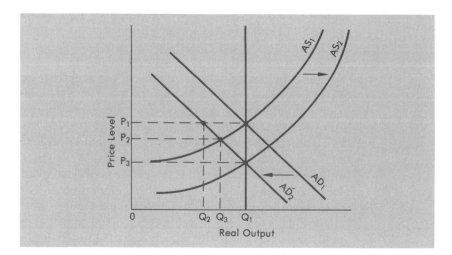

FIGURE 20-10

off AS_1) is still $0Q_1$, while the aggregate quantity demanded is now only $0Q_2$. This will surely cause sellers to cut back on their production by laying off some workers.

Now if the recessionary gap story is to be the mirror image of the inflationary gap story, we could argue that logically the first workers laid off would be those who are least productive so that the labor cost per unit of product *falls* when they leave. And this, in turn, would lead to a cut in the price level to $0P_2$ which will cause the aggregate quantity demanded to rise via the wealth and interest rate effects to $0Q_3$. As before, one might then argue that the equilibrium reached at $0P_2$ and $0Q_3$ will be short-lived. This is so because the surplus of workers must sooner or later lead to a cut in money wage rates and that will shift the aggregate supply curve down to the right, further lowering the price level. Finally, the entire adjustment reaches a new "long-run" equilibrium at the full-employment level of real output, $0Q$, with the price level all the way down to $0P_3$.

Does such a scenario with its implied automatic cure for recession and cyclical unemployment make sense? As a logical proposition, yes. All the mechanisms and corrective tendencies of the price system do, indeed, *exist*. But they are only tendencies and recent experience with recessionary periods offers no evidence and precious little grounds for hope that future recessions will automatically generate a sufficiently large *fall* in the price level (as distinct from a decline in the rate of increase) to restore full employment.

The fact is that, whereas wages and prices do move freely in the upward direction, they tend to be exceptionally sticky and resistant to pressures tending to lower them. The result is that many economists, doubtful of the practical usefulness of the long-run corrective mechanism described, would dismiss it almost as cavalierly as Keynes did in his most quoted phrase, "In the long run we are all dead." [4]

---

[4] Although many economists would agree with Keynes's recommendation of discretionary government stabilization policy to moderate the effects of recession, a significant number, especially the monetarists, do not accept this prescription. We consider the monetarist view in the next chapter.

Discretionary Monetary and Fiscal Policy as Stabilization Tools

We learned in the preceding chapter that monetary policy is a more effective tool for altering total intended spending and money GNP, the steeper is the total demand for money (steeper the LM) curve and the flatter the MEI (flatter the IS) curve. Conversely, fiscal policy will have more impact on total intended spending and money GNP the flatter the total demand for money (flatter the LM) curve and the steeper the MEI (steeper the IS) curve. Now it can hardly be denied that these conclusions are important for comparing the effectiveness of these two prime stabilization weapons. However, the ultimate payoff for stabilization weapons is not really their effect on money GNP but rather their specific effect on either real GNP or on the price level.

More explicitly, expansionary monetary or fiscal policy is aimed at raising real GNP. To the degree that it also pushes up the price level, its overall beneficial effects are compromised. Similarly, contractionary monetary or fiscal policy measures are aimed primarily at holding down a rising price level. To the extent that they also cut real output and employment, their desirability is reduced. To comment on the appropriateness of stabilization policies, therefore, we must be able to say something about the conditions under which they will impact primarily on their target variable. Fortunately, that is just what aggregate demand and supply curves are designed to do.

Expansionary monetary-fiscal policies "work" by shifting the aggregate demand curve out to the right. Their effectiveness in achieving their goal of raising real output and employment, however, depends greatly on the slope of the aggregate supply curve in the area affected. Let us look at the possibilities in Figure 20-11.

In part (a) of Figure 20-11, the aggregate demand curves cross the aggregate supply curve in the completely horizontal segment of the AS curve. Here, in depression or deep recession, expansionary policies are most effective since the entire impact of the increased spending goes to raise production and none of it is wasted in raising the price level.

FIGURE 20-11

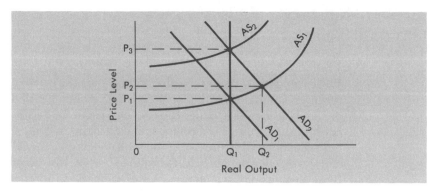

FIGURE 20-12

In part (b), the reverse is the case. Here the entire effect of the increase in aggregate demand raises prices and none of it is successful in raising employment and production. Clearly, expansionary stabilization policy is to be avoided in such circumstances.

Finally, in part (c) we depict the most common situation faced by policymakers. Here, in the upsloping, but not vertical, portion of the aggregate supply curve, the results of expansionary monetary-fiscal actions are mixed, partly the desired effect of increased real output and partly the unwelcome by-product of a higher price level.

Note, however, that even the modest gain in real output depicted in part (c) of Figure 20-11 cannot be maintained in the long run if the potential or full-employment level of output is less than $0Q_2$. Figure 20-12 shows why.

Here the only difference from part (c) of Figure 20-11 is that a vertical line has been inserted at output $0Q_1$ to indicate that this is the potential level of output. In this case, we do get the rise in output from $0Q_1$ to $0Q_2$ noted earlier, but it is only a short-run gain. For in the long run, money wage rates will be bid up, shifting the aggregate supply curve up and to the left until we are back to $0Q_1$ again. This seems to imply that only in the horizontal portion of the aggregate supply curve are expansionary monetary-fiscal policies of long-run benefit.

The evaluation of contractionary monetary-fiscal policies involves examining the flip side of all this. The object is to cut back on a potentially excessive level of aggregate demand to prevent, or at least moderate, inflationary pressures. Note, however, that the goal here might be considered more modest than is the case for expansionary policy. Whereas expansionary policy succeeds if it actually raises real output above the level it would have otherwise reached, contractionary policy does not seek to actually *lower* the price level. It merely aims at moderating an expected rise.[5]

Consider Figure 20-13. Suppose an initial equilibrium of $0Q_1$ and $0P_1$, de-

---

[5] As stabilization weapons, both expansionary and contractionary policies are aimed at preventing or moderating unfavorable changes in real output and the price level. However, while reversing an unfavorable change in real output would be considered beneficial, actually *lowering* the price level after it had risen would not. Changes in the price level in any direction impose unfair, capricious redistributions of income and wealth and are, therefore, to be avoided.

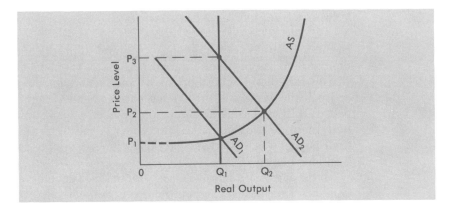

FIGURE 20-13

termined by AD_1 and AS_1, is disturbed by a sudden upsurge in consumer spending which if not combated would shift the aggregate demand curve to AD_2. In the absence of government stabilization action, there would be a short-term equilibrium reached at $0Q_2$ and $0P_2$, but in the longer term, money wage rate increases would shift the aggregate supply curve back to the left with output being reduced back to $0Q_1$ and the price level rising further to $0P_3$. Skillful use of contractionary monetary-fiscal policies (i.e., shifting the AD curve back to AD_1) could conceivably *avoid* this inflation (as well as the temporary hike in real output) and produce a marked improvement in society's welfare.

Adjustments Initiated by Shifts in Aggregate Supply

Until fairly recently, instability in real output or the price level was almost exclusively considered to be the product of aberrant shifts in the level of aggregate demand. And, as a corollary, discussion regarding means of dealing with inflation or unemployment centered almost entirely on such demand management measures as monetary and fiscal policy employed to counter the undesirable shifts in aggregate demand.

This approach served reasonably well until the mid-1970s when our first real encounter with serious stagflation (rising prices and rising unemployment) sent economists scurrying for new explanations. If the double-digit inflation we were experiencing was caused by excess aggregate demand, why then was production and employment falling? If we were to use conventional monetary-fiscal policy measures to combat the inflation, presumably contractionary policies, wouldn't that worsen the unemployment? Suddenly it seemed that the world had been detached from its economic moorings to such an extent that some critics wrote freely about the alleged ongoing "repeal of the laws of supply and demand." No such repeal had occurred, of course. It was just that the problem had been initiated by an undesirable shift in aggregate supply rather than demand and that produced an unpleasant, as well as unfamiliar result.

"Supply Shocks" and Stagflation

In the mid-1970s several events combined to produce a sudden and unprecedented increase in production costs. First, a rare run of unfavorable weather sharply raised agricultural prices. Secondly, and much more significantly, a majority of the world's oil-producing nations banded together in an organization called OPEC and used their monopoly power to quadruple the price of oil. Since both these developments had the effect of raising producers' resource prices, their impact was to shift the nation's aggregate supply curve up and to the left. Consider Figure 20-14.

If the aggregate supply curve prior to these developments was AS_1, then the equilibrium price level and output levels, respectively, would be $0P_1$ and $0Q_1$. A shift of the aggregate supply curve to AS_2, however, would produce a higher price level, $0P_2$, and a lower output (and employment) level, $0Q_2$. So the result is classic stagflation.

However, that is not the end of the matter. If the $0Q_1$ level of output was the full-employment level (as indicated by the vertical line sketched in there) then the equilibrium reached at $0Q_2$ and $0P_2$ is only short run, subject to change in the long run.

What we have now is a recessionary gap not significantly different from the one depicted in Figure 20-10. That situation produces a *tendency* for money wages to fall, shifting the aggregate supply curve back to the right again until a new longer-run equilibrium is reestablished at $0P_1$ and $0Q_1$ again. In effect, the rise in oil and agricultural prices is just offset in the long run by the decline in money wages and we end up after some unemployment and inflation back at the original levels.

As noted earlier, however, the well-documented rigidity of wages and prices in the downward direction makes the long-run adjustment suggested in the preceding paragraph so painfully slow as to be of limited practical significance. Are there any alternatives or must an economy hit by unfavorable aggregate

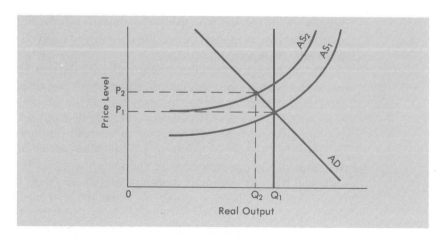

FIGURE 20-14

supply shifts simply "grin and bear it," suffering through long-term excess unemployment in the meantime?

There is an alternative, but as is so often the case, it is not without costs in its own right. What the nation's government could do after $0P_2$ and $0Q_2$ are reached is to institute an expansionary monetary-fiscal policy aimed at shifting the aggregate demand curve sufficiently far to the right to bring production back to $0Q_1$. Such a policy is generally described as one of *accommodation.* It can succeed in ameliorating the unemployment, but in doing so it will cause the price level to rise further, above $0P_2$.

Which approach is better? There is no right or wrong answer. A policy of no accommodation to supply shocks reduces the inflation problem but guarantees longer, more serious losses from unemployment. Accommodation reduces the deadweight loss from unemployment, but forces the price level up even higher. The appropriate choice obviously depends on the society's values and its assessment of the relative costs of inflation and unemployment.

Supply-Side Governmental Policies

Shifts to the left in the aggregate supply curve, as we have seen, inflict a double dose of misery on the community—both inflation *and* unemployment. Given this, it does not require any special genius or insight to recognize that if a way could be found to shift the aggregate supply curve to the *right* (without at the same time shifting the aggregate demand curve), we could reap the double benefit of lower prices and higher output.

This knowledge, coupled with recognition of the fact that the conventional demand-shifting stabilization weapons of monetary and fiscal policy were ill equipped to deal with both sides of the stagflation problem, led in the early 1980s to popularization of an approach that came to be called supply-side economics.

In general, the objective of supply-side economics is to shift the aggregate supply curve to the right via measures aimed at improving productive incentives along with other measures directed at causing people to act on those incentives by actually producing more. For example, it was argued that reductions in personal income tax rates would cause people to substitute work for leisure by raising the after-tax return for added labor.[6] Similarly, special cuts in taxes on the income from saving, coupled with such business tax changes as accelerated depreciation and investment tax credits, were aimed at simultaneously increasing saving and investment spending, thereby stimulating a faster rate of capital formation.

What can be said in evaluation of such supply-side efforts as these? First, few economists, be they supply-siders, Keynesians, or monetarists, doubt that the effect on the aggregate supply curve will be in the desired direction. On the other hand, most nonsupply-siders would argue that these favorable effects are likely to be relatively small and realizable only in the long run. Furthermore, skeptics contend that the effects of such tax cuts on the aggregate *demand* curve are likely to be both quicker and stronger. If so, measures taken with the intent of combat-

[6] It should be noted that for this effect to be as desired, the substitution effect must be stronger than the income effect.

ing inflation could very well (via the impact of the rightward shift in the aggregate demand curve) exacerbate it.

In summary, it seems fair to say that while selected supply-side measures do have a legitimate role to play in our overall policy mix, few if any professional economists look upon them as a panacea.

Review Questions

1. "To assume a stable price level until the full-employment level of production is reached is to assume that there are no trade-offs to be encountered in the use of expansionary monetary and fiscal policy." Explain.

2. What are the determinants of the slope of the aggregate demand curve? Contrast these with the determinants of the slope of a demand-for-a-single-good curve.

3. Draw appropriately labeled graphs to illustrate the relation between the aggregate expenditures line and the aggregate demand line.

4. Explain the factors that can cause a rightward shift in a nation's aggregate demand curve. Make clear your understanding of the relationship between the vertical rise in aggregate expenditures and the rightward shift in aggregate demand. (Hint: remember the multiplier?)

5. Carefully explain the logic behind the differing slopes of the three major segments of the aggregate supply curve.

6. What are the determinants of the level of the aggregate supply curve?

7. Using appropriately labeled aggregate demand and aggregate supply curves, explain how the price system may automatically eliminate an inflationary gap.

8. "In theory, a recessionary gap will tend to cure itself." Explain. Comment on the practical usefulness of such a "cure."

9. "The effectiveness of demand management weapons in stabilizing production without destabilizing the price level depends heavily on the slope of the aggregate supply curve in the area affected." Explain carefully.

10. Explain how supply shocks can affect the economy and what policy measures are available to government to deal with these effects.

11. Explain the purpose of supply-side governmental measures and then, to the extent that you can, evaluate them.

The Modern Quantity Theory and the Monetarist – Post-Keynesian Debate

It is a tribute to the genius and enduring influence of J. M. Keynes that the theoretical model presented in Chapters 16 through 19 is, despite updating modifications, essentially the same structure as that put forth by the Cambridge master almost 60 years ago. Surely it is not an overstatement to describe the upheaval in economic thought associated with the publication of the *General Theory* as a Keynesian revolution.

But revolution sometimes begets counterrevolution. During the past 35 years, an influential group of economists, originally based primarily at the University of Chicago, has emerged to challenge some of the theory and much of the policy that since Keynes had become almost the accepted dogma of the economics profession. These neoclassical economists led by Professor Milton Friedman have reformulated and refurbished an old classical idea which almost, but not quite, died under the Keynesian onslaught. Their special concern is with the quantity theory of money, restyled in a new theoretical format and supported by impressive new empirical data.

The Keynesian Position — A Variable Velocity and a Role for Fiscal Policy

It will be recalled that a central tenet of the older versions of the quantity theory was the assumption that the velocity of spending is essentially fixed, leading inevitably to the corollary proposition that changes in the money supply lead to equal percentage changes in total spending. If MV' is equal to total spending and V' is a constant, a change in M is both a necessary and a sufficient condition for an alteration in total intended spending.

The fixed velocity assumption ultimately fell victim to both fact and theory. The facts alone, which revealed velocity as a number that varied both cyclically and secularly, were enough to undermine the foundations of the old theory.

It was left to Keynes to provide a theoretical base for a varying velocity. This he provided with his speculative demand-for-money concept. To Keynes, the reader will recall, the demand for money $(1/V')$ varied not only with the level of income (the transactions demand) but also with the rate of interest (the speculative demand). The relation to the interest rate was the crucial factor.

For if the public was now thought willing to hold essentially idle money balances for speculative purposes, as well as active transactions balances, a number of previously unexplored possibilities were opened up.

In the first place, money supply increases no longer were seen as necessarily guaranteeing total spending increases. Under normal conditions, part (but not all) of any increase in the money supply was absorbed into idle, speculative balances. Because that portion of the money supply increase went unspent, velocity fell. If, for example, the money supply were $100 with a velocity of 4 per year, a $50 increase in M, half of which was spent 4 times per year in transactions balances and half of which was held idle in speculative balances, would result in a new velocity figure of $3\frac{1}{3}$. That is,

$$\frac{(100 \times 4) + (25 \times 4)}{150} = \frac{500}{150} = 3\frac{1}{3}$$

Total spending would have risen (to $500), but by a smaller percentage than the money supply.

Under abnormal conditions, however, money supply increases might not raise spending at all! This, of course, could happen if the liquidity trap had been reached. In such a case, *all* of any money supply increase is absorbed into speculative balances, leading to a reduction in velocity exactly equivalent to the rise in M.[1]

Second, and perhaps of greater significance, the introduction of a speculative money demand with its resulting variability in velocity provided a means by which total spending could be raised *without* any change in the money supply. For policy purposes, this represented a monumental change because it allowed the introduction of fiscal policy as a stabilization tool.

---

[1] Some have chastised Keynes for developing a model in which the liquidity trap is a crucial and necessary element. Such criticism has taken on added meaning in recent years when empirical investigation has been unable to locate any such trap in the U.S. economy.

Whatever the sins of some of his followers, Keynes himself does not appear guilty of overstressing the liquidity trap notion. Indeed, he considered an infinitely elastic demand-for-money curve as only a possibility.

"There is the possibility, for the reasons discussed above, that, after the rate of interest has fallen to a certain level, liquidity preference may become virtually absolute in the sense that almost everyone prefers cash to holding a debt which yields so low a rate of interest. In this event the monetary authority would have lost effective control over the rate of interest. But whilst this limiting case might become practically important in the future, I know of no example of it hitherto." John Maynard Keynes, *General Theory of Employment, Interest and Money* (London and New York: Macmillan, 1936), p. 207. For a different view on Keynes's emphasis on a liquidity trap, however, see Milton Friedman, "Comments on the Critics," *Journal of Political Economy*, September–October 1972, pp. 945–946.

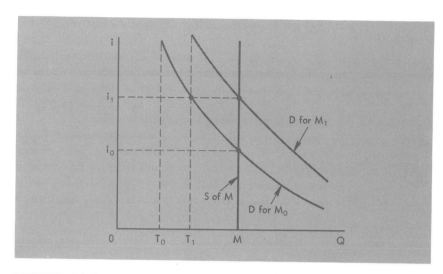

FIGURE 21-1   Increased transactions demand raises velocity

It is not difficult to see what is involved here. Prior to Keynes, pure fiscal policy where the government's budget is altered without a change in the money supply had not been thought capable of affecting spending. For if aggregate demand is MV′ and V′ is a constant, only measures that raise M can raise demand.[2]

Now, however, assuming the existence of idle, speculative money balances, things looked quite different. A rise in government spending (or a cut in taxes) *could* raise aggregate spending by the simple expedient of pulling that part of the existing money supply needed to finance transactions out of idle, speculative balance into active, transactions use.

Look at Figure 21-1. Suppose that government spending has been increased, raising the equilibrium income level and that that, in turn, has increased the transactions demand for money from OT_0 to OT_1. This raises the total demand for money from D for M_0 to D for M_1 and increases the interest rate from i_0 to i_1. Now, in this Keynesian case, the rise in interest rates will *not* be enough to cut investment spending back by as much as government spending initially rose because it is moderated by the existence of speculative money balances. Notice that before the interest rate rose, transactions balances totaled only OT_0, with T_0M held idle in speculative balances. After interest rises to i_1, transactions balances are increased to OT_1, with only T_1M being kept idle. What this means is that a larger percentage of the existing money supply is now being spent to buy goods and services; velocity has been raised.

---

[2] The rationale for this attitude was simple. If all existing money is already being used to finance all the expenditures it can, what can, for example, a rise in government spending without a rise in the money supply do? The added money spent by government is necessarily acquired from the public by the sale of new government bonds. This, in the classical view, merely pushes interest rates up high enough to cut back private investment spending by the amount government spending rose. Fiscal policy under these circumstances is simply a means of determining what percentage of resources will be used publicly and what percentage privately, but *not* a means of affecting the total amount actually used.

Keynes's *General Theory* thus not only tended to undercut the hitherto implicit faith in the effectiveness of money supply changes but laid the foundation for fiscal policy as a potentially more useful stabilization weapon. When these theoretical developments were combined with actual experience in the 1930s of massive excess reserves, record low interest rates, but persistent widespread unemployment, the impotency of monetary policy seemed to have been clearly demonstrated in actual practice.[3]

The result of all this was that many economists, especially during the 1940s, overreacted. Fiscal policy was elevated to the throne and monetary policy demoted to the role of handmaiden. Professor Friedman, in reference to some of Keynes's followers, put it this way: "His disciples, as disciples will, went much farther than the master. The view became widespread that 'money does not matter.'"[4]

The Theoretical Foundation of the Modern Quantity Theory

While all this was going on in the majority of the economics profession, the "oral tradition" of the quantity theory continued at the University of Chicago. Finally, in the mid-1950s, Professor Friedman offered a "restatement of the quantity theory — in modern terms."[5] The result was not only a new and more sophisticated version of the quantity theory, altered from the old "crude" theory, but one set up in a form subject to empirical testing. Let us look first at the theoretical framework.

Friedman's prime concern was to show that velocity (or its inverse, the demand for money) was not a "will-o'-the-wisp," dancing around in unpredictable fashion to the tune of hundreds of undeterminable variables but, rather, was a stable function of a limited number of key variables. This point deserves stress. Friedman does not consider — as did some of the older quantity theorists — that velocity is a stable, predictable *number* but, rather, that it is a quantity that bears a stable, predictable *relationship* to a limited number of other important factors.

Unlike Keynes, Friedman does not begin with an analysis of the motives for

---

[3] This interpretation of the experience of the Great Depression has been sharply challenged by the monetarists who point out that despite the low interest rates and excess reserves, the money supply was permitted to fall dramatically.

[4] Milton Friedman, *Employment Growth and Price Levels*, Hearings Before the Joint Economic Committee, 86th Cong., 1st sess., May 25–28, 1958. In some ways it is strange that this overly negative attitude toward the role of money in the economy should have developed following the *General Theory*, for Keynes himself had developed a theoretical model in which money (barring a liquidity trap) *did* play an important role. Before the *General Theory*, classical theory had relegated money to the role of determining only the price level. Keynes made it a variable that could affect production and employment also. For an excellent statement to this effect, see Lawrence S. Ritter, "The Role of Money in Keynesian Theory," in *Banking and Monetary Studies*, ed. Deane Carson (Homewood, IL: Richard D. Irwin, 1963).

[5] See Milton Friedman, "The Quantity Theory of Money: A Restatement," in *Studies in the Quantity Theory of Money* (Chicago: University of Chicago Press, 1956).

holding money. He takes it as an observable fact that people *do* hold money (velocity is not infinite) and concentrates on the determinants of *how much* money will be held.

Money, to Friedman, is one of a number of forms in which people can choose to hold their wealth. An individual may decide to hold durable goods, to hold stocks, or to hold bonds, but he or she may also opt to hold money. The question is, "What determines how much money he or she will choose to hold?" "What are the determinants of an individual's demand for money?"

The approach employed should be quite familiar to economics students. The demand for money is treated in exactly the same fashion as the demand for any good. How do we approach the demand for, say, automobiles? The quantity demanded, we say, will depend on the car's price, the prices of other, related goods that might be purchased instead, the amount of income available, and consumer tastes and expectations. The ordinary, demand-for-good X function thus could be represented as

$$D_x = f(P_x, P_y, P_z, Y, t)$$

where P_x is the price of good X, P_y and P_z are the prices of alternative related goods, Y is income, which represents a constraint on the ability to purchase good X, and t represents tastes and expectations.

The almost completely analogous demand-for-money function suggested by Professor Friedman is[6]

$$M_d = f\left(r_b, r_e, \frac{1}{P}\frac{dP}{dt}, W, t\right)$$

where

r_b = the interest return available on bonds

r_e = the dividends (and capital gains) available on equities or direct ownership of capital goods

$\dfrac{1}{P}\dfrac{dP}{dt}$ = the expected rate of price change

W = wealth

t = tastes and preferences

[6] Actually this is an oversimplification of Friedman's function. The wealth variable preferred by Friedman is what he calls "permanent income" rather than the usually defined wealth magnitude. In addition, Friedman includes another variable that is omitted entirely. This variable is the ratio of nonhuman to human wealth.

Friedman's inclusion of this variable is based upon the totally logical position that the usual measure of wealth — nonhuman wealth — understates total wealth. If wealth is any asset on which income can be earned, then the productive capacities of human beings (present discounted value of future wage and salary payments) is just as properly considered wealth as a stock or bond. When a person is making a decision as to the form in which he or she will hold his or her wealth, that person has, in addition to the option of holding it in the form of money, stocks, or bonds, the possibility of using it (through further education or training) to enhance his or her human wealth. The logic of including it seems unassailable and it is omitted in the text solely for the sake of simplicity.

Let us see if we can put this rather imposing expression into commonsense language. It says that the quantity of money that is demanded (M_d) will tend to be

1. Lower, the higher the return that could be earned by buying bonds (r_b).
2. Lower, the higher the return that could be earned by buying equities (r_e).
3. Lower, the more rapid the rate of expected price increase $\left(\dfrac{1}{P}\dfrac{dP}{dt}\right)$.
4. Higher, the greater the amount of wealth available to be apportioned (W).
5. Higher or lower, as affected by tastes and preferences (t).

This then is the function that Professor Friedman believes to be reasonably stable. Velocity (or the demand for money) is not a fixed quantum but varies in a fairly predictable fashion with the return on bonds and stocks, price expectations, wealth, and tastes.

Now up to this point there is little dispute. Almost everyone — monetarist and Keynesian alike — would be likely to accept, with perhaps minor modification, such a formulation of the demand for money. To quote Friedman once again, "Almost every economist will accept the general lines of the preceding analysis on a purely formal and abstract level, although each would doubtless choose to express it differently in detail." [7]

The differences enter in when the stability of the relationship itself and the direction and degree of influence of the independent variables are considered. Some opponents of the modern quantity theory would include other independent variables in the equation and argue that their omission results in an unstable function. In addition, they would place considerable weight and significance on the relation between interest rates and the demand for money. Friedman, on the other hand, saw the function itself as stable and, barring the development of hyperinflation, only wealth as a variable likely to cause significant changes in velocity. [8]

From this beginning, the debate between the monetarists and the Keynesians has developed over several decades into a major controversy of the greatest importance for economic policy. Skipping over the decades of debate, let us attempt to abstract the essence of the monetarist position as it appears to stand today.

The Essence of the Monetarist Position

It is exceedingly difficult, if not impossible, to summarize the position of all advocates of the modern quantity theory. The monetarist position, like its counterpart the Keynesian position, has been built up over the years by a large group of highly competent individual scholars who, though in general agreement regarding the basic role of money in the economy, differ in many ways as to detail

---

[7] Friedman, "Quantity Theory of Money: A Restatement."

[8] Although in his earlier work Professor Friedman did argue that interest rates were of minor significance, in more recent articles he appears to have changed this position.

and as to specific policy prescription. In the following discussion, we shall, in the main, overlook the relatively minor differences among individual monetarists to bring out the common elements that distinguish the views of the group as a whole from their Keynesian adversaries.[9]

The Basic Tenets of Monetarism

The fundamental convictions all the modern monetarists appear to share include the following propositions.[10]

1. A capitalistic economy is basically quite stable and, when disturbed by some change in basic conditions, will fairly quickly readjust on its own. In general, the monetarists look upon a private enterprise economy as inherently stable with a strong built-in propensity to recover quickly from disturbing forces and "naturally revert to its long-run growth path."[11] This should not be taken to mean that the monetarists visualize a completely laissez-faire economy as one in which disturbances can never cause disagreeable effects on output, employment, and prices. What is argued is that such disturbances, if not exacerbated by misguided government policy, will tend automatically and reasonably promptly to correct themselves.

As a corollary to this point, monetarists typically take the position that serious, long-lasting economic maladjustments in the nation's past have resulted largely from governmental mismanagement. A vivid example of this position is the claim by some monetarists that the severity of the Great Depression of the 1930s is attributable, in large part, to the Federal Reserve System's failure to keep the money supply from falling.

2. The supply of money is the single most important determinant of money GNP. Specifically, the monetarists argue that the supply of money is the "dominant, though not exclusive" determinant of both the level of physical output and the price level in the short run and of the level of prices in the long run. The long-run level of physical output is taken to be uninfluenced by the supply of money but dependent, instead, on such real factors as technology and the quantity and quality of productive resources.

Now statements such as these, though perhaps formally correct, are almost devoid of significance unless something can be said about *how* "dominant" the monetarists perceive the money supply to be and *how* "nonexclusive" it is as a determinant of economic activity. Perhaps quotations from two prominent monetarist position advocates regarding the extent of their faith in the money supply as the dominant determinant can put some meat on this barebones statement.

Professor Friedman has expressed his views as follows: "I regard the descrip-

---

[9] Needless to say, the Keynesian group is no more monolithic than the monetarists with regard to detail and specific policy prescription.

[10] Much of this section follows the statement by Leonall C. Andersen, "The State of the Monetarist Debate," *Review*, Federal Reserve Bank of St. Louis, September 1973. See also William Poole, *Money and the Economy: A Monetarist View* (Reading, MA: Addison-Wesley, 1978) and Thomas Mayer, *The Structure of Monetarism* (New York: W. W. Norton, 1978).

[11] Andersen, "The State of the Monetarist Debate," p. 7.

tion of our position as 'money is all that matters for changes in *nominal* income and for *short-run* changes in real income' as an exaggeration but *one that gives the right flavor to our conclusions.*" [12]

In a similar vein, monetarist Leonall C. Andersen has concluded that "the key proposition is that changes in money dominate other short-run influences on output and other long-run influences on the price level and nominal aggregate demand." [13]

And, more recently, David Laidler has put it this way.

> The characteristic monetarist belief that variations in the supply of money are the "dominant impulse" (to borrow Brunner's phrase) causing fluctuations in money income is clearly related to this traditional version of the quantity theory, but modern monetarists are more clearcut in their attribution of a dominant causative role to the money supply than were quantity theorists of earlier vintages. [14]

In short, although factors other than the money supply can have an impact on the nominal level of GNP (that is, on the level of production, employment, and prices) in the short run, such effects are distinctly subordinate to that exerted by the supply of money. Change the supply of money, say the monetarists, and you will inevitably cause the price level and/or the level of production to rise in the short run; in the longer run, the effect will be entirely on prices.

This position would appear to go far beyond the mere denial of the more extreme early Keynesian arguments that a liquidity trap or an excessively inelastic MEI curve may negate the effects of money supply changes altogether. It posits not only that changes in the money supply always work (in the sense that they always affect aggregate demand in the same direction) but that they are the *dominant* cause of *any* change in aggregate demand. That is, not only do money supply changes inevitably (albeit with some lag) alter P and Q but, whereas other factors can have temporary and subordinate effects, *P and Q* (in the short run) *are not likely to be changed significantly without some prior change in the money supply providing the driving force.*

3. Money supply changes affect aggregate demand through effects on a range of assets much broader than that implied by the Keynesian theory. The monetarists feel that Keynesian theory involves an unnecessarily narrow transmission mechanism between money supply and aggregate demand changes. Specifically, it is argued that in the Keynesian system, money supply increases that do not at the same time raise income will be spent on bonds, thereby lowering interest rates and ultimately permitting an increase in investment spending because of a lowered cost of borrowing.

The monetarist position is that excess money balances produced by an increase in the money supply will lead to spending on a much broader range of assets than the "bonds-only" model of Keynes. Professor Friedman has put it as follows:

[12] Milton Friedman, "A Theoretical Framework for Monetary Analysis," *Journal of Political Economy*, March–April 1970 (emphasis added).

[13] Andersen, "State of the Monetarist Debate," p. 3.

[14] David Laidler, "Monetarism: An Interpretation and an Assessment," *The Economic Journal*, March 1981, p. 5.

The attempt by holders of money to restore or retain a desired balance sheet after an unexpected increase in the quantity of money will tend to raise the prices of assets and reduce interest rates, which will encourage both spending to produce new assets and spending on current services rather than on purchasing existing assets. This is how an initial effect on balance sheets gets translated into an effect on income and spending.

The difference between us and the Keynesians is less in the nature of the process than in the range of assets considered. The Keynesians tend to concentrate on a narrow range of marketable assets and recorded interest rates. We insist that a far wider range of assets and interest rates must be taken into account—such assets as durable and semi-durable consumer goods, structures and other real property. As a result, we regard the market rate stressed by the Keynesians as only a small part of the total spectrum of rates that are relevant. . . . [15]

4. Fiscal policy, without changes in the money supply, has little or no effect on aggregate demand or the level of GNP. This proposition follows, of course, as a logical consequence of the second proposition. If the government raises its spending and/or reduces taxes, financing the budget deficit thereby created by sale of securities to the nonbank public, the money supply is unchanged. Such a fiscal policy measure, argue many monetarists, will have little or no effect on aggregate demand.

This extreme conclusion—that fiscal policy by itself is virtually impotent—does seem to have been reached by Professor Friedman. In a debate focusing on the relative merits of monetary and fiscal policy, Friedman says, "in my opinion, the state of the budget by itself has no significant effect on the course of nominal income, on inflation, or deflation, or on cyclical fluctuations." [16]

The Friedman position on fiscal policy is obviously of profound importance. If it is correct, much of what has been taught in economics courses and much of government policy in the past 50 years is simply wrong. A policy position of such basic significance deserves a closer look.

The "state of the budget by itself," of course, refers to tax and/or government expenditure changes that are *not* accompanied by money supply changes. Let us follow the reasoning as applied to a tax cut, with the deficit financed by sale of securities to the public.

Such a fiscal move would be intended to raise aggregate demand. As it does not involve a money supply increase, total spending (MV′) can only be increased if the fiscal action somehow raises velocity.

In the simplest version of the Keynesian system, this rise in velocity is made possible by the existence of idle, speculative money balances. When consumer spending is increased as a result of the tax cut, income rises. This raises the demand for money, which, in turn, increases the interest rate. The rise in interest rates then pulls part of the existing money supply out of asset balances (where it had a zero velocity) into transactions balances where it is spent. It is true, of course, that the higher interest rate cuts back somewhat on investment spending, thereby partially undercutting the expansionary effects of the policy, but this

[15] Milton Friedman, *A Theoretical Framework for Monetary Analysis*, Occasional Paper 112 (New York: National Bureau of Economic Research, 1971), pp. 27–29.
[16] M. Friedman and W. W. Heller, *Monetary Versus Fiscal Policy* (New York: W. W. Norton, 1969), p. 51.

(second-round) effect is thought of only as diminishing the good effects — not eliminating them.

Professor Friedman does not accept this line of reasoning. He would grant that a tax cut would lead to an initial increase in consumer spending. That is, to put it in the terms of Chapter 19, the first-round effect would be as desired. However, it is his view that the second-round effects — the increase in the interest rate induced by financing the deficit in a manner that creates no new money — would be likely to undo all, or almost all, the accomplishments of the first round.

To many Keynesians, such a position — that second-round interest rate changes would completely offset or crowd out the favorable first-round effects — necessarily implied the assumption that the demand-for-money curve was perfectly inelastic (i.e., vertical). Such an assumption, if indeed it did lie beneath the Friedman conclusions, would be contrary to a very considerable amount of empirical evidence already available.[17]

Many attempts have been made to measure the relation between the rate of interest and the quantity of money demanded. In every study, with the single exception of an early one by Professor Friedman, it was determined that there was indeed a significant negative relation between interest and the demand for money. (That is, the total demand-for-money curve was found to have some degree of negative slope rather than being vertical.)

In reference to these data, Professor Lester Chandler observes that "It is highly significant that Professor Friedman stands almost alone in contending that income velocity and demands for cash balances are not significantly affected by changes of interest rates. Virtually all other investigators have found very significant effects."[18] Similarly, David Laidler reports, "there is an overwhelming body of evidence in favor of the proposition that the demand for money is stably and negatively related to the rate of interest. Of all the issues in monetary economics, this is the one that appears to have been settled most decisively."[19]

These empirical results are, of course, of potentially great importance. If velocity does vary with interest rates, monetary changes are not necessarily the only avenue to altering income levels. Fiscal policy can also play a role. Professor Paul A. Samuelson put it this way:

> There is every plausible reason in terms of experience, in terms of rarified neo-classical theory, for the velocity of circulation to be a systematic and increasing function of the rate of interest; and the minute you believe that, you have moved from the right of the spectrum — that of monetarism — to that noble eclectic position which I hold, the post-Keynesian position.[20]

[17] Indeed the only empirical results that showed no relation between the interest rate and the quantity of money demanded were those of Professor Friedman himself in his earlier article, "The Demand for Money — Some Theoretical and Empirical Results," *Journal of Political Economy*, June 1959.

[18] Lester V. Chandler, "Standards for Guiding Monetary Action," Hearings Before the Joint Economic Committee, 90th Cong., 2d sess., May 1968, p. 158.

[19] David E. W. Laidler, *The Demand for Money: Theories and Evidence* (Scranton, PA: International Textbook Co., 1969), p. 97. For excellent reviews of the results of basic research articles on this point and others in the quantity theory area, Laidler's book is superb. See also R. L. Teigen, "The Demand for and Supply of Money," in *Readings in Money, National Income and Stabilization Policy*, ed. Ronald L. Teigen (Homewood, IL: Richard D. Irwin, 1978), pp. 54–81.

[20] Paul A. Samuelson, "The Role of Money in National Economic Policy," *Controlling Monetary Aggregates*, Federal Reserve Bank of Boston, 1969, p. 12.

Professor Friedman, however, is unmoved by such evidence. He has stated in rebuttal that he sees "no 'fundamental issues' in either monetary theory or monetary policy [that] hinge on whether [the demand for money depends on interest rates]." [21] Rather, he attributes his anticipated strong second-round reduction in spending to the fact that "the categories of spending affected by changes in interest rates are far broader than the business capital formation, housing construction, and inventory accumulation to which the neo-Keynesians tend to restrict 'investment.' " [22]

That this latter position fails to satisfy many Keynesians is evidenced by the following statement from two distinguished members of that school: "most monetarists disavow the interest inelasticity of the demand for money but still do not believe in the efficacy of fiscal policy. How they can have it both ways is not clear." [23]

And more recently Professor James Tobin has observed, "If monetarist propositions about the effects of monetary and fiscal policies on output and prices are at stake, the only reasonable way to make sense of this dictum is to take full employment, in the sense of cleared markets for labour and capital services, as the assumed state of the economy." [24]

5. The determinants and direction of interest rate movements are different from those stressed by Keynesians. The monetarists argue that the simple Keynesian model covered in the preceding chapter leads to erroneous conclusions regarding the effects of money supply changes on interest rates. Worse yet, they maintain, these "erroneous conclusions" have tended to cause the Federal Reserve authorities to misinterpret the magnitude, and sometimes even the direction, of the monetary policy they were implementing.

To the monetarists, money supply increases affect interest rates in three different ways. First, there is a *liquidity effect* which causes a very-short-run reduction in interest rates. It is comparable to the first-round effect discussed in Chapter 19. Second, there is an *output effect*, a tendency for interest rates to rise because of the rise in production and demand for money resulting from the first round. This is approximately equivalent to the "round 2" offsetting effect. Finally, there is a *price expectations effect*. In a period of generally rising prices, spenders quite naturally develop expectations of future inflation. When this inflation occurs in conjunction with money supply increases (as, of course, monetarist doctrine insists that it must), these inflationary expectations may well be triggered by the money supply increases themselves. In that case the inflationary expectations will tend to raise nominal interest rates.

Let us consider this argument in more detail. Suppose, for example, that

[21] Milton Friedman, "Interest Rates and the Demand for Money," *Journal of Law and Economics*, October 1966, p. 85.

[22] Milton Friedman, "Comments on the Critics," *Journal of Political Economy*, September– October 1972, pp. 915–916. In this statement Professor Friedman appears to be relating his views on fiscal policy strongly to those on the transmission mechanism discussed in proposition 2. For a similar view on this point, see Karl Brunner, "Commentary on 'The State of the Monetarist Debate,' " *Review*, Federal Reserve Bank of St. Louis, September 1973.

[23] Alan S. Blinder and Robert M. Solow, "Analytical Foundations of Fiscal Policy," *The Economics of Public Finance* (Washington, D.C.: The Brookings Institution, 1974), p. 62.

[24] James Tobin, "Comment on the Paper by Professor Laidler," *The Economic Journal*, March 1981, p. 56.

lenders were willing to lend their funds to someone else for a year for a 5 percent return, *assuming that prices remained stable* so that the dollars they would get back were worth just as much as those they lent. In this case, we would say the *real* rate of interest is 5 percent. Now if in fact lenders really expect the price level to rise by, say, 6 percent during the year, they would insist on receiving a *nominal* interest return of 11 percent (5 percent for lending the money plus another 6 percent to protect themselves from the effects of inflation).

The net effect is that money supply increases could very well lead to *increases* in the nominal interest rate if the combined impacts of the output and price expectations effect are greater than the liquidity effect.

The implications of all this for the conduct of monetary policy are profound. For many years, as we have seen, the Fed used short-term interest rates as its immediate policy target. During that period, a rise in nominal interest rates was taken as evidence of a contractionary monetary policy, whereas interest rate declines were seen as resulting from expansionary policy. But this, according to the monetarists, led to some serious policy mistakes.

Throughout much of the inflationary 1970s, monetarists argued, nominal interest rates were rising — not because the Fed was applying "appropriately" contractionary monetary policy but because they were permitting the money supply to rise too rapidly. And during the deflationary Great Depression of the 1930s, the situation was reversed. Nominal interest rates were, it is true, at historic lows, but to conclude from this that the Fed was employing a desperately needed expansionary policy would be to ignore the fact that the supply of money actually declined by one third during the decade.

To conclude, if money supply changes can cause nominal interest rates to change in the same direction, the monetarists insist that the Fed must switch from targeting interest rates to targeting the money supply itself.[25]

The Monetarist Evidence

In support of the positions just sketched, the modern quantity theorists have amassed a considerable volume of empirical data. This evidence includes (1) time series data showing the relation between money and income in the United States for nearly a century; (2) extensive historical case studies purporting to show that external factors were responsible for most of the money supply changes — not the change in income itself; (3) least squares regression analysis aimed at demonstrating that monetary factors explain a much larger percentage of the variation in income levels than do fiscal factors; and (4) real-world experience, especially in 1966–1967 and 1968–1970, which was widely interpreted as supporting their case.

The Time Series Data   A substantial part of the time series data cited by the monetarists comes from a prodigious work by Professor Friedman and Anna J. Schwartz, entitled *A Monetary History of the United States, 1867–1960*, and a

---

[25] For an argument that the Keynesian model is perfectly consistent with the possibility of money and interest rates moving in the same direction, see Ronald L. Teigen, "A Critical Look at Monetarist Economics," *Review*, St. Louis Federal Reserve Bank, January 1972, pp. 19–20.

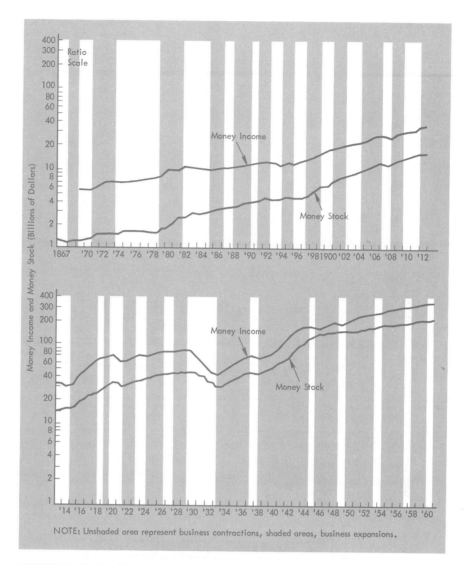

FIGURE 21-2 Money stock and money income, 1867–1960

companion piece by the same two authors, entitled "Money and Business Cycles."[26]

The impressive long-run relationship between money and money income that they have uncovered can be seen in Figures 21-2 and 21-3.

Note in Figure 21-2 that the shaded areas represent periods of business contraction and the unshaded areas show expansion periods. The similarity in the two series is clear, especially during major periods of expansion and contraction.

[26] M. Milton Friedman and Anna J. Schwartz, *A Monetary History of the United States, 1867–1960* (Princeton, NJ: Princeton University Press, 1963); and "Money and Business Cycles," *Review of Economics and Statistics,* February 1963.

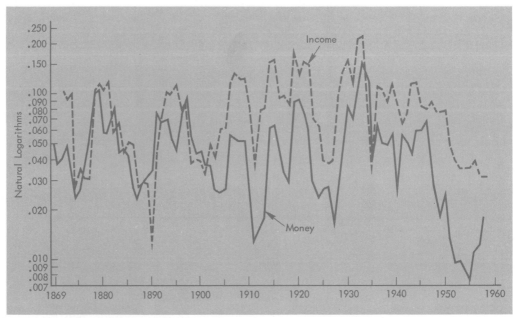

Source: M. Friedman and A. Schwartz, "Money and Business Cycles," *Review of Economics and Statistics*, February 1963.

FIGURE 21-3   Money and business cycles: moving standard deviation of annual rates of change in money, 1869–1958, and in income, 1871–1958, four-term series

Figure 21-3 depicts moving standard deviations of annual rates of change in money and income from 1871 to 1958. These are simply "measures of the variability of the rates of change, in the one case of money and in the other case, of income."[27]

Bringing the evidence a bit more up to date, Figures 21-4 and 21-5 chart comparative changes in GNP, M1, and M2 from 1960 through 1986. Two things of significance should be noted in these graphs. In the first figure (Figure 21-4), which traces the absolute amounts of the three series, it is clear that the M2 pattern much more closely approximates that of GNP. This reflects a fact pointed out by many monetarists in recent years — that the velocity of M2 has been much stabler in the past two decades than has the velocity of the M1 money stock.[28]

Second, especially evident in Figure 21-5, is the apparent tendency for the change in money stock series to turn down prior to declines in the change in GNP series. This is particularly notable in 1965–1966, 1968–1969, 1972–1974, and 1978–1980 and 1981–1982. Although grossly oversimplified, this behavior coincides impressively with the conclusions of the monetarist theory.

The Case Study Data   Friedman and Schwartz, as well as a number of other quantity theorists, offer a voluminous list of historical instances where observed

[27] Friedman and Schwartz, "Money and Business Cycles," p. 40.

[28] It should be noted, however, that this impressive degree of stability of V_2 is *not* evident prior to 1960. For evidence on this point see Figure 21-6.

FIGURE 21-4   GNP, M1, and M2, 1960–1986

changes in the money stock could not have been induced by the associated change in income levels. This evidence is intended to show that it has been the money variable that has been the driving force causing most of the major observed income changes.

For example, they point out that the long expansion from 1897 to 1914 reflected an increase in gold production. Similarly, large gold inflows to the United States during the two world wars are considered contributory to those money stock increases. In 1920, 1931, and 1936—all periods of sharp monetary and income contraction—specific Federal Reserve actions are singled out as independent causes of monetary change. In 1920 and 1931, very large increases in the discount rate are focused on; in 1936, a doubling of reserve requirements is cited as the culprit.[29]

This evidence is especially significant in light of one of the major arguments advanced by the opponents of the modern quantity theory. Known as the reverse causation thesis, it involves the proposition that time series data showing close relationships between M and GNP could just as easily be a result of GNP *causing*

[29] Friedman and Schwartz, *A Monetary History,* pp. 686–95.

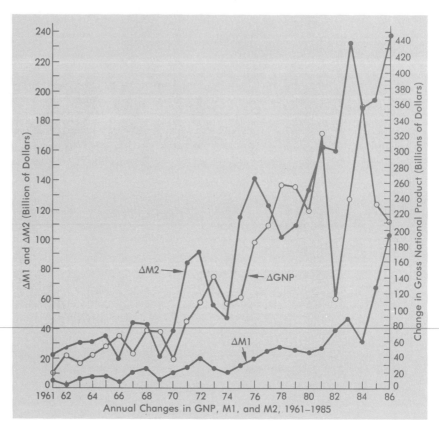

FIGURE 21-5   Annual changes in GNP, M1, and M2, 1961–1986

M as M *causing* GNP. The latter direction of causation is, of course, crucial for the monetarists. We return to this point in the concluding section of this chapter.

The Regression Analysis Evidence   A somewhat different approach to illustrating and confirming the importance of monetary factors (and the alleged insignificance of fiscal factors) is the use of multiple correlation techniques. This approach was adopted first by Professor Friedman and Professor David Meiselman in a 1963 article and was later refined and carried further in a series of papers presented by the St. Louis Federal Reserve Bank.[30]

Friedman and Meiselman regressed data for the money supply and autonomous expenditures against consumption for a number of years. Their results showed that the money supply was an important and statistically significant "predictor" of consumption, but not so their autonomous expenditures. The conclusion drawn by Friedman and Meiselman was that the demand for money

---

[30] Milton Friedman and David Meiselman, "The Relative Stability of Monetary Velocity and the Investment Multiplier in the United States, 1897–1958," in a Commission on Money and Credit Report entitled *Stabilization Policies* (Englewood Cliffs, NJ: Prentice-Hall, 1963). The basic paper of the St. Louis Federal Reserve Bank effort is Leonall C. Andersen and Jerry L. Jordan, "Monetary and Fiscal Actions: A Test of Their Relative Importance in Economic Stabilization," *Review*, St. Louis Federal Reserve Bank, November 1968.

(velocity) was more stable than the Keynesian multiplier and, consequently, that money supply changes are a more reliable method of controlling national income than fiscal changes.

Critics found the Friedman-Meiselman paper unconvincing, partly because of the technique used and partly because of the choice of variables. Subsequently, in 1968, Leonall Andersen and Jerry Jordan of the Federal Reserve Bank of St. Louis published their own research results from an econometric model of the economy now popularly referred to as the St. Louis model. Profiting from reviews of the Friedman-Meiselman effort, Andersen and Jordan (A–J) chose their variables carefully to avoid some of the earlier criticisms.

The A–J results, nonetheless, were in substantial agreement with the Friedman-Meiselman conclusions. Fiscal policy, the A–J model indicated, has only minor and temporary effects on GNP. For example, an early version of the model predicted that a $1 million rise in government spending would raise GNP by $400,000 in three months and by $900,000 in six months. By the end of one year, however, the second-round crowding out phenomenon would have reduced the increase in GNP to a mere $100,000. In other words, the government expenditure multiplier after one year would be a paltry one-tenth. In sharp contrast to its fiscal results, the St. Louis model predicted that a $1 million rise in the money supply would lead to a $1.6 million rise in GNP within three months, a $3.5 million increase after six months, and a full $6.6 million by the end of one year![31]

The St. Louis model created a not inconsiderable stir among economists of both the monetarist and the post-Keynesian camps. The methodology employed in construction of the model has been, as we shall see shortly, severely criticized by the Keynesians. Even more significant, the model's ability to predict GNP movements, which was impressive for earlier years, deteriorated markedly during the 1970s and 1980s.[32]

The Experience of the Late 1960s as Monetarist Evidence   It is probably fair to say that all this research left the majority of the economics profession intrigued and impressed—but unconvinced. "Of course money matters—perhaps more than we had recognized," seemed to be the general reaction, "but so do a lot of other things, including fiscal policy. We can accept much of the evidence testifying to the crucial role of money, but not the conclusions that money alone matters or that fiscal policy doesn't."

This attitude may well be the dominant one today, but some real-world events of the latter 1960s gave the monetarist case a considerable boost. It will be recalled that prices rose rapidly after 1965. In 1966, with the federal budget still in deficit, the Federal Reserve System clamped down hard on money supply increases. Some monetarists predicted that, despite the budget deficit, this monetary action would shortly produce a recession. In fact, the economy did not go into recession, but it did level off sufficiently in 1967 to produce what some have called a "minirecession." The quantity theorists pointed to this experience as

[31] The data cited in this paragraph are taken from the excellent review article by Richard G. Davis, "How Much Does Money Matter? A Look at Some Recent Evidence," *Monthly Review*, Federal Reserve Bank of New York, June 1969.

[32] See, for example, Stephen K. McNees, "A Comparison of the Forecasting Accuracy of the Fair and St. Louis Econometric Models," *New England Economic Review*, Federal Reserve Bank of Boston, September–October 1973.

evidence supporting their position; their opponents have cited the absence of a full-fledged recession as a quantity theory failure. This episode shows up clearly in Figure 21-5.

But more was to come. Inflation accelerated once again in late 1967 and 1968. In an effort to control it, Congress at long last passed, in June 1968, a 10 percent personal income tax surcharge.

This fiscal measure, which was primarily responsible for transforming a fiscal year 1968 budget deficit of $25 billion into a fiscal year 1969 budget surplus of over $3 billion, was widely expected to dampen the inflationary pressure in relatively short order. Federal Reserve authorities, in fact, were so confident of the tax measure's contractionary impact that they — in order to avoid a feared contractionary overkill — allowed the money supply to be increased more rapidly in the latter part of 1968. The result was that for a number of months in late 1968 and early 1969 we had a rare real-world test case. Fiscal policy had turned sharply restrictive while monetary policy continued in an expansive direction.

What happened? Consumer prices rose during 1969 by 5.6 percent while the unemployment rate stayed under 4 percent for the entire year. The fiscal policy either did not work or, at best, worked only with an intolerably long lag. Finally, in early 1969, the Federal Reserve System reversed its expansionary money policy and during that year curtailed monetary expansion very sharply. By the end of 1969 the economy began weakening, and in early 1970 the nation's fourth post–World War II recession was upon us.

The monetarists, quite naturally, claimed a major victory. Professor Friedman had stated publicly in early 1967, "I do not share the widespread view that a tax increase which is not matched by higher government spending will necessarily have a strong braking effect on the economy." [33] In summary, they pointed out that (1) when fiscal policy was restrictive and monetary policy expansive, the economy did not slow down, but (2) when restrictions were placed on the rate of growth in the money supply in 1969, it was not long before the boom ended. This, they argued, is precisely what the monetarist theories predicted.

There can be little doubt that these events gave the monetarists a powerful shot in the arm, and their opponents, considerable food for thought. But despite all this, the disagreement continued. The monetarists have unquestionably made real headway in convincing some of their detractors. They probably still represent, however, a minority within the economics profession. We shall consider the views of the unconvinced majority in the final section of this chapter. Before doing so, however, it seems appropriate to draw together the main policy prescriptions advocated by the monetarists.

The Policy Prescriptions of the Monetarists

If the monetarists had complete control of the nation's economic affairs, how would they conduct policy? The following prescriptions would no doubt be the result.

[33] M. Friedman, *Newsweek*, January 23, 1967.

Rely on Control of the Money Supply to Stabilize Cyclical Fluctuations

In the short run, the monetarists argue, the supply of money is the dominant determinant of both the price level and the level of output (and along with it, presumably, the level of employment). In terms of the equation of exchange, this says that velocity (V') is, though not a constant, sufficiently stable to permit us to have great confidence that proper control of the money supply will provide reasonable stability in employment and prices. Fluctuations would still occur, but they would be relatively minor and relatively quickly corrected.

Eliminate Pure Fiscal Policy as a Stabilization Tool

Because fiscal policy that does not have the effect of altering the money supply cannot be expected to have much impact on aggregate demand, it should be abandoned. This does not necessarily require acceptance of the "annually balanced budget" philosophy, as most monetarists do not appear to oppose unbalanced budgets as such. What it does mean is that if government spending is to be increased and/or taxes decreased to raise aggregate demand, the deficit thereby created must be financed with newly created money if it is to have any real impact. And even in that case, it is the increase in M rather than the fiscal actions that provides the driving force to raise aggregate demand.[34]

The Money Supply, Not Interest Rates, Should Be the Guide to Policy

As noted, the monetarists feel that the level or direction of movement of interest rates is *not* an appropriate guide for policy. In their view, high or rising interest rates may well be a reflection of an expansionary, rather than a contractionary, policy. For example, they frequently cite the experience of the Great Depression when, despite *extremely* low interest rates, the money supply was permitted to fall by about one-third. Had we focused on the supply of money rather than on interest rates, they argue, the severe income contraction of the 1930s might not have occurred.

It seems fair to say that the monetarists have been at least partially successful in effecting this policy change. When the Federal Reserve in October 1979 switched from aiming at direct control of the Federal Funds rate to nonborrowed reserves, it was widely interpreted as a movement toward the monetarist position. The monetarists themselves, however, while applauding the decision to allow the Federal Funds rate to move more freely, are still less than enthusiastic about the conduct of monetary policy. This was the case in the mid- and late-1980s when the Fed switched to the borrowed reserves target and began, once again, to place emphasis on interest rate changes in determining policy.

---

[34] Again, not all monetarists would necessarily subscribe to this policy prescription.

Eliminate the Discretion of the Monetary Authorities and Replace It with a Money Supply Rule

A final most important policy position accepted by most monetarists has to do with time lags—the period of time between a money supply change and its resultant effect on the level of income.

One might suppose that as the monetarists are so confident of the potency of monetary changes, they would be ardent champions of discretionary monetary policy as the ideal stabilization device. Such a supposition, though understandable, would be quite wrong.

For a policy weapon to be an effective stabilization tool, not only must it affect income in the desired *direction* but it must do so at the right *time*. If the problem is recession and unemployment, it is not enough to know that money supply increases will, sooner or later, raise aggregate demand and income. It must do so quickly enough to raise demand while that is what is still needed. Money supply increases that do not raise demand until the recession has already ended clearly do more harm than good by adding to succeeding inflation.

In their empirical work, Professor Friedman and others have found that the money supply (or the rate of change therein) affects GNP only after long and variable lags.[35] For example, in one of his works with Anna Schwartz, it was determined that the money supply series leads the GNP series by periods varying from 6 to 29 months at business cycle peaks and from 4 to 22 months at the troughs.[36]

The policy conclusion that most monetarists reach from evidence such as this is simple. Potent though monetary policy is, it is not appropriate for "fine tuning." Discretionary monetary action taken to combat a cyclical downswing (upswing) may very easily result in an addition to (contraction in) demand in the succeeding phase of the cycle, where it simply makes matters worse. Indeed the quantity theorists feel that our past experience with discretion in monetary policy has had just this effect—causing more instability than it has combated.

In line with this view, Professor Friedman has called for an *end to discretion in monetary policy*. In place of the judgment of the monetary authorities, he would substitute a rule requiring an annual fixed percentage increase in the money supply. Although Friedman is not adamant about any exact rate of increase, he has suggested a rate in the 3- to 4-percent-per-year neighborhood as one that reasonably closely approximates the economy's past average annual rate of growth in real output.

The fixed money supply increase rule is not represented as a cure-all for the business cycle. The monetarists are quite aware that the nation would still suffer from cyclical fluctuations, even with this kind of rule. What is claimed, however, is that the more stable monetary environment produced by such a rule would provide a more stable economy than we have had (or are likely to have in the future) with discretion. As Professor Friedman puts it, "money is too important to be left to central bankers."[37]

[35] This evidence is obviously in some conflict with the Andersen-Jordan "St. Louis model," which, as we have seen, forecasts not only large but very rapid response to money supply changes.

[36] Friedman and Schwartz, "Money and Business Cycles," pp. 37–38.

[37] Milton Friedman, "M1's Hot Streak Gave Keynesians a Bad Idea," *The Wall Street Journal*, September 18, 1986.

The Views of the Opposition

Without question, the modern quantity theory represents a major challenge to what had become economic orthodoxy. A sophisticated theoretical framework has been buttressed by an impressive array of empirical data in support of the policy positions just discussed. A distinguished group within the economics profession has been convinced of the general validity of the monetarist view. Some elements of the press and of Congress have been similarly persuaded.

And there is no doubt that they have made progress. There is, for example, general agreement among monetarists and post-Keynesians alike (1) that money supply changes *do* have significant effects on GNP; (2) that there is no evidence in support of Keynes's suggestion that the demand-for-money curve may, at some low interest rate, become perfectly elastic — that is, there is no evidence of a liquidity trap; (3) that although the quantity of money demanded does, in fact, increase as the interest rate falls, the degree of elasticity is small; (4) that the so-called crowding out effect of the interest rate consequent to a pure fiscal policy measure is of sufficient size to markedly reduce its effect on aggregate demand; and (5) that more attention should be paid to the rate of growth of monetary aggregates such as the money supply than had been given previously.

Despite the gains of its adherents, the more extreme version of the monetarist position probably remains a minority view within the economics profession. Many distinguished economists representing the Keynesian viewpoint have spoken out in opposition to the basic tenets and the policy prescriptions of the monetarists. In general, these advocates have praised the monetarists for their professional skill and diligence in shedding new light on the role of money in the economy. But with regard to the key proposition of monetarism that "money is the *dominant* determinant of short run GNP changes," many would subscribe to the blunt retort of Professor Lawrence Klein — "I don't believe a word of it." [38]

The Keynesian counterattack has taken place on a broad front. *First,* the evidence presented by Friedman and others to the effect that historically the money supply and GNP have been closely correlated (or, alternately expressed, that velocity has been remarkably stable) has been criticized both as to the degree of correlation and as to the direction of causation. *Second,* the statistical models of the monetarists such as the Andersen-Jordan St. Louis model have been sharply criticized on grounds of methodology and challenged as to predictive capability. *Third,* the post-Keynesians have strongly supported their continuing faith in fiscal policy as, along with monetary policy, a viable stabilization weapon. *Fourth,* the monetarists have been severely chastised for their failure to provide a precise, detailed definition of the transmission mechanism they believe so powerfully transmits monetary changes to GNP.

Criticism of the Monetarists' Money-GNP Relationship

In this area, the Keynesians have expressed their skepticism along two different lines. In the first place, a number of critics have argued that, even using the monetarists' own data, the historical relationship between money and GNP has

---

[38] Lawrence R. Klein, "Commentary on 'The State of the Monetarist Debate,'" *Review,* Federal Reserve Bank of St. Louis, September 1973, p. 10.

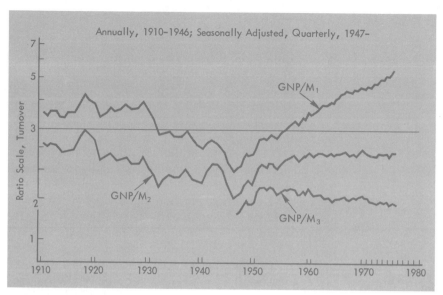

Source: Paul S. Anderson, "Behavior of Monetary Velocity," *New England Economic Review,* Federal Reserve Bank of Boston, March–April 1977.

FIGURE 21-6   Velocity of M1, M2, and M3, 1910–1976

not been sufficiently close to support monetarist policy prescriptions. Second, it has been pointed out via the reverse causation argument that mere correlation between two variables does not necessarily imply causation. Perhaps it has been GNP changes that have caused money changes rather than the other way around.

Velocity Is Not Stable Enough   Although it cannot be denied that the Friedman-Schwartz evidence shows that historically the stock of money and the level of GNP have tended to move together, the issue — if monetarist policy prescriptions are to be adopted — is, *How* close is the relationship? Or, to ask the same question the other way around, just *how* stable is velocity in fact?

As we have seen in Chapter 15 (Table 15-1), velocity in the United States not only rose from 2.04 in 1947 to over 6 in the 1980s but tended to vary procyclically. That is, in each postwar recession, V has declined, whereas in boom periods it has invariably increased. Post-Keynesian critics argue that this hardly represents the "extraordinary empirical stability and regularity" Professor Friedman claims income velocity demonstrates.

Nor, if a long enough period is considered, does the velocity of the more broadly defined M2 money stock seem to show extraordinary stability. It is true that this variable has been quite stable since 1960, but prior to that year, as Figure 21-6 makes clear, it too was subject to significant variability.

In addition, the Friedman-Schwartz data themselves have often been cited as providing evidence of a variable velocity. Much stress, for example, is placed on the following statement: "the observed year-to-year change in velocity was less than 10 percent in 78 out of 91 year-to-year changes from 1860 . . . to 1960.[39]

[39] Friedman and Schwartz, *A Monetary History,* p. 682.

The monetarists offer this as one summary piece of evidence supporting their view that the money supply and income tend to move closely together. Many Keynesians read it quite the other way around. "Since a 10 percent difference in money income is the difference between inflation and recession, these figures are not very reassuring" is the opinion of one authority.[40] Another critic puts it this way: "a difference of 10 percent in the velocity of a given money stock, at today's level of the money stock, would result in a difference of about $80 billion in GNP. The Council of Economic Advisers gets roasted when errors in its annual forecasts are a fraction of that amount."[41]

Finally, as we shall soon consider in more detail, the behavior of velocity in the face of the massive financial innovation of the 1980s was anything but "stable and predictable."

The Reverse Causation Argument   Even a closer fit of the money supply and GNP would probably not satisfy many Keynesians. For, as they have pointed out many times, correlation does not imply causation. Money and GNP could move together because, as the monetarists argue, the money supply basically determines GNP. But they could also move together for the reverse reason—because changes in GNP cause the money supply to move accordingly. This is the reverse causation argument.

The monetarists argue that the supply of money is an exogenous variable, one determined outside their model by the monetary authorities. This need not always be the case. If the monetary authorities and the banking system follow the practice of accommodating the demands for credit, we may find them expanding the money supply *because* production, income, and the demand for credit have picked up. If so, this would involve GNP changes causing money supply changes rather than the other way around.[42]

The Defense of Fiscal Policy

Keynesians also reject the views expressed by Friedman and the Andersen-Jordan St. Louis model evidence to the effect that fiscal policy is virtually useless as a means of affecting GNP.

In denial, they cite the overwhelming body of evidence showing that the demand for money is negatively related to interest rates and that, therefore, total spending (MV') can, indeed, vary without a change in M. In the short run at least, they contend, pure fiscal policy can change V enough to permit desired changes in spending.

The fiscal multiplier included in the St. Louis model (which, it will be re-

---

[40] James Tobin, "The Monetary Interpretation of History," *American Economic Review*, June 1965.

[41] Daniel H. Brill, "Can the Government 'Fine-Tune' the Economy?" Address to American Statistical Association, February 1968, reprinted in *Standards for Guiding Monetary Action*, Hearings Before the Joint Economic Committee, 90th Cong., 2d sess., May 1968, p. 158.

[42] On this point, see Raymond Lombra and Raymond Torto, "Federal Reserve Defensive Behavior and the Reserve Causation Argument," *Staff Economic Studies*, Board of Governors of the Federal Reserve System, 1972. Lombra and Torto argue that defensive open-market operations by the FOMC "confirm the interdependence of the supply and demand for money" and provide persuasive evidence of the validity of the reverse causation argument.

membered, shows the effects of fiscal measures virtually disappearing at the end of one year) is in sharp contrast to those included in many other econometric models of the economy constructed in accordance with the Keynesian position. As Professor Lawrence Klein puts it,

> Most American models, other than the St. Louis model, imply fiscal multipliers that rise fairly quickly to values between 2.0 and 3.0. They fluctuate in a narrow range for a number of years and then decline. . . . For the only period of policy relevance (before many other changes, besides the original fiscal policy change, have taken place) the fiscal multipliers are estimated to be substantial by a broad consensus.[43]

As noted, the monetarist camp itself is divided on the issue of the potency of fiscal policy, but Professor Friedman and the architects of the St. Louis Fed's Andersen-Jordan model both appear to occupy the extreme position of denying any significant fiscal effects beyond fleeting changes for no more than six months. The St. Louis model's published fiscal multiplier has drawn an important challenge from Harvard's Professor Benjamin Friedman. In an article entitled "Even the St. Louis Model Now Believes in Fiscal Policy," Friedman presents the results of his reestimation of the St. Louis equation using data through mid-1976. What he finds is that

> the St. Louis equation, reestimated to incorporate the most recent available data, now indicates that fiscal policy unaccompanied by changes in the stock of money *does* matter. Furthermore, the indicated first-year cumulative multiplier of government spending on nominal GNP is about one and one-half—a value not surprising intuitively to believers in fiscal policy, and not very dissimilar to the values reported by familiar nonmonetarist models.[44]

In response, Keith Carlson of the St. Louis Federal Reserve Bank has argued that the inclusion of data from 1975 and 1976 makes "the form in which the St. Louis equation was specified . . . no longer statistically appropriate." [45] Carlson presents a recalculation of the St. Louis equation substituting rate of change for absolute dollar change data and argues that the results reaffirm the original St. Louis conclusions regarding the effects of fiscal policy.

Whatever the St. Louis equation concludes about fiscal policy, however, the majority of Keynesians insist that the fiscal multipliers implied by the vast majority of existing econometric models come closer to the true values and, as a result, conclude that fiscal policy, while not so potent as they once believed, possesses significant stabilization potential.[46]

[43] Klein, "Commentary on 'The State of the Monetarist Debate,' " pp. 10–11. For details on the fiscal multipliers of a large number of econometric models, see Gary Fromm and Lawrence Klein, "A Comparison of Eleven Econometric Models," *American Economic Review*, May 1973.

[44] Benjamin M. Friedman, "Even the St. Louis Model Now Believes in Fiscal Policy," *Journal of Money, Credit and Banking*, May 1977, p. 365.

[45] Keith M. Carlson, "Does the St. Louis Equation Now Believe in Fiscal Policy?" *Review*, Federal Reserve Bank of St. Louis, February 1978.

[46] The post-Keynesians go to pains to point out that their defense of fiscal policy should not be taken to indicate any lack of faith in monetary policy. For example, Professor Tobin has said, "One thing the nonmonetarists should *not* be called is 'fiscalists.' The debate is not symmetrical. Whereas neo-Keynesians believe that both monetary and fiscal policies affect nominal income,

Criticisms of the Statistical Approach
of Monetarist Models

The form of the statistical models employed by both Friedman and Meiselman in their earlier work and by Andersen and Jordan in setting up the St. Louis model has come under sharp criticism. Whereas all recognized econometric models of the Keynesian variety are structural models, which include equations specifically describing how monetary, fiscal, and other variables affect aggregate demand, the monetarist models are "reduced form" equations, which make no attempt to explain the underlying interconnections or transmission mechanisms. As Professor Tobin has put it,

> What I mean by a pseudo-reduced-form is an equation relating an ultimate variable of interest, like GNP, to the supposedly causal variables, but one which doesn't come out of any structure at all. Instead, the investigator just says, "Here are the effects and here are the causes, let's just throw them into an equation." The form and content of the equation — the list of variables and the lag structure — are not derived from any structural model. That is what we have presented to us as the main evidence for the supposed superiority of monetary variables in explaining GNP.[47]

Professor Klein has also pointed out that whereas the Keynesian structural econometric models of the economy do perform in a manner consistent with the real world, the same cannot be said for the monetarist models:

> Simulations of econometric models built along post-Keynesian lines do show important business cycle characteristics. It is a strong claim on the part of such model builders that these systems are capable of generating the cycle, as it has been historically measured, when the models are subjected to repeated shocks in stochastic simulations. I regard this as a basic validation feature of contemporary econometric model building research, and this is an integral part of my challenge to the monetarists, to see whether they can do as well in reproducing accepted measures of cyclical characteristics from simulations of their models. I am disappointed in their not following this line of econometric research.[48]

Monetarist Transmission Mechanism
Must Be More Clearly Explained

The monetarists have charged the Keynesian models with requiring money to work its way through to its effect on aggregate demand via a transmission mechanism that is much too narrow. The Keynesians respond with the charge that the monetarists have been unable or unwilling to make clear just what the specifics of their own transmissions mechanism are. As Professor Klein has put it, the

---

monetarists believe that only monetary policies do so." James Tobin, "Friedman's Theoretical Framework," *Journal of Political Economy*, September–October 1972, p. 852.

[47] James Tobin, "The Role of Money in National Economic Policy," *Controlling Monetary Aggregates*, Federal Reserve Bank of Boston, 1969, p. 23.

[48] Klein, "Commentary on 'The State of the Monetarist Debate,'" p. 12.

Keynesian models are all "specific about the channels of monetary influence in a structural way. They stand as challenges to the monetarist points of view."[49]

In short, it is argued, the monetarists have made the claim that the supply of money is the dominant determinant of GNP and have offered considerable empirical evidence in support of the view. But beyond a few very tentative and preliminary descriptions, they have done little to specify exactly *how* and *through what channels* money has such powerful effects on economic activity.[50]

Without such further specification, many Keynesians find the logic following from the monetarist propositions quite unacceptable. "How," many ask, "can we accept the proposition that a $100 increase in the money supply will have roughly the same effects on GNP no matter what else happens (changes in technology, changes in consumer and investor psychology) and no matter what the procedure through which the money is created (open-market sale to the public, government borrowing as a result of increased government spending or tax reduction, loans to business, or bank purchases of securities from the public)?" Here, then, lies the heart of much of the debate.

Financial Innovation, the Changing Meaning of Money, and Effects on Velocity

The innovative financial environment of the 1980s, whatever its other effects, has not been exactly hospitable to the monetarist advocacy of stable, nondiscretionary "monetary rules," for to argue that the nation should commit itself to a fixed rate of increase in the money supply requires that the concept of money and components of the money supply stay reasonably fixed. As we have seen earlier, that requirement has not been met in recent years.

Keynesians have been quick to point out the problems financial innovation has created for monetarist policy prescription. As Professor Alan Blinder has put it,

> Monetarism is now an anachronism. Monetarism simply makes no sense in a world where financial reform and innovation are wreaking havoc upon their demand functions. One result of all these financial innovations . . . is that no one knows what concept of M today corresponds to what we used to think of as M1 or M2 a few years ago.[51]

As Figure 21-7 (a duplicate of Figure 1-3) makes vividly clear, the early 1980s produced unprecedented declines in velocity. Although (significantly) these precipitous velocity reductions were not predicted in advance, it seems clear that financial innovation and sharply declining interest rates were the major causes.

It has been in response to these dramatic velocity declines that the Fed has twice in recent years found it advisable to abandon its own targets for annual M1 growth. It did so in 1982, in the midst of the nation's most severe post–World War II recession, and abandoned an M1 target altogether starting in the mid-

---

[49] Klein, "Empirical Evidence on Fiscal and Monetary Models," p. 49.

[50] This point is granted by a well-known monetarist. "Monetarists must spell out, in greater detail than up to now, the channels by which money influences nominal GNP, the price level, and output." Andersen, "State of the Monetarist Debate," p. 8.

[51] Alan S. Blinder, "Monetarism Is Obsolete," *Challenge*, September–October 1981, p. 39.

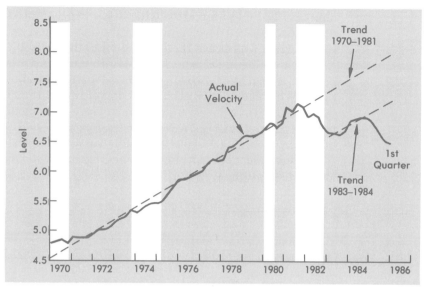

Source: Federal Reserve System.

FIGURE 21-7 Velocity of M1 (GNP/M1)

1980s. The problem with M1 target setting in this period is depicted in Figure 21-8.

Note that an M1 growth range of 4.0 to 7.0 percent for 1985 had been set in late 1984. By midyear, the actual M1 level was so far above the upper 7 percent

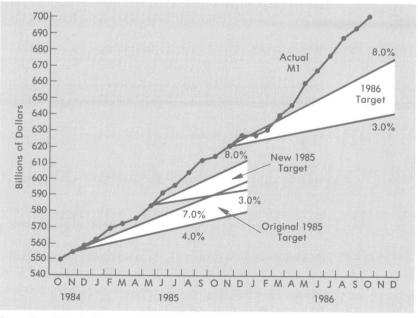

Source: Federal Reserve System.

FIGURE 21-8 M1: levels and targets, 1985–1986

limit that the FOMC found it advisable to scrap their original target and establish a broader 3.0 to 8.0 percent range for the rest of the year. Despite this, actual M1 rose at a rate well above the upper limit of the revised 1985 target.

In November 1985, the 1986 M1 growth target was again set at 3.0 to 8.0 percent. Actual M1, however, once more soared well above the upper limit of the range. What does all this mean? It seems clear that the FOMC, in recognition of the sharp dive in velocity and accompanying softening of the economy, decided to use its discretionary power to "lean against the wind." In doing so they were, of course, diverging sharply from monetarist principles.

In any case, real-world experience in the 1980s did little to support the monetarist position.

Where Do We Stand Now in the Monetarist – Post-Keynesian Debate?

Despite continuing differences of major import, substantial progress has been made toward narrowing the gulf between these two groups of economists over the past 20 years. Today, indeed, there appear to be few *theoretical* differences of substance that divide the more moderate monetarists from the more moderate post-Keynesians. As one prominent Keynesian put it, "there are no significant differences of analysis between able, intelligent openminded monetarists and nonmonetarists." [52]

In what areas have the two groups tended to come together in recent years? On the one hand, the Keynesians appear to have moved measurably toward the monetarist position on the key issue of the role of the money stock as a determinant of aggregate demand. This movement has come in two stages.

The first stage, a movement largely unrelated to monetarist prodding, constituted a rather general disavowal of the more extreme "money matters hardly at all" position some Keynesians seemed to have adopted in the 1940s and early 1950s. Thus when the monetarist–post-Keynesian debate heated up in the mid-1960s, the majority of post-Keynesians already accepted the money supply as an important determinant of aggregate demand (albeit, not necessarily the *dominant* determinant).

The second stage consisted of a veritable mountain of empirical evidence that has piled up since the battle was really joined in the 1960s, tending to reinforce the importance of the money stock as well as the magnitude of the crowding out effects connected with fiscal policy. As a result, the Keynesians have adjusted their position further toward the direction of the monetarists. This evidence, as incorporated in the essentially Keynesian M.I.T. – Penn – Social Science Research Council econometric model, implies a relatively steep demand-for-money curve and "pervasive and substantial" interest rate effects on demand. As one economist has recently put it, the "Keynesians have moved to occupy the strategic middle ground, having been flexible enough to incorporate

[52] Franco Modigliani, "The Monetarist Controversy," *Economic Review Supplement*, Federal Reserve Bank of San Francisco, Spring 1977, p. 6.

a major role for money in the Keynesian schema, thus leaving to monetarists the role of defending a more extreme position. The ultimate verdict on the debate *may* well be the victory of a moderate monetarism dressed in Keynesian clothes.''[53]

At the same time a significant number of the more moderate monetarists refuse to accept the extreme position vis-à-vis fiscal policy adopted by some of their colleagues. For example, monetarist David Fand has observed that

> to deny any short run stabilization effects to fiscal actions, one must be prepared to argue that surpluses (or deficits), irrespective of magnitude, have no direct effect on spending through changes in disposable income and that they have no indirect effect through changes in desired real balances or desired liquidity, and on velocity. But this can be true only in the exceptional case of a completely (interest) inelastic demand for money.[54]

And monetarists Karl Brunner and Allan Meltzer, in commenting on two of Professor Friedman's papers, observe that

> One of the more striking features of Friedman's analysis is that . . . the fiscal role of government is mentioned only once and only to be dismissed. Changes in government expenditures and taxes, apparently, have so little effect that they can be ignored entirely.
>
> We know of no evidence to support this conclusion. The empirical work done by Friedman and Meiselman, Keran, Andersen and Jordan, and others frequently identified as "monetarists" provides no evidence that changes in the government expenditure and taxation have no effect on output.[55]

It seems, then, that many Keynesians have accepted a very important role for money and have somewhat tempered their claims for fiscal policy while a number of monetarists have granted that the interest elasticity of the demand for money does, indeed, permit some variation in velocity and, consequently, a stabilizing role for fiscal policy. But while the gap between the two groups has been narrowed by these developments, substantive differences on these and other important issues remain.

Perhaps the most fundamental of these is their divergence of views on the government's capacity to moderate cyclical swings via discretionary monetary and fiscal policy. Here the debate continues and the policy implications are profound.[56]

On this issue, the monetarists see the private economy as fairly stable — that is, as not subject to major and continuing disturbance from external shocks (such as large and variable shifts in the MEI curve, the demand-for-money curve, or

---

[53] Thomas Mayer, "Some Reflections on the Current State of the Monetarist Debate," in *Readings in Money, National Income and Stabilization Policy*, 4th ed., ed. Ronald L. Teigen (Homewood, IL: Richard D. Irwin, 1978), p. 83.

[54] David I. Fand, "A Monetarist Model of the Monetary Process," *Journal of Finance*, May 1970, p. 286.

[55] K. Brunner and A. H. Meltzer, "Friedman's Monetary Theory," *Journal of Political Economy*, September–October 1972, p. 842.

[56] For an excellent recent article on monetarism see David Laidler, "The Legacy of the Monetarist Controversy," *Review*, Federal Reserve Bank of St. Louis, March–April 1990.

international trade patterns). To the extent that such external shocks do disturb the economy's stability, monetarists generally see strong and reasonably prompt correction via such neutralizing devices as the interest rate effects that we have labeled the second-round effects. As a consequence, they not only see little need for the government to enter in with discretionary stabilization programs to attempt to ameliorate the relatively minor problems caused by such shocks but, indeed, see such attempts as likely to make matters worse. This is the case, in their view, because given the long and variable lags involved before such measures affect aggregate demand, we are unable to apply them at the appropriate time to have the desired effects. On the contrary, monetarists believe that well intentioned, but ill-advised and badly timed, discretionary stabilization attempts in the past have been a large part of the *cause* of the instability we have suffered.

Keynesians, in the main, view our world quite differently. They do see the potential for serious instability from external shocks and, while granting that the economy does contain built-in stabilizing tendencies that will, in time, lessen the problem, they conclude that "the *interim* response is still of significant magnitude and of considerable duration, basically because the wheels of the offsetting mechanism grind slowly."[57] The Keynesian response to the monetarist contention that discretionary stabilization policy can only make matters worse is to contrast the relative stability of the post–World War II era (where discretionary policy has been employed) with the pre–World War II period (where it was not).

One example of a view most Keynesians would accept was offered some years ago by Professor Don Patinkin:

> In brief, even if monetary policy could be depended upon to ultimately restore the economy to full employment, there would still remain the crucial question of the length of time it would need. There would still remain the very real possibility that it would necessitate subjecting the economy to an intolerably long period of dynamic adjustment: a period during which wages, prices, and interest would continue to fall, and—what is most important—a period during which varying numbers of workers would continue to suffer from involuntary unemployment. Though I am not aware that he expressed himself in this way, this is the essence of Keynes' position. This is all that need be established in order to justify his fundamental policy conclusion that the "self-adjusting quality of the economic system"—even when reinforced by central-bank policy—is not enough, and that resort must be had to fiscal policy.[58]

Thus, the core of the issue may well be differing views on Keynes's oft-quoted statement that "In the long run we are all dead." The Keynesians argue that we can minimize our "short-run illnesses" with appropriate discretionary stabilization policy without jeopardizing the long-run health of the economy. The monetarists feel that the medicine prescribed by the Keynesians for short-run ills will make the patient sicker in the short run as well as threaten his long-run welfare.

---

[57] Franco Modigliani, "The Monetarist Controversy, or, Should We Forsake Stabilization Policies?" *American Economic Review*, March 1977.

[58] Don Patinkin, "Friedman on the Quantity Theory and Keynesian Economics," *Journal of Political Economy*, September–October 1972, pp. 901–902.

Review Questions

1. Compare the conclusions of the modern monetarists with those of the "old" quantity theory covered earlier. In what respects do the two differ?

2. Carefully explain how the inclusion of a speculative (or asset) demand for money by Keynes in his interest theory may be said to make it possible for pure fiscal policy to affect aggregate demand.

3. How would you characterize the monetarist position on the crowding out effects of fiscal policy?

4. The monetarists argue that the use of interest rates as a prime monetary policy target is not only inappropriate but may lead to procyclical monetary policy. Carefully explain this view.

5. Many monetarists would argue that fiscal policy as a stabilization weapon should be eliminated because it is ineffective; they would eliminate discretionary monetary policy not because it is ineffective but because they consider it subject to long and variable time lags. Carefully explain both positions.

6. Explain the reverse causation argument.

7. In terms of the four-diagram model employed in Chapter 20, the monetarists might be said to consider the second-round effects to be very powerful. Explain what this means for the slopes of the curves involved and how such slopes would lead to monetarist conclusions.

8. To the monetarists, a rise in the supply of money may well lead to a *rise* in interest rates. Explain carefully.

9. What events in the late 1960s gave a major boost to the monetarist case?

10. "One thing the nonmonetarists should *not* be called is 'fiscalists.' The debate is not symmetrical." Explain the point of this quote from Nobel laureate James Tobin.

11. Carefully outline the major elements of the post-Keynesians' opposition to the monetarist positions and policy prescriptions. What are the implications of financial innovation and the changing definition of money for monetarist policy conclusions?

12. "The behavior of velocity during the 1980s significantly weakened the monetarists' position." Do you agree? Explain carefully.

U.S. Economic Activity Since 1965 — The Phillips Curve, Stagflation, and Inflationary Expectations

Introduction

Economists' faith in Keynesian theory and policy prescriptions undoubtedly reached its peak in the mid- to late 1960s. Then, partly as a result of empirical evidence offered by the monetarists and partly as a result of the accelerating inflation and stagflation encountered during the chaotic 1970s, an agonizing reappraisal seemed in order.

In Chapters 20 and 21, we have considered some effects of this reappraisal. In this chapter we carry that consideration a bit further by introducing the effects of price expectations on the business cycle.

The Pre-1970s View of the Business Cycle and the Role for Stabilization Policies

As we have already noted, the idealized world in which policymakers simply pull the appropriate levers to raise aggregate demand when there is unemployment and reverse the dosage when there is inflation never has existed. There have always been phases of the business cycle during which it was known that an expansion of demand aimed at fuller employment would likely raise prices somewhat and other periods where it was to be expected that demand restriction aimed at combating inflation would probably lead to some unemployment also. While some degree of trade-off between unemployment and inflation has been a problem confronting policymakers for many years, prior to the disturbing events of the 1970s, it was generally considered quite manageable.

The Phases of a Typical Business Cycle — The Pre-1970s View

From 1945 to 1970, U.S. business cycles, though each was different in cause, length, and amplitude, followed a pattern sufficiently similar to permit one to summarize a typical path. This is done in Figure 22-1, where money GNP is measured off on the vertical axis and time on the horizontal axis. The assumption, of course, is that increasing (decreasing) aggregate demand raises (lowers) GNP and that the composition of the GNP change (as between real production and employment on the one hand and prices on the other) varies with the phase of the cycle.

At the initial trough of the typical (pre-1970s) recession (point A in Figure 22-1), one might have expected to find unemployment in the 6 to 7 percent range with the price level essentially stable. Then, when aggregate demand was increased, the initial response (A to B in Figure 22-1) could be expected to be primarily increases in production caused by a callback of laid-off workers with little or no price increase. Thus, no trade-off problem existed, for the effects of rising demand were almost entirely the good ones of increased production and employment. This, of course, is comparable to the horizontal portion of the aggregate supply curve introduced in Chapter 20.

After a while, however, possibly as the overall unemployment rate approached 5 percent, further increases in aggregate demand were expected to produce mixed results (from B to C in Figure 22-1). For even though full employment for the entire economy had not yet been reached, in certain industries and in the markets for certain skills capacity had already been reached and the pressure of excess demand in specific sectors began to produce more and more price increases. Indeed, the closer the approach to the overall full-employment level, the greater the effect on prices and the less on employment and production.

Comparable to the upsloping part of the aggregate supply curve, the B to C range was where policymakers encountered their first serious trade-off decisions. If unemployment is now at a 5 percent rate and prices are currently rising at 2 percent per year and we know (although, we are never really sure) that the demand increases needed to reduce unemployment to the 4 percent rate then conventionally accepted as full employment will push the inflation rate up to 4 percent per year, should we do it? Are the benefits of reducing the unemployment rate by 1 percent greater than, or less than, the costs of causing a 2 percent increase in the rate of price increase? Here, policymakers generally must rely on their own value judgments, for economists have little to offer them in the way of concrete evaluation of these costs and benefits.

Once full employment has been achieved, further increases in demand, while still capable of generating some moderate short-run increases in output, must have the bulk of their impact on the price level. Here is where we have the classical demand-pull inflation case that is so often described as "too much money chasing too few goods."

While the appropriate direction of stabilization policy is clearer in the C to D range than in the B to C range (Figure 22-1), the policymaker must be ever mindful of the possibility that an *excessive* cut in demand may not only halt the inflation but also shove the economy over the peak into a new recession.

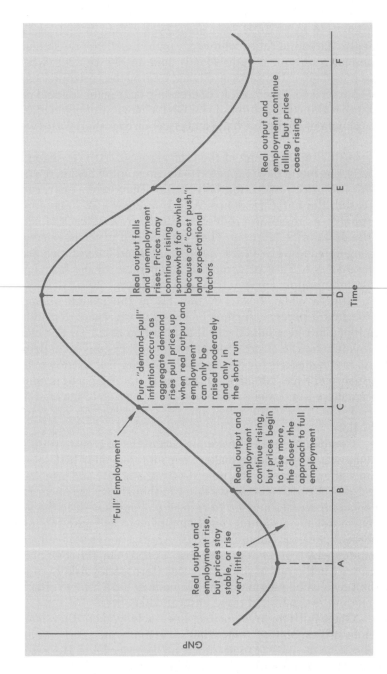

Real output and employment rise, but prices stay stable, or rise very little

"Full" Employment

Real output and employment continue rising, but prices begin to rise more, the closer the approach to full employment

Pure "demand–pull" inflation occurs as aggregate demand rises pull prices up when real output and employment can only be raised moderately and only in the short run

Real output falls and unemployment rises. Prices may continue rising somewhat for awhile because of "cost push" and expectational factors

Real output and employment continue falling, but prices cease rising

GNP

Time

A   B   C   D   E   F

FIGURE 22-1   Stages of the typical U.S. business cycle (pre-1970s view)

Whether as a result of overzealous policy, structural dislocations built up within the economy, or demand cutbacks for other reasons, periods of excess demand inflation in the United States have almost invariably been followed by downturn and recession. The first results of such a downturn (D to E in Figure 22-1) have generally consisted of increases in unemployment and cutbacks in production, but very little price relief.

Indeed, even before the 1970 recession and our experience with serious stagflation problems later in that decade, it was widely recognized that prices may continue rising for a time even while employment and production are falling and a full-blown recession is getting underway.

Why might prices continue upward when aggregate demand has fallen off sufficiently to cause rising unemployment? Because of a combination of inequities built up during the preceding boom and expectations, both of which tend to stimulate the development of cost-push, or sellers, inflation.

Cost-push inflation, according to the usual definition, consists of a markup in prices by sellers who possess sufficient market (monopoly) power simply to increase their own prices, *in the absence of an excess of demand.* This type of inflation, which is a variety not readily controllable by stabilization policies, is generally aided and abetted by inequities and expectations built up during the cycle.

While prices in general have been rising in the preceding boom phase of the cycle, it is inevitable that some wage recipients, perhaps tied in to long-term contracts without escalator clauses, will have suffered real income reductions. If their union contracts then come up for renegotiation during the D to E phase of the cycle, their union can be expected to use its bargaining power despite developing unemployment to attempt to at least restore its members' relative purchasing power by demanding wage increases at least equal to the inflation plus productivity increases. And such action, by raising sellers' costs further, will likely trigger further price increases.

Catching up with past cost-of-living increases may not be the end of it. If prices have been rising over some considerable time period, the experience is quite likely to generate expectations that inflation will continue. If so, one should not be surprised to find industry and unions pushing up wages and prices by enough, not only to catch up with perceived past inequities but also to attempt to protect themselves against future erosion of their purchasing power. Expectations thus may reinforce the inflationary process both through generating a (cost-push) wage-price (or price-wage) spiral and through engendering a (demand-pull) buy-now-and-beat-the-price-rise psychology.

In any case, even before the experience of the 1970s, some inflation accompanying falling employment and production in the early portion of the recession phase of the business cycle was a widely recognized phenomenon. It was not, however, considered to be a major source of concern, since, in those days, experience seemed to dictate that the increasing slack in labor markets and the unsold inventories in product markets would fairly expeditiously bring the inflationary forces to heel. And although downward rigidity in wages and prices was recognized as sufficiently strong to prevent actual wage-price declines, the pre-1970 expectation was for roughly stable prices by the time the recession bottomed out.

Source: A. W. Phillips, "The Relation Between Unemployment and the Rate of Change of Money Wage Rates in the United Kingdom, 1861–1957," *Economica,* Vol. 25, No. 100, November 1958, p. 285.

FIGURE 22-2   The original Phillips curve

The Phillips Curve

The general tendency for higher levels of aggregate spending to stimulate rises in prices coupled with declines in unemployment rates would naturally lead one to expect inflation and unemployment rates to be inversely related. In the 1950s, this observation led a British economist, A. W. Phillips, to carry out an empirical study of the British economy over a period of nearly a century aimed at investigating the relationship.[1]

The result of his study was a graphical device called the *Phillips curve,* which sums up neatly the typical (indeed, historical, as Phillips's and other similar curves are derived from actual experience with unemployment and inflation in the past) relation between unemployment rates and inflation rates for an economy during a given time period.

Phillips's original curve is shown in Figure 22-2; an early adaptation for the United States, using the rate of change of prices on the vertical axis, is shown in Figure 22-3. Both illustrate the expected negative relationship between unemployment rates and rates of wage (price) change.

It is important to recognize that both these curves are based on experience prior to 1960 and neither claims to represent the available trade-offs for more

[1] A. W. Phillips, "The Relation Between Unemployment and the Rate of Change of Money Wage Rates in the United Kingdom, 1861–1957," *Economica,* November 1958. As the title of his article indicates, Phillips's work was done with wage rates rather than price-level changes. Because it is normally assumed that money wage rates and price levels tend to move together, it has since become more common to use the so-called Phillips curve to relate unemployment rates with rates of price increase.

recent periods. With that qualification in mind, let us consider briefly the implications of Figure 22-3.

What it suggests is that, *given the structure of the U.S. economy during the years studied,* government policymakers could through the use of monetary and fiscal policy to alter aggregate demand choose among a wide variety of unemployment-inflation combinations. For example, if stable prices are to be achieved, aggregate demand must be low enough to allow 5.5 percent unemployment (point A). Achieving a 4 percent unemployment rate, however, would have required that aggregate demand be raised enough to generate about a 2 percent per annum rate of inflation (point B). If it was desired to push the unemployment rate down to as low as 2 percent (a level only achieved in the United States during World War II), aggregate demand would have had to have been raised sufficiently to cause an inflation rate between 7 and 8 percent.

Conceptually, then, the Phillips curve device implied the existence of a more or less stable menu of unemployment-inflation combinations available to policymakers. Expansionary monetary-fiscal measures raising aggregate demand would be expected to shift the economy up to the left along its existing curve, reducing unemployment rates but, at the same time, generating more rapid inflation. Contractionary measures would shift us downward to the right, cutting the inflation rate but raising unemployment.

Nor was movement along the curve in response to aggregate demand changes the only way in which government policymakers might affect the nation's economic fate. Since the level (distance from the origin) of any given Phillips curve depends partly upon the structural imperfections of the economy,

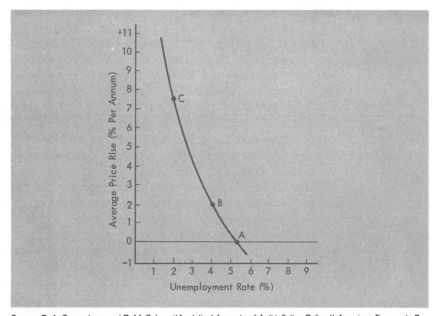

Source: P. A. Samuelson and R. M. Solow, "Analytical Aspects of Anti-inflation Policy," *American Economic Review,* May 1960.

FIGURE 22-3 Modified Phillips curve for the United States it seemed entirely possible, *in the long run,* to move toward shifting the curve itself leftward to a position offering a more attractive set of short-run trade-offs. Such measures as manpower training programs and policies aimed at reducing monopolistic restrictions were considered appropriate ways of reducing structural unemployment and minimizing cost-push inflation, thereby in the long run tending to shift the Phillips curve leftward to a level closer to the origin.

All in all, the Phillips curve device seemed to constitute a clear as well as a fairly realistic way of summing up the options open to government for influencing employment and prices, and in the 1960s its use spread rapidly. But just as it was gaining widespread acceptance, developments in the late 1960s and early 1970s cast serious doubts on its viability. Let us consider the facts of that period.

U.S. Unemployment-Inflation Relationships After 1965

After a long period of remarkably stable prices but excessive unemployment in the early 1960s, monetary and fiscal policy were brought to bear in the mid-1960s to raise aggregate demand and reduce unemployment. At about the same time, the Vietnam conflict began to escalate into a major U.S. commitment, which added markedly to the increase in demand. The result was as might well have been expected. Unemployment fell from 5.2 percent in 1964 to 4.5 percent in 1965 and on down to 3.8 percent by 1966. It stayed at or below the 3.8 level through 1969. Concurrently, the consumer price index began to rise. From an annual percentage increase of 1.7 during 1965, it went up by 2.9 percent in 1966, 2.9 percent in 1967, 4.2 percent in 1968, and 5.4 percent during 1969.

All this should not have been surprising. The United States was involved in a lengthy demand-pull inflationary boom, which implied that we had moved to the left and upward on our Phillips curve. The government unwisely postponed action to curb the developing inflation for several years.[2]

Finally, in late 1968 for fiscal policy and 1969 for monetary policy, a concerted governmental effort was made to cut down on demand with the aim, of course, of slowing down the accelerating inflation. The result was a rapid increase in unemployment (to 4.9 percent) as the nation slid into the 1970 recession but an astonishing 5.9 percent rise in prices at the same time!

Now, as noted, *some* continuing increase in prices from cost-push and other such factors, as unemployment initially rose, would not have been surprising. But there can be no doubt that virtually everyone — government policymakers and economists alike — was surprised to see inflation continue at such a rapid rate despite the strong action that had been taken to curb demand.

There were explanations after the fact, of course. That long period of unchecked demand-pull inflation, it was pointed out, had undoubtedly generated inflationary expectations that would take some time to subside. And cost-push

---

[2] Although the Federal Reserve did attempt to cool things off with an extremely restrictive monetary policy during part of 1966.

inflation, it had always been argued, was an inherently short-run phenomenon that could not continue for much longer with aggregate demand held down.

This latter point is a simple one. Certainly, it was granted, monopoly forces *can* raise prices in the absence of excess demand. But when their action (in the absence of a rise in aggregate demand to sustain or accommodate the inflation) results in large unsold inventories and unemployment, they will reasonably quickly reassess their position and hold back on further price markups. "Just give it time," was the general refrain, "and things will straighten out."

Time passed, but things did not really straighten out. In 1971, unemployment rose to 5.9 percent while the consumer price index went up another 4.3 percent. This unsettling experience (along with alarming developments in the nation's balance of international payments) led a reluctant President Nixon to implement powers granted him earlier by Congress by instituting a 90-day general price and wage freeze in August 1971.

The price freeze was followed, starting in November 1971, with a policy under which prices and wages were still directly controlled by governmental authority, but wages were permitted to be increased at a 5.5 percent annual rate and price increases had to be justified by cost increases. This policy was continued throughout 1972, and, for that year, the record showed unemployment averaging 5.6 percent (but falling) and the consumer price index up by only 3.3 percent.

Somewhat encouraged, the administration greatly relaxed controls in January 1973. Explicit controls over price increases were lifted from all but the food, health, and construction industries, but the federal government retained the power to establish control over others whose price increases were considered excessive.

What happened during 1973 is a matter of record. Unemployment fell to an average of 4.9 percent during the year, but the consumer price index for the year shot upward by over 6 percent. And all this happened despite another overall 60-day price freeze in mid-1973 and reinstitution controls for the balance of the year.

Following this brief and relatively unsatisfactory fling at wage and price controls, the federal government, alarmed by the startling resurgence of accelerating inflation, returned to more conventional means for combating it. From mid-1973 to mid-1974, for example, the federal funds interest rate was allowed to rise from just over 7 percent to more than 13 percent as the Fed launched what appeared to be an all-out attack. But the results this time were not only disappointing but spectacularly so.

During 1974 not only did the unemployment rate climb back to an average of 5.6 percent but the consumer price index shot upward by an astonishing 11.0 percent. In 1975 the recession deepened, with the unemployment rate soaring above 9.0 percent and averaging 8.5 percent for the year as a whole. And contrary to the very essence of the Phillips curve analysis, the inflation rate, far from being modified by the excessive slack in the economy, rocketed upward by another 9.1 percent! Clearly something quite new was occurring, and the Phillips curve promise of stable trade-offs between inflation and unemployment was brought into serious question.

There was hope, of course, that one benefit of undergoing what, up to that time, was the worst recession since the Great Depression of the 1930s, would be

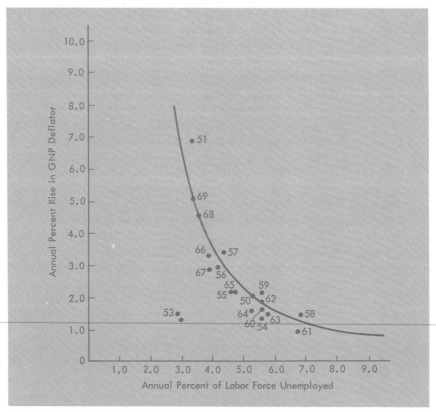

Source: U.S. Department of Labor, *Economic Report of the President,* various issues.

FIGURE 22-4   **Relationship between rate of price increase and rate of unemployment, 1950–1969**

to snuff out the inflationary pressures that had been battering the economy for nearly a decade. The rate of increase in the consumer index did dip sharply to 4.8 percent during 1976, but the respite was only temporary as it shot up again to 6.8 percent in 1977 and 9.0 percent in 1978 before reaching the double-digit level again in 1979 and 1980 with disheartening 13.3 and 12.4 percent performances. And while the economy's unemployment rate did fall steadily from its 1975 average of 8.5 percent to as low as 5.8 percent by 1979, two successive recessions in 1980 and 1982 brought it right back up again to unprecedentedly high rates in the early 1980s. Indeed, by late 1982 the monthly unemployment rate was well over 10 percent for the first time since 1940.

     Probably the best way to illustrate the deterioration in performance of the U.S. economy since 1970 is via the Phillips curve type diagrams in Figures 22-4 and 22-5. In Figure 22-4, data for the unemployment rate and the inflation rate (as measured by the implicit GNP deflator) for 1950 to 1969 are plotted and a Phillips curve is sketched in to illustrate the relationship.[3]

[3] It should be noted that the curve in Figure 22-4 is not statistically fitted to the data but rather is simply drawn in by "eyeballing" the data.

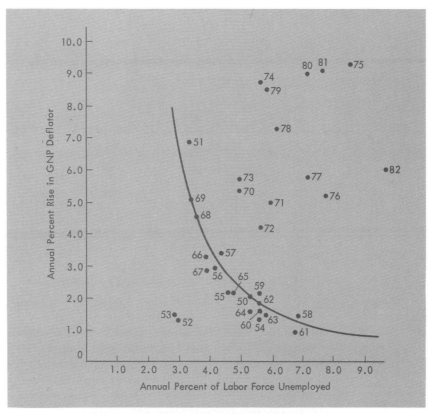

Source: U.S. Department of Labor, *Economic Report of the President,* various issues.

FIGURE 22-5 Relationship between rate of price increase and rate of unemployment, 1950–1982

What stands out here is the fact that (except for the Korean war–price control years of 1952 and 1953) this performance produces a fairly regular pattern quite consistent with the Phillips curve hypothesis.

Figure 22-5 then adds observations for the economy's performance from 1970 through 1982. Two things fairly leap out at one from this diagram. First, it dramatically portrays the worsened performance of the economy after 1969. Second, it provides ample reason for questioning the concept of a stable Phillips curve-type trade-off. How might one explain these startling developments?

Attempts to Explain the Unemployment-Inflation Experience After 1969

Even before the disasters of the 1970s, some economists had begun to doubt the concept of a stable Phillips curve. For although rising aggregate demand in the 1966–1969 period did reduce the unemployment rate to the 3.5 to 3.8 percent

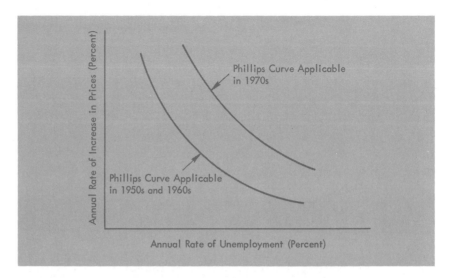

FIGURE 22-6   The shifting worsening Phillips curve view

neighborhood, it became apparent that it stayed there only at the cost of *increasing* rates of inflation each year. Although one might have explained this experience as the result of reaching full employment and, thus, the essentially vertical (left) portion of an existing Phillips curve, a number of economists took the position that it reflected that the nation's Phillips curve itself had shifted to the right (that is, to a *less* satisfactory position).

The Shifting Phillips Curve View

Whatever the interpretation of the experience of the latter 1960s, it was quite evident that the 1970s and 1980s represented something quite new. Among a number of attempts to explain it was the notion that structural and institutional changes in the economy had combined to shift the U.S. Phillips curve sharply to the right. This view of the situation is depicted in Figure 22-6 where the post-1970 curve implies that a higher level of inflation was associated with each achievable rate of unemployment. There were at least two sets of reasons for this view.

Changing Structure of Labor Force   Several economists put forth the view that a changing structure of the U.S. labor force was at least partially responsible for a shift to the right in the nation's Phillips curve and the consequent worsening of trade-off terms.[4] It was their position that the nation had undergone changes in

[4] See, for example, George L. Perry, "Changing Labor Markets and Inflation," *Brookings Papers on Economic Activity*, Vol. 1, No. 3 (Washington, D.C.: The Brookings Institution, 1970); and Charles L. Schultz, "Has the Phillips Curve Shifted? Some Additional Evidence," *Brookings Papers on Economic Activity*, Vol. 2, No. 2 (Washington, D.C.: The Brookings Institution, 1971).

TABLE 22-1 Percentage of civilian labor force employed, by sex and age, 1950–1980

	1950	1955	1960	1965	1970	1975	1980
Males, total	70.6%	68.5%	66.7%	65.1%	62.2%	59.7%	57.6%
Females, total	29.4	31.5	33.3	34.9	37.8	40.3	42.4
Both sexes, 16–19	6.3	5.8	6.1	7.0	7.8	8.3	7.9

Source: U.S. Department of Labor, Bureau of Labor Statistics, *Employment and Earnings,* various years.

the labor force composition such that the achievement of any given overall unemployment rate, say, 4 percent, would require a higher level of demand and therefore a higher rate of inflation than had been the case earlier.

The labor force of the 1970s and 1980s contained a much larger percentage of teenagers, females, and part-time workers than in earlier years. These are groups of workers who traditionally experience higher unemployment rates than others, but in the 1970s their employment experience had gotten even worse.[5] Evidence to this effect is contained in Tables 22-1 and 22-2.[6]

A similar view was taken by the President's Council of Economic Advisers in 1977 when changes in labor force structure were cited as the reason for a change in the base on which the full-employment budget figures were computed. In effect, the council stated that the same degree of inflationary pressure was now to be expected at a 4.9 percent rate of unemployment as had previously been encountered at a 4.0 percent unemployment rate. In essence, then, the council was attributing unemployment totaling about 1 percent of the labor force to the changed labor force composition.[7]

Undoubtedly there is validity to this position. It has been challenged, however, on two grounds. First, it has been pointed out that other factors affecting

TABLE 22-2 Unemployment rates, by age and sex, 1950–1980

	1950	1955	1960	1965	1970	1975	1980
Males, 20 and over	4.7%	3.8%	4.7%	3.2%	3.5%	6.8%	5.9%
Females, 20 and over	5.1	4.4	5.1	4.5	4.8	8.0	6.4
Both sexes, 16–19	12.2	11.0	14.7	14.8	15.3	19.9	17.8

Source: U.S. Department of Labor, Bureau of Labor Statistics, *Employment and Earnings,* various years.

[5] For example, in 1955 teenage males had unemployment rates 3.7 times as high as those of adult males. By 1969, their unemployment rate was 6.8 times as high as that of older males. See Charles Schultz, "The Inflation-Unemployment Dilemma: Has It Worsened?" in *Charles Schultz on Economics,* December 4, 1972 (New York: Appleton-Century-Crofts, 1972).

[6] For an excellent earlier discussion of the facts of these changes, see Sharon P. Smith, "The Changing Composition of the Labor Force," *Quarterly Review,* Federal Reserve Bank of New York, Winter 1976.

[7] *Economic Report of the President, 1977* (Washington, D.C.: Government Printing Office, 1977), pp. 48–51.

the structure of the labor force have worked the other way around.[8] Second, it seems clear that the structural changes in the labor force cited, though important, could not possibly have had sufficient impact to completely explain the nation's dismal trade-off situation in the 1970s.

Increased Level of Benefits to the Unemployed   A second reason that was cited as working toward a rightward shift in the nation's Phillips curve was the increased level and duration of government benefits available to the unemployed. This is especially the case for unemployment compensation benefits, but some of the nation's welfare programs were also singled out for criticism along the same lines.

A distinguished Harvard economist, Professor Martin Feldstein, presented evidence indicating that increased unemployment compensation benefits produced additions to the unemployment rolls that may well have totaled .75 percent of the labor force.[9] The point here, of course, was that rising benefit levels —as well as their increased duration—led some unemployed workers to be a bit more casual and selective in their job search than was previously the case.[10]

Although the estimates are the subject of disagreement, there can be no question that if both Professor Feldstein and those who cite changes in the structure of the labor force as a source of increased unemployment are correct in their judgment, the two factors could account for a substantial shift in the Phillips curve. Taken together, these two factors have been cited as being responsible for unemployment among 1.75 percent of the labor force—a very significant total indeed.

Supply Shocks as a Cause of Stagflation

Although the nation's economic performance might be characterized as subpar ever since 1970, the 1974–1975 years and the 1979–1980 years stand out as exceptionally bad. Is there a way of explaining these unusually bad years?

One common element in both periods was an enormous increase in the price charged for oil imported from the OPEC nations. The oil price increases (along with sharp food price rises during the same periods) have been singled out as solely responsible for much of the exceptional surge of inflation during these two periods.[11]

These oil price increases, along with unusual worldwide food price rises, can

---

[8] These include the fact that the 1970s labor force was better educated than that of the 1950s and that a number of governmental manpower training programs have improved the employability of a significant number of workers in recent years. See Edgar L. Feige, "The 1972 Report of the President's Council of Economic Advisers: Inflation and Unemployment," *American Economic Review*, September 1972; and Sylvia S. Small, "Statistical Effect of Work-Training Programs on the Unemployment Rate," *Monthly Labor Review*, September 1972.

[9] Martin S. Feldstein, *Lowering the Permanent Rate of Unemployment*, A Study for the Joint Economic Committee, 93rd Cong., 1st sess., 1973.

[10] A somewhat different, but nonetheless related, objection has been raised by others regarding the effects that rising legal minimum-wage levels have on teenage and minority unemployment.

[11] For estimates of the size of their impact, see Charles L. Schultz, "Some Macro Foundations for Micro Theory," *Brookings Papers on Economic Activity*, February 1981; and Alan S. Blinder, "Monetarism Is Obsolete," *Challenge*, September–October 1981.

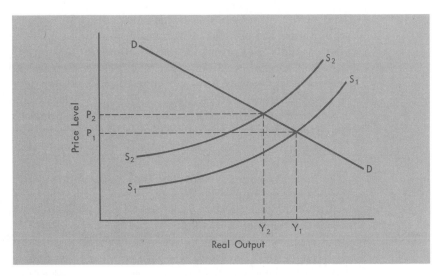

FIGURE 22-7 Short-run effects of supply shocks on the economy

be looked upon as generating an exceptional burst of cost-push inflation, although currently it is fashionable to refer to them as "supply shocks." Their effects can best be depicted, as in Figure 22-7, as a leftward shift in the economy's aggregate supply curve.

The result, of course, was the unprecedented jolt of stagflation referred to earlier. As noted in Chapter 20, policymakers were then confronted with the uncomfortable choice between combating the inflation via demand cuts (thereby worsening the unemployment) or "accommodating" by permitting demand to increase (thereby worsening the inflation).

It would be foolish to deny that the series of severe supply shocks that befell the U.S. economy in 1974–1975 and again in 1979–1980 had significant effects. Unquestionably they did, but one cannot explain a decade-long experience solely on the basis of a number of random (however severe) supply shocks suffered along the way. One factor we have not yet touched upon that, in the opinion of all observers, played a key role in price-unemployment experience during the 1970s and early 1980s has been that of price expectations. The remainder of the chapter considers this vitally important matter.

The Role of Price Expectations

After a lengthy period of relative stability, the price level began rising alarmingly in the mid-1960s in response to the excess demand generated during the Vietnam war. It was the beginning of an inflationary surge that persisted throughout the next decade and right on into the 1980s. It had long been understood that years of continued inflation could generate price expectations that, in and of themselves, could sustain the process and, indeed, even accelerate it. Buyers, after all, expecting price increases, would tend to buy more now to beat the rise, and price setters such as unions and corporations would attempt to protect themselves against loss of purchasing power by pushing up wages and prices more rapidly. But prior to the end of the 1960s, the implications of these developments for stabilization policy had not been considered in any detail. During the past two decades, however, much effort has been devoted to that area and, as a result of these studies, the concept of a "natural" unemployment rate, the so-called "accelerationist" theory, and the "rational expectations" argument have been developed to deal with the effects of price expectations and, to some extent, further challenge advocates of discretionary stabilization policies.[12]

The Natural Unemployment Rate Hypothesis and the Accelerationist View   Difficulties in relating the Phillips curve concept to the facts of the 1970s have led many economists to the conclusion that Phillips curve-type trade-offs between inflation and unemployment exist only in the short run and only because of transitionary differences between the expected and actual rates of inflation. In the longer run, however, when consumers have had sufficient experience to adapt their price expectations fully to the actual rate of inflation, all opportunity for trade-offs via alterations in aggregate demand disappears. To this "accelerationist" group, then, the long-run Phillips curve is a vertical line implying that changes in aggregate demand can only alter the price level with no lasting effect on the employment level. This long-run Phillips curve can be looked upon as very similar to the vertical line referred to as the potential level of output in Chapter 20.

The accelerationist view is based upon the concept of a "natural" rate of unemployment. The natural rate of unemployment may be defined as *that rate of employment at which the rate of inflation being experienced equals the rate of inflation that was expected.* It is thus an equilibrium rate of unemployment, in the sense that, at that rate, everyone is receiving the real wage they expected when they entered into their current wage contract. A rate of unemployment lower than the natural rate can be achieved, but only as a result of workers being fooled into working for a lower real wage than they had expected. Such a lower unemployment rate is not an equilibrium because ultimately workers will learn that they have been fooled and will readjust their labor offerings accordingly.

This natural (or equilibrium) unemployment rate is not considered to be a fixed datum, established by some natural laws for all time, impervious to any efforts to alter it. Rather, it is determined by the number of structural impediments to employment built into an economy. For example, restrictive licensing as an obstacle to entry into a field, minimum wage laws, inadequate employment information, deficiencies in manpower training, and arbitrary restrictions on apprenticeships by unions would all work in the direction of establishing a high natural rate of unemployment.[13]

---

[12] The following two sections owe much to two excellent articles by Thomas M. Humphrey. See Humphrey, "Changing Views of the Phillips Curve," *Monthly Review*, Federal Reserve Bank of Richmond, July 1973; and "Some Recent Developments in Phillips Curve Analysis," *Monthly Review*, Federal Reserve Bank of Richmond, January–February 1978. For more technical surveys, see Robert J. Gordon, "Recent Developments in the Theory of Inflation and Unemployment," *Journal of Monetary Economics*, April 1976; and Helmut Frisch, "Inflation Theory 1963–1975: A 'Second Generation' Survey," *Journal of Economic Literature*, December 1977.

[13] See Milton Friedman, "The Role of Monetary Policy," *American Economic Review*, March 1968.

Let us consider this natural rate–accelerationist view in some detail. As noted, its proponents do not deny that, *in the short run*, unemployment can be reduced below the natural rate and the rate of inflation increased by increases in demand. That, is, they grant that there do exist some very short-run Phillips curves along which shifts (and trade-offs between unemployment and inflation) are possible. But, they argue, the price increases resulting from such an effort will quickly generate a higher level of inflationary expectations on the part of the public which, in themselves, will tend to shift the (short-run) Phillips curve up to the right. Consider the graphic illustration in Figure 22-8.

Suppose, for example, that the natural rate of unemployment for the economy depicted there is 5 percent and that the country is initially at point **A**, where unemployment is 5 percent and prices are stable. (By way of example, we might assume that the current price level is $2.00 per unit, while the current money wage rate is $8.00 per hour. This would produce a real wage rate—money wage/price level—of $4.00 per hour, which, for equilibrium, we must assume satisfies both employers and employees at the current employment level.)

Now assume that the government decides to raise aggregate demand via monetary-fiscal policies so as to lower unemployment from 5 to 3 percent. Such a rise in demand will, it knows, increase the rate of price increase from its current zero rate to a rate of 4 percent. In Figure 22-8, this means the government action moves the economy along the short-run Phillips curve labeled S_1 to point **B**.

It is worth considering why more workers are hired (97 rather than 95 percent of the labor force) after this governmental measure. From the employers' point of view, it is easy to see. They are now receiving prices for the goods they sell that are rising at 4 percent per year, but (initially, anyway) their money wage costs are hardly rising at all. This means that the real wage they pay has fallen so they can readily *afford* to hire more workers.

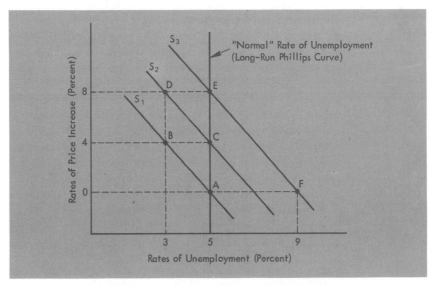

Source: Adapted from similar figure in Thomas M. Humphrey, "Changing Views of the Phillips Curve," *Monthly Review,* Federal Reserve Bank of Richmond, January–February 1978, p. 10.

FIGURE 22-8   The accelerationist view of unemployment-inflation trade-offs

And what about the workers? Initially, they are fooled into offering more labor by what appears to them as *higher* real wages. Having recently experienced stable prices, they have come to expect more of the same. If they now start receiving money wages going up at a rate of, say, 1 percent, that rise, taken together with the expected stability of product prices, appears to them (errone-ously, of course) as a higher real wage.

But they are not likely to be fooled this way for long. Once they begin to experience the actual 4 percent rate of price increase, their price expectations will be changed, and they will, of course, act to protect themselves. That is, they will insist on *money* wage increases at a rate of at least 4 percent to keep up with prices and eliminate the cut in real wages they have temporarily undergone.

These changes in price expectations, causing, as they must, increases in money wages at a faster rate, will *shift the nation's short-run Phillips curve to the right.* Indeed, once a 4 percent per annum inflation comes to be fully expected, the short-run Phillips curve will shift to S_2, at which point (because money wages have now risen enough to raise real wages back to their original level) employers will, as at point A, find it worthwhile to hire only 95 percent of the labor force. We are back to the natural rate of unemployment once again but find ourselves still experiencing a 4 percent annual inflation rate (point C).

If, however, the government is determined to maintain the level of unem-ployment at the 3 percent rate, it can do so only at the cost of ever-accelerating price levels. Look again at Figure 22-8. Once the public has come to anticipate an inflation rate of 4 percent, the short-run Phillips curve becomes S_2. From here, unemployment can once again be driven down to 3 percent via aggregate de-mand increases (along S_2) until we arrive at point D. We can only stay at point D (with 3 percent unemployment and 8 percent inflation) so long as the public *expects* prices to rise 4 percent per year. As soon as the public adjusts its expecta-tions to the new circumstances and comes to expect 8 percent inflation, the real wage rises once again and the short-run Phillips curve shifts up once more to S_3. And, again, unemployment will rise back to its natural level (to point E).

So what is to be done now? The government has attempted to trade off price stability for reduced unemployment but has succeeded in purchasing only brief episodes of fuller employment while people were adapting their price expecta-tions to reality. In the end, it finds itself back at the same old 5 percent unem-ployment level but saddled with a continuing 8 percent inflation rate. The accel-erationist prescription is simple. Since, except briefly, it cannot achieve an unemployment rate below its natural 5 percent rate without perpetually accel-erating the inflation rate, its optimum course is to accept the inevitable 5 percent of unemployment and do what it can to work its way back to the more desirable S_1 short-run Phillips curve where, at least, prices are stable. This simply requires a reversal of direction of its demand management tools of sufficient magnitude and duration to squeeze out the inflationary expectations built up earlier. It could, for example, enact sufficiently restrictive monetary and fiscal policies to move the economy southeasterly along its current short-run Phillips curve (by assumption, S_3) to point F.

This, of course, will extract a price — a rise in the unemployment rate to 9 percent. But that unhappy situation cannot last. The S_3 short-run Phillips curve implies expectations of 8 percent price rises built up from the past. Since these expectations now *exceed* the actual rate of inflation, the short-run Phillips curve must ultimately shift downward until, when all inflationary expectations have been squeezed out, the nation can return to the best position open to it — point **A** on short-run Phillips curve S_1.

The accelerationist conclusion, then, is that the long-run Phillips curve is the vertical line drawn in at the 5 percent unemployment rate in Figure 22-8. Alterations in demand by those charged with stabilization policy can move us off it, but only temporarily and only because people overestimate or underestimate the inflation rate. In the long run, we are foredoomed to the natural unemployment rate, and all that variations in aggregate demand can do is alter the rate of inflation.

The policy implications of the accelerationist view are, of course, of profound importance. Monetary and fiscal policy measures to reduce unemployment below the natural rate through raising aggregate demand are seen as being actually counterproductive because, while they may permanently raise the rate of inflation, they can only temporarily reduce unemployment below its natural rate. The only rational course for an economy suffering from the combined ills of inflation and unemployment is intentionally to worsen the latter for a period sufficiently long to eliminate the inflationary expectations underlying the former. And once that is accomplished, we must launch the long-run task of reducing the structural impediments to employment — the majority of which are alleged to have been erected by government in any case — which keep the so-called natural unemployment rate so high.

The Rational Expectations Hypothesis   As if the natural unemployment rate and accelerationist thesis were not a sufficient challenge to those favoring an activist government stabilization program, a small but distinguished group of economists has gone them one better in recent years by denying the possibility of any inflation-unemployment trade-off *even in the short run.* These economists, who have been dubbed the **rational expectationists,** have concentrated particularly on the way in which people arrive at their expectations.

In essence they argue that the assumption, implicit in the accelerationist hypothesis, that people's price expectations are formed solely on the basis of past inflation experience is naïve and unrealistic. It will be recalled that according to that hypothesis, increases in demand can have short-run effects on employment only because workers tend to underestimate the degree of price increase, thereby settling for money wage increases that permit a decline in the real wage (because actual product prices rise faster than wages) and therefore provide an incentive to employers to increase hiring. Only after experiencing a given rate of inflation for some time are workers assumed able to adapt their expectations to the true rate of inflation thereby upping their wage demands (or quitting to seek higher pay elsewhere) and wiping out the profit margin that permitted the rise in employment.

According to the rational expectationists, the notion that people form their price expectations solely from past inflation experience is equivalent to assuming that people are irrational. If they start out this way (during a period when, in fact, the rate of price increase is rising), they will soon learn that they were wrong. On learning this, rational people will not slavishly keep committing the same error in the future but, rather, will use all information at their disposal to forecast future inflation more accurately. Assuming that all relevant information is available to them, this should permit them to rapidly improve the accuracy of their price forecasts, thereby minimizing the period during which they underestimate the inflation.

The policy implications of the rational expectations view are indeed extreme. Not only do they envision no long-run trade-off between unemployment and inflation, but they see virtually none in the short run either. If correct, what this means is that governmental monetary and fiscal policies are totally incapable of influencing real magnitudes such as the level of production and employment. This, in turn, would imply that stabilization policy as we have known it for over a half-century should be summarily discarded as being unworkable!

Conclusion

When John Maynard Keynes wrote his *General Theory*, it represented an attempt to offer policy solutions to serious economic problems with which the then-dominant theory seemed incapable of coping. His central message was that government could, through judicious use of monetary and fiscal policy, contribute mightily to stabilization, at acceptable levels, of prices, employment, and production. To a generation desperately seeking solutions to the worst economic collapse the nation had ever experienced, it was a heartening message. No longer need we stand by helplessly while forces heretofore thought to be beyond our control buffeted us about. At long last mankind had both the will and the means to control its own economic destiny!

Most of our experience in the following three decades seemed to confirm the validity of Keynes's observations. Business cycles continued in the post–World War II period, but they were relatively mild, short-lived affairs. By the mid-1960s, especially after the 1964 tax cut along with supportive monetary expansion restored the nation to full employment in near-textbook fashion, many economists became convinced that serious unemployment and inflation problems had finally been eliminated.

But by the end of the 1960s, and especially in the 1970s, things began to become unstuck. Not only were we unable to establish full employment with stable prices, but—Professor Phillips notwithstanding—we proved singularly unsuccessful in any efforts to trade off unemployment against inflation. Clearly something was amiss, and economic scholars around the country went back to the drawing boards to attempt to uncover explanations.

The preceding sections on the natural rate of unemployment and its corollary, the accelerationist hypothesis, as well as the more recent rational expectations hypothesis, briefly describe the position of some highly respected members of the economics profession in the 1990s. It would be less than accurate to say that they as yet form a new consensus. While recognizing the existence of new limitations on stabilization policy via aggregate demand management, many economists still see a substantial role for them. Many, indeed, would readily subscribe to the following statement of Professor Modigliani:

We must, therefore, categorically reject the Monetarist appeal to turn back the clock 40 years by discarding the basic message of the General Theory. We should instead concentrate our efforts in an endeavor to make stabilization policies even more effective in the future than they have been in the past![14]

Despite their appeal as a way of explaining the role played by expectations in the inflation of the 1970s, the accelerationist and rational expectations hypotheses have been criticized as requiring unrealistic assumptions and as failing, in any case, to "fit the facts" of the U.S. economy.

Based as they are, on a foundation of neoclassical microeconomics, many versions of the accelerationist hypothesis appear to assume competitive markets, to envision downward as well as upward flexibility of wages and prices, and to treat the labor market as an auction market in which a homogeneous product is bought and sold.[15] This leads to a number of peculiarities not the least of which is the position that all unemployment above the natural rate is seen as voluntary. When demand falls in a competitive world, prices and money wages must fall as a consequence. If, however, workers fail to forecast the decline in prices accurately, they will interpret the cut in money wages as a decline in their real wage. And since it is assumed that the quantity of labor they will offer varies positively with the real wage, they will react to the perceived cut in their real wage by cutting back the quantity of labor supplied. In this version of the accelerationist logic we are thus left with the startling conclusion that ". . . output falls not because of the decline in demand but because of the entirely voluntary reduction in the supply of labor, in response to erroneous perceptions."[16] Mindful of the well-documented fact that voluntary quits tend to *fall*, rather than rise, during periods of declining demand and of the demonstrated downward stickiness of wages and prices, many economists find themselves unable to accept this logic.

Further skepticism regarding the accelerationist hypothesis is aroused by the fact that its conclusions, especially regarding events during periods of declining demand, appear to be inconsistent with the evidence from U.S. experience. When the actual unemployment rate rises above the natural rate, no stimulative boost from the demand side (via expansionary monetary-fiscal policies) is said to be needed because — after some (presumably tolerable) time lag — workers will recognize that prices are no longer rising as fast as before and will modify their wage demands accordingly. Indeed, in the strict logic of the accelerationist hypothesis, "an accelerating deflation should occur when the rate of unemployment increases above the 'natural' rate."[17] But during much of the Great Depression, the long slack period from 1958 to 1964, and the more recent episodes in 1974–1975, and 1981–1982 — all of which are surely periods where the unemployment rate rose well above the natural rate — little evidence of such a development can be seen.

---

[14] Franco Modigliani, "The Monetarist Controversy, or, Should We Forsake Stabilization Policies," *American Economic Review*, March 1977, p. 18.

[15] Ibid., pp. 6–7.

[16] Ibid., p. 4.

[17] Frisch, "Inflation Theory 1963–1975," p. 1297.

As might be expected, there is even more opposition to the more extreme rational expectations hypothesis as applied to macroeconomics. Opponents point out that people actually do have imperfect knowledge with which to predict future price levels — less, surely, than the stabilization authorities — and that, in any case, our experience does not confirm the price flexibility and speedy return to the natural rate of unemployment that the hypothesis implies.

What seems clear as we struggle into the 1990s is that, while much has been learned from the stagflation of past years and several plausible hypotheses have been offered, the economics profession is, unhappily, not yet in a position to fully explain it, much less advise policymakers on just how to prevent its recurrence.

Review Questions

1. Define and contrast demand-pull and cost-push inflation.

2. What does the conventional (short-run) Phillips curve purport to show?

3. The performance of the U.S. economy during the 1970s led some observers to argue that the nation's Phillips curve had shifted to the right. What reasons have been given in support of this view?

4. What are supply shocks? How have they tended to affect U.S. economic performance, especially during the 1970s?

5. Define the natural rate of unemployment. What factors can cause increases in the natural rate? What must ultimately happen if the actual rate of unemployment is driven down to below the natural rate?

6. According to the accelerationist hypothesis, increase in demand to reduce unemployment below the natural rate can only succeed temporarily as a result of workers underestimating the actual rate of inflation. Explain carefully why unemployment is reduced in the short run and why this gain will tend to be wiped out in the long run.

7. "In the long run, a nation's Phillips curve is vertical." Explain, making clear in the process the policy implications of such a viewpoint.

8. What is the major position of the so-called rational expectationists? For policy purposes, what does this view imply about the costs, in terms of increased unemployment, of cutting inflation via decreased levels of aggregate demand?

The Channels of Monetary Policy and Some Alleged Weaknesses

Introduction

The simplified, essentially Keynesian, income determination model presented in Chapter 19 provides an excellent framework for analyzing many macroeconomic problems of major significance. Partly because of the simplified form in which it was presented, however, it is ill suited for dealing directly with a number of policy issues that must be considered more explicitly.

As we have presented it in this book, for example, the Keynesian model implicitly seems to provide only one channel through which money supply changes can affect spending—that of the changing cost of capital (interest cost to borrowers), which raises or lowers the interest cost of financing real investment projects.[1] Such a narrow view of the channels through which monetary policy works is universally considered inadequate, and we shall attempt to broaden our conception of the transmission mechanism of monetary policy in the first part of this chapter.

Following this discussion we briefly consider a number of the alleged weaknesses of monetary policy as a stabilization weapon. Here we depart from the oversimplification implicit in any purely theoretical discussion to consider the effects of existing structural and institutional imperfections on the real-world impacts of monetary policy.

---

[1] It will be recalled that this is an important charge made by the monetarists against reliance on the Keynesian model.

The Channels of Monetary Policy

While monetary economics and opinion regarding the efficacy of monetary policy are now in a state of flux, this is hardly a novel situation. Indeed, it is no overstatement to describe the field as having been in such a state for the past half-century.

Time and again since the 1920s, students concerned with *how* monetary policy works and how *well* it works have had to reorient their thinking in response to new theoretical developments, new empirical evidence, and the hard facts of experience. The result has been a whole series of changes in attitude toward monetary policy, some of them approximating 180° turns.

Faith in the powers of the monetary authorities probably reached its zenith in the 1920s. In that period, a near-hypnotic spell cast by a booming economy, along with a firm conviction that all that was required to keep things moving ever onward and upward was a reasonably intelligent handling of the discount rate, convinced many an observer that a new and permanent "plateau of prosperity" had been achieved. Fiscal policy was as yet unknown and, in any case, "unneeded." Monetary policy — indeed a mere fraction of what we now call monetary policy — was sufficient to handle any problems that might crop up. Or, at least, so it was believed at the time.

The 1930s, of course, irreparably shattered the rose-tinted glasses. Not only had we fallen off the prosperity plateau, but monetary policy seemed utterly incapable of doing anything whatever about it! Truly, a reassessment of the potentialities of monetary policy was in order.

As might have been expected, the reaction went too far. The same policy weapon that some had looked upon as a virtual panacea 10 years earlier now appeared next to useless. Not only had the experience of the 1930s seemed to show it incapable of easing a depression, but empirical evidence that began to appear regarding the lack of responsiveness of investors to interest rate changes (the alleged inelasticity of the MEI curve) seemed to cast serious doubt on its usefulness in either direction.

There the matter stood until after World War II. Monetary policy had reached its lowest ebb. To its opponents, it represented an exercise in futility; and even its staunchest defenders admitted to very serious weaknesses.

The Availability Thesis and Credit Rationing

But a revival was already underway. In the late 1940s and early 1950s — well before the monetarist upsurge — the defenders of monetary policy developed a new thesis to explain how monetary restriction could achieve its objectives no matter how unresponsive investors might be to interest rate increases. This new approach, popularly entitled the *availability thesis*, focused on the effects of monetary restriction on lenders, rather than on borrowers.

In essence, the availability thesis argued that monetary restriction by the central bank (the Fed) would lead lenders to not only raise interest rates (and thereby eliminate some potential borrowing and spending via increases in the cost of capital) but also *ration credit to potential borrowers via nonprice devices.*

The main point of the availability thesis was fairly simple. It was argued that lenders, seeing their reserves (and lending capacity) cut by Federal Reserve action, would not necessarily allow the price of credit (the interest rate) to rise to a market-clearing level but rather would rely on *authoritative, nonprice rationing* (via such mechanisms as more stringent collateral requirements, higher compensating balances, or favoritism to old, valued customers) simply to deny credit to prospective borrowers who were perfectly willing to pay the going market interest rate.[2]

The availability thesis was intended primarily as a response to (1) those who felt that the MEI curve was very inelastic and (2) those who felt that monetary restriction works only via raising the cost of capital (the interest rate). To the extent that it is valid, it matters little that borrowers (potential spenders) cut back only slightly on the quantity of credit demanded as market interest rates rise (that is, it does not really matter if the MEI *is* inelastic), for lenders will simply refuse to lend to many who would be willing to borrow at the going (presumably higher) market rate of interest.[3]

Wealth Effects

A third channel (in addition to the cost of capital and credit rationing channels) through which monetary policy works to affect aggregate demand is what has come to be called the wealth effect of money and credit supply changes.

In essence, the wealth effect channel involves the tendency for money supply increases to increase consumer wealth, which in turn induces a rise in consumer spending. There are two generally accepted elements of the wealth effect channel — the *real balance effect* and an *equity effect.*

The Real Balance Effect   The real balance effect, the careful reader will recall, was introduced in Chapter 20 as a determinant of the slope of the aggregate demand curve. What we said there was that "as the price level falls, the real value of certain types of wealth, like money, rises, thereby raising consumer spending." Here we have reference to the same phenomenon but, instead of a fall in the price level raising the real value of a fixed nominal money supply, we are thinking of an increased nominal money supply with a fixed price level.

---

[2] Another important strand of the availability thesis was the argument that rising interest rates, caused by Federal Reserve restraint, would lower the market value of the U.S. securities in bank portfolios and, because they would then allegedly be unwilling to sell them and realize capital losses, "lock in" banks to their present holdings of U.S. securities. This, it was argued, would keep banks from selling U.S. securities to the public (and absorbing largely idle money) to acquire the excess reserves needed to support an expansion of loans to business (which would surely be active money). If the argument is valid, the "locking-in" effect would prevent banks from promoting an increase in velocity via changes in their earning asset portfolios. Data on the behavior of banks during tight-money periods throw considerable doubt on the potency of the "locking-in" effect.

[3] For an excellent summary of the literature on the availability thesis and credit rationing, see Benjamin M. Friedman, *"Credit Rationing: A Review,"* Staff Economic Studies of the Board of Governors of the Federal Reserve System, 1972. See also Paul S. Anderson and James R. Ostas, "Private Credit Rationing," *New England Economic Review,* Federal Reserve Bank of Boston, May–June 1977.

Although there can be no doubt that increases in the money supply do affect consumption spending in this way, many economists doubt that the effect is very large.

The Equity Effect Of substantially greater impact is the equity effect of money supply changes. This might best be explained as follows.

Suppose that initially society is just satisfied with the relative quantities of money, bonds, stock, and real assets that make up its wealth portfolios. Then assume that the Federal Reserve upsets this equilibrium with an open-market purchase that "inflicts" more money on the public while taking away some bonds.

Clearly the community has no *more* assets or income than before, but the relative proportions have been changed. If the public was "just satisfied" with the proportions of money, bonds, stocks, and real assets before the open-market purchase, it now must have relatively too much money and too few bonds.

That sort of disequilibrium is easily set to rights. The public can simply use the excess money to buy more bonds. But of course there are no more bonds to be had, so their action will raise bond prices and lower interest rates. So far so good and, one may well add, nothing new either.

Note that, although the rise in bond prices may have raised bond values to the level desired to go along with the higher quantity of money, we now have too high a value of bonds and money relative to stocks and real assets. So some more balance sheet reshuffling must go on, with some of the new money spilling over into the stock market and the market for real assets (consumer durables, maybe?). If and when the latter happens, the monetary policy has already raised aggregate demand somewhat.

That isn't all there is to it. Note that along the way, during all these attempts to reestablish desired proportions of money, bonds, stocks, and real assets, the demand for a fixed quantity of bonds and stock has risen. Necessarily their prices must have risen in response. What do these price increases mean to their holders?

Security holders, especially stockholders, will find that the money (market) value of their holdings will have increased. In other words, their net worth—their personal wealth holdings—will be greater than before. Now, of course, wealth is not the same as income and people would not be expected to spend (on consumption) nearly as large a fraction of their increase in wealth as of an equivalent increase in their incomes. Nevertheless, such an improvement in wealth positions has been shown to lead to significant boosts in consumption.[4]

The Exchange Rate Effect

An additional important channel through which monetary policy affects aggregate demand is via effects on exchange rates.

The rationale here is straightforward. Contractionary monetary policy in this country raises U.S. interest rates. That, in turn, causes foreigners to demand more dollars (to "financially" invest here) which causes the dollar to appreciate

---

[4] For a more thorough discussion of this area, see Roger W. Spencer, "Channels of Monetary Influence: A Survey," *Review*, Federal Reserve Bank of St. Louis, November 1974. See also Frederic S. Mishkin, "Liquidity, and the Role of Monetary Policy in Consumer Durable Demand," *New England Economic Review*, November–December 1976.

vis-à-vis the currencies of our trading partners. This increase in the international value of the dollar makes foreign goods and services cheaper to Americans, raising our imports and American goods and service more expensive to foreigners, cutting our exports. The net result is a decline in the "net export" component of total spending.

The Relative Importance of the Monetary Policy Channels   Econometric studies carried out at the Federal Reserve Board indicate that monetary policy works its way through to exert significant effects on total spending. A 1 percent reduction in the federal funds rate, for example, is estimated to increase total spending by $15.3 billion after one year with the impact rising to over $43 billion after three years.[5]

It is interesting to consider the relative importance of the different channels in producing this effect on spending. Two decades ago it was estimated that 50 percent of the effect on spending came via the cost-of-capital route, 33 to 44 percent via the wealth effect, with the remaining 6 to 17 percent attributable to the credit-rationing channel.[6]

That result, however, was estimated in an era when exchange rates were being held stable by government action, and Regulation Q ceilings on interest rates were contributing significantly to periodic episodes of disintermediation. In recent years the elimination of Regulation Q and the flexibility of exchange rates has caused the exchange rate channel to replace the credit rationing channel. Consequently, in a 1990 estimate, after three years, 46 percent of the impact of monetary policy on spending is attributed to the cost-of-capital channel, 31 percent to the wealth channel, and 24 percent to the exchange rate channel.[7]

Problems with Monetary Policy

By now virtually all economists, monetarist and Keynesian alike, are convinced that the money supply is a very important determinant of the level of aggregate demand. But not even its staunchest supporters believe that monetary policy, especially given the institutional structure within which it is implemented, is anything close to a panacea for the nation's problems with economic instability. This section considers some of the alleged weaknesses of monetary policy as it is currently constituted.

Doubts About Expansionary Monetary Policy

For years it was popular to sum up the relative effectiveness of monetary policy in recession and inflation with that overworked cliché: "You can pull on a string but you can't push on it." The obvious inference, of course, was that monetary

---

[5] See Eileen Mauskopf, "The Transmission Channels of Monetary Policy: How Have They Changed," *Federal Reserve Bulletin*, December 1990.

[6] See Frank DeLeeuw and Edward M. Gramlich, "The Channels of Monetary Policy," *Federal Reserve Bulletin*, June 1969.

[7] Mauskopf, "The Transmission of Monetary Policy," p. 987.

restriction to counter inflation has more chance of success than does monetary ease to combat recession. Some years ago, in fact, there was almost universal agreement on this generality.

In recent years, however, as a result of both theoretical developments and new empirical evidence, there has been a noticeable change of attitude regarding the capacity of money supply changes to generate expansion as well as contraction of demand. Today it is likely that only a relatively few economists still cling to the nonsymmetrical view of monetary policy. Nevertheless, since it is a position still held by some, we consider it briefly.

Their reasoning runs something like this. There can be little doubt that the Federal Reserve has sufficient power to force a reduction in spending because the impact of substantial money supply reductions surely cannot be *indefinitely* offset by increases in velocity. But the effects of monetary expansion, especially when the economy is mired in a deep recession or depression, may be less certain.

In such a situation the Fed can, of course, provide the banks with sufficient excess reserves to *permit* expansion. But whether and how soon such action will result in substantial increases in spending, it is alleged, is open to question. After all, it is not completely inconceivable that increases in the monetary base might be partially offset by a decrease in the size of the money multiplier caused by a sharp rise in desired excess reserves under such conditions.

True, the interest rate (cost of capital) will be forced down by such action, but if the MEI curve has shifted to the left and become more inelastic (as has been argued typically happens during recession), interest rate reductions may lead to little increase in investment spending. Indeed, if the recession is sufficiently severe and profit prospects sufficiently bleak, even a *zero* rate of interest may be inadequate to call forth sufficient additional investment spending.

And how about monetary policy's so-called wealth effect? No doubt it would work in the desired direction, but its magnitude under severe recession conditions is open to question. Given a pessimistic outlook, wealth holders may choose to hold a large proportion of their wealth in idle money form (thereby reducing velocity). And given the typical performance of the stock market during recession, it is difficult to conceive of a very substantial rush to purchase stocks and drive up the market value of equities.

All this must not be carried too far. Those who consider an expansionary monetary policy during recession to be weak (relative to its potential to curb excessive spending during a boom) do not deny that it does work in the desired direction. Their view, rather, is that to achieve recovery, reliance on monetary policy *alone* may require an unacceptably long time period to do the job. Perhaps their attitude could best be summed up as arguing that in such circumstances monetary expansion is "necessary, but by no means sufficient."

The Problem of Cost-Push (Sellers') Inflation or Supply Shocks

As does fiscal policy, monetary policy works by affecting aggregate demand. If the problem happens to be demand-pull inflation wherein prices are being pulled up via an excess of aggregate demand at full employment, a reduction in demand via monetary restriction is entirely appropriate, since it gets at the core of the problem—excessive aggregate demand.

But if the source of the inflationary pressure is not excessive demand but rather the exploitation of monopoly power by sellers—that is, cost-push, or sellers', inflation—monetary restraint may not be a viable remedy at all. Let us see why this is so. Cost-push, or sellers', inflation has been defined as *a rise in the price level that is initiated by price (or wage) setters employing monopoly power to simply mark up the prices of the goods or services they sell, in the absence of an excess of aggregate demand.* It may be initiated by unions using their bargaining power to push up wages, which, by raising production costs, leads to a rise in prices; by management employing its market power to increase profit margins; or, as we have seen, by outsiders such as the OPEC nations exploiting cartel power to quadruple oil prices.

Whatever the identity of its originators, cost-push inflation constitutes a dilemma for government policymakers. In Chapter 20 we considered this dilemma using the aggregate demand-aggregate supply format. Let us look at it here in the context of the equation of exchange.

Assume, for purposes of illustration, that initially M equals $200 billion, V′ equals 3, P equals $4, and Q equals 150 billion—a full-employment level of output. Obviously this is a favorable situation in which we have equilibrium in the production of goods and services (total spending equals production) at the full-employment level. Now suppose that some price setters with sufficient monopoly power to implement it decide to raise their prices to a level sufficiently high to increase the overall average price to $5 per unit. What is the situation now? Clearly,

$$MV' < PQ$$

$$(\$200b \cdot 3) < (\$5 \cdot 150b)$$

That is, aggregate demand now falls short of aggregate supply, since $600 billion of spending will not purchase 150 billion units priced at $5 each. If conditions stay exactly as they are, only 120 billion units will be purchased with the current level of demand and the immediate effect of the unsold inventory of 30 billion is likely to be a layoff of workers. Unemployment, then, will coexist with inflation.

What can government do about it through monetary (or fiscal) policy? If it employs the same sort of contractionary policy called for to combat demand-pull inflation, that is, cutting aggregate demand *below* the present $600 billion level, it will surely *worsen* the unemployment problem while, in the short run at least, accomplishing little toward reducing the inflationary pressure. If, on the other hand, it chooses to combat the rising unemployment by implementing a *rise* in aggregate demand to $750 billion, while all 150 billion units can now be purchased at the $5 price, it will have dealt with the unemployment problem by *ratifying* (or accommodating) the inflation already experienced.[8]

What seems clear is that monetary policy (as well as fiscal policy) is ill equipped to deal with inflation that is not initiated by excess demand. Monetary

---

[8] And, indeed, by "bailing out" sellers with unsold inventories, set itself up for further likely rounds of inflation.

policy's stabilization potential is effectuated through aggregate demand, and if that is not the source of the problem, the Fed's ability to combat it is, in the short run at least, severely constrained.

The Problem of Time Lags

Among the most serious of the attacks against monetary policy as it is now employed is the charge that, because of time lags involved in its operation, it actually reinforces the business cycle. That is, discretionary monetary policy, aimed at minimizing inflation and unemployment, misses the mark by such a margin that it makes them worse.

There is nothing complicated about the logic involved and, indeed, as we have already seen, it has led to one important monetarist policy position. It starts from the universally recognized fact that monetary policy measures do not affect aggregate demand instantaneously. There is a process involved that takes time to work. Those who believe that discretionary monetary policy is positively destabilizing simply argue that the time required for this process to work itself out is very long — so long, indeed, that policy measures undertaken to combat ongoing inflation are only likely to come to fruition (cut aggregate demand) some months after the inflationary pressure has disappeared and the economy has turned to recession. In that case, of course, the monetary policy will only make the recession worse.

Similarly, in their view, monetary action undertaken to raise aggregate demand to combat recession can also be expected to make matters worse, because by the time aggregate demand is actually increased by monetary measures taken many months previously, the economy may have recovered and be well on the road to inflation. The antirecession measure would thus merely magnify the succeeding inflation.

The relevant time lags have, for purposes of discussion, been divided into three types. The first, the *recognition lag,* is the time between the development of a need for action in the economy and recognition of that need by policymakers. Unless and until forecasting techniques provide much more dependable results, this period will be, almost certainly, several months long. Second, there is an *administrative lag,* the time between the recognition of need for action and the action's execution. For monetary policy, with the seven-member semi-independent Board of Governors in the driver's seat, this lag is probably very short.

Finally, there is an additional period, which has been called the *operational lag,* between action by the policy agency and its final effect on demand in the economy. For monetary policy, for example, this would be the time between an actual sale of securities on the open market and its intended reduction in spending.

Everyone agrees that monetary policy involves time lags. Where there is disagreement is on the length and variability of those lags. As we have seen, Professor Friedman sees the lags as both long and variable. This, indeed, is the basic reason for his advocacy of the elimination of discretion in monetary policy in favor of a law requiring a fixed rate of increase in money each year.

The measurement of policy time lags, however, is an extremely difficult task, and, as we have seen, both the St. Louis Federal Reserve Bank and the Federal Reserve–M.I.T.–Penn econometric models conclude that money supply changes tend to begin affecting GNP rather quickly. Other investigators have come up with still different lag measurements.[9]

None of these studies claims to have the last word, the definitive answer, on the length of these lags. But elusive though it is, that answer is of crucial importance. For if the lag *is* relatively short, then discretionary monetary policy can be relied on to make some contribution toward business-cycle stabilization. If, on the other hand, it is as long and variable as some investigators believe, then it follows logically that discretionary monetary policy should be abandoned altogether.

Implementing the Friedman proposal would, of course, require far-reaching changes in the U.S. monetary machinery. The present discretionary power possessed by members of the Board of Governors to employ their tools as they see fit would be abolished in favor of a law requiring the Federal Reserve to take such action as would raise the money supply by a fixed percentage each year, come what may. The present monetary managers would thus become mere technicians instead of policymakers.

Such a change, if it were to be made, could be defended by its advocates as a purely pragmatic act, based solely on the evidence from the past that discretion has not done an adequate job. Yet there would be important philosophical overtones. Long before the evidence cited earlier was developed, Friedman and his illustrious predecessor at the University of Chicago, Professor Henry Simons, had argued for an end to discretion in economic policy on more fundamental and philosophical grounds.

For example, over 50 years ago Professor Simons said,

> A democratic, free-enterprise system implies, and requires for its effective functioning and survival, a stable framework of definite rules, laid down in legislation and subject to change only gradually and with careful regard for the vested interests of participants in the economic game. It is peculiarly essential economically that there should be a minimum of uncertainty for enterprisers and investors as to monetary conditions in the future — and, politically that the plausible expedient of setting up "authorities" instead of rules, with respect to matters of such fundamental importance, be avoided, or accepted only as a very temporary arrangement. The most important objective of sound liberal policy, apart from the establishment of highly competitive conditions in industry and the narrow limitations of political control over relative prices, should be that of securing a monetary system governed by definite rule.[10]

It thus seems evident that, although part of the steam behind the proposals to eliminate discretion in monetary policy comes from empirical evidence indicat-

[9] See, for example, Thomas Mayer, "The Inflexibility of Monetary Policy," *Review of Economics and Statistics,* November 1958; A. Ando, E. C. Brown, R. Solow, and J. Karaken, "Lags in Fiscal and Monetary Policy," *Stabilization Policies,* Commission on Money and Credit (Englewood Cliffs, NJ: Prentice-Hall, 1963); and Michael J. Hamburger, "The Lag in the Effect of Monetary Policy," *Monetary Aggregates and Monetary Policy,* Federal Reserve Bank of New York, 1974.

[10] Henry C. Simons, "Rules Versus Authorities in Monetary Policy," *Journal of Political Economy,* February 1936.

ing that time lags have kept discretion from working well in the past, part of it is also based on a more fundamental distrust of discretionary policy, in principle.

General Credit Controls Apply Capriciously to Groups of Spenders; the Charge of Unplanned Selectivity

Another major set of criticisms centers not on whether spending is cut or by how much it is cut or when it is cut but rather on *whose* spending is deterred by monetary restraint. To state the issue directly, it has been argued that tightening of general credit controls has a disproportionately severe effect on the spending plans of certain groups while leaving other groups of spenders relatively unscathed. The result is, these critics argue, an unplanned, capricious, and, in substantial degree, undesirable selectivity in the impact of general credit restraint.

Let us run through the essence of the argument from the beginning. Credit restraint, if it is to work at all, must have a bite. Some people who would have carried out added spending in the absence of the policy must now find it unwise or impossible to do so. The question with which we are concerned is the identity of those groups whose spending is inhibited.

In a first approximation, this would not seem to be too difficult a problem. General credit restraint reduces the total supply of credit available. This tends to raise its price — in this case, the rate of interest. The prime function of this higher interest rate is to ration out the smaller amount of credit available. If there is a perfect market, those who desire to use credit for purposes that will most satisfy consumer desires will be able to afford the higher interest cost and still obtain it, and those who would have borrowed for less socially desirable purposes will be *rationed out* of the market. Consequently, so the argument runs, it is those who desired credit for the least socially desirable purposes who will find themselves unable to obtain it. And surely, because for the restrictive policy to work at all, *someone's* spending must be cut, this is the optimum result.

But, say the proponents of the *unplanned selectivity* thesis, this argument grossly oversimplifies the situation. To begin with, the credit market is far from a *perfect* market. It is not just the rise in the price of credit that impersonally rations out the smaller supply but — and this comes from no less avid supporters of monetary policy than the developers of the availability thesis themselves — also a significant amount of authoritative (nonprice) credit rationing by individual lenders. Although both Borrower A and Borrower B may be willing and able to pay the higher interest rate required, the lender may now arbitrarily decide to grant the request of one and refuse that of the other. How can we be sure that this provides an optimum allocation? Then, too, are there not a number of structural imperfections that could have the effect of diverting credit from one sector to another to the detriment of the general welfare?

It is, by now, rather generally accepted that three sectors of the economy have tended to bear disproportionately heavy burdens from general credit restraint. These are the residential construction sector, the state and local government sector, and small and new businesses. Let us consider each of these in turn.

The Residential Home Construction Sector   It has become increasingly apparent that monetary restraint hits the home construction industry with special severity.[11] It requires only a cursory glance at the home construction data for the past 30 years to arouse one's suspicions.

Since the end of the bond-support program during and immediately after World War II, there have been six well-defined periods of monetary restraint of sufficient duration to be recognized as such. These include 1956–1957, 1959, 1966, 1969, 1974–1975, and 1980–1982. In four of these tight-money periods, the residential housing industry slumped perceptibly.

From 1955 to 1957, single-family dwelling starts fell off from 1,194,400 to 872,000. Such a decline in an economy with rapidly rising incomes, population, and family formation can hardly be a mere random fluctuation. A closer look at the mid-1950s data reveals that almost the entire decrease in housing starts occurred in homes financed with government-guaranteed mortgages.

Why the special impact on FHA- and VA-financed homes? Almost certainly, it was largely a result of unrealistic interest rate limitations on such mortgages. At the time, lenders financing home building with FHA or VA mortgages were permitted to charge no more than 4.5 percent. As long as alternative opportunities are earning no more than this, a 4.5 percent interest rate ceiling has no effect at all. But 1956–1957 was a tight-money period and interest rates generally were rising. Lenders, who had more takers for the available credit than they could accommodate, quite naturally began to back away from taking mortgages on which they could charge only 4.5 percent when numerous alternative opportunities offered them 6 and 7 percent. The result, hardly surprising, was a dramatic cutback in housing starts financed with government-guaranteed mortgages.

In the 1960s, 1970s, and 1980s, as Table 23-1 makes abundantly clear, each of the especially tight money periods, 1966, 1969, 1974–1975, and 1980–1982, exhibited notable decreases in single-family homes started.

In these more recent periods, however, the chief culprit appears to have been *disintermediation.* As interest rates generally rose, governmental authorities, via Regulation Q and its companion pieces applying to savings and loan associations and mutual savings banks, kept interest rates that savings institutions were permitted to pay time depositors well below the alternatives open elsewhere to savers. The result, as might well have been expected, was a sharp decline in the flow of funds to savings and loan associations, savings banks, and commercial banks savings departments, leading to a dramatic restriction in mortgage money available.

The problem, and its relation to monetary policy, was put most succinctly by Professor James S. Duesenberry of Harvard, in his capacity as chairman of the President's Commission on Mortgage Interest Rates:

if we did not know it before, it is now clear that homebuilding does bear an excessive share of the burden of a restrictive monetary policy. That is so partly because

---

[11] For a contrary view, see N. M. Bowsher and L. Kalish, "Does Slower Monetary Expansion Discriminate Against Housing?" *Review*, St. Louis Federal Reserve Bank, June 1968.

TABLE 23-1   New single-family housing starts, 1960–1989 (thousands)

Year	Number of houses started	Year	Number of houses started
1960	995	1975	892
1961	974	1976	1,163
1962	991	1977	1,451
1963	1,021	1978	1,433
1964	972	1979	1,194
1965	964	1980	852
1966	779	1981	705
1967	844	1982	663
1968	900	1983	1,067
1969	814	1984	1,084
1970	813	1985	1,072
1971	1,151	1986	1,179
1972	1,309	1987	1,146
1973	1,132	1988	1,081
1974	888	1989	1,003

Source: Federal Reserve Bulletin.

homebuilding is financed mainly with debt and partly because of some special features of our mortgage market.

Of these special features, the most important are the excessive reliance of the mortgage market on funds raised through thrift institutions and the adverse effects of the ceiling on insured and guaranteed mortgages.[12]

The elimination of Regulation Q as a result of the Monetary Control Act of 1980 plus a reasonably strong tendency to remove or moderate legal interest rate ceilings seem likely to reduce sharply monetary contraction's heretofore disproportionate effect on the housing sector. How much, only time will tell.

State and Local Government Capital Expenditures   Experience in the mid-1950s and once again in the decade of the 1960s also led to a strong conviction that state and local government capital outlays were disproportionately restricted by monetary restraint.

The essence of this problem was well stated over two decades ago by Tilford Gaines, economist for Manufacturers Hanover Trust:

Almost equally troubling is the impact that tight money and credit conditions in 1969 have had upon the ability of state and local authorities to finance themselves in the municipal bond market. In this case, the fact that credit policy has been

[12] J. S. Duesenberry, testimony on the Mortgage Interest Rate Commission Report, Hearings Before the Committee on Banking and Currency, U.S. Senate, 91st Congr., 1st sess., September 1969, p. 3.

centered upon the ability of the commercial banks to increase their loans and investments, and given that banks account for the bulk of all net purchases of such securities, implies that primary responsibility for the shortage of funds in the tax-exempt market does rest with Federal Reserve policy. To the extent that public expenditures that have had to be deferred because they could not be financed would have been on non-essential projects, the market's allocative process has made a useful contribution to restraining spending and restoring price stability. But the market usually allocates money on the basis of credit worthiness not essentiality, and it is more than likely that some essential schools, public health and other facilities have been delayed.[13]

In the tight money period of the mid-1950s, a sharp reduction in the sales of state and local government securities in 1955 and 1956 led to speculation that monetary restriction was playing special havoc with state and local borrowing at that time. As Table 23-2 indicates, the same sort of evidence showed up again in the 1966 and 1969 tight-money years. In 1974–1975, however, the data are less persuasive, but a similar pattern reappears in the 1979–1981 period.

As in the case of housing, some significant structural peculiarities of the state and local bond market go a long way toward explaining that sector's apparent sensitivity to credit restraint.

One institutional factor of no small significance in the past was the practice, by most states, of limiting by law the interest rate local governments can pay. For many years, such limits had been set at 5 or 6 percent. At those levels, no real

TABLE 23-2 New issues of state and local government general obligations, 1962–1989 (millions of dollars)

Year	New securities sold	Year	New securities sold
1962	5,582	1976	18,040
1963	5,855	1977	18,042
1964	6,417	1978	17,854
1965	7,177	1979	12,109
1966	6,804	1980	14,100
1967	8,985	1981	12,394
1968	9,269	1982	21,094
1969	7,725	1983	21,566
1970	11,850	1984	26,485
1971	15,220	1985	52,622
1972	13,305	1986	44,801
1973	12,257	1987	30,589
1974	13,563	1988	30,312
1975	16,020	1989	35,774

Source: Federal Reserve Bulletin.

[13] Tilford Gaines, "Federal Reserve Policy Review," *Economic Report* (New York: Manufacturers Hanover Trust Company, November 1969).

problem was encountered during the 1930s, 1940s, and early 1950s, as the market interest rates local governments were required to pay were usually well below the legal limits.

As interest rates began rising in the late 1950s, and especially during the 1960s, however, market interest rates began more and more frequently to edge above legal limits for many governments, and this meant real problems. Many local governments, seeking to borrow money within their own legal limits, found no lenders willing to accommodate them. As a result, especially in 1966 and 1969, many local government projects had to be postponed.

A second important factor in the municipal bond market is the fact that interest on state and local government securities is federal income tax exempt. Now normally, of course, the tax-exemption feature is an advantage to these governments, allowing them to borrow at lower interest cost than would be possible without it. But it does create an odd market for municipal securities, which makes it especially susceptible to monetary restraint.

The prime buyers of state and local securities are high-income individuals and commercial banks. High-income individuals have an obvious interest in the tax-exemption feature, and commercial banks, until recent years the most heavily taxed of the financial institutions, have found them attractive for the same reason.

During periods of monetary restraint, however, commercial banks, pressed for reserves, have withdrawn almost completely from the municipals market. This means that, at such times, many more state and local securities must be absorbed by individuals. The market for state and local obligations is thus drastically narrowed as a result of credit restriction. The result is that, to entice enough lower-income individuals to purchase the municipal securities seeking placement, very sharp increases in interest yields are necessary. State and local governments, therefore, may find themselves paying rates that are up by 50 percent when other rates have only increased by 25 percent. In the early 1960s, for example, interest rates on state and local securities were about 70 percent of taxable corporate bond yields. By January 1970, they had risen until they were 80 percent as high. Put another way, the average interest yield on state and local bonds more than doubled between 1965 and January 1970, while that on corporate bonds rose by less than 80 percent. And from 1973 to tight money 1975, while corporate bond yields were rising just about 20 percent, municipal bond interest rates shot up by a full 35 percent.

All this seems to show quite clearly that state and local government *borrowing* has been noticeably affected by monetary restraint. But borrowing and spending are two different things. Despite the apparent impact on their borrowing, state and local government capital *expenditures* in tight-money years do not appear to be cut so sharply. This was true in all recent periods of restraint. For example, the Federal Reserve found that in 1966, although large government borrowing was apparently cut by $1.4 billion, the capital spending reduction was estimated at only $250 million.[14] Apparently, by short-term borrowing and using

[14] P. F. McGouldrick, and J. E. Petersen, "Monetary Restraint and Borrowing and Capital Spending by Large State and Local Governments in 1966," *Federal Reserve Bulletin*, July 1968, pp. 522–571.

funds borrowed in earlier periods but not yet spent, governments were able to go ahead with spending programs with little reduction.[15]

Conclusions, therefore, are difficult to draw on this point. Monetary restriction surely has notable effects on state and local government borrowing as well as on their interest costs, but the extent to which this carries over to spending is not quite so clear.

Borrowing by Small and New Businesses　Another sector said to be uniquely susceptible to the cutting edge of a tight-money policy is that of new and small businesses. The argument here is intuitively appealing, although, once again, we have little reliable quantitative evidence to document it.

When credit is restricted, it is argued, the market power of lenders permits them authoritatively to *ration* credit, granting the credit requests of some while refusing others. It is to be expected, when there is not enough to go around, that the large, well-known, long-established concern will have preference over the small, newly established credit applicant. Thus, in the view of the critics, the larger, well-established firms will suffer little deprivation from credit rationing, while the new, unknown firm will bear the burden. To make matters worse, the newer firms, having little or no retained earnings, are the ones most urgently in need of external financing.[16]

Although this result may or may not be justifiable from the viewpoint of relative risks, its effect on the nation's economic growth could be undesirable because new products and new ideas, as often as not, are introduced by new firms struggling to establish themselves. If a tight-money policy shuts them out, the ultimate cost could be considerable.[17]

---

[15] A survey of smaller governments showed that a larger percentage of borrowing postponements led to expenditure postponements than was the case for the larger governments. See J. E. Petersen and P. F. McGouldrick, "Monetary Restraint, Borrowing, and Capital Spending by Small Local Governments and State Colleges in 1966," *Federal Reserve Bulletin,* December 1968.

[16] Some evidence of this effect was cited by *The Wall Street Journal*, December 10, 1969:

> Times are getting uncomfortably difficult for many small companies.
>
> Turning a profit has recently grown harder for business in general. But problems that are only beginning to trouble big corporations already are severely hurting many small firms. The list of woes includes super-tight money, scarce and costly skilled labor and slow payment of bills by some customers. Owners of some small firms, convinced that still more difficult times lie ahead, are reluctantly selling their businesses, usually through exchanges of stock, to big corporations. . . .
>
> A few statistics clearly indicate that small companies are faring worse than their big brothers. Last month a *Wall Street Journal* survey of 436 large corporations found that after-tax profits in the third quarter were 3.7% higher than a year earlier. But a later Commerce Department survey of *all* corporations, small as well as large, found that after-tax profits in the third quarter were no higher than in the 1968 period.
>
> "Obviously, the smaller companies dragged the total down," says a Commerce Department economist.

[17] For a survey of this and other aspects of bank nonprice rationing, see Paul S. Anderson and James R. Ostas, "Private Credit Rationing," *New England Economic Review*, May–June 1977. Anderson and Ostas conclude that credit rationing "may be characterized as one of the costs of contracyclical monetary policy, with the highest price paid by new and high-risk ventures." (p. 37)

Monetary Restraint Does Cut Aggregate Demand, but Its Effect May Be Weak or Hard to Predict

The reputations of some of those who argue that monetary policy is destabilizing and some of those who argue that general credit controls are seriously discriminatory are such as to command solid respect and careful consideration. But respect and consideration do not necessarily imply agreement.

The majority of economists today are neither so pessimistic regarding the time lags involved as to be prepared to eliminate discretion nor so convinced of the capriciousness of quantitative controls as to be willing to abandon them. Judiciously administered monetary policy still seems capable, in the minds of most, of making positive contributions toward stabilization of economic activity.

But among this large group, the degree of faith in monetary policy varies widely. At one end of the spectrum are those whose confidence in the potency of credit control is very firm. Not so for many others, however. For them the record reveals too many disappointing experiences to justify implicit and unreserved faith. "Of course monetary restraint is helpful," they seem to say, "but we need to guard against expecting too much from it. Let us make use of monetary policy, by all means, but let's also be aware of its limitations."

Let us now consider two additional factors that may operate so as to weaken the effectiveness of monetary restraint.

Increasing Interest Rates May Not Greatly Restrict Some Investment Projects   The effect of higher interest rates on the investment spending of many firms may be disappointingly small for a number of reasons.

One may be the fact that a very large percentage of investment spending is financed with internal funds rather than those borrowed on the capital market. In 1990, for example, when gross private domestic investment totaled $745 billion, depreciation allowances and corporate retained earnings combined provided over $591 billion of the needed funds. Therefore, just over 20 percent of the funds needed to finance the year's investment spending had to be borrowed from external lenders.

In theory, the interest cost involved should be considered roughly the same whether borrowed externally (with a consequent out-of-pocket interest payment) or obtained from internal sources through the firm's own saving. For, as noted earlier, there is an implicit interest cost involved in the use of internally generated funds to purchase capital goods directly which is equal to the interest return given up by not lending them out to someone else at the going market rate.

Despite the airtight logic involved in this argument, there is some room for doubt that all firms *do* maximize profits by recognizing that increases in market interest rates necessarily raise the opportunity cost of internally generated funds.

To the extent that this is the case, a rise in the market rate of interest from 10 to 15 percent, as a result of credit restriction, may not really be looked upon as an increase in investment cost. Certainly, a firm that refuses to use internal funds for any purpose other than financing its own investment outlays, and possesses ample amounts for its needs, will be less responsive to market rate increases than will one forced to rely solely on external funds. And the fact that a preponderance of investment is financed internally may add significantly to the alleged insensitivity to interest rate changes.

Also, the market power of some firms may play a role in explaining borrower insensitivity to interest rate increases. To oligopolistic firms, the rise in credit costs, not unlike a hike in taxes, may provide just the impetus needed to permit a comparable price increase. If this is the case, the burden of the interest rate increase will fall on consumers rather than reducing investors' profit prospects. Such shifting of the burden to consumers is even easier for regulated public utilities selling a distinctive service subject to highly inelastic demand. Here the firms need merely show the regulatory agency evidence that their costs have been raised to justify a rate increase. And if consumer demand is sufficiently inelastic, little, if any, cutback in expenditures would be expected.

Shifting Commercial Bank Portfolios May Permit Partially Offsetting Velocity Increases   Although no economists today would expect money supply decreases to be totally offset by equivalent velocity increases, there is a good deal of evidence indicating that, for a variety of reasons, monetary authorities must be prepared for *some* weakening in their effects from this source. A restriction in the supply of money leads quite naturally to ingenious efforts on the part of the public and the financial community to make the smaller money supply "do more work" than before.

No better evidence of this ingenuity exists than the development of the federal funds market, which, after all, is little more than a device to make an existing supply of bank reserves stretch a bit farther. When the credit restraint screws are tightened, the banking system does not idly accept its fate but rather seeks to make the reserves it has go as far as possible. The effect is to lessen, to some degree, the impact of the restraint policy. The striking pace of financial innovation in the late 1970s and 1980s serves well to illustrate this phenomenon.

Another example of the banking system's response to a restriction of reserves is the now familiar practice of unloading U.S. securities during tight-money periods to acquire the excess reserves needed to make more business loans. If, for example, a member bank sells U.S. securities to a member of the public who pays by check, the transaction reduces demand deposits and, consequently, required reserves for the system. As total reserves are unaffected, the net effect is a rise in excess reserves. These excess reserves, then, provide the basis for an increase in loans to business.

Note that such a portfolio switch alters neither total bank reserves nor the size of the money supply. But if the old demand deposit given up by the purchaser of the U.S. securities was largely idle money in asset balances or resulted from an effort to economize on transactions balances while the new demand deposit created to lend to the business investor is active money likely to be spent (as is almost certain), then the bank's action has fostered a rise in total spending (MV') by facilitating an increase in velocity.[18]

---

[18] One part of the availability thesis is the argument that increases in interest rates induced by a "tight-money" policy will, by driving down the market value of U.S. securities, "lock in" banks to their current security portfolio because they will be reluctant to sell them and realize capital losses on them. The data in Table 23-3 provide some grounds for doubting the effectiveness of this "locking-in" argument.

TABLE 23-3 Loans and U.S. securities at commercial banks, 1953–1985 (billions of dollars)

Year	Loans	U.S. securities	Change in loans	Change in securities
1953	66.2	$ 62.2	—	—
1954	69.1	67.6	+$2.9	+$5.4
1955	80.6	60.3	+11.5	−7.3
1956	88.1	57.2	+7.5	−3.1
1957	91.5	56.9	+3.4	−0.3
1958	95.6	65.1	+4.1	+8.2
1959	110.5	57.7	+14.9	+7.4
1960	116.7	59.9	+6.2	+2.2
1961	123.6	65.3	+6.9	+5.4
1962	137.3	64.7	+13.7	−0.6
1963	153.7	61.5	+16.4	−3.2
1964	172.9	60.8	+19.2	−0.7
1965	198.2	57.1	+25.3	−3.7
1966	213.9	53.5	+15.7	−3.6
1967	231.3	59.4	+17.4	+5.9
1968	258.2	60.7	+26.9	+1.3
1969	279.4	51.2	+21.2	−9.5
1970	292.0	57.8	+12.6	+6.6
1971	320.9	60.6	+28.9	+2.8
1972	378.9	62.6	+58.0	+2.0
1973	460.5	58.5	+81.6	−4.1
1974	520.1	53.6	+59.6	−4.9
1975	517.4	82.2	−2.7	+28.6
1976	555.0	100.8	+37.6	+18.6
1977	632.5	99.8	+77.5	−1.0
1978	747.0	93.8	+114.5	−6.0
1979	849.9	94.5	+102.9	+0.7
1980	915.1	110.0	+65.2	+15.5
1981	974.9	110.9	+59.8	+0.9
1982	1,042.3	130.9	+67.4	+20.0
1983	1,122.7	188.8	+80.4	+57.9
1984	1,314.7	183.4	+192.0	−5.4
1985	1.449.7	192.2	+135.0	+8.8

Source: Federal Reserve Bulletin.

To what extent do banks actually alter their earning asset portfolios in such a manner and thereby partially offset the intended effect of Federal Reserve policy? Quite a bit, as Table 23-3 makes clear.

Note especially the years 1955–1956, 1965–1966, 1969, and 1973–1974. All were periods of more or less tight money when the Federal Reserve was attempting to restrict demand. In all five periods, banks sharply increased their loans — *partly as a result of excess reserves provided by the sale of U.S. securities.* Glance also at the years 1958–1959, 1966–1967, 1970–1971, 1975–1976, and 1983. These were, in general, easy-money years during which the FRS was providing the banking system with substantial additional reserves. What is striking is the unmistakable impression that banks tend to load up on U.S. securities in easy-money years and then sell them off to permit a larger increase in business loans during tight-money episodes. When they do so, they tend to facilitate undesired (by the FRS) shifts in velocity.

Review Questions

1. Carefully explain the three channels through which money supply changes are said to affect total spending.

2. "Cost-push inflation creates a dilemma for policymakers." Explain carefully, making clear your understanding of the nature of cost-push inflation as well as the problems involved in controlling it via monetary and fiscal policy.

3. What are the three time lags associated with monetary and fiscal policy? Which of the lags would you expect would be longer for monetary policy, and which for discretionary fiscal policy? What bearing do the duration and variability of these lags have on monetarist policy prescriptions?

4. How might one defend selective credit controls as, in practice if not in theory, more appropriate than general credit controls? What impact would you expect financial deregulation, such as was included in the Monetary Control Act of 1980, to have on the efficiency of general credit controls?

5. Carefully explain how market imperfections have, in the past, made the housing sector peculiarly susceptible to monetary contraction.

6. Discuss the factors that expose state and local government borrowing to monetary restraint. Do you think tax exemption on the income from municipal securities is a good idea? Why or why not?

7. In what way may changing commercial bank earning assets play a role in modifying the intended effects of monetary policy?

Alternatives to Monetary Policy for Economic Stabilization

Aside from those advocating the most extreme form of the monetarist position, economists generally recognize that monetary policy alone is likely to be inadequate to provide an entirely satisfactory degree of economic stability and growth. This chapter briefly considers the major policy alternatives.

Fiscal Policy

The prime complement to monetary policy is *fiscal policy*. Let us define fiscal policy as *alterations in tax revenue and/or government expenditures that are intended to affect the level of aggregate demand.*

This definition is sufficiently broad to cover both *discretionary fiscal* policy and the nondiscretionary variety, popularly known as the *automatic stabilizers*. Discretionary fiscal policy requires action by the legislature to change tax laws or government expenditure programs with the intent of altering aggregate demand.[1] The automatic stabilizers, on the other hand, are laws already on the books (such as the personal income tax, the corporate profits tax, and the unemployment compensation program) that operate automatically in such a manner as to increase (decrease) the amount of tax revenue collected and/or decrease (increase) the amount spent by government when the nation's income is rising (falling). Before looking into these two types of fiscal policy in more detail, let us attempt to separate fiscal policy from other government actions involving tax/expenditure changes.

[1] Properly speaking, discretionary fiscal policy also encompasses action by the executive to speed up or slow down the completion of already authorized programs.

What Is and What Is Not Fiscal Policy

It is important that the student see clearly the distinction between fiscal policy and other activities of government. One source of confusion that sometimes arises is failure to recognize that although discretionary fiscal policy does entail alterations in tax laws or expenditure programs, not every tax or expenditure change should be considered a fiscal policy action.

Discretionary fiscal policy per se should be thought of as changes in taxes or government expenditures *that are undertaken primarily for their effect on aggregate demand.* It is entirely possible, for example, for government to launch a new program calling for increased spending, providing at the same time for sufficient added tax revenue to forestall any rise in aggregate demand. Such action would simply represent an attempt to increase the size of the public sector rather than a fiscal policy measure, as the term is customarily used.

In this connection, it is useful to keep in mind the distinction between different economic activities of government drawn by Musgrave.[2] First, there is the allocation branch, which uses taxes, expenditures, and other devices to reallocate resources, both between the public and private sectors and within the private sector itself. Second, there is a distribution branch, which may use taxes and expenditures to alter the distribution of income. Finally, there is the stabilization branch, the function of which is to use taxes and expenditures to achieve the proper level of aggregate demand. Fiscal policy, as we are using the term, consists of the activities of the stabilization branch alone.

Another distinction that should be drawn here is that between fiscal and monetary policy. As many activities involve them both and as the aims of both are the same — the pursuit of major economic goals via alterations in aggregate demand — there is sometimes a tendency to confuse them. For purposes of this chapter, we shall define a pure monetary policy measure as one carried out by the monetary authorities with the specific intent of altering the *degree of liquidity* of the community's wealth. Most often this would be accomplished by increasing or decreasing the money supply. For example, an open-market purchase from the public would be a pure monetary policy measure because its initial effect is simply to substitute money for bonds previously held by the public. The public's wealth is not directly changed in amount, but it has been made more liquid.[3]

On the other hand, as discussed in Chapter 19, a pure fiscal policy measure would involve altering taxes or expenditures, *without changing the money supply.* A reduction in taxes, with the resulting budget deficit financed by sale of securities to the public, would be an example, as there is no change in the money supply.

Many stabilization policy measures involve a combination of monetary and fiscal effects. For example, a tax cut creating a budget deficit, with the deficit financed by sale of securities to the banks, involves both. The tax cut by itself would be a fiscal measure, but when it is combined with a sale of securities to the banks, the money supply rises also, adding a monetary element. The same thing would be true of the hypothetical case of increasing the public's money supply by

[2] R. A. Musgrave, *The Theory of Public Finance* (New York: McGraw-Hill, 1959).

[3] Of course, such a policy would, nevertheless, affect aggregate demand through its effects on the cost of capital, consumers' wealth position, and credit rationing.

simply running the printing presses and passing out an extra $1,000 to each person. Such an action *sounds* for all the world like pure monetary policy. But it is not. Of course it *does* involve monetary effects because it increases the supply of money. But it also involves fiscal effects because the passing out of such money (without taking away something in exchange) constitutes a rise in government transfer payments.

How Discretionary Fiscal Policy Works

The potential role of fiscal policy should be clear from the material covered in Chapters 16 through 19.[4] If the requirement is to raise production and employment, aggregate demand must be increased. Fiscal authorities can choose any of three methods.[5] They may raise government spending on goods and services without altering taxes, raise government transfer payments without changing taxes, or lower taxes without reducing government spending.

The first approach will raise aggregate demand directly, as government spending on goods and services is a part of aggregate demand. The other two alternatives work (raise aggregate demand) only slightly less directly. In both cases disposable income (plus perhaps business saving) is directly increased with the expectation that a rise in private spending C, and/or I, will be forthcoming.

In all three cases, the initial rise in demand will trigger a multiplier, which will magnify the final effect. On the other hand, if we assume no increase in the supply of money (deficit financed by sale of bonds to the public), the expansionary effects of all three will be tempered by the rise in the rate of interest that must be induced by the increased transactions demand for money.

Let us now briefly consider the chief characteristics of each fiscal device.

Raising Government Spending on Goods and Services, Taxes Unchanged

This approach has an initial advantage over the other two in that total spending will initially go up by the full amount of the increase in government spending. Raising transfer payments or lowering taxes merely gives private spenders more to spend. If their marginal propensity to spend is less than 1, the initial rise in spending will be less than the amount of the tax cut (or transfer increase).

On the other hand, the time lag involved in this case may be a serious detriment in comparison with the other two. It takes time to organize public works projects (even after Congress has acted), but tax cuts and/or transfer payments programs can be instituted and affect the spending stream almost immediately.[6] Another potential problem with raising government spending is the fact that much of the initial effects may fall on the construction industry and

---

[4] In this chapter we shall overlook the position of some monetarists and assume throughout that fiscal policy *does* alter aggregate demand.

[5] Or, of course, any desired combination of the three.

[6] Experience with a tax increase, for example, the income tax surcharge of 1968, has led to doubts about the speed with which tax changes affect aggregate demand.

its suppliers. Now if this is one of the industries suffering with excess capacity, the effect is good. If, however, the unemployment is more widespread and the construction industry is near capacity, the initial effects of the government spending may be partly dissipated through raising construction prices and costs.

Raising Transfer Payments, Taxes Unchanged

As just noted, unless the recipients of increased transfer payments happen to have a marginal propensity to spend of 1, $1 billion of added transfers will raise spending initially (before the multiplier effects are considered) by something less than $1 billion. However, as the average transfer payment recipient is generally in the lower part of the income scale, his or her MPC will probably be quite high. If so, the initial effect on demand will be only slightly less favorable than is the case for goods and services expenditures.

To the degree that the added transfer payments are designed as additions to unemployment compensation, this approach has the additional virtue of reaching, reasonably quickly, those probably in most need of aid.

On the other hand, depending upon the extent and duration of the program, one might object to the possible incentive effects of transfer payments. Public works projects, it might be argued, possess the advantage of requiring the recipient of government paychecks to work for them, thereby avoiding the risk that the government's fiscal policy action will undercut the incentive to work.

Reducing Taxes, Government Expenditures Unchanged

Lowered taxes, by providing households and businesses with enlarged disposable incomes, lead to increased private spending. Of course, the amount of increase depends heavily on whose taxes are cut as well as on taxpayers' perceptions as to the permanence of the cut. If the beneficiaries of tax relief are heavy marginal spenders, the boost given spending will be significant. If, however, individuals with low MPCs or businesses with little incentive to invest are the affected parties, the fiscal action will be less successful. In addition, the effectiveness of a tax cut would normally be lower if taxpayers perceive it as temporary rather than permanent.

One criticism often made of this variant of fiscal policy is that, if it is the income tax that is cut, the only immediate beneficiaries are those who are still employed and earning sufficient income to benefit from the reduction. The unemployed, currently earning little or no income, derive little or no immediate relief.[7] In addition, as noted, it is likely that it will affect total spending less, per dollar of fiscal action, than would increased expenditures on goods and services.[8]

---

[7] They do, of course, benefit indirectly via the multiplier effects if the measure has its desired effect.

[8] As long as transfer payment programs are concentrated among the unemployed and lower-income groups, where MPCs can be expected to be high, they too probably raise spending more than tax cuts.

Government Expenditure Changes Versus Tax Changes as Resource Reallocation Devices

One important difference between tax and government expenditure changes not yet discussed is the resource allocation effect.[9] If the problem is recession with unemployed resources, either government expenditure increases or tax cuts can help put those resources back to work. But *where* they will work — on public or private goods — will differ in the two cases.

Suppose, for example, that we have an economy, with an MPC of two-thirds, that is going along at a production level $30 billion short of full employment. The unemployment can be eliminated, we would say, by *either* a $10 billion rise in the level of government spending or by a $15 billion cut in taxes. Either of these two fiscal policy actions will (when the multiplier has worked itself out) raise production by the required $30 billion.[10]

But the additional goods produced in the tax-cut case will be all consumer goods; in the government expenditure increase case, one-third ($10 billion) will be government (social) goods and the remaining two-thirds will be consumer goods. If taxes are cut, in other words, *all* the presently unemployed resources will be allocated toward producing goods in line with voluntarily expressed consumer preferences. If government expenditures are increased, only two-thirds of these resources will react to voluntarily expressed consumer demand; the other one-third will be allocated directly by government to the production of social goods.

It has been argued that this difference favors the tax change approach. The "stabilization branch" should not involve itself in decisions that are the proper province of the "allocation branch."[11] The proportion of resources devoted to producing social (government) goods should be determined by a comparison of their marginal benefits with marginal benefits from private goods. Stabilization activities aimed at establishing a level of aggregate demand just adequate for full employment should not be used in a manner that alters the allocation of resources established by the allocation branch. Hence, so this argument goes, lowering taxes and allowing consumers to determine the added goods produced has an edge.

Automatic Fiscal Policy — the Built-in Stabilizers

Up to this point we have considered only discretionary fiscal policy where Congress acts to pass a new tax law or new government expenditure program to push aggregate demand in the desired direction. We must now take note that certain

---

[9] As increased transfer payments are like reduced taxes in that both result in a rise in disposable income (indeed transfer payments are commonly referred to as negative taxes), comments in this section referring to tax changes could apply equally well to transfer payment changes.

[10] This, of course, is only the first-round effect in the Chapter 19 sense. It ignores offsetting interest rate changes.

[11] The reference, of course, is once again to Musgrave's breakdown of governmental economic activities. See Musgrave, *Theory of Public Finance.*

laws *already on the books* act in such a manner as to produce budget deficits automatically during recession and surpluses during inflationary booms. These are the built-in or automatic fiscal stabilizers.

Any tax law qualifies as an automatic stabilizer if it automatically (without specific legislative action) collects more tax revenue when GNP is rising (during the expansion phase of the business cycle) and automatically collects less tax revenue when GNP is falling (during the recession phase of the business cycle). Any government expenditure program (law) is an automatic stabilizer if it operates in such a way as to automatically increase the amount spent during recession and to cut back on the amount spent during inflation. The personal income tax and corporate profits tax laws are powerful tax stabilizers. The unemployment compensation program is an important expenditure stabilizer.

In the boom phase of the business cycle, when incomes are rising rapidly, tax revenue from the existing personal income tax law automatically goes up — both because people must pay tax on more income and because, with progressive tax rates, some must pay higher rates of tax. Because corporate profits generally rise more rapidly than GNP in expansion periods and fall more rapidly during recessions, corporate profits tax revenue also increases automatically in booms and falls off sharply in recessions. Both taxes, therefore, act as powerful stabilizers.

The unemployment compensation program calls for tax payments into the unemployment compensation fund by employers, out of which laid-off employees who qualify are paid weekly benefits for specified time periods. Weekly benefit payments to the unemployed are, of course, government transfer payments. As the program is set up, the amount of these government transfers automatically rises dramatically during recession periods when many workers are laid off and automatically is cut back in the expansion phase of the cycle as full employment is approached.

The role played by the automatic stabilizers is perhaps best described as "shock absorbers." They do not *prevent* recessions and inflations nor do they help the economy to get out of already existing recessions. What they do accomplish is a reduction in the severity of business cycles. Referring, for example, to Figure 24-1, the solid line depicts the movement of GNP over the course of a business cycle if there are no automatic stabilizers combating the movement. The dashed line is intended to show the lesser amplitude of business cycles because of the automatic stabilizers.

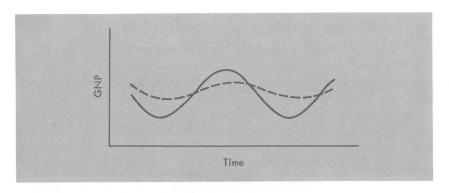

FIGURE 24-1 Effect of automatic stabilizers

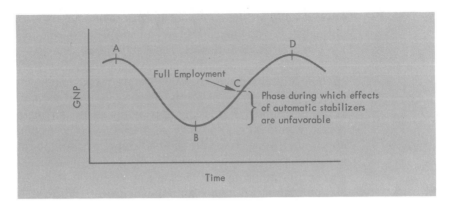

FIGURE 24-2   Deficiencies of automatic stabilizers during recovery from recession

It seems clear that, on balance, the effects of the automatic stabilizers are overwhelmingly favorable. They tend to produce deficits in recessions and surpluses (or lower deficits) in a boom, and they do it automatically, without the long delay often required for Congress to take discretionary action. This is no mean accomplishment.

But despite virtues that have led some to argue that we should dispense with discretionary fiscal policy altogether, the stabilizers are not perfect.[12] In the first place, as noted, they cannot eliminate the business cycle; they simply reduce its severity.

Second, and considerably more objectionable, their effects are not *always* favorable. What the stabilizers do is combat *any* change in the level of income. Over most of the business cycle, such action is obviously in the desired direction and is to be applauded. But this is not so for recovery from existing recession.

Look, for example, at Figure 24-2. The stabilizers' opposition to the changes in income in phase AB and in phase CD deserves unreserved praise. But how about phase BC? At point B, the bottom of the recession has been reached and, over the BC range, the economy is climbing back toward full employment. Clearly this is a movement in income that is desirable, yet the automatic stabilizers — *which automatically combat any change in income* — make this recovery more difficult than it would be in their absence.

The Determinants of the Degree of Effectiveness of Discretionary Fiscal Policy

Most economists believe that intelligently administered fiscal policy can play a significant role in achieving economic stability. But we must be on guard against allowing oversimplification to distort our evaluation.

As a first approximation it is often argued that the first-round effects of fiscal

[12] For an early statement favoring sole reliance on the automatic stabilizers, see Committee for Economic Development, *Fiscal and Monetary Policy for High Employment* (New York: Committee for Economic Development, 1962).

policy on the equilibrium level of production and income can be read from the following simple expression:[13]

$$\frac{1}{1 - \text{MPC}} \times \begin{array}{c} \Delta \text{ Government spending} \\ \text{on goods and services} \end{array} = \begin{array}{c} \Delta \text{ Equilibrium level} \\ \text{of production} \end{array}$$

or

$$\frac{1}{1 - \text{MPC}} \times (\text{MPC} \times \Delta \text{ Taxes}) = \begin{array}{c} \Delta \text{ Equilibrium level} \\ \text{of production and income} \end{array}$$

or

$$\frac{1}{1 - \text{MPC}} \times \left(\text{MPC} \times \begin{array}{c} \Delta \text{ Government} \\ \text{transfers} \end{array} \right) = \begin{array}{c} \Delta \text{ Equilibrium level} \\ \text{of production and income} \end{array}$$

While there is nothing wrong with putting it this way as a simplified first approximation, the alert student will recognize that this does involve considerable abstraction from reality. Although we cannot, within the scope of this book, exhaustively treat fiscal policy, it does seem in order to carry it a bit further than these expressions permit. What are the determinants of the degree of effectiveness of fiscal policy?

To keep the discussion within manageable proportions, we shall consider only the stabilization effects of fiscal policy. And to avoid unnecessary duplication, let us concentrate on only one side of the stabilization task—fiscal action to deal with unemployment. What will determine *how* effective a given fiscal program will be, in its goal of raising employment?

As the following list indicates, it is convenient to break the discussion down into two major categories. Because the aim is to raise employment through increases in aggregate demand, we must first consider the factors that determine the effect of the fiscal policy on spending. Then, because the increase in demand is means rather than end, we must go on to discuss the circumstances under which demand increases are likely to cut unemployment.

Factors Determining the Degree of Effectiveness of Antirecession Fiscal Policy[14]

I. Determinants of the effect of the fiscal policy aggregate demand
   A. How does the government spend its funds?
      1. On goods and services or transfers?
      2. In an area where the initial recipients of funds spent by government have a higher or lower MPC than the average for the community?

[13] Some economists prefer to differentiate between a tax multiplier and an expenditure multiplier. For example, if b stands for the MPC, the expenditure multiplier would be as given, $1/(1 - b)$, but the tax (or transfer) multiplier would be $-b/(1 - b)$, which would then be multiplied directly times the tax (or transfer) change. Obviously these are alternative ways of saying the same thing, it being a matter of pedagogical taste whether the multiplier or multiplicand should be altered.

[14] Obviously this contains a different list of factors than those included in the table in Chapter 19. In fact, both lists matter, but many included here bear on the slopes of the curves referred to in Chapter 19.

    B. How does the government raise the funds it spends?
       1. By taxing or borrowing?
       2. If by taxing, what is the MPC of the particular taxpayers affected?
       3. If by borrowing,
          a. To what extent, if any, do the lenders cut their consumer spending to lend to government?
          b. To what extent does the government's added use of loanable funds raise the rate of interest and, thereby, indirectly cut private spending (i.e., How much crowding out is there?)?
    C. Does the fiscal policy itself cause offsetting cuts in private spending for any other reasons?
    D. If taxes are altered, do those affected view it as a permanent change or a temporary, one-shot affair?

II. Given the rise in aggregate demand, what determines its effectiveness in eliminating unemployment without raising prices?
    A. How near to full employment are we?
    B. How near to full employment are the industries most directly affected by the government policy?
    C. How closely do the areas of unemployment and added government spending coincide geographically?
    D. How long does it take for aggregate demand to be affected?
    E. To what extent does the unemployment result from deficient aggregate demand rather than from structural factors in the economy?
    F. What is the current state of consumer expectations regarding price-level increases?

Regarding the first question of the effect on aggregate demand, the variables are numerous. A given-sized fiscal program will raise demand more, other things being equal, the more government spending is devoted to goods and services expenditures rather than transfers, where there is a possible leakage resulting from the MPS of transfer recipients. In addition, the second round of the multiplier effect may differ somewhat depending on the particular MPCs of those paid by the government. For example, a $10 billion rise in government spending on goods and services raises demand by a full $10 billion in the first instance. Even if the MPC for the average citizen is four-fifths, however, there is no guarantee that the rise in consumer spending resulting in the next period will be $8 billion. For the recipients of the money spent by government may not be average. They could conceivably be well-paid contractors and construction workers with an MPC well below the average for the community. If so, the full effect on aggregate demand will be less than the $50 billion the simple formula would predict.[15]

---

[15] If the MPC for the average member of the community is $\frac{8}{10}$, but that of the group initially receiving the $10 billion extra spent by government is only $\frac{1}{2}$, the ultimate rise in the equilibrium income level will be $35 billion rather than $50 billion. Looking at it on a period-by-period basis, we would expect

Period 1	Period 2	Period 3	Period 4	Period 5	
+$10 billion	+$5 billion	+$4 billion	+$3.2 billion	+$2.56 billion	etc.

If the fiscal action takes the form of added government spending, the ultimate effect on demand depends heavily on the method used to finance the added expenditures. If taxes are increased to pay the tab, the expansionary influence of the rise in government spending will be in large measure (but not entirely) offset by the contractionary effect on private consumer spending of the tax hike.

If the government borrows the funds via sale of securities, we must consider the remote possibility that those who lend the money (buy the securities) may cut their consumer spending in order to do so. This hardly seems likely. Unlike taxpayers, whose incomes and private wealth positions are cut when the government takes more, bond buyers simply agree voluntarily to accept government securities in exchange for their loanable funds. Neither their incomes nor their wealth positions are cut, so there is no obvious reason to expect them to reduce their consumption. To argue otherwise is to imply that bond buyers decide voluntarily to save more (consume less) and lend the funds to the government simply because the government is trying to borrow. What seems very much more likely is that the bond buyers decide to divert funds that they had already decided to save away from private borrowers to the government.

But this too has its implications for aggregate demand. Even if we agree that those who lend to the government will not directly cut their spending in order to do so, the fact that government borrowing may reduce the funds available for business may indirectly cut private spending. If, for example, the government finances deficit spending by sale of securities to the nonbank public, the increased demand for loanable funds—with no rise in the supply—will raise interest rates, cutting back investment spending somewhat. The reader will remember from the theory section that the expansionary effects of a rise in government spending will, assuming no rise in the money supply, be partially offset by a rise in interest rates.

As we noted then, this need not happen if the deficit is financed by sale of securities to the banks. For, in that case, the increase in the demand for money (or for loanable funds) may be just offset by the rise in the supply of money (or loanable funds), so that the interest rate need not rise. The conclusion from all this is that the net increase in aggregate demand will be greatest if increased government spending is financed by borrowing from the banks; less if the funds are borrowed from the nonbank public; and least of all if they are raised via taxation.

In addition, we must recognize the possibility that the expansionary effects of fiscal action could be partially offset by the direct reactions of private spenders to the fiscal policy. For example, if there are investors who (rationally or not) are sufficiently fearful of a rise in the national debt to cut their outlays because of it, their doing so will certainly nullify part of the beneficial effects on aggregate demand.

It does not seem likely, however, that such a negative response to fiscal

---

The increase in period 1 is the rise in government spending; that in period 2 is the added consumer spending done by the group that initially receives the funds spent by government. From period 3 on, it is assumed that new income is dispersed to the community at large, where the average MPC, $\frac{8}{10}$, applies.

action would amount to very much. First, the modern business community is, in the main, too knowledgeable to react in this way. Second, there must be set off against such a response the favorable effects of the fiscal policy on the expectations of those investors who understand its purposes and believe in its effectiveness. Those who expect the policy to succeed in raising demand would, on that account, probably increase their investment spending, reinforcing the policy.

Finally, it is generally recognized that the impact of tax changes on spending will be greater if those affected perceive it as a permanent change than if they consider it temporary. This is based on those consumption theories that regard people's so-called permanent income as a more reliable predictor of their consumption spending than any given year's income.

So much for the determinants of the effect of the policy on aggregate demand. This takes us half the way. But if the objective is to raise employment, we must go on to consider the conditions under which increased demand will accomplish the objective, instead of spilling over into such undesired results as price increases. This, of course, depends upon a number of factors and is an area about which there is much current debate. First, most economists would argue that the farther from full employment we now are (the greater the slack in the economy), the more likely it will be that demand increases will increase employment rather than prices. The distribution of the unemployment matters too. If the industries most immediately affected by the fiscal action (for example, the construction industry) are near capacity, prices there may well be driven up even though there is considerable unemployment in the rest of the economy. Similarly, if the unemployment is geographically concentrated and the fiscal policy raises demand more generally throughout the economy, part of the added spending will be dissipated via undesirable price increases.

Another factor of real significance is the state of consumer expectations regarding future prices. One does not have to subscribe to the accelerationist view of the Phillips curve to grant the crucial importance of expectations in determining whether demand increases will raise employment or prices. Without question, a nation that has been experiencing roughly stable prices for some years preceding expansionary fiscal action has more reason for confidence in the success of its policy than one that has been undergoing substantial inflation in the past.

The time factor also matters. There is little benefit to demonstrating that, *if other things remain the same*, a given fiscal policy measure will ultimately raise aggregate demand by x billion dollars if that result would only be achieved after ten years. If we are attempting to combat the business cycle, it matters little that aggregate demand could be raised by x billion dollars in ten years, other things being equal, if there is good reason to expect the "other things" to change markedly long before five years. Perhaps, for policy purposes, we should concentrate more on the expected rise in demand within a 12- to 18-month period rather than on an equilibrium result that will never be realized anyway.

Finally, we must consider the possibility that the unemployment is not of the sort a rise in demand can easily eliminate. If the unemployment is structural in nature, resulting, for example, from a work force whose training and skills simply do not meet the needs of employers with job openings, increased aggregate demand alone may do little to solve the problem.

The Weaknesses of Fiscal Policy
Relative to Monetary Policy

Fiscal policy, whatever its strengths, is no panacea. Even its most enthusiastic adherents acknowledge that it has weaknesses, although there is, of course, disagreement regarding their severity.

One of the most serious drawbacks to discretionary fiscal policy, given the present institutional structure in the United States, is the time lag involved between the recognition of the need for action and the time when action can be taken. Because discretionary fiscal policy is entirely up to Congress to enact, delays of many months can be expected while the legislature considers action.

In this respect, fiscal policy contrasts sharply with monetary policy. Because monetary policy is in the hands of the seven-person, uniquely independent Board of Governors, it can be initiated immediately once the need for action has been determined. Clearly, with the existing U.S. governmental structure, monetary policy is superior to fiscal policy in terms of this particular time lag.[16]

Another disadvantage of the fiscal arm relative to its monetary counterpart is its inflexibility. Monetary policy, especially open-market operations, can easily be reversed when conditions dictate. Fiscal policy, though not totally inflexible, is substantially more difficult to reverse. This is especially true of the public works variant of fiscal policy, which, once turned on, is particularly difficult to stop before completion of the project.

A third problem with fiscal policy appears to be the political problem involved with its use to combat excessive demand. Fortunately, good economics coincides with good politics in a recession. A tax cut or an increase in government expenditure projects makes economic sense, then, as well as being attractive politically. Unhappily, this is not so in the inflation phase, where good economics—a tax increase or a reduction of government services—may be political poison. The result may well be that fiscal action to combat excessive demand may only be taken after even longer lags and in the most extreme cases.

In this respect, monetary policy again has a relative advantage. Although so-called tight-money policies are by no means free of opposition and political pressures, the policymaker, the Federal Reserve Board, is far better insulated from the immediate threat of political retribution than are its fiscal counterparts. The result, almost certainly, is a speedier initial response to inflationary tendencies.

A majority of economists, while granting these deficiencies of discretionary fiscal policy, still feel that it can play a significant role in the nation's stabilization policy. Some others, however, have become so impressed with the problems that they advocate abandoning discretionary fiscal policy altogether, relying only on the so-called automatic fiscal stabilizers to supplement monetary policy. It is their feeling that the lags involved in discretionary policy are so long and variable that fiscal action is more likely to reinforce the cycle than to combat it. The most

---

[16] It should be noted that this advantage of monetary policy is not an inherent one. It exists because we have chosen to place the administration of monetary policy with seven-person board rather than directly with Congress. If fiscal policy should ever be similarly administered, as has been recommended, its time lag problem would be markedly lessened.

extreme position on fiscal policy, of course, has been taken by the monetarists, some of whom, as we have noted, deny that fiscal policy has *any* significant effects on aggregate demand.

Debt Management

It has become traditional to refer to debt management as a third policy alternative, to be used along with monetary and fiscal policy. Although we shall abide by the strictures of tradition, there is room for questioning the validity of treating debt management as an activity entirely distinct from monetary and fiscal policy, for debt management activities are so closely intertwined with monetary and fiscal actions that they often seem to merge.

Debt Management Defined

For our discussion, we shall accept the definition of debt management employed by the late Warren L. Smith. *Debt management* includes "all actions of the government, including both the Treasury and the Federal Reserve, which affect the composition of the publicly held debt." [17]

By this definition, the *amount* of new debt to be sold by the Treasury is in the fiscal policy province. Only the determination of its *composition* (the types of securities to be sold) involves debt management. Similarly, the amount of securities to be sold (or bought) by the Federal Reserve is a monetary policy decision; the decision about the type of security to be sold (or bought) is one of debt management.

The lion's share of debt management decisions, however, is involved in the Treasury's efforts to refund the national debt. As outstanding securities mature, the Treasury (assuming no tax surplus exists) must sell new ones to raise the money to pay off the holders of those coming due. [18] The choice of the type of new issue is, once again, a debt management decision. Some sense of the enormity of this refunding responsibility can be obtained from the fact that, as of mid-1990, about $600 billion of the outstanding federal securities were within a year of maturity.

The Objectives of Debt Management

What can and what should be accomplished via debt management? Opinions on this question have varied widely over the years. [19] In the years prior to the 1930s,

[17] Warren L. Smith, "Debt Management in the United States," Study Paper Number 19, *Study of Employment, Growth and Price Levels* (Washington, D.C.: Joint Economic Committee, 1960), p. 2.

[18] In fact, refunding usually consists of an exchange offering of new securities to the holders of maturing obligations, rather than a sale for cash and then use of the cash to retire the old securities. Because the effect is the same in either case, we shall ignore the distinction.

the major aim of debt management appears to have been simply to keep the then-small federal debt in as long term a form as possible, thereby minimizing the Treasury's refunding difficulties. Then, as now, the prime consideration was protection of the government's credit. Long-term debt, it was felt, was the soundest means of accomplishing this end.

The Great Depression and World War II changed all this. The former experience markedly intensified concern for economic stabilization; the latter gave us a large federal debt to manage. Debt management had become a major activity, and considerable interest developed in employing it contracyclically, as a stabilization weapon to supplement monetary and fiscal policy.

In general terms, the idea was to shift (in refunding) toward long-term securities in periods of excess demand and then back toward short-term obligations during recessions. Lengthening the maturity of the debt structure during cyclical upswings was expected to help in at least two ways. First, selling more long-term debt would tend to raise-long-term interest rates. This, it was hoped, would hold down on investment expenditures somewhat. Second, by replacing highly liquid short-term obligations with less liquid long-term securities, the total liquidity of the public's wealth would be reduced so that, one would hope, further restrictions on demand would be forthcoming. The reverse, of course, follows in recession.

Later, however, the notion that debt management should be employed as a third stabilization weapon encountered increasing opposition.[20] Considerable doubt was expressed regarding the magnitude of the effect on demand of such cyclical switches in the debt's maturity structure. In addition, it was pointed out that whatever can be accomplished through these means to combat the business cycle can probably be done more efficiently through intensification of monetary policy itself. Third, the attempt to lengthen the maturity of the debt during booms runs some risk of undermining Federal Reserve policy, as the Treasury sometimes requires support from the Federal Reserve when it attempts to place long-term issues. Such support, taking as it must the form of Federal Reserve open-market purchases, could require (at least temporarily) abandonment of a policy of restraint. Finally, borrowing long during booms, when interest rates are typically high, and short during recessions, when they are usually low, implies higher borrowing costs to the Treasury.

In the light of all these problems with a contracyclical debt management policy, more and more economists appear to have moved toward the view that it does not really constitute an effective stabilization weapon. There is widespread agreement that the maturity of the debt should be lengthened, but not just during the boom phase of the cycle. Indeed, some would argue that the bulk of the long-term securities should be sold during the recessions, thereby taking advantage of the generally easier market conditions prevailing, and the short terms during the booms. This would reduce the cost of servicing the debt while generally easing the Treasury's refunding task. It would then be left entirely to the monetary and fiscal policymakers to take whatever action is needed to modify business cycle swings.

---

[19] For a good discussion of these changing attitudes, see the article by William E. Laird, "The Changing Views on Debt Management," *Quarterly Review of Economics and Business*, Autumn 1963.

[20] See, for example, Smith, "Debt Management."

Incomes Policies

For many years economists and government policymakers, while recognizing that the ideal of full employment with stable prices was not fully realizable even with the most skilled use of monetary and fiscal policy, were more or less content to rely solely on these two prime instruments of demand management to produce a roughly satisfactory approximation to the desired results. Events of the 1960s and 1970s, however, shattered much of this complacency and provided an environment within which many governments found it necessary to resort to wide-ranging experimentation with a different set of policies — those that we now call *incomes policies.*

What Are Incomes Policies?

Incomes policies involve direct action by government (as opposed to the indirect thrust of monetary and fiscal policy through aggregate demand) to attempt to hold down excessive rates of inflation. It is almost impossible to provide a specific definition of these policies because they include a vast array of governmental actions varying all the way from mere verbal exhortation to tightfisted, ironclad, authoritative, across-the-board price and wage freezes backed up by the threat of heavy fines and/or imprisonment for violators.

For purposes of our discussion, we consider incomes policies to include the following sorts of governmental actions:

1. *"Jawboning."* Here the government merely appeals to labor and management to use restraint in raising wages and prices but applies no specific sanctions to the noncooperative. This approach usually implies reliance on the force of public opinion to hold price setters in line and often involves singling out the most visible large companies and unions for special verbal admonition.

2. *"Arm-Twisting."* In this technique the government carries its pressures on key price setters to the point of threats of withdrawals of governmental benefits or other active reprisal. Such actions might include withholding government contracts from offenders, threatening to unload government stockpiles of strategic materials so as to force down the price, reducing subsidies including removing tariff protection, or threatening more intensive antitrust prosecution.

3. *Voluntary Price and Wage Controls.* This consists of the federal government formally announcing guidelines or standards specifying maximum acceptable rates of price and wage increase. Such guidelines are voluntary in that the executive has no legal power to enforce them directly. As a result, they are almost invariably accompanied by considerable jawboning and arm-twisting to induce compliance. Examples of their use include the guidelines established by the Kennedy administration in the early 1960s and President Carter's program in the late 1970s.

4. *Authoritative Price and Wage Controls.* Involved here is a whole range

of possible activities whereby government places direct mandatory limits on the rate at which prices and/or wages may be increased. Both the coverage and the degree of authority employed may vary widely. "Phase II" of President Nixon's policy during 1972, wherein wage rates were permitted to increase at a rate of 5.5 percent per year and profits margins in excess of the average of the best two of the three years immediately preceding August 1971 were forbidden, was an example.

5. *Price and Wage Freezes.* An across-the-board price and wage freeze is the most extreme form of control wherein prices and wages are for a specified time period simply not permitted to rise at all above levels established during a previously designated time period. An example of this for the U.S. was the 90-day price and wage freeze in the fall of 1971.[21]

The Opposition to Incomes Policies

Incomes policies as a means of dealing with inflation are highly controversial. Many economists oppose them altogether on a variety of grounds.

First, there is the charge that such direct governmental involvement in price setting inevitably involves interference with the price system and with the very shifts in relative prices that are relied upon as signals of changes in consumer preferences, in technology, and in resource availability. In short, it is argued, such measures will inevitably lead to a distortion of resource allocation. Most economists oppose *long-run* price freezes on these grounds.

Second, there is the not insignificant matter of time loss through the bureaucracy involved in authoritative price and wage controls. Not only does proper administration of such a program require a considerable administrative hierarchy at the governmental level, but it also causes firms under control to spend substantial amounts of time complying with the regulations.

Third, freezing prices and wages at given levels or allowing them to rise only at some prescribed uniform maximum rate inevitably creates inequities. Workers who got their raises just before imposition of the program are at an advantage as compared with those who did not. Firms whose prices had not previously been raised as rapidly as their costs are similarly disadvantaged. And if the less formal approaches referred to as jawboning and arm-twisting are resorted to, critics point out that, by their very nature, they will apply selectively only to the most visible of price setters, thereby discriminating unfairly against certain segments of the business community or of organized labor.

Fourth, but by no means of least significance, many economists do not believe that incomes policies can succeed in their objectives anyway. Prices and wages held down by fiat can be raised by subterfuge by changing job titles or product quality. Black markets are a distinct threat, especially if controls are

---

[21] This list presents a narrower view of incomes policies than many observers would prefer. A broader definition might include governmental activities to improve labor markets (such as manpower training, job information, and relocation subsidies) and programs aimed at improving the structure and competitiveness of markets (such as more intensive antitrust action, eliminating barriers to entry, lowering tariffs and minimum wage laws).

applied during a period of excess demand. Excess demand, repressed during a period of controls, is very likely to resurface once they are removed and, in the long run, possibly raise prices to a level just as high as if controls had not been applied in the first place. And as the clincher, opponents say, incomes policies have been tried in this country and a number of others, and the evidence shows they simply have not worked. For example, two researchers who made a careful study of experience with incomes policies in Western Europe conclude that: "In none of the variations so far turned up has incomes policy succeeded in its fundamental objective, as stated, of making full employment consistent with a reasonable degree of price stability." [22]

The Case for Incomes Policies

Despite the still formidable opposition among economists to attempts at authoritative control of prices, a considerable number support renewed use of incomes policies in the future.[23] Those who support them do not see them as a panacea and do not deny the existence of problems. However, in the troubled times of the 1990s, they see them as capable of making some positive contribution toward the solution of our economic problems.

> Advocates of incomes policies do not deny that such policies are a "second-best" approach to the problem of inflation control. They recognize that restoration of competition in markets would help to reduce inflationary pressures. But they think that such an ideal procompetitive policy would be politically or technologically impossible to achieve in the foreseeable future. Thus, in view of the unavailability of a "first-best" procompetitive policy, a "second-best" incomes policy must be relied upon.[24]

Advocates of incomes policies do not generally favor permanent price and wage controls under any and all circumstances. Most agree that when inflation is being caused by excess demand, the proper solution is not authoritative controls but effective monetary-fiscal restraint on demand. Nor do they differ from their opposition in their support for immediate efforts to remove obstructions to freer markets and the improvement of labor markets via retraining, better job information, and the like. And they, like most economists, would countenance across-the-board price freezes only for relatively short periods, as a form of shock therapy to, it is hoped, shatter developing inflationary expectations (or during such extreme emergencies as an all-out war).

In the main, however, the incomes policies advocates read the evidence of the 1960s, 1970s, and 1980s as prima facie proof that satisfactory performance of

[22] Lloyd Ulman and Robert J. Flanagan, *Wage Restraint: A Study of Incomes Policies in Western Europe* (Berkeley: University of California Press, 1971), p. 216.

[23] See, for example, Gardner Ackley, "An Incomes Policy for the 1970s," *Review of Economics and Statistics,* August 1972; John Sheahan, "Incomes Policies," *Journal of Economic Issues,* December 1972; Sidney Weintraub, "Incomes Policy: Completing the Stabilization Triangle," *Journal of Economic Issues,* December 1972.

[24] Thomas M. Humphrey, "The Economics of Incomes Policies," *Monthly Review,* Federal Reserve Bank of Richmond, October 1972. Humphrey's survey article is an excellent source for those who wish to further explore the incomes policy issue.

market economies now requires something more than the standard monetary-fiscal policy duo can offer. It is their position that serious structural imperfections and the long period of inflationary excesses have now laid the groundwork for a higher level of structural unemployment along with a firmer basis for intolerable cost-push inflation, aided and abetted by inflationary expectations.

What of the charges that past incomes policy experiments have failed? Incomes policy advocates read the record somewhat differently. For example, in response to the summary judgment of Western Europe's experience by Ulman and Flanagan cited earlier, John Sheahan says,

> [their] judgment seems more negative than the facts warrant. . . . All these attempts broke down eventually because of emerging patterns of excess demand. It seems somewhat arbitrary to emphasize the inability to stop inflation at full employment more than the fact that some of these programs did achieve reductions in the rates of inflation associated with low levels of employment for periods of one to several years.[25]

As for the U.S. experience with incomes policies, some observers argue that inflation during the earlier 1960s was indeed reduced as a result of that period's "Guideposts" program. Despite the high levels of inflation in the United States during the early 1970s, the argument has also been made that the situation would have been even worse had the administration not instituted its control program.[26] The Joint Economic Committee of the Congress, for example, states, "What evidence is available suggests that the Phase I and Phase II controls of 1971–72 reduced the rate of increase in prices and wages as much as one or two percentage points."[27]

In addition, a number of observers have argued that the early 1970s control experiment might well have been more successful had it been better administered. The short duration of the initial price freeze, the fact that spenders were told well in advance when it would end, and the alleged bad timing of the removal of controls are among the specifics often cited. Then, too, it has been argued, the control policy of the 1970s was initiated and run by an administration whose chief economic advisers had been among the most outspoken opponents of incomes policies. As one former head of the Council of Economic Advisers has put it, "The record is one of political expediency, of an absence of clear plan or firm intention, and unresolved ideological tensions within the Administration."[28]

---

[25] Sheahan, "Incomes Policies," p. 12.

[26] See, for example, Peter Fortune, "An Evaluation of Anti-inflation Policies in the United States," *New England Economic Review,* January–February 1974. The amount of inflation there "would have been" without control programs is, of course, extremely difficult to measure. Opponents of incomes policies offer the 1971–1973 U.S. experience as further evidence of the failure of controls.

[27] The *1974 Joint Economic Report,* Joint Economic Committee of the 93rd Cong., 2d sess., March 24, 1974, p. 37.

[28] Gardner Ackley, in testimony before the Joint Economic Committee, quoted in the *1974 Joint Economic Report,* p. 38. For an interesting account of the 1971 to 1973 U.S. incomes policy experience, see Arnold R. Weber, *In Pursuit of Price Stability,* Studies in Wage-Price Policy (Washington, D.C.: The Brookings Institution, 1973). See also Robert H. Floyd, "Incomes Policies: A Quick Critique," *Monthly Review,* Federal Reserve Bank of Atlanta, for a brief review of earlier experience in other countries.

Proposals for a Tax-Based Incomes Policy

In the 1990s, it seems clear that the vast majority of economists, business leaders, and much of organized labor would oppose reinstitution of the more authoritative varieties of incomes policies for the United States. Despite this general atmosphere of disapproval, however, concern about a return to inflation has generated substantial interest in an earlier proposal for an incomes policy based upon the tax system.[29]

In essence, the idea is to attempt to keep wage increases related to the increase in labor's productivity by raising the corporate profits tax rate on employers who grant inflationary wage settlements. It might work as follows.

Suppose that the productivity of labor rises at a rate of 3 percent per year and, assuming ongoing inflation, that it is expected that the average firm will offer wage increases averaging 5 percent. To implement the program, the top-bracket corporate profits tax could be reduced from the 46 percent level ruling in 1986 to 40 percent, but then each corporation would have a surcharge added on to the basic 40 percent rate that would be *a multiple of the amount its wage settlement exceeded the 3 percent productivity growth.* If, for example, the multiple chosen was 3, and corporation A agreed to an average 5 percent wage settlement, corporation B settled for an above-average 8 percent wage rise, and corporation C offered only a 3 percent wage boost, the corporate profits tax applying to each firm would be as follows:

> Corporation A would pay the basic 40 percent plus a surcharge equal to three times its 2 percent excess, or a total of the same corporate tax it paid at the 46 percent rate.
> Corporation B would pay the basic 40 percent plus a surcharge equal to three times its 5 percent excess, or a sharply increased corporate tax of 55 percent.
> Corporation C would be rewarded for its restraint by paying only the basic 40 percent rate, 6 percent less than previously.[30]

Such a plan, once it was initially adopted, would have the advantage of operating automatically, thereby avoiding the administrative bureaucracy that often is necessary to implement other types of incomes policies. In addition, it would put no absolute barrier on any industry. Growing firms and industries would be free to grant wage increases in excess of any arbitrary standard but would be penalized as far as taxes are concerned for doing so. Despite this, the plan's authors believe that it would involve less interference with the price system than would other possible plans.

There are, of course, problems. First, success would depend upon the assumption that the corporate profits tax cannot be shifted forward to consumers via increased prices — an assumption about which economists are in disagreement. Second, its success would presuppose an appropriate monetary fiscal policy so that aggregate demand would not be excessive. And last, but of consider-

---

[29] See H. Wallich and S. Weintraub, "A Tax-Based Incomes Policy," *Journal of Economic Issues,* June 1971. For a critical review of the Wallich-Weintraub proposal, see Nancy A. Jianakoplos, "A Tax-Based Incomes Policy (TIP): What's It All About?" *Review,* Federal Reserve Bank of St. Louis, February 1978.

[30] The particular multiple chosen could be varied according to how severe a penalty was desired.

able importance, there would probably be real difficulties in enlisting the support of organized labor for such a plan, since it would directly restrain wages but not prices.

The first official recommendation for a tax-based incomes policy in the United States came from President Carter in late 1978. Recognizing that the cooperation of organized labor was an essential prerequisite to the success of its anti-inflation program, the Carter administration proposed an innovative combination of voluntary wage-price guidelines buttressed by a type of tax-based incomes policy that quickly came to be known as "real wage insurance."

Under this proposal key price setters were asked to keep their rate of price increase down to a level .5 percent less than that during the 1976–1977 period (but in no case, more than 9.5 percent) while wage and salary increases were to be held to a maximum of 7 percent. The unique feature of the plan was the recommendation that Congress enact a tax rebate scheme under which workers whose wage increases were within the 7 percent guideline during fiscal 1979 would be protected from losses in real income should the cost-of-living increase exceed 7 percent. If, for example, the cost of living should rise by 9 percent in 1979, the proposal was to pay workers who had stayed within the 7 percent wage increase standard a tax rebate equal to the 2 percent difference. The intent, of course, was to forestall another round of inflationary wage increases based upon the premise that larger wage increases were necessary to keep pace with the cost of living. This proposal, however, was flatly rejected by Congress.

Tax-based incomes policies are not, of course, a panacea. But for all their weaknesses, they offer an interesting alternative to dealing with the problem of inflation that seems to merit serious study. The relevant comparison, after all, is not between their admittedly imperfect effects and an ideal situation but rather between them and the inequity and misallocation caused by the current degree of inflation.

Review Questions

1. Not all changes in government expenditures and taxes constitute fiscal policy measures. Some are undertaken for allocation purposes and others for distribution purposes. Explain.

2. Carefully distinguish between the three main types of discretionary fiscal policy. How do they compare in terms of their effects on the level of total spending?

3. How do the automatic stabilizers tend to affect the economy? Can you identify any possible unfavorable effects?

4. Aside from the views of the monetarists, what are some of the major weaknesses of fiscal policy in comparison with monetary policy?

5. Explain and evaluate debt management as a stabilization weapon.

6. What are incomes policies? What are the fundamental differences in approach between incomes policies and monetary and fiscal policies as means of controlling inflation? Explain.

7. List the pros and cons of incomes policies.

8. Carefully explain how a tax-based incomes policy based on alterations in the corporate profits tax might work. What advantages does a tax-based incomes policy have over other types?

CHAPTER 25

Introduction to International Finance

Simplification is the real goal of economic theory. Consequently it was not only acceptable but necessary to proceed within the comfortable confines of an imposing list of simplifying assumptions as we made our way through the income determination model sketched in Chapters 16 through 19.

But the luxury of the simplifying assumption carries with it a heavy obligation. The theorist who would say something useful about the world in which we live must be ever mindful of the need to approach reality, even though never really getting there.

The purely domestic aspects of money and banking are, no doubt, of dominant importance, especially for the U.S. economy. But the problems facing an open economy—one involved in trade with other nations—are of great and growing significance. This section of the book considers the complexities and problems of international finance.

The Case for Free Trade

No nation is an island unto itself. Some, it is true, are so lavishly endowed with natural resources and other needed factors of production that they *approach* a state of self-sufficiency. But no nation, however wealthy, can be as well off without trade as it would be with it.

The case for free, unobstructed international trade is, of course, a simple one. Indeed, it can be justified on substantially the same grounds as money itself. Just as the existence of an efficiently operating money system permits fuller exploitation of the advantages of specialization, so too does free unrestricted international trade.

The reader is no doubt familiar with the time-honored principle of comparative advantage. Given peaceful conditions and ignoring transportation costs, each nation will be better off (that is, have a higher real level of living) by specializing in the production of those goods and services in which it has a comparative advantage while trading for the other things it needs. In its essence, the principle of comparative advantage simply states that a nation should obtain its goods and services wherever they cost least in terms of its own resources. If a nation can obtain more units of Product X from abroad by producing Product Y and trading it to obtain X than it could by using a similar amount of its resources to produce X at home, it clearly gains by specializing in Y and importing X.

The real gains available to all nations from the fullest possible exploitation of worldwide specialization in production are unquestionably very large. Unfortunately, however, in the world as it is, these gains are not easily obtainable. We are not "one world," unreservedly committed to the betterment of mankind in general, but a large group of separate nations—all too often given not only to trade warfare but, sadly, to outright military conflict as well.

The result has been myriad obstacles to free international exchange and the higher living standards it would make possible. Now, we cannot begin to consider all these obstacles in the short space of three chapters, and in any case, many of them go beyond the normal scope of a money and banking text. One area, however, is not only appropriate but essential. It has to do with the financial side of international trade.

Our prime concern in this section will be with the many problems involved in the use of scores of different national moneys to complete transactions across borderlines. For example, how can an American, who has only dollars, buy a product produced by a German who presumably wants only Deutsche marks? How can the United States buy more from other nations than it sells to them? What institutional structures, private and governmental, have been set up to facilitate the freest possible international exchange? Finally, how effectively do all these international monetary institutions function as mechanisms for the promotion of worldwide specialization? These fundamental questions of international finance will be our concern in this and the following two chapters.

The U.S. Role in International Trade and the Importance of International Transactions to the U.S. Economy

If one were to adopt the parochial viewpoint that the U.S. economy is our only interest, data on international trade might seem to imply that U.S. international transactions are relatively unimportant and that devoting several chapters to this topic overstates its importance to us. For example, it might be noted that, in 1990, the *net* effect of international trade on U.S. aggregate demand was just over $31 billion—or less than one-half of 1 percent of the total. Or again, it could be pointed out that *gross* U.S. exports of goods and services during 1990

TABLE 25-1 U.S. imports of goods and services as a percentage of U.S. GNP, 1960–1990	
1960	5.0
1965	5.0
1970	6.0
1975	8.0
1980	12.0
1985	11.0
1990	13.3

Source: U.S. Department of Commerce

equaled $649 billion, an impressive figure in itself, but one that represented only about 12 percent of the nation's GNP.

Such data, however, should not lead to the thoroughly unwarranted conclusion that international trade is of minor significance for the U.S. economy. In fact, it is of critical and growing importance.

For many years the U.S. economy has been heavily dependent on other countries for critical supplies of highly strategic materials. Far more than half of U.S. supplies of asbestos, tin, nickel, chromium, rubber, industrial diamonds, and cobalt must be imported from our trading partners. And, as we learned to our chagrin in the 1970s, and again in the early 1990s, it is difficult to overstate the importance to our economy and our living standards of imported oil.

But U.S. reliance on foreign countries for critical minerals and raw materials has been large for decades. More recently, the nation has begun to import greatly increased portions of its manufactured goods from abroad, a trend that has done more than anything else to bring U.S. involvement in the world economy home to the average American worker and consumer. Evidence of the internationalization of the U.S. economy in recent years is presented in Table 25-1.

Note that since the early 1970s, U.S. dependence on foreign products has more than doubled. Whereas throughout the quarter-century immediately following World War II, this country imported goods and services equal to only about 5 percent of its total GNP, by 1990 that figure had more than doubled! Certainly as any U.S. farmer, autoworker, or steel worker can attest, the U.S. economy is now heavily dependent on international markets.[1]

But despite the growing significance of the world economy to the United States, it is still true that our involvement in international trade, relatively speaking, is small compared to most of our trading partners. That this is the case is vividly illustrated by the data in Table 25-2. There, exports of goods and services

---

[1] For an excellent account of this trend, see Jack L. Hervey, "The Internationalization of Uncle Sam," *Economic Perspectives*, The Federal Reserve Bank of Chicago, May–June 1986.

TABLE 25-2 Exports of goods and services as percentage of GNP for selected industrialized nations, 1989

Belgium	73
Canada	25
France[a]	23
Germany	35
Italy	19
Netherlands	58
United Kingdom	24
United States	12

[a] Gross domestic product is used instead of GNP.

Source: International Financial Statistics, Yearbook, 1990, International Monetary Fund.

as a fraction of GNP for 1989 is reported for eight industrialized nations. If one interprets these figures as a rough measure of the percentage of each country's jobs that are dependent on sales to foreigners, the enormous implications of trade for the economic welfare of many of these countries become readily apparent.

Methods of Making International Payments

For our purposes, the really different aspect of an international transaction is that two different kinds of money are involved. Whereas a transaction between Americans can be simply settled by the buyer handing dollars over to the seller, a transaction between an American and an Englishman is not quite so simple. For in this case, assuming that the American is the buyer, the English seller wants his own currency, pounds, in payment, but the American buyer normally possesses only dollars.

What solution is available? Stripped to its bare essentials, what is required is a mechanism through which dollars can be exchanged for pounds with a minimum of inconvenience to both parties. Such a mechanism exists in the form of the *foreign exchange market.*

The foreign exchange market, like any other market, is made up of buyers, sellers, and middlemen. The object of sale, foreign exchange, consists of foreign currency, demand deposits in foreign banks, and other highly liquid short-term claims payable in foreign money. It is, to put it briefly, the nation's supply of foreign money, plus very-short-term claims to it. The buyers of foreign exchange (from the American viewpoint) are all those Americans who desire to purchase goods or services or perhaps securities from foreigners — essentially, U.S. importers. The sellers of foreign exchange (still from the U.S. viewpoint) are those Americans who, through the sale of goods or services or securities to foreigners, have acquired foreign money that they would like to convert into dollars — essentially, U.S. exporters.

The middlemen involved in this market are of special concern. It is, of course, their function to bring buyers and sellers together. These middlemen, in the majority of cases, are large commercial banks located in the nation's financial center (New York, for the United States), acting in the capacity of exchange dealers or brokers.

The commercial banks that perform this vital middleman function in the foreign exchange market arm themselves for their task by establishing a correspondent relationship with their counterparts in the financial centers of the other countries of the world. The role of the correspondent is an important one. Generally, the American bank will maintain a checking account in its foreign correspondent in the form, of course, of the other country's money. And, in the usual case, the foreign correspondent will reciprocate by maintaining a deposit, in dollars, in the U.S. bank. Besides holding demand deposits for one another, correspondents perform a number of other important services, some of which will be noted in the paragraphs that follow.[2]

So much for the institutional structure of the foreign exchange market. Our immediate concern is to get some feel for how it works — that is, how international payments are actually made. In what follows, we shall make no attempt to describe all the possible means of making such payments. They are many and varied and, indeed, they change as world trade patterns, competitive conditions, and the like change. What we shall attempt is a description of two of the most prominent mechanisms of payment, leaving greater detail for more specialized treatments. These two will then be relied on as examples for our further consideration of international finance.

Let us consider, for our example, a transaction between an American and a British company where the value involved is $200,000 (or, alternatively, if the exchange rate between the dollar and pound is $2 per £1, £100,000). The mechanism and effects of payment for a U.S. import will be considered in two ways, and then we shall turn everything around for a look at the mechanism and effects of payment for a U.S. export.

Payment for a U.S. Import

Bank Draft   By far the simplest payment instrument in use in international finance is the *bank draft*. A bank draft is merely a special kind of check — an order to pay — that one bank draws on its account at another bank.

Here the American importer would go to one of the large New York banks

---

[2] We shall oversimplify in this chapter in several respects. First, we ignore the great and growing significance in the foreign exchange market of branches of U.S. banks located in foreign countries. Second, for the moment, we ignore the dollar's status as an international reserve currency, similar in many respects to gold. Thus, though in fact most transactions with the United States are settled by increasing or decreasing dollar balances owned by foreigners in the United States, we proceed in this chapter as if adjustments in foreign money balances owned by U.S. banks are equally as important.

that deals in foreign exchange[3] and "buy a draft" that the New York bank would draw on its account at its correspondent bank in London. The U.S. importer, for example, would write a check for $200,000 (plus a service charge) on its own checking account and turn it over to the New York bank in exchange for the draft, which is a check the New York bank makes out for £100,000 on its account at its London correspondent, made payable to the British exporter. The draft is then sent to the exporter, who deposits it in her own account in London.

Let us take a look at the T-account effects of all this. Assuming that the U.S. importer keeps an account at the same New York bank from which the draft is purchased, the effect of its purchase on the New York bank would be as follows:

New York Bank

Demand deposit owned at London correspondent − $200,000 (worth of £s)	Demand deposit of U.S. importer − $200,000

When the draft is received and deposited by the British exporter in the London correspondent bank, the effects on that bank are

London Bank

	Demand deposit of New York correspondent bank − £100,000
	Demand deposit of British export company + £100,000

And that is all there is to it. The U.S. importer has used his dollars to buy pounds from the middleman, the New York bank, and has transferred these pounds to the British exporter to pay his bill. Sometimes such payments are made immediately on receipt of the goods being shipped, but often, especially if the importer is well known, the goods are shipped on a 30-day *open account*. This simply means that payment, by the same means as those just described, does not have to be made until the end of the 30-day period.

Bill of Exchange   The other mechanism of payment is a bit more complicated. In this case the payment process is initiated, not by the importer, but by the exporter. In our example, the British exporter would draw up a *bill of exchange*, a document described by some as a "You owe me." In simplest terms, it is a paper that states on its face that certain goods are being shipped to a specific U.S. company, for which payment of $200,000 is expected. This bill of exchange can then be taken by the British exporter to her London bank and "sold" to it for pounds at the going exchange rate (less a discount to account for the fact that the London bank will not be immediately repaid). The exporter thus gets her payment in pounds immediately and her London bank has the bill. The London bank will immediately send the bill to its New York correspondent bank, which will, in turn, present it to the U.S. importer for "acceptance."

The U.S. importer accepts the obligation stated in the bill by simply signing

---

[3] It would not really have to go directly to one of these, as its own local bank may have a correspondent relationship with a New York bank. It is simpler, however, for purposes of exposition to assume that the U.S. importer is located in New York.

"accepted" on the face of it. In the usual case, other documents associated with the shipment, most importantly the bill of lading, are attached to the bill of exchange. Upon acceptance, the bill of lading, which gives the holder the right to go to the docks and claim the goods that have been shipped, is detached by the bank and is turned over to the importer.

Sometimes the bill will call for immediate payment by the importer, and sometimes it will call for payment 60 or 90 days hence. In the latter case, the New York bank that now holds it can do one of two things, depending on instructions from its London correspondent. It can hold the bill (an "acceptance" now that it has been signed) until maturity, at which time the U.S. importer must meet his obligation for the face value of the acceptance by writing a check for $200,000 and placing it in the account the London bank holds at its New York correspondent.[4] In this case, the London bank is providing the credit involved.

If, on the other hand, the London bank does not choose to finance the transaction, it will instruct its New York correspondent to rediscount the acceptance in the New York money market. This simply involves finding an American lender who will purchase it at its discounted value and hold it for 60 to 90 days to earn the interest involved.

If the U.S. importer is small and not widely known, it may have received advance permission from its own New York bank to have the British exporter draw the bill of exchange on the bank, rather than the importer. Then, when the bank accepts it, the acceptance is much more readily salable in the money market because it is the bank's own promise to pay. Such an instrument is typically referred to as a *banker's acceptance.*

What are the T-account effects with the bill of exchange? When the British exporter sells the document to her London bank, the entries would be

London Bank

Discounts and acceptances +£100,000	Demand deposit of British exporter +£100,000

If the London bank chooses to remain the owner of the acceptance until its maturity, the effects of final payment by the U.S. importer on the two banks involved would be

New York Bank		*London Bank*	
	Demand deposit of U.S. importer −$200,000	Demand deposit owned at New York correspondent bank +£100,000 (worth of dollars)	
	Demand deposit of London correspondent bank +$200,000	Discounts and acceptances −£100,000	

[4] The London bank, which paid the British importer £100,000 less a discount, receives the full $200,000, the difference being the interest it earns for financing the 60 or 90 days of credit. It should be pointed out that the original purchase price agreed upon between the two companies would be such that the discounted amount received by the British exporter would fully compensate it. The American importer, who is really getting the 60 or 90 days' credit, bears the interest cost.

Payment for a U.S. Export

Bank Draft   When the United States exports, as might be expected, everything is reversed. If we assume, once again, that a $200,000 sale is involved, the British importer could pay most directly by purchasing a bank draft from her London bank for approximately £100,000 and sending it directly to the U.S. exporter, who deposits it in his New York bank. In this case, the T-account entries are

London Bank		*New York Bank*	
Demand deposit owned at New York correspondent bank −£100,000 (worth of dollars)	Demand deposit of British importer −£100,000		Demand deposit of U.S. exporter +$200,000 Demand deposit of London correspondent bank −$200,000

Bill of Exchange   On the other hand, if a bill of exchange is used, the U.S. exporter would draw it up and have it discounted at his New York bank. The New York bank would send it to its London correspondent, who would present it to the British importer for acceptance and, if the New York bank requested, hold it there until maturity. At maturity, the British importer would, of course, pay in pounds, thereby increasing the New York bank's foreign balances. The T-accounts (once again ignoring the interest involved) would look like the following: (1) when the bill is originally discounted at the New York bank,

New York Bank	
Discounts and acceptances +$200,000	Demand deposit of U.S. exporter +$200,000

and (2) when the importer pays at maturity,

New York Bank		*London Bank*	
Demand deposit owned at London correspondent bank +$200,000 (worth of £s) Discounts and acceptances −$200,000			Demand deposit of British importer −£100,000 Demand deposit of New York correspondent bank +£100,000

The Foreign Exchange Effects of Imports and Exports — A Summary

Again, the two types of payment just discussed are included only as examples for future reference. Many other payment methods might be described if techniques and instruments of international payment were our prime concern. In fact, of course, they are not.

What is of the greatest importance for the student's undertaking of upcoming material is not the details of international payment transactions themselves but the effects of such payments on the quantities of foreign exchange (foreign money) owned by the nations involved and, in turn, the tendency for such changes to affect *exchange rates.*

An exchange rate, of course, is simply *the price of foreign money in terms of your own.* From the U.S. viewpoint, for example, the dollar price of a British pound (as of December 1990) was about $1.93; the price of a German Deutsche mark was $0.67 and that of a Japanese yen was a bit over one-half of a cent.

As with any price, exchange rates tend to move in accordance with supply and demand.[5] Let us make use of the two examples of payment already discussed to trace through the basic exchange rate effects.

When an American imports British goods, as we have seen, the payment process must either reduce the supply of pounds owned by U.S. banks (if a bank draft is used) or increase the supply of dollars owned by British banks (if a bill of exchange is employed). In either case the result will be a tendency for the dollar price of pounds to rise (or, equivalently, the pound price of dollars to fall). For if pound balances owned by U.S. banks fall (the bank draft case), this constitutes a reduction in the supply of pounds and a tendency for their dollar price to rise. Conversely, if dollar balances owned by British banks rise (the bill of exchange case), that rise in the supply of dollars will tend to lower the pound price of dollars.[6]

Consequently, we can conclude that U.S. imports from Britain will

1. Either lower the supply of pounds owned by U.S. banks or raise the supply of dollars owned by British banks.
2. Tend to raise the dollar price of pounds [which is commonly referred to as *depreciating* the dollar (and *appreciating* the pound)].

American exports have exactly opposite effects. If payment is made by a British importer via a bank draft, the supply of dollars owned by British banks will fall. If a bill of exchange is used, the payment process will result in an increase in the supply of pounds possessed by U.S. banks. In either case, the dollar price of pounds will tend to fall (meaning, of course, that the pound price of dollars rises). Therefore we can conclude that U.S. exports to Britain will

1. Either raise the supply of pounds owned by U.S. banks or lower the supply of dollars owned by British banks.
2. Tend to lower the dollar price of pounds *appreciating* the dollar (and *depreciating* the pound).

---

[5] As we shall see, however, government intervention into the foreign exchange market has often been employed to "peg" exchange rates at levels other than the equilibrium rates private supply and demand would have established.

[6] If the exchange rate initially is $1.90 per £1, and an increase in U.S. imports tends to push it to $2.00 per £1, this change (from the U.S. viewpoint) represents a *rise* in the number of dollars required to buy a pound. From the British viewpoint, the same $2.00 per £1 rate represents a *reduction* in the number of pounds needed to buy a dollar.

The Balance of Payments

In any year, of course, there are many transactions between Americans and foreigners such as those just described. It is obviously useful, for policy purposes, to know something about their total and composition for the nation as a whole. This is the purpose of the *balance of payments*, compiled regularly for the United States by the Department of Commerce.

A thorough understanding of the logic, concepts, and organization of the balance of payments is an indispensable first step to any discussion of international trade problems. And yet, such understanding does not always come easily.

Let us begin at the beginning with a working definition. The U.S. balance of payments can be defined as *a listing of both sides of every economic transaction between American residents and foreign residents during the year, grouped according to the direction of payment required*. One way of presenting a balance-of-payments statement is shown in Table 25-3.

TABLE 25-3   U.S. balance of payments statement

Import items: Transactions requiring payments by Americans to foreigners (debits)	*Export items: Transactions requiring payments to Americans by foreigners (credits)*
1. Imports of goods	1. Exports of goods

2. Imports of services
    Examples:
    a. Foreign ships transport U.S. goods.
    b. American tourists spend money abroad.
    c. Value of the services of foreign capital used by Americans during the year (equal in amount to interest, dividends, and profits received by foreigners on investments in the United States).
	2. Exports of services
	    Examples:
	    a. U.S. ships transport foreign goods.
	    b. Foreign tourists spend money in the United States.
	    c. Value of the services of American capital used by foreigners during the year (equal in amount to interest, dividends, and profits received by Americans on foreign investments).

3. Unilateral transfers (gifts from Americans to foreigners).	3. Unilateral transfers (gifts from foreigners to Americans).

4. Change in U.S.-owned private assets held abroad
    a. Purchase by Americans of stocks, bonds, and short-term IOUs issued by foreign firms and governments.
    b. Purchase by Americans of plant and equipment abroad ("direct" investment).
    c. Americans increase ownership of demand deposits in foreign banks (or foreigners reduce ownership of demand deposits in U.S. banks).
	4. Change in foreign-owned private assets held in the U.S.
	    a. Purchase by foreigners of stocks, bonds, and short-term IOUs issued by U.S. firms and governments.
	    b. Purchase by foreigners of plant and equipment in the U.S. ("direct" investment).
	    c. Foreigners increase ownership of demand deposits in U.S. banks (or Americans reduce ownership of demand deposits in foreign banks).

5. Change in U.S. official reserve assets held.	5. Change in foreign official reserve assets held.

Before we look at the various categories of transactions within the balance of payments in somewhat more detail, one point should be stressed. It is an accounting statement, based upon the fundamental premise that there are *two* sides to every transaction. When the balance of payments is presented as in Table 25-3, every transaction between Americans and foreigners will affect it in two places, one on each side, reflecting the two sides of the transaction.

Suppose, for example, that the U.S. exports $100 million worth of goods to foreigners and that payment is made via a bill of exchange increasing American bank holdings of demand deposits in foreign banks. The two sides of this transaction are (1) the shipment of goods from us to them and (2) their payment for these goods by giving our banks increased deposits in their banks. The first side of the transaction — the $100 million shipment of goods to foreigners — would clearly be entered on the right-hand side of the U.S. balance of payments as a "Transaction Requiring Payment to Us" (see Table 25-3). We have sent them something of value, and that flow of goods to them establishes an obligation for them to send us something equivalent in return. That "something equivalent in return" — the payment of $100 million in the form of an increase in U.S. banks' holdings of deposits in foreign banks — is entered on the left-hand side of the statement under the heading "Change in U.S.-owned private assets held abroad" (see Table 25-3, item 4c). Their payment for our goods, then, is listed separately as a type of "Transaction Requiring Payment by Americans."

The point that merits stress and also, unfortunately, often creates confusion is that *each side of every transaction is entered on the side of the balance-of-payments statement that reflects the direction of the obligation incurred.* The fact that we happen to know that in this particular case the left-hand entry merely represents payment for goods we have sent them should not be permitted to obscure the fact that their sending us increased claims on their banks does represent something for which we must pay (and *have* paid, in the form of the goods sent).

In going through the details of the balance-of-payments statement presented in Table 25-3, students will be well advised to ask themselves the following questions about any transaction:

In this transaction, what are the "things of value" we are sending foreigners (goods, services, securities, deposits in our banks, gold)? The value of such things is entered on the right-hand side. What are the "things of value" they are sending us in return (goods, services, securities, bank deposits, gold)? The values of these things are left-hand entries in our balance-of-payments statement.

Let us now consider some of the details of Table 25-3.

1. *Exports and Imports of Goods.* There is little problem in understanding and properly locating these. When we export goods, we clearly send out something of value for which we expect payment; and when we import goods, the reverse is true.

2. *Exports and Imports of Services.* Only slightly greater difficulty is encountered here. If U.S. ships transport foreign goods or if foreign tourists enjoy U.S. hotels, restaurants, and recreation facilities, U.S. citizens are providing valuable services for foreigners for which the U.S. citizens expect payment. Such items will therefore be right-hand entries, representing exports of services. On the other hand, to the extent that foreign ships transport U.S. goods and to the considerable extent that U.S. tourists spend money traveling abroad, foreigners are providing services for U.S. citizens for which the foreigners must be paid. These, then, are left-hand entries.

Students sometimes have difficulties with another item that we list as a part of exports and imports of services — investment income. This represents interest, dividends, and profits earned during the year on investments owned abroad. The *dollar amount* of the payment of interest, dividends, and profits to Americans, earned on securities and branch plants owned abroad, is considered to represent *the value of the services of American capital* exported during the year and, as such, appears on the right-hand side of the balance of payments. The dollar amount of interest, dividends, and profits, paid by Americans to foreign owners of U.S. corporate or government securities or branch plants here, is treated as an import of the services of foreign capital, a left-hand entry.

How does this treatment fit in with our prior classification of right-hand entries representing things of value done by Americans for foreigners, requiring payment to Americans, and left-hand entries representing things of value done by foreigners for Americans, requiring payment by Americans? Very simply. The item that goes on the right-hand (export) side represents the *value of the services* U.S. capital invested abroad has performed for foreigners during the year, for which Americans expect payment. This entry is *not* the payment itself (although it is equal to it in amount) but the value of the services rendered for which payment (which will show up elsewhere on the left-hand side) is due. Similarly, the amount of interest, dividends, and profits paid by Americans to foreigners is taken to represent the *value of the services* performed by foreign capital invested in the United States, a service for which Americans must pay.

3. *Unilateral Transfers.* The unilateral-transfer entry in the balance-of-payments statements is somewhat more difficult to explain. The problem is that, by their very nature, *unilateral* transfers are not two-sided, quid pro quo, transactions. They represent gifts between Americans and foreigners which *have* only one side.

Since such gifts are one sided, and the balance of payments is an accounting statement that must always balance, a fictitious "other side" — unilateral transfers — is employed to keep things in balance. An example might help make this clear.

Suppose the U.S. government makes a $1 billion gift to a foreign government in the form of a dollar deposit in New York banks. The effect of such a transaction on the U.S. balance of payments would be:

Transactions Requiring Payment by Americans	*Transactions Requiring Payment to Americans*
Unilateral transfers $1 billion	Foreigners increase ownership of demand deposits in U.S. banks $1 billion

It is fairly easy to justify placement of imports of goods and services on the left-hand side as "Transactions Requiring Americans to Pay Foreigners," since in these cases we are clearly receiving things of value for which payment is surely required. In the case of unilateral transfers, however, it is stretching things a bit to say that when we make gifts to foreigners, we receive something of value for which we are obligated to make payment. Perhaps in this case we had best call the unilateral-transfer entry what it is — a balancing item needed to provide an "other-side" entry to balance the gift.

4. *Change in U.S.-Owned and Foreign-Owned Assets Held Abroad.* It is a natural but serious mistake to think only of imports and exports of goods and services when considering a nation's international transactions. These transactions do constitute the bulk of what is called the "current account," but they ignore altogether the international investment transactions included in the "capital account."

In any given year, Americans "invest" abroad by buying long-term securities issued by foreign firms and governments (such as stocks and bonds), by buying shorter-term IOUs of foreigners, and by purchasing outright plants located abroad (generally referred to as direct investment). At the same time, foreigners are investing in the U.S. by buying stocks and bonds and shorter-term IOUs issued by U.S. firms and governments, as well as by purchasing directly productive facilities within the U.S.

There is nothing unusual or surprising about that, of course. However, their treatment in the balance-of-payments statement is often the source of confusion. Many people have difficulty understanding the fact that when Americans invest abroad, the transaction is included on the same side as imports of goods, as a "Transaction Requiring Payment by Americans to Foreigners."

The logic of this treatment is really quite simple. When Americans invest abroad they receive valuable pieces of paper — the stocks, bonds, shorter-term IOUs, or deeds to foreign plants — for which they must pay. Looking at the transaction in this way, it is clear that the entry on the left-hand (import) side is intended to reflect the *value of the paper claims American investors get* (import); the actual "capital export" or the actual *payment* by the Americans for these paper claims (stocks, bond, etc.) appears somewhere on the right-hand (export) side.

Similarly, when foreigners purchase claims (stocks, bonds, etc.) issued by U.S. firms and governments, the purchase appears on the right-hand (export) side of the U.S. balance of payments because, in truth, when foreigners invest here Americans *are* exporting valuable IOUs to foreigners for which they have a right to expect payment. The actual payment, or "capital import" if that phrase is desired, will show up on the left-hand (import) side.

To illustrate, suppose bonds issued by foreign companies are paid for by an American purchasing a draft from a New York bank. How will this transaction affect the U.S. balance of payments?

Transactions Requiring Payment by Americans	Transactions Requiring Payment to Americans
Imports of stocks and bonds $100 million	American banks' ownership of demand deposits in foreign banks is reduced $100 million

The left-hand entry depicts the shipment of bonds to U.S. investors. The right-hand entry reflects the payment for them.

A word of caution before we go on. The reader should take care to avoid confusing interest and dividends earned with new investments. The payments for the former, of course, represent income from the services of capital invested in past years. Expenditures on the latter, on the other hand, permit an *increase* in the stock of capital that Americans have invested abroad and lay the basis for even greater interest and dividend payments in future years. The volume of U.S. foreign investment and the volume of interest and dividends received are both, over the long run, related. It is, however, important to recognize their fundamental differences.

5. *Change in U.S. and Foreign Official Reserve Assets.* U.S. official reserve assets consist of four assets possessed by the U.S. government: gold, regular drawing rights at the IMF, special drawing rights at the IMF, and foreign currencies. We postpone discussion of these assets until Chapter 27.

Why the Two Sides of the Balance of Payments Must Balance— Some Further Examples

Having stressed the double-entry nature of the balance of payments, it should be obvious that when all transactions are considered, the two sides must be equal. This, of course, follows from the fact that every single transaction that affects the statement has offsetting effects on each side. The balance of payments always balances, numerically, by definition. It, like the equation of exchange, is a truism.

This definitional equality of the two sides of the entire balance-of-payments statement does not hold for any single part or parts of the statement, however. That is, there is no reason why exports of goods should necessarily equal imports of goods or that goods and services exports should not exceed or fall short of goods and services imports. Although the sum of *all items* on the left-hand side is defined as equal to the sum of *all items* on the right-hand side, no such equivalence holds for any of the parts of the statement.

We conclude this section with a list of examples of the balance-of-payments effects of particular transactions in the hope that (1) they will further illustrate that every transaction has offsetting entries, thereby requiring that the balance of payments must balance and (2) they will help to clarify some of the areas of difficulty in the preceding material.

1. An American company sells $100,000 worth of goods to a British company, payment being made on a bill of exchange that increases the balances owned by New York banks at their London correspondents:

Transactions Requiring Payment by Americans	*Transactions Requiring Payment to Americans*
Increase in U.S.-owned private assets held abroad $100,000	Exports of goods $100,000

2. American owners of securities issued by a British firm receive $50,000 of dividend payments, the mechanism of payment raising the balance owned by New York banks at their London correspondents:

Transactions Requiring Payment by Americans	Transactions Requiring Payment to Americans
Increase in U.S.-owned private assets held abroad $50,000	Exports of services $50,000

3. Americans purchase $250,000 of the common stock of a British company, the payment process raising the dollar balances of London banks owned at their New York correspondents:

Transactions Requiring Payment by Americans	Transactions Requiring Payment to Americans
Change in U.S.-owned private assets held abroad $250,000 (import of the stock)	Change in foreign-owned private assets held in the U.S. $250,000 (increased dollar deposits owned by British banks)

4. The U.S. government makes a gift of $500,000 to a foreign government in the form of dollar deposits in New York banks:

Transactions Requiring Payment by Americans	Transactions Requiring Payment to Americans
Unilateral transactions $500,000	Change in foreign-owned private assets held in the U.S. $500,000

5. The foreign government spends these dollars to buy goods from U.S. companies, thereby reducing its claim on U.S. banks:

Transactions Requiring Payment by Americans	Transactions Requiring Payment to Americans
Change in U.S.-owned private assets held abroad $500,000 (foreigners reduce ownership of deposits in U.S. banks)	Exports of goods $500,000

The U.S. Balance of Payments for 1990

Preliminary data for the U.S. balance of payments for 1990 are presented in Table 25-4. We use this table as a basis for defining a number of summary relationships that are of significance in evaluating the U.S. performance in international transactions for the year.

The Balance of Merchandise Trade

The difference between a nation's exports of goods and its imports of goods is called its balance of trade. If the nation's goods exports exceed its goods imports, it is said to have a *balance-of-trade surplus.* If, on the other hand, imports of commodities exceed exports of commodities, the nation is said to have incurred a *balance-of-trade deficit.*

TABLE 25-4 U.S. balance of payments, 1990 (billions of dollars)			
Imports of goods	$498.0	Exports of goods	$389.3
Imports of services	228.9	Exports of services	259.5
Unilateral transfers, net	21.1		
Change in U.S.-owned private assets held abroad[a]	59.1	Change in foreign-owned private assets held in U.S.	56.8
Change in U.S. official reserve assets	2.2	Change in foreign official reserve assets	30.8
		Statistical discrepancy	73.0

[a] Includes some government-owned assets other than official reserve assets.
Source: Survey of Current Business, U.S. Department of Commerce.

As Table 25-4 indicates, the United States ran a large balance-of-trade deficit in 1990, a total of just under $109 billion. Indeed, as Table 25-5 makes clear, the 1980s produced a series of unprecedented trade deficits for the United States, a development to which we return in Chapter 27.

The Balance on Goods and Services

When the sum of our imports of goods *and services* is subtracted from the sum of our exports of goods *and services,* the result is referred to as the nation's balance on goods and services. Despite the fact that U.S. exports of services exceeded imports by over $30 billion in 1990, the nation incurred a goods and services deficit of over $78 billion.

It should be noted that although Americans earned interest, dividends, and profits of almost $130 billion on their foreign investments during the year, foreigners earned over $121 billion on their investments here. The dramatic rise in foreign earnings here is a direct result of the large U.S. deficits during the 1980s.

The Balance on Current Account

The balance on current account results from adding net unilateral transfers to the balance on goods and services. That is, the sum of U.S. imports of goods and services plus U.S. gifts to foreigners is subtracted from the sum of U.S. exports of goods and services plus foreign gifts to Americans. In 1990, as is clear from the data in Table 25-5, the United States had a deficit in its balance on current account of just under $100 billion.[7]

---

[7] The nation's balance on current account plus any allocations of special drawing rights during the year is equal to net foreign investment in the U.S. national income and product accounts. The balance on goods and services is similar, but not quite identical to, net exports in the national income accounts. The latter excludes U.S. government interest payments to foreigners, while the balance on goods and services includes them.

TABLE 25-5 U.S. international trade performance, 1946–1990 (billions of dollars) deficit = negative

Year	Balance of trade	Balance on goods and services	Balance on current account	Year	Balance of trade	Balance on goods and services	Balance on current account
1946	6.7	7.8	4.9	1969	0.6	3.4	0.4
1947	10.1	11.6	9.0	1970	2.6	5.6	2.3
1948	5.7	6.9	2.4	1971	−2.3	2.3	−1.4
1949	5.3	6.5	0.9	1972	−6.4	−1.9	−5.8
1950	1.1	2.2	−1.8	1973	0.9	11.0	7.1
1951	3.1	4.4	0.9	1974	−5.3	9.3	2.1
1952	2.6	3.1	0.6	1975	9.0	22.9	18.2
1953	1.4	1.2	−1.3	1976	−9.3	9.4	4.4
1954	2.6	2.5	0.2	1977	−30.9	−9.5	−14.1
1955	2.9	2.9	0.4	1978	−33.8	−9.7	−14.8
1956	4.8	5.2	2.7	1979	−27.3	5.1	−0.5
1957	6.3	7.1	4.8	1980	−25.3	8.3	1.5
1958	3.5	3.1	0.8	1981	−28.0	11.1	6.3
1959	1.1	1.2	−1.3	1982	−36.5	−1.1	−9.2
1960	4.9	5.1	2.8	1983	−67.1	−37.1	−46.6
1961	5.6	6.3	3.8	1984	−112.5	−94.3	−106.5
1962	4.5	6.0	3.4	1985	−124.4	−102.7	−117.7
1963	5.2	7.2	4.4	1986	−147.7	−125.4	−140.6
1964	6.8	9.6	6.8	1987	−160.3	−140.5	−154.0
1965	5.0	8.3	5.4	1988	−127.0	−113.9	−128.9
1966	3.8	6.0	3.0	1989	−114.9	−95.4	−110.0
1967	3.8	5.7	2.6	1990	−108.7	−78.2	−99.3
1968	0.6	3.6	0.6				

Source: Department of Commerce.

The Significance of International Deficit and Surplus Measures

As we have seen, the United States encountered sharply accelerated deficits in all of its major balance-of-payments summary measures during the 1980s. We turn now to consider the implications of these deficits for the nation's current and future economic welfare.

First, it should be recognized that the balance on merchandise trade, while readily available and widely publicized, can be a misleading indicator and, by itself, has relatively little significance. While it does, of course, accurately portray the balance of goods trade, it has the deficiency of tending to "emphasize excessively the distinction between goods and services, which is of little economic significance." [8]

[8] See "Report of the Advisory Committee on the Presentation of Balance of Payments Statistics," *Statistical Reporter*, June 1976, p. 227.

The balance on goods and services, however, has the advantage of being very closely related to the net export component of the national income and product accounting system and, more fundamentally, provides an accurate measure of the net transfer of real productive resources to or from foreigners as a result of the year's trade. A goods and services surplus, for example, implies that, on balance, a portion of the output of a nation's resources was exported to foreigners, whereas a deficit signifies that, on balance, part of the output of foreign resources was imported during the year. What Table 25-5 tells us then is that during most of the 1980s, the United States was to a considerable and, indeed, unprecedented extent living off the rest of the world.

In many ways, the balance on current account is the most meaningful of the three summary measures we have defined. What do current account deficits of over $100 billion really mean? They measure the extent to which the United States went into debt to the rest of the world during those years.

The reader is asked to recall the balance-of-payments statement as presented in Table 25-3. Note that the current account encompasses items 1, 2, and 3 on both sides of the balance sheet. A $100 billion current account deficit means that the sum of items 1, 2, and 3 on the left-hand (import) side exceeds the sum of items 1, 2, and 3 on the right-hand (export) side by $100 billion. The nation has imported $100 billion more goods and services than it has exported and since item 3 takes account of any gifts in either direction, we necessarily still owe foreigners for them.

Indeed, the reader should recognize that as a matter of definition, **any current account deficit must be matched by an equal capital account surplus.** That is, if the sum of items 1, 2, and 3 on the left-hand side exceeds the sum of items 1, 2, and 3 on the right-hand side (since the balance-of-payments statement as a whole balances by definition), the sum of items 4 and 5 on the right-hand side (which measure increasing debt by Americans to foreigners) must exceed the sum of items 4 and 5 on the left-hand side. To paraphrase a statement made many years ago by a famous economist, "if we import more goods and services than we export, and they haven't given them to us (item 3 in the balance of payments) then we necessarily still owe them for them" (items 4 and 5 in the balance of payments).

Attitudes Toward International Deficits and Surpluses

To understand the meaning of equilibrium in the level of production is to know that it is not necessarily a good situation, merely a sustainable or stable one. It may be bad or good depending, among other things, on the level of employment.

Does the same thing hold for equilibrium (the absence of deficits or surpluses) in a nation's balance of payments? Is it necessarily a "good" position? The question is a difficult one, not readily subject to a yes or no answer. Nor, for practical purposes, does it really need to be answered because equilibrium is, at best, a transitory phase in the real world, seldom really reached, retained only momentarily. For most nations, living reality usually consists of either a deficit or a surplus. What of these? Is one good and the other bad, or must we resort to that time-honored hedge, "It all depends"?

We have come a long way since the days when the early British economists devoted themselves to battling the then-dominant philosophy of the mercantilists regarding the goal of international trade. To the mercantilists, the measure of success of an economy was the size of its stock of precious metals, and the prime means of increasing this stock was via the development of a balance-of-payments surplus. In their view, then, a surplus was good and a deficit, bad.

Entrenched though it was, this mercantilist philosophy could not long hold up under the determined onslaught of the earlier classical economists. But although the "free trade" disciples won the day in the minds of the intellectuals of their time, the mercantilist ideas died hard in the minds of the general public. Indeed, it is probably fair to say that these ancient fallacies are still very much alive in some circles.

Of course, as the years went by, the arguments in support of the proposition that surpluses were good and deficits bad took on new sophistication. The emphasis on the accumulation of gold, as in and of itself a major virtue, soon gave way to stress on objectionable employment, wage rate, or other such effects of deficits. But the implications for policy purposes were not much changed.

In more recent years, a simple erroneous analogy may be as responsible as anything else for the popular conception of surpluses as good and deficits, bad. This is the pervasive, yet grossly misleading, habit of identifying the nation and its goals with those of a single business firm. Its simple application to international trade problems is clear and straightforward. "A firm is better off when it sells more (takes in more revenue) than it buys (pays out in costs). Therefore, a nation that is able to sell more to the rest of the world than it buys from it is clearly better off too."

Whatever the appeal of the deceptively simple logic in the preceding quotation and however much it may seem to be in accord with common sense, it is neither logical nor sensible. The analogy drawn between the firm and the nation is simply faulty, and policy measures based on it are likely to be equally faulty. Indeed, it would be difficult to find a more important single source of economic illiteracy than the tendency to equate the nation and the firm.

Consider, for example, the implications of a current account surplus. The nation that achieves one does so only by sending out to foreigners, through export, more of its own goods and services than it receives from abroad.[9] In return, the surplus country accumulates short- and long-term IOUs. Now this result may very well be fine for a while. But the effects of such a surplus are not good in and of themselves. What, after all, is so good about sending useful products out to other countries and receiving back promises to pay? Clearly, the IOUs add to the nation's real economic welfare only if they are used up in later years to finance added imports. And that amounts to saying that the good thing about a surplus is the fact that it permits a country to enjoy the fruits of a later deficit. Obviously, a national policy aimed at perpetual balance-of-payments surpluses would be a shortsighted one!

We are forced to the conclusion that it is not really possible to classify surplus and deficit under a "good" or "bad" tag. On the one hand, there is nothing especially good, from a nationalistic economic point of view, about a nation aiming at the perpetual support of other nations (which is what a permanent surplus on current account implies). On the other hand, a nation cannot expect to

---

[9] Ignoring, for the moment, unilateral transfers.

reap the short-run benefits of a deficit without, sooner or later, having to settle up accounts. Every nation, over a period of time, must experience both surpluses and deficits, and a conscious public policy that aims at the perpetuation of either one must certainly be mistaken.

And yet, entirely aside from erroneous viewpoints based on mistaken analogies or mercantilist reasoning, it is quite clear that in most countries there is more worry, more immediate pressure to "do something about it," in the case of a deficit. Indeed, a main focus of the succeeding discussion will be on what can be done to eliminate deficits.

Such an attitude is perfectly natural. A nation with a current account surplus is accumulating other countries' IOUs. As long as it is willing to accept these in exchange for the extra goods and services it is shipping out, it does not have to worry about corrective steps. If, on the other hand, it is operating at a deficit, no such long-run arrangement is possible. For a while, of course, it can get along by using up its current supply of internationally accepted reserves in payment. But this is at best a temporary solution, since no nation possesses an unlimited supply of international reserves. Once they are lost, if the deficit persists, its only option is to issue IOUs payable in its own currency. But this too is likely to be a limited source of relief, since, except for the case of a "key currency" country whose domestic currency *is* a form of international reserves, such IOUs are likely to be of only limited acceptability.

The certain knowledge that deficits can only be financed for limited periods, and that failure to curb them may ultimately require major readjustments within their domestic economy with serious implications for their citizens' living standards, quite naturally induces most governments to take long-term, chronic deficits quite seriously. In the next chapter we shall consider what mechanisms and measures exist to correct or adjust such international payments imbalances.

Review Questions

1. Compare the effects on the financial institutions involved and on the pound-dollar exchange rate of payment for a U.S. export to Britain by a bank draft and by a bill of exchange.

2. Carefully explain why the two sides of a nation's balance of payments must always balance.

3. "When Americans invest abroad, the effect on the U.S. balance of payments is similar to that of a U.S. import of goods." Explain.

4. Define and compare
   a. Balance-of-trade deficit.
   b. Balance on goods and services surplus.
   c. Balance on current account deficit.

5. Explain why a national policy aimed at a permanent balance of payments

surplus would not only be virtually impossible to achieve but probably very foolish.

6. From a strictly nationalistic viewpoint it could be argued that, if either were possible, a perpetual goods and services deficit would be vastly superior to a perpetual goods and services surplus. Comment.

7. "Since the balance of payments must always balance, a nation incurring a current account deficit must be importing capital." Explain.

8. In the period from 1976 till 1982, the U.S. regularly ran balance-of-trade deficits but, in most years, had goods and service surpluses. What balance-of-payment entry was most responsible for these surpluses?

9. Speculate on the effect of continuing over $100 billion dollar current account deficits on the economic welfare of future generations of Americans.

CHAPTER 26

International Payments Systems and Their Functions

It is the existence of political boundaries dividing the world into a large number of sovereign nations that makes some sort of *system* to facilitate international exchange a necessity. If all countries used the same type of money and none had the power to obstruct movement of goods or resources across their borders, international economic transactions would be in no significant way different from purely domestic ones. For good or ill, however, our world is not that sort of world, and some sort of international monetary system has been deemed a necessity for generations.

What Is the Function of an Ideal International Monetary System?

Just as most purely national economic systems are aimed at maximizing consumer satisfaction in the nation as a whole, the ideal international monetary system would be one that promoted an allocation of limited world resources that would maximize the satisfaction of all mankind. More specifically, such a system should facilitate the freest possible movement of goods and resources so as to permit (1) the widest possible degree of world specialization of production in accordance with comparative advantage and (2) a free flow of capital from the wealthier, better developed countries to the poorer, lesser developed nations.

Achieving this laudable goal, however, would require a system so structured as to (1) encourage producers and consumers around the world to participate freely and willingly in international commerce and (2) make it unnecessary for sovereign national governments to resort to trade barriers and obstructions to the free flow of capital to protect their own national interests. Such a system, in turn, would seem to necessitate the existence of each of the following:

1. An effective balance-of-payments *adjustment mechanism*
2. An adequate supply of internationally accepted money, or, to use the more common phrase, *international liquidity*
3. A sufficiently *stable international economic environment* to minimize the risk of those who might participate in international trade

Before we discuss several possible types of international monetary systems, let us look at some of the implications of these three requirements.

An Effective Adjustment Mechanism

As we have seen, chronic current account deficits tend almost inevitably to generate governmental action aimed at restoring equilibrium. Such actions, unfortunately, have often taken the form of trade barriers, capital controls, and other measures that seriously hamper free trade and the maximization of world living standards. Consequently it is most important that the international monetary system contain within it some automatic mechanism for promptly and effectively eliminating chronic deficits so that such destructive discretionary national measures do not become necessary.

How can a current account deficit be adjusted — that is, eliminated? By the creation of conditions under which the deficit nation can reduce its imports and/or raise its exports, of course. And what are the determinants of a nation's imports and exports? Basically, a nation's imports will be larger (1) the higher its income, (2) the lower the level of foreign domestic prices relative to its own, and (3) the lower the cost of the foreign money in terms of its own (the exchange rate). Similarly, its exports will be larger (1) the higher the level of foreign incomes, (2) the lower its own domestic price level relative to its trading partners, and (3) the lower the cost of its money to foreigners.

It should be apparent that the first two determinants of imports and exports just itemized — the level of national income and domestic price levels — are to a considerable degree controllable via appropriate changes in aggregate demand in the deficit and surplus countries. A country's imports can be reduced if its aggregate demand is held down, causing its own income to fall (and thus reducing its ability to buy foreign goods). Its exports can be increased if its domestic price level can be restrained sufficiently to make its goods relatively more attractive, as far as price is concerned, to foreigners.[1]

But note that something quite similar can result from an exchange rate change. The cost of the deficit country's goods to foreigners is dependent on *both* that country's domestic price level and the cost of its money. If the British price of

---

[1] At the same time, increases in aggregate demand in countries with balance-of-payments surpluses can raise their incomes, permitting them to buy more from the deficit country and increase their domestic price levels, thereby reducing the attractiveness of their exports (the deficit country's imports).

Scotch is £3, and the exchange rate between the dollar and the pound is $3 to £1, a bottle of British Scotch costs an American importer $9. If a cut in the British aggregate demand should lead to a cut in the domestic price to £2, Scotch would cost the American only $6. But the same result could be achieved by depreciation of the pound to $2 per £1. In this case, even if the British price of Scotch stays at £3, the American can obtain it for only $6 because the £3 required to buy it costs only that much.

Therefore, "adjustment" of payments deficits can be accomplished either through a reduction in aggregate demand in the deficit country relative to that of its trading partners or through a reduction in the value of its money relative to that of other nations (that is, a change in its exchange rate). In evaluating the three international monetary systems discussed in the paragraphs that follow, we shall need to consider carefully the effectiveness of the built-in adjustment mechanism in each case.

Sufficient International Liquidity

When a nation incurs a payments deficit, as we have seen, it generally covers the deficit by an appropriate short-term capital movement. If its banks happen to own sufficient deposits in the banks of the nations to which it owes money, it can, of course, use those deposits for payment. If, however, it owes some countries more than the total of its banks' accumulation of their particular currencies, it may have to pay up with a form of money generally accepted by all nations — so-called international reserves. Gold, of course, has for years been an important part of the world's international reserves. So too, for almost five decades, has the U.S. dollar.[2]

Now as there can be no doubt that under any international monetary system, some countries will at all times be incurring deficits, it is essential that there be a sufficient supply of international reserves (or liquidity) available to let them get by until the deficit can be eliminated. And, because the volume of trade grows every year, it must be expected that the volume of deficits that must be covered will grow also. This means, if world trade is not to be hampered by inadequate liquidity, that the international monetary system must include some dependable means of increasing the volume of international reserves at a rate commensurate with the growth of international commerce.

Incidentally, the quantity of international reserves required is directly related to the efficiency of the adjustment mechanism discussed earlier. As we shall see, the quantity of international reserves required for the successful operation of a payments system calling for relatively stable exchange rates tends to be much larger than that needed in a system permitting freely floating exchange rates. Under stable exchange rate systems, not only are adequate supplies of international reserves essential for implementation of the mechanism stabilizing ex-

---

[2] As the U.S. dollar has been accepted as a form of international reserves, the U.S. has been able to cover its long string of deficits by allowing foreign countries to build up short-term dollar claims in this country. This approach, however, has not been open to most other nations. Other forms of international reserves such as IMF borrowing rights and special drawing rights are considered in the next chapter.

change rates but relatively inefficient adjustment mechanisms may often lead to longer periods of deficit to be financed.

A Stable Economic Environment with Minimum Risk

A third requirement for an effective international monetary system, in the eyes of many, is a set of arrangements whereby individual participants in international trade will be protected from unusual risks resulting solely from the fact that their business is international. For many years the chief issue in this area has been the degree of *stability of exchange rates*. Relatively stable exchange rates, it has been argued, have the advantage of lessening risk to traders and international investors, thereby encouraging more international transactions and permitting a fuller exploitation of the advantages that accrue to all from greater worldwide specialization.

It is not difficult to understand the argument here. If an American importer agrees to pay £100,000 for British goods 60 days from the date of sale, a sharp increase in the price of pounds during the 60-day period could turn a potentially profitable deal into a financial disaster. If the cost of pounds was $2.00 per £1 when he made an agreement, he expected his cost to be $200,000. But if the exchange rate jumps up to $2.50 per £1 at the end of the 60 days, he will be required to pay $250,000, a figure that may more than wipe out his expected profit. Now, if our importer is not a speculator, willing to gamble on the possible equal chance that he may gain by a reduction in the cost of pounds, as well as lose by a rise, he may simply shy away from international trading altogether, preferring to concentrate on less risky domestic trade. Consequently the volume of international trade, and its important attendant advantage of fuller specialization, may be impeded.

Whatever the merits of this argument for stability in exchange rates, it must be recognized that—to a degree at least—it tends to conflict with the requirement for an effective adjustment mechanism. As we have seen, the adjustment of a balance-of-payments deficit can be aided either through a reduction in aggregate demand in the deficit nation or through a change in its exchange rate. Clearly, then, a system that attempts to provide a stable economic environment through arrangements to maintain relatively fixed exchange rates does so at the expense of one of the factors that promotes adjustment. This issue of fixed versus fluctuating exchange rates has long been an area of serious conflict among experts on international finance, and we shall consider it in great depth at a later point.

Three Alternative International Monetary Systems

Although many variations are possible, three distinct types of international monetary systems have been predominant in the past century. These include the full international gold standard, the system in effect from 1945 to 1971, which we shall refer to as the Bretton Woods system, and the freely floating exchange rate system. Let us consider the characteristics of each of these in turn.

The Full International Gold Standard

The full international gold standard, under which much of the world operated for many years prior to the 1930s, required a nation to observe certain rules. Specifically, each government was required to

1. Define its monetary unit as being equivalent to a fixed amount of gold (for example, prior to 1933, one U.S. dollar was defined to equal 23.22 grains of gold).
2. Stand ready to exchange its monetary unit for gold, or gold for its monetary unit, in unlimited amounts with anyone, at that price.
3. Allow gold flows out of the country to automatically reduce the nation's money supply and gold flows in to automatically raise the money supply.

Defenders of the gold standard argued that such a system would not only provide the advantage of stable exchange rates but also offer an effective automatic adjustment mechanism. Let us see how it was expected to work.

Stable Exchange Rates Under the Gold Standard   Suppose that the United States has defined the dollar as equivalent to 23.22 grains of gold and that England has defined the pound as being the same as 113 grains of gold.[3] Now, as both monies are defined in terms of a common substance, gold, they are related to one another. This relationship, called the *mint part of exchange,* is obtained by dividing the gold content of the dollar into the gold content of the pound. The result of this operation is approximately 4.87, indicating that the mint par of exchange between the pound and the dollar under these arrangements was $4.87 per £1.[4]

If, for purposes of furthering the example, we assume that the cost of transporting 113 grains of gold across the Atlantic in either direction is 2 cents, we can state definitely that the cost of British pounds can never exceed $4.89 per pound or be less than $4.85 per pound. The exchange rate, in other words, can fluctuate only within the relatively narrow limits of $4.85 per £1 and $4.89 per £1.

The force that assures this high degree of exchange rate stability is the self-interest of traders. No American importer (needing pounds to make payment) will pay more than $4.89 to obtain a pound because she does not need to. Any tendency for the price of pounds to rise (as a result of a U.S. deficit that makes the U.S. demand for pounds exceed the supply) is limited by the gold standard mechanism itself. No American importer would be willing to pay more than $4.89 to get the pound she needs because she can always take (or, more

---

[3] These are the actual relationships set by the two governments during much of the heyday of the international gold standard.

[4] It should be noted that this is not, in and of itself, an exchange rate, but simply the arithmetical result arrived at by dividing the statutory gold content of the dollar into the statutory gold content of the pound. It merely said that the British government had defined the pound as being worth as much gold as the American government had said $4.87 was worth.

likely, her bank will take for her) $4.87 to the U.S. Treasury and get 113 grains of gold, ship the gold to England, and exchange it at the British Treasury for one pound. The cost of shipment being 2 cents, our U.S. importer's total expense for her pound is $4.89. Under these gold standard arrangements, she need never pay more to get it.

Similarly, the British importer, if he is a profit maximizer, will never accept anything less than $4.85 for his pound when he uses it to obtain the dollars he needs to make payment. For he too has the option of taking his one pound to the British Treasury, exchanging it for 113 grains of gold, shipping the gold to the U.S. Treasury, and swapping it there for $4.87. As he pays 2 cents transport cost, he realizes a minimum of $4.85 for his pound. He need not accept less.

Thus, with the conditions as stated, the exchange rate between the dollar and the pound can only fluctuate within the narrow limits of $4.85 per £1 and $4.89 per £1. When a U.S. deficit raises our demand for pounds above our supply of them, the price of pounds can only rise to $4.89 per pound, at which point it will be cheaper for American importers to pay by shipping gold to England. The upper limit, the $4.89 per £1 rate, is called the *U.S. gold export point.* On the other hand, when a British deficit (necessarily a U.S. surplus in a two-country world) increases the U.S. supply of pounds above the U.S. demand for them, the price of pounds for Americans will fall toward $4.85 per pound (the cost of dollars to the British will rise to the point where they get only $4.85 for each pound), beyond which it becomes cheaper for British importers to obtain their dollars by shipping gold to the United States. The $4.85 per £1 rate is, thus, the *U.S. gold import point.*

The Adjustment Mechanisms Under the Gold Standard

The "Indirect, Money Supply" Mechanism When a country on the full gold standard incurs a balance-of-payments deficit, payment for that deficit will automatically tend to cause both its and the surplus countries' money supplies to change in the direction required to reduce the disequilibrium. Suppose, for example, that the U.S. has developed a trade deficit with Britain. Payment for the excess U.S. imports will (because our demand for pounds exceeds the supply of pounds being provided by our exporters) initially tend to drive up the dollar price of pounds. Under the gold standard, however, the price of pounds can only rise slightly to the U.S. gold export point, after which gold will flow out of the U.S. to pay, in effect, for the deficit.

Now the loss of gold must have some effects on the economy of the deficit country. It represents, after all, the base of its money supply under the gold standard. When the U.S. Treasury sells gold, not only the money supply but also commercial bank reserves go down by the amount of the sale. This means, in a fully "loaned-up" banking system, the domestic money supply may be cut by several times the amount of the gold loss.

But that is not all. The money supply reduction that results automatically from the gold loss must, in turn, other things being equal, raise the rate of interest and, in greater or less degree, cut down on aggregate demand.[5] And a reduction

---

[5] Indeed, under the unwritten but generally understood "rules of the game" of the gold standard, the central bank was expected to reinforce the effects of the gold loss by raising its discount rate to raise interest rates even more.

in aggregate demand must reflect itself in lowered prices and/or reduced employment, production, and income.

How does all this tend to reduce the deficit that started it all? Very simply. To the extent that the deficit country's prices are cut, it becomes a cheaper market for foreigners (as well as its own citizens) and it may therefore expand its exports. If, as is likely with the "sticky" prices with which we are familiar today, the cut in aggregate demand lowers incomes, the deficit country, having less to spend both at home and abroad, will import less. In either case, the effect is to lessen the deficit.

While all this is going on in the deficit country, the surplus country or countries are feeling the reverse effects. There, gold flows in, bank reserves and the money supply are increased, interest rates tend to be reduced, aggregate demand rises, and prices and/or incomes are raised. As a result of the price and/or income increases, the surplus countries' exports are cut and their imports raised, intensifying the corrective effects both there and in the deficit country. This chain of effects for both countries can be summarized as follows.

Deficit country	*Surplus country or countries*
1. Imports > exports	1. Exports > imports
2. Demand for foreign money > supply of foreign money	2. Demand for foreign money < supply of foreign money
3. Price of foreign money rises to gold export point	3. Price of foreign money falls to gold import point
4. Gold flows out	4. Gold flows in
5. Bank reserves and money supply cut	5. Bank reserves and money supply rise
6. Interest rates rise	6. Interest rates fall
7. Aggregate demand falls	7. Aggregate demand rises
8. Prices and/or incomes fall	8. Prices and/or incomes rise
9. To extent prices fall, exports rise; to extent incomes fall, imports fall	9. To extent prices rise, exports fall; to extent incomes rise, imports rise

The Direct Effects on Aggregate Demand   In addition to the adjustment effects generated automatically through money supply changes, there are certain *direct* effects on aggregate demand that should be noted.

When foreigners spend money to buy currently produced goods and services from a nation's export industries, it is clear that they, no less than the domestic investors, government, and consumers, are adding to the demand for the output of its industry. For an open economy, then, total spending equals not just $C + I + G$, as we assumed in chapters 16 through 20, but rather $C + I + G + X$, where X equals a nation's exports of newly produced goods and services.[6]

---

[6] A word of clarification is in order at this point. The more generally accepted way of defining total spending is $C + I + G + (X - M)$, where C, I, and G are defined to include *total* purchase of consumer, investment, and government goods from home and abroad. When defined this way, the imports must be subtracted out somewhere to avoid overstating the demand for domestic production. Our procedure here will diverge from the usual in that C, I, and G will be used to refer to purchases from *domestic producers only*. With this definition, there is no need to subtract expend-

As an element of total spending, exports are very much like investment and government spending in that their amount is largely unrelated to the domestic level of income. How much a nation is able to sell as exports is pretty much dependent on such external factors as *foreign* tastes and incomes and relative prices and only slightly and indirectly influenced by the domestic income level. Consequently we treat it, as we do investment and government spending in the main, as an autonomously determined element of the demand for a nation's goods and services.

A nation's imports of goods and services, on the other hand, are, in most essential ways, like saving and taxes. For, like saving and taxes, they are an element of income earned from the current production of the nation, which *is not* spent to buy its newly produced goods and services. They represent, that is, an additional leakage. Consequently, when the theoretical material covered earlier is modified to allow international trade into the picture, instead of saying that all income earned from production is split into three parts, $C + S + T$, we must recognize that it is divided into *four* parts, $C + S + T + M$, where M stands for imports.

Imports of goods and services are like saving and taxes in still another way. All three are directly related to the level of income. This is especially true to the extent that a country's imported goods are consumer goods, because in this case, just as a country is able to spend more for domestically produced consumer goods when its income rises, it also tends to spend more on foreign-produced items.[7]

When exports of goods and services are admitted as an element of total spending for a nation's output, and imports of goods and services are recognized as a leakage from its incomes, we must amend the conditions for stable, rising, and falling production listed earlier for a closed economy only. Now, we must say

1. Condition for stable production (equilibrium):

$$when \ C + I + G + X = C + S + T + M$$

2. Condition for rising production:

$$when \ C + I + G + X > C + S + T + M$$

3. Condition for falling production:

$$when \ C + I + G + X < C + S + T + M$$

It is these new conditions that reveal most clearly the second automatic corrective mechanism to which we referred as the direct effects. A country that

---

itures on imports, as they are never included in the first place. Total spending on U.S.-produced goods and services then can be expressed as $C + I + G + X$, and a shift from buying imported consumer goods to buying domestically produced consumer goods will raise the U.S. consumption function.

[7] Indeed, just as we were able earlier to talk about a marginal propensity to consume and a marginal propensity to save, we could now talk in terms of a marginal propensity to import, defined as $\Delta M/\Delta GNP$.

incurs a balance-of-payments deficit (where the deficit is caused by an excess of goods and services imports) is, on that account, leaking more out of its income stream than foreigners are adding to it through their purchases. Consequently, *in addition to the corrective mechanism that works indirectly through affecting the money supply,* we have a direct cut in the nation's total spending through its international trade. Whenever imports of goods and services exceed exports of goods and services, the nation's involvement in international trade directly reduces its total spending. Conversely, an excess of goods and services exports over imports adds to total spending.

Now for our deficit country, this direct cut in aggregate demand puts further downward pressure on its prices and/or income, resulting in even greater increases in its exports and reductions in its imports than the indirect, money supply corrective mechanism alone would produce.

How Effective Were the Gold Standard's Adjustment Mechanisms?   Just how effective were those adjustment mechanisms? In a world with extremely flexible prices, they might well be quite effective, because the reduction in total spending induced by the balance-of-payments deficit would have its impact primarily on domestic prices rather than on income and employment.

In the modern world, however, prices tend to be extremely rigid in the downward direction, so that reductions in demand initially fall largely on physical output, income, and employment. Although, as we have seen, reductions in a deficit nation's income *will* tend to reduce its deficit, the corrective mechanism involved actually works by requiring the deficit nation to undergo recession and unemployment. This was a prime reason for abandoning the international gold standard in the 1930s. The major countries involved, already reeling under the devastating effects of worldwide depression, decided that the gold standard's "medicine" of unemployment was worse than the "disease" of international payments deficits. We must therefore conclude that in a world in which government policymakers are constrained from condoning periodic recession and excessive unemployment, the gold standard's automatic adjustment mechanisms would be unacceptable.

The Bretton Woods System of Stable, but Adjustable, Exchange Rates — 1945 to 1971

Before World War I, the international gold standard served admirably; after that war, however, the reestablished gold standard floundered and finally collapsed amid the chaos of the early 1930s. As a consequence, it was decided, after World War II, to abandon the "discipline of gold" in favor of a new system, which, it was hoped, would retain the gold standard's major advantages while eliminating its most glaring drawbacks.

Under the new system established at the Bretton Woods Conference in 1944, most of the world's nations bound themselves to the regulations of the newly established International Monetary Fund. IMF member nations were required to define their currencies in terms of a fixed amount of gold (or dollars — the dollar being already defined in terms of gold) to set up initial postwar exchange rates.

Gold, therefore, was still destined to play a key role in international monetary matters. It was, however, no longer a dominant role. The old link between the gold supply and the domestic money supply had been abolished. The fixed commitment to pay out gold for domestic currency in unlimited amounts to anyone had been universally eliminated. Indeed, only the United States agreed to exchange gold for its domestic currency, and even that pledge was open only to foreign governments. Clearly, many of the features of the old gold standard had disappeared.

The founders of the IMF sought a mechanism that would retain the gold standard's virtue of relatively stable exchange rates but not its vice of requiring deficit nations periodically to abandon their domestic commitment to the maintenance of full employment. The system that emerged, often described as a system characterized by "adjustable pegs," required that exchange rates be kept quite stable except in cases of chronic deficit. In these cases, *devaluation* of the currency (that is, a once-and-for-all official change in its exchange rate, lowering the value of its money relative to that of other countries), was to be relied on to facilitate adjustment.

Exchange Rates Under the Bretton Woods System   Exchange rate stability was maintained in the following manner. The United States, which owned about 75 percent of the "free-world" gold supply when the system was first introduced, was expected to keep the dollar tied to gold by freely exchanging it for dollars held by foreign governments at a fixed rate of $35 per ounce. Other member nations, having announced an official exchange rate between their currencies and the dollar, were expected to use national *exchange stabilization funds* to peg the exchange rate at that level.

The exchange stabilization funds, in theory at least, operated very simply. They were equipped (by their governments) with supplies of gold, foreign exchange, and their own domestic money. When the exchange rate between theirs and another country's currency threatened to exceed the limits set, it was the task of the stabilization fund to enter into the other side of the market and halt the undesired change.

Suppose, for example, that the British government had set the par value for the pound at £1 per $2.40.[8] Under the rules of the IMF, the British Exchange Stabilization Fund was required to take action to limit actual variations in the dollar-pound exchange rate to within 1 percent on either side of the stated par value. Roughly speaking, this meant the pound-dollar exchange rate was pegged by the British Exchange Stabilization Fund within the limits of £1 per $2.38 and £1 per $2.42.

Within these narrow limits, of course, the exchange rate was subject to the same supply-demand forces as a freely floating rate. If British imports rose, the demand for dollars rose, pushing the price of dollars up (the rate approached the £1 to $2.38 limit). If British exports increased, the supply of dollars rose, lowering the cost of dollars to English citizens (the rate approached the £1 to $2.42 limit).

All this may perhaps best be illustrated by Figure 26-1. Suppose that the par value of the Belgian franc in terms of the dollar has been set at 50 francs per dollar. From the Belgian viewpoint, assume that the initial demand for dollars (on

---

[8] This was the official par value of the pound from 1967 to 1971.

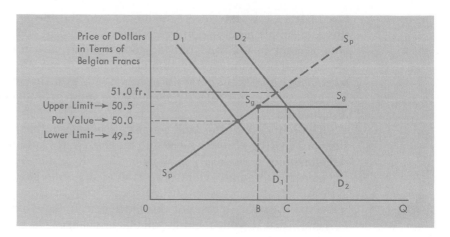

FIGURE 26-1   Stabilization of exchange rates under IMF

the part of Belgian importers) is D_1D_1. If the initial supply-of-dollars curve (provided by Belgian exports) is S_pS_p, the actual initial exchange rate will be 50 francs = $1.

Now assume that Belgian tastes change in favor of products from the United States, raising the demand-for-dollars curve to D_2D_2. If the Belgian Exchange Stabilization Fund did not intervene, the cost of dollars would rise to the level at which D_2D_2 and S_pS_p intersect — 51 francs per dollar. Under its IMF obligation, however, the Belgian government could not permit this — a 2 percent rise in the price of dollars — to occur. Its Exchange Stabilization Fund would enter into the foreign exchange market to keep the increase in the price of dollars within 1 percent (no higher than 50.5 francs per dollar).

When the Belgian Exchange Stabilization Fund is brought into the picture, the supply-of-dollars curve becomes the kinked line $S_pS_gS_g$. The S_gS_g portion of the curve depicts dollars coming on to the exchange market from the Belgian government. To keep the exchange rate pegged within permissible limits, the Belgian Exchange Stabilization Fund would have to use up BC of its available supply of dollars.

If, on the other hand, the franc price of dollars was tending to fall below 49.5 francs per dollar, the Belgian authorities would enter on the other side of the market — buying dollars with francs — to maintain the required degree of exchange rate stability.

The Adjustment Mechanism Under the Bretton Woods System   As already noted, it was the intention of the framers of the International Monetary Fund that countries with chronic balance-of-payments deficits should rely primarily on devaluation of their currencies (lowering their stated par value with respect to the dollar) to provide needed balance-of-payments adjustment. Although the devaluation device was employed quite frequently between 1945 and 1971, it turned out to be something of a disappointment in practice for two main reasons.

First, deficit countries tended to be reluctant to employ it except as a last resort. Defense of the international value of their currency (that is, the current par value with respect to the dollar) was unfortunately permitted to assume domestic political overtones of such significance that governments of deficit countries came to look upon devaluation as a last-ditch, desperation measure accompanied by substantial loss of political face. Second, among the most serious deficit situations was that of the United States, which — because the U.S. dollar was an important part of the world's supply of international reserves and because the United States did not directly control exchange rates between the dollar and other national currencies — did not consider devaluation a measure open to it.[9] The result of all this was that the devaluation device as the basic adjustment mechanism never adequately fulfilled the expectations of the IMF's founders.

What other adjustment mechanisms besides devaluation existed under the Bretton Woods system? The "indirect, money supply" mechanism discussed under the gold standard amounted to very little under the IMF. Even if a payments deficit did, in and of itself, reduce the deficit country's money supply and bank reserves, there was no commitment to avoid offsetting those effects with an expansionary discretionary monetary policy. Under the full gold standard, it was clearly understood that the rules of the game forbade a domestic monetary policy that offset the changes in money caused by international disequilibrium. Under the IMF system, there was no such outright commitment.

The same direct effect adjustment mechanism discussed under the gold standard still existed. A nation with a deficit resulting from importing more goods and services than it exported could expect this to directly reduce its aggregate demand and, through this, its income and/or prices. It should be stressed, however, that this mechanism only helped when the deficit showed up in the nation's balance on goods and services. A deficit such as the United States ran regularly between 1950 and 1970 was accelerated, rather than combated, by these "direct effects." For, as we have seen, the United States consistently exported more goods and services than it imported in every post–World War II year prior to 1971, its deficit being balanced by long-term investment abroad and unilateral transfers. Consequently, American involvement in international trade *raised*, rather than lowered, U.S. aggregate demand for almost 20 years.

In summary, it is generally agreed that the Bretton Woods system contained automatic adjustment mechanisms that were quite weak, too weak in the opinion of many critics to do the job of correcting serious and chronic payments imbalances.

The Freely Floating Exchange Rate System

A system of freely floating exchange rates involves the most direct extension of the institutions of the free market into the settling of international transactions. Under such a system, exchange rates are determined solely by supply and demand with, in theory at least, no intervention by government. Unlike the other two types of systems discussed, it cannot boast of a long history of use, as it has

[9] The United States controlled only the relation between the dollar and gold, whereas *other* countries controlled the exchange rates between their currencies and the dollar. As we shall see, the United States *did* finally devalue the dollar in 1971 and again in 1973, but the essence of the IMF system was markedly changed before this could be accomplished.

generally been resorted to only for relatively short periods after a fixed rate system has broken down. After the downfall of the gold standard in the early 1930s until World War II, a variant of a floating rate system existed. Similarly, since March 1973, when the attempt to maintain stable exchange rates under the IMF setup was abandoned, much of the world has been operating with floating rates. In both cases, however, national governments have intervened considerably into foreign exchange markets, producing a "managed" or "dirty" float rather than the "clean" float envisioned in theory by many of the backers of the freely floating exchange rate system.

Determination of Exchange Rates Under a Freely Floating System   Under a freely floating exchange rate system, commercial banks or other foreign exchange dealers would (as they do now) act as middlemen in the foreign exchange market, buying foreign money (primarily in the form of deposits in foreign banks) from those who have it to sell and selling foreign money to those wanting to buy it for dollars. The price that these banks charge for a unit of foreign money, that is, the exchange rate, would depend solely on supply and demand.

The demand for foreign money — let us say, pounds — would clearly come from those Americans who need pounds to make payment for goods and services bought in Britain. U.S. importers then would be the source of the demand for pounds. The supply of pounds, on the other hand, would come largely from British importers who need to get hold of dollars or, what amounts to the same thing, U.S. exporters who earn pounds through their sales to the British.

Given a competitive foreign exchange market and no interference from government, the price of pounds would then continually move toward an equilibrium level, where the demand on the part of importers just equaled the supply coming from exporters. If, at the current exchange rate, the quantity of pounds demanded exceeded the quantity supplied, the dealers (banks) would simply raise the price. If the quantity supplied should exceed the quantity demanded, the price of pounds would tend to fall. Under a freely floating exchange rate system, then, the price of foreign money would tend to rise as imports rise and to fall when exports rise.

The Adjustment Mechanism with Freely Floating Exchange Rates   Opponents of a freely fluctuating exchange rate system object strenuously to the instability that they believe is injected into the international payments scene by rates free to move without limit. Supporters of floating rates, however, see freedom to move as a major virtue. For the change in exchange rates itself constitutes an automatic adjustment mechanism which can quickly and efficiently reestablish international payments equilibrium.

The mechanism in this case is impressively simple. Let us refer to Figure 26-2 to work it through. Suppose, as before, that the initial equilibrium exchange rate between the Belgian franc and the U.S. dollar is 50 francs to 1 dollar, with Belgian importers' demand for dollars being depicted by D_1D_1 and the supply of dollars being earned by Belgian exporters shown as S_1S_1. Note that at this initial equilibrium, the quantity of dollars demanded by importers (OA) exactly equals the quantity of dollars supplied by exporters. An equilibrium exchange rate means that the value of exports equals the value of imports — equilibrium in the balance of payments.

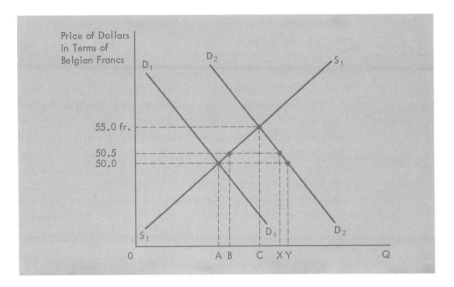

FIGURE 26-2 Reestablishing equilibrium via floating exchange rates

Now, as before, suppose that Belgian tastes change in favor of American goods, raising Belgian imports from the United States and shifting the demand-for-dollars curve out to D_2D_2. Such a development means that initially (at the 50 francs to 1 dollar rate) the quantity of dollars demanded exceeds the quantity supplied by **AY**. And imports exceed exports by the same amount.

But this is a simple supply and demand case. The sellers of dollars (Belgian banks), facing an excess demand and seeing their inventory of dollars being drawn down, will quite naturally move to raise the franc price of dollars. Under the two systems previously discussed, this rise in the franc price of dollars could only proceed for a short distance before gold flows or exchange stabilization fund activity would stop it. For example, as noted, under the old IMF rules, the exchange rate could only rise to 50.5 francs per dollar before being halted by the government. Accomplishing this would not only drain the stabilization fund's dollar resources by an amount equal to BX but would leave Belgium with imports still exceeding exports.

Contrast this result with the floating exchange rate result. In this case, with no government intervention, Belgian banks will continue raising the franc price of dollars as long as demand exceeds supply. Only when the new equilibrium rate of 55 francs per dollar is reached will the rise stop.

More important, consider what this rise in the exchange rate does to Belgium's balance of payments. As the franc price of dollars rises, American goods, on that account, become more expensive to the Belgians, so their imports are reduced (by an amount equal to **CY**). Conversely, as an increase in the franc price of dollars means a *decrease* in the dollar price of francs, Belgian goods have been made *less* expensive to Americans who will buy more (in an amount equal to **AC**). The rise in the exchange rate, therefore, completely and automatically eliminates Belgium's balance-of-payments-deficit.

Summary: The Pros and Cons of the Three Types of Systems

What can we say in general summary about the relative merits of the three types of systems just covered?

The full international gold standard does have the advantage of stable exchange rates, but, given the downward rigidity of prices and the general reluctance of modern nations to put up with excessive unemployment, it seems clear that its adjustment mechanisms—whatever their intrinsic merits—would not be permitted to work. In addition, with gold itself as the sole form of ultimate international reserve, there is considerable question whether such a system would be capable of generating an adequate degree of liquidity to handle expanding world trade. In any case, the full gold standard as described here is currently an issue of only historical and academic importance. There is little interest in returning to it.

The Bretton Woods system in effect from 1945 to 1971 also had the merit of relatively stable exchange rates and appeared—on paper at least—to offer a somewhat better adjustment mechanism than the gold standard. In practice, however, as we have seen, the reluctance of deficit countries to avail themselves of the devaluation weapon more frequently undercut much of its potential for adjustment. The system did adapt itself reasonably well over the years to the international liquidity problem. Not only gold, but billions of U.S. dollars pumped out during years of American deficits, have provided ample liquidity. Also, a third source of international reserves—special drawing rights—was created by international agreement through the IMF. Consideration of special drawing rights will be postponed to the next chapter.

The freely floating exchange rate system, of course, must receive high grades for its adjustment mechanism and, given that advantage, cannot be faulted on grounds of international liquidity. However, the uncertainty generated by daily and unlimited changes in exchange rates is still a matter of concern for some observers. And, as we have learned in the mid-1980s, the effects of capital movements on exchange rates may sometimes push them in the opposite direction from that needed to produce a current account equilibrium. We return to the fixed versus flexible exchange rate issue in the concluding chapter.

Discretionary Government Policy Measures to Deal with International Payments Deficits

In the preceding section we have seen that no matter what the institutional arrangement, international payments deficits generate some of the seeds of their own destruction. Unfortunately, however, with the exception of the freely floating exchange rate case, none of the automatic mechanisms is vigorous enough to go all the way and completely wipe out the deficit that triggered them, unless severe unemployment is passively accepted.

The result is that the government in an economy with a chronic deficit, and a limited supply of foreign exchange to finance it, faces enormous pressure to "do something" about it. If automatic forces built into the international monetary system are inadequate to handle the adjustment task, then almost inevitably governments of such deficit-plagued nations turn to authoritative, discretionary policy to deal with it. The remainder of this chapter briefly considers four lines of discretionary action:

1. Erection of trade barriers
2. Reduction of governmental spending abroad and of governmental aid programs to foreign nations
3. Restrictive monetary and fiscal policy at home (coupled with pressure on surplus nations to enact more expansive monetary and fiscal policies)
4. In the case of a stable exchange rate system — devaluation

The Use of Trade Barriers

Trade barriers are as old as nations themselves. They include a wide variety of restrictive devices ranging from tariffs and such nontariff barriers as subsidies to exporters, "health and safety" standards discriminatory toward imported goods, and coerced "voluntary" agreements between governments to limit certain types of internationally traded items to more overt limitations such as explicit import quotas and exchange controls. Most are aimed at reducing imports, but a few constitute attempts to boost exports.

Tariffs are really a special form of excise tax placed upon the importation of foreign goods and services and, in some cases, securities. Quotas can be very much more restrictive in that they involve an absolute barrier to imports beyond a certain point rather than simply a hurdle that can be overcome. Exchange control can be the most extreme of all because, in this case, a governmental agency simply "takes over" all foreign exchange earned by the nation's exporters (by requiring its sale for domestic currency at a fixed exchange rate) and then rations it out to favored importers according to some scale of national priorities, thereby effectively eliminating excessive potential importers who would otherwise contribute to the deficit.

The trade barrier method of dealing with a balance-of-payments deficit is held in very low regard by most authorities. It should be, in the opinion of most, employed extensively only as a last resort. Its widespread unpopularity among economists results from the fact that it impedes international specialization and that it is unlikely to succeed in its objective in any case. The more fundamental economic objection to a raising of trade barriers is clear-cut. By interfering with the patterns of trade, such barriers limit the degree of international specialization and thereby lead to a misallocation of resources that reduces world production. On a more practical level, it is even to be doubted whether these objectionable results will, to any significant degree, be counterbalanced by a favorable effect on the nation's balance of payments. Trade barriers that work by cutting down a nation's imports necessarily reduce another nation's exports. It is extremely unlikely that the injured nation will simply sit there and take it; it will almost certainly retaliate quickly by raising its own trade barriers, thereby canceling out whatever balance-of-payments advantage the deficit nation had obtained from its own action. We must conclude that this course is, in general, to be avoided, although, as we shall see, it has not been.

Cutting Foreign Spending by the Government

A second discretionary approach available to cut a balance-of-payments deficit is for the government itself to reduce its foreign spending. To the degree that it imports goods and services, it could cut these; and to the degree that it makes gifts to foreigners, it could reduce these.

But even this apparently more direct approach is not without its problems. In the first place, whatever good effect it would have on the balance of payments might come at quite a cost. If, to solve a balance-of-payments deficit, a nation should sacrifice programs of foreign spending that seem important to its own security, the remedy might well be worse than the disease. In any case, a risk of undetermined magnitude exists.

In the second place, the good effects of this approach on the deficit country's balance of payments may be substantially less than would appear at first glance. When a government spends or gives its money to foreigners, the complete effect of this action on its balance of payments depends partly on what foreigners do with the funds they receive. If foreigners use money acquired in this manner to buy goods and services they would not otherwise purchase, from the deficit country, eliminating the gifts and/or government foreign purchases will reduce the goods and services exports of the deficit country along with the reduction in import items. To the degree that this happens, the deficit would be unchanged and the action, ineffective.

Restrictive Monetary and Fiscal Policy

Given the problems associated with the two discretionary policies already discussed, it would be ideal if the remaining tools could represent all virtue and no vice. Such, however, is not the case for restrictive monetary and fiscal policy.

This classical medicine to cure payments deficits works primarily by reinforcing the automatic mechanisms of fixed exchange rate systems. It consists of a tight-money policy and budget surpluses to raise a nation's interest rates and lower its prices and/or incomes. To the extent that short-term interest rates are raised, it is hoped that the nation will be the beneficiary of an inflow of short-term capital. To the extent that the nation's prices are reduced relative to others, it is expected that it will be able to sell more to foreigners. To the extent that its incomes are reduced, it is hoped that it will cut back on its imports.

There can be no doubt that sufficiently restrictive monetary and fiscal policies *can* eliminate a balance-of-payments deficit. But how this is accomplished is a matter of no little concern. If we lived in a world of very flexible prices — prices that would easily and quickly fall as a consequence of a cut in aggregate demand

— this policy would have much to recommend it. But, unfortunately, that is not our world. A reduction in aggregate demand resulting from restrictive monetary and fiscal policies would, given the downward inflexibility of prices in the modern world, almost certainly lower employment, production, and income in the deficit country. And that, of course, means that the real price of battling a payments deficit in this way is the creation of a domestic recession.

Recognizing these problems, a more popular approach in recent years has been for deficit countries to try to convince surplus countries to implement more expansive monetary and fiscal policies in the hope that the resultant rise in foreign demand and prices will accomplish the same effect at much less cost to the deficit nation.[10]

Devaluation of the Currency

If the international monetary system is such as to rely upon stable exchange rates pegged at certain levels by governmental action (as under the gold standard or Bretton Woods system), one further discretionary measure is available — devaluation of the currency.

Under any stable rate system, a nation's monetary unit must be defined by law as equivalent to a fixed amount of either some commodity such as gold or some other country's currency that is generally accepted as a form of international reserves. Such legally established par values may then be changed by the government involved when circumstances require it.[11] For example, under the Bretton Woods system, the British devalued the pound with respect to the dollar from $2.80 per pound to $2.40 per pound in 1967. And the United States devalued the dollar with respect to gold in both 1971 and 1973, changing the official gold price from $35.00 per ounce to $42.22 per ounce.

The purpose of devaluation is clear. By lowering the price of a nation's currency relative to others, it hopes to raise its exports. At the same time, because devaluation makes foreign money (and therefore foreign products) more expensive to its citizens, the devaluating nation hopes to cut its own imports.[12]

There is, however, no guarantee that it would work that way. In the first place, this action, as is true of an increase in trade barriers, is subject to retaliation on the part of the nation's trading partners — a development that could render it

---

[10] The reluctance of the United States to attack its 1977 current account deficit via restrictive aggregate demand policies was explicitly expressed in the 1978 *Economic Report of the President:* "Especially for large countries like the United States, where the economic cost of changing domestic growth is large relative to the improvement in the current account that would result, it is not appropriate to modify domestic objectives for economic growth in order to reduce the current account deficit" (p. 125).

[11] When the stated par value of a currency is reduced relative to other currencies (or gold) by a specific act of that nation's government, the currency is said to have been *devalued.* When the value of a currency falls relative to others as a result of supply and demand market pressures (as under a floating exchange rate system), the currency is said to have *depreciated.*

[12] The term *revaluation* has often been used to describe the reverse action — where a country *raises* its currency's value relative to others. This action might appropriately be undertaken by a country with substantial balance-of-payments surpluses and, perhaps, inflationary pressure.

totally ineffective. Nor is this the only problem. Even in the absence of retaliation, devaluation will only succeed in reducing the deficit if demand elasticities
are favorable.[13]

The point here is complicated, but important. Assume that the United States
has a deficit and that Great Britain represents its sole trading partner. If the
United States should devalue the dollar so that the exchange rate rises from $2
per £1 to $3 per £1, the action would certainly reduce the number of pounds
Americans purchase to pay for imports from Britain. So long as the U.S. demand
for British imports were anything other than *perfectly inelastic* (in which highly
unlikely case, Americans would purchase the same number of pounds at the
higher price), the devaluation would reduce the quantity of pounds (and, therefore, the quantity of imports) demanded by Americans and help to reduce the
U.S. deficit.

On the other side, however, things are not so clear-cut. American goods are
now cheaper for Britons because dollars cost less. But whether this would lead
them to spend more pounds on American goods depends upon the degree of
elasticity of the British demand for U.S. goods.

If their demand were of greater than unit elasticity, they would spend more
pounds on U.S. goods than before and the U.S. deficit would be further reduced.
If their demand were of unit elasticity, they would spend the same number of
pounds as before the devaluation and, although this would not help to cut the
U.S. deficit, the fact that Americans were buying fewer pounds from the British
would reduce it. If, however, the British demand for U.S. goods were of less than
unit elasticity, the devaluation would lead them to spend fewer pounds to buy
U.S. goods, which would, in and of itself, tend to worsen the U.S. deficit.

Under circumstances of highly inelastic demands in both countries, it would
be possible for devaluation to worsen the U.S. deficit. Because, if the American
demand were highly inelastic, the favorable effects of cutting the American
demand for British goods would be small. If the British demand for U.S. goods
were also highly inelastic, the unfavorable effects of cutting their demand for
U.S. goods would be large. In such a situation, devaluation would not only not
help, but it would worsen the U.S. deficit.

Summary of Discretionary Policies to Deal
with International Payments Deficits

Perhaps the best way of summarizing the points made in this section is to restate
the central lesson of economics. *As long as resources are scarce, getting more of
one thing requires giving up something else.* The same general point can be made
about any economic policy measures. *As long as our economic goals are in partial
conflict with one another, we may be able to achieve one only by losing some ground
in our progress toward another.*

A balance-of-payments deficit might be ended by trade barriers, but to do so
would impair the worldwide allocation of resources. It might be ended by reduc-

[13] Elasticity of supply in the affected countries is also a factor that is relevant in determining the
effectiveness of devaluation. To simplify as much as possible, we shall ignore this added complication in our discussion.

ing foreign spending by government, but to do so might jeopardize the national security. It might be countered by devaluation of the currency, but then again this might not work. Or finally, it could be fought with restrictive monetary and fiscal policy, but only at the likely cost of increasing unemployment.

The economic arena, it seems, is not one of blacks and whites, but one of grays. Economic policy measures are not classifiable into good and bad in any absolute sense, but almost all require a delicate balancing of the good effects against the bad. We must recognize that there are few policy measures that advance us toward one of our goals without, to some degree, conflicting with another.

Review Questions

1. "Ultimately, adjustment of a goods and services deficit can be accomplished either through lowering the external value of the deficit nation's currency or through reducing the rate of growth in the deficit nation's domestic prices and income." Explain.

2. Carefully explain why international liquidity tends to be more important with a stable exchange rate system than with a flexible exchange rate system.

3. Explain how, under a full international gold standard system
   a. Exchange rates were kept stable.
   b. Payments deficits generate changes that automatically tend to reduce the deficit.

4. Explain how, under the Bretton Woods system
   a. Exchange rates were kept stable.
   b. Nations with chronic payments deficits were expected to eliminate the deficits.

5. Explain how, under a freely floating exchange rate system
   a. Exchange rates are determined.
   b. Adjustment of a payments deficit would occur.

6. List and evaluate the discretionary measures available to policymakers to attempt to deal with international payments deficits.

Recent History and Current Problems in International Finance

The past century's experience in organizing and managing international monetary affairs provides painfully clear evidence indicating that there is no one perfect international monetary system ideally suited for all time and all situations. As patterns of trade, techniques of payment, degree of industrialization, and the like have changed over the years, international monetary institutions have been forced to adapt. The result has been a continuing evolutionary process that provided us with some experience with each of the types of systems described in the preceding chapter. If perfection in this complex area exists, the world has not yet found it. But the search goes on, right into the 1990s.

In this concluding chapter, we attempt to trace through the highlights of this process of change. The first section briefly comments on developments from 1870 to the end of World War II, during most of which the international gold standard played the central role. The second section reviews the 1945–1973 period, during which the Bretton Woods system implemented by the International Monetary Fund withstood, with varying degrees of success, a seemingly unending series of challenges and monetary crises. The concluding section deals with the massive upheavals that led to the abandonment of the Bretton Woods system in 1973 in favor of the current system of "managed" floating exchange rates and the problems since that time.

The Past — Mid-Nineteenth Century Through World War II

The Golden Era: 1870–1914

The period from about 1870 to 1914 has often been characterized as the *golden era.* During most of those years the world was untroubled by the vast upheavals associated with major wars, and the full international gold standard held the center of the stage.

It was in many ways an idyllic era, and the gold standard seemed to many to be the ultimate in sane and stable economic arrangements. Although such faith in the now discarded system may seem, with the invaluable aid of hindsight, to have been overdone, one can hardly deny that it worked amazingly well.

The unquestioned financial center of the world at the time was that staunch citadel of free trade, Great Britain. She played her key role well. As a developed industrial giant, Britain permitted less fully developed nations to finance trade deficits by making long-term loans abroad. As the heart of the financial world, she played an important role in fostering the development of freer trade with a minimum of trade barriers and restrictions. And, along with most other nations, her monetary authorities obeyed, reasonably faithfully, the rules of the gold standard game whereby monetary policy was tightened in the face of a payments deficit and eased to combat a surplus.

But it took more than skillful management to make the system work so well. Other conditions favored it greatly. In the first place, wages and prices were considerably more flexible than they are today. This had the important effect of permitting the drop in demand associated with payments deficits to lower prices rather than income and employment—a much preferred result. In addition, public and official attitudes had not yet reached the point where "doing something about unemployment" was considered a proper area for governmental action. Hence, the policy conflict that has worried us so much since—between policy to deal with inflation and a payments deficit and policy to deal with unemployment—was largely absent.

One does less than justice to the international gold standard if one does not recognize its solid record of accomplishment prior to World War I. And yet one does a certain violence to history if one does not recognize that the ideal conditions for its efficient operation largely evaporated under the extreme pressures of World War I and its aftermath.

The Unsettled Years: 1918–1930

Not that an attempt was not made to return to the "good old days" of the prewar gold standard after that conflict. Most major countries went back "on gold" as soon as possible. But the conditions of the nineteenth century, fortunately or unfortunately, were gone forever. The institutional trappings of the gold standard were restored, but the conditions necessary to make it a viable, efficient system of world financial order had simply disappeared.

A full discussion of the problems of the between-the-wars gold standard is not permitted by the scope of this book. We can, however, mention some of the chief causes of difficulty: unrealistic reparation demands imposed on vanquished Germany; an attempt by the British to reestablish their pound at the same relationship with gold as that maintained in prewar days—a clear overevaluation; excessive use of the protective tariff by the emerging industrial giant, the United States; and, finally, the growing recognition, especially after the experience of mass unemployment in the 1920s and 1930s, that the strict discipline of the gold standard required the sacrifice of what was rapidly emerging as the major domestic policy goal—restoring and maintaining full employment.

The combination of all these factors produced, if not a hostile climate, at least a less than ideal environment for a smoothly functioning gold standard. And when, in the early 1930s, the public's confidence in the ability of its governments to honor their pledge to pay gold on demand to all comers dipped sharply, country after country, drained of its gold supply through payments deficits, public hoarding demands, and speculative short-term capital movements, was forced to abandon the standard.[1]

The Chaotic 1930s

The decade of the 1930s was indeed a turbulent period in international finance. This period was marked not only by the abandonment of the gold standard by most nations but also by a wild scramble of unilateral devaluations, increased tariff barriers, and a whole range of actions calculated to impede the restoration of normal, free international exchange. It was an economically sick world that girded itself for the second all-out war of the century in 1939.

U.S. actions during the interwar period were, at times, deplorable; at other times, exemplary. The nation at first enabled the post–World War I reparations arrangements to work by, in essence, lending Germany sufficient amounts to enable the Germans to pay reparations to England and France, which countries, in turn, used these proceeds to pay off part of their war debts to the United States. U.S. lending to permit this triangular deal, however, was made necessary partly by its own greatly increased tariff barrier in the 1920s, which made it all but impossible for the Germans to earn the reparation payment through exports.

When the U.S. stock market crash in 1929 put a virtual end to long-term U.S. lending, and when the United States followed up this calamity with the new Smoot-Hawley tariff bill, establishing the highest tariff rates in its history, the Germans were simply unable to meet their obligations. And, in turn, the British and French were unable to keep up with scheduled repayments on their war debts to the United States. The result was that the United States had no choice but to declare a moratorium on payment of inter-Allied war debts, and, of course, the Germans were forced to default on much of their reparation burden.

Only in the latter 1930s did the United States begin to demonstrate its awareness of the futility of unilateral competitive trade restrictions. During this period the historic Reciprocal Trade Agreements Act was passed, providing for substantial reductions in U.S. tariff barriers; the Tri-Partite Agreement with England and France was signed, forming the basis for an end to competitive devaluation; and the Export-Import Bank was established to provide long-term loans to some of the trading partners of the United States.

These more enlightened, constructive policies were followed up during and after World War II with all-out efforts to avoid the mistakes of unilateralism of the 1920s and 1930s. No heavy reparations were demanded of the defeated Axis powers; no large inter-Allied debts were built up during the war, largely as a result of the U.S. Lend-Lease Program; the basis for large-scale international monetary cooperation after the war in the form of the International Monetary Fund was established at the historic 1944 conference at Bretton Woods; and the rebuilding of the economies of the war-ravaged Western Allies was speeded up

---

[1] It would be incorrect, however, to say that the U.S. decision to go "off gold" in 1933 was forced by any immediate shortage of gold reserves.

immeasurably by the unprecedented, far-sighted Marshall Plan. The lessons learned at such heavy cost in the interwar period had provided the basis for the far more enlightened multilateral approach of the late 1940s and 1950s.

The Bretton Woods System and the "Gold Exchange" Standard: 1945–1971

The international monetary system that emerged in the quarter-century following World War II was shaped primarily by two fundamental institutional developments — the implementation of the Bretton Woods agreement and the emergence of a "gold exchange" standard. Let us consider the essence of both of these developments before taking a look at how well they worked out in practice.

The Original Bretton Woods System and the International Monetary Fund

As already noted, the heart of the Bretton Woods agreement was the establishment of the *International Monetary Fund*. Its initial purposes, as clearly stated in its *Articles of Agreement* promulgated in 1944, were to (1) promote the growth of world trade through international cooperation, (2) work toward eliminating the widespread network of exchange controls in existence in the late 1940s, (3) establish a system whereby exchange rates could be kept relatively stable without returning to the shackles of the old full gold standard, and (4) provide a new source of loans of foreign exchange to assist member nations undergoing temporary or cyclical balance-of-payments deficits. The system is perhaps best described by the steps taken to implement the last of these two objectives.

The "Stable, but Adjustable" Exchange Rate System Established by the IMF   As we saw in the preceding chapter, exchange rates were to be kept stable primarily by the pegging activities of governmental exchange stabilization funds. The United States (possessor of a majority of the world gold supply in the late 1940s) was committed to maintaining a fixed relationship between the dollar and gold by standing ready to convert all dollars obtained by foreign governments to gold at a fixed ($35 per ounce of gold) price. Other member nations, then, were formally to announce a par value for their currencies with respect to the dollar (thereby setting up an official exchange rate with the dollar) and to intervene directly into the foreign exchange market to keep fluctuations in that exchange rate within 1 percent on either side.

The IMF's framers were not so naïve as to believe that a fixed and rigid set of exchange rates could be maintained for all time regardless of changes in productivity, resources availability, inflation rates, and the like. Rather, as we have seen, they set up a system whereby nations suffering from chronic deficits caused by a fundamental disequilibrium could, upon consultation with IMF authorities, devalue their currencies in an effort to restore payments equilibrium. It was, then, a system under which exchange rates were pegged by governmental action, but the pegs were adjustable over time in response to changing circumstances.

IMF "Drawing Rights"—Loans to Assist Member Nations with Short-Term Deficits While devaluation was considered an appropriate way to combat a chronic, long-term payments deficit, those deficits that arose from random or seasonal factors or as a result of the business-cycle were expected to be dealt with by other measures. For example, a cyclical payments deficit resulting from excess demand in the deficit nation was thought to be most effectively combated by more appropriate (i.e., restrictive) domestic monetary-fiscal measures.

To help member nations withstand deficits of this sort while corrective measures were taking effect, the IMF established a loan facility offering members so-called drawing rights under carefully specified conditions. To set up the loan fund, the IMF originally assessed each member nation a quota (based roughly on the relative size of the country in the world economy), 25 percent of which was to be paid in the form of gold and the rest in the form of its own domestic currency. Payment of its quota entitled a country to drawing rights (the right to borrow) on the foreign exchange held in the IMF loan fund.

As originally established, any member country could borrow any other country's currency (by exchanging an equivalent amount of its own domestic currency for it) in an amount up to 25 percent of its own quota (often referred to as its *gold tranche*) at any time and without question. Beyond that, it could borrow (or, more correctly, buy with its own currency) additional yearly amounts not exceeding 25 percent of its own quota until the fund had accumulated its domestic currency in an amount equivalent to 200 percent of its quota. These added amounts, however, were *not* automatically available on simple request and were made available only with sufficient justification to IMF authorities.

Over the years the national quotas (and therefore the size of the loan fund) have been raised several times and the conditions for borrowing have been altered, but the drawing rights facility still exists in essentially its original form. Also, in a recent change, no gold payments are required to meet the quota. It should be noted, however, that it is a fund of limited size, intended only to help with temporary deficit problems. Nations with large, chronic deficits were expected to deal with their problems through more fundamental alterations in their competitive status.

The Rise of the "Gold Exchange" Standard

While the Bretton Woods system was the result of carefully thought-out international planning, another main feature of the post–World War II international monetary structure—the so-called gold exchange standard—simply evolved naturally without any preconceived planning. The basic structure of the International Monetary Fund, along with the earlier predominance and strength of the U.S. economy, provided the foundation for this development. Perhaps the most fruitful way to go about explaining the emergence of the gold exchange standard is to comment briefly on the balance-of-payments experience of the United States during the late 1940s and the 1950s.

Developments in the 1940s and the 1950s In the immediate post–World War II years the United States, already the possessor of about 70 percent of the free world's gold supply, ran heavy balance-of-payments surpluses while the leading nations of Western Europe had to contend with substantial deficits. From 1946 through 1949, for example, the U.S. surplus on goods and services averaged over $8 billion, an enormous amount in terms of the prices of that earlier period. It was a situation that many felt would continue indefinitely, and, indeed, methods of dealing with what was assumed to be a very-long-term "dollar shortage" problem dominated discussion.

A look back at the events of the late 1940s and early 1950s, however, provides a much better perspective of what was happening than was possible at the time. The *dollar gap*, which was the cause of so much concern, was rapidly being bridged by developments all around. The role of Marshall Plan aid has already been mentioned in this regard. Not only did it permit a temporary bridging of Western Europe's balance-of-payments gap but it also aided the rebuilding and modernization of European industry to the point where it could better compete in world markets. And when the Marshall Plan ended, the intensification of the cold war provided justification for continuance, on a long-term basis, of heavy U.S. foreign aid to its allies abroad.

In the meantime, Western Europe was acting on its own to recover its share of world trade. Not only was it modernizing its productive equipment, but it acted firmly and boldly to achieve a degree of economic integration through the Schuman Plan, the European Economic Community, and the Common Market, which gave it trade advantages it had never before possessed. Finally, the nations of Western Europe acted, in 1948 and 1949, to devalue their currencies sharply with respect to the dollar to curtail their then-heavy deficits.

While the United States was occupied with the Korean war and then, later, a postwar boom in the first half of the 1950s, vast changes in its international economic position were taking place almost without notice. What had been considered a dollar gap had already disappeared. But the relatively small U.S. payments deficits that had begun to show up caused no alarm whatsoever because foreigners were quite content to hold the bulk of their excess dollar earnings in dollar form. This, in turn, was a consequence of the rapid development of the *gold exchange standard* for which the pound and the dollar were the key currencies.

As we have seen, the gold exchange standard was not the result of any worldwide planning. Rather, it spread as a result of decisions on the part of individual nations to hold part of their international reserves in dollar form (or pounds, for the sterling bloc) as well as in gold.

That this should have happened is hardly surprising. The rapidly expanding volume of trade in the period required greatly increased international reserves to finance it (i.e., to enable deficit nations to continue pegging their exchange rates). Clearly some method had to be found for making the too-small and maldistributed world gold supply stretch farther. One partial answer to the problem was for many nations to begin counting their dollar holdings (which were, after all, readily convertible into gold) as an additional form of international reserve. And that is what a gold exchange standard is — a system whereby a strong national currency, adequately backed by, and convertible into, gold, permits an otherwise inadequate world gold supply to support a much larger supply of internationally accepted reserves.

The advantages to other countries from this arrangement are obvious. Instead of tying up all their monetary reserves in the nonincome-earning form of gold, they could hold substantial portions in the form of short-term dollar assets, which not only earned interest but were, as long as the U.S. honored its promise to make them convertible into gold, "as good as gold" itself. For the United States, on the other hand, it meant that its deficits during the early and middle 1950s led only to a piling up of more short-term dollar obligations to foreigners who were, in the main, more desirous of expanding the dollar-asset portion of their monetary reserves than of taking out gold.

During this period, therefore, the dollar became a true world currency in the sense that it performed, for all nations of the world, the three basic functions of money. It was then, and is still, widely used as a "vehicle" currency in that a very large percentage of world trade is actually transacted with the use of dollars. Thus it acted as a *medium of exchange* for most international transactions. Second, it served as a *unit of account* as all other IMF member nations expressed the value of their currencies in terms of U.S. dollars.[2] And, of course, it also served as a *store of value* for the countries acquiring it.

Experience Under Bretton Woods: 1958–1970

The almost unnoticed U.S. deficits of the mid-1950s mushroomed suddenly in 1958 to a scale that seemed to demand not only attention but action from responsible authorities. It was a combination of two developments that rang the warning bell.

First, the reasonably comfortable surplus on goods and services the United States had enjoyed in the mid-1950s fell precipitously. Indeed, when net long-term investment abroad by Americans was added to the U.S. current account balance, it was clear that in both 1958 and 1959, foreigners acquired some $3.5 billion to $4.0 billion in short-term dollar claims from their transactions with the United States.

Second, foreign nations that had been willing, in the past, to accept the proceeds of their surpluses with the United States almost entirely in the form of increased holdings of short-term dollar claims suddenly switched tactics and withdrew over $2 billion of gold. This sudden change in foreign attitudes undoubtedly resulted from a combination of two factors. On the one hand, some of them, having already built up their dollar reserves to the tolerable limits, felt obliged to take gold to keep a balanced proportion of gold and dollars in their monetary reserves. Others, however, probably reacted to the sharply expanded U.S. deficit as a danger sign and, on the chance that the United States might be forced to devalue, took the defensive speculative action of withdrawing gold. Note in Table 27-1 that the U.S. gold stock, which had been almost $23 billion as late as 1957 (with only a little over $8 billion of liquid liabilities owed to foreign governments), fell steadily throughout most of the 1960s.

---

[2] Specifically, these par values were expressed in terms of the U.S. dollar *with a gold content as of 1944.* When the United States finally devalued in the early 1970s (by lowering the gold content of the dollar below that of 1944), the other nations had to decide whether to allow their currencies' relationship to the dollar to stay the same (thereby changing it with respect to the dollar's 1944 content).

TABLE 27-1 U.S. balance-of-payments performance, 1959–1971 (billions of dollars)

Year	Balance on goods and services	Current account plus net long-term capital movements	Liquid liabilities owed to foreign governments	Gold stock
1959	1.2	−4.1	10.6	19.5
1960	5.1	−1.2	11.9	17.8
1961	6.3	0	12.6	17.0
1962	6.0	−1.0	13.6	16.1
1963	7.2	−1.3	15.2	15.6
1964	9.6	0	16.2	15.5
1965	8.3	−1.8	16.2	14.1
1966	6.0	−1.7	14.6	13.2
1967	5.7	−3.3	16.7	12.1
1968	3.6	−1.4	13.6	10.9
1969	3.4	−3.0	13.0	11.9
1970	5.6	−3.0	20.6	11.1
1971	2.3	−9.6	48.2	11.1[a]

[a] Value of gold stock raised via devaluation of dollar.

Source: Federal Reserve Bank of St. Louis and *Federal Reserve Bulletin.*

The U.S. reaction to this balance-of-payments experience and its attendant gold drain was many faceted. In accordance with its commitment to the IMF, the United States regularly reaffirmed its pledge to maintain the convertibility of foreign government–held dollars into gold. Early in the period this was an eminently credible promise, since the U.S. gold stock was larger (until 1964) than the short-term dollar claims of foreigners. But as the "gold drain" continued and the volume of foreign-owned short-term dollar claims grew, it became clear that some sort of discretionary action would be needed.

Throughout the 1960s, the U.S. government employed every discretionary measure available with the exception of devaluation. For example, there can be little doubt that governmental spending abroad was held down and that domestic monetary and fiscal policy were kept less expansive than the unemployment levels in the early 1960s might otherwise have dictated.[3]

---

[3] Evidence of this is the following observation on President Kennedy's view of the balance-of-payments problem by one of his chief advisers:

> The balance of payments remained a constant worry to Kennedy. . . . He used to tell his advisors that the two things which scared him most were nuclear war and the payments deficit. . . . He had acquired somewhere, perhaps from his father, the belief that a nation was only as strong as the value of its currency; and he feared that, if he pushed things too far, "loss of confidence" would descend and there would be a run on gold.

Arthur M. Schlesinger, Jr., *A Thousand Days: John F. Kennedy in the White House* (Boston: Houghton Mifflin, 1965), pp. 654–655.

In addition, it instituted a whole range of measures that properly belong under the heading of trade barriers. These included cutting the duty-free allowance for American tourists abroad from $500 to $100, restricting Defense Department purchases to U.S. firms only unless the U.S. price was more than 50 percent higher than the foreign price, implementing more stringent action to require recipients of U.S. foreign aid to spend it on U.S.-produced goods, levying a 15 percent tax (called the "interest equalization" tax) on purchase of foreign securities by Americans, limiting direct lending to foreigners by U.S. financial institutions, and controlling the amount and method of financing direct investment abroad.

How well did all this work? As Table 27-1 indicates, it did reduce the size of U.S. deficits and, through the 1960s at least, held down on the foreign accumulation of short-term dollar claims. But these successes were not sufficient to restore full confidence in the dollar, and the "gold drain" continued. And as the 1960s drew to a close, the acceleration of the Vietnam war and ever more serious inflation combined to almost wipe out the accustomed surplus on goods and services, pushing the entire U.S. balance of payments into heavy deficit and paving the way for an extremely rapid buildup of foreign-held short-term dollar claims. The result was that by 1971, with foreign government short-term dollar claims approaching five times the level of the U.S. gold stock, it was obvious to all that the American promise to maintain the convertibility of the dollar had become an essentially empty pledge.

Why, one might reasonably ask, did the United States take so long before resorting to devaluation? The answer is rather complex but worth our consideration.

In the first place, under the Bretton Woods rules, the United States on its own actually lacked the power to devalue the dollar *with respect to other currencies.* It could devalue the dollar in terms of gold (raise the dollar price of gold) but, it will be recalled, it was other nations (and their exchange stabilization funds) that established and maintained exchange rates between the dollar and other national currencies. And since the only way devaluation could help restore equilibrium to the American balance of payments was by lowering the value of the dollar relative to other national currencies, cooperation from U.S. trading partners was essential.

But there were more fundamental barriers to a dollar devaluation than mere mechanics. The dollar, after all, was an international reserve currency, and its relationship to gold was the cornerstone of the Bretton Woods system. The United States not only had formally committed itself to converting dollars held by foreign countries into gold at a $35-per-ounce price but had publicly pressured friendly governments to do their bit to keep the Bretton Woods system afloat by forgoing their option to conversion. Some had acquiesced, opting to retain their short-term dollar claims rather than take out gold, but others had rejected the American plea and had taken out large quantities of gold. Devaluation under these circumstances (raising the dollar value of gold) would consequently reward those who had refused to cooperate at the expense of those who had gone along and kept the bulk of their reserves in dollar form. For all these reasons, devaluation of the dollar was considered a last-ditch alternative, to be resorted to only in the most critical of circumstances. Therefore, it was not until December 1971, four months after the suspension of the convertibility of the dollar, that the first devaluation came about.

An Aside: The Authorization of Special Drawing Rights

Long before the events of 1971 brought about the suspension of the dollar's convertibility signaling the eventual demise of Bretton Woods' stable exchange rate system, international monetary authorities were wrestling with a dilemma of a different sort—how to maintain an adequate flow of international reserves after the United States eliminated its chronic deficits.

Despite official concern over the string of U.S. deficits in the 1950s and 1960s, they did have one important redeeming feature. During a period when world trade was expanding rapidly but official gold stocks were hardly rising at all, there was a pressing need for an expansion of international reserves. This need was met during these years primarily by the outpouring of U.S. dollars in consequence of this nation's deficits.

But helpful though it was, this method of enlarging international reserves was a hazardous one. Its continuance depended solely on continuance of American deficits. And continuance of those deficits seemed certain, eventually, to undermine foreign nations' *confidence* in the dollar as an appropriate international reserve asset. Clearly, the longer the United States continued to incur large deficits, pumping out more and more short-term dollar claims, the less credible would be its promise to convert those dollars to gold on demand. As short-term dollar claims owned by foreigners mushroomed while the U.S. gold stock dwindled, it seemed inevitable that the U.S. would eventually be forced to suspend the convertibility of the dollar and/or devalue it (both of which, of course, it did in 1971).

Given this situation, it was apparent that a new form of international liquidity was needed. After much study, the International Monetary Fund authorized the creation of *special drawing rights*, first issued in 1970.

Special Drawing Rights   Special drawing rights (or SDRs) are claims on the IMF that have been issued to member countries in proportion to their quotas but separate and *additional* to those quotas. As of late 1990, 21.4 billion of SDRs had been issued with a dollar value of about $30 billion.[4]

Countries receiving these added claims against the IMF incur no added liability. The IMF simply created new international money in establishing them.

A country with a balance-of-payments deficit may use its SDRs to purchase convertible currencies from other participant nations. Participant nations are obligated to accept such increases in their SDR accounts until their total holdings equal three times their original SDR allocation. For those nations who acquire additions to their SDR accounts in this manner, the IMF pays interest.

Suppose, for example, that the United States finds it necessary to acquire $500 million worth of Deutsche marks to settle a deficit. It could transfer $500 million of its SDR account to Germany, in return for which it would receive an equivalent value in marks. Germany, now holding its original allotment of SDRs plus the $500 million obtained from the United States, would receive interest on the $500 million.

---

[4] When the SDRs were first authorized, one SDR equaled one dollar. Since then the dollar has been devalued (and depreciated) with respect to the SDR, so that while there were a total of SDR 21.4 billion outstanding in 1990, their dollar value had risen to well above that figure.

At the time of their authorization, it was expected that SDRs might eventually become the dominant type of international reserve, supplanting both gold and such foreign exchange reserves as the dollar. However, while the *absolute* amount of SDRs increased sharply in the 1970s and 1980s, they still constituted less than 5 percent of total reserves held by all nations in the late 1980s.

The Transition to a New Exchange Rate System: 1971–1973

When the United States suspended the convertibility of the dollar in August 1971, the cornerstone of the "stable, but adjustable" exchange rate systems established at Bretton Woods was removed. In the immediate aftermath, most industrial countries suspended their efforts to peg their exchange rate to the dollar. "By the end of August, all major currencies except the French franc were floating, but exchange controls were in widespread use and central bank intervention was substantial." [5]

There was at the time a widespread desire to return to a stable exchange rate system as soon as possible. All recognized, however, that any new exchange rate structure set up must involve a substantial devaluation of the dollar — especially relative to the Japanese yen and the German mark — if the United States was to be able to curb its burgeoning balance-of-payments deficits. There were, however, sharp differences, especially between the United States and France, as to how this should be accomplished.

The American position was for the world's major surplus nations to *re*value their currencies with respect to the dollar but to leave the dollar price of gold unchanged. The French, on the other hand, insisted that any realignment of exchange rates include a devaluation of the dollar with respect to gold. After months of debate, a compromise was reached in the Smithsonian Agreement of December 1971.

In that document it was agreed that most industrialized countries would revalue their currencies with respect to the dollar. For example, relative to the U.S. dollar, the Japanese yen was raised 16.7 percent, the German mark 13.6 percent, and the French franc 8.6 percent. In return, the United States agreed to devalue the dollar with respect to gold by 8.57 percent, thereby raising the dollar price of gold from $35 to $38 per ounce. [6]

The raising of the official gold price represented a political compromise by the United States, but its economic significance was really minimal. Since the dollar remained inconvertible into gold in any case, it is difficult to see what was gained by the action aside from the purely political accomplishment of forcing

[5] Robert Solomon, *The International Monetary System, 1945–1976* (New York: Harper & Row, 1977), p. 189. This section relies heavily upon Solomon's excellent account as well as on Gerald M. Meier's *Problems of a World Monetary Order* (New York: Oxford University Press, 1974).

[6] Other parts of the Smithsonian Agreement included removal of a temporary 10 percent surcharge on imports by the United States and agreement that exchange rates would be permitted to fluctuate above and below the newly established levels by 2.25 percent rather than the old 1 percent limit.

the Americans to swallow the same devaluation medicine that its Western European trading partners had had to accept in the past. After all, as one observer put it, "it made no real difference whether the U.S. was not buying or selling monetary gold at $35 per ounce or whether it was not buying or selling it at $38 per ounce."[7]

Nevertheless, hopes were high that the realignment of exchange rates between world currencies would permit a long-term return to a stable exchange rate system. Indeed, in what turned out to be a classic overstatement, President Nixon hailed the Smithsonian Agreement as "the most significant monetary achievement in the history of the world."

With the aid of hindsight, it would be an almost equally classic understatement to point out that it turned out to be no such thing. By early 1973, just a little over a year after the signing of the Smithsonian Agreement, international monetary markets were once again in chaos. Accelerating U.S. inflation and discouraging balance-of-trade reports led to renewed speculation against the dollar. Italy, France, and Belgium broke away from the Smithsonian agreements to allow their currencies to float for capital transactions. Switzerland also floated its franc. And the West German government was forced to absorb billions of U.S. dollars to maintain the mark-dollar exchange rate agreed upon at Smithsonian.

In the face of all this, the United States announced a second dollar devaluation—this one by 10 percent—in February 1973.[8] The action helped little to stay the immediate crisis. The following day the Japanese yen was allowed to float. The flow of dollars to Germany accelerated at such a rate that on March 1 alone the West German government had to absorb almost $3 billion! Amid these chaotic conditions, European foreign exchange markets were closed and an emergency meeting among major industrial countries was called in Paris in early March. Out of that Paris meeting came an agreement to scrap the remnants of the Smithsonian guidelines and turn to general floating. Not only Smithsonian but the long-cherished stable exchange rate system had been abandoned for the indefinite future.

The exchange rate system adopted in the spring of 1973 (and retained to the present) was not a pure floating system wherein exchange rates fluctuate solely in accordance with private demand and supply factors. Rather, it was (and is) a managed floating system wherein private supply and demand (by exporters and importers) are the dominant exchange rate determinants but in which governments feel free to intervene directly any time they consider a nudge to the exchange rate appropriate.

Efforts at Reform Since 1973

Even before the Smithsonian Agreement broke down in early 1973, the International Monetary Fund had set into action a group charged with planning a thorough reform and overhaul of the international monetary system. The members of

---

[7] Ernest Olson, "Devaluation of the Dollar," *Monthly Review*, Federal Reserve Bank of San Francisco, June 1972, p. 7.

[8] This action raised the official price of gold from $38.00 per ounce to the current $42.22.

this group, popularly known as the *Committee of Twenty*, were chosen to represent all segments of the world community and instructed to report back to the IMF Board of Governors with their recommendations by July 1974. Singled out as critical areas requiring study were the exchange rate mechanism, a means of restoring worldwide convertibility of currencies, the proper role in the revised system for foreign exchange reserves, gold, and SDRs, the appropriate steps to control disequilibrating capital movements, and techniques for providing more aid to lesser developed nations.

In its early deliberations it seems clear that the Committee of Twenty considered the managed floating exchange rate system resorted to in March 1973 as a temporary arrangement to be superseded, when plans were completed, by a return to a stable rate system. For example, in an interim report issued in September 1973, the committee recommended that reform should include measures aimed at "establishing an exchange rate system based on stable but adjustable par values, with temporary floating to be considered an acceptable method of changing par values."

Whatever the merits or demerits of this professed intent to return to a stable rate system, it has since been abandoned in the wake of a series of international economic upheavals of sufficient severity to convince even the most adamant of stable rate proponents that, for the foreseeable future, we must learn to live with floating.

The major developments that convinced world monetary leaders that the managed floating system in effect since 1973 must remain for the indefinite future were the extraordinary hikes in OPEC oil prices beginning in late 1973 and the continuing acceleration of worldwide inflation. With unprecedented international payments imbalances caused by widely differing dependence on imported oil and major differences in the rates of inflation of various nations, it has become clear to all that the adjustment potential of floating rates is currently an indispensable ingredient for the maintenance of reasonably free international commerce.

In recognition of all this, agreement was reached in 1976 on a proposed change in the IMF's Articles of Agreement, which specifically authorized member countries to adopt any exchange rate system for their currency they choose so long as they "avoid manipulating exchange rates on the international monetary system in order to prevent effective balance-of-payments adjustment or to gain an unfair advantage over other members." Under this new article, which was ratified by the required number of member nations in early 1978, the IMF proposes to exercise "firm surveillance over the exchange rate policies of members" and to "adopt specific principles for the guidance of all members with respect to those policies." So as we proceed through the 1990s, the exchange rate procedures first established in the early 1970s remain much the same. Some currencies are floating with only occasional interventions by their governments to influence their movement; many (by the individual choice of their governments rather than by IMF rules) are pegged at a stable rate with the dollar (especially the developing countries); and some (such as most of the nations in the European Economic Community) are held roughly stable among one another but float as a group with respect to the dollar. This is what has come to be called the current managed floating system, and it is likely to be with us for some time.

How Well Has the Managed Floating System Worked?

The current exchange rate system, as we have seen, was adopted more or less out of necessity in the wake of the breakdown of the "stable, but adjustable, peg system" instituted initially by the Bretton Woods agreement. Although it seems clear that momentous changes in underlying conditions forced the abandonment of the stable rate system, the current managed floating system has since been officially sanctioned by the International Monetary Fund through a change in its Articles of Agreement that currently approves virtually any exchange rate system that does not involve "manipulating exchange rates . . . in order to . . . gain an unfair competitive advantage over other members."

In effect, then, the 1970s featured a dramatic turnaround from a stable rate to a more or less flexible rate system. It therefore seems appropriate that we conclude this chapter by first considering the alleged pros and cons of stable and flexible rate systems and then briefly discussing how the new system has worked in terms of U.S. international payments experience.

The Case for Stable Exchange Rates

Stable exchange rate advocates, while recognizing the effectiveness of exchange rate flexibility as a balance-of-payments adjustment mechanism, argue that (1) this benefit is more than offset by a number of potentially unfavorable side effects from fluctuating rates and (2) it is possible to develop quite satisfactory alternative mechanisms for adjustment without accepting the risks inherent in a market-determined exchange rate system.

One of their major points, noted in the preceding chapter, is the fear that exchange rate flexibility may impose so much *added risk* that some prospective traders will avoid international transactions altogether. While they recognize that it is possible to hedge against this risk by purchasing forward exchange (buying foreign exchange for delivery at a specified future time at a currently guaranteed exchange rate), they point out that such hedging itself might be quite expensive and that forward commitments might conceivably be impossible to obtain for such very-long-term transactions as long-term investments.

Second, there is the alleged risk of *destabilizing speculation*. What is envisaged here is the possibility that a movement of exchange rates in any one direction will generate expectations that a further move in that direction is likely, leading to actions that fulfill the expectation. Exchange rates movements, then, might become self-generating in the same sense that prices are during hyperinflation or the stock market is during a crash.

With completely flexible exchange rates, it may well also be that capital movements will cause wide swings in exchange rates that are entirely inappropriate for dealing with the nation's current account. Such a possibility would be especially damaging to a nation whose dependence on imports is such as to expose it to major changes in its cost of living as a result. And, as we shall see shortly, for "key currency" countries such as the United States, enormous capital flows possess the potential of causing exchange rate swings of such magnitude as to inflict periodic episodes of very painful reallocation of resources.

Finally, advocates of stable exchange rates point to experience with floating rates in the 1970s as evidence in support of their conviction that flexible exchange rates may contribute heavily to *worldwide inflation.* One point here is that, whereas with a stable rate system domestic inflation causes a loss of reserves that serves as a signal that the inflation must be arrested, with flexible rates the only international result of inflation is exchange rate depreciation. In other words, a flexible rate system may undermine the discipline required to combat inflation.

Another part of the inflation argument involves the potential feedback on the cost of living in a deficit country whose currency is undergoing rapid depreciation. Depreciation of the currency, it is argued, will necessarily make imported goods more expensive in the deficit country, which will not only raise the cost of those items still imported but — in so doing — shelter domestic producers of goods that are also imported from competition which would otherwise hold down on their prices. And, so the argument runs, those cost-of-living increases may, in turn, trigger a further wage-price spiral as labor and management attempt to protect themselves from inflation-induced reductions in their living standards.

Such an inflationary result, it is argued, is all the more likely in a world in which wages and prices are highly resistant to downward changes. What is to be expected, then, is a rise of prices in the deficit country (whose currency is depreciating) but no equivalent fall in prices in the surplus country (as a result of currency appreciation).

The Case for Flexible Exchange Rates

Without question, the most fundamental advantage claimed for a flexible exchange rate system is its alleged capacity to adjust or eliminate international payments imbalances automatically through market-induced alterations in the external value of the currency.

As the flexible exchange rate advocates see it, the adjustable peg system established at Bretton Woods (or, indeed, any feasible system relying on stable exchange rates) contains some serious deficiencies that are an inevitable result of the exchange rate stability itself.

If, for example, a nation develops a chronic payments deficit under a stable exchange rate system, it is likely to react as follows:

1. Initially, in the short run, it will be forced to use up part of its precious supply of international reserves to finance the deficit and keep its currency pegged at the current level. This means, as noted, that such a system requires far more concern for the development of procedures for generating large and growing supplies of international reserves than is the case for a flexible rate system.

2. If the deficit is truly chronic, the use of international reserves to finance it can do no more than buy time until more fundamental corrective measures can be taken. And experience has shown that these measures are very likely to consist of (a) the erection or intensification of trade barriers and (b) the use of contractive monetary-fiscal meas-

ures at home to hold down on both the domestic demand for imports and domestic export prices, as well as to raise short-term interest rates in the hope of attracting foreign capital. Trade barriers (even if they do succeed in reducing the deficit) constitute a clear-cut impediment to the maximization of world living standards, while contractive monetary-fiscal policies are almost certain to result in an undesired rise in unemployment.

3. Therefore, devaluation of the currency is likely to become the only viable solution. But, as we have seen, this step is likely to be postponed until defense of the currency has been allowed to become a major political issue. And the delay plays directly into the hands of speculators who, recognizing the need for, and eventual certainty of, devaluation are presented with a "can't lose" situation. They can sell their supplies of the deficit country's currency with a strong likelihood of a profit (when the devaluation does occur) but no chance (given a rate pegged within narrow limits) of loss. And this speculative activity only makes matters worse for the deficit nation. With it all, when the devaluation finally comes, the devaluing government will have no clear-cut indication as to *how much* to lower the international value of its currency, and it is more likely than not — to be sure that the painful action does the job — that they will overshoot the mark.

How much simpler and more sensible it is, say the flexible rate advocates, to let market forces guide the rate down automatically to the appropriate market-clearing (equilibrium) level!

And what about the stable rate adherents' charge that a flexible rate system may introduce an added element of uncertainty into the picture that will cause risk averters to back away from international transactions? The flexible rate advocates point out that it is perfectly possible for a trader to protect himself against the risk of an exchange rate change by hedging. And as to the longer-run international transactions, they note that under a stable rate system, the risk of the imposition of exchange controls and of devaluation itself produces at least as much uncertainty as anticipated rate changes under a flexible system.

The charge that a flexible rate system may break down under the pressure of destabilizing speculation is also denied by the flexible rate camp. Pointing out that such a development (where speculators expect a currency to depreciate and sell it — thereby not only contributing to the depreciation but fostering the expectation that it will continue, requiring even further sales and even more depreciation) implies that speculators must lose money. For the only way that speculation *can* be destabilizing is if the participants, on average, sell when the currency is low in price and buy when it is high.

Finally, it is pointed out that the Bretton Woods stable rate system tended to spread the disease of worldwide inflation. According to this view, the United States allowed overly expansive monetary-fiscal policies in the late 1960s to generate excessive price rises in the United States, which, in turn, contributed to heavy American payments deficits. This, in turn, required surplus nations, under their IMF commitment to maintain stable exchange rates with the dollar, to buy up billions of excess dollars with their domestic currencies. But the very act of doing so inflated their own domestic money supplies and subjected them to inflation also! Thus, it is argued, the stable rate system acted as a mechanism whereby inflation was spread from one nation to another. To resort to an old cliché, it was simply one more example of a case where "when Uncle Sam sneezed, the rest of the world caught pneumonia."

The Managed Floating System and the U.S. Balance of Payments in Recent Years

In light of the claims of flexible exchange rate advocates, it seems appropriate to take a brief look at how effective a job the new, more flexible system launched in 1973 has done in terms of U.S. balance-of-payments performance. In assessing the evidence available, it is important to bear in mind that the world does not now have a *perfectly* flexible exchange rate system. As noted, many countries (by their own choice) still keep their exchange rates stable with respect to the dollar. In addition, among those that do not, direct governmental intervention into the foreign exchange market to at least prevent "disorderly markets" has been com-

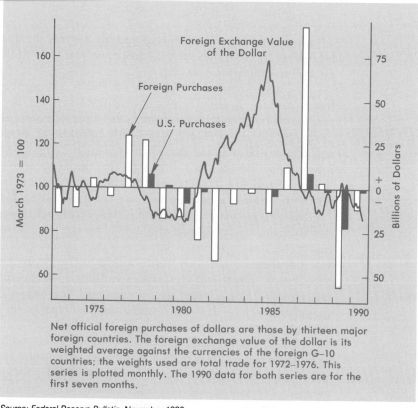

Net official foreign purchases of dollars are those by thirteen major foreign countries. The foreign exchange value of the dollar is its weighted average against the currencies of the foreign G–10 countries; the weights used are total trade for 1972–1976. This series is plotted monthly. The 1990 data for both series are for the first seven months.

Source: Federal Reserve Bulletin, November 1990.

FIGURE 27-1　Net official purchases of dollars and the foreign exchange value of the dollar, 1973–1990

TABLE 27-2   U.S. balance on goods and services and
exchange rate changes 1973–1990

Year	Balance on goods and services (billions of dollars)	Index of weighted average exchange value of U.S. dollar (March 1973 = 100)
1973	11.0	99.1
1974	9.3	101.4
1975	22.9	98.5
1976	9.4	105.6
1977	−9.5	103.3
1978	−9.7	92.4
1979	5.1	88.1
1980	8.3	87.4
1981	11.1	102.9
1982	−1.1	116.6
1983	−37.1	125.3
1984	−94.3	138.2
1985	−102.7	143.0
1986	−125.4	112.2
1987	−140.5	96.9
1988	−113.9	92.7
1989	−95.4	98.6
1990	−78.2	89.1

Source: U.S. Department of Commerce and Federal Reserve System.

monplace.[9] But despite all this, there can be no doubt that the current system contains exchange rates that are much more flexible than those of past systems, so for evaluative purposes it seems reasonable to take a look at the record.

The record is presented in Figure 27-1 and Table 27-2. Figure 27-1 shows the changes in the foreign exchange value of the dollar vis-à-vis the value of a weighted average of the currencies of 10 of the prime trading partners of the United States. In addition, it shows the degree to which the U.S. and foreign governments intervened directly into the foreign market to attempt to alter exchange rates. Table 27-2 presents yearly average data for the dollar exchange

[9] The definition of disorderly markets is, at best, vague. The congressional Joint Economic Committee has offered the following interpretation:

> Disorderly markets are characterized by an unusually low volume of transactions and abnormally wide spreads between bid and asked prices for at least some currencies, i.e., there is a heavy supply of some currencies but virtually no purchasers, while other moneys are in strong demand but only small amounts are offered. When markets are disorderly, exchange rates are likely to fluctuate erratically.

"Living with the Trade Deficit," Report of the Subcommittee on International Economics of the Joint Economic Committee (Washington, D.C.: Government Printing Office, November 18, 1977), p. 8.

rate from 1973 to 1990 plus the U.S. balance on goods and service over the same period.

Other things equal, one might expect an appreciation of the dollar, with some lag, to push the nation's balance on goods and services toward a deficit while depreciation should move us in the direction of a surplus. While "other things" were anything but equal over the period since 1973, the data in Table 27-2 would seem to roughly corroborate this hypothesis. An appreciation of the dollar in the mid-1970s is followed by sharp deficits in 1977 and 1978, and the dollar's depreciation in the latter 1970s is succeeded by rather sizable goods and service surpluses in 1980 and 1981.[10]

But the truly dramatic changes have taken place since 1980. Starting in 1980 and continuing almost without interruption until reaching its peak in February 1985, the dollar rose in value, relative to the average value of the currencies of 10 major industrial nations, from a position 10 percent below the 1973 benchmark to one almost 60 percent above it. Since that time, the dollar has depreciated sharply until by December 1990, it was well below the 1973 relationship. In effect had other conditions remained unchanged, the 1980–1985 appreciation of the dollar would have raised the cost of American goods to foreigners by over 50 percent (while lowering the cost of foreign goods to Americans equivalently) while the 1985–1990 dollar depreciation would have reversed matters. Let us consider these two episodes in somewhat greater detail.

How can we explain the unprecedented goods and service deficits that developed in the mid-1980s? One contributing factor was the fact that the U.S. economy recovered more rapidly from the 1982 recession than did our trading partners, with the result that the U.S. demand for imports of goods and services shot up relative to the foreign demand for our exports.

Taken by itself, however, that *should* have led to a dollar *de*preciation which, in line with the argument that flexible exchange rates provide an effective adjustment mechanism, would have tended to moderate the goods and service deficit. Instead, as we know, the dollar *ap*preciated wildly. All this leads to two important questions: (1) Why didn't the dollar depreciate? and (2) what are the implications of this episode for the adjustment potential of flexible exchange rates?

The answer to the first question is fairly easy. The increased American demand for foreign goods did not lead to a dollar depreciation because its effects were overwhelmed by an enormous foreign demand for U.S.-issued securities. That is, an enormous capital flow into the U.S. from abroad had the effect of pushing the value of the dollar to historic highs. And that, in its turn, played the major role in producing our $100 billion-plus deficits. Consider Figure 27-2.

Assume that in 1982 we had essentially an equilibrium on goods and services as depicted by the intersection of the furthest-to-the-left demand and supply curves. That would have produced $0P_1$ as the international value of the dollar and exports of goods and services would equal imports of goods and services at 0A. The more rapid U.S. recovery from the 1982 recession would shift our demand curve to the right which, had that alone happened, would have depreciated the

[10] Obviously, to attribute changes in the U.S. balance of payments solely to exchange rate movements is to oversimplify grossly. Clearly, such factors as oil prices, comparative rates of inflation and comparative income levels are also critically important.

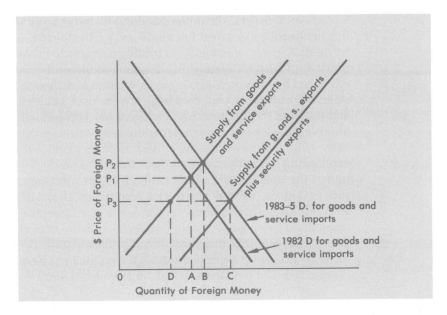

FIGURE 27-2

dollar to $0P_2$ (where foreign money costs more dollars than at $0P_1$). That, in turn, would have ultimately generated an equality between goods and service exports and imports at 0B. But now suppose that at the same time a large inflow of foreign capital (to purchase IOUs in the United States) shifts the supply curve out to the right and that this, in turn, overwhelms the effect of the shift of the demand curve and causes the international value of the dollar to *ap*preciate to $0P_3$. This appreciation will raise U.S. imports of goods and services by BC (since foreign goods are now cheaper to Americans) and cut U.S. exports of goods and services by BD (since U.S. goods are now more expensive to foreigners). The result will be a deficit on goods and services equal to DC at the equilibrium international value of the dollar.

Now if this scenario is correct, if it is true that an enormous capital inflow into the United States caused an overvalued dollar which in turn produced our enormous international payments deficits, we need to take one final step and ask what caused the capital inflow. One answer seems to be that foreign investors in the 1980s found the United States to be a "safe haven" in which to invest. Our economy appeared healthy and stable and there seemed very little risk that their funds might be appropriated by the state or that access to them might be blocked by such measures as exchange controls.

But there was a more positive lure to foreign investors and that was the fact that the rate of return on investment in the U.S., the real rate of interest, was appreciably higher than that available in other developed economies. Part of the reason for these unusually high real interest rates was the "crowding out" caused by the financing of the equally unprecedented federal government budget deficits. From a policy viewpoint, then, our budget deficits were an important cause of our balance-of-payments deficits and reducing the latter depends partly on a reduction in the former.

As noted earlier, the dollar has depreciated sharply since early 1985, partly due to a decline in interest rates here and partly due to discretionary action taken by the U.S. government and our trading partners to drive it down. Although this sharp drop must ultimately result in a moderation of U.S. payments deficits, this effect has been surprisingly slow in surfacing. Although, as noted earlier, substantial time lags are expected between the time a currency begins depreciating and the time this depreciation produces marked reductions in its deficits, most observers have been surprised that the very significant dollar depreciation since early 1985 had not yet reduced U.S. deficits a full five years later. Part of the explanation lies in the fact that there has not actually *been* that large a depreciation of the dollar with respect to some of our most important trading partners such as Canada, Taiwan, and Korea. Also, although the depreciation of the dollar with respect to the Japanese yen has been very large, the Japanese have thus far maintained their large surplus with the U.S. by apparently cutting domestic prices and accepting sharply reduced profit margins. Despite all this, however, the dramatic dollar depreciation and the recession seem all but certain to lead to sharply reduced payments deficits in the early 1990s.[11]

Review Questions

1. How did the gold exchange standard arise during the 1950s?

2. What is the purpose of IMF drawing rights?

3. "Under Bretton Woods, the United States really was not in a position to devalue the dollar with respect to other currencies in order to deal with its payments deficits." Explain carefully.

4. What are SDRs? Why were they initially issued by the IMF?

5. "The early 1970s devaluations of the U.S. dollar with respect to gold, taken by themselves, were of very little significance." Do you agree? Explain.

6. Carefully explain the case for and against flexible exchange rates.

7. Explain the circumstances which forced the United States to abandon its offer to pay gold for dollars to foreign governments in 1971.

8. How would you characterize the international exchange rate system of the world since 1973?

9. Carefully explain how one might relate the U.S. current account deficits of the mid-1980s to the large deficits in the federal government's budget.

10. When a nation's currency depreciates as the dollar has since early 1985, it sometimes takes many months before that change produces a turnaround in its current account. What might explain this lag?

[11] For an excellent review of post-1973 exchange rate policy, see B. Dianne Pauls, "U.S. Exchange Rate Policy: Bretton Woods to Present," *Federal Reserve Bulletin*, November 1990.

Index